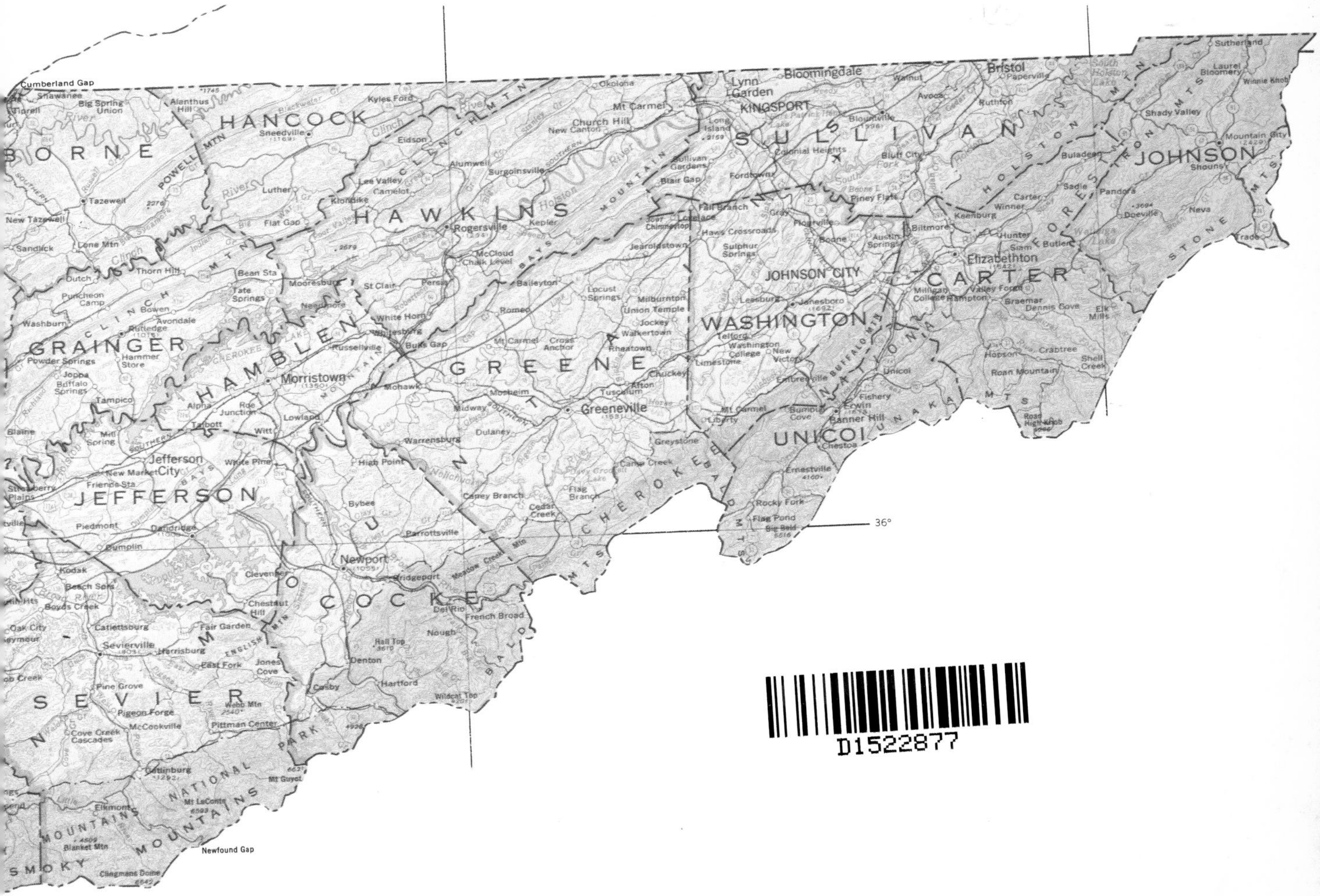

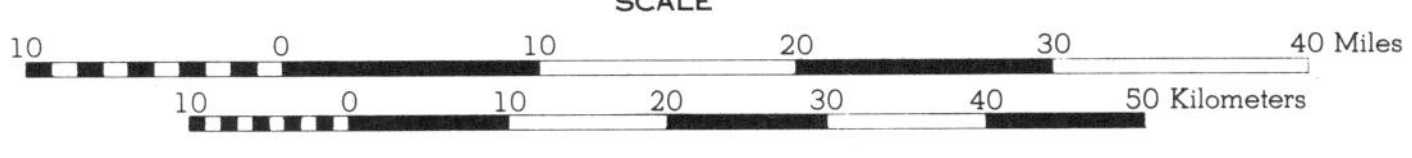

EAST TENNESSEE

SCALE

10 0 10 20 30 40 Miles

10 0 10 20 30 40 50 Kilometers

LEGEND

- County seat
- City, town, or village
- Scheduled service airport
- Built-up area shown for towns over 10,000 population
- County boundary
- National park
- Interstate highway
- U.S. highway
- State highway
- Other principal roads
- National forest
- National wildlife refuge

POPULATION KEY

KNOXVILLE........more than 100,000

JOHNSON CITY...... 25,000 to 100,000

Crossville...............5,000 to 25,000

Sevierville ....2,500 to 5,000

Elkmont.................. less than 2,500

population indicated by size of letters

Based on State of Tennessee map by U.S. Geological Survey, Reston, Virginia 22092
REVISED 1973

AN ENCYCLOPEDIA *of* EAST TENNESSEE

AN ENCYCLOPEDIA *of* EAST TENNESSEE

Edited by Jim Stokely and Jeff D. Johnson

Children's Museum of Oak Ridge
Oak Ridge, Tennessee
1981

The publication of this book, a project of An Appalachian Experience at the Children's Museum of Oak Ridge, was funded by a Cultural Institutions Programs grant from the National Endowment for the Humanities.

An Appalachian Experience was made possible by a grant from the National Endowment for the Humanities (NEH), a Federal agency. The Children's Museum of Oak Ridge is an NEH Learning Museum.

The findings, conclusions, and points of view expressed in *An Encyclopedia of East Tennessee* do not necessarily represent the view of the Endowment.

The editors gratefully acknowledge permission to reprint from "English Footprints in Tennessee," by Vera T. Dean, in *Country Scene*, V.3, No.1, by permission of Ideals Publishing Company; from *Prophet of Plenty: The First Ninety Years of W.D. Weatherford*, by Wilma Dykeman, by permission of The University of Tennessee Press; from *Night Comes to the Cumberlands: A Biography of a Depressed Area*, by Harry M. Caudill, by permission of Little, Brown and Co. in association with The Atlantic Monthly Press; from "Loyston in the 1930's," by Michael J. McDonald and John Muldowny, in *Tennessee Valley Perspective*, V.2, No.3, by permission of the Tennessee Valley Authority; from "Demise of the One-Room School," by Dan Crowe, in *Tennessee Valley Perspective*, V.8, No.3, by permission of the Tennessee Valley Authority; from "Norris—First Planned City," by Alberta Brewer, in *Tennessee Valley Perspective*, V.4, No.1, by permission of the Tennessee Valley Authority; from "The Maturing of a Planned New Town—Norris, Tennessee," by Aelred J. Gray, in *The Tennessee Planner*, V.32, by permission of the Tennessee State Planning Office; from "The Appalachian Experience," by Cratis Williams, in *Appalachian Heritage*, V.7, No.2, by permission of *Appalachian Heritage*; from "The Graysville Melungeons: A Tri-Racial People in Lower East Tennessee," by E. Raymond Evans, in *Tennessee Anthropologist*, V.4, No.1, by permission of the Tennessee Anthropological Association; from "Miners' Insurrections/Convict Labor," ed. by Fran Ansley and Brenda Bell, in *Southern Exposure*, V.1, No. 3&4, by permission of the Institute for Southern Studies; from "The Pottery Patriarch," by David Kent Miller, in *The Tennessee Conservationist*, V.37, No.11, by permission of the Division of Information and Education, Tennessee Department of Conservation; from *A History of Navigation on the Tennessee River System*, by J. Haden Alldredge, Mildred Burnham Spottswood, Vera V. Anderson, John H. Goff and Robert M. LaForge, by permission of the Tennessee Valley Authority; from *Greeneville: One Hundred Year Portrait, 1775-1875*, by Richard Harrison Doughty, by permission of Richard Doughty; from "Libraries: Tools of Learning," by Jesse C. Mills, in *Tennessee Valley Perspective*, V.3, No.3, by permission of the Tennessee Valley Authority; from "Wilma Dykeman—*Tennessee: A Bicentennial History:* An Essay Review and an Appreciation," by Sam B. Smith, in *Tennessee Historical Quarterly*, V.35, No.1, by permission of the Tennessee Historical Commission; and from "Folktales Told in Tennessee," by Leonard Roberts, in *Tennessee Folklore Society Bulletin*, V.21, No.2, by permission of the Tennessee Folklore Society.

Second Printing

Library of Congress Catalog Card Number 81-68545

ISBN 0-9606832-0-8

Printed in the United States of America at Kingsport Press

Introduction

This book is for you. If you are from outside the region, we hope that *An Encyclopedia of East Tennessee* will stimulate your interest in both this area and your own portion of the world. If you now live in, or grew up in, one of the 38 counties we have chosen to call East Tennessee, we hope that you will learn from—and enlarge upon—what we have done here. If this *Encyclopedia* sends out any message, it is that knowledge is carried by all the people, that education is the responsibility of all the people, and that informed action is crucial to the humane survival of all the people.

When the CHILDREN'S MUSEUM OF OAK RIDGE (see entry) received a major National Endowment for the Humanities program grant in April of 1978, we knew that much work lay ahead of us. As an NEH Learning Museum, with funding for "An Appalachian Experience" through 1981, we posited the goal of "putting aspects of Southern Appalachian life into a balanced perspective from which Appalachian people can derive a greater awareness of their past, pride in themselves, and self-confidence for the future." Toward this general end, we committed ourselves to the following specific objectives: (1) producing weekly lectures or "courses", open to both credit-seeking students and the general public, at the Children's Museum; (2) producing similar talks, workshops and forums in a 16-county area surrounding OAK RIDGE and KNOXVILLE; (3) producing eighteen half-hour programs for educational television; and (4) publishing an anthology of Appalachian materials as well as an Appalachian studies teacher's manual.

By the end of 1978, the anthology had evolved into *An Encyclopedia of East Tennessee*, with the probability of course learners and other area volunteers contributing entries on local communities, personalities, and subject categories. My primary responsibility would be the text of the *Encyclopedia*; its photographs and design would be in the hands of Assistant Director Jeff Johnson. I wrote the NEH in January of 1979: "As a participatory endeavor, and as a concrete outlet for citizens' humanistic concerns, the *Encyclopedia*—complete with photographs, cross-references, and a list of contributors' names—promises to be as exciting as any part of the entire Experience." During the spring of 1979, we bulk-mailed our first *Encyclopedia* brochure, listing possible topics and calling for contributions on a voluntary basis. Along with our eight-person Advisory Committee for An Appalachian Experience, composed of Marguerite Carson, William Countess, WILMA DYKEMAN, John Rice Irwin, Loyal Jones, JEFF DANIEL MARION, Jim

Wayne Miller and Selma Shapiro, we began discussing the range, depth, and format of the *Encyclopedia*.

Our initial contributors—students, homemakers, local historians—were soon joined by college professors and other teachers. Dozens more followed suit. As we approached the last day of the year, our entry total neared fifty. But it was during the first months of 1980 that the project seemed to quicken and gel. Articles came in steadily from many quarters. A second and final brochure, pinpointing sixty untaken topics necessary to the *Encyclopedia*, went through the mails in the spring and elicited a wholly positive response. Throughout 1980, this backlog of articles took shape into a book of even more exciting dimensions than I had anticipated. In November, our entry count passed the 200 mark. In the meantime, Jeff Johnson was carefully selecting photographs from a variety of area sources, including the TENNESSEE VALLEY AUTHORITY, the McClung Museum at THE UNIVERSITY OF TENNESSEE, the McClung Room at the Lawson McGhee Library in downtown Knoxville, the Archives of APPALACHIA at EAST TENNESSEE STATE UNIVERSITY, and scores of individuals.

Most of our contributors were East Tennesseans; several are now dead. All of the contributors wrote articles free-of-charge. Taken together, as we have listed them at the back of this volume, they span a broad spectrum of vocations and interests. I would suggest that their common denominator was their gracious energy, their willingness to give talent and time to a promising venture. In this sense, the best sense, they were true believers. Just what we all were believing in revealed itself not only as the manuscript developed, but also as the writers showed enthusiasm in their research, and as prospective readers voiced desire for such a book.

These attitudes appeared to me as the visible expression of more-or-less unspoken needs—needs over time which the *Encyclopedia* was filling in all three modes of past, present, and future. In terms of the past, the book was unearthing a rich vein of personal knowledge acquired over many years and recorded nowhere else, as well as discovering some of the most arresting photographs of the region. In terms of the present, the participatory nature of the project was stimulating a wide variety of persons to write and to research further their personal and regional history and culture. In terms of the future, the *Encyclopedia* was making it more possible to (1) help students and the generally curious delve into particular topics of interest, (2) acquaint newcomers with East Tennessee, and (3) serve as a model for similar or more comprehensive studies.

The above modifier, "more comprehensive", is not used lightly. *An Encyclopedia of East Tennessee* is not comprehensive. Given the existence of East Tennessee as a full third of one of our fifty states, no single volume of this sort can ever be comprehensive or even pretend to be definitive. With this in mind, I do believe that the *Encyclopedia* is representative, demonstrative, and suggestive.

Most of the entries in the *Encyclopedia* are meant to be representative; that is, they give examples of area-wide developments or ways of living. For this reason, we have not tried to replicate BRADLEY COUNTY WAR HEROES or CAMPBELL COUNTY IN THE 1850

FEDERAL CENSUS for each of our 38 East Tennessee counties. Likewise, PRIVATE EDUCATION IN SWEETWATER treats only a small portion of a regional concern, CLEAR BRANCH BAPTIST CHURCH indicates the method of growth of the Baptist denomination in East Tennessee, and MAPLEHURST PARK offers the history and meaning of one urban neighborhood. Our inclusion of midwife HATTIE HARRISON GADDIS and miner-farmer LEVI COLLINS should not be taken as a judgment against other particular midwives or mountaineers. Conversely, we hope that the absence here of a Howard Baker or a Lamar Alexander is mitigated somewhat by the presence of Estes Kefauver, Ben W. Hooper, and other political leaders whose stories have already entered history.

Some of the entries, in and of themselves, demonstrate facets of East Tennessee life. The list of FESTIVALS AND EVENTS, for instance, shows a surprising continuity throughout the calendar year. Our numerous entries on writers and colleges evidence a certain variety and cultural community. LEWIS HINE's photographs stand for themselves, while a tale like JACK AND THE BEANSTALK shows an interesting money motif prevalent in narrative folklore. Entries on DANIEL BOONE and DAVID CROCKETT give the facts of these legends' lives. And, like a few other personal entries, John Rice Irwin's MUSEUM OF APPALACHIA is a distinctive and specifically oriented memoir.

It will remain for the reader to determine the suggestiveness of this *Encyclopedia*. Even so, because of space restrictions, we have deliberately attempted to suggest selected correlations and avenues for further research. In our chart of POPULATION CHARACTERISTICS, the number of doctors choosing to practice in various East Tennessee counties seems to be directly related to such quality-of-life indices as school years completed and family income in those locations. And in my short bibliographical essays scattered throughout this volume, I have attempted to provide a brief scan of introductory works.

As a last word, I refer the reader to two books of great help to me: Sam B. Smith's exemplary *Tennessee History: A Bibliography* (Knoxville: University of Tennessee Press, 1974), which aided in many *Encyclopedia* citations; and the Tennessee Historical Commission's *Tennessee Historical Markers* (Nashville: Tennessee Historical Commission, Sixth Edition, 1972), which served as the basis for much of the individual county information, and which lists many East Tennessee personalities, buildings and events absent from the *Encyclopedia*. These two books point the way to many productive research opportunities. Realizing such possibilities, I must apologize in advance for the deficiencies of *An Encyclopedia of East Tennessee*. But I must also invite you to search in these pages for the information and inspiration contributed here, and after so gleaning, to use that grain for larger purposes.

Jim Stokely, Director
An Appalachian Experience
Children's Museum of Oak Ridge
March, 1981

Acknowledgements

Thanks must go, first and foremost, to Terry Krieger — whose Cultural Institutions Program at the National Endowment for the Humanities made all of this possible — and to the more than two hundred individuals who contributed articles and/or photographs for this volume.

Our own research was aided immensely by Connie Battle and her staff at the Oak Ridge Public Library; by Paul Bartolini, William MacArthur, and the staff at the Knoxville-Knox County Public Library; by Jesse Mills, Robert Kollar and others at the Tennessee Valley Authority; by David Harkness, John Dobson, Joan Worley, Patricia Hudson and others at The University of Tennessee's libraries; by Richard Kesner at East Tennessee State University's Archives of Appalachia; by John Rice Irwin at The Museum of Appalachia; by Martha Lou Coile in Jefferson County and Kathleen Graves in Union County; and by Wilma Dykeman in Newport.

Finally, every reader who finds value in this book should thank Judy Lewis, Office Manager of An Appalachian Experience, who typed the manuscript and, given our time constraints, made attainable its publication.

Jim Stokely and Jeff Johnson

James Agee (November 27, 1909 - May 16, 1955), poet, author and film critic, was born in KNOXVILLE. His father, Hugh Agee, died in an automobile accident in 1916, when James Rufus was six years old. His mother, a devout Episcopalian who had friends at St. Andrew's School on the southern Cumberland Plateau west of CHATTANOOGA, spent the summers of 1918 and 1919 there with her son and younger daughter Emma. James attended St. Andrew's from 1919 to 1924, and he became an acolyte at the school's Episcopal chapel. When his mother's father became ill in early 1924, James returned with his family to Knoxville. He attended high school in the city during the 1924-25 academic year, then went on to Phillips Exeter Academy, a private boarding school in New Hampshire.

At Exeter, Agee edited the *Monthly* and developed his interest in writing. In 1928 he entered Harvard University, where he was President of *The Harvard Advocate*. Through the efforts of *Fortune* writer Dwight McDonald, a fellow Exeter graduate, Agee went to work for the magazine a month after graduation from Harvard in the spring of 1932. Poet Archibald MacLeish also worked at *Fortune*. With MacLeish's influence, Agee's *Permit Me Voyage* was published as the 1934 award of the Yale Series of Younger Poets.

After a six-month leave of absence from *Fortune,* Agee returned to the magazine and drew an assignment which led to his most memorable book. *Fortune* sent Agee and photographer Walker Evans to Alabama during the summer of 1936 in order to photograph and write about the plight of tenant farmers in the Deep South. Both men spent two months in Alabama, attempting to record as best they knew how the situation and meaning of the three tenant families they came to know. Agee had already conceived, from the day of the assignment, a book-length work on the subject, and when *Fortune* declined to publish his article in late 1936, he spent the next thirty months writing what would become *Let Us Now Praise Famous Men.*

Even before *Let Us Now Praise Famous Men* was published in 1941, James Agee began reviewing books in *Time* magazine. During the 1940's he reviewed movies for both *Time* and *Nation* and wrote a regular film column in the latter magazine. Because Agee was one of America's first critics to look

Helen Levitt / Print courtesy Ross Spears

James Agee, 1945.

at films seriously and intensely, his *Nation* column exerted a wide influence. In 1948, he resigned from *Time* and *Nation* and adapted into film scripts more than one of Stephen Crane's stark, acutely felt stories. Two years later, in California, Agee collaborated with director John Huston on the script for *The African Queen*. He suffered a heart attack in January of 1951, but he recovered, and within three months Houghton Mifflin published his *The Morning Watch*. Agee set this long story of maturation and religious sensibility at an unnamed Episcopal school in Tennessee. Through the early 1950's, Agee continued to work on a novel about his father's death, a work planned since Exeter days and actually begun as early as 1935. Before he could finish the final draft, however, James Agee died from a heart attack in New York City.

A Death in the Family, edited by Agee's fellow St. Andrew's graduate David

McDowell, was published in 1957. The novel won the Pulitzer Prize in 1958, and its adaptation for the stage—entitled *All the Way Home*—won another Pulitzer two years later. *A Death in the Family* is a partially autobiographical and particularly unsentimental novel. It deals less with a child's response to growing up than with universal response to irrevocable change. There are at least three major kinds of death at work in this novel. Jay Follet's physical death rends the family structure and provides the narrative basis of the book. Jay's death by car suggests a second type of death: the passing, in East Tennessee, of a former way of life. The turn-of-the-century industrialization of Knoxville and the Cumberland Plateau vastly transformed the rural patterns of the area. This social transition gave Agee a complex background against which to portray characters from the old world and the new, as well as those caught in between.

But Agee's deepest focus in *A Death in the Family* is the challenge of death-in-life. Through the eyes of six-year old Rufus Follet, we confront the Follet alcoholism, inadequate communication among human beings, and the dangers of religious reductionism. In all his work, Agee wanted his readers to worry about these sorts of problems. Agee's special talent lay in successfully grafting such broad concerns onto a large number of specific situations. Because of the precision of his detail, the inclusiveness of his vision, and the power of his language, James Agee was one of the greatest writers America has ever produced.

Jim Stokely

Refer to: James Agee, *A Death in the Family*, New York: McDowell, Obolensky, 1957, and *The Morning Watch*, Boston: Houghton Mifflin, 1951; James Agee and Walker Evans, *Let Us Now Praise Famous Men*, Boston: Houghton Mifflin, 1941; Robert Coles, *Irony in the Mind's Life: Essays on Novels by James Agee, Elizabeth Bowen, and George Eliot*, Charlottesville: University Press of Virginia, 1974; Robert Fitzgerald, ed. *The Collected Poems of James Agee* and *The Collected Short Prose of James Agee*, Boston: Houghton Mifflin, 1968 and 1969; David Madden, ed. *Remembering James Agee*, Baton Rouge: Louisiana State University Press, 1974; Genevieve Moreau, *The Restless Journey of James Agee*, New York: William Morrow, 1977; *Agee on Film: Reviews and Comments* (V.1) and *Agee on Film: Five Film Scripts* (V.2), New York: McDowell, Obolensky, 1958 and 1960; and *The Harvard Advocate Commemorative to James Agee*, V.105, No.4 (February 1972).
See also: APPALACHIAN LITERATURE

Agriculture was the vocation of most early East Tennessee settlers. Farming's social and cultural ramifications in antebellum APPALACHIA form the basis of Ronald D. Eller's "Land and Family: An Historical View of Preindustrial Appalachia" (in *Appalachian Journal*, V.6, No.2, Winter 1979, pp.83-109). WILMA DYKEMAN's *The French Broad* (New York: Rinehart, 1955) shows the importance of hogs and other livestock in East Tennessee before the CIVIL WAR. This Rivers of America volume also recounts the war's devastation of East Tennessee and western North Carolina. Contemporary observer John Trowbridge (Gordon Carroll, ed. *The Desolate South, 1865-6*, Boston: Little, Brown, 1956, Chapters 16-18) also describes agricultural destruction in post-war East Tennessee.

A massive work entitled *Introduction to the Resources of Tennessee* (J.B. Killebrew, J.M. Safford, C.W Charlton, and H.L. Bentley, Nashville: Tavel, Eastman and

Billy Glenn / Courtesy TVA

Farmer, Cherokee Lake, July 29, 1943.

Howell, 1874), undertaken by the Tennessee Bureau of Agriculture, includes a county-by-county evaluation of soils, crops, and prospects for immigration and for resource development. *Resources* also contains a general assessment of area farming, in which the authors state that "the characteristic of East Tennessee agriculture is *diversity of products.* This characteristic is strengthened by the prevalence of small farms. According to the census returns of 1870, there are, in East Tennessee, 26,331 farms. Of these only nine are reported to amount to, or exceed, 1,000 acres, only seventy amount to 500 acres and over, while 6,379 are between 100 and 500 acres, leaving the large proportion of 19,873 under 100 acres."

Turn-of-the-century agrarian politics are explored in Daniel Merritt Robinson's *Bob Taylor and the Agrarian Revolt in Tennessee* (Chapel Hill: University of North Carolina Press, 1935), as are agricultural settlement patterns in Selmer R. Neskaug's "Agricultural and Social Aspects of the Swiss Settlement in Grundy County, Tennessee" (University of Tennessee thesis, 1936). Later changes in East Tennessee farming practices, usually implemented in the service of larger scale and productivity, are chronicled by Charles Miller Strack ("Agricultural Changes in the TVA Area, 1930-1945", University of Iowa dissertation, 1950), Norman I. Wengert (*Valley of Tomorrow: The TVA and Agriculture,* Knoxville: University of Tennessee Record, Extension Series, V.28, No.1, 1952), and Larry M. Boone (*Changes in Tennessee Agriculture by Counties, 1954-1964,* Knoxville: University of Tennessee Agricultural Experiment Station Bulletin 435, 1967).

From 1959 to 1974, harvested acreage in a 21-county area in East Tennessee decreased almost 40%, from 609,575 acres to 380,557 acres. Such facts of urban life prompted Wendell Berry to write *The Unsettling of America: Culture and Agriculture* (San Francisco: Sierra Club Books, 1977), a scathing reaction against the careless modernization of the country's landscape and way of life. Two years earlier, government accountants had already published recommendations for benefitting small farms through the state universities and the agricultural extension services (*Some Problems Impeding Economic Improvement of Small Farm Operations: What the Department of Agriculture Could Do,* Washington, D.C.: U.S. General Accounting Office, 1975). Throughout this period, Eliot Wigginton and his Foxfire students in

Marshall A. Wilson / Courtesy TVA

M.U. Weaver's threshing machine at the home of George Woods, Andersonville, August 20, 1935.

Emil Sienknecht / Courtesy TVA

Portable thresher developed by TVA for small farms, upper East Tennessee, September 1941.

AGRICULTURE

Marion Post / Courtesy Farm Security Administration

Plowing a tobacco field, northeastern Tennessee, May 1940.

E.E. Exline / National Park Service

Tobacco in bloom.

Rabun Gap, Georgia, were recalling the daily routine of the earliest southern mountain settlers by publishing mountaineers' working knowledge and methods of farming on a small scale. See, for example, "Gardening" in Eliot Wigginton, ed. *Foxfire 4* (Garden City, N.Y.: Anchor Press/Doubleday, 1977, pp.150-193).

Jim Stokely

Alcoa. The name Alcoa, an acronym for Aluminum Company of America, was adapted for the city before it became the familiar designation for the company. Lucy Rickey, wife of the company's ranking engineer in the field, first coined the title for a base camp along the Little Tennessee River. Later the title was applied to the North Maryville plant site, then to the city when it was incorporated in 1919.

Edwin S. Fickes, chief engineer of the ALUMINUM COMPANY OF AMERICA, and Robert F. Ewald, a company hydraulic engineer, drew the plans for the city. These were predicated on 7500 acres with provision for an eventual population of 40,000 to 60,000. Parks and playgrounds were to be allocated on the basis of one acre for every 100 people. The city was divided into four sections: Bassel, for G.M. Bassel, company engineer employed in construction of the reduction plant; Springbrook, for the stream that ran through that section; Hall, for Charles M. Hall, discoverer of the electrolytic

Cutting sugar cane, and hauling cane by sled, Great Smoky Mountains, late 1930's.

E.E. Exline / National Park Service

process for reduction of aluminum from its ore; and Vose, the maiden name of Mrs. C.L. Babcock. Shortly before the Aluminum Company's arrival, Babcock Lumber and Land Company had built about 150 houses for its employees at a sawmill and finishing mill in North Maryville. Babcock became the city's first mayor.

By 1920, with ALCOA's annual payroll running over $3 million, the townsite boasted 700 houses, a population of 3358, and a labor force of 3672. Presiding as city manager over the commission-type government of the fledgling municipality was Victor J. Hultquist, who was destined to hold his post for almost thirty years. Hultquist and Arthur B. Smith, city recorder-treasurer-judge, worked in close harmony in city administration and in ALCOA's local hierarchy as well, since both were company employees. On sites donated by ALCOA, Alcoa built Springbrook School in 1921, Bassel School in 1923, Charles M. Hall School in 1926, Alcoa High School in 1939, new Alcoa High School in 1964, and Alcoa Elementary School in 1971. Present permanent population, excluding ALCOA's work force, is about 8,000.

Russell D. Parker

Refer to: Russell D. Parker, "The Black Community in a Company Town; Alcoa, Tennessee, 1919-1939," in *Tennessee Historical Quarterly*, V.37, No. 2; Russell D. Parker, "Alcoa, Tennessee, 1919-1939; The Early Years," in East Tennessee Historical Society's *Publications*, V.47 (1976); and Russell D. Parker, "Alcoa, Tennessee, 1940-1960; Years of Change," in *Ibid.*, V.48 (1977).

Aluminum Company of America (ALCOA). The Pittsburgh Reduction Company, organized in 1888, changed its title in 1907 to the Aluminum Company of America and began its venture in East Tennessee in quest of low cost power. The concept of an integrated network of dams to utilize the full electrical potential of a total watershed was a new one in 1910 when ALCOA began buying riparian rights along the Little Tennessee River. Three years later ALCOA reached a decision regarding location of a plant site and bought up land in North Maryville, some thirty-five miles north of its hydroelectric power source. Construction of a reduction (smelting) plant and about 150 houses in North Maryville began in 1914. When World War I ended in 1918, the Maryville facility was expanded to include a rolling mill; the sheet mill (West Plant) was in operation by August, 1920.

There was some question in the early 1920's whether Tennessee Operations would prosper, but newly discovered uses for the light metal assured the plant's permanence. The 1930's were marked by depression and by labor strife as the New Deal gave workers the right to bargain collectively through representatives of their own choosing. World War II spelled massive prosperity for ALCOA, and Tennessee Operations was greatly expanded to include a work force of 12,000. The North Plant at ALCOA, constructed in 1940-41, covered 55 acres and was the largest plant under one roof in the world. Company and community supported the war vigorously. By 1945 the company's fifteen power plants in East

Tennessee and western North Carolina were furnishing 50 percent of its power requirement, while the TENNESSEE VALLEY AUTHORITY supplied the other half.

ALCOA eventually decided, in view of TVA's preeminence in the power market, to turn its utilities over to the municipality of Alcoa. The company's economic impact on the city, and on BLOUNT COUNTY and all of East Tennessee, would be difficult to overstate. Beginning in 1958, ALCOA published annual impact statements pointing up payroll benefits, goods and services purchased in the state, electric power purchased from TVA, city taxes (almost $750,000 in 1975), Blount County taxes (almost $1 million), MONROE COUNTY taxes (over $100,000), various state taxes, freight and transportation expenditures, and hospital and life insurance claims. A general statement in 1960 observed that Blount County had risen from 85th (of 95 counties) in assembled wealth in 1913 to the top ten, and that in 1950 Alcoans could boast the highest median family income of any Tennessee city in a similarly sized county.

Russell D. Parker

See also: TENNESSEE EASTMAN

Anderson County
Size: 335 Square Miles (214,400 acres)
Established: 1801
Named For: Joseph Anderson, U.S. Senator from Tennessee
County Seat: Clinton

Boy plowing a potato field with mule and bull-tongue plow. J.W. Melton farm near Andersonville road, Anderson County. October 24, 1933.

Lewis Hine / Courtesy TVA

Other Major Cities, Towns, or Communities:
OAK RIDGE
Lake City
NORRIS
Briceville
Andersonville
Medford
Norwood
Fraterville
Rosedale

Refer to: Katherine B. Hoskins, *Anderson County*, Memphis: Memphis State University Press, 1979.
See also: CHILDREN'S MUSEUM OF OAK RIDGE
CLEAR BRANCH BAPTIST CHURCH
CLINTON SCHOOL DESEGREGATION
LEVI COLLINS
WILL G. AND HELEN H. LENOIR MUSEUM
LOWER WINDROCK MINING CAMP
THE MUSEUM OF APPALACHIA
WHEAT

Appalachia. Southern Appalachia begins with the southern border of Pennsylvania and extends like a huge thumb into the heart of the South, terminating in northern Georgia and northeastern Alabama. It includes West Virginia and parts of Maryland, Virginia, North Carolina, South Carolina, Georgia, Tennessee, and Kentucky. As Harry Caudill has pointed out, it is one of the richest regions in natural resources in the world and at the same time has more POVERTY in it than any other region in America.

Approximately thirteen million people now living were born in Appalachia. Nine million are living in the region now, and four million born there have migrated, mostly to northern industrial cities where they have tended to gather in ghettos of poverty but, according to observers who live along the highways leading out of Appalachia, try to get back "down home" every weekend. Of the thirteen million Appalachians, approximately 94% of them are descended from ancestors who were living along the border at the time of the American Revolution. It has been estimated that not more than 30 million of our country's total population of approximately 220 million are descended through all lines from pre-Revolutionary American ancestors. Of these, 43% are natives of Appalachia.

Appalachian people, while far from being homogeneous, are much like one another throughout the region. The Eastern Kentuckian is more like a North Georgian than he is like a native of the Bluegrass region of his own state. The North Carolina mountaineer is more like a West Virginian or an Eastern Kentuckian than he is like a North Carolinian from east of Greensboro. One of the tragedies of Appalachia, parceled out as it is among southern states, is that the South has not been willing to admit that culturally, socially and politically Appalachia is not a part of the South.

Mountain folk in the mass had done well before the CIVIL WAR. They had established schools, retained their literacy, and related themselves in comfortable ways to the land on which they lived in the open settlement pattern of their ancestors. Basically "country people", Appalachian folk had few towns and cities of any size. Travellers through the mountains, however, reported that there was more evidence of culture, industry, and even

Billy Glenn / Courtesy TVA

Wear's Valley, April 9, 1964.

gracious living among mountain folk than there was among the average of plantation owners in Alabama and Mississippi.

Generally, the mountaineers shared neither the culture nor the concerns of the plantation South. They had helped to forge a new nation in which they had enjoyed, for three generations, more freedom and independence than their ancestors had known for a thousand years, and they had rushed to the support of that nation in the War of 1812 and the War with Mexico. It is not surprising that when the Civil War came, large numbers of mountain men refused to join the armies of the Confederacy and either hid in cliffs and caves in the mountains or slipped through the forests at night and joined Union armies in East Tennessee or Kentucky. That mountain folk were supporting the Union was not generally understood during the War by either the North or the South.

By the time political power in the South had been restored to antebellum leadership following the period of Reconstruction, however, the position the mountain men had taken was known. Although they had not supported Abraham Lincoln for president in 1860, they joined the ranks of the Republican Party and supported him in 1864, thereby becoming political minorities in states controlled by the Democratic Party. From the point of view of Southerners, the mountaineers had been traitors to the "noble cause".

Prostrated in anguish and poverty, the South was unwilling to share any of its meager benefits with the traitorous mountain folk. Such road funds and "literacy" funds as the states sharing Appalachia had were spent to reward the faithful. Mountain folk, unable to pay taxes on land of little value and with no other tax base, could no longer support schools. Roads became worse than they had ever been. In many mountain counties, schools that closed in 1861 did not open again for twenty-five years. As population continued to grow in the hills, poverty and illiteracy increased. By 1890 up to 90% of Appalachian people could not read or write. Animosities generated by the Civil War and by its depredations and raids inflamed the feud spirit. Upwards of 200 feuds had developed in the region by 1900.

Echoes of the bloody feuds reverberated across the nation. Writers and newspaper reporters came gathering information about them. Mountain folk, unacquainted with the word feud, referred to the vendettas as "troubles" or "wars", but seldom revealed any knowledge of them to outsiders. Unable to learn much about the feuds, writers turned to the old-fashioned mountain folk themselves as subjects for their quaint journalism. They reported the crude pioneer conditions in the mountains; the social habits, manners and behavior patterns of the archaic people who lived there; the religious beliefs and practices of the hardline church congregations; the curious dialect spoken in the region; and the poverty, health problems and illiteracy of the over-crowded population struggling for survival in a subsistence economy.

Moved by compassion and pity for the mountain folk who had fated their doom

Charles Grossman / Courtesy National Park Service

Plowing Cosby, April 12, 1937.

by supporting the Union during the Civil War, church leaders in the North declared the "Appalachian South" a missionary region, thereby identifying it as a geographical entity apart from the "South" and relegating it to a colonial status, the first of many ruinous efforts in Appalachia. Up to 200 church-related "collegiate institutes" had been established throughout the region by the time the mountain counties were able to maintain their own public high schools in the 1920's. Literature used in the appeals for the financial support of the "institutes" often magnified and emphasized poverty, ignorance, immorality, disease, and degeneracy in the overpopulated and deeply isolated coves and hollows. Overselectiveness of material for public relations of the institutes, together with quaint journalism and the overblown fiction of sentimental "realists", effectively established stereotypes, more caricature than real, of mountain folk that have survived even into our own generation.

The missionaries, dedicated and capable, brought enlightenment and aid to people no longer able to help themselves. Many thousands of Appalachian young people received education that proceeded from a base of rejection of their Appalachian identity to preparation for life as successful middle class people outside the region, for the education they received qualified them for jobs that did not exist in the mountains. Methods of instruction began with rejection of hard-shell RELIGION, mountain music, country dance, oral traditions, Appalachian speech and manners, and the Appalachian identity. The teachers, mostly from the North, proceeding from the assumption that only they spoke correct English, excoriated mountain boys and girls who spoke the Appalachian dialect. Thus, in time, mountain people came to feel ashamed of their traditions and to resist the incursion of outsiders who might laugh at their old-fashioned ways and write unpleasant things about them.

By the time institutes were fairly well established, other invasions had begun. Industrialists from the outside, including ruined plantation owners from the South and northern and British capitalists, began to buy timber rights and broad deeds for mineral deposits for an infinitesimal fraction of their worth from illiterate landowners to whom every fifty cents an acres seemed like wealth. By working in collusion with political leaders from outside the mountainous regions of the states that share Appalachia and by corrupting county governments, the outsiders were successful in preventing the imposition of local taxes on minerals extracted or timber removed that might have supported educational and social programs in the counties being exploited. The industrialists invaded Appalachia and exploited it as if it were a colony imbedded within the nation itself and left its people demoralized and in poverty.

Until the 1930's most of those who spoke for and wrote about Appalachia were outsiders. Tending to present in stereotypes the visible aspects of mountain folk, their homes and institutions, they represented spittle-bearded mountain folk as dressing in homespun, carrying long-barrel RIFLES and toting jugs of moonshine whiskey, living in log cabins, engaging in feuds, and speaking the prototypical dialect long after such things were representative. Beginning with such native writers as Jesse Stuart, James Still, and Harriette Arnow, Appalachian folk began to be presented as real persons with cultural identities, traditions, problems and concerns that are peculiarly their own. Individuals rather than pasteboard cutouts, characters rather than caricatures, occupy the stage, no longer hung with those strings of shucky-beans and festoons of pepperpods that were the perennial props of the outsiders who wrote about us.

In recent years we have as a nation become concerned about our subculture. Our media threatened to destroy our dialects and reduce our national speech to that strident nasal inflection, sometimes touted as the Great American Dialect, spoken by people of the Midwest. Our American grammar provided few options for the rich, colorful idiom of some of our subcultures. Rhetorical styles of Appalachian oral traditions became an endangered species. Cultural traditions of our mountain folk were becoming subsumed by television culture. Our school curricula, established by and dictated from central offices in our states, were providing no room for cultural pluralism.

Now that cultural pluralism has been recognized and accepted, we are in position to save our culture, to learn and write our history, to define our identity, to write our own books, compose our own music, develop our own art, solve our own social problems, manage our own institutions, and build our own economy. We can achieve these things best, not as the Appalachian South but as Appalachia, and not as a people subservient to the outside exploiter or

E.E. Exline / National Park Service

George Lamon and his bees, Great Smoky Mountains, late 1930's.

the greed-impelled Judas within our own ranks but as Appalachians who have risen from our long fast in the mountains, the agony of our neglect and abuse, and the sharp thorns of perfidy that have been our anguish, and are now shaking our hides and flexing our muscles as we reach for the control box that determines our destiny.

Cratis Williams

Refer to: John C. Campbell, *The Southern Highlander and His Homeland*, New York: Russell Sage Foundation, 1921; Wilma Dykeman, "Appalachian Mountains," Macropaedia, V.1, *Encyclopaedia Britannica*,

Chicago: Encyclopaedia Britannica, 1979; Bruce Ergood and Bruce E. Kuhre, eds. *Appalachia: Social Context Past and Present*, Dubuque, Iowa: Kendall/Hunt, 1978; and Helen Matthew Lewis, Linda Johnson, and Donald Askins, eds. *Colonialism in Modern America: The Appalachian Case*, Boone, N.C.: The Appalachian Consortium Press, 1978.

See also: AGRICULTURE
APPALACHIAN GLOSSARY
APPALACHIAN LITERATURE
THE BROAD-FORM DEED
COAL MINING
EAST TENNESSEE TALK
JOHN FOX, JR.
MARY MURFREE

Appalachian Glossary (Some Characteristic Words and Phrases). No word list or glossary can pretend to be either complete or exclusively representative. Certainly this one cannot. It simply offers a list of words and phrases that many native speakers of the dialect under consideration use or recognize and assess as being in some way typical of the area. These abbreviations are used: *n., noun; v., verb; vb. ph., verb phrase; a., adjective; adv., adverb.*

acrosst: Across.

aim to: *vb. ph.* Intend to. "I been *aimin' to* go for a year."

ain't: Am not, are not, is not.

anywheres: Anywhere.

ary: E'er a. "Have you got *ary* egg?"

ast: Asked.

ax: Ask.

bad to: *Bad to* plus an infinitive indicates habitual action. "I'm *bad to* forget." The phrase occurs in inflected forms, also, as in "She was the *worst* I ever seen *to* tell stories."

baking powders: *n.* plural.

beal: *v.* Gather, fester, suppurate; to cause to swell.

bird-work: *v.* Move hastily or busily, usually with awkward movements. "Look at that guy move; he's really *bird-workin'*."

biscuit: *n.* Biscuits. "It don't pay me to make *biscuit*, now there's just me and him."

blind tiger: Site for the illegal sale of whiskey. Typically, it was a small building with no windows, constructed so that there were either one or two drawer-like receptacles for the transactions to be carried out. A customer placed money in a drawer, then closed it, after which the whiskey appeared in it or another drawer.

blowed: Blew. "It *blowed* hard that day."

borned: Born. "I was *borned* in Newton County."

boughten: Bought. "We went to buyin' *boughten* bread then."

bound to: Must. "I'm *bound to* have one."

bullet: The developed bean pod (as opposed to the hull) of any bean that might be eaten shelled. "Cook'em until the *bullets*'ll mash."

can't hardly: Can hardly.

Chat'nooga: Chattanooga.

childern: Children.

clum: Climbed. "He *clum* the tree last week."

creel: *v.* Swell.

corn squeezin's: Illegally manufactured corn whiskey.

diddle: *n.* Baby chick or duckling. (Cf. *doodle, weedie.*) Also appears as *dibbie, diddie, diddlie,* and *diddlier.* Not to be confused with the verb.

diddle: *v.* Copulate. There are many such terms.

don't care to: *vb. ph.* Don't mind, don't object. "I *don't care to* work hard."

doodle: *n.* Baby chick or duckling. (Cf. *diddle, weedie.*) Also appears as *doodie* and

doodlier.
dope: *n.* Canned or bottled carbonated non-alcoholic beverage. "Coke." Occasionally appears as *doper.* "I want a *brown doper* (Coca-Cola)." An *orange doper* is an orange drink, etc.
everwhat: Whatever.
everwhen: Whenever.
everwho: Whoever.
et: Ate.
far: Fire.
fit: Fought.
frog-strangler: A hard rain. (Cf. *gully-washer* and *toad-strangler.*)
go to: Intend to, mean to. "I didn't *go to* do it."
growed: Grew.
gully washer: A hard rain. (Cf. *frog-strangler* and *toad-strangler.*)
half-a-quarter: Half of a quarter of a mile. "Hit's about a *half-a-quarter* from here."
hain't: Has not, have not, am not, are not, is not.
heered: Heard.
hern: Hers.
het: Heated.
hippins: Diapers.
hisn: His.
hit: It.
holp, holped: Helped.
hope how soon: *vb. ph.* Hope (that) soon. "I *hope how soon* the corn comes in" = "I hope the corn comes in soon."
hunderd: Hundred.
hunker: Squat. Sometimes *hunker down.*
infare: *adj.* A wedding celebration. "The *infare* dinner was held at their house." Also written *infair.*
ingern: Onion.
inspignent: *adj.* Fraught with possibility. "That's an *inspignent* idea."
jackleg: *adj.* Untrained, amateurish. "He wasn't nothin' but a *jackleg* preacher." Not to be confused with the next entry.
jake-leg: *n.* Paralysis of a lower extremity caused by drinking a certain variety of regionally available illegally manufactured whiskey. "He's got the *jake-leg.*" Not to be confused with the above entry.
jedge: Judge.
kindly: *adj.* Sort of, somewhat. "She been *kindly* sickly, seems like."
lasty: *adj.* Long-lasting. Can be inflected. "But the *lastiest* back sticks we ever git is black gum."
Law!: An exclamation expressing astonishment. "*Law,* I reckon!"
law: *v.* To go to court, to sue. "I never *lawed* nobody."
mater: Tomato.
molassi: *n. sing.* Back-formation from *molasses.* "We used to make a lot of *molassi* candy."
middlin': *adj.* Tolerable. "Fair to *middlin'*" is a common response to the question, "How are you?"
Murrville: Maryville.
nary: Ne'er a. "No need to ast him. He ain't got *nary* none."
nowheres: Nowhere.
offen: Off of. "That's where we got our cow—we bought him *offen* our uncle."
oncet: Once.
ortent: Ought not. "You *ortent* to do that."
ourn: Ours.
out-doin'est: Out-doingest. Most extraordinary with respect to activity. "That's the *out-doin'est* woman I ever did see."
pezzle: Puzzle.
pizen: Poison.
poke: Small sack or bag. "Just gimme a

poke to put this in, and I'll be on my way."
poke sallet: A wild green.
pone: *v.* Swell up, burst.
pop-skull: Illegally manufactured corn whiskey.
ramp: *n.* A wild edible plant with a strong and easily identifiable taste and odor.
reckon: *v.* Suppose, guess. "I *reckon* so."
red as a fox's ass in pokeberry time: Representative of the vividness and literal accuracy of many of the descriptive phrases used in the area.
red-eye: Whiskey.
right smart: *n.* or *adj.* A considerable amount or distance.
rotgut: Illegally manufactured corn whiskey.
school: *v.* Pay for the education of. "He *schooled* my oldest boy."
sech: Such.
Sequatchie: *n.* Inhabitant of Sequoyah Hills, a fashionable residential area in Knoxville. Used disparagingly.
Sevurrville: Sevierville.
s'I: Says I. Used in narration. "I says to him, *s'I*..."
slow-pokin': Idling, working at a slow pace. "Now don't be *a-slow-pokin'* around."
smoke: Paint thinner consumed as alcohol.
'spec: Expect.
'spose: Suppose.
Straw Plains: Strawberry Plains.
'tater: Potato.
theirn: Theirs.
they's: There are. "*They's* some men come over there to see about it."
toad-strangler: A hard rain. (Cf. *frog-strangler* and *gully-washer.)*
tobaky: Tobacco.
tommy-toe: Cherry or plum tomato. Sometimes used for any variety of tomato.
tuck: Took.
twicet: Twice
us'uns: We.
white lightning: Illegally manufactured corn whiskey.
yander: Yonder.
yarb: Harb.
yieldy: High-producing. Can be inflected. "They's a bunch bean that I think's the most *yieldinest* bunch bean I ever seen."
young'uns: Young ones. Children.
yourn: Yours.
you'uns: You.
you'unses: Your.

Bethany K. Dumas

Appalachian Literature. If Southern literature is American literature with a difference, Appalachian literature may be considered Southern literature—with a difference. Appalachian literature may be understood as the Frontier tradition in Southern literature.

Non-Fiction

James Adair's *History of the American Indians* is the first book written west of the Appalachians. When it was published (1775), Adair had already lived forty years among the CHEROKEES and other southern tribes. John Haywood, a member of an antiquarian society which flourished in Tennessee when the state was still in its pioneer and settlement phase, wrote Tennessee's first history. It is reported that Judge Haywood wrote his *Civil and Political History of the State of Tennessee* (1823) sitting on a bull's hide spread beneath a tree, his books and documents stacked around him. This mix of civilization and frontier conditions is reflected in *The Life of David Crockett of Tennessee* (1834).

Early travel accounts were written by William Bartram, Francis Asbury, James Kirk Paulding, Frederick Law Olmstead, and John Muir. After the turn of the century, important non-fiction accounts of the Appalachian region came from EMMA BELL MILES, Horace Kephart, and John C. Campbell. More recent works of non-fiction by WILMA DYKEMAN AND JAMES STOKELY, Harry Caudill, Jack Weller, Robert Coles and Neil Peirce have stressed both APPALACHIA's plight and its promise.

Prose Fiction

Before 1880, mountain people were generally not distinguished—in fiction or non-fiction—from pioneers. In fiction they were depicted by imitators of James Fenimore Cooper. After 1850, as a result of Longstreet's *Georgia Scenes*, mountain people began to be presented in a humorous vein along with other plain people of the South.

Yet, Appalachian literature has been closely identified with (and often considered synonymous with) the figure of the mountaineer. The beginnings of the mountaineer, as a fictional type, can be seen in the early fiction. George Tucker (*The Valley of the Shenandoah*, 1824) was the first writer of fiction to identify and label a mountaineer. Elizabeth Haven Appleton's "A Half-Life and Half a Life" (*The Atlantic Monthly*, 1864) is the first short story to deal with the life of the mountain people. Sidney Lanier's *Tiger-Lilies* (1867) is the first novel in which the mountaineer is treated as a distinct regional type. Other early works, in which mountain people are presented as distinct from the frontiersman or pioneer, are William Gilmore Simms' *Guy Rivers: A Romance of Georgia* (1834), Hardin E. Taliaferro's *Fisher's River Scenes and Characters* (1859), and *Sut Lovingood. Yarns Spun by a "Nat'ral Born Durn'd Fool"* (1867) by KNOXVILLE author GEORGE WASHINGTON HARRIS.

Charles Egbert Craddock (pseudonymn of MARY MURFREE) established the mountaineer as a distinct fictional type. Her imitators manipulated but did not add to the types and motifs found in such works as *In the Tennessee Mountains* (1884) and *The Prophet of the Great Smoky Mountains* (1885). Other notable writers from this period of "local color" were JOHN FOX JR., Will N. Harben, Lucy Furman, and Charles Neville Buck. The latter's *Flight to the Hills* (1926) helped initiate a new attitude toward Appalachia, for in this novel Buck considers aspects of traditional Appalachian life superior to life outside the region.

The years since the late 1920's have seen the emergence of many writers native to the Appalachian region. Important authors include Elizabeth Madox Roberts, Thomas Wolfe, Jesse Stuart, Harriette Arnow, MILDRED HAUN, James Still, Byron Herbert Reece, JAMES AGEE, Romulus Linney, Mary Lee Settle, John Ehle, and Wilma Dykeman. The novels of Ehle and Dykeman present a panorama of life in the Appalachian region from the pioneer period to the present. Recent and worthwhile fiction includes novels and short stories by John Foster West,

RICHARD MARIUS, CORMAC McCARTHY, Gurney Norman and Fred Chappell.

Poetry

While most of the poetry of Appalachia has been produced by native writers since 1930, this poetry draws much of its strength from the folk culture or the "invisible part of the baggage" which, according to Donald Davidson, was brought by settlers into the mountains along with the Bible and Shakespeare. A mix of indigenous folk materials and mainstream influences can be found in poetry written by Roy Helton, Jesse Stuart, Byron Herbert Reece, James Still, Louise McNeill, Bernard Stallard, Billy Edd Wheeler, Jonathan Williams, Lillie Chaffin, John Beecher, Robert Morgan, Don West, Fred Chappell, Jim Wayne Miller, P.J. Laska, JEFF DANIEL MARION, GEORGE SCARBROUGH, Lee Pennington, and Muriel Dressler. Several journals and magazines attest to the vigor of poetry in the region. Some of the younger poets appearing in these publications are Rudy Thomas, Robert Baber, Billy Greenhorn (pseudonymn of Robert Snyder), Rodney Jones, Jim Stokely, and Mary Joan Coleman.

Folk Literature/Oral Tradition

The oral literature—riddles, beliefs, sayings, songs, ballads, stories—and the folk culture which preserved that literature continue to be a source of renewal and stimulation for scholars, prose writers, poets and musicians. Impressive collections have been made by Cecil Sharp (1917), James Aswell (1940), Richard Chase (1943, 1948, 1956), May Justus (1952), and Ruth Ann Musick (1965, 1970, 1977). Leonard Roberts' *South From Hell-Fer-Sartin* (1955), *Up Cutshin and Down Greasy* (1959), and *Sang Branch Settlers* (1974) combine the art of the taleteller with the painstaking care of the scholar. The delightfully unself-conscious diary of WILLIAM A. McCALL, *I Thunk Me a Thaut* (1975), vividly reflects the folk culture of East Tennessee in the late 19th and early 20th centuries. As both poet and musician, Jean Ritchie, author of *Singing Family of the Cumberlands* (1955) and *Celebration of Life: Jean Ritchie, Her Songs, Her Poems* (1971), discovers continuing vitality in the folk culture. Recent interest in oral history is reflected in such works as Lynwood Montell's *The Saga of Coe Ridge* (1970), the *Foxfire* books edited by Eliot Wigginton (1972 ff.), *Our Appalachia* edited by Shackelford and Weinberg (1977), and Verna Mae Slone's *What My Heart Wants to Tell* (1979). By publishing his modern folk tale, "Ancient Creek", on record (Appalshop, 1976), Gurney Norman also emphasized the validity of oral literature in the region.

The growth and development of American literature can be viewed as a process in which writers have discovered the land and life of different geographical and cultural regions: New England, the South, the Midwest, the Far West. The writers and their works have then been discovered by the country, with the result that the country has come to know itself better. Appalachian literature, which is, according to Wilma Dykeman,"as unique as churning butter, as universal as getting born," is a part of this ongoing discovery of America.

Jim Wayne Miller

Refer to: Donald Davidson, *The Tennessee* (Two Volumes), New York: Rinehart, 1946, 1948, and *The Attack on Leviathan*, Gloucester, Mass: Peter Smith, 1962; Wilma Dykeman, "The Literature of the Southern Appalachian Mountains," in *Mountain Life and Work*, V. 40 (Winter,1964); Robert J. Higgs and Ambrose N. Manning, eds. *Voices From the Hills: Selected Readings of Southern Appalachia*, New York: Frederick Ungar, 1975; Jim Wayne Miller, "Appalachian Literature," in *Appalachian Journal*, V. 5,No. 1 (Autumn 1977), pp. 82-91; Charlotte T. Ross, ed. *Bibliography of Southern Appalachia*, Boone, N.C.: Appalachian Consortium Press, 1976; W.D. Weatherford and Wilma Dykeman, "Literature Since 1900," in Thomas Ford, ed. *The Southern Appalachian Region: A Survey*, Lexington: University of Kentucky Press, 1962; and Cratis Williams, "The Southern Mountaineer in Fact and Fiction," New York University dissertation, 1961.
See also: POETRY MAGAZINES

Archaeology (Prehistoric). The objective of prehistoric archaeologists is to describe and explain the ways in which groups of people lived before written records were made of them. Evidence of these lifeways consists primarily of concentrations of material used by people in adapting to the natural environment at specific geographic locations, or sites. Such material includes abandoned, or broken, tools, equipment, and associated data which indicate patterns of human activity. These data may include the remains of structures, food, burials, hearths, storage or refuse pits, and rituals. When all these data are compiled, the archaeologists attempt to reconstruct the lifeways, or cultures, which they represent. The cultures which have been described for East Tennessee reflect changes in CLIMATE, land forms, FLORA and FAUNA as well as changes in technology and influences from other groups.

The archaeological record extends some 10,000 years into the past. There is evidence that prehistoric populations in the area interacted with populations in adjacent states, especially those portions of states which share the same river valleys. As they approached the present day, cultures became more complex and increasingly utilized the environmental resources. These increases are marked by the appearance of culturally significant data in the archaeological record. Certain of these data have been selected by archaeologists to establish segments, or sets of cultural assemblages, in the continuum of lifeways. Archaeologists refer to these segments as the Paleo-Indian, Archaic, Woodland and Mississippian periods. The following summaries give significant elements of these periods, some of the sites, and inferences they permit regarding patterns of living.

Paleo-Indian Period (c. 10,000 - 15,000 years ago)

This was the period during which the initial human occupation of the area took place. After a migration of people across the Bering Strait region, bands (groups of 50-60 individuals) dispersed into much of North America, ultimately reaching the area of our concern. These bands established base camps to which they returned from their hunting and foraging trips. Shelters, if any, were probably screens of brush or skins to protect them from the wind. Fire was used for warmth. The principal food resource was game animals, but these were probably supplemented by smaller animals and the gathering of plant foods.

Courtesy Frank H. McClung Museum, University of Tennessee

Bird effigy pipe from Zimmerman's Island of the French Broad River (now inundated by Douglas Lake). The pipe is 44.3 cm long, 7.4 cm wide, and 9.4 cm high at the bowl.

No camp sites, or base camps, of these people have been located in East Tennessee, but in adjacent areas a few have been identified and excavated. The principal indication of this occupation is a specific tool type fashioned of chipped stone and referred to as a fluted point. Such points probably served as spear tips and possessed the unique technological characteristic of a flute, or single flake scar, extending from the base of the point toward its tip. Such point types, designated as Clovis and Cumberland, have been recovered as isolated finds on the surface of the ground along rivers and streams in East Tennessee. The skilled artisans who produced them also prepared other chipped stone tools: scrapers, burins, and knives. Bone and wooden implements were probably used, but they have not been preserved.

Archaic Period (c. 3,000 - 10,000 years ago)

The Indians became well-adapted to a forest environment during this period. Food resources being exploited included numerous plant and animal species, including fish and shellfish. Depending upon the season of the year, bands of people moved from one part of their home range to another. The chipped stone technology continued from the Paleo-Indian period with only minor changes in forms. These changes and some additional data permit the identification of three parts in the Archaic Period.

Early Archaic sites indicate that Indian bands established camps on the developing second terraces of rivers, presumably during the fall of the year since quantities of acorns and hickory nuts were found in the deposits. Along the Little Tennessee River, one series of camps was located at the Icehouse Bottom Site, another on Rose Island. At each of these sites, superimposed cultural levels were separated by sterile flood deposits, thereby providing a sequence of projectile point types: Kirk Corner Notched (earliest), St. Albans, and LeCroy (latest). Similar sequences occur in West Virginia and North Carolina. In addition to these point types, other chipped stone tools include scrapers, drills, bipolar flakes, and knives. Pitted cobblestones and a multipurpose hammerstone-muller-anvil are also present in the assemblage. Of particular interest is the association of hearths on prepared clay, some of which bear impressions of woven basketry. A burial of cremated human bone is also associated with the Early Archaic material.

Middle Archaic sites indicate a continuation of seasonal occupations on developing second terraces along the rivers. Nuts, including walnuts, served as part of the Indians' diet. Projectile points include the Stanley and Morrow Mountain types. Net weights and spear-thrower weights appear in the assemblages for the first time.

Late Archaic materials occur in the second terraces along rivers as well as other locations in the general area. The seasonal movement of Indian bands continued, but the materials indicate an increase in the population density which probably reduced the mobility of the bands. Trade networks were established between bands occupying areas with differing resources. Shelters were constructed by placing small poles upright in the earth to form a semicircular enclosure. Additions to the tool inventory and equipment include ground stone axes, stone (steatite) bowls, bone fishhooks and awls.

Woodland Period (c. 3,000 - 1,000 years ago)

More permanent settlements were established during this period. Woodland Indians practiced limited cultivation of plants such as squash, sunflower, goosefoot, and sumpweed. Structures were completely enclosed and built by placing cut saplings vertically in the ground with the tops bent to form the wall-roof frame. Bark strips or thatch covered these oval to rectangular structures. Trade networks extended into other regions. Differences in social status within the society were recognized, and earthen mounds were constructed in which to inter the dead. Chipped and ground stone tools continued to be used, and the making of pottery vessels began. Three levels of the Woodland Period have been identified.

Early Woodland occupations have been located along rivers in the area. Extensive deposits of refuse representing such occupations include the Camp Creek Site along the Nolichucky River in GREENE COUNTY and the Rankin Site in COCKE COUNTY. Additional sites are along the French Broad, Holston, Little Tennessee, Clinch and Tennessee rivers. Chipped stone points in this culture are simple triangles, possibly arrow tips. Ground stone articles include birdstones and gorgets of slate. The pottery was tempered with crushed stone and has conoidal bases. The exterior surface of these vessels was impressed with twisted cords, or corded fabrics.

Middle Woodland occupations are represented by ceramic vessels tempered with crushed limestone or sand. Their surfaces were impressed with stamped designs, presumably applied by pressing carved wooden paddles into the soft clay before firing the vessel. This surface treatment reflects influences from the Georgia area. Extensive trade networks existed and linked East Tennessee sites with sites in western North Carolina and those of the Hopewell culture in Ohio. Such linkages are indicated in the assemblage representing this level of occupation at the Icehouse Bottom Site, where prismatic blades of chalcedony (Ohio) and mica (North Carolina) were recovered.

Late Woodland sites of the Hamilton culture reveal that the seasonal round of hunting and gathering continued, even though maize had been added to the plants being cultivated in gardens. The refuse of these seasonal camps sometimes contains shell mounds, indicating that the camps were occupied during the winter or early spring. Burials of prominent members, possibly entire lineages, of the society were in earthen mounds constructed for this purpose. Such mounds have been recorded on the Clinch River, in the Tellico Reservoir area, and along the Tennessee River from MARION COUNTY into KNOX COUNTY. One such mound can be been on the campus of THE UNIVERSITY OF TENNESSEE College of Agriculture in KNOXVILLE. Pottery bowls and jars were tempered with crushed limestone. Gorgets and beads were made of stone and some ornaments were fashioned of shell obtained in trade from the Gulf Coast. Chipped stone articles include projectile points, knives, and scrapers.

Mississippian Period (c. 1,000 - 300 years ago)

Intensive cultivation was developed during this period in the alluvial bottoms of the larger rivers. Cultigens included maize, squash and beans. Hunting, fishing and the gathering of wild plants continued to provide a substantial portion of the diet. Semi-permanent villages surrounded by palisades were also located in the bottoms. These consisted of several family dwellings around a central plaza with at least one community building, frequently on a flat-topped mound, at one end of the plaza.

Five phases of this period have been identified. The Emergent Mississippian phase is represented in the Tellico Reservoir area and possibly the Norris Reservoir area. It is the earliest phase and is currently considered the product of internal culture change developing within the Hamilton phase of the preceding Woodland period. The Emergent Mississippian phase is succeeded by the Hiwassee Island phase, which is represented by villages on Hiwassee Island, in the Tellico Reservoir area, and on the Powell River. Some cultural elements may have reached East Tennessee from the middle Mississippi River valley. The Dallas phase is more recent than the Hiwassee Island phase and is represented by the Hixson and Citico Sites near CHATTANOOGA, Hiwassee Island, the Toqua Site in the Tellico Reservoir area, and the McMahan Site in Sevierville. A fourth phase is designated Mouse Creek. Sites of this phase are on the Hiwassee River. Community plans, architecture, burial customs, and pottery distinguish it from the Dallas phase, with which it coexisted.

Construction techniques changed with time. Structures of the Hiwassee Island phase were oblong to square and were formed by vertically placed saplings with their tops bent to form the wall-roof frame. This framework was covered with flexible materials, and the wall portion was covered with clay. The roof was thatched. In the Dallas phase, structures were rectangular to square and consisted of walls formed by vertically placed poles. The roof was supported by four posts placed within the enclosed area. Circular structures were constructed to serve as community buildings. The walls were interlaced with split cane or other flexible materials and then covered with clay. The roof was of thatch. Mouse Creek structures were semisubterranean with poles forming the exposed portions of the walls.

Some villages were larger than others and probably served as ceremonial centers. Social differentiation existed in Dallas society, and the centers may be identified with chiefdoms which controlled some of the activity in several satellite villages.

Pottery vessels were tempered with crushed shell and were fashioned into bowls, jars, bottles, pans, and effigy forms. The surfaces were usually smooth, with decoration often confined to the rim areas. Designs were executed with incised lines, modeling, or painted lines and zones. Chipped stone tools served utilitarian and ceremonial purposes. Stone axes (celts) and chisels were prepared by grinding stone. Ornaments were fashioned from shell obtained in trade from the Gulf Coast. In the Dallas phase these ornaments included circular gorgets engraved with designs representing the turkey, rattlesnake, spider and humans. Additional shell ornaments included earplugs and "face masks" bearing an engraved "weeping eye" motif. Some ornamental use was made of copper and mica.

The Cherokee culture represents the latest and fifth phase of the Mississippian period. During the last few centuries of prehistory, Indians with this culture lived in the Southern Appalachian area and expanded their territory into East Tennessee. Before the CHEROKEES were removed to the West during the early 19th century, Cherokee villages were located along the Holston, French Broad, Little Tennessee and Tennessee rivers.

Alfred K. Guthe

Refer to: Charles H. Faulkner, "The Mississippian-Woodland Transition in the eastern Tennessee Valley," in *Bulletin No. 18*, Memphis, Tenn.: Southeastern Archaeological Conference, 1975, pp. 19-30; Alfred K. Guthe, "The eighteenth-century Overhill Cherokee," in *Anthropological Papers of the Museum of Anthropology, University of Michigan*, V.61 (1977), pp.212-229; Thomas M.N. Lewis and Madeline Kneberg, *Hiwassee Island*, Knoxville: University of Tennessee Press, 1946; articles in the University of Tennessee Department of Anthropology *Report of Investigations*, Nos. 10, 13, 14 and 18 (1973, 1975, 1977); and articles in *Tennessee Archaeologist*, V.13, No.1 (1957), pp.1-48, and V.24, No.2 (1968), pp.37-91.
See also: ARCHAEOLOGY (HISTORICAL)

Archaeology (Historical). Archaeology as a means of studying past human endeavors is not limited to the sites left by native Americans and their ancestors. The investigation of historic period sites has much to offer students of history. Archaeological information derived in this manner is independent of the kinds of biases often found in historical documents, and it is of a nature that is rarely mentioned in historical accounts. Although the specific artifacts differ from those found on prehistoric sites, the overall objective is the same: to illuminate the kinds of activities which took place in the past and thus to understand, in a limited way, the development of human society.

The discussion of previous archaeological research in APPALACHIA can be organized in a number of ways. This account has selected a division by the kinds of related activities—domestic, military, manufacturing, transportation, and education/religion. Domestic sites include a full range of activities, from those of individual families to a whole community. Much of the emphasis has been placed on the sites associated with "historical" persons, the small percentage of persons recognized as instrumental in the development of our state and nation. Examples include excavation of part of the ANDREW JOHNSON House in Greeneville, the Davy Crockett Birthplace in GREENE COUNTY, the J.G.M. RAMSEY House in KNOX COUNTY, and KINGSPORT's Preston Farm/Exchange Place, a typical mid-19th century farmstead.

But as we all recognize, since most persons living at any point in time are not the "movers and shakers", it is important to understand what the majority was doing. Relatively little work has been done on this aspect. The Davy Crockett State Historical Area excavation, however, also included work on the remains of an average family farmstead dating from 1824 to 1968. The construction of the Tellico Dam on the Little Tennessee River inundated the remains of the early town of Morganton in LOUDON COUNTY. Archaeological investigations were carried out to correlate the town plan with archaeological data, thus producing material from a number of houses on the same street. All Federal construction projects require identification of historic period sites; two such surveys were done in the OAK RIDGE area of Roane and Anderson counties.

Military sites have always played a key role in the study of history, and this importance is also reflected in the amount of work done by archaeologists. FORT LOUDOUN, a British colonial fort built in MONROE COUNTY in 1756 and occupied until 1760, has seen many archaeologists come and go. The fort was reconstructed in the 1930's by Works Progress Administration workmen and archaeologists. Other work was done in the 1950's and in 1960. Prior to flooding by the TENNESSEE VALLEY AUTHORITY's Tellico Dam Reservoir, the Fort Loudoun site was completely excavated by the Tennessee Division of Archaeology. Other excavated military sites associated with the early exploration of East Tennessee are the Tellico Blockhouse (1794-1807) in Monroe County and Fort Southwest Point (1792-1807) at Kingston. The CIVIL WAR in East Tennessee has not received very much attention from archaeologists, but one study looked at the remains of a camp site used by northern reporters on Lookout Mountain in CHATTANOOGA.

One sub-field in historic sites archaeology specializes in the excavation of sites associated with manufacturing, processing, or procuring natural and mineral resources. A statewide survey of 163 sites associated with the manufacture of earthenware and stoneware pottery has produced important information on this family-oriented cottage craft industry from 1800 to 1940. Iron making was an important industry in East Tennessee, and several studies have looked at individual sites in Hamilton and Roane counties, as well as surveying sites in CARTER COUNTY. Grist and saw mills also played a key role in each area community, but archaeological research is just beginning on this aspect of history. The 1979 excavation of a mill on South Chickamauga Creek in Chattanooga provided information on early mill wheel innovations. One unusual type of excavation resulted from folk fishing techniques; a 1978 study described a historic fish trap on the lower Holston River near KNOXVILLE.

The development of transportation has been an integral part of our history. Archaeological investigations related to this aspect have included excavation of a wayside inn located in Kingsport, and a survey of Cumberland Gap National Historical Park. The excavation of Chattanooga rail yards south of the old Union Station has produced remains of early railroad buildings, turntables, and rail bed construction techniques.

Other types of archaeological research have looked at the SAM HOUSTON Schoolhouse in Maryville and the first building at THE UNIVERSITY OF TENNESSEE at Chattanooga. Prehistoric archaeologists have excavated burial sites for many years, but historical archaeologists seldom get the chance to investigate historic cemeteries. The relocation of a German Lutheran cemetery in MORGAN COUNTY involved excavation of twelve burials and

Swimming at the Monday Island fish trap, on the lower Holston River near Mascot, May 30, 1915.

William J. McCoy Sr. (Knoxville professional photographer, 1898 - 1955) / Courtesy William J. McCoy Jr.

associated grave artifacts.

The archaeological research done on historic period sites has provided the study of Appalachian culture with a time depth beyond the recent past. Although many of the sites which have been excavated were associated with the rich and powerful, the emphasis is shifting to the sites of the everyday person. We have learned that the Appalachian areas of Tennessee show a strong continuity with the past; many of the agricultural and architectural practices studied by folk culture scholars have not changed a great deal since first settlement. Archaeology has given us an appreciation of where we have been and where we are today. It may even help chart the proper course for the future.

George F. Fielder, Jr.

Refer to: Jeff Brown, "The Camp Site Beneath the Cravens House Porch" and James E. Cobb, "Historic Fish Traps on the Lower Holston River," in *Tennessee Anthropologist*, V.3, No. 1 (Spring 1978), pp.6-13 and pp.31-58; D. Bruce Dickson, "Archaeological Test Excavations of the Sam Houston Schoolhouse," in *Tennessee Anthropologist*, V.2, No.1 (Spring 1977), pp. 81-97; George F. Fielder, Jr., Stevan R. Ahler, and Benjamin Barrington, *Historic Sites Reconnaissance of the Oak Ridge Reservation, Oak Ridge, Tennessee*, Oak Ridge: Oak Ridge National Laboratory, 1977; Carl Kuttruff and Beverly Bastian, "Fort Loudoun Excavations: 1975 Season," in *The Conference on Historic Site Archaeology Papers 1975*, V.10, Part 1, pp.11-23; Richard Polhemus, "Archaeological Investigations of the Tellico Blockhouse Site," *Tennessee Valley Authority Reports in Anthropology No. 16* and University of Tennessee Department of Anthropology *Report of Investigations No. 26*, 1980; Samuel D. Smith, "Historical Background and Archaeological Testing of the Davy Crockett Birthplace State Historic Area, Greene County, Tennessee," *Tennessee Division of Archaeology Research Series No. 6*, 1980; Samuel D. Smith and Stephen T. Rogers, "A Survey of Historic Pottery Making in Tennessee," *Tennessee Division of Archaeology Research Series No. 3*, 1979; Prentice M. Thomas, ed. *Archaeological Investigations at Fort Southwest Point*, Nashville: Tennessee Historical Commission, 1977; and John W. Walker, *Assessment of Archaeological Resources of Cumberland Gap National Historical Park*, Tallahassee, Florida: National Park Service, 1975.

See also: ARCHAEOLOGY (PREHISTORIC)
CHARLES FREDERICK DECKER
RAILROADS
STATE PARKS

Architecture. The beginning of European architecture in East Tennessee was the building of FORT LOUDOUN on the Tennessee River (at the site not far from the present-day town of Vonore in MONROE COUNTY) in 1757. Carpenters and soldiers from Charleston erected a frame barrack and guard house, along with squared-log storage houses, and began to construct the fortifications designed for the fort by the English engineer William Gerhard De Brahm. Between the fall of Fort Loudoun to the CHEROKEES in 1760 and the establishment of settlements on the Watauga River about 1770, there continued a steady trickle of immigration, mostly by traders. These frontier merchants, outposts of a system of commerce which ran to Richmond, Charleston, and London, often built stores, probably frame or squared-log, like John Carter's near the Holston River (at the site of Church Hill in HAWKINS COUNTY) and dwellings like Cornelius Dougharty's near Hiwassee Old Town. Fort Patrick Henry near the Long Island of the Holston, Fort Caswell at Sycamore Shoals of the

Courtesy Rocky Mount Historical Association

Rocky Mount.

Watauga, and a dozen other forts popularized the squared-log construction which before 1770 had usually been employed in the southern colonies only in the building of barns.

During the late eighteenth and early nineteenth centuries architecture in the upper counties (Sullivan, Hawkins, Washington, Greene, Blount, Sevier, Jefferson) was determined by the faithfulness of carpenters to the house types familiar on the seaboard and in the Shenandoah Valley. Apart from rough cabins built hastily for temporary use, the first dwellings were of neatly hewn logs, of stone, or frame. The earliest mention of brick chimneys occurs in a letter of Abashai Thomas written to John Gray Blount in 1794, though brick were probably fired much earlier. Glass and pigment were imported from Philadelphia, and later from Baltimore. Nails were forged locally, and sawmills were probably at work before 1780. Surviving examples typical of late eighteenth-century architecture include Rocky Mount, a squared-log house of the 1780's (at Piney Flats in SULLIVAN COUNTY); the stone house Thomas Embree built in WASHINGTON COUNTY (near present-day Telford) about 1790, and the Buckingham house, a brick hall-and-parlor house built in SEVIER COUNTY about 1795. Before the end of the century, East Tennessee had stylish late-Baroque houses with handsome architectural details: the Carter house (1775?) at Watauga Old Fields (ELIZABETHTON), with its elegant panelling executed in the style of the

1760's; Stony Point (ca. 1788), William Armstrong's brick central-passage house in Hawkins County (near Surgoinsville), perhaps originally a five-part design; and the stone house Francis A. Ramsey built near KNOXVILLE about 1797.

After 1800 this post-colonial style gave way to Federal. Among the great East Tennessee examples were the William Deery house in Blountville (ca. 1813), the Alfred Moore Carter house in Elizabethton (ca. 1819), and the Earnest house near Chucky in GREENE COUNTY (ca. 1820). Towns like DANDRIDGE, Maryville, Rogersville, Madisonville, and Athens were full of plain Federal examples, and Greeneville, Blountville, and JONESBORO still have something of the character of early nineteenth-century towns. The best known East Tennessee house carpenter of this period was Thomas Hope (ca. 1757-1820), who came to Knoxville from Charleston about 1797, and who built at least six fine houses in the upper counties, among them the Joseph C. Strong house and the F.A. Ramsey house in KNOX COUNTY, and Frederick Ross's Rotherwood near KINGSPORT.

East Tennessee had little distinguished Greek Revival architecture, though the Rogersville Branch of the Bank of the State of Tennessee (1839) by Thomas Jones, now the Masonic Hall, and the Tennessee Institution for the Deaf and Dumb (1851), until 1980 the Knoxville City Hall, were representative of that style. Indeed, East Tennessee proved

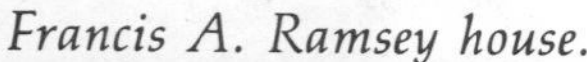

Francis A. Ramsey house.

Courtesy Thompson Photographs, C.M. McClung Historical Collection, Lawson McGhee Library

largely impervious to the romantic revivals. Before the war there was little Italianate, though Lucknow (1861), later renamed Melrose, and Bleak House (ca. 1850), both built in Knoxville, were exceptions. Among the few antebellum Gothic buildings were St. John's Episcopal Church, Knoxville (1846), St James' Church, Greeneville (1849), and St. Andrew's, Four Mile Point (near Vonore), an Upjohn design completed in 1857. The free classicism characteristic of the decade immediately preceding the CIVIL WAR was also poorly represented in East Tennessee, though a few plantation houses such as Fair View near Jefferson City and River View near White Pine were built in that manner. It was characteristic of East Tennessee thoughout the first half of the nineteenth century that a rather plain Federal predominated.

After 1865 Knoxville experienced the boom that incessant westward emigration and the transfer of the capital to Middle Tennessee after 1817 had forestalled. Architectural practice was dominated by Joseph F. Baumann (1844-1920), who built an important group of Knoxville churches—of which Immaculate Conception Catholic Church on Summit Hill is the only survivor—as well as office buildings and stores. Another important architect of the post-war period was A.C. Bruce (1835-1927), who was especially noted during his Knoxville years (1866-1879) for his Second Empire courthouses at Loudon, Morristown, Athens, and CHATTANOOGA. In 1890 George F. Barber (1854-1913) opened the Knoxville drafting rooms from which thousands of designs for Queen Anne houses would be mailed across the United States, to Japan, and to Canada.

Style during the period 1865-1900 consisted of a playful and mannered development of historical themes: Second Empire (or French Renaissance), Romanesque, Gothic. At the close of the nineteenth century there was a return, foreshadowed by Alfred B. Mullet's Italianate Knoxville Custom House (1874), to a beaux-arts classicism called Second Renaissance Revival. It is characteristic of East Tennessee during this period that while a sophisticated neo-medieval and neo-classical architecture flourished in the cities, a tradition of building with logs, related to both eighteenth-century house types and to mid-century vernacular styles derived perhaps ultimately from the designs of A.J. Downing, persisted in the coves.

During the late nineteenth century Chattanooga, which before 1861 had been only a village, blossomed as a manufacturing center. The architecture of that city soon reflected its new-won size and importance. The most important Chattanooga architects of this period were Reuben Harrison Hunt (1862-1937), whose Second Presbyterian Church (1891) is a good example of his Romanesque designs, and Samuel McClung Patton (1852-1897), who designed such landmarks as the Mountain City Club (1890) and the Lookout Mountain Hotel (1889) during the brief years (1888-1897) of his Chattanooga practice. Hunt practiced until 1936, and in Knoxville Albert B. Baumann (1861-1942) and Albert B. Baumann, Jr. (1897-1952) perpetuated the family practice until the 1950's.

Custom House in downtown Knoxville, April 28, 1934.

Granville Hunt / Courtesy TVA

Ron Childress / Used by permission of Frederic S. LeClercq

J.V. Henderson House on Kingston Pike in Knoxville. Designed by Charles Barber in 1925.

Charles I. Barber (1887-1962) inherited his father's love of architecture and his abilities, and many of the splendid eclectic designs along Kingston Pike and in Sequoyah Hills are the work of the younger Barber's Knoxville firm.

After 1945 new industrial developments and new transportation patterns changed the face of East Tennessee. The TENNESSEE VALLEY AUTHORITY began in the 1940's to create an architecture of its own, and Federally sponsored towns like NORRIS and OAK RIDGE brought to the region its first examples of large-scale planning. Architects of great ability and distinction perpetuated the tradition of fine building begun by Thomas Hope, and designers like Bruce McCarty, Robert B. Church, III, Patrick James, William Moorefield, and James R. Franklin will have a place in future histories of the regional architecture. After 1965 Knoxville had a School of Architecture (part of THE UNIVERSITY OF TENNESSEE) which was able to offer its services in research as well as teaching.

James Patrick

Refer to: Richard H. Doughty, "The Architecture and Furniture of Greeneville," in *Greeneville: One Hundred Year Portrait, 1775-1875*, Greeneville, Tenn., 1975, pp. 268-297; William R. McNabb, "Architecture," in *Heart of the Valley: A History of Knoxville, Tennessee*, Knoxville, Tenn.: East Tennessee Historical Society, 1976, pp. 414-422; and James Patrick, *Architecture in Tennessee, 1768-1897*, Knoxville: University of Tennessee Press, 1981.

Edward Westcott

Oak Ridge, 1944.

Anne W. Armstrong (September 20, 1872 - March 15, 1958) was a business woman and writer who spent much of her life in East Tennessee and southwest Virginia. She was born in Grand Rapids, Michigan, the daughter of Henry and Lorinda Wetzell. When she was quite young, her family moved to KNOXVILLE. This she vividly recalled in an unpublished autobiography, *Of Time and Knoxville,* a portion of which was published in *The Yale Review* (March, 1938) under the title, "The Branner House". She attended Mount Holyoke College and the University of Chicago and in 1905 married Robert Franklin Armstrong. In 1915 she published anonymously her first novel, *The Seas of God,* which deals with the theme of the young girl from the provinces.

Near the end of World War I, Anne Armstrong began a career in business, serving from 1918 to 1919 as personnel director of National City Company of New York City. From 1919 to 1923, she was assistant manager for industrial relations for Eastman Kodak Company of Rochester, New York. She was the first woman to lecture before the business schools of Dartmouth and Harvard. Later in the 1920's she retired to the Big Creek section of SULLIVAN COUNTY, where she wrote *This Day and Time* (1930) and where she lived until forced to move by completion of the South Holston Dam. She then lived variously in BRISTOL, Tennessee; Lafayette, Louisiana; and Asheville, North Carolina, before moving in the late forties or early fifties to the Barter Inn at Abingdon, Virginia. There she lived until her death.

Mrs. Armstrong may legitimately be regarded as a pioneering woman in the world of business. In addition to working as a business executive, she lectured widely on the subject and recorded her views on business in practically every major periodical in the nation. She is also remembered as a personal friend of Thomas Wolfe, who visited her at Big Creek. Her "As I Saw Thomas Wolfe" (*Arizona Quarterly,* Spring, 1946) has been recognized for some time as a genuine contribution to the understanding of Wolfe's nature. Her perspective on social change taking place in the mountains in the thirties, including the TENNESSEE VALLEY AUTHORITY, can be found in "The Southern Mountaineers" (*The Yale Review,* March, 1935).

Mrs. Armstrong's most significant accomplishment, however, is likely to remain *This Day and Time,* an artistic and accurate account of life in the East Tennessee mountains immediately before the advent of TVA. The novel is remarkable for its detailed descriptions of mountain customs, dialect, and violence. Moreover, it may well be the first novel in the region to deal with the now familiar theme of the damming of the waters. *This Day and Time* was made into a play and perfomed at the Barter Theatre in 1958 under the title, *Some Sweet Day.*

Robert J. Higgs

Refer to: Anne Armstrong, *This Day and Time,* New York: Knopf, 1930 (Reprinted 1970, Johnson City, Tenn.: Research Advisory Council, East Tennessee State University, with a personal reminiscence by David McClellan).
See also: APPALACHIAN LITERATURE

Courtesy Smithsonian Institution National Anthropological Archives, Bureau of American Ethnology Collection

In 1730, Alexander Cuming brought seven Cherokee Indians to London. Attakullakulla, here called Ukwaneequa, is at the far right. Engraving by Isaac Basire, after a group portrait commissioned by the Duke of Montagu.

Attakullakulla, who was known to whites as Little Carpenter, was one of the principal chiefs of the CHEROKEES during the second and third quarters of the eighteenth century. He was born between 1700 and 1712 on the Big Island of the French Broad River, later called Sevier's Island. He was raised in the Cherokee villages along the banks of the Little Tennessee River. These were called the Overhill towns because they lay across the mountains from the Cherokee settlements in what are now the Carolinas. Throughout his life, Attakullakulla strove to establish and maintain the supremacy of the Overhills over both the Middle Settlements in southwestern North Carolina and the Lower Towns in upper South Carolina.

As the son of an important family, Attakullakulla probably was trained at an early age in the mysteries of statecraft and tribal tradition, but nothing is definitely known of him before 1730. In that year Attakullakulla, then a young man known as Okoonaka or White Owl, was among seven Cherokees who accompanied Sir Alexander Cuming to London to conclude a treaty of friendship and commerce with the British Crown. Attakullakulla arrived at Dover, England, on May 4, 1730. At Windsor Castle he was presented to King George II. He visited Canterbury Cathedral, the Tower of London, the Tottenham Court and Smithfield fairs, a fashionable spa, and other attractions. He also posed for a group portrait by Markham, which was engraved by Isaac Basire and sold as a print. On October 7, 1730 he embarked for America.

Attakullakulla had been greatly impressed by the power of Great Britain, and in 1736 he helped his people to resist overtures from the French. But three or four years later he was captured by the Ottowas, allies of the French, and was taken to Canada, where he remained in honorable captivity for seven years. When he returned to his homeland his Anglophilia had been neutralized. Attakullakulla came to believe that it was in the best interests of the Cherokees to play off the British and French against each other. The French, however, were chronically unable to supply the trade goods upon which the Indians had come to depend. Therefore Attakullakulla had to deal with the British, but he resolved to play off the British colony of Virginia against the British colony of South Carolina. At that time the latter had a monopoly on trade with the Cherokees, which had resulted in high prices, irregular supply, and dishonesty in the use of weights and measures.

In 1751 Attakullakulla traveled to Williamsburg in search of a new trading partner. Virginia did not respond, but the effort made South Carolina more responsive to Cherokee demands. In July of 1753, Attakullakulla met Governor Glen of South Carolina. Glen made promises which he did not keep, so Attakullakulla again approached Virginia, but without success. In June of 1755, he again met Glen. The Cherokees formally ceded their lands to the British Crown in exchange for Glen's promise to build a fort in the Overhills to facilitate trade, to confirm the supremacy of the Overhills in the Cherokee nation, and to offer protection against the French and their Indian allies. When Glen was unable to secure funds from his legislature to build a fort, Attakullakulla once again approached Virginia. The outbreak of the French and Indian War, and especially General Braddock's defeat, had made Virginia desperate for Indian assistance, so Virginia agreed to open trade with the Cherokees and to build a fort in the Overhills.

A small fort was built. But when Attakullakulla learned that the Virginians were not going to garrison it, he again turned to South Carolina. Governor Glen finally secured the money to build a fort, and in July of 1756 Attakullakulla met the fort-building expedition sent from Charleston. He escorted a portion of them to the Overhills, where construction began. Attakullakulla helped select the location of the fort, which was called FORT LOUDOUN. In 1757 he visited Governor Lyttelton, who had replaced Glen, and negotiated an agreement whereby Cherokee warriors would assist the British and colonials on the Virginia and Pennsylvania frontiers in exchange for improved trade and control by the

Overhills of all British gifts and supplies. Attakullakulla also agreed to undertake personally an expedition against the French on the Ohio River.

As time passed, Attakullakulla's predominant position in the tribe came to depend upon the continuance of the British alliance. Attakullakulla prevented a French alliance from being concluded, which raised him in the estimation of the British to such an extent that his reception in Charleston in January of 1758 was truly regal. But Anglo-Cherokee relations began to deteriorate. As Cherokee warriors passed to and from the Virginia and Pennsylvania frontiers, they often clashed with backcountry British settlers. The Cherokees stole horses and frightened settlers, and some Cherokee were killed in retaliation. Attakullakulla himself joined the British expedition across Pennsylvania to capture Fort Duquesne (Pittsburgh), but he had an immediate falling out with the British commander, General John Forbes, over what presents the Cherokees and other tribes were to receive. Attakullakulla finally left the expedition and was called a deserter by Forbes. Nonetheless, Attakullakulla favored continuation of the British alliance and kept his people fighting the French. He led a successful expedition against the French in the Illinois country.

While Attakullakulla was away on these expeditions, clashes between Cherokees and British settlers mounted. Attakullakulla negotiated a treaty with the British, but he could not enforce it because Cherokee hostility to the British was too intense. War soon broke out. To show his disapproval of Cherokee policy, Attakullakulla and his family went into the woods to live. Later he moved into Fort Loudoun, which was under siege by the Cherokees, and he contrived to get provisions smuggled into the fort. On June 2, 1760, he had to leave the fort, and that same day he was expelled from the Cherokee council. On August 7 Fort Loudoun capitulated, and two days later many of the survivors were massacred. At great expense Attakullakulla ransomed Captain John Stuart, the only British officer to survive the massacre. Then Attakullakulla and Stuart escaped to Virginia.

The British retaliated against the Cherokees in 1761 by destroying most of the Lower Towns and the Middle Settlements. Attakullakulla was recalled to power to negotiate a peace, which he did. He also persuaded the British Crown to appoint John Stuart as Superintendent for Southern Indian Affairs. In 1767 Attakullakulla traveled by land and sea to upstate New York, where he negotiated a peace with the Iroquois Confederacy, which had been at war with the Cherokees for several years. He returned by way of Fort Pitt, where he made peace with several western tribes.

After 1763, numerous whites crossed the Appalachians and settled on Cherokee lands. Attakullakulla resisted these encroachments whenever possible, but in 1772 he reluctantly agreed to lease land to THE WATAUGA ASSOCIATION. In March of 1775, he played a principal role in the sale of Kentucky and Middle Tennessee to Richard Henderson's Transylvania

Company. He reasoned that the whites would seize the land anyway if it was not sold to them, and he hoped to divert white settlement away from the Overhills. One Cherokee who bitterly denounced the sale was Attakullakulla's son DRAGGING CANOE. During the American Revolution Attakullakulla supported the British, who were not the threat to Cherokee civilization that the American settlers were. But when the heavy hand of American might reached deep into the Overhills, Attakullakulla was among those who agreed to peace at the Long Island of the Holston River in July of 1777. The last reference to Attakullakulla is in a letter dated 1778. It is believed that he died in 1780 or 1781.

One of Attakullakulla's objectives was to break the South Carolina trade monopoly. That was achieved at the end of the Cherokee War. Another objective was to insure that the leaders of the Overhill towns were accepted as the national leadership of the Cherokee nation. In that, too, Attakullakulla was successful. Another objective, adopted as early as 1750, was to avoid fighting the British, whom he had learned were best able to supply his people's needs. Here his success was mixed, but had he not prevented the Cherokees from joining the French during the early years of the French and Indian War, the result of that conflict might well have been different. When the Cherokees did fight the British, the French were already beaten. During the American Revolution, a civil war, it proved impossible to avoid fighting one element of the British: those who called themselves Americans.

Attakullakulla, a man of small stature and slightly built, had some command of English. He was a man of peace rather than of war. His success was built on diplomacy and oratory. Pleasant Henderson thought that "he was the most fluent, most graceful and eloquent orator he had heard." One authority has called him the only truly "noble savage" on the Southern colonial frontier. *The South Carolina Gazette* wrote that Attakullakulla's rescue of Stuart "evinced that an Indian can be friendly and humane in the strongest manner." On the racially troubled frontier, that was an important demonstration. His achievements were many and his fame was widespread. One contemporary recollected that in 1775 Attakullakulla had been "the most celebrated and influential Indian among the tribes then known."

James C. Kelly

Refer to: John R. Alden, *John Stuart and the Southern Colonial Frontier,* Ann Arbor: University of Michigan Press, 1944; John P. Brown, *Old Frontiers,* Kingsport, Tenn.: Kingsport Press, 1938; David Corkran, *The Cherokee Frontier: Conflict and Survival, 1740-1762,* Norman: University of Oklahoma Press, 1962; James C. Kelly, "Attakull-akulla," in *Journal of Cherokee Studies,* V. 3, No. 1 (Winter 1978), pp. 3-34; and William MacDowell, ed. *Colonial Records of South Carolina,* series 2, *Documents Relating to Indian Affairs, May 21, 1750 - August 7, 1754,* Columbia: South Carolina Historical Commission, 1958, and *Documents Relating to Indian Affairs, 1754-1765,* Columbia: South Carolina Historical Commission, 1962.

Austins Mill was one of HAWKINS COUNTY's earliest settlements. The community derived its name from the Austin family, owners of the flour mill on the Holston River, about one mile upstream from the bridge on the Rogersville-BULLS GAP branch of the Southern Railway. After selling the mill to E.M. Spears, the Austins moved from the county. Mr. Spears sold the mill to Alex McDonald, who came from nearby GREENE COUNTY around 1908, and the McDonalds operated the mill until the coming of the TENNESSEE VALLEY AUTHORITY. For a few years there was a generating plant at the mill, serving part of Rogersville's needs.

The greater part of activity around Austins Mill developed from the operation of a nearby concentration yard and shipping point. Lumber was rafted down the river from sawmills at KINGSPORT and Church Hill, then banked at the "Lumber Landing" on the farm of my great-uncle Alex Steele. His sons, Henry and George, loaded the lumber on wagons and hauled it a half-mile to the railroad station, no easy task in wet weather. Once, a wayward raft struck one of the piers of the railroad bridge, causing suspension of service until repairs could be made. Other unsawed timber was rafted past the Steele landing to KNOXVILLE.

The coming of the railroad from Moccasin Gap to Coran, paralleling the river, put a stop to the rafting of lumber. The landing, being of easy access, was in later years a favorite spot for Sunday afternoon baptizings in the then relatively unpolluted water. This custom gave way to the encroachment of Lake Cherokee. Another victim of the changing times was the ferry midway between the mill and the railroad bridge, operated by James Woods and his sons Hugh and "Chute". The building of a highway bridge at this site made the ferry obsolete. The Woods brothers remained at the site, fishing the river, and were a dependable source of supply for fresh catfish.

The community church, Spears' Chapel, was located on the Steele farm about a half-mile up the railroad from the station. It was on the Rogersville Circuit of the Methodist Church. The single-room Cedar Grove School was one of the early public schools of Hawkins County; Alex Steele was its first teacher. The school was only three miles from Rogersville, but later teachers boarded at the home of my grandmother, Mrs. Joseph J. Beal, returning to Rogersville only on weekends. Teachers' pay was low in those days, and travel difficult.

The mill, station, school and church are all gone. The railroad and bridge are still there, but the rails and steel work are rusted. The river is no longer a free flowing stream, but I have nostalgic memories of being lulled into restful sleep by the distant roar of the mill dam and the nearer murmur of the shoals below the bridge. The sound of live water is better than sleeping pills.

J.H. McCrary

See also: ALFRED BUFFAT HOMESTEAD AND MILL
THE HARRIS MILL
LOG RAFTS
LOYSTON
THE ONE-ROOM SCHOOL
RAILROADS
RELIGION

B

Bruce Barton (August 5, 1886 - July 5, 1967), cousin to Red Cross founder Clara Barton, was the eldest son of Rev. William E. Barton, a writer, historian, and circuit riding preacher in the service of the American Missionary Association. William Barton graduated from Berea College in June of 1885 and married Esther Treat Bushnell, a teacher from Ohio, the next month. The bride and groom made their new home in the small mountain community of Robbins, Tennessee, which Barton had visited two months earlier. Bruce was born in the Bartons' two-story white cottage.

The elder Barton's parish extended from Lancing to Pine Knot, Kentucky. He preached in almost every community where the trains stopped and in many others accessible only by horseback. In order to relieve part of his wife's burden, he frequently took Bruce on his travels. Thomas Hughes, seven miles away in RUGBY, once accompanied them to a black revival in a tobacco barn. The Bartons established the Pilgrim Congregational Church in Robbins in 1885 on land and with lumber donated by A.C. Ellis. The white frame church, with its belfry and tall spire, was the only church building in the immediate town until the Baptist Church was built in 1926.

The Bartons left Tennessee and moved to Oberlin, Ohio, when Bruce was one year old. Later the family moved to Boston, where Bruce attended grammar school. He went to high school in Oak Park, Illinois, and became the editor of the school paper as well as a successful distributor of his uncles' maple syrup. For his freshman year, Bruce attended Berea College in Kentucky, where he and his cousin began a school magazine called "The Josher." Barton spent his remaining college years at Amherst. There he edited the school magazine and was head of the student government association and the college's Christian Association. He declined both valedictorian honors and a fellowship for graduate study.

After work in Montana as a construction timekeeper, Bruce Barton went to Chicago as an advertising salesman for a group of household magazines. The company failed, and Barton traveled on to New York. He worked for *Collier's* in several capacities and became widely known for his editorials. He volunteered for World War I and organized massive charity drives for such organizations as the Y.M.C.A. and the Salvation Army. Barton is credited with the slogan, "A man may be down, but he is never out."

In 1919 Bruce Barton, Roy S. Durstine, and Alex F. Osborne pooled their experience in advertising and opened their own agency with a $10,000 loan. They merged in 1928 with George Batten to form Batten, Barton, Durstine and Osborne, Inc. Their success soon placed them as the fourth largest advertising agency in the world. Barton was a U.S. Representative from Manhattan's East Side "Silk Stocking" District between 1937 and 1941. His opposition to New Deal policies, along with that of House Speaker Joseph Martin and Rep. Hamilton Fishall, earned the enthusiastic enmity of Democrats. President Roosevelt referred in speeches to the mythical firm of "Martin, Barton, and Fish."

Bruce Barton never became the minister his father had hoped for, yet he did "minister" in a different way. He was a prolific writer of books and articles. His *The Man Nobody Knows* (1924), a biography of Christ written as an analysis of a modern-day business executive, headed best seller lists for two years. Other books included *The Book Nobody Knows* (1926) and *What Can A Man Believe* (1927).

Bruce Barton never forgot his East Tennessee roots. In 1926 the community of Robbins broke ground for a new church. Dr. William Barton was present to lay the cornerstone of the building that would bear his name, Barton Chapel. The ceremony began in the Robbins School auditorium, with Rev. F.P. Ensminger, state superintendent, presiding. The student body, faculty, and friends then marched to the church site. There Dr. Barton presented the building fund two $500 checks, one from himself and the other from his son.

Dr. Barton died in New York in 1930. Bruce Barton retired as Chairman of the Board of Batten, Barton, Durstine and Osborne in 1961, but maintained an office in the agency's Madison Avenue headquarters. The last surviving founder of the agency, Barton died in his New York home at the age of 80.

Jean K. Phillips

Refer to: Bruce Barton, *The Man Nobody Knows*, Indianapolis: Bobbs-Merrill, 1924 and *The Autobiography of William E. Barton*, Indianapolis: Bobbs-Merrill, 1932.
See also: RELIGION

Beersheba Springs, a renowned summer resort whose heyday was in the late 1850's, has been called "queen of the hill country in Tennessee," for its elegance far surpassed other summering places in the state during that era. This mid-19th century spa was developed in Tennessee's lower Cumberland Mountains and had several brilliant seasons before the War Between the States stopped its growth. The small community, 20 miles southeast of McMinnville and on the edge of GRUNDY COUNTY's Broad Mountain, now has 560 permanent residents. Summer visitors, however, continue to swell the population as they did more than a century ago, and the old hotel and about twenty spacious cottages built in the mid-1850's have been preserved.

Beersheba Springs began when a

prominent McMinnville merchant, John Cain, built several log cabins near a large iron springs in 1834. This chalybeate spring, found by Cain's wife Beersheba in 1833, became noted in a short time for its medicinal value, and early settler William Dugan sold adjacent property for a rough tavern and additional cabins. Other settlers also moved into the Collins River Valley in the early 1800's. Old Indian trails, including the famous Chickamauga Trace which ran a short distance from Beersheba, were used by arriving pioneers, and it is thought that Mrs. Cain followed an Indian path on the mountain to discover the famous spring. Tennessee's General Assembly incorporated Beersheba Springs' 1,000 acres in 1839 and authorized a turnpike between the resort and present-day CHATTANOOGA.

Guests' accommodations were fairly primitive until John Armfield of Virginia acquired the resort in 1854. A former slave trader, Armfield became absorbed in developing Beersheba Springs; he built elegant summer cottages in addition to the 400-guest white-pillared hotel which still stands. At the hotel, Armfield employed a French chef, servants, and a French band from New Orleans. This band played at dances and as guests came by public coach up the mountain's sharp turns and steep grades. At rests for the horses, the coachman sounded his horn for each arriving guest so that accommodations would be ready. Private coaches also brought wealthy families and their retinue to enjoy the famous spa and the mountain air. Available entertainments included fox hunts, card games, billiards, dancing, bowling, walks, and association with the other visitors.

Beersheba Springs became a refuge for many people during the CIVIL WAR, for the community's location halfway between Chattanooga and Nashville placed it in both armies' line of march. Unwelcome intruders were bushwhackers from both armies who invaded Beersheba at frequent intervals with great damage to the hotel and cottages. On one occasion, horsemen rode pell-mell up and down the hotel's long lower gallery. Area people pillaged the empty hotel and those cottages not occupied.

The resort has fascinated writers for over a century. Many stories and books have been based on the area and its people. One of the best known authors, a summer resident for many years, was MARY MURFREE, who wrote under the pen name of Charles Egbert Craddock. Murfree's books and short stories, with Beersheba as a model, were international favorites in the late 1880's. Mrs. Lucy Virginia French, Miss Will Allen Dromgoole, Elizabeth Wilkins Purnell, Blanche Spurlock Bentley, Alfred Leland Crabb, and Isabel Howell have written about Beersheba Springs. Poets exalting the area have included Robert Sparks Walker and contemporary Beersheba native, Leonard Tate.

Beersheba Springs has been touched by nearby communities and their people. In 1867, a Swiss farming colony located at nearby Gruetli. Captain E.H. Plumacher, colony founder, built his home at Beersheba; his descendents still live there. Through John Armfield's influence, the UNIVERSITY OF THE

SOUTH was located at nearby Sewanee in 1860. Epsicopal bishops Leonidas Polk and James H. Otey owned cottages at Beersheba, and the charter of the university was drawn up at the resort in the summer of 1859. When Grundy County was first formed in 1844, even the county courts were held at Beersheba until a permanent county seat was selected.

Today, Beersheba has a library, a post office and several businesses. The old iron spring has had little water flow since road building in the 1920's. Due to landslides, White's Spring behind the Armfield house no longer flows, but Indian Spring on Backbone Road still produces water. The hotel was bought in the early 1940's by the Tennessee Conference of the United Methodist Church and is operated as an assembly ground.

The back of the hotel, with its Brick Row, Log Row, Cross Row, Smoky Row, and Post Office Row, forms an open courtyard where activities occurred during the resort's prosperity. This courtyard is now the scene of Beersheba Springs' Annual Arts and Crafts Show. Legends of Beersheba tell of Armfield's slave, Nathan, buried near his master; of the letter written by a Federal soldier and hidden in a cabin wall; of the slave cemetery disturbed when a modern chicken house was built; of slaves dancing in a building over the iron spring; of valuables hidden from marauders, and of Beersheba's haunted house. Beersheba Springs is listed in the National Register of Historic Places, and a local historical society is being formed. Despite modern inroads, perhaps the relics and recollections of the past will remain so that future generations can better understand and cherish the history of Beersheba Springs.

Patricia A. Shirley

Refer to: Will Allen Dromgoole, *The Sunny Side of the Cumberland: A Story of the Mountains*, Philadelphia: J.B. Lippincott, 1886; Georgianna D. Overby, ed. "Historical Beersheba Springs," *Warren County News*, October 15, 1979, pp. 1B-4B; and Elizabeth Wilkins Purnell, *John Gamp: Or, Coves and Cliffs of the Cumberlands*, Nashville: Gospel Advocate Publishing Company, 1901.

See also: DUPONT SPRINGS
THE UNINVITED

Big Orange Football. In 1899 *Harper's Weekly* complained that college football was no longer amateur, that schools were plagued by eligibility problems and that amateur ideals were being subverted. The desire to win, said the magazine, was too great. Sound familiar? Of course. Intercollegiate football started in 1869 when Rutgers defeated Princeton, 6-4. The game has been in turmoil almost ever since.

Major universities and colleges periodically deplore football's bigness and its influence on the alumni. But only occasionally has anyone taken strong action against the sport. In 1939 Dr. Robert M. Hutchins thought he had the only solution: abolish football, which he did at the University of Chicago. In 1906 President Theodore Roosevelt told the schools to clean up the sport and to cut out the mayhem and brutality, or else he would eliminate it. That led to the forward pass and more finesse. College football mushroomed in the wild and high-stepping 1920's, in the heyday of the speakeasy, easy money, Al Capone,

Courtesy Neal O'Steen, University of Tennessee

The University of Tennessee's second football team, 1892.

Babe Ruth and Bobby Jones. Huge football arenas were built. Notre Dame went "national" with Knute Rockne and the Four Horsemen, and Illinois featured Red Grange, the Galloping Ghost. And the most coveted prize in the football world was an invitation to the Rose Bowl in Pasadena.

Football at the UNIVERSITY OF TENNESSEE surfaced 90 years ago, as a sort of club team that struggled along as best it could. The first real prominence came in 1914 when the Volunteers under Coach Zora G. Clevenger first defeated Vanderbilt, 16 to 14. The Vols defeated Vanderbilt again in 1916, skipped the World War I years, then reorganized with so-so success in the early 1920's. But as the game grew, the interest of Tennessee fans was strongly kindled for the first time. A stadium was built and 3,200 seats erected. In 1925 Coach M.B. Banks hired an end coach from West Point, one Robert Reese Neyland, an Army captain who doubled as an ROTC instructor. Captain Neyland replaced Banks as head coach in 1926, a development that was to have a profound effect on football at the school, in the South, and, as we shall see, the nation. Neyland's first product in 1926 lost one game, that to Vanderbilt, 20-3. Tennessee did not lose again until 1930, an 18-6 setback to Alabama. The third loss did not come until 1933. From 1926 to 1932, Tennessee lost just two games out of 68. By 1932, Neyland had established himself as the scourge of southern football. Never again was Vanderbilt a bar to football success as far as Tennessee was concerned. In fact, victories over Vanderbilt became routine, and Alabama supplanted the once-mighty Commodores as *the* game on the Tennessee schedule.

Tennessee, it so happened, had hired a man gifted in the stratagems of football. The wiry Texan, a 1916 graduate of West Point, had soaked up the fundamentals of the game from his superiors at his alma mater, where he had also served as an aide to the Superintendent, General Douglas MacArthur. Taking over in 1926 at the age of 34, Neyland quickly applied to football the tactics and strategy of the military. His bedrock was the belief that the young men who play football make dozens of mistakes, just as soldiers do in fighting a war. His job, he figured out, was to (1) eliminate all mistakes possible, (2) accept those you do make, and (3) be ready to capitalize on the mistakes of the foe. Neyland made the point over and over that the team must have the poise and character to rise above the inevitable mistakes, accept them as part of the game, and be even tougher in such trying moments. Neyland was the master of the psychology of football. In addition, he stressed speed, mobility, the surprise thrust, and the defense that bends but does not break. Bear Bryant, Alabama and Kentucky coach who failed to beat Neyland in eight tries, once observed, "General Neyland doesn't throw the ball much but when he does he hurts you."

Neyland coached Tennessee for 21 years, missing 1935 on military duty in Panama, and 1941-45 in World War II. He retired after the 1952 season, remaining as athletic director. Coach Neyland died 10 years later. His legacy was a single wing offense that was the picture of precision and timing, plus a defensive philosophy that was to be copied all over the country. Also, he produced dozens of head coaches: Bobby Dodd at Georgia Tech; Bowden Wyatt at Wyoming, Arkansas and Tennessee; Murray Warmath at Mississippi State and Minnesota; Herman Hickman at Yale; John Barnhill at Arkansas; Phil Dickens at Wofford, Wyoming and Indiana; Bill Meek at Kansas State, Houston and Southern Methodist; Harvey Robinson at Tennessee; Bill Barnes at UCLA; Ray Graves at Florida; Beattie Feathers at North Carolina State; Ralph Hatley at Memphis State; Allyn McKeen at Mississippi State; and Jim Myers at Iowa State and Texas A & M.

Neyland's 1951 team won the national championship, and his teams appeared in all of the major bowls. Tennessee football success was hit-or-miss in the Wyatt years, 1955-62, after which Jim McDonald handled the team for one year. Doug Dickey gave Tennessee excellent teams in 1966-69, beating Alabama three times and going to four bowl games. The 1970's left Tennessee football sagging. In Bill Battle's seven-year stint the Vols slid badly, mainly at the hands of Alabama, which won nine straight from UT during the decade. John Majors, who came in as head coach in 1977, is charged with putting Tennessee back on top. Meanwhile, the football faithful have run a true course. The arena that began modestly with a capacity of 3,200 now seats 91,249, second largest in the country behind only Michigan.

College football becomes more of a mania each year. Periodically, educators admit the game has gotten too big for its britches, but talk of reform is about like "balancing the budget". After the great football surge of the 1920's the Carnegie Foundation, in its famous Bulletin 23, recommended that schools cut back, use student coaches, and concentrate more on education and less on filling the stadium. But nothing came of that. Every few years now, a spate of evil doing (falsifying transcripts, recruiting excesses, etc.) brings the educators out of their leather-padded swivel chairs. But they soon sit back down, knowing that their own alumni would be most upset by drastic reform. Football today is a national obsession, and almost nowhere is it more of an obsession than at Tennessee—where football income, for the most part, funds an athletic budget of $7.5 million, where football-mad alumni are among the most generous givers in the nation, and where the record over the years indicates that the school's program is one of the cleanest in the nation.

Tom Siler

Refer to: Thomas T. Siler, *Tennessee: Football's Greatest Dynasty*, Knoxville: Holston, 1961 and *Tennessee's Dazzling Decade, 1960-1970*, Knoxville: Hodge, 1970.

Big Orange Football action during Volunteer - Yellow Jacket homecoming game, November 9, 1957. Final score: Tennessee 21, Georgia Tech 6.

Courtesy University of Tennessee Photo Services

The Blacksmith Preacher. One of the most famous turn-of-the-century evangelists in East Tennessee was the Rev. J. T. "Tom" Sexton, who was known as the "Blacksmith Preacher". A native of BLOUNT COUNTY, Sexton began his ministry within six months after his conversion in 1888 at age 32. While preaching over much of East and Middle Tennessee and holding evangelistic meetings in Kentucky, Virginia, and Texas, Sexton claimed the conversion of over 8,000 souls. He stated his method as follows: "I call people to the altar and let them and their God settle it."

In his 1906 autobiography, *From the Anvil to the Pulput,* Sexton described his conversion at a revival meeting in Morganton, a small LOUDON COUNTY town on the Little Tennessee River. Sexton had been living with his family in the county seat of Loudon, where he operated a successful blacksmith business. Mrs. Sexton persuaded her husband to move to Morganton, because he had a heavy drinking problem and the town of Loudon had many saloons. The Sextons lived at Morganton for almost two years before the Rev. John Kittrell came to hold a meeting at the small community church. Morganton's church was located near Sexton's shop. Sexton later wrote that he told a friend, "Kittrell might hold his meetings, but I will hold my jug and blacksmith shop." During daytime services Sexton would beat his anvil, even when he had no work to do, in order to drown out the preacher's voice.

Many people urged Tom Sexton to attend Kittrell's meetings, and he finally did. He went to the mourner's bench at several services before he was finally saved. Soon after his conversion, his wife began to teach him to read the Bible. Not long afterward, he began his fruitful ministry as the "Blacksmith Preacher." During the first year of his ministry, Sexton alternated between preaching for two weeks and shoeing horses for two weeks in order to support his family. His preaching that year earned him $32. Finally he gave up his shop and became a full time evangelist.

A large portly man, Sexton was a powerful figure in the pulpit. A colleague described Sexton's preaching in this way: "Some of his character pictures and illustrations are vivid as lightning and as powerful as a moral cyclone. He does not stick to his text, but he sticks to his crowd and always moves them." During the course of his ministry, Sexton and his family moved to KNOXVILLE. There he became a member of the First Baptist Church, and eventually of Broadway Baptist Church. His autobiography contains many testimonials from friends, including Governor Robert L. Taylor.

Beulah A. Davis

Refer to: Rev. J.T. Sexton, *From the Anvil to the Pulpit,* Knoxville: S.B. Newman and Company, 1906.
See also: RELIGION
BOB AND ALF TAYLOR: KNIGHTS OF THE ROSES.

Bledsoe County
Size: 404 Square Miles (258,560 acres)
Established: 1807
Named For: Anthony Bledsoe, Major in the American Revolution

County Seat: Pikeville
Other Major Cities, Towns, or Communities:
Pailo
Brayton
Sampson
Melvine
Old Cumberland
See also: STATE PARKS

Courtesy Tennessee State Library

William Blount

William Blount (March 26, 1749 - March 21, 1800), pioneer speculator and politician, was born and raised near New Bern in eastern North Carolina. William Masterson, in his masterful biography of Blount, states that Blount's life and interests typify, above all, those of the American businessman. Blount was the son of Barbara Gray Blount, daughter of Scotsman John Gray, and of Jacob Blount, an Episcopalian farmer, miller, and slaveowner. In May of 1771, William, his brother John Gray, and his father Jacob participated in the Battle of Alamance—on the side of the British Crown, against the frustrated "Regulators" from the West. Four years later, as the Blounts moved cautiously to join America's thrust for independence, William traveled west and bought acreage in his friend Richard Henderson's Transylvania enterprise. During the Revolutionary War, William prospered in his various roles as paymaster, commodity merchant, and land speculator.

In 1778, William Blount married Mary Grainger, daughter of a merchant, and moved to Martinsborough. Three years later, he began his political career as a representative in the North Carolina legistature. His and his brother's land speculations continued, and by the end of the Revolution, their interest in business expansion and personal profit coincided with veterans' desire for western land and with the young country's thirst for development. Throughout the 1780's, William Blount capitalized on such frontier connections as JOHN SEVIER, who with Blount pushed legitimation of their land acquisitions and corresponding subjugation of the CHEROKEES; John Haywood, North Carolina Treasurer, who preferentially lent state funds to Blount; and John Donelson, who with his son Stockley Donelson was Blount's partner and land agent-surveyor.

In June of 1790, President George Washington appointed Blount Governor of the Territory South of the River Ohio. The next June, Blount effected THE TREATY OF HOLSTON at White's Fort. This fort was the site of Blount's new territorial capital, which he named KNOXVILLE. He and his wife moved to a log house there early the next spring. Their two-story frame mansion, overlooking the Tennessee River, was completed later in 1792. Governor Blount secretly sanctioned a 1794 military expedition against the Chickamaugas. This expedition, led by Major James Ore yet surreptitiously organized by General James Roberston, dealt a death blow to the power of DRAGGING CANOE'S successor John Watts and his fighting Cherokee remnant. Blount also supported statehood, and following a 1796 constitutional convention assembled in Knoxville for this purpose, Blount exchanged his territorial governorship for a seat in the U.S. Senate.

As one of Tennessee's first two Senators, William Blount set into motion what has become known as "the Blount conspiracy". Anxious to preserve his western lands from the threat of French control, Blount interested British officials, as well as powerful friends up and down the frontier, in attacking New Orleans. Unfortunately for Blount, political enemies discovered one of his letters outlining the scheme. In July of 1797, the U.S. Senate heard this letter, and Blount was soon expelled from that body. Blount returned to Knoxville and, aided by such henchmen as Andrew Jackson, Charles McClung, James White and son Hugh Lawson White, reforged a state political base. Blount died in a fever epidemic and was buried in the cemetery of the First Presbyterian Church.

Jim Stokely

Refer to: William H. Masterson, *William Blount,* Baton Rouge: Louisiana State University Press, 1954.

Blount County

Size: 575 Square Miles (368,000 acres)

Established: 1795

Named For: William Blount, Governor of the Territory South of the River Ohio.

County Seat: Maryville

Other Major Cities, Towns, or Communities:

ALCOA
FRIENDSVILLE
Rockford
Townsend
Shooks Gap
Louisville
Walland
Chilhowee

Refer to: Inez Burns, *History of Blount County, Tennessee, from War Trail to Landing Strip, 1795-1955,* Nashville: Tennessee Historical Commission, 1957.

See also: ALUMINUM CORPORATION OF AMERICA
THE BLACKSMITH PREACHER
CADES COVE
GREAT SMOKY MOUNTAINS NATIONAL PARK
MARYVILLE COLLEGE
WILLIAM A. MCCALL

Bluegrass Music is an acoustical string-band type of music which usually features a prominent three-finger Scruggs style banjo and some combination of guitar, fiddle, mandolin, and string bass. Many groups also feature the resonator or Dobro guitar played in an Hawaiian style. Solo vocals may vary from a smooth country sound to a high lonesome mountain wail. The musicians sing frequent duets, trios, and sometimes quartets. The range of

Courtesy Will Parham Photographs, C.M. McClung Historical Collection, Lawson McGhee Library

Maryville, 1921.

bluegrass songs may extend from traditional ballads to modern rock.

Bluegrass represents a modernization of the older tradition of mountain string bands. Bill Monroe, a western Kentucky native who in the late 1930's played on RADIO stations in the Carolinas with his brother Charlie, is generally considered the major innovator in the development of the music. By 1945 the style had evolved in Monroe's band while playing at WSM Nashville. The Blue Grass Boys then consisted of Bill Monroe on mandolin, Chubby Wise on fiddle, Howard Watts on bass, and Lester Flatt (from Sparta, Tennessee) on guitar. Although some Carolina bands had earlier moved in a direction approaching bluegrass, the Monroe sound reached a national audience and gave the music a wide following. Other musicians rather quickly emulated that sound. While working at WCYB Bristol, the Stanley Brothers from Virginia altered their format slightly and by 1947 became the second bluegrass band.

East Tennessee, which already possessed a rich traditional folk music heritage, rapidly became a major center of bluegrass. Knoxville's two radio stations—WNOX and WROL—already featured generous amounts of live country entertainment and, like WCYB Bristol, became a key base for several early groups and individual musicians. Some of these bands, with a prior existence as tradition-oriented country aggregations, simply evolved into bluegrass. Among the first to do so were the Bailey Brothers (Charlie and Danny) and their Happy Valley Boys. Natives of HAWKINS COUNTY, the Bailey Brothers worked from 1939 onward as professional musicians at radio stations in BRISTOL, KINGSPORT, ELIZABETHTON, KNOXVILLE, and Nashville. By 1947, the Baileys added a banjo and went bluegrass. Although they did not record extensively, Charlie and Danny achieved tremendous popularity on radio and in personal appearances. They have been credited with merging the smooth harmony duet tradition of the 1930's with bluegrass. The Baileys also served notable radio stints in Raleigh, Roanoke, and Wheeling.

Carl Story and the Rambling Mountaineers constituted another early band which evolved into a bluegrass format. Story, a North Carolina native, tended to alternate his major base among the cities of Asheville, Charlotte, and Knoxville. But he undoubtedly enjoyed his peak years in the latter location, where he performed on WNOX's Mid-Day Merry-Go-Round and the Tennessee Barn Dance. The group became especially known for high quality quartets and helped to bring to prominence such outstanding musicians as William "Red" Rector, Claude Boone, and the Brewster Brothers. Unlike the Baileys, Carl Story managed to record quite extensively. Carl and J.P. Sauceman and their Hillbilly Ramblers/Green Valley Boys made up another pioneer bluegrass group which worked extensively on both Knoxville and Bristol radio. The Saucemans from GREENE COUNTY did not record extensively, but they managed to get on some major labels as well as the small but influential Rich-R—Tone label which waxed several East Tennessee groups. In 1948, Lester Flatt teamed up with Earl Scruggs to form the most popular band of all. Flatt and Scruggs gained their reputation and first fame on stations like WCYB and WROL prior to their Grand Ole Opry and Martha White Show stardom.

Numerous other key musicians either came from East Tennessee backgrounds or gained valuable experience in radio at Knoxville and Bristol. Those in the former category are led by Sneedville's Jimmy Martin. After a brief experience in Knoxville, Martin worked several years with Bill Monroe, then went on his own, and subsequently became one of the music's most significant lead singers. Sparta's Benny Martin ranks among the most influential bluegrass fiddlers, despite his frequent forays into more contemporary forms of COUNTRY MUSIC. Dobro expert Josh Graves worked on WROL for several years with the Esco Hankins band.

Those key musicians in the latter category include Virginians like Mac Wiseman, who gained valuable early experience on both Bristol's Farm and Fun Time and Knoxville's Mid-Day Merry-Go-Round prior to his later successes in Richmond and Nashville; fiddler Clarence "Tater" Tate, who worked many years as a sideman with several of the aforementioned groups; and Jim and Jesse McReynolds, who also worked at both WCYB and WNOX. Although gaining most of their fame in country music, both Carl Butler and Don Gibson came from Knoxville bluegrass backgrounds. Speedy Krise, a West Virginian playing at WNOX with Jack Shelton and his Greene County Boys and recording with Carl Butler in 1950, apparently introduced the Dobro into bluegrass, although Josh Graves popularized it some years later as a member of the Flatt and Scruggs band. East Tennessee songwriters like Arthur Q. Smith and Ruby Moody have composed some of the best bluegrass lyrics ever written.

In more recent years, a variety of older and newer musicians have continued to maintain East Tennessee's reputation as an important center for bluegrass music. Television shows sponsored by Cas Walker utilize the talents of mandolin virtuoso Red Rector along with Danny Bailey, Claude Boone, comedian Fred Smith, and banjoist Dave West. An important husband-wife duet, Bonnie Lou and Buster Moore, have for some 35 years featured a mixture of bluegrass and country music on Knoxville radio, JOHNSON CITY television, the syndicated Jim Walter Jubilee shows, and their live concerts at the Pigeon Forge Coliseum. Among newer groups the Pinnacle Boys, made up of a combination of established musicians like Larry Mathis and Bud Brewster together with younger ones

Courtesy Country Music Foundation Library and Media Center, Nashville, Tennessee

Carl Story and the Rambling Mountaineers at the WIVK radio studios in Knoxville, 1956. Left to right: Willie Brewster, Claude Boone, Carl Story, Bud Brewster.

such as Jerry Moore, Randall Collins and Jim Smith, have attained a wide following. Most recently, the youthful Knoxville Grass have attracted much attention and have successfully toured Europe. One can easily conclude that, from the very beginning, East Tennessee as a region—with its musical heritage and talented vocalists and creative instrumentalists—has been a major factor in the continuing development of bluegrass music as a uniquely American folk-art form.

Ivan M. Tribe

Refer to: Bob Artis, *Bluegrass,* New York: Hawthorn Books, 1975.

Daniel Boone. Although Daniel Boone is most closely connected with the history and settlement of Kentucky, the famous frontiersman explored and lived in many other regions as well. Born in Berks County, Pennsylvania in 1734, he ventured as far south as Pensacola, Florida about the time of his thirty-first birthday, and he died in Missouri in 1820 after residing for twenty-one years in that territory. Together with Virginia, North Carolina, and Detroit as boundaries, these areas roughly delineate that portion of the United States which can lay claim to Daniel Boone.

Relatively speaking, Boone spent few of his eighty-six years in East Tennessee. It was, however, one of his favorite hunting grounds before the outbreak of the Revolutionary War, his place of residence by 1772, and the scene of one of his most significant accomplishments—the bringing of the Indians to the Treaty of Sycamore Shoals to negotiate with Richard Henderson and his Transylvania Company for the purchase of Kentucky.

Boone's first documented hunting trip into East Tennessee occurred in 1760. Because of Indian hostilities he had previously moved with his wife Rebecca and his two young sons, James and Israel, from their home on Sugar Tree Creek in the Yadkin River region of North Carolina to the safety of Culpepper County, Virginia. Daniel, however, always appeared to be too restless to enjoy the farmer's or tradesman's life that was his lot in Virginia. During a temporary cessation of hostilities, he plunged into his beloved wilderness and made his first journey across the Blue Ridge, penetrating as far as Boone's Creek in present WASHINGTON COUNTY, Tennessee. About a hundred miles from the Cherokee towns on the Little Tennessee River, he carved the now famous 14-by-19-inch inscription: "D. Boon cilled a Bar on tree in the year 1760." The hunting was fine.

Boone soon joined Colonel High Waddell in a campaign against the CHEROKEES and was present on November 19, 1760, for the signing of the peace treaty at Fort Robinson, a newly constructed outpost on the Long Island of the Holston River. Daniel indulged in another hunt after Waddell's regiment disbanded. At the head of a group of Yadkin men, he again roamed through East Tennessee and then into southwestern Virginia until the spring of 1761. One of his companions was Nathaniel Gist, the son of Christopher Gist, Washington's famous scout.

Sometime after his return to North Carolina from his trip to Florida on Christmas day, 1765, Boone made the acquaintance of Benjamin Cutbirth, who married his niece, Elizabeth Wilcoxen. Boone, a lover of solitude, found in his new relative one of his few compatible hunting companions. They ranged far and wide in the North Carolina-Tennessee-Virginia area and frequently met parties of Indian hunters who were angered by their trespassing and by the duo's considerable success in killing game. On one such trip, after they had completed an exceedingly fine hunt, a party of Cherokees attacked their camp on Roane's Creek, a tributary of the Watauga in East Tennessee, and robbed them of everything they possessed. It was a risk all hunters knowingly took when they plunged into the wilderness; this time Boone and Cutbirth lost their wager with luck, but escaped unharmed.

Another interesting anecdote recounts one of Daniel's easier escapes during a 1768 hunting foray into the Watauga region. One winter night, camping alone near the present city of JONESBORO in East Tennessee, he was aroused from a deep sleep when his snow-covered blanket was gently raised by a Cherokee brave. The warrior recognized Boone and delightedly exclaimed "Ah, Wide-Mouth, have I got you now?" Undaunted, Daniel got up and gave each of the band a hearty handshake and stated how happy he was to see his red brothers. After exchanging civilities, news and comments on the hunting, Boone was

Courtesy Tennessee State Library

Engraving of Daniel Boone.

allowed to depart. He lost no time in putting a considerable distance between himself and his "brothers".

The ensuing period from May 1, 1769, when Boone and his party set out to explore Kentucky, until his return in the summer of 1771, comprises a well-known history that needs no further comment. The expedition was a mixed blessing. When Daniel arrived back in the Upper Yadkin to greet his family, he had seen Kentucky and recognized its potential, but was deeper in debt than when he left to find the Cumberland Gap.

Little information has survived about the next two years in Boone's life. He farmed and in season often went hunting with an old weaver named Joe Robertson, who owned a celebrated pack of bear dogs. They hunted in the Brushy Mountain and Watauga areas and once ventured as far as the French

Lick (Nashville) on the Cumberland before returning with a load of skins. Daniel no doubt also sounded the Cherokees' willingness to sell Kentucky and became convinced that the country could be purchased. Daniel had changed his residence by 1722 to Sapling Grove in what is now Tennessee, but he eventually moved back to the Yadkin. Store accounts indicate that his food purchases in Tennessee were for a family. They also dispel the contention of Boone's early biographer, John Mason Peck, that the pioneer never indulged in strong drink. An entry for January 25, 1773 read "2 quarts of Rum."

In the autumn of 1774, Henderson and Captain Nathaniel Hart visited the Cherokee nation and confirmed Boone's reports that Kentucky could indeed be purchased. Henderson's Transylvania Company wished to buy twenty million acres of land, nearly all of the present states of Kentucky and Tennessee, and to found the fourteenth colony, to be called Transylvania. Matters progressed swiftly in negotiations. February or March was set as the time for the bargaining groups to meet to sign a treaty at Sycamore Shoals on the Watauga River. Chief ATTAKULLAKULLA (Leaning Wood), renowned for his wisdom, accompanied the Transylvania partners to Cross-Creek (now Fayetteville, North Carolina) to examine the goods offered for the land. The merchandise was shipped to the Watauga on December 6.

During the winter, Boone toured the Cherokee towns and convinced a thousand to twelve hundred Indians to attend the March treaty. Daniel negotiated the boundaries of the purchase and was sure enough of the completion of the sale to have begun assembling woodsmen at the Long Island of the Holston River in order to cut the Wilderness Road.

At Sycamore Shoals, the goods were set in plain sight and, although no inventory has survived, were said to have "filled a house." Henderson anticipated no dissent and was taken aback when DRAGGING CANOE, an influential young chief, spoke out vehemently against the treaty. His keen eye had seen that the offered treasure, the equivalent of 10,000 pounds sterling or about $50,000, was not a fair price for the land. The next day, March 15, Dragging Canoe and the other opposing chiefs gave in to the demands of the young braves for the finery and some quantity of ammunition that lay tantalizingly before them. The treaty-deed, called "The Great Grant," was signed on March 17, 1775. It gave "Henderson and company the tract of country from the mouth of the Kentucky or Louisa River to the head spring of its most northerly fork, thence south-easterly to the top of Powell's Mountain, and thence, first westerly, and then north-westerly, to the head spring of the most southerly branch of the Cumberland River, and down that stream, including all its waters, to the Ohio, and up the Ohio to the mouth of the Kentucky." Henderson then stated that he wished to purchase a right-of-way from the Holston River to "The Great Grant" and, after some brief haggling, terms for "The Path Deed" were also agreed to.

At one point early in the negotiations,

when the purchase seemed sure, Boone was taken aside by Dragging Canoe and told: "Brother, we have given you a fine land, but I believe you will have much trouble in settling it." To this prophetic chief was also attributed the remark that "There was a dark cloud over that country." No one recognized how true the two statements would prove to be. Boone, undaunted, left for the Long Island of the Holston to mobilize his axmen before the treaty was ratified.

Thirty armed backwoodsmen warmly greeted Boone's arrival. Among those present were Squire Boone, Michael Stoner, Benjamin Cutbirth, Colonel Richard Callaway, David Gass, William Bush, Captain William Twitty, and Felix Walker, who chronicled the expedition. When on March 10, 1775, the woods began to resound with the ring of axes, the Wilderness Road began, but Daniel Boone's last documented stay in East Tennessee came to an end. He undoubtedly wandered and hunted again in this region before his remove to Missouri in 1799, but he left no evidence of such visits. Nonetheless, his fifteen-year intermittent association with East Tennessee was a significant and fruitful phase of his gradual migration to the west. As in other areas, he took his living and his pleasure from these lands and, though retreating from civilization, paved the way for future pioneers who would share in the same bounty of nature that he once enjoyed.

Michael A. Lofaro

Refer to: John Bakeless, *Daniel Boone: Master of the Wilderness,* New York: William Morrow, 1939 (reprinted 1965, Harrisburg, Pennsylvania: Stackpole Books); Lyman C. Draper, Mss. Collection, State Historical Society of Wisconsin, 486 Volumes (See especially Series B, Draper's "Life of Boone," 5 Volumes); and Michael A. Lofaro, *The Life and Adventures of Daniel Boone,* Lexington: University Press of Kentucky, 1978.
See Also: DAVID CROCKETT

John Bowers (March 12, 1928 -), writer, son of Tip Richard and Stella Swafford Bowers, was born in Lenoir City, Tennessee, in a house on Third Avenue. At the age of three, he moved with his family to JOHNSON CITY. He attended public schools there. When he was about 14, he saw the most popular girl in school looking over a classmate's shoulder, admiring the latter's handwritten story. Bowers read the story, liked it, and decided that he wanted to be a writer. When his mother learned that her son wanted to write, she bought him a typewriter and took him to a local business school so that he could learn to type.

Bowers graduated from THE UNIVERSITY OF TENNESSEE in 1951. During the late 1950's, he worked in Washington as a personnel officer for the U.S. State Department. He later moved to New York City, did magazine work, and wrote three novels published during the 1970's. *The Colony* describes life in a writer's colony. *No More Reunions* is about growing up in East Tennessee. *Helene* concerns itself with Washington, D.C. John Bowers married Liz Harris, who reviewed *No More Reunions* for *The New Yorker* magazine. They presently live in Greenwich Village with their two sons.

Jim Stokely

Refer to: John Bowers, *The Golden Bowers,* New

York: Tower Publications, 1971; and Bowers, *No More Reunions,* New York: E.P. Dutton, 1973.
See also: APPALACHIAN LITERATURE

Bradley County
Size: 334 Square Miles (213,760 acres)
Established: 1836
Named For: Edward Bradley, Colonel of Tennessee Volunteers in the War of 1812.
County Seat: CLEVELAND
Other Major Cities, Towns, or Communities:
Charleston
Black Fox
McDonald
Eureka
Georgetown
Tasso
Chatata Valley
Chilcutts

Refer to: Roy G. Lillard, *Bradley County,* Memphis, Tennessee: Memphis State University Press, 1980.
See also: BRADLEY COUNTY WAR HEROES
COMMUNITY COLLEGES
LEE COLLEGE
RED CLAY COUNCIL GROUND

Bradley County War Heroes. BRADLEY COUNTY had no native sons in the Revolutionary War or the War of 1812. Veterans of those wars, however, later came to the county. The Mexican War was the first war in which the United States engaged after the organization of Bradley County, and at least 31 men from this county served in that war. Bradley County was very much involved in the CIVIL WAR and furnished eight units for the Confederacy as well as seven units for the Federal Army. Records indicate that at least 47 veterans of the Spanish-American War lived in Bradley County. More than 600 Bradley Countians participated in World War I, more than 3,100 engaged in World War II, and approximately 275 fought in Korea. Bradley Countians participating in the Vietnam struggle totaled 2,650 and today almost 8,000 veterans of all U.S. wars reside within the county.

There are many gallant soldiers among the Bradley Countians who have served in our wars, and many have made the supreme sacrifice. Corporal Clarence L. Richmond has been designated as Bradley County's most decorated soldier. For his service during World War I, Corporal Richmond was awarded the Distinguished Service Cross, the Navy Cross, and the French Croix de Guerre. Corporal Richmond, a member of the Marine Corps, was given the awards for his service during operations near Blanc Mont Ridge on October 3, 4 and 5, 1918. As a stretcher-bearer, he never hesitated to go through the heaviest barrage of machine gun bullets or shrapnel in his efforts to assist the wounded.

Bradley County's two outstanding heroes of World War II were Corporal Paul B. Huff and Major Paul Jones. Paul M. Jones, a graduate of West Point who had already been wounded, was one of the first men captured by the Japanese on Bataan and possibly Corregidor. A recipient of the Purple Heart and Silver Star, Major Jones was held prisoner for three years. Paul B. Huff, a 25-year old corporal, received the Congressional Medal of Honor, the nation's highest decoration, for gallantry in action as a parachute-infantryman against the

Germans near Carano, Italy, February 8, 1944. On June 5 of that year, *The Chattanooga Times* wrote, "In action almost paralleling that of Sgt. Alvin York, Cpl. Huff, single-handed, advanced 350 yards under heavy artillery, mortar and machine gun fire through an enemy mine field and wiped out a German machine gun crew. He deliberately drew enemy fire on himself to determine the strength and location of the enemy and led his six-man patrol to safety after the German unit was annihilated." The citation to the Medal of Honor said simply, "For conspicuous gallantry and intrepidity at risk of life above and beyond the call of duty."

Roy G. Lillard

Refer to: Roy G. Lillard, ed. *The History of Bradley County,* Cleveland, Tennessee: Bradley County Chapter, East Tennessee Historical Society, 1976; and Clarence L. Richmond, "World War I Diary," unpublished, Cleveland Public Library, Cleveland, Tennessee.
See also: ALVIN YORK

Bristol, with a population of 50,000, is a twin city of Tennessee (27,500) and Virginia (22,500). It is located in SULLIVAN COUNTY, in the Great Valley between the north and south forks of the Holston River. Bristol was originally the site of a large Cherokee village known as "Camp Big Meet", so called because deer and buffalo met there to feast on canebreaks after licking salt and sulphur in nearby licks.

In the early eighteenth century, the CHEROKEES sold the future site of Bristol as part of 50,000 acres to the Loyal Land Company of England in return for horses, flintlock rifles, wampum and "fire water". The original Bristol tract, known as Sapling Grove, was first surveyed in 1749 and sold to Colonel James Patton for fifty dollars. Evan Shelby and Isaac Baker later purchased Sapling Grove, with Shelby assuming the southern portion and Baker the northern portion. In 1772, Shelby opened a store on the land and thereby established one of the first commercial enterprises in what was to become Tennessee. During the Revolutionary War, some of the strategy for the Battle of Kings Mountain was planned at Shelby's Fort.

Following the War Colonel James King, who had migrated to Virginia in 1769 and had acquired some 50,000 acres near Sapling Grove, built an early iron works and nail factory. Cannon balls used in the War of 1812 were made at King's furnace, and his shipping point for iron on the Holston River was later named KINGSPORT. Evan Shelby's son Isaac, who moved to Kentucky and became that state's first governor, conveyed the Shelby tract in 1814 to Colonel King. Rev. James King, Jr. acquired the property in the 1830's.

Joseph R. Anderson, son-in-law of Reverend King, foresaw the industrial potential of the location. In 1852, he purchased from his father-in-law one hundred acres of meadowland: 48 acres in Tennessee and 52 in Virginia. Anderson named his development Bristol after the English manufacturing city. The Tennessee Legislature incorporated the Town of Bristol on February 22, 1856. The East Tennessee and Virginia Railroad soon came to Bristol, and the town grew rapidly. The

Tennessee-Virginia state line, located in the center of Bristol's State Street, became the focus of numerous controversies. The line was finally established by a 1903 decision of the U.S. Supreme Court and is now marked with brass markers. Bristol has continued to grow and establish a stimulating and healthy economy based on a strategic geographical location, good highways, TENNESSEE VALLEY AUTHORITY electricity, the modern Tri-Cities Airport, diversified manufacturing, exceptional medical facilities, and distinguished educational institutions.

Amelia Copenhaver

Refer to: Carl W. Holland, "Educational Facilities and Economic Development of Bristol, 1930-1950," East Tennessee State University thesis, 1956; and Robert S. Loving, *Double Destiny: The Story of Bristol, Tennessee-Virginia*, Bristol, 1956.
See also: BLUEGRASS MUSIC
COUNTRY MUSIC
RADIO
RAILROADS (NORTHEASTERN)

The Broad-Form Deed (Copyright 1962, 1963 by Harry M. Caudill). During the late 1800's, gentlemen arrived in the county-seat towns of the Cumberland Plateau for the purpose of buying tracts of minerals, leaving the surface of the land in the ownership of the mountaineers who resided on it. The Eastern and Northern capitalists selected for this mission men of great guile and charm. They were courteous, pleasant, and wonderful storytellers. Their goal was to buy the minerals on a grand scale as cheaply as possible and on terms so favorable to the purchasers as to grant them every desirable exploitive privilege, while simultaneously leaving to the mountaineer an illusion of ownership and the continuing responsibility for practically all the taxes which might be thereafter levied against the land.

Hardly more than 25% of the resulting mineral deeds were signed by grantors who could so much as scrawl their names. Most of them "touched the pen and made their mark," in the form of a spidery X, in the presence of witnesses whom the agent had thoughtfully brought along. Usually the agent was the notary public, but sometimes he brought one from the county seat. Unable to read the instrument or able to read it only with much uncertainty, the sellers relied upon the agent for an explanation of its contents—contents which were to prove deadly to the welfare of generations of the mountaineer's descendants.

Sometimes the instrument was what lawyers in later years called "the short-form deed," merely passing title to the minerals underlying the land "together with all the usual and ordinary mining rights and privileges thereunto appertaining." But the great majority of these deeds were the "broad-form" and, in addition to the minerals, conveyed a great number of specific contractual privileges and immunities.

The broad-form deeds passed to the coal companies title to all coal, oil and gas and all "mineral and metallic substances and all combinations of the same." They authorized the grantees to excavate for the minerals, to build roads and structures on the land and to use the surface for any purpose "convenient or necessary" to the company and its successors in title. Their wordy covenants passed to the coal men the right to utilize as mining props the timber growing on the land, to divert and pollute the water and to cover the surface with toxic mining refuse. The landowner's estate was made perpetually "servient" to the superior or "dominant" rights of the owner of the minerals. And, for good measure, a final clause absolved the mining company from all liability to the landowner for such damages as might be caused "directly or indirectly" by mining operations on his land.

Under ordinary mining methods prevailing throughout the region during the years after 1913, the operating coal companies were able to recover from one thousand to fifteen hundred tons of coal per acre foot. This means that a seam of coal five feet thick produced a minimum of five thousand tons per acre! Where more than one seam was mined, a single acre sometimes yielded fifteen or twenty thousand tons! Even this prodigious recovery left thousands of tons underground–plus the oil, gas, and other minerals. For this vast mineral wealth the mountaineer in most instances received a single half-dollar.

Harry M. Caudill

See also: COAL MINING

Broadside TV. Until October of 1978, when it finally slipped into bankruptcy, Broadside TV of JOHNSON CITY was a communications phenomenon virtually unique in contemporary American culture. It was a distinctively hybrid phenomenon. Its parents were, on the one side, the alternative media movement—popularly termed "Guerrilla TV"—which developed in the late sixties in the wake of the advent of portapac and small format video technology; and on the other side, the romantic mystique of Appalachian folk culture which has challenged the imagination of generations of missionaries and other similarly motivated Americans from outside the region.

Broadside TV was born in the mind of its founding director, Ted Carpenter. Himself born in Nova Scotia, Canada, raised and educated in New England, Carpenter's first direct encounter with the South and with APPALACHIA was as a VISTA volunteer. Assigned to head the VISTA program in Nashville, he was called upon to fill in briefly for the VISTA worker in Cookeville, Tennessee. Carpenter was intrigued by the people and the region around Cookeville, and later took a VISTA opening in Monterey, Tennessee, supervising community development programs for several surrounding counties. In November, 1972, with the aid of a two-year grant from the Appalachian Regional Commission administered through the First Tennessee-Virginia Development District, he founded Broadside TV.

With Broadside TV, Ted Carpenter proposed a pattern of self-enlightenment which would allow mountaineers to teach themselves their own culture, and thus eliminate, so to speak, the middleman — the teacher, the missionary, the filmmaker. "We assume," Carpenter wrote during the early 1970's,

> that people in the region already have access to experience, language, and ideas when it comes to their own vital interests. We assume, too, that they are willing to share this experience through tape with someone like themselves... In this sense we motivate problem-centered dialogues among people in a region, instead of showing curriculums or films. We create a disciplined exchange that allows people to generate the material for their own learning.

By providing the medium for Appalachians "to generate the material for their own learning," Broadside would at the same time allow mountaineers to participate in their own culture, and so to become themselves. Instead of thinking of his organization as a little TV station, Carpenter took for his model the community newspaper—hence the name "Broadside" TV. The advantage of this model was that it freed him from the necessity of tying each of his programs to a dollar, just as each article in a newspaper, unlike each program of a station, does not have to have an individual financial sponsor.

Primary cable TV markets such as Appalachia, where television reception is relatively poor, had been "wired" decades before most urban regions got cable services. The cable industry in East Tennessee had heavily penetrated the market, and was long and well established in the region. Carpenter reasoned that he could ground the economic viability of Broadside in the healthy cable industry in the region by stressing a governmental (Federal Communications Commission) mandate that cable operators produce locally-originated programming. Because of this mandate, local stations were eager to delegate locally-originated programming responsibility to Broadside. Carpenter convinced the local cable operators not only to turn over their production budgets to him (about $25,000 apiece annually), but also to allow him discretionary powers in the use of these funds. This revenue amounted to a sizeable block of unrestricted production money. In return for his discretionary power, Carpenter promised to produce a certain number of hours of wrestling and BLUEGRASS MUSIC, which previously had been the cable operators' standard fare. The result of this strategy was a considerably expanded and diversified spectrum of locally-originated programs via cable, ranging from wrestling and bluegrass to documentary and journalistic programming.

Forming a network of the cable stations in the FTVDD, Broadside TV at its peak provided 20 hours of programming per week to some 12,000 homes. The programs it produced included a series of nine 30-minute tapes involving wildlife habitat, water quality, astronomy, and weather for use in area school systems; a 25-part series relevant to the needs of senior citizens, ranging in focus from nutrition to transportation, health screening, housing and recreation; a series of programs on career education, history, environmental studies, and Appalachian appreciation; coverage of local area school board meetings, city commission meetings, and other local hearings; The Southern Appalachian Video Ethnography Series (SAVES), a comprehensive library of tapes which explored, documented, and thereby preserved on video traditional mountain music, crafts, and lifestyles; tapes on health careers, in-service training, and local health problems for area hospitals; and All-Star Wrestling.

But like any highly specialized organization, Broadside TV was extremely vulnerable to any changes in the communications environment. In 1974, a change was wrought in that environment which ultimately spelled Broadside's doom. The Federal government simply did away with its requirement that cable operators provide locally-originated programming. Inasmuch as this regulation had been virtually the only incentive for the production of such programming by the cable industry, the ruling had the effect of wiping out local programming virtually overnight, not just in East Tennessee but throughout the nation. Within one year of the Federal Communications Commission ruling, funding for locally-originated programming from cable corporations was cut in half and within two years it was completely gone.

Broadside was faced with the collapse of its operational and economic strategy. Carpenter left in 1975 to head the newly formed Citizens Committee for Broadcasting, and a new breed of directors succeeded him. In the end it proved a no-win situation, but even in the face of a hostile environment, Broadside had established such a strong presence and identity among funding agencies and foundations that it managed to keep the doors open for an additional three years.

Did Broadside really offer the opportunity to create a new community and new culture in Appalachia? It did not, but it quite possibly could have. The problems Broadside had in fulfilling its potential in this regard were perhaps more in its organizational support and management than in its concept. Certainly it was naive in its acceptance of a homogeneous folk-society view of Appalachia, though this is certainly an honored tradition and one come by quite honestly. It would be easy to write off Broadside's attempts at social change as romantic and trivial.

There remains those early tapes of Carpenter's, where he indeed went from hollow to hollow with portapac in hand and did indeed talk with farmers about farming and shopkeepers about shopkeeping. There is indeed contained in these tapes "self-enlightenment", and, more importantly, a valid and viable communications process for bringing it about. And there is also the fact that an "electronic community", as it were, composed of fourteen communities, seventeen public school systems, several colleges and universities and even for a time the TENNESSEE VALLEY AUTHORITY, was indeed forged, and that this electronic community constituted a social alignment of institutions and people never before put together in Appalachia, and that this alignment had the potential at least, however poorly realized, for profound and radical social change.

Ferdinand Alexi Hilenski

Refer to: Ted Carpenter and Mike Clark, *Challenge for Change/Society Nouvelle Access,* Nov.

11, 1973; and Charles Childs, "Portable Videotape and CATV in Appalachia," in *Educational and Industrial Television*, June, 1973.

Harvey Broome (July 15, 1902 - March 8, 1968). From Ireland in the 1770's came John Adair and his family to East Tennessee. Adair was a public entry-taker who collected money for the sale of lands. He relied on his conscience during the American Revolution to justify turning over public monies, without authorization, to finance the battle of Kings Mountain. From England in the 1870's came George Broome and his family to East Tennessee. Broome, a wheelwright and carpenter, was a tenant who had been evicted by his landlord for doing what he thought "every Englishman had a right to do, vote according to the dictate of his own conscience."

Harvey Benjamin Broome, a fifth-generation descendant of his maternal ancestor John Adair, and a third-generation descendant of his paternal ancestor George Broome, was born in KNOXVILLE. He graduated from THE UNIVERSITY OF TENNESSEE and from Harvard Law School. In 1935, with seven other persons, he organized The Wilderness Society. From 1948 to 1968, he was a trustee for the Robert Marshall Wilderness Fund. He served as president, at various periods, of The Wilderness Society, the Smoky Mountains Hiking Club, and the East Tennessee Historical Society. It has been written that the law was Harvey Broome's way of making a living, but wilderness was his way of life. The latter way was opened to him in 1917 when he accompanied three uncles on a two-week camping trip to the Great Smoky Mountains. That event began a 50-year hiking career; on his last hike, in November of 1967, he went with a friend to Charlies Bunion in the Smokies. The 1917 camping trip also led to years of outdoor writing and to Harvey Broome's role as a leader in wilderness preservation. His first published writing was an article entitled "Great Smoky Mountain Trails," which appeared in the January 1928 issue of *Mountain Magazine*.

In January of 1941, Harvey conceived a project of keeping a journal in the manner of Henry David Thoreau, whose journals he read with dedication. This concept materialized when he received, in the Christmas mail, a 5" x 8" notebook from a business friend. He filled 26 such notebooks and a portion of the 27th. He did not make notes while hiking; "fact underfoot and thought overhead" had to be carried in his memory until time could be found at home to write. Sometimes this would be the day after a mountain trip; sometimes there would be a lapse of a week or more. These journals, plus a "black notebook" containing thumbnail sketches of his hikes, provided the text for two of his three posthumously published books.

Like Thoreau, Harvey constructed a box to house the journals. Thoreau's chest was handmade of pine and stained brown, with a front hinged at the bottom and a lock at the top. Harvey made his chest of walnut, from a tree on his property. It had a sliding front with thumbnail indentation and was hand-polished with wax.

As president of The Wilderness

Courtesy Anne Broome

Harvey Broome, 1952.

Society, Harvey was requested in 1964 to write a letter predicting the status of forest conservation a hundred years hence. He wrote that forests will be pressed for survival against the effects of overuse, forest disease, and air pollutants; that plastics and metals will have largely displaced the structural use of wood; and that the quantity and quality of first-growth trees will have vanished, except in such wilderness preserves as have survived. His letter is to be opened by the President of the United States on October 24, 2064.

With his heritage of conscience, his love of nature, and his power of articulation, Harvey Broome was deeply spiritual. He had an understanding of human relationships and human values. His faith, he wrote, was in life itself.

Anne Broome

Refer to: Harvey Broome, *Out Under the Sky of the Great Smokies: A Personal Journal,* 515 Mountain Crest Drive, Knoxville, Tennessee: Greenbrier Press, 1975, *Faces of the Wilderness,* Missoula, Montana: Mountain Press Publishing Company, 1972, and *Harvey Broome: Earth Man,* Knoxville, Tennessee: Greenbrier Press, 1970.

See also: GREAT SMOKY MOUNTAINS NATIONAL PARK

Parson Brownlow. William Gannaway Brownlow (August 29, 1805 - April 29, 1877), son of Joseph Brownlow and Catherine Gannaway Brownlow, was born in Wythe County, Virginia. Following the War of 1812, the family moved from Virginia to Blountville in SULLIVAN COUNTY. Shortly after both parents died in 1816, the orphaned Brownlows were farmed out to relatives, William going with his paternal uncle and later serving in Abingdon, Virginia, as a carpenter's apprentice. During a Methodist camp meeting, young Brownlow underwent a conversion to Methodism that embarked him on a career of circuit-riding criticism of the men and institutions of his time. Seldom did a Methodist conference occur without him in the midst. This, along with a burning desire to educate himself, consumed his energies for ten years.

Early in his evangelic career, the vitriol exuding from his pulpit began to appear in print, and he was promptly sued for libel--an action to which he quickly became accustomed. By 1839 he was publishing the *Tennessee Whig* in ELIZABETHTON. It was politically biased, scathingly pious, and described by peers as "dull, vapid and without a singularly redeeming feature." This description, however, did not last, as Brownlow's political leanings and his diatribes

Parson Brownlow

against Baptists, Quakers and other disagreeing with him became fair game for his poisonous pen. His colorful phrases, both from the pulpit and the editor's desk, caught the fancy of most of the frontiersmen of East Tennessee. During the 1840's, he edited the JONESBORO *Whig and Independent Journal*, and the 1850's found him at the influential desk of the KNOXVILLE *Whig*.

Enjoying the sobriquet "Parson" by which he is still referred to today, Brownlow furiously entered national politics in 1844 in support of presidential hopeful Henry Clay from nearby Kentucky. After returning to Tennessee from the Whig convention, the parson campaigned vigorously for Clay, despite the fact that his fellow Tennessean James K. Polk was Clay's opponent. Polk lost Tennessee, but carried enough votes elsewhere to be elected. Brownlow himself was defeated for Congress by ANDREW JOHNSON, thus making a mortal enemy for the Knoxville editor. This hatred lasted throughout the lives of both men. The Parson, through his Whig editorials and preachings, also castigated the non-Unionists before the CIVIL WAR and was bitterly opposed to secession. Though he bore no great love for the Negro, he believed "that in a Southern Confederacy the freedom of speech and of the press will be denied." During the Civil War, when Knoxville fell to the Confederates, Brownlow escaped the city for SEVIER COUNTY. Tradition has it that Brownlow tossed his moveable type into the Tennessee River as he was fleeing Knoxville with his newspaper equipment.

The fire-breathing editor was elected Governor of Tennessee in 1865 and supposedly "saved" the state from carpetbag rule during the Reconstruction. Some observers, however, felt that Tennessee would have fared better at the hands of the dreaded invaders from the North. Brownlow, with his violent hatred for the Confederacy, believed the South should be severely punished for its past crimes. In 1869 Brownlow was elected U.S. Senator, only to be replaced later by his old enemy Andrew Johnson, who having stepped down as President, returned to his previous seat in the U.S. Senate. In 1877, with editorials in the *Whig* appearing less frequently, the parson fell ill at his East Cumberland Avenue house in Knoxville. He died at home and was interred in Gray Cemetery, among soldiers from his revered Union Army. There William Brownlow still rests, the former editor, prisoner of war, fighter of duels, libeler of persons, governor, senator, and most of all, Parson.

James A. Young

Refer to: William G. Brownlow, *Helps to the Study of Presbyterianism,* Knoxville, Tenn.: Heiskell, 1834, and *Sketches of the Rise, Progress, and Decline of Secession,* Philadelphia: Childs, 1862; and Merton E. Coulter, *William G. Brownlow: Fighting Parson of the Southern Highlands,* Chapel Hill: University of North Carolina Press, 1937 (reprinted 1971, Knoxville: University of Tennessee Press).
See also: RELIGION

Browntown, near Harriman, was a coal mining town that was founded in 1891 when the Brown Mining Company began digging ore from Walden's Ridge. It was a typical mining town, consisting roughly of 150 four-room houses, a commissary, and a boarding house. School was held in the boarding house until 1896, when a one-room schoolhouse was built. The school soon became an active center for the miners' social gatherings. On Saturday nights the citizens often met for box suppers, dances, and an occasional play performed by the children. On Sundays the school served as church.

Most of the mining families were large, and their meager wages barely covered the cost of food and rent. To supplement their incomes, most planted gardens and raised hogs and chickens. Whenever a river boat made its way from CHATTANOOGA to Harriman, the miners took their excess produce to trade for household goods, clothing, and staples such as flour, sugar, and salt. Browntown's water was supplied completely by a large rock spring at the foot of Walden's Ridge. Former citizens of the town sadly recall the year 1918, when influenza swept through the area and nearly wiped out the town. At the peak of the epidemic, bodies were stacked on top of one another and removed by wagon at midnight.

In 1925, the mining company closed operations. Many of the miners moved their families on to the rich coal fields of Kentucky. Most of the houses were sold to Harriman residents, who moved them or tore them apart for lumber. The rest were left to be demolished by age and neglect. The old spring remains as our only reminder of Browntown.

Jo Stafford

See also: COAL MINER'S SON
LOWER WINDROCK MINING CAMP

Alfred Buffat Homestead and Mill. In 1848, seeking religious and economic freedom in the New World, Professor Pierre Francois Buffat, his wife Sylvia Tauxe Buffat, and their four small children endured a stormy voyage from LeHavre, France, to New York City. From New York they sailed to Charleston, South Carolina, and ultimately disembarked from a Tennessee River packet at the foot of KNOXVILLE's Market Street on the Fourth of July. The eldest of their children was 8-year old Alfred Buffat.

The family soon purchased a 300-acre farm to the northeast of the city, fronting the Washington Road (now Millertown Pike) and extending easterly to Big Creek (now Love's Creek). Choosing among three traditional family skills brought from Switzerland —cheesemaking, winemaking, and watermilling—the Buffats soon decided to erect a large grist mill on Big Creek on the back side of their farm. In 1861 they began grinding corn and wheat, with 21-year old Alfred as the operator and his uncle, Gus Truan, as the miller. The "Spring Place" mill soon became the thriving center of a pioneer community complex on the Buffat lands which also included Spring Place School, the manor house, the miller's house, a granary, public wagon scales, a blacksmith shop, a small orchard and vineyard, several barns and a general farming operation. Meal and flour from the Buffat Mill supplied many of the stores and households of Knoxville and East KNOX COUNTY for sixty years or more. Regular teamster deliveries into Knoxville necessitated the construction of Buffat Mill Drive between the mill and the city.

The Buffat Homestead was erected near the mill in 1867 for Alfred's bride, Eliza Bolli. Named "The Maples" by Eliza, the 9-room frame house was constructed of timbers harvested on the homeplace and sawed into lumber at a water-powered sawmill operated in conjunction with the grist mill. It was there, in the early days, where the freedom-seeking Swiss-American Protestants met regularly to worship according to the dictates of their conscience. It was there, also, where Alfred Buffat conducted his farming and milling operations, officiated as a Justice of the Peace, and functioned as school director, an elected member of the Knox County Quarterly Court, and Trustee of Knox County. Squire Buffat died of a stroke there in December 1908 and was buried nearby in the cemetery of Spring Place Presbyterian Church.

Today, the mill site in Spring Place Park is marked by the same stone pillars which once supported the overshot water wheet. The Alfred Buffat Homestead, listed on the National Register of Historic Places, has been privately preserved as a physical symbol and reminder of the culture, life style, influence and community prominence of the many Swiss immigrants who colonized Knox County in the 19th century.

John Alfred Parker

See also: THE HARRIS MILL

Bulls Gap. Since earliest Indian and pioneer days, the pass through Bay's Mountain known as Bull's Gap has served as a natural opening or gateway to the West. Bull's Gap was named for John Bull, the earliest and one of the influential settlers of the strategic area. In 1792, Bull paid 27 or 28 shillings for 55 acres at the gap of Bay's Mountain. He began operating a stage line and gunsmith shop there. He made a long-barrelled cap-and-ball rifle which was said to have been a very good rifle. His sons all became gunsmiths. James Parker, second oldest settler of Bull's Gap, lived as a hermit in the gap of the mountain. He knew the location of a lead mine not far from his home, sold lead as a private enterprise, and could have made Bull's Gap very famous if he had revealed the location of the mine.

Bull's Gap was perhaps the most

bitterly contested CIVIL WAR point in upper East Tennessee, and it changed hands several times between the opposing armies. Through Bull's Gap had been built the east-west wagon road and, in 1857, one of the most important RAILROADS in the South: the East Tennessee and Virginia Railroad between BRISTOL and KNOXVILLE. So important was Bull's Gap in the strategy of each army that in official correspondence and communiques written in and about the progress of the war in this area, it was often referred to simply as "The Gap". From the autumn of 1863 until the close of the war in the spring of 1865, this strongly fortified spot was the scene of many battles and skirmishes.

In August of 1864, for example, with the Gap under Confederate control, Military Governor of Tennessee ANDREW JOHNSON appointed General Alvin C. Gillem commander of a force to be known as the "Governor's Guard". This command, composed mostly of loyal East Tennesseans, was ordered to the area for the protection of citizens against pillage and depredations by straggling soldiers and bands of criminals. With the help of the Union Army, the "Governor's Guard" retook Bull's Gap. Soon after establishing fortifications at the Gap, the Federals learned that General John H. Morgan, the dreaded Confederate cavalry leader,

Farm home near Bulls Gap, October 22, 1933.

Lewis Hine / Courtesy TVA

was in Greeneville. Operating from Bull's Gap on the night of September 3, the Federals sent two companies by way of Warrensburg and Timber Ridge into Greeneville, where they surprised and killed the famous raider.

As the area attempted to repair itself after the War, the Rogersville and Jefferson Railroad constructed a branch railroad line from Bull's Gap to Rogersville across the Holston River. Bull's Gap became the supper stop on the main line. The Smith House, run by Peter Smith during the 1880's, handled all the travelers' business for many years. One traveler described it as "one of the best hotels on the line of the E.T.V. and G. Railroad, and there is not, perhaps, in the state a landlord who enjoys a greater or more deserved popularity. His fine four-story brick building is within a few rods of the depot at the junction of the E.T.V. and G. and Rogersville and Jefferson Railroads and is a modern, first-class establishment in all that the term implies. The surroundings are all pleasant, and from the broad verandas and halls magnificent views of mountain and valley are to be had, and order, system, and cleanliness pervade every department."

In 1912, according to a Board of Trade pamphlet printed by the town of Bulls Gap, the local population numbered "over twelve hundred hustling people." The community had a high school and an eight-month elementary school with free tuition. Fourteen passenger trains passed through daily. Today, the population of Bulls Gap is approximately 850. Most working residents commute by automobile to industries in or near surrounding county seats, including American Enka (synthetic fibers) at Lowland near Morristown, Magnavox (electronic equipment) in Greeneville, and I.P.C. Dennison Co. (cards and labels) in Rogersville. The Bulls Gap High School has been consolidated into a new county-wide school between Bulls Gap and Rogersville.

Allen D. Swann

See also: RIFLES
THE THREE STATES OF EAST TENNESSEE

Frances Hodgson Burnett (November 24, 1849 - October 29, 1924) was born in Manchester, England. Through her *Little Lord Fauntleroy*, translated into twelve languages, she became internationally famous. Although poor during her early years, she amassed wealth and eventually lived in a villa on Long Island overlooking Manhasset Bay. She also became a cosmopolite, crossing the Atlantic at least thirty-three times. When she was fifteen, Frances moved from England to New Market in JEFFERSON COUNTY. This move, made in 1865, came when Frances Hodgson's widowed mother decided to improve her financial status by coming to the United States. Here they lived for a short time in a two-story log house. Frances and her sister Edith operated a "select seminary", a barter school in which most students paid tuition with farm produce. Frances, who had already started writing, picked blackberries and sold them in order to get money for paper and postage. Her first stories,

Courtesy C.M. McClung Historical Collection, Lawson McGhee Library

Frances Hodgson Burnett

written in a Lancashire dialect and published by *Godey's Lady's Book*, were English in tone, idiom and setting. In essence, she was an English writer in an Appalachian setting.

The Hodgson family moved to KNOXVILLE in 1869, where Frances was to live for six years. In 1873 she married Dr. Swan Burnett, a specialist in ophthalmic and aural surgery. Dr. Burnett later joined the medical faculty of Georgetown University in Washington, D.C., where the family resided for several years during the 1870's. Already Mrs. Burnett's stories in national literary magazines were widely acknowledged. She experienced her greatest success, however, with the publication of *Little Lord Fauntleroy* in 1886. Possibly a counterpart of her son Vivian, Fauntleroy was a small, charming, courteous, thoughtful lad, a little gentleman in a velvet suit with lace collar and cuffs. Mrs. Burnett had created, in him, the ideal of many mothers. Following a play and a film based on this novel, fashions for little boys boomed, especially the Little Lord Fauntleroy suits. More than a dozen other Burnett stories were turned into plays. One of Mrs. Burnett's chief successes, *A Lady of Quality*, had long runs in New York and London. Of her more than forty novels, the most well known are *Sara Crewe*, *Little Saint Elizabeth*, *Little Lord Fauntleroy*, and *The Secret Garden*. The latter two remain in print.

Success in writing, however, did not guarantee Mrs. Burnett a satisfying personal life. In 1898, following several years of separation, the Burnetts were divorced. Their son Lionel had already died. Vivian, the other son, suffered as Fauntleroy incarnate. Two years following her divorce, Mrs. Burnett married Stephen Townsend, a London doctor, who was her business manager. Within months this marriage ended, and Mrs. Burnett returned to the United States, where she built her villa at Plandome, Long Island. Here landscape artists created her own "secret garden". She lived here until her death.

Mrs. Burnett's novels embodied the usual hallmarks of feminine fiction of the mid-19th century: artificiality, sentimentality, layered romanticism. But her juveniles, the fairy tales of real life, gave her a permanent niche in popular literature. Even now, Jefferson Countians reflect pride in their "First Lady of Literature". In 1955, the Jefferson County Chapter of the Association for the Preservation of Tennessee Antiquities sponsored a

Frances Hodgson Burnett Celebration. They also placed a marker on the lawn of the Frances Hodgson Burnett House, which still stands on Highway 11E. A section of highway near the house was named the Frances Hodgson Burnett Drive. A portrait of Mrs. Burnett, painted by Knoxville artist Eleanor M. Wylie, hangs in the historical room of the Jefferson County High School Media Center.

Ruth Osborne Turner

Refer to: Frances Hodgson Burnett, *In Connection with the De Willoughby Claim*, New York: Scribner's, 1899; Vivian Burnett, *The Romantick Lady*, New York: Scribner's, 1927; and Ann Thwaite, *Waiting For the Party: The Life of Frances Hodgson Burnett*, New York: Scribner's, 1974.

C

Cades Cove. When John Oliver, a veteran of the War of 1812, arrived with his wife and young child in Cades Cove during the early autumn of 1818, CHEROKEES still occupied this fertile elliptical valley surrounded on all sides by the Great Smoky Mountains. Called Tsiyahi, or otter place, by the Cherokee, the cove intersected several major Indian trails and contained a small Indian settlement, perhaps only a hunting camp. Two Cherokee chieftains, Kades and Old Abraham of Chilhowee, gave their names to the cove and to its major stream, Abram's Creek. Despite hostility to earlier white encroachment, the cove Indians took pity on the lone Oliver family and actually brought them food — dried pumpkin — which enabled them to survive near-starvation in the winter of 1818-1819.

By 1821, other families from CARTER COUNTY joined the Olivers, and the rich limestone soil of the cove basin provided abundant harvests of traditional pioneer crops — corn, wheat, potatoes, and beans. Although the cove would remain an island of cultivated land surrounded by mountain wilderness, its early development was in the mainstream of the American westward movement. As early as 1827, the Cades Cove Bloomery Forge was being operated by Daniel D. Foute, an ambitious and restless entrepreneur. Even though the local iron ore soon proved too poor in quality to continue production profitably, by the 1850's five roads out of the cove had been constructed largely through Foute's efforts. These roads connected the cove with regional markets in nearby KNOXVILLE and Maryville, and allowed a thriving market economy to develop.

The 1840's and 1850's saw new waves of immigrants from other states and from many foreign countries enter the cove and enrich the community life by their diversity. Among these newcomers was Dr. Calvin Post, a physician, scientist, abolitionist, and mineralogist representing Northern mining interests. Although Post was never able to convince his employers to invest large sums in prospective gold and copper mines, considerable mining activity nevertheless occurred in the surrounding mountains. This vast wilderness also provided recreation for cove farmers who hunted deer and bear and trapped for fur in the forests after their crops were gathered.

The CIVIL WAR found most of the

Courtesy East Tennessee Development District

Cades Cove in winter.

cove inhabitants staunchly loyal to the Union, despite their proximity to Confederate North Carolina. Unionism was strong because of the absence of slavery, the older loyalties to Jacksonian democracy, and the transference to politics of conservative values from the Primitive Baptist Church, the cove's largest organized religious group. For their loyalty, covites paid dearly. Marauding bands of rebel North Carolina guerrillas systematically terrorized the community, attacking suddenly from the cover of the mountains, murdering, harassing, and robbing the civilian population of all visible food supplies.

The postwar community emerged dramatically altered from the prosperity and progressive development which had characterized the entrepreneurial spirit of the 1850's. Families shared in the impoverishment and retrogression of the larger region of East Tennessee. Constant harassment and starvation had made people afraid of strangers, embittered against anyone who fought for the Confederacy, and even suspicious of former neighbors and friends. The postwar community became increasingly introspective as prewar markets failed to revive.

In this new environment, the extended family or kinship structure assumed disproportionate importance. During the war, one's family often proved the only trustworthy source of information or assistance. By 1870, the prewar diversity among the cove population had disappeared; almost everyone now was related to one or more of the cove's large extended families. Out of this closeness developed an authentic folk culture, characterized not by isolation, as later writers erroneously assumed, but rather by the cove people's intimate knowledge of everyone in the community and a precise common knowledge of the cove's landscape. This folk culture in some degree compensated by its inner variety and beauty for the outward barrenness and POVERTY of the reconstruction years.

By 1900, some degree of prosperity had returned to the community as regional markets revived. Cove farmers grazed their cattle in the surrounding mountains in the summer and sold their crops in Knoxville during the fall. Contact with the outside world had never been broken, and by 1910 progressivism swept Cades Cove as it engulfed the rest of the United States. Led by John W. Oliver, cove farmers sought new methods through modern scientific AGRICULTURE to improve virtually every aspect of farming. The progressive emphasis on education led cove citizens in 1915 to construct the first modern consolidated schoolhouse in BLOUNT COUNTY. The years immediately before American entry into World War I were characterized by progressive optimism and endeavors to improve life in many areas — health, education, agriculture and home demonstration projects.

The 1920's witnessed a sudden regression as agricultural prices — high before and during the war — suddenly dropped, leaving many cove farmers in desperate financial straits. National prohibition in 1919 suddenly highlighted the advantages of the cove's geographic isolation for distilling illicit whiskey. Distilling had always occupied a small fraction of the community before, but by 1920 many mainstream, respectable citizens turned to moonshining in desperation as farm prices continued to fall. The community was torn with dissension. The dominant Primitive Baptist Church strongly opposed illicit distilling, and older progressives deplored the social havoc wrought among cove families by increasing alcoholism. Murders resulting from drunken brawls sharply increased. In 1921, both the barn of John W. Oliver, a leading advocate of prohibition, and the barn of his elderly father, a Primitive Baptist minister, were burned in reprisal.

In 1927, a larger external threat to the community suddenly appeared. The movement for the GREAT SMOKY MOUNTAINS NATIONAL PARK planned to include Cades Cove within its bounds and seize all private property there by eminent domain. Most cove residents found it extremely difficult to articulate or convey to outsiders the deeper significance of the cove to families who had lived there over a hundred years. The land was intertwined with their lives and history; fields, streams, and meadows all had particular emotional and symbolic value in their folk culture. Most were horrified at the prospect of forced removal. The original John Oliver's great-grandson, John W. Oliver, fought a heroic and lonely series of court battles at his own expense to forestall eviction. After appealing his case three times to the Tennessee Supreme Court, he was finally forced to concede defeat. Thus the birth of the new national park signaled the death of this historic community.

Durwood Dunn

Refer to: Inez E. Burns, *History of Blount County*, Maryville, Tenn., 1957; Durwood Dunn, "Cades Cove During the Nineteenth Century," University of Tennessee dissertation, 1976; Jean M. Jones, "The Regional English of the Former Inhabitants of Cades Cove in the Great Smoky Mountains," University of Tennessee dissertation, 1973; and Randolph A. Shields, *The Cades Cove Story*, Gatlinburg, Tenn.: Great Smoky Mountains National History Association, 1977.

See also: COAL MINING
GEOGRAPHY
GRASSY COVE

Campbell County

Size: 451 Square Miles (288,640 acres)
Established: 1806
Named For: Arthur Campbell, Colonel in the American Revolution
County Seat: Jacksboro
Other Major Cities, Towns, or Communities:
LaFollette
Jellico
Caryville
Habersham
Elk Valley
White Oak
Fincastle

Refer to: James Hayden Siler, *A History of Jellico, Tennessee, Containing Historical Information*

Jellico's main street, 1920's.

Courtesy Thompson Photographs, C.M. McClung Historical Collection, Lawson McGhee Library

on Campbell County, Tennessee, and Whitley County, Kentucky, Jellico, 1938.
See also: CAMPBELL COUNTY IN THE 1850 FEDERAL CENSUS
JOHN FOX, JR.
THE JELLICO EXPLOSION
GRACE MOORE

Campbell County in the 1850 Federal Census. Gleanings from old census returns are often instructive for the social historian and for other scholars. Those from CAMPBELL COUNTY, Tennessee, are no exception. They provide interesting insights into a typical Appalachian county in the decade preceding the CIVIL WAR. The population of Campbell County in 1850 was 5,750, including 97 "free colored" persons and 318 slaves.

The Census Bureau in 1850 instructed its census takers that both "personal" and "real" property were to be evaluated. However, only one figure is given as the "worth" for a Head of Household, and it is impossible to ascertain whether this was a composite of both kinds of property. Only 296 out of approximately 700 Heads of Household were even assigned a worth. Based on the values attributed to these, the average worth of the Heads of Household was $1,118. This is a considerably higher figure than that of Campbell's northern neighbor, Whitley County in Kentucky, and may be accounted for by the more fertile Powell's Valley area of Campbell, where farmers show consistently higher sums by their names. The "millionaire" of Campbell County in 1850 was a farmer, John Kincaid, worth $76,500. The next highest figure, however, shows only $9,000. Thirty-two Heads had values in the $1,000 range, and seventeen show property of $100 or less.

As to occupation, farmers were the predominant group, 609 of them. The recapitulation at the end of the census lists 481 farms in the county. Some young sons still under the parental roof are also designated as farmers. Only one listing as "medecine" is to be found, with a worth of $1,000. Three lawyers are met with, only one showing a worth, and that is set at $2,000. There are eight schoolteachers, only one of whom has any value ascribed, at $300. There are five merchants, with two having property valued at $5,000. Two men are listed as "selling goods."

Following farmers, the highest occupational group in Campbell County in 1850 was that of blacksmiths, who numbered fifteen. Waggoners numbered five, hammermen three, cabinetmakers three. Only one preacher is encountered in the census, but four millers appear, as well as four saddlers, two brick layers, two tanners, and two shoemakers. The following occupations count one each, according to the returns: hatter, clerk, housepainter, carpenter, gunsmith, stock dealer, stone mason, stone cutter, iron maker, tailor, trader, and "slay maker".

Two Heads of Household told the enumerator that their occupation was "stilling", but their financial success at this business is not shown. There were four colliers in Campbell County in 1850, one listed with a worth of $150. Presumably, they could be the same four responsible for the 160 tons of coal mined in Campbell in 1854 and 1855, the first years for which figures are available. These four colliers would probably have been amazed at the 1,802,413 tons of coal mined in Campbell's peak year of 1912. Finally, one Head of Household — proudly, we may assume — listed one of his older sons as a "student".

James Hayden Siler

See also: COAL MINING
POPULATION CHARACTERISTICS

Charles Warner Cansler (May 15, 1871-November 1, 1953) was a prominent KNOXVILLE black educator, civic leader, and member of a distinguished family. He was very learned in history, literature, law and politics. He had exceptional skill in rapid mathematical computation. He served the Knoxville City Schools for over forty years, twelve as a teacher and the balance as Principal of Knoxville Colored High School. He had the capacity to form relationships with prominent persons, and this enabled him to accomplish many improvements for the colored race, as it was known in his day. During his lifetime he was recognized by many as Knoxville's foremost black citizen.

Charles Cansler attended MARYVILLE COLLEGE and the Quaker Freedmen's Normal Institute in Maryville. He then decided to study law privately under Judge William C. Kain, a Yale graduate who had been a Judge Advocate in the Confederate Army. Cansler passed the state bar examination in 1892 and entered the practice of law. He was a Republican candidate from KNOX COUNTY for the state legislature in 1894. In 1896 he attended the Republican National Convention, and in 1897 he attended various social activities in Washington upon the occasion of the inauguration of President William McKinley.

In spite of a promising law career and his interest in political affairs, Charles Cansler developed a powerful urge to devote himself to quality education for blacks, even at a modest salary. After passing a Federal civil service examination, he experienced personal discrimination and unequal treatment in seeking and gaining employment in the postal service and in a Navy yard. He recognized that Negroes, as they were known then, would have to be superior to their white counterparts in competing for quality positions.

Throughout his career Charles Cansler sought ways to improve opportunities and civil rights for blacks. He was impressed with a form of discrimination in Tennessee law in which cousins, nephews, and nieces of ex-slaves could not inherit property from the ex-slaves, whereas such white relatives could inherit property from their white ancestors. He thus drafted a bill to correct this inequity and arranged through his close association with two state senators to have it passed in the Tennessee legislature. Through the same channels, he was also instrumental in getting a private act passed which provided playgrounds and parks for blacks in Knoxville. As principal of the "colored" high school, he persuaded the city to move the school from a blighted to a respectable neighborhood and to add five cents to the tax rate for vocational education.

Charles Cansler left the Knoxville

community a great legacy in the publication of a book entitled *Three Generations: The Story of a Colored Family in East Tennessee.* This book traces the life and thought of Cansler and his family from the time of the Nat Turner Insurrection in 1831 to the time of the writing of the book in 1939. The book provides an excellent interpretation from a black perspective of the status of free Negroes before emancipation.

Charles Cansler's maternal grandparents, free Negroes of mixed heritage, migrated from North Carolina to Knoxville in 1847. Shortly after arriving, the family settled in FRIENDSVILLE upon a Quaker's invitation. The family moved to Knoxille during the CIVIL WAR because of the threat of a Confederate raid. Cansler's grandfather later published *The Colored Tennessean,* the first Negro newspaper in Tennessee. Cansler's mother was instructed during the war by Dr. Thomas Humes, an Episcopal rector and later President of East Tennessee University (THE UNIVERSITY OF TENNESSEE). Cansler's father, Hugh Lawson Cansler, was the offspring of a MONROE COUNTY plantation owner's daughter and one of his slaves.

It is difficult to contemplate Charles Cansler without realizing the importance he attached to his ancestry and to the transmission of this heritage to his descendants. He revered both of his parents as paragons of virtue, devoted to the love and intensive training of their large family. His father was an artisan. His mother was a scholar and distinguished teacher in her own right. Cansler Elementary School in Knoxville is named for her. Charles

Courtesy Beck Cultural Center

Charles Cansler

Cansler married Miss Lillian Webber of Tate Springs. They had one child, a daughter who graduated from KNOXVILLE COLLEGE and married Dr. J. Herman Daves, a prominent TENNESSEE VALLEY AUTHORITY personnel official. From this union came three children. A daughter married a Knoxvillian, Dr. John Reinhardt, a career diplomat who became U.S. Ambassador to Nigeria and later Director of the U.S. International Communication Agency.

Lowell Giffen

Refer to: Charles Cansler, "Negro Life in Knox County and Knoxville," in Mary U. Rothrock, ed. *The French Broad-Holston Country,* Knoxville: East Tennessee Historical Society, 1946, pp. 308-325; and Charles Cansler, *Three Generations: The Story of a Colored Family in East Tennessee,* Kingsport: Kingsport Press, 1939.
See also: NIKKI GIOVANNI

Carson-Newman College, owned by the Tennessee Baptist Convention and located in Jefferson City, was founded in 1851. At that time, the town was known as Mossy Creek, and the college was called Mossy Creek Missionary Baptist Seminary. The seminary later became Carson College. Since 1889, when it merged with Newman College for women, it has been known by the present name. Except for an interruption during the CIVIL WAR, Carson-Newman has been in continuous operation. From the beginning the college has been a four-year liberal arts school, though during most of its nineteenth-century history and until the mid-1920's, it included a preparatory department for those needing sub-collegiate instruction.

Brought into being to prepare an educated clergy and an informed area public, Carson-Newman has always served the immediate area. But its emphasis has not been just regional, for students attend from every Southern state, all major national regions, and some foreign countries. Carson-Newman encourages individual growth in a Christian setting. The student body of approximately 1600 is taught by more than 100 faculty members, whose approach to learning is personal: seminars, individual conferences, independent study, small classes. A good number of courses, programs, and surveys are devoted to the many aspects of APPALACHIA. Generally, more than 50% of students pursue graduate study, particularly in the health sciences, RELIGION, education, law, business, home economics, social work, and the arts. The influence of the school is carried by more than 10,000 alumni.

Robert Randolph Turner

Refer to: Isaac Newton Carr, *History of Carson-Newman College: Survey History, 1851-1959*, V. 1, Jefferson City, Tenn.: Carson-Newman College, 1959.

Carter County

Size: 348 Square Miles (222,720 acres)

Established: 1796

Named For: Landon Carter, Secretary of State of THE STATE OF FRANKLIN

County Seat: ELIZABETHTON

Other Major Cities, Towns, or Communities:

Hampton
Milligan College
Roan Mountain
Valley Forge
Biltmore
Braemar
Stony Creek
Elk Mills

Refer to: Frank Merritt, *Early History of Carter County, 1760-1861*, Knoxville: East Tennessee Historical Society, 1950.
See also: PETERS HOLLOW

Catholicism. The preliminary development of the Southern Appalachian coal fields coincided with the heaviest influx of the "new" immigration, principally Catholics and Jews from Southern and Eastern Europe. Hundreds, perhaps thousands, of Italians, Hungarians, Poles, Slavs, and other white ethnics as well as American Blacks from the Deep South answered advertisements of the coal barons for cheap labor and carried their religious needs with them to the remote mountain wilderness. In less than forty years, the conditions that produced the brief flowering of Catholicism in Southern APPALACHIA collapsed, resulting in its return to an inconspicuous existence. Its brief interruption of a rather monolithic cultural environment can be attributed almost totally to outside influence: capitalists from the North, priests mostly of German ancestry, and immigrants from Hungary and Italy. Protestantism, which had never been seriously challenged, retained its steadfast hold on the southern mountains.

A few Catholics had been among the early settlers of Southern Appalachia. Most of these had lost touch with their faith, but there were some small concentrations in some of the towns. For example, during the 1840's, priests from Wytheville, Virginia, held occasional services for scattered Catholics in southwest Virginia. The itinerant brothers were obliged to take the train as far as Hilton in Scott County and then climb the trail over Clinch Mountain to a small chapel near Snowflake where people assembled every couple of months for Mass. Two churches were established in East

Students and teachers in front of Catholic High School, Knoxville, September 1934.

Courtesy Thompson Photographs, C.M. McClung Historical Collection, Lawson McGhee Library

Tennessee during 1852: Immaculate Conception at KNOXVILLE and Sts. Peter and Paul at CHATTANOOGA.

Beginning during the 1880's, industrial development in the southern mountains led to a stronger Catholic presence. The alterations that have occurred in the ethnic composition and religious make-up of Southern Appalachia have been more pronounced since that time, when Yankee and foreign investors realized the potential mineral wealth waiting to be exploited. This industrial development, with the establishment of coal camps, lumber camps, and RAILROADS, opened a great missionary field; for the laborers recruited by the capitalists were to a considerable degree "new" immigrants from European Catholic countries.

The greatest problem confronting the operators was how to secure and retain an adequate labor supply. Some company officials claimed that native whites were "at least two hundred years behind the civilization of the more densely populated sections of the United States." Whatever the merits of this argument, the native whites were not all that numerous; they were not yet ready to abandon their hillside farms to work underground (which may attest to their innate intelligence); consequently immigrants were brought into the region. Having acquired laborers, company officials usually made every reasonable effort to keep earnings as well as working and living conditions at a level to retain them. Recognizing the religious needs of their employees as well as more mundane requirements for existence, the companies encouraged Catholic priests to live in the coal towns and camps, constructed sanctuaries for the congregations, and provided housing for the clergy.

Father Ryan, writing of the Covington diocese, identified two trends in progress there during the 1880's that brought a number of Catholics into the southwestern part of the diocese. First, around the Kentucky-Tennessee border town of Jellico, a railroad was under construction and COAL MINING development was about to take place. Catholic laborers were engaged for construction work. In 1882, Reverend Francis T. Marron of Immaculate Conception Parish at Knoxville was requested to visit the area and offer mass for Catholics in the vicinity. Jellico soon became the center of a busy mining district which employed Italians, Irish, Germans, some Frenchmen, as well as other groups. Second, a few Swiss, German, and Austrian settlements were being made in Kentucky in the area around London. These families were interested in land ownership and farming. A priest from Louisville offered his services to these groups.

Jellico became the mission center for the southeastern part of the diocese. The church dedicated to St. Boniface became the mother parish. Reverend Clarence Meyer, a Benedictine priest who worked this locale from 1926 to 1932, had the following recollection:

> They (the immigrants) did not have the facilities to practice their religion formally but they considered it a must to have their children baptized and to marry and be buried in the Catholic Rite. The church in Jellico, Tennessee with its adjoining Catholic cemetery was unofficially their religious center and they considered laying to rest the remains of their

deceased in that cemetery an obligation. I myself officiated in the commitment of many who were killed in the mines. Since the people could not come to the priest by reason of lack of churches, transportation, etc., the priest would do the best to come to them. My practice was to pack my bags, hitch a ride on a railroad as far as I could and then walk the railroad track or ride a mule to wherever my destination was and then have religious services in some home.

Ironically, Catholicism provided a bridge from the past to the future for these immigrants in a Protestant nation. The opportunity to practice their religion left them with an important remnant of their Old-World heritage as they attempted to adjust to a new environment. Although it is possible to argue that Catholicism aided the coal companies that impeded assimilation in this remote part of America through their paternalism, one could also contend that urban political bosses did the same. Before immigrants could assimilate, they needed a sense of group identity. It was in American cities that many thousands of immigrants from the rural villages of Europe first developed a consciousness of their national origins; they were Hungarians, Italians, Germans, Slavs, and Poles rather than peasants from isolated villages. The development of this consciousness represented a vital step in their adjustment. To a certain extent, Catholicism fostered this phenomenon in the coal camps because it provided perhaps the only social nucleus around which the immigrants could cluster as distinctive groups.

During the 1920's, the symbiotic relationship between the Catholics and the coal companies collapsed. Developments of that decade rendered the Catholic Church a needless expense. Foreigners who worked in the Southern Appalachian coal camps had always been a highly transient group, but until World War I, they had been relatively easy to recruit and their numbers justified the companies' support of Catholicism. Following the war, economic difficulties beset the coal industry and many mines closed. Mines at Keokee, Virginia, for example, remained inactive from 1924 to 1927. Faced with unemployment at worst and an insecure situation at best, the majority of the immigrant generations fled the coal fields for the opportunities of northern cities. Even if the company had needed foreigners, it would have been unable to hire them. Restriction of immigration had been effected, and older immigrants had made their adjustment elsewhere. These ominous developments of the 1920's, followed by the stark realities of the 1930's served as the backdrop for the declining Catholic influence in Southern Appalachian coal camps.

To attempt to counteract the decline of Catholicism, the Church undertook, during the 1940's and 1950's, the establishment of missions at county seats, conducted "outdoor preaching" and RADIO preaching, dispersed used clothing to the needy, and visited door-to-door in the communities. Catholic hospitals were established. Also, educational work was launched by Catholic nuns on a more extensive scale than previously.

In East Tennessee, in particular, several missions and new churches have been established in the last few decades. This trend is partially in response to Catholic needs in such new towns as

KINGSPORT, ALCOA, NORRIS, and OAK RIDGE where "outsiders" have settled, and partially to meet the demands of the influx of Catholics into older, established towns of the area. If Americans continue to be the mobile people that they traditionally have been, then Southern Appalachia will undoubtedly harbor a more heterogeneous population in the future. Consequently, it would not be foolhardy to predict a continued Catholic presence in the region.

Margaret Ripley Wolfe

Refer to: Reverend Paul E. Ryan, *History of the Diocese of Covington, Kentucky,* Diocese of Covington, Kentucky, 1954; and Margaret Ripley Wolfe, "Aliens in Southern Appalachia: Catholics in the Coal Camps, 1900-1940," *Appalachian Heritage,* V.6, No.1 (Winter 1978), pp. 43-56.
See also: DEER LODGE
RELIGION
VINELAND

Chattanooga, located on the Tennessee River in HAMILTON COUNTY in southeast Tennessee, is a city of varied manufactures and much scenic and historical interest. It is near the point where the states of Tennessee, Georgia and Alabama come together. The 1980 Federal census gave Chattanooga's population as 169,565, and that of Hamilton County as 287,740.

Hamilton County was established in 1819, but the section south of the Tennessee River at this point remained in the hands of the CHEROKEES until the late 1830's. Only a few white traders and agents crossed the river from the county side to "Indian country" at Ross's Landing. The Landing was named for JOHN ROSS, Cherokee chief who was one of the sons of the Scottish trader Daniel Ross and the grandson of John McDonald, another early Scottish trader in this vicinity. Despite a valiant struggle led by Chief Ross, the Cherokees were rounded up at a Ross's Landing stockade and deported west. Immediately, whites began moving into the beautiful section at the Landing, and the town of Chattanooga was formed in 1838. The adoption of this Indian title for the little log-cabin settlement was made official by the Legislature in December of 1839.

Due to its strategic location at several mountain passes, Chattanooga's river trade continued to grow. Numerous STEAMBOATS could often be seen at the city wharf. However, it was the RAILROADS that assured Chattanooga's prominence. The Western and Atlantic Railroad from Georgia reached the city in 1849, and the Nashville and Chattanooga Railroad began operation between the two cities in 1854. The East Tennessee and Georgia Railroad, furnishing a connection to KNOXVILLE, also built a spur line to Chattanooga before the CIVIL WAR. Colonel James A. Whiteside was the leader in the city's rail endeavors.

Chattanooga was a focal point in the Civil War. The two armies realized the strategic importance of the city as a railroad center and gateway to the South. General Braxton Bragg occupied Chattanooga for the Confederacy, but he retreated on September 9, 1863. Soon after the Federals took over Chattanooga, the bloody Battle of Chickamauga was fought just south of town. It ended with a Federal retreat

Courtesy John Wilson

View, from Lookout Mountain, of Moccasin Bend and Chattanooga.

back to Chattanooga and the beginning of a long Confederate siege. Generals U.S. Grant, William T. Sherman and Joseph Hooker arrived to relieve the nearly starved Federals and drive the Confederates away with dramatic November victories at Lookout Mountain and Missionary Ridge.

Chattanooga was devastated by the war and by a record flood in 1867. It was hit by another flood in 1875, by several financial panics, and by scourges of cholera (1873) and yellow fever (1878). But General John T. Wilder, Captain Hiram S. Chamberlain and other men of means from the North lent their financial resources to rebuilding the city. They aimed especially at developing the rich mineral resources of the area. A real estate boom in 1887 led to the development of suburbs across the river and to the east and south of the old downtown section. Lookout Mountain, long a delight to the tourist and nature lover, began to be filled with handsome homes. Rock City and Ruby Falls attractions were later developed on the mountain. The Chickamauga and Chattanooga National Military Park was formed in 1895 at the point of Lookout Mountain, at battle sites in several sections of the city, and at Chickamauga. Chattanooga gained a horsecar line in 1875, and it had electric streetcars by the late 1880's. These rail lines radiated throughout the city area and also were built to the increasingly important residential section at Signal Mountain by the tireless Charles James.

The young Adolph Ochs came down from Knoxville in the late 1870's to build the struggling *Chattanooga Daily Times*. He departed in the mid-1890's to take over *The New York Times*. Zeboim Cartter Patten, a Union veteran from Illinois, started the Chattanooga Medicine Company and the Volunteer State Life Insurance Company. His son-in-law, John T. Lupton, secured great wealth upon making a wise investment in the bottling of the soft drink Coca-Cola. The plant at Chattanooga that opened in 1899 was the first franchised bottler of Coca-Cola.

By the close of World War II, many of Chattanooga's older residential sections were deteriorating, abandoned by those who chose mountain or suburban homes. It was decided to level the top of Cameron Hill downtown by the river, and to convert it into the Golden Gateway development. An interstate

Market Street, downtown Chattanooga, 1920's.

Courtesy John Wilson

highway system was then built into town through Missionary Ridge and around the Moccasin Bend of the river. No longer did streetcars and passenger trains serve Chattanooga. The city's historic Union Station was torn down in 1973, but the Terminal Station on South Market Street was converted to the Chattanooga Choo-Choo restaurant and family entertainment complex. Also during the 1970's, a new public library and other modern structures went up near the Union Depot site and the historic Read House hotel. In this same vicinity, work began in 1980 on a huge TENNESSEE VALLEY AUTHORITY solar-heated complex. The TVA has been an important force in Chattanooga since its establishment in the 1930's.

The University of Chattanooga, which began in 1886 as a Methodist-supported school, was merged in 1969 with THE UNIVERSITY OF TENNESSEE system. Chattanooga State Technical Community College and Tennessee Temple Schools are also located in Chattanooga. The city's oldest Baptist church is now located in the Golden Gateway, while the two oldest Methodist groups united and in 1973 opened the First-Centenary United Methodist Church on McCallie Avenue. The oldest Presbyterian church is also on McCallie Avenue. The oldest Catholic church has long stood on East Eighth Street, and there are several Jewish congregations as well as those of other denominations. Wiley Memorial Methodist Church and the First Baptist Church (Eighth Street) are historic black churches.

The city's two daily newspapers, the *Times* and the *News-Free Press*, entered into a merger arrangement in 1980 after the *Times* filed as a "failing newspaper". The *News-Free Press* was led by Roy McDonald, a native Chattanoogan who also established the old Home Store grocery chain and Blue Cross-Blue Shield of Tennessee. Today, over 600 manufacturers in the Chattanooga area employ 57,300, with an annual payroll of over $481 million. These firms produce more than 1,500 classified products or materials, including textiles, fabricated metals, chemicals, primary metals, food products, machinery, apparel, paper products and leather goods.

Courtesy Tennessee State Library

Adolph Ochs

John Wilson

Refer to: Zella Armstrong, *The History of Hamilton County and Chattanooga, Tennessee*, 2 Volumes, Chattanooga: Lookout, 1931;

Courtesy TVA

Contemporary Chattanooga, with the Hunter Museum of Art in the left foreground and Lookout Mountain in the background.

Gilbert E. Govan and James W. Livingood, *The Chattanooga Country, 1540-1951: From Tomahawks to TVA*, New York: Dutton, 1952 (Revised edition 1963, Chapel Hill: University of North Carolina Press; Third edition 1977, Knoxville: University of Tennessee Press); Charles D. McGuffey, ed. *Standard History of Chattanooga*, Knoxville: Crew & Dorey, 1911; and John Wilson, *Chattanooga's Story*, Chattanooga: *Chattanooga News-Free Press*, 1980.
See also: COMMUNITY COLLEGES

Cherokees, to the pioneers fighting them and to most early historians of Tennessee, were simply "Indians" or "savages" — a menace to Caucasian settlers and an abomination on the face of the earth. But the Cherokees were a nation, a people proud and distinguished and worthy of their name *Ahiyunwiya*, which in English means Principal People. Prior to 1700, the Cherokees lived in about eighty towns scattered along the waterways of southern APPALACHIA. These towns extended in a rough arc from the head of navigation in South Carolina, where Fort Prince George was built, to the vicinity of FORT LOUDOUN on the Little Tennessee River. The towns were in four groups: the Lower Towns in South Carolina and northern Georgia; the Middle Towns and Valley Towns in the mountains and along the streams of western North Carolina; and the Overhill Towns in East Tennessee.

Towns, of more or less importance according to their sizes and the characters of their individual chiefs, were divisions within the clans of the Cherokees. The chiefs in several of the larger towns could act independently in military, civil and religious affairs, and most of the business of government was conducted by them. They were not necessarily priests, as the tribal chief was, but they had certain religious duties in connection with the lesser festivals. Succession was in the female line, and all children belonged to the mother's clan regardless of who the father was. Traditional beliefs and customs crumbled under the impact of European occupation, as both groups learned that the Cherokees possessed two assets of commercial value: land and animal skins or furs. The Cherokees' riches were their undoing.

Lillian Perrine Davis

Clear overviews of the early history and culture of the Cherokees can be found in Charles Hudson's *The Southeastern Indians* (Knoxville: University of Tennessee Press, 1976) and in Henry T. Malone's *Cherokees of the Old South: A People in Transition* (Athens: University of Georgia Press, 1956). Cherokee prehistory and archaeology are well covered by Roy S. Dickens, Jr. (*Cherokee Prehistory*, Knoxville: University of Tennessee Press, 1976), Bennie C. Keel (*Cherokee Archaeology*, Knoxville: University of Tennessee Press, 1976), and Burton L. Purrington ("The Status and Future of Archaeology and Native American Studies in the Southern Appalachians," in *Appalachian Journal*, V.5, No.1, Autumn 1977, pp.40-54).

Cherokee beliefs, medicinal plant formulas, and other cultural patterns were first presented in James Mooney's famous "The Sacred Formulas of the Cherokees" and "Myths of the Cherokees" (Bureau of American Ethnology *Seventh Annual Report, 1885-1886*, pp. 301-397, and *Nineteenth Annual Report, 1897-1898*, Part 1, pp.3-576, Washington, D.C.: Smithsonian Institution, 1891 and 1900) and can now be found in various reprints. Contemporary observations stemming from early white contact include trader James Adair's *The History of the American Indians* (London: Edward and Charles Dilly, 1775; edited 1930 by Samuel Cole Williams, Johnson City, Tenn.: The Watauga Press, pp.237-273), botanist William Bartram's *Travels* (Philadelphia: James and Johnson, 1791; reprinted 1928, New York: Dover), and Lieutenant Henry Timberlake's *Memoirs* (London: Timberlake, 1765; edited 1927 by Samuel Cole Williams, Johnson City: Watauga).

Cherokee history during the late 18th and early 19th centuries has for years been the subject of close and extensive study. Standard overviews have been Grace Steele Woodward's *The Cherokees* (Norman: University of Oklahoma Press, 1963) and John P. Brown's *Old Frontiers* (Kingsport, Tenn.: Southern, 1938), which concentrates on the life and times of Dragging Canoe. Charles C. Royce's "The Cherokee Nation of Indians" (in Bureau of American Ethnology *Fifth Annual Report, 1883-1884*, Washington, D.C.: Smithsonian Institution, 1887; reprinted 1975, Chicago: Aldine) focuses on the many treaties negotiated between the whites and Cherokees, while Samuel Carter III provides a very readable history of the rise and removal of Cherokee civilization during the early 1800's

(*Cherokee Sunset: A Nation Betrayed*, Garden City, N.Y.: Doubleday, 1976).

Among those studies dealing with more modern history of the Eastern Band of the Cherokees, William H. Gilbert, Jr.'s *The Eastern Cherokees* (Bureau of American Ethnology Bulletin 133, Washington, D.C.: Smithsonian Institution, 1943) is a fairly comprehensive beginning. John Gulick's *Cherokees at the Crossroads* (Chapel Hill: University of North Carolina Institute for Research in Social Science, 1960; 2nd edition, 1973) serves as an update and extension of Gilbert's work. The *Appalachian Journal*'s Special Cherokee Issue (V.2, No.4, Summer 1975) also treats the Eastern Cherokees and includes essays on modern cultural identity, plant uses, and drinking patterns. The *Journal of Cherokee Studies*, published by the Museum of the Cherokee Indian in Cherokee, North Carolina, has devoted issues to the real story of Tsali, based on primary evidence; to contemporary newspaper accounts of Cherokee events; to primary documents concerning the Cherokee removal; and to diaries as well as linguistic and biographical articles. Much recent Cherokee scholarship has been collected in book form by *JCS* editor Duane H. King (Duane H. King, ed. *The Cherokee Indian Nation: A Troubled History*, Knoxville, Tenn.: University of Tennessee Press, 1979). Finally, Raymond D. Fogelson's *The Cherokees: A Critical Bibliography* (Bloomington: Indiana University Press, 1978) offers a wealth of reading to anyone interested in East Tennessee's Indian heritage.

Jim Stokely

See also: ARCHAEOLOGY (PREHISTORIC)
DEERSKIN TRADE OF THE CHEROKEE
ATTAKULLAKULLA
FORT LOUDOUN
NANCY WARD
DANIEL BOONE
DRAGGING CANOE
THE TREATY OF HOLSTON
RED CLAY COUNCIL GROUND
SEQUOYAH
JOHN ROSS
RATTLESNAKE SPRINGS

Children's Museum of Oak Ridge. From the day its doors first opened, the Children's Museum has filled a very special need, that of bringing together people of all ages and all walks of life. Where else but the Children's Museum can one find an aged cooper and a world renowned scientist working side by side? Where else can one explore a pioneer dog-trot cabin, and within a few short steps, see an exhibit of Japanese Kokeshi dolls?

The present Children's Museum was preceded by a one-room museum in early OAK RIDGE, opened in 1948 and maintained for twenty years by a group of teachers serving as the Association for Early Childhood Education. In 1972 the Senior Girl Scouts, under the direction of Mrs. Joyce Maienschein, again assessed the needs of the community and found a need for a place where both young people and adults could learn and share together. From the beginning, part of the philosophy and plan was for the museum to be a family learning experience as well as a place for individuals and classes. After identifying the need the Senior Scouts sought and obtained a $500 Reader's

Digest Foundation grant awarded for Senior Scout projects which initiate a needed community service. With much hard work, the Girl Scouts and enthusiastic members of the community gathered stored artifacts from the former museum, obtained new exhibits, received donations of craft supplies, and located the museum in the library of the vacant Jefferson Junior High School building on Kentucky Avenue. An afternoon open house on Girl Scout Sunday, March 11, 1973, marked the formal opening of the Children's Museum by members of Troop 69.

As soon as the doors were opened, a class schedule was set up and a special program slated. The museum kept regular hours each day after school and Sunday afternoons. The first summer, limited hours were established and summer classes organized. The response from the community was favorable. In September of 1973, Lorin Costanza was named director and Selma Shapiro was hired as program coordinator. Two months later, the museum's nine-member Board of Trustees named Mrs. Shapiro director, with responsibility for the administration of all museum programs. From the time she initially joined the staff, Selma Shapiro, who had been a Girl Scout leader, identified with the project. A transplanted Bostonian with four grown children, she had come with her engineer husband to Oak Ridge in October of 1945. Her charm and vitality quickly became a part of the Children's Museum. Her Yankee ingenuity and deep respect for the people of APPALACHIA, the mountains and heritage, have combined as a strong asset to the museum's development. Selma Shapiro is a director who does not acknowledge defeat.

Late in 1973, the Children's Museum became incorporated. Early in 1974, the museum was moved from the 2500 square feet of area in which it opened to a new 10,000 sq. ft. location in the empty Highland View Elementary School building. On March 23, 1974, the Tennessee Committee for the Humanities awarded a $6000 grant to the museum to hold a four-part colloquium on "Strip Mining in Appalachia—the Past, the Present and the Future." The programs brought together representatives of coal companies and of the TENNESSEE VALLEY AUTHORITY, philosophers, environmentalists, state legislators, and people who lived in strip-mining areas.

From the beginning, the Children's Museum of Oak Ridge has had a "hands on" policy where visitors can touch, explore and participate in the exhibits. In the spring of 1974, Troop 69 received a second $500 Reader's Digest grant for the Pioneer Living section of the Museum. During May, the Scouts reconstructed a dog-trot log cabin, complete with furnishings typical of the time and place, in the Pioneer Living area inside the Museum. During the summer, a Children's Museum Guild was formed and has continued to support the work of the museum. The year 1975 saw both the addition to the Pioneer Living area of a log smokehouse from Lake City, and the new Coal Mining Room, with exhibits related to the story of COAL MINING in East Tennessee.

In the Pioneer Living area, Children's Museum of Oak Ridge.

Also in 1975, the Children's Museum was selected to officially kick off Oak Ridge's Bicentennial celebration with a spring festival. The spring Appalachian Music and Craft Festival has continued as an annual event. It brings together some of the best craftsmen, musicians, dancers and storytellers from the Appalachian region. Through the arrangements for the smokehouse, Selma Shapiro had met the late Beulah Brummett Braden, author of a manuscript chronicling middle class life in this area at the turn of the century. In 1976, the Children's Museum joined with *The Oak Ridger* and *The Clinton Courier-News* to publish *When Grandma Was a Girl* as a Bicentennial project. The museum celebrated a Bicentennial Weekend in April of 1976 with a festival entitled "Spirit of '76: Reflections—Projections." The festival commemorated the 200th anniversary of the ride of Paul Revere and the Battle of Lexington.

In September of 1977, the museum established an Orff music program as a continuing project. Also in September, the Children's Museum was one of ten arts organizations in the state which received the Governor's Award in the Arts. A month later, Southern authors and poets came together at the museum for "Appalachia in Print", a first-ever gathering for writers in East Tennessee. The following spring, the National Endowment for the Humanities designated the Children's Museum as one of the few Learning Museums in the country. On April 14, 1978, NEH awarded the museum a grant of $394,000 for a three-year public educational project entitled "An Appalachian Experience". This project, which began in June of 1978, undertook a broad-based exploration of Appalachia involving outreach to a 16-county area in East Tennessee.

Since its inception, the Children's Museum of Oak Ridge has seen phenomenal growth in owned collections, including a collection of Japanese Kokeshi dolls presented by the Smithsonian Institution. There has been a significant increase in staff and financial support. The museum, which is an agency of the United Way, reaches more than 100,000 persons annually and offers services to schools in some 20 counties. Youth programs include a Youth Advisory Council and a Junior Curator program. The Children's Museum has also become a cultural development center. It is dedicated to promoting interest in the arts, sciences and humanities, with major emphasis on the folklore and history of the Southern Appalachian region. In so doing, the museum has served as a catalyst in generating an exchange of knowledge between the city of Oak Ridge and the surrounding countryside. The Children's Museum is, finally, people—people working together and learning together.

Dorothy Senn

Refer to: Beulah Brummett Braden, *When Grandma Was a Girl*, Oak Ridge, Tenn.: *The Oak Ridger* and *The Clinton Courier-News*, 1976; Aalbert Heine, "Making Glad the Heart of Childhood," in *Museum News*, V. 58, No. 2 (November-December 1979), pp. 23-25; and *An Appalachian Studies Teacher's Manual*, Oak Ridge, Tenn.: Children's Museum of Oak Ridge, 1981.

See also: MUSEUM OF APPALACHIA
MUSEUMS

Civil War (Battles and Raids). For both sides in the Civil War, East Tennessee held great strategic importance. The Confederacy needed the food supplies produced by the rich Tennessee River Valley; its factories required the saltpeter, copper, and other minerals found in the region. Of additional importance, one of the South's few continuous RAILROADS ran from BRISTOL to CHATTANOOGA and linked the upper Confederacy to the Mississippi Valley. For the Confederate armies, this railroad was to be a main conduit for troops and supplies. Union forces not only had to stop the flow of Confederate supplies from East Tennessee, but needed to seize the railroad and occupy the key cities of KNOXVILLE and Chattanooga. The latter was the strategic point for launching an invasion of the lower South. President Lincoln and his generals came to believe that control of the Nashville-Chattanooga-Atlanta corridor would sap Confederate strength and hasten the end of the war.

For many East Tennesseans, General Felix Zollicoffer and the Confederate forces that moved into the area in the summer of 1861 were the enemy. Staunchly Unionist, the majority of the people resented the "occupation" of their land and gave little support to their self-proclaimed guardians. Indeed, violent resistance soon flared. Believing that they were preparing the way for Union troops to move into East Tennessee from Kentucky, well-organized Unionists on the night of November 8, 1861, burned railroad bridges all along the Bristol - Chattanooga route. Confederate authorities retaliated by arresting suspected bridge-burners and trying them before military courts. Two men were hanged, and others were sent to prison. Alerted to the "disloyalty" in East Tennessee, Confederates proceeded to occupy Chattanooga.

With Confederate troops in the major cities and most of the surrounding counties, Unionists suffered greatly during the first two years of the war. After the Confederacy imposed a conscription law in April of 1862, many Union men sought to avoid the draft by fleeing to the Union lines in Kentucky. It was a hazardous journey for the men. The hills and mountains presented formidable barriers, but Confederate patrols posed the most danger. Those caught by the patrols were often subjected to physical abuse and imprisonment.

To guide their fellow Unionists to safety, a number of "pilots" and scouts volunteered their services. From CARTER COUNTY, DANIEL ELLIS led hundreds of Union sympathizers to the Union camps beyond the Cumberland Gap. In the Sequatchie Valley area, another pilot, Richard Flynn, conducted Unionists from as far away as Georgia and Alabama to the Kentucky havens. Nicknamed the "Red Fox", Flynn became a master at evading the Confederate forces sent to destroy his escape routes.

The horrors of a particular kind of civil war came early to East Tennessee. Guerrilla warfare, often pitting neighbor against neighbor, made life precarious and property vulnerable to seizure or destruction. Roving bands of these irregular soldiers, with many giving only lip service to the Confederate or Union cause, raided the farms and towns, confiscated food, stole valuables, and left death and ruin in their wake.

Two of these guerrilla groups were especially active on the western border of the region. Operating from a base in the Calfkiller River Valley of White County, the Champ Ferguson band upheld the Confederate cause by raiding suspected Unionists all along the Cumberland Plateau. Ferguson, who boasted that he personally killed over one hundred men during the war, sometimes led his bushwhackers even farther afield, attacking on one occasion a Federal supply post near Strawberry Plains and, late in the war, taking part in the battle of Saltville, Virginia. His counterpart in irregular warfare was a FENTRESS COUNTY Unionist, "Tinker Dave" Beatty. Harassed by Ferguson and other Confederate sympathizers, Beatty began retaliatory raids of his own in early 1862. By keeping the Confederate guerrillas occupied with their forays, Beatty and his men were of particular help to the Union forces after they entered East Tennessee in 1863. Beatty emerged from the war as a local hero; Federal authorities hanged Ferguson in October of 1865.

Suffering from the depredations of guerrilla bands and property

Courtesy TVA

Chattanooga, a strategic rail and water transport center, during the Civil War.

confiscations by Confederate troops, East Tennessee Unionists finally received relief in the summer of 1863. Conducting a raid to disrupt Confederate defenses, Colonel William Sanders and 1500 Union cavalrymen left Kentucky for East Tennessee in June. The raiders routed Confederate troops at Wartburg, seized military supplies at Lenoir's Station (Lenoir City), and engaged in a brief artillery duel with Confederate forces in Knoxville. Farther east, Sanders' men destroyed bridges near Strawberry Plains before returning to Kentucky.

In August of 1863, having maneuvered General Braxton Bragg and his Confederate army out of Middle Tennessee, General William Rosecrans directed his Union forces to move against Chattanooga. On August 21, General Ambrose Burnside with 15,000 men from his Army of the Ohio began the northern invasion of East Tennessee. To help Bragg stop Rosecrans's army, General Simon Bolivar Buckner and his 6,000 soldiers evacuated Knoxville and joined the Confederate forces near Chattanooga. On September 1, Burnside's advance guard reached Knoxville. Two days later, Burnside and his remaining forces arrived. After more than two years of Confederate control, East Tennessee once again was in Union hands. Confederate sympathizers fled into hiding; large crowds of Unionists hailed Burnside and his soldiers as their deliverers.

While Knoxville celebrated, Rosecrans's army was well on its way to taking control of the second link in the Nashville - Chattanooga - Atlanta corridor. Through adroit maneuvers by the Union forces and inadequate responses by the Confederate commanders, Bragg's army was forced to abandon Chattanooga on September 7. Two days later, Rosecrans occupied the city without a battle. With Bragg's forces still in the vicinity, Union control of the area remained insecure.

The gateway to Atlanta was too valuable for the Confederates to give up without a fight. In early September Bragg asked for and received reinforcements from other Confederate commands. From Virginia came General James Longstreet and 11,000 troops. From the Alabama - Mississippi area 9,000 infantrymen arrived. Rarely had Confederate armies cooperated with one another so well, but rarely had the prize of battle been so important.

On September 19-20, the Union and Confederate forces clashed in the Battle of Chickamauga, ten miles south of Chattanooga. Longstreet's soldiers poured through a gap in the Federal lines and caused two corps of Union troops to panic and flee toward Chattanooga. Rosecrans himself became unnerved and abandoned the field. A Union rout was averted only because General George Thomas rallied his troops and held them together against ferocious Confederate assaults. Thomas's stand permitted the bulk of the Union forces to reach Chattanooga safely.

Chickamauga produced a desperately needed victory for the Confederacy, but at a high cost. Bragg's army suffered some 21,000 casualties, about forty percent of its strength. Rosecrans's losses numbered about 17,000. The Confederates, however, did have the enemy bottled up in Chattanooga. His control of the railroad and river routes to Chattanooga made Bragg decide to starve the Federals into abandoning the city. By early October food shortages afflicted soldiers and civilians alike in Chattanooga.

To avoid further setbacks west of the Appalachians, President Lincoln appointed General Ulysses S. Grant as the supreme commander of Union forces in the region. General Thomas, "Rock of Chickamauga", replaced Rosecrans as commander of the Chattanooga forces. Acting swiftly, Grant directed reinforcements to converge on the beleaguered city, forced open a new supply route, and laid plans to rout the besieging Confederate forces occupying Missionary Ridge and Lookout Mountain. The Confederate generals inadvertently aided Grant by quarreling among themselves and dividing their army. In early November, Bragg sent Longstreet with about one third of the Confederate troops on an expedition to retake Knoxville.

On November 23-25, Grant's forces struck the Confederates besieging Chattanooga. After two days of heavy fighting, the Southern army had been driven into a defensive position on Missionary Ridge. Late on November 25, Thomas ordered his troops to create a diversion by assaulting the Confederate rifle pits at the bottom of the ridge. This accomplished, the exultant soldiers, without waiting for new orders, dashed up the ridge, routed the Confederate defenders, and sent them fleeing in panic. Missionary Ridge thus fell into Union hands. Bragg's army, victors only two months before, straggled deeper into Georgia. Chattanooga was now secure; the lower

South lay exposed to Union invasion.

Ignoring Bragg's plight, Longstreet continued his operations in East Tennessee. Burnside's scattered forces gave ground and slowly retreated toward Knoxville, where a stand against Longstreet's forces could be better made. On November 29, Longstreet launched an assault against Fort Sanders, the city's northwestern bastion. The attack went badly from the beginning. In the predawn darkness, Confederate soldiers became entangled in the wire strung along the ground in front of the fort and then plunged unexpectedly into a deep ditch at the base of the fort's wall. Makeshift grenades and rifle fire from the fort tore into the men in the ditch. The battle lasted only twenty minutes, but this was enough time for the Federal defenders to inflict terrible losses on the Confederates. Longstreet's forces retreated to avoid more carnage, but left behind 813 casualties. The defenders had suffered only five killed and eight wounded.

Hearing that Union reinforcements were moving toward Knoxville, Longstreet lifted the city's siege on December 4. Russellville became the site of his winter headquarters. In April of

General Ulysses S. Grant, lower left, on Lookout Mountain a few days after General Joseph Hooker's successful assault. (November 24, 1863).

Courtesy National Archives (111-BA-2276)

1864, Longstreet's army quietly rejoined Lee's forces in Virginia.

The departure of Longstreet's soldiers marked the end of major military operations in East Tennessee. For the remainder of the war, Union forces, divided into small detachments, consolidated their hold on East Tennessee by destroying pockets of Confederate resistance and routing hostile guerrilla bands. John Hunt Morgan, the famous Confederate cavalry leader, became the victim of one of these Union forays. In September of 1864, Federal troops killed Morgan and captured his staff in Greeneville.

By the summer of 1865, peace had finally returned to East Tennessee. But the war would not be soon forgotten. Ruined farms, damaged cities, the many families that had suffered violence and death provided proof of civil war's horrors. The soldiers' graves offered additional testimony that the war had been indeed a costly one. For East Tennesseans, the Civil War had finally meant a legacy of bitterness and sadness.

Larry H. Whiteaker

Refer to: Thomas L. Connelly, *Civil War Tennessee: Battles and Leaders,* Knoxville: University of Tennessee Press, 1979; Thurman Sensing, *Champ Ferguson, Confederate Guerilla,* Nashville: Vanderbilt University Press, 1942; and Digby Gordon Seymour, *Divided Loyalties: Fort Sanders and the Civil War in East Tennessee,* Knoxville: University of Tennessee Press, 1963.

See also: BEERSHEBA SPRINGS
CADES COVE
FARRAGUT

Civil War (Civilian Life and Institutions). Throughout the secession crisis of 1861, East Tennessee displayed a fervid loyalty to the Union, refusing to follow Governor Isham G. Harris's calls for secession. Even after Tennessee had officially seceded, most East Tennesseans never accepted the authority of the Southern Confederacy.

Even though the majority sympathized with the Union, a sufficient number of East Tennesseans supported the Confederacy to create a civil war within a civil war. Both sides seemed bent on rooting out or destroying those who would not conform to the appropriate cause. Neighbors, classmates, and even fellow worshippers at local churches were suddenly turned into the bitterest of enemies. As a result, life for the people of the region became one of fear, distrust, deprivation, and often extreme misery. Contributing to their predicament was the fact that East Tennessee, like the rest of the state, experienced immediate military action. Moreover, unlike many areas of the lower South that saw little or no armed clashes until the waning months of the war, the eastern counties of Tennessee were torn by fighting even after Lee's surrender at Appomattox. Whether on a large scale, such as the KNOXVILLE and CHATTANOOGA campaigns of 1863, or the smaller — but in many ways more terrifying — scale of almost constant guerrilla warfare, the area remained in the vortex of war.

Just as the war touched the lives of the people of East Tennessee, it also affected the institutions that were the threads in the fabric of their society. Because of the divisive nature of the conflict, all formal institutions — local government, schools, churches, and slavery — were severely strained during the decade of the 1860's.

Local government continued to operate throughout the war, but its regular functioning was frequently interrupted and it quickly became a tool of both Confederate and Federal authorities to aid in the war effort. In many ways the role and function of local government grew to unprecedented levels in response to the stresses of war. Chattanooga and Knoxville city governments expanded their police forces to assure the maintenance of law and order amid rapidly increasing and constantly fluctuating populations. When citizens experienced shortages of salt, corn, hay, and even firewood, city and county governments alike appointed agents and appropriated funds to acquire these needed commodities. This expansion in services, coupled with a marked decrease in revenues taken into city and county coffers, brought local government to near bankruptcy in much of the region. For the governments of Chattanooga and Knoxville, where local economies recovered soon after the war, city treasuries quickly filled; but county governments in rural areas suffered the effects of war for many years.

Education was unable to withstand the strains of conflict. College classrooms emptied rapidly, and the already limited funds available for public schools quickly dried up. Private academies, especially female institutes, managed to function on a diminished scale until the disruptions of Federal occupation and the growing intensity of the war after 1863. Many children, however, obtained the basics of an education in their own homes. In the last months of the war, small private classrooms opened and met with overwhelming responses. The colleges faced an enormous task of recovery. Most had suffered not only losses of students, but also extensive physical damages caused by occupying armies. Fortunately, almost all were able gradually to resume instruction by the end of the 1860's.

Of all institutions, the church most visibly revealed the acrimony that troubled East Tennessee's population. Even though the marching to and fro of the armies disrupted churches and even demolished many places of worship, the most destructive force was internal division. For decades, the various denominations in the region had warred among themselves and within themselves over theology and church policy. But the political questions of the 1860's tore the churches asunder, irrespective of denomination. Unlike other parts of the South, the East Tennessee clergy was not overwhelmingly in favor of the Confederacy. Yet a large enough element was pro-Rebel so as to cause divisions within the denominations. The governing bodies of Methodist and Presbyterian churches at one time or another prescribed national loyalty to the Confederacy and later to the Union as a test for the ministry and in some cases for church membership. Individual congregations split into Unionist and Rebel factions, and even though the armies laid down their weapons in 1865, the conflict within many church bodies continued for years. Unionist-dominated congregations insisted that communicants who had been Confederates must confess their "sins" or suffer excommunication. Usually the ex-Rebels refused to recognize their wartime loyalties as a sin, and rather than return to their former churches, they banded together to create new congregations with persons of compatible wartime sympathies. Such bodies inevitably joined the Southern wing of their denomination, such as the Methodist Episcopal Church, South or the Southern Presbyterian Church.

One institution, slavery, did not survive the war. Although blacks were only a small percentage of the East Tennessee population, at times all whites felt threatened by the freedom of the slaves. Initially all Unionists pledged loyalty to the Federal Government, but still maintained that slavery must be preserved. The disruptions of war and certain Federal policies such as the conscription of Negroes caused the *de facto* death of slavery by 1864. The slave issue, however, split the Unionist coalition as Radicals sought the institution's end as a means of weakening the Confederacy and punishing Rebels. Because most whites had little interest in uplifting the freedmen, agencies such as the Freedmen's Bureau and Northern benevolent aid societies met with a hostile reception. As in the rest of the South, a policy of segregation was instituted soon after the war.

East Tennessee's war experience reveals that its people and institutions were profoundly affected. The population suffered not only from the presence of contending armies, but most of all from a malicious internal struggle that pitted citizen against citizen. The internal conflict presented a microcosm of the struggle that divided the nation as a whole.

Charles F. Bryan, Jr.

Refer to: Charles F. Bryan, Jr., "The Civil War in East Tennessee: A Social, Political, and Economic Study," University of Tennessee dissertation, 1978; Thomas W. Humes, *The Loyal Mountaineers of Tennessee*, Knoxville: Ogden, 1888; and Oliver P. Temple, *East Tennessee and the Civil War*, Cincinnati: R. Clarke, 1899.

See also: PARSON BROWNLOW
UNIVERSITY OF THE SOUTH
WASHINGTON COLLEGE ACADEMY

Claiborne County

Size: 444 Square Miles (284,160 acres)
Established: 1801
Named For: William Claiborne, U.S. Representative from Tennessee
County Seat: Tazewell
Other Major Cities, Towns, or Communities:
New Tazewell
Harrogate
Clairfield
Arthur
Cumberland Gap
Speedwell
Hopewell

Refer to: John Gaventa, *Power and Powerlessness: Quiescence and Rebellion in an Appalachian Valley*, Urbana: University of Illinois Press, 1980; and Robert L. Kincaid, *The Wilderness Road*, Indianapolis: Bobbs-Merrill, 1946 (reprinted 1966, Middlesboro, Ky.).

See also: LINCOLN MEMORIAL UNIVERSITY

Philander Priestley Claxton
(September 28, 1862 - January 12, 1957)

was born in a one-room log cabin in Bedford County, Tennessee, during the chaos of the CIVIL WAR. He went on to become an outstanding educator, a United States Commissioner of Education, a university president, and an ardent and vocal supporter of public education. Philander started school when he was four years old, having learned his ABC's and the numbers 1 to 100 from his mother. The only text at his first school was Webster's *Blue Back Speller*. The public school system was very sporadic after the Civil War, so Philander attended several small schools at which he progressed through text books at his own speed.

When Claxton was seventeen, his father borrowed money so that Philander could attend THE UNIVERSITY OF TENNESSEE. He entered U.T., in January of 1880, with $37.50 that he had earned by hauling lumber. A state agricultural scholarship paid his tuition, and Claxton took a double load of courses. He graduated in 2½ years at the age of nineteen. His dream was to study law at Vanderbilt, but the offer of a teaching position in Goldsboro, North Carolina, changed his plans. Claxton taught in Goldsboro, and in 1883 he accepted the post of superintendent of schools in Kinston, North Carolina. During the next two years, he did graduate work in education at Johns Hopkins University.

Claxton married Varina Moore from Blowing Rock, North Carolina, in December of 1885. They honeymooned in Germany, where Claxton spent much time observing the highly organized school system. He noted how strong government support, intensive teacher training, and the public's high regard for teachers all worked together to produce superior schools. He was impressed by how German teachers spent their class time in discussion, review, and synthesis of facts, rather than in the memory drills and recitations used by American teachers. Upon his return to Baltimore, Claxton applied for a teaching position but could not provide the political influence necessary to land the job. He went to North Carolina and became superintendent of schools in Wilson and, later, in Asheville. The University of Tennessee awarded him a masters degree for his study in Baltimore and in Germany.

Philander Claxton believed that the most important function of a superintendent was the promotion of good teaching. His teacher meetings were forums for the discussion of new ideas and methods in education. He initiated phonics, field trips, kindergartens, and the elimination of corporal punishment in his schools. Because only 40% of school-age children attended schools in North Carolina, Claxton fought for a compulsory attendance law. He also believed in public education for all children without regard to their race or social standing. This was doubly unpopular in many towns, for wealthy families resented the idea that their taxes would provide as good an education for poor children as they would be able to purchase for their own children.

In 1902, University of Tennessee president Charles W. Dabney invited Claxton to Knoxville as the chief of the Bureau of Investigation and Information for the Southern Education

Board. Claxton was also to organize a summer school for teachers and to organize and head a department of education at the university. Claxton's summer schools became overwhelming successes and continued for many years. The department of education began with four teachers and 75 students; today's College of Education at U.T., based in a building named for Claxton, offers advanced degrees in many areas of education.

Philander Claxton was appointed in 1911 as the United States Commissioner of Education. For the next decade he averaged 75,000 miles of travel and more than 200 speeches per year. In these talks and in many articles, Claxton advocated consolidation of rural schools, summer schools for students, and adult and vocational education. President Harding removed Claxton from his Commissionship in 1921, but Philander soon became Provost of the University of Alabama. He later was superintendent of schools in Tulsa, Oklahoma, and president of Austin Peay Normal School in Clarksville, Tennessee. When Philander P. Claxton died at the age of 94, he left behind him a lifetime of work devoted to making sure that all children receive their rightful due: a free public education. Some have called him the South's Horace Mann; he was, at the least, a prolific writer, courageous crusader, and outstanding educator.

Diane Bohannon

Refer to: Philander P. Claxton, *Some Rights of Children and Youth,* 1953; and Charles Lee Lewis, *Philander Priestley Claxton: Crusader For Public Education,* Knoxville: University of Tennessee Press, 1948.

See also: WILLIAM A. McCALL
THE ONE - ROOM SCHOOL

Clear Branch Baptist Church of Coal Creek, now Longfield Baptist Church of Lake City, exemplified in its early history much of the pre-CIVIL WAR character of East Tennessee religious life. Logs from one of the church's old meeting houses are now on display as a reassembled smokehouse at the CHILDREN'S MUSEUM OF OAK RIDGE.

Clear Branch Baptist Church came into being through the preaching ministry of Chesley H. Boatwright. After Boatwright came from Virginia to GRAINGER COUNTY in 1817, he was deeply influenced by his father-in-law, Hughes Owen Taylor, a well-known pioneer Baptist preacher in East Tennessee. When Boatwright moved to KNOX COUNTY in 1824, he and his wife Louisa lost no time in joining Mt. Hebron Baptist Church. In 1831, he was licensed by that church to preach. Bethel Baptist Church in ANDERSON COUNTY ordained him to the ministry.

Brother Boatwright came to Coal Creek in the fall of 1831. Throughout the winter, he preached at night to small groups in various homes of the community. As the weather grew warmer, he preached at the schoolhouse. During the spring of 1832, Boatwright asked Elder Joshua Frost to assist him in his preaching ministry, and a spontaneous revival took place. Frost suggested that the resulting congregation of 30 people petition his Zion Baptist Church to instate them as a missionary arm. They did so, and from 1832 to 1834 the congregation constituted an "arm of Zion at Coal Creek."

By 1834, the "arm" was strong enough to ask Zion to make it a separate body. Zion appointed a "presbytery" consisting of Elders Joshua Frost, John Clark, and Chesley Boatwright to attend to a constitution for the new body. The missionary arm drew up articles of faith and rules of decorum, which the elders studied and found to be consistent with Baptist beliefs. The elders charged the arm to remain faithful to the articles and then officially declared it as Clear Branch Baptist Church.

Each member was expected to be baptised by immersion, and infants were not accorded baptism. Baptisms were held in several nearby creeks, but the favorite place for conducting the ordinance of baptism was Lindsay's Mill, later covered by the waters of Norris Lake. Baptisms sometimes took place in the dead of winter, and ice had to be broken to conduct the ceremony. In addition to being baptised, each member was expected to attend the monthly business meeting held on a particular Saturday, and to attend the worship services on the following Sunday. The member was expected to remain faithful to the articles of faith, abide by the rules of decorum, keep the Ten Commandments, and observe the unwritten moral code of good behavior. If a member strayed from the faith or broke the rules, he was subject to "exclusion". Exclusion was sometimes called "being churched" or being "turned out". Exclusion meant only that the person was no longer considered a member of the church; it did not mean that he or she was no longer considered a Christian.

Exclusion proceedings were conducted according to a set pattern. At a monthly meeting in 1838, for example, Brother Canady (Kennedy) "proffer-red" a charge against Brother Elisha Adkins for getting drunk at muster on New River. The moderator appointed Brother Canady to "cite" Brother Adkins to attend the next business meeting in order to answer the charge. If Brother Adkins did not respond to the citation, he could be excluded automatically for "contempt of the church". If he came to the meeting, he had to face witnesses against him. He had either to prove his innocence or to acknowledge his guilt. If he was shown guilty, he was subject to exclusion. Brother Adkins came to the meeting and answered the charge by expressing his deep sorrow for getting drunk. The church accepted his statement and forgave him. Soon afterward, Adkins was again charged with drunkenness. This time the church excluded him. Several months later, Adkins attended church again and made a satisfactory statement of repentance before the congregation. The church received him by "recantation" and restored him to full membership in the church.

Exclusion did not always have this result. Sometimes the excluded member was so humiliated and angered that he never returned to church. Some typical cases of exclusion were Brother Carroll for fighting, Brother Disney for covenant breaking, Sister Johnson for telling a scandalous lie, Sister White for refusing to cook her husband's supper and separating from him, Brother

Reynolds for participating in a shooting match, Sister Marlow for cursing and swearing, Brother Wilson for getting drunk, Sister Smith for fornication, Brother Adkins for stealing his brother's cattle and leaving town, Sister Duncan for having frolics (parties) at her house, and Brother and Sister Huckaby for not being able to prove that they were legally married. Gradually the practice of exclusion was discontinued. The members came to realize that those proffering charges were guilty of sins themselves. By the 1940's, the custom became almost non-existent.

In 1839 the church itself experienced exclusion. Powell Valley Association, organized in 1818 and second oldest Association of Baptists in Tennessee, took an anti-mission stand. Clear Branch Baptist Church belonged to this Association, but the majority in the church did not agree with the anti-mission stand. Powell Valley Association excluded the majority and retained the minority. The minority faction, led by Michael Spessard, continued to call itself Clear Branch Baptist Church for nearly fifteen years thereafter. But in November of 1839, the Clear Branch majority joined with other congregations excluded from the Powell Valley Association and met at Glade Springs Baptist Church in CAMPBELL COUNTY. They formed another area association called the Northern Association of Baptists. Clear Branch was a member of this Association until 1854, when it became a charter member of the Clinton Association and changed its name to Longfield Baptist Church. From 1839 to 1854, then, there were two churches in Anderson County which called themselves Clear Branch Baptist. Powell Valley Association and its churches became known as "Primitive Baptists", while Northern Association churches were known as "Missionary Baptists". The distinction still exists.

For the next hundred years, Longfield Baptist Church certainly lived up to its name "Missionary". Its influence became widespread in Anderson, Campbell, Morgan, and Scott counties. During this period Longfield established eight churches and six missionary arms in these counties. Churches established included Union (1846) near Wartburg, Macedonia (1847) and Cherry Bottom (1914) near the Anderson-Campbell county line, Beech Fork (1856) across Caryville Mountain from Caryville, Coal Creek (1872, now The First Baptist Church) and Main Street (1928) in Lake City, and Beech Grove (1873) and Island Ford (1892) in Anderson County. Missionary arms were located at Smokey Creek near Smokey Junction (1852, a church in 1873), Deep Ford in Campbell County (1860, a church in 1913, later disbanded because of Norris Lake), the Swag on Vowell Mountain (1860), and John Huckaby's (1872), Mill Springs (1874), and Big Springs (1878) in Anderson County.

During the Civil War, nearly all of the churches and arms formed by Longfield were seriously affected. Smokey Creek Arm evidently disbanded for the duration. Although no major battles were fought near these churches, the danger was so great that meetings were discontinued. Longfield did not send delegates to the Association during this time, but it continued its worship services.

The women who were members of Longfield did no preaching from the pulpit, but they did much work in their supportive role. Sally Leach, for example, made bread for church use in the ordinance of the Lord's Supper. Louisa Riggs practically made a career out of feeding Saturday and Sunday dinner to visiting preachers and delegates from the Association. Many housewives provided clean and comfortable lodgings for the visiting officials. Their contribution may seem small and undistinguished by today's standards. But in those days, clean lodging, good meals, and food supplies were all the church members could afford to give in payment for the labors of their pastors and missionaries.

Few of these latter received much pay. Most made their living by farming or COAL MINING. But the preachers did not complain. Most of them were like William Webb, who donated land for Longfield Baptist Church in 1854. It is recorded in that deed that Webb gave the land to the church because of his love for the church and for the Redeemer's Kingdom.

Edith Wilson Hutton

Refer to: James Jehu Burnett, *Sketches of Tennessee's Pioneer Baptist Preachers*, Nashville: Marshall and Bruce, 1919.
See also: RELIGION

Clerking for the L & N. I was born in 1901. I grew up in Coal Creek (now Lake City) and graduated from Coal Creek High School in 1918. Shortly after World War I, thinking it would be good for my health to work out in the open for a while, I took a job on the Louisville and Nashville railroad section. F. P. Flinchum was the foreman. Our work consisted of putting in cross ties, laying steel rail, surfacing the track, and grassing the roadbed. Our means of transportation was a hand lever car.

Later, I quit the section and gained a job in the L & N depot as warehouseman or helper. This was the real beginning of my railroad career — not in the mechanical or transportation part but in the clerical part. I learned to make freight bills, bills of lading, and waybills, file tariffs, sell passenger tickets, check baggage and bill express shipments. I also had to do the janitor work, handle freight, and unload baggage and express from the trains. I worked at Coal Creek from 1920 to 1925, when I was transferred to LaFollette.

During this decade, known as the Roaring Twenties, I had steady work except for a brief layoff in 1921. This period was truly the heyday of railroading, with passenger trains numerous, travel good, and practically everything shipped by freight or express. In those days the railroad employed many people in many different categories of work. On the trains, there were engineers, firemen, conductors, flagmen, brakemen and baggage men. In the depots, there were agents, operators, clerks, and warehousemen. In the track department, there were the section workers, extra gangs that maintained the tracks, and signal men, telephone repairmen, carpenters, and painters. Some of the gangs had camp cars, where they cooked, ate, and slept when out on the road.

Business with the RAILROADS was good until the stock market crash of 1929. The Depression did not affect me until the middle of 1931, when I was sent to Maryville. I worked there about eight months before an older clerk claimed my job. The next two or three years, in the depth of the Depression, were lean years. There was no Social Security, no unemployment insurance, no welfare, no relief, no food stamps, no work, and no money. We had to struggle through the best we could, yet we managed to get food, and I got a few days extra work now and then. In the fall of 1936, I bid in a job as clerk at Athens. I worked there until 1942, with the exception of a six-month layoff in 1938. The job was abolished in 1942, and I took the clerk's job at ALCOA. Business was good during World War II due to the making and shipping of aluminum to various aircraft companies.

I worked at Alcoa from 1942 until I retired in 1965. In the meantime, the L&N discontinued using the steam locomotive and substituted the diesel locomotive. The diesel with extra units could pull longer and heavier trains at less expense. It enabled the railroad to do away with coaling stations and water towers. During the early 1960's, the L&N Railroad established piggy-back tractor trailer service and automobile car racks. This increased their business a great deal. They also built spur tracks and ramps so that they could load and unload trailers, thereby providing direct service from factory to warehouse. The railroads will always be needed to haul heavy and bulky articles for long distances. I hope that America will continue to use the railroads, and use them more as time goes by, since they have contributed so much to the prosperity of our country.

Verlin A. Wilson

See also: OAKDALE
SOUNDS OF RAILROADING

Cleveland. The legislative act which created BRADLEY COUNTY on February 10, 1836, provided that the county seat, when established, should be named Cleveland. The name was to honor Benjamin Cleveland, a veteran of the Revolutionary War, who had seen action at King's Mountain. Bradley County was fashioned out of the Ocoee District, which had been a part of the Cherokee Nation. With the future of the CHEROKEES destined mostly for west of the Mississippi River, white settlers in 1835 began to settle in the area, near the present-day post office. Early settlers faced a choice between "Taylor's Place" and land owned by Deer-in-the-Water. Taylor's Place was chosen by a majority of one vote, due to an abundant water source.

In 1838 the Tennessee legislature authorized a group of commissioners to survey the town, assign site numbers, and sell lots at public auction. Proceeds from the sale were to pay the state for two sections of land upon which the town was to be located, and to raise an additional amount of up to $8,000 to build a courthouse and jail. Among the first buildings to be constructed in 1836 was a log courthouse located on the central square. In 1840, Thomas

Emil Sienknecht / Courtesy TVA

Picking strawberries near Cleveland, May 1940.

Crutchfield erected a brick building on the site. The state legislature incorporated Cleveland two years later. The first election, for a mayor and six aldermen, was held Monday, April 4, 1842. The first city officers are not known, but three of the early mayors were G.W. Parks, W.J. Campbell, and J.C. Brown.

In 1837 the Methodists and Cumberland Presbyterians established church congregations in Cleveland, thereby beginning a community tradition as a religious center. That same year, Oak Grove Academy was granted a charter. By 1838, Cleveland reported a population of 400 and was rapidly becoming a popular trading center. Miss Rosine Parmentier of New York City visited Cleveland in 1852 on her way to visit the Old Dutch Settlement (VINELAND) in POLK COUNTY. Her diary recorded that Cleveland had a population of about 1,000 and was "well laid out," with streets that were "wide and straight, many of them planted with trees." The real growth of the town came in the 1850's with the railroad and newspapers. The first newspaper was the *Cleveland Dispatch*, a Whig journal, which premiered two weeks before its Democratic rival, the *Cleveland Banner*. The town's first financial institution, the Ocoee Bank, was chartered in 1854 and continued to do business until the CIVIL WAR.

As the strength of the Union was tested in 1861, the city and county voted to remain with the United States. Other events, however, determined that Tennessee would cast her lot with other southern states. The community experienced little military action, but there was stress within the community, because feelings ran strong among supporters of the respective sides. Cleveland recovered slowly after the Civil War; in 1866, population was reported at 1,500. By the 1870's, however, more economic and cultural activity was manifest. Among the buildings erected around the courthouse square was Craigmiles Hall, popularly known as Craigmiles Opera House, constructed by Walter Craigmiles in 1878. Besides serving as Cleveland's first cultural center, the Opera House hosted a number of social, political, and religious gatherings. For a brief time it also served as a skating rink. Another member of the same family, John H. Craigmiles, was a leading contributor in the completion of St. Luke's Episcopal Church, a Gothic structure of native stone and locally made bricks.

By the late 1870's, the community was participating in the industrial emphasis that was engulfing the country. Hardwick Stove Company, the city's oldest industry, was established in 1879. Other industries, such as Cleveland Woolen Mill in 1880 and Cleveland Chair Company in 1884, were soon to follow. During the 1880's, the town experienced a flurry of interest in real estate. A number of individuals bought land and erected residences, while a number of business facilities began operation. The 1880 census showed a population of 1,812; by 1900 the size of the town had doubled to 3,643. Colonel R.M. Edwards, an early observer of events in Cleveland, reported that in 1890 there were nine practicing physicians, twelve attorneys, eleven general mercantile establishments, fourteen grocery stores, two millinery establishments, three hardware stores, three drug stores, six butcher shops, one shoe store, seven licensed saloons, two hotels, and three livery stables.

In 1886 the city's first public transportation system was inaugurated. It was a mule-drawn trolley car which ran from the depot up Inman Street to Cleveland National Bank, where it turned north on Ocoee Street and ended near the monuments. Other improvements came. In 1891 a local observer reported that "Cleveland is fast putting on city airs. We now have a street car line, a telephone exchange, a water works system secured, and are now to have free mail delivery. The next step will be electric lights. With our fine schools, there is not a more desirable location for a home in the South than in Cleveland." By 1895 electricity was locally available. The present downtown profile was established in the thirty-five year period from 1880 to 1915. Most of the buildings have kept their exterior physical appearance, with modifications being made inside for lighting, heating, cooling, and space arrangements.

In 1954 a period of industrial growth was stimulated by the location in nearby

Calhoun, Tennessee, of a major Bowater Southern Paper Corporation plant, which drew personnel from the Cleveland area. Presently, there are more than 80 manufacturers in the Cleveland-Bradley County area, including manufacturers of gas and electric ranges, upholstered FURNITURE, garments, chemicals, batteries, printing, and auto and truck brake linings. These industries employ more than 15,000 workers. A Chamber of Commerce was inaugurated in 1925. The government of Cleveland, last modified in 1977, is now composed of a mayor and four commissioners.

Higher education has been a part of the cultural tradition of Cleveland since 1885 when Centenary Female College, a Methodist institution, was chartered. In 1933 the campus was acquired by Bob Jones College. LEE COLLEGE, founded by the Church of God in 1918, acquired the property in 1947. Tomlinson College, sponsored by the Church of God of Prophecy, was established in 1966. Cleveland State, one of Tennessee's COMMUNITY COLLEGES, was begun in 1967. Kent College was started in 1976 by The Church of God (Jerusalem Acres). Cleveland now serves as the international headquarters for the Church of God, the Church of God of Prophecy, and The Church of God (Jerusalem Acres). Each denomination has local publishing facilities for state newspapers and literature. During the 1970's, special efforts were made to revitalize the downtown district. A Historic Zoning Steering Committee is presently working on the concept of historic zoning for downtown, which would encourage improvement and maintenance of the architectural heritage of the area.

William R. Snell

See also: ARCHITECTURE
RAILROADS (SOUTHEASTERN)

Climate. The climate of East Tennessee is influenced by the enormous air masses which, having their origin in the north or south, move across the state west to east. Cold air masses invade Tennessee in the winter from the north and west, lowering temperatures everywhere. These fronts may bring in rain or snow, and after the storm passes, they may be followed by clearing skies. During much of the year, however, area air temperatures are determined more by winds from the south, which result in East Tennessee's generally mild climate. Temperatures vary with elevation. Maxima in July on the Cumberland Plateau and at low to middle elevations in the Unaka Mountains are often eight degrees Fahrenheit below those in the Valley; on the high mountains of the Unakas, they average 20 degrees lower. The growing season varies from 150 to 210 days, depending upon elevation; at high elevations, it may be as few as 100 days.

The moisture of precipitation generally reaches East Tennessee from the Gulf; however, as the air passes over the Unaka Mountains to the east and Cumberland Plateau and Mountains to the west, moisture is lost as rain or snow. Precipitation is as high as 60 inches per year on the Plateau, and rises above 80 inches on the high mountain

Elizabeth Settlemyer

Winter in the Bradbury Community of Roane County, 1979-80.

peaks. The Great Valley, in the rain shadow from these ridges, receives 40-52 inches per year. In all of these areas, total precipitation and flooding probability increases southward, and snowfall increases northward. Precipitation varies monthly. Highs are reached in winter and midsummer (July); annual droughts occur in May and August through October. Strong winds such as tornadoes, very heavy rainfall or snowfall, and ice storms occur only occasionally.

Small features of terrain exhibit microclimatic features of importance. The amount of solar radiation, determining soil and air temperatures and moisture stress in plants, varies greatly with latitude, time of year and terrain features such as slope angle, aspect (whether the slope faces the sun) and protection (whether the slope is shielded form direct radiation by an intervening ridge). In addition, on clear windless nights, the cool air that forms at the earth's surface flows downhill into valley bottoms; thus stream valleys and sinkholes experience more frost than do uplands.

H.R. DeSelm

See also: GEOGRAPHY

Clinton School Desegregation. Clinton, a small county seat town in ANDERSON COUNTY, was an unlikely candidate for the headlines that spread across the world in 1956, 1957, and 1958. These headlines reported the violence that accompanied the integration of the local high school, the sending in of the National Guard, the arrest and conviction of segregationists, and finally the dynamiting of the school. The catalyst for this came after the 1954 U.S. Supreme Court decision ordering equal schooling for all as opposed to "separate but equal" facilities. Federal District Judge Robert Taylor, who had earlier ruled in KNOXVILLE against black children entering Clinton High School, was reversed. In January of 1956, Judge Taylor ordered Clinton officials to register black students in the fall.

Clinton in 1956 enjoyed relatively good black-white relations. For years black citizens had served on juries, participated in joint religious and civic activities, and owned homes in the white section of town. Blacks were respected, and even during the height of the disorder, the conflict was not between blacks and whites, but between whites who opposed integration and whites who believed the court order should be obeyed. For months during the spring and summer, the local Board of Education, PTA, and school staff worked with the county's feeder communities to prepare citizens for the fall school opening. When that day came, it appeared they had done their job well.

There was no trouble until John Kasper of New York came on the scene. Going from door to door, he stirred up some of the people. He showed them a picture of black soldiers kissing white girls, and asked them if that was what they wanted for their daughters. He warned that unless integration was stopped, we would have a mongrel society. He said that the Supreme Court did not make the laws, that the people did, and the courts, officials, and others who failed to listen to the people should be opposed.

For days people gathered at the high school, and by night at the courthouse, to hear Kasper and other out-of-town segregationists. They threatened to burn down the courthouse and the mayor's home. This brought first the Tennessee Highway Patrol and then the National Guard. After a ban on incoming travel at night ended the crowds and the trouble, the Guard left. But harassment at the high school continued. The Rev. Paul W. Turner, a white Baptist minister, was beaten as he walked down the hill from the black community with some of the children. U.S. Marshals arrested seventeen people, including Kasper, for violating Judge Taylor's order not to interfere with the orderly integration of the school. In July of 1957 Kasper and most of the other people charged were convicted, but only Kasper went to jail. The others were placed on probation, and the trouble was apparently over.

That fall and through the 1957-8 academic year, minor problems arose in the high school. The children of unhappy segregationists annoyed black students in an unsuccessful effort to discourage them from attending school, but this soon ended. Then, on October 5, 1958, in the early morning hours of that Sunday, three separate blasts tore the school apart. Only the gymnasium, auditorium, and music and home economics departments were left standing. Gone were the language arts areas, the science laboratory, the offices, and the cafeteria.

Determined that they would not be without a school, local officials began to search for other quarters. The OAK RIDGE Board of Education and the Atomic Energy Commission offered the vacant Linden Elementary School, and this offer was accepted. Students and others salvaged what they could from the dynamited building, and on Thursday, just three days after the elementary school was made available, high school classes resumed in Oak Ridge. That first morning was an exciting one, for the Oak Ridge High School band gathered in front of the Linden School and played as school buses brought the Clinton students to their new "home". The students remained two years at Linden while the damaged structure was repaired.

Drew Pearson, nationally syndicated Washington columnist, began a campaign for "Bricks of Love". Contributions from school children, adults, and foundations poured in from all over the world. Pearson raised more than $50,000 and came to see the building after it was rebuilt. He received the thanks of the community, expressed in a plaque hanging in the entry way of the school. As for the students themselves, black graduates from Clinton High School have gone on to take their place in responsible jobs and in the professions. Now black athletes are student heroes, and there are many who have forgotten—if they ever knew about—the problems of the late 1950's.

Horace V. Wells, Jr.

Refer to: Margaret Anderson, *The Children of the South*, New York: Farrar, 1966.
See also: CHARLES CANSLER

Coal Miner's Son. My dad, William Taylor Henry, was born in Barbourville, Kentucky, on May 22, 1884. He died on March 19, 1962, from the ravages of emphysema, tuberculosis, and lung cancer.

My parents were married in 1922. They had seven children: four boys and three girls. Dad went to work in the coal mines in 1898, when he was fourteen years old. For twenty years, he worked at various mines in Virginia, Kentucky, and Tennessee. From 1918 until 1926, Dad worked for the Southern Railroad. In 1926 he returned to the coal mines and worked fifteen more years. In 1941 he suffered a broken back which totally disabled him for many months. Dad spent a total of 35 years of his days underground.

I was born in the mining camp at Gatliff, Kentucky, in 1929. I was the third oldest child. We moved from Gatliff when I was very young, and I remember very little about the place. The other mining camp we lived in was at Clairfield, Tennessee. I was ten years old when we moved there in 1939, and I remember it very well. Very well indeed.

We lived in a part of the camp called "Ball Diamond Hill". The houses were all alike: four rooms and a path, unpainted—pathetic, really, but we didn't know it at the time. We did have electric lights for the first time, and that was a marvel. There was one water pump in the middle of the camp which everyone used. On wash days we had to stand in line.

The company commissary was at the foot of the hill. All our trading was done there. Every miner had a card which could be used to draw scrip for trading, as an advance on his wages. The company deducted rent, utilities, doctor's fees, and more from the miner's wages. If there was anything left after the deductions, the family could eat. Prices at the commissary were terribly inflated, but the miners were paid in the company's own scrip, not U.S. currency. They were trapped and cruelly exploited.

Life on "Ball Diamond Hill" was a bit on the seamy side. You seemed to need a vice or two in order to be at ease with your peers. I learned to chew "Brown Mule" and roll my own cigarettes with "Bugler". I heard my first off-color jokes there and learned Halloween pranks which are X-rated to this very day. Kids around the mining camp took their amusement where they found it. Some of the ways we entertained ourselves seem pretty bizarre as I look back on it.

There were always boys around the commissary bumming pennies for "B-B Bats" or "Guess Whats". Occasionally a soft touch might treat a kid to a big Pepsi Cola, which cost a nickel and really burned going down. The ultimate treat was a bag of salted peanuts to pour into the Pepsi. Every boy carried a knife, a pocket full of marbles, and a slingshot around his neck. We called the slingshots "flip-jacks". Marbles and mumblety-peg were daily fair weather rituals. The flip-jacks were for plunking at tin cans, birds, and occasionally each other.

We made yo-yos by driving a nail through two buckeyes. Our darts were straight pins tied onto kitchen matches. We made like Tarzan on grapevine swings in the woods. We also played with insects. By tying strings onto the legs of June bugs, we had a flying pet. We would harass tumblebugs by taking their dung balls from them with twigs. On rainy days we could crawl back under the porch and, in the dust there, call doodlebugs from their cone-shaped traps. We would get down close to the cone and chant:

Doodlebug, doodlebug, fly away home,
Your house is on fire and your children are alone.

This would bring them out almost every time.

When we ran out of anything else to do, we might do the following. Take about two feet of twine string. Keep one end free, but wad the rest into a small ball. Put the ball into your mouth, but hold on to the end. Now drink some water and swallow the ball. Pull the string out slowly, and it will tickle your throat. But don't pull too fast; it may be looped around something down there. For showfare on Saturday, we would go into the woods near the camp and cut the biggest dead chestnut tree we could drag home. This we sold for fifteen cents in scrip, as it could be used for kindling.

The houses were all fire traps, and occasionally one would burn. I don't recall one ever being saved. When a house caught fire, a bucket brigade from the pump would form quickly, but little could be done. Once, while a house burned, the family living next door began carrying water to wet down their own house. They weren't helping to fight the fire. This made sense, really, but it seemed awfully selfish at the time. It made the other folks mad as hornets. But the kids would have a ball after the ashes cooled. There would always be weird melted glass shapes and twisted metal.

Doctor Rogers was the company doctor. He drove a Dodge business coupe and always had a box of John Ruskin cigars on the seat of his car. He liked me and would often take me with him on his rounds. It made me proud to ride with him, smoke his cigars, and carry the grip which held his instruments and pills. We answered a call one day where a boy had cut his big toe badly. He had taken two soft drink bottles and had broken the small glass ring from the mouth of one by using the other. This was a trick we did often, but this time the ring, as sharp as a razor, had fallen on his toe. Doctors used metal clamps to close such wounds in those days. I'll never forget how that kid screamed when Doctor Rogers clamped that wound. Rather often, Doctor Rogers would have what he called a "granny case". This meant that he had a baby to deliver. I could not go with him at these times.

We lived in Clairfield for two years, and things went reasonably well with us for quite a while. We were as poor as Job's turkey, but practically all our neighbors were no better off than we were. Dad purchased a second-hand RADIO on the installment plan. We enjoyed "Gang Busters" and "The Inner Sanctum". Jim and I had learned to ride Cletus Brown's bicycle, and the Carlisle Family with "Hot-Shot Elmer" were coming to the Little Tennessee Theater the next Saturday night. Then Dad had his accident, and our flimsy world began to fall apart.

I don't remember the details of the accident. We've always called it a broken back. It may have been a ruptured disk; I don't know. I do know it was a severe back injury, and figuratively, at least, it broke our backs. Times were never really good for miners' families, but they were called good when work was steady. When work was interrupted, or ceased altogether, catastrophe was immediate. Our card which had worked its weekly magic at the commissary lost its power. Installment purchases were repossessed. We were in a sort of limbo.

Dad tried through the United Mine Workers of America to exact some sort of monetary settlement with the company. To my knowledge, this produced not one cent. We were still occupying company property, but as things heated up, our presence there became more precarious. Dad brought a lawsuit against the company. At the appointed time, we trooped to Tazewell to see justice done. It didn't take long. Judge Brown summarily threw Dad's case out of court.

Shortly thereafter, a company truck backed up to our door. Everything we owned was put aboard. The truck proceeded off Ball Diamond Hill and to the edge of town. There, along the shoulder of State Route 90, the Henry's pitched camp. We draped our old linoleum rugs over the furniture and made a tent of sorts. The weather was good, and we kids had a great time living our gypsy life. We frolicked in the woods during the day, catching ground squirrels in sugar sacks. I made a bit of change picking up beer and soft drink bottles in the ditch along the road, then selling them at Granny Rozier's beer joint.

These things occurred during the summer of 1941. We moved back to Jellico and piled up with my sister and brother-in-law. After awhile, we found a small place to live. Dad was flat on his back for a year or more. Mom worked as a cook at the bus station and took in washing. My older brother Jim delivered groceries from Mr. White's store. I sold kindling, cut grass, and was general flunky for another family at fifteen cents per hour. The younger kids stayed home with Dad and did chores.

In the midst of all this, the family dog "Boss" was killed by a train. Then my younger brother Tom and I were badly hurt in a bicycle-car accident that was my fault. Three of our legs were broken; two were compound fractures. We were in the hospital for a month and on crutches for many weeks. During this time, Mom sold all her fruit jars to buy food. And we finally washed the carbide from our seed beans and ate them. We had put carbide with seed beans to keep them free of bugs; to this day, pinto beans are called "life savers" in our family.

Dad finally began to recover, and by wearing a back brace, could do light work. He, Mom, and Jim took factory jobs in KNOXVILLE, and we moved there in 1943. The Manhattan Project, started in 1942, was booming. Dad soon took a job in OAK RIDGE as a time keeper for the Roane-Anderson Company. We moved into a new flat top, #Q-1220, on February 29, 1944. The streets were mud, and there was construction all around us, but we were settled in the only new home we had ever known. To us, Oak Ridge seemed like the promised land.

You may wonder why I have written this rather stark account of my early years. The fact that it is true is reason enough, but more than that, I feel that statements like this should be made. My family's case was not unique. My Dad is gone, but there remain thousands of human derelicts in the southeastern coal fields who left their family farms for work in the coal mines. They were crippled, broken, totally used up and left to wheeze their very lives away on welfare and in POVERTY. And there are thousands of their children who, like myself, remember how things were and would like the story told. My parents didn't have a lot of education and fewer material things, but they kept us together, did the best they could—and we got by.

Bill Henry

See also: BROWNTOWN
COAL MINING
LOWER WINDROCK MINING CAMP

Coal Mining. Although the entire Cumberland Plateau in East Tennessee is laden with coal and coal mines (see *Coal Reserves of Tennessee,* Cincinnati: Southern Railway, October 1964), books and articles concerned directly with coal mining in the area are relatively scarce. One work on the history of these mines is Allen McCormick's "Development of the Coal Industry of Grundy County, Tennessee" (George Peabody College thesis, 1934). John Gaventa's *Power and Powerlessness: Quiescence and Rebellion in an Appalachian Valley* (Urbana: University of Illinois Press, 1980) focuses on the rise of the coal industry in the Clear Fork Valley of CLAIBORNE COUNTY and CAMPBELL COUNTY. Gaventa also gives valuable information on the history of labor in the East Tennessee coal fields.

The labor history of coal mining has traditionally been more desperate and more violent than that of most other industries. Fran Ansley's and Brenda Bell's "East Tennessee Coal Mining Battles" (in *Southern Exposure,* V.1, Nos. 3 and 4, Winter 1974, pp.112-159) discusses both THE CONVICT LABOR (COAL CREEK) WARS of the 1890's and the Davidson-Wilder Strike of 1932-33, including oral history by participants. Reasons for such struggles are suggested by *"...in the mines, in the mines, in the Blue Diamond Mines..."* (Knoxville, Tenn.: Coal Company Monitoring Project, 1979), a short study of KNOXVILLE-headquartered Blue Diamond Coal Company, its history since 1915, and its post-1960 record in labor relations, mine safety, and surface mining.

Surface or strip mining (as opposed to deep or underground mining) works from the surface down, stripping away soil and PLANT COMMUNITIES (the "overburden") to expose coal seams. Tennessee's enforcement, during the 1970's, of state anti-pollution requirements and other regulations having to do with strip mining was examined by attorney William A. Allen in *A Study of Tennessee Strip Mine Enforcement, 1972-1977* (Save Our Cumberland Mountains and East Tennessee Research Corporation, 1978). Following Congressional passage in 1977 of the Surface Mining and Reclamation Act, a portion of strip mine regulation came under Federal control. This act created the Office of Surface Mining, which in turn established Knoxville headquarters for its important Region 2 (Kentucky-Tennessee) field office. Almost immediately, OSM came under attack by coal industry representatives. Recent coal activity and controversy in ANDERSON COUNTY and elsewhere in East Tennessee were explored by *The Oak Ridger* reporter Lucy Smyser ("Coal in Our Counties", in *The Oak Ridger*, June 9-20, 1980; reprinted September 12, 1980).

More general works on coal mining in APPALACHIA help explain coal mining in East Tennessee. Harold Wilson Aurand's *From the Molly Maguires to the UMW* (Philadelphia: Temple University Press, 1971) and Joseph E. Finley's *The Corrupt Kingdom: The Rise and Fall of the United Mine Workers* (New York: Simon and Schuster, 1973) chronicle this important union up through the aberrant reign of Tony Boyle, whose henchmen from District 19 in East Tennessee murdered political rival Jock Yablonski. Trevor Armbrister's *Act of Vengeance: The Yablonski Murders and Their Solution* (New York: Saturday Review-Dutton, 1975) includes a closer look at the East Tennessee participants. Early heroes of the southern mountain labor movement come alive in *The Autobiography of Mother Jones* (Chicago: Charles H. Kerr, 1925; reprinted 1969, New York: Arno) and in Saul Alinsky's *John L. Lewis: An Unauthorized Biography* (New York: Putnam, 1949), although Brit Hume's *Death and the Mines: Rebellion*

Courtesy John Rice Irwin

Charley Woods
Said to he was saved
if he never lived to
See the outside again
he would meet his
Mother in heven
if we never live to
git out we are not
hurt but only perishing
for air there is but
a few of us here and
I dont know where
the other men is
Elbert Said
for you all to
meet him in
heaven all of the
of the children
to meet us both

At 7:30 on the morning of Monday, May 19, 1902, just after the day's work had begun in the Fraterville mine at Coal Creek, a methane (coal dust) explosion killed 184 miners. The death count included 11 blacks and a number of boys. Some of the men and boys were killed immediately by the explosion; some were trapped in smaller rooms and lived for a short time; some crawled to those passages farthest from the source of the explosion. Here, at the least contaminated headings deep within the mine, small groups of miners survived for as long as eight hours before succumbing to suffocation, to heat, or to "afterdamp" (an increase in carbon monoxide resulting from imperfect combustion of coal during the explosion). During these final hours, several miners wrote letters to their loved ones. Jacob L. Vowell, whose body was later recovered and was buried at Longfield Baptist Church, wrote his wife Ellen on behalf of both himself and his son Elbert. A fragment of Vowell's letter appears here.

Courtesy TVA

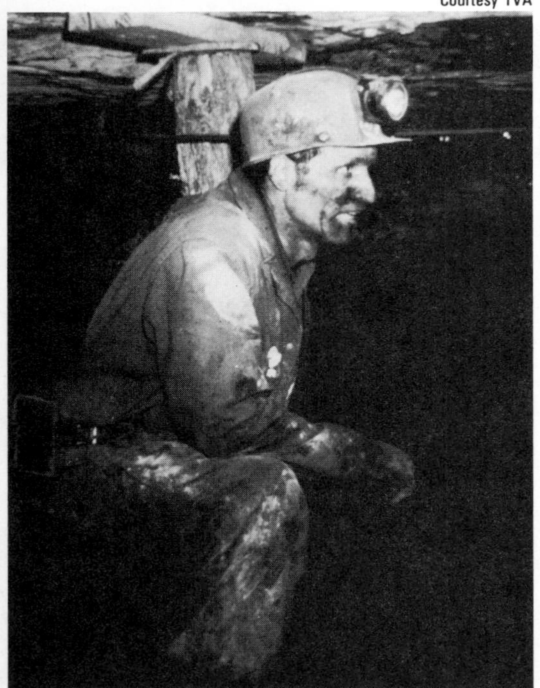

Underground coal miner, East Tennessee, ca. 1976.

and Murder in the United Mine Workers (New York: Grossman, 1971) portrays a John L. Lewis during the 1950's in collusion with coal management.

John Sayles, in his novel *Union Dues* (Boston: Atlantic-Little, Brown, 1977, pp.32-35), gives a brilliant picture of the bathhouse routine of coal miners. George Vecsey's non-fiction portrait (*One Sunset a Week: the Story of a Coal Miner*, New York: Saturday Review-Dutton, 1974) also describes the miner's daily life. John Fetterman's *Stinking Creek* (New York: Dutton, 1967) shows life in a valley dependent on coal, while Bryan Woolley's and Ford Reid's *We Be Here When the Morning Comes* (Lexington: University of Kentucky Press, 1975) captures the anger, insecurity, and brotherhood of a coal strike. The history and meaning of coal mining songs are

Coal town, 1970's.

Courtesy TVA

James P. Blair

Red Oak Mountain above Caryville in southwest Campbell County, ca. 1975.

introduced by Guy and Candie Carawan's *Voices From the Mountains* (New York: Knopf, 1975), and Archie Green analyzes some of these songs in detail in *Only a Miner: Studies in Recorded Coal Mining Songs* (Urbana: University of Illinois Press, 1972.)

Coal mining in East Tennessee and Southern Appalachia has always given rise to issues involving health and land. James Davitt McAteer and a team of researchers present health issues in *Coal Mine Health and Safety: The Case of West Virginia* (New York: Praeger, 1973), as do Juliet Merrifield and a similar team in *We're Tired of Being Guinea Pigs!* (New Market, Tenn.: Highlander Research and Education Center, 1980). This latter handbook covers a wide spectrum of environmental health challenges in Appalachia, and it contains much valuable information concerning East Tennessee. *Land Ownership Patterns and Their Impacts on Appalachian Communities: A Survey of 80 Counties* (Appalachian Land Ownership Task Force, 1981), an Appalachian Regional Commission report, examines the close and often tragic relationship among coal companies, the land, and its inhabitants. Finally, John Calhoun Wells, Jr.'s "Poverty Amidst Riches: Why People Are Poor in Appalachia" (Rutgers University dissertation, 1977) is a primer for anyone truly interested in the political economy of the region.

Jim Stokely

See also: BROWNTOWN
COAL MINER'S SON
LOWER WINDROCK MINING CAMP

Cocke County

Size: 424 Square Miles (271,360 acres)
Established: 1797
Named For: William Cocke, U.S. Senator from Tennessee
County Seat: Newport
Other Major Cities, Towns, or Communities:
Cosby
Parrottsville
Del Rio
Hartford
Reedtown
Bybee

Refer to: Ruth Webb O'Dell, *Over the Misty Blue Hills: The Story of Cocke County, Tennessee,* 1951.

See also: WILMA DYKEMAN AND JAMES STOKELY
GRASSY FORK STRING BAND
GREAT SMOKY MOUNTAINS NATIONAL PARK
HOMER HARRIS
THE HARRIS MILL
MILDRED HAUN
BEN W. HOOPER
GRACE MOORE
SUNSET GAP COMMUNITY CENTER

Levi Collins was born "on the other side" of Pine Ridge in an isolated hollow known as Bear Creek Valley, a place later chosen as the site of the Y-12 atomic energy plant in what is now OAK RIDGE, Tennessee. His home was directly across the ridge from our place, formerly the old Jim McKamey place, and he and his cousins often walked across the mountain and over our farm on their way to the old John Key store located where the Senior Citizen's Center now stands in Oak Ridge.

At the Key store, they could buy patent medicines and turpentine as well as their coffee and sugar. Sometimes they would walk across the ridge to

Courtesy Gene Branam

Downtown Newport, looking east on Broadway, April 4, 1970.

"Scabber" town, more properly Scarboro, a community located in the present area of THE UNIVERSITY OF TENNESSEE Comparative Animal Research Laboratory.

Levi attended a one-room school called Valley Grove, but dropped out after only a few months, when he was in the second grade. One of his teachers was T.L. Seeber, who was later to become mayor of Clinton, county judge, and one of East Tennessee's most successful businessmen.

As a small lad, Levi went to work as farm hand, saw mill helper, or on any odd job he could get. He worked 10-12 hours per day at a daily rate of 50¢. He learned from his father and from his grandfather the ways of the mountains: how to do blacksmith work; how to farm, hunt, fish, trap; and other frontier-pioneer customs still practiced in the early part of this century. When he was old enough, he went to Illinois where he raised a crop. For shucking corn in the fall, he received 2¢ per bushel. He returned home during the winter, but returned to Illinois a few

Frank Hoffman / Courtesy John Rice Irwin

Levi Collins, 1978.

years later for two additional years.

Like many young men of this area, Levi went to the mines where "good" money was being paid, and he worked as a miner in Anderson and Campbell counties for 29 years. He left the mines temporarily to work on "the project", later called Oak Ridge, but the lure of the mines caused his Oak Ridge stay to be brief. He returned to the mining life.

Levi Collins now lives in a narrow hollow off the public road a few miles north of Lake City, in a place call Cherry Bottom. Here he operates a small grist or corn grinding mill, a blacksmith shop, and a farm of several acres. Levi, who plays the old mountain-style banjo, has an affinity for MUSICAL INSTRUMENTS, guns, mining tools and frontier-pioneer artifacts. He has a collection of each. His lifestyle today is little changed from his early days in Bear Creek Valley.

John Rice Irwin

Community Colleges. The community college movement represents the culmination of a trend in American higher education that has been developing since colonial time. Because colonial colleges were few, small, highly selective, expensive, and concerned almost exclusively with classical education, they served mainly to educate the elite. Typically, the modern community college is none of these things, but like its colonial forbear, the community college strives to meet the needs of the society of its time.

The hundreds of contemporary community colleges nationwide are as diverse and different as the work and needs of the communities they serve, but generally they aim toward three goals: to provide two years of traditional college work for the transfer student, to provide career-vocational-technical training of a post-secondary nature for those who want to enter the job market immediately, and to provide courses and programs of a community service-continuing education nature. The community colleges are known for "open door" admission policies, low fees, and diverse course offerings. Perhaps as much as any social institution, the community college offers equality of opportunity to those who seek further education and training.

The nascence of the community college movement in Tennessee was marked by a tripartite cooperation between the national, state and local governments. The need for expanding the system of higher education was pointed up by the 1957 Pierce-Albright Report to the General Assembly, which suggested that a public college should be within an hour's drive of as many citizens as possible. The idea needed only money and leadership to become a reality.The leadership was provided by Governor Frank G. Clement, State Education Commissioner J. Howard Warf, and several members of the Legislature. The money was a fine example of cooperation. The national government, through the 1963 Higher Education Facilities Act, provided some $10 million for the original construction; the state, over the years, has provided nearly $70 million; and the local communities were required to contribute $250,000 and at least 100 acres of land if they were to have a college. Four of Tennessee's ten community colleges have been located in East Tennessee: Cleveland State Community College in BRADLEY COUNTY, Walters State Community College in HAMBLEN COUNTY, Roane State Community College in ROANE COUNTY, and Chattanooga State Technical Community College in HAMILTON COUNTY.

Cleveland State was opened in CLEVELAND in the fall of 1967. The first president, Dr. D.F. Adkisson, shepherded the institution from an initial 681 students, 16 faculty members, 12 programs of study, and 65 courses through the college's first ten years until there were 3,966 students, 94 faculty members, 29 programs, and 710 courses. Dr. Adkisson's administration was, obviously, one of great growth. In 1978 a new president, Dr. L. Quentin Lane, assumed leadership of what was by then a stable and mature institution and focused his attention on the challenges of quality education and fiscal accountability. The majority of Cleveland State's students come from the thirteen county area in southeastern Tennessee. Compared with senior institutions, the students at Cleveland State are more likely to be parttime (68.8 percent), older (mean age 27) and female (54 percent). These figures are typical of most community colleges, and they reflect an important mission: to make higher education available to students who have perhaps neither the time nor the money to leave their communities to attend a regional or state university. This may well be one of the greatest accomplishments of the community college system in Tennessee.

Walters State was the second community college to open its doors in East Tennessee. It is named for former U.S. Senator Herbert S. Walters and is located on 134 acres of land in Morristown, the geographical center of upper East Tennessee. Established in 1970 with Dr. James W. Clark as president, Walters State began with 414 students. In 1978, with Dr. Jack E. Campbell as president, the college had a total enrollment of 3,393 students, a profile of whom was quite similar to those of the other community colleges. Walters State has developed an innovative approach to computer science education and is the state's only community college to offer a production horticulture technology program.

In 1971, Roane State opened its doors to 323 students in Harriman. The original president, Dr. Cuyler A. Dunbar, continues to guide the institution which served 3,233 students in1978. In addition to the usual transfer, career, and continuing education curriculums, Roane State works with Department of Energy officials in OAK RIDGE to offer courses related to alternative sources of energy and coal mine training. In cooperation with the Department of Corrections, Roane State offers programs at Brushy Mountain State Prison and plans to expand into other regional facilities.

The final community college established in East Tennessee was Chattanooga State. CSTCC is unique in that it was originally opened in 1965 as Chattanooga State Technical Institute, the state's first technical institute, before being converted to community college standing in 1973. President Charles W. Branch's institution is, because of its past, more firmly rooted in careers education, but the college today offers a full comprehensive program. It serves in excess of 4200 students, most of whom come either from CHATTANOOGA, the city which ranks twelfth nationally in manufacturing employment as a percentage of total population, or from the four rural surrounding counties: Sequatchie, Bledsoe, Marion, and Rhea. Chattanooga State truly looks in several directions to meet the needs of its students.

The community colleges are governed and financed primarily at the state, and not the local, level. With the exception of THE UNIVERSITY OF TENNESSEE system, all public higher education is governed by the State Board of Regents through the Office of the Chancellor. Another board, the Tennessee Higher Education Commission, coordinates the efforts of the Board of Regents, the U.T. Board of Trustees, and the Board of Vocational Education in order to prevent duplication and overlap of programs. Community colleges are financed mainly by state tax dollars plus student fees and campus auxiliary enterprises. There is no local tax support, yet when a college like

Cleveland State spends $5 million annually in its area, that community college is a boon not only to its students but to many others as well.

Jerome G. Taylor

Refer to: Roy S. Nicks, ed. *Community Colleges of Tennessee: The Founding and Early Years*, Memphis: Memphis State University Press, 1979; James W. Thornton, Jr. *The Community Junior College*, New York: John Wiley and Son, 1972; and *Higher Education in Tennessee: A Statewide Master Plan, 1979-1984*, Nashville: Tennessee Higher Education Commission, 1979.

Concord, approximately 15 miles west of KNOXVILLE, began in 1854 after the East Tennessee and Georgia railroad (later the Southern Railway) first built its link between Knoxville and CHATTANOOGA. The railroad ran near the Tennessee River and bypassed the busy community of FARRAGUT by two miles. Thus the new business center of Concord was surveyed and "laid off" beside the railroad on land given by James M. Rogers. In addition to the handsome brick depot, a post office, hotel, and many retail businesses were established at Concord. Both business and population were lured away from neighboring Farragut as people wanted to be part of the growing railroad town.

In the 1880's Concord became the center of a large marble business. Local quarries produced some of the finest varieties of marble to be found in East Tennessee, and Concord was the shipping point from which the marble was sent throughout America. By 1887, Concord was the largest town in KNOX COUNTY outside of Knoxville. As the terminal point where river cargo was unloaded from barges and shipped by rail to Knoxville and the East, Concord's industrial and commercial activity brought many newcomers into the area. Two large fair grounds attracted special interest in fine horseshows, displays of canned foods, crafts and various competitions.

As the marble industry moved toward Knoxville, Concord's growth waned during the early twentieth century. In 1942, the TENNESSEE VALLEY AUTHORITY completed Fort Loudoun Dam at Lenoir City. The waters of Fort Loudoun Lake covered most of Concord, forcing the railroad to be relocated and many remaining businesses to close. However, during the 1950's and 1960's, recreational acreage bordering the lake became a sound investment. Families of long standing sold their farms to investors to be developed into subdivisions. Again newcomers moved in, this time looking for pleasant suburban living within easy reach of Knoxville or OAK RIDGE. They brought city culture and values into the rural atmosphere, and because of that mix, life in Concord continues to flourish.

Vera T. Dean

See also: RAILROADS (SOUTHEASTERN)

The Convict Labor (Coal Creek) Wars. Among the most dramatic events in the history of the Southern Appalachian coal fields were the East Tennessee miners' insurrections of the 1890's, still known as "the wars" by many people around the coal camps of the areas. In a series of massive armed confrontations the coal miners of Tennessee rose up against the state convict leasing system to defend their jobs which the coal companies were trying to fill with convict laborers.

The convict lease system first began in Tennessee in 1866, as part of a wave of such legislation which swept through the South and Midwest after the CIVIL WAR. A Nashville furniture company built workshops on the grounds of the penitentiary, fed and clothed the men, and paid 43¢ a head per day to the state. One year later, the prisoners burned the workshops to the ground in protest over the treatment they were receiving. From that time on, prisoners have waged battles to win decent working conditions and fairer wages. Meanwhile, the labor movement agitated for an end to convict labor, though usually on the grounds of unfair competition rather than of justice for convicts. When the Mechanics and Manufactors Association of Tennessee took a stand against convict labor, the bulk of convicts was soon switched to the coal and iron mines and to farms in order to avoid competition with the mechanical trades.

By the time of the miners' insurrections, all of Tennessee's convicts were leased by the Tennessee Coal, Iron & Railroad Co., a corporation based in New York. TCI leased about 1600 men from the state for $101,000 annually or approximately $63 per year per man. Some of these men worked in TCI mines in GRUNDY COUNTY; some were sub-leased by TCI to other coal companies mining as far north as ANDERSON COUNTY, near the communities of Coal Creek and Briceville. The convict lease system built TCI's fortune, and the highly successful company became a subsidiary of U.S. Steel in 1907. Besides the huge profits TCI made off its convicts, the company was also able to use the convicts as an ace-in-the-hole strike deterrent against free miners. The state, also, had a vested interest in the system. Between 1870 and 1890, Tennessee made a total net profit of $771,000 from its convict leasing.

What follows is a short chronology of the Convict Labor Wars in East Tennessee. During the course of their fight against the convict leasing system, the miners were forced by the logic of the situation to ignore more and more the distinctions between themselves (as law-abiding, predominantly white citizens) and the convicts (as law-breaking, predominantly black criminals). To the extent that the miners ignored these distinctions in a massive and popularly supported way, they succeeded in winning their demands.

Chronology of Convict Labor Wars

1871: First convict miners brought to Tracy City and Sewanee.
1876: First strike of miners at Coal Creek.
1877: First convicts brought to Coal Creek.
1884: The Tennessee Coal, Iron and Railroad Company (TCI) signs a five-year contract for all Tennessee convicts.
1887: Law guaranteeing miners the right to elect a checkweighman is passed in Tennessee.

1889: TCI signs a second six-year contract.
1890: United Mine Workers of America founded.
April, 1891: The Tennessee Coal Mining Company at Briceville fires their men's checkweighman and demands that the men sign an "ironclad" agreement promising never to join a union. The men refuse, and the company locks them out.
July 4, 1891: The company announces it has signed a contract with TCI for convicts to work the Briceville mine. (There had been some convicts at Coal Creek before, but never at Briceville.)
July 14, 1891: First Insurrection. Three hundred armed miners and citizens march on the Briceville stockade, walk the convicts to Coal Creek, and put them on a train for KNOXVILLE. They send a telegram to the governor explaining their actions and appealing for his help in ridding the state of the convict lease system.
July 16, 1891: Governor John Buchanan arrives with the convicts and with state militia to install and protect the convicts. He addresses a mass meeting and urges law and order.
July 17, 1891: Much public support for the miners appears, including members of the militia units.
July 20, 1891: Second Insurrection. Miners pour into Anderson County from throughout the East Tennessee Cumberlands. They march quietly and with discipline to the Briceville stockade. Two thousand armed men line the surrounding ridges. The miners again send convicts to Coal Creek and on to Knoxville. Miners then march on the Knoxville Iron Company mine at Coal Creek, sending those convicts off as well. Not a shot is fired. Women give out sandwiches to miners and to soldiers while they march. The governor mobilizes all 14 companies of the Tennessee militia.
July 24, 1891: After negotiation, the governor says the convicts must return, and he will call a special session of the legislature to consider taking action on the convict lease law.
August, 1891: Legislature meets and, instead of repealing the law, reinforces it by increasing the governor's "emergency powers", thus making it a crime to lead a protest group or to interfere with the work of a convict.
October 28, 1891: Miners' committee resigns, saying it has done all it can.
October 31, 1891: Third Insurrection. Secret meetings are held in the dark in the mines at Briceville and Coal Creek. That night, 1500 men march on the stockades, the leader disguised in a 'kerchief. They set the convicts free and burn the stockade at Briceville. At Coal Creek they spare the stockade because the warden's wife is sick, but they burn everything else and release the prisoners. Citizens help convicts escape by giving them food and clothes.
November 1, 1891: Men march for the first time to Oliver Springs, where convicts are also being worked. The miners release the convicts and burn the stockade there. The governor offers cash rewards for leaders and participants.
January, 1892: A company of militia returns convicts to Coal Creek and establishes a military occupation, including a fort and Gatling guns.
Spring, 1892: At Coal Creek, Tracy City,

and Oliver Springs, work is slack for free miners, but convicts work full time.
July, 1892: Tracy City miners, who have suffered under the convict system the longest but have not yet rebelled, are cut to half-time work.
August, 1892: Fourth Insurrection. A miners' committee at Tracy City takes the keys to the stockade at gunpoint and puts the convicts on a train to Nashville. The committee intercepts a trainload of guards sent to nearby Inman and disarms them. Coal Creek citizens, already upset by the soldiers' occupation, grow more restless. An attack is made unsuccessfully on the Oliver Springs stockade. The governor orders more troops and calls for volunteers. For Coal Creek's final showdown, miners pour in and put Fort Anderson under siege. The soldiers finally break the siege and arrest 300 within ten days. Miners in Briceville are forced to sign an "iron-clad" agreement.
April, 1893: Fifth Insurrection. At Tracy City, 50 to 100 men stage an unsuccessful attack on the stockade. Troops are sent in to hunt for the leaders. Most miners are forced to sign a disclaimer of involvement in any convict release.
1896: Despite the appearance of the miners' defeat, the TCI contract expires and is not renewed. Convict leasing in Tennessee is abolished by the legislature. As an alternative policy, the same legislature buys land and establishes a state-run convict mine near Petros.

Fran Ansley
Brenda Bell

Refer to: Fran Ansley and Brenda Bell, "East Tennessee Coal Mining Battles," in *Southern Exposure,* V.1, Nos. 3 & 4 (Winter, 1974), pp.112-159; James Dombrowski, "Fire in the Hole," unpublished manuscript (ca. 1940, approx. 200pp.) plus transcripts of interviews and other notes, Tuskegee Institute, Tuskegee, Alabama; Archie Green, *Only a Miner: Studies in Recorded Coal-Mining Songs,* Urbana: University of Illinois Press, 1972; and A.C. Hutson, Jr., "The Coal Miners' Insurrections, 1891-1892," University of Tennessee thesis, 1933 (See, for condensed version, Hutson in *East Tennessee Historical Society Publications,* Nos. 7 and 8, 1935 and 1936).
See also: COAL MINER'S SON
COAL MINING

The Copper Mines. Tucked into the southeastern corner of POLK COUNTY lies the Copper Basin, an area of approximately one hundred square miles. A commercial and mining area covers about twenty-five square miles of the Basin. In August of 1843 a Mr. Lemmons, prospecting on a branch of Potato Creek, found a reddish brown and blackish decomposed rock he thought was gold. He called in his neighbors, sent for whiskey, and celebrated all night. The next morning the gold proved to be red oxide of copper in crystals. In 1850 the first of several copper mines began operations at Ducktown. Copper and supplies were transported by famous "copper haulers" over a rough wagon road cut through the Ocoee River gorge to CLEVELAND, some 40 miles west. It has been said that these mines supplied the Confederacy with 90% of their copper, or some two million pounds.

Mining growth continued with only a brief halt caused by the occupation of Cleveland by Union troops during the CIVIL WAR. New impetus was received after 1865 from the introduction of the diamond drill and dynamite. By 1871 twelve mines were in operation: the Polk County mine operated by Polk County Copper Company, Eureka and Isabella by J.E. Raht, Burra Burra and Hiawassee by the Burra Burra Copper Company, Culchote by private parties, Tennessee by the Township (for schools), and Mary, Callaway, Loudon, Cherokee, and East Tennessee by the Union Consolidated Mining Company. By 1878, the high cost of hauling copper ingots to Cleveland via wagon road forced a shutdown of facilities until completion of a railway to KNOXVILLE in 1890.

The Tennessee Copper Company, forerunner of today's Basin Operations, was formed in 1899. From 1936, when TCC purchased the Ducktown Chemical & Iron Company, until 1963, Tennessee Copper operated all mining and processing facilities in the Basin. Cities Service Company became owner of all TCC holdings in 1963 and has since implemented a significant modernization program which has made the processing plants among the most advanced in America. Beginning in 1970, at a cost of over $70 million, four iron roasters were constructed along with an ore pelletizing plant, an electric furnace and related copper smelting facilities, and an additional sulfuric acid

Housing at Copperhill, 1930's.

Courtesy Frank H. McClung Museum, University of Tennessee

plant. Shortly after, additional improvements were made at a cost of $40 million. In addition to copper, products now produced include: sulfuric acid, iron and zinc, copper sulfate, copper carbonate, and tri-basic copper sulfate.

From the 1850's until 1907, open-air smelting of copper was the accepted practice. Using wood for fuel, workers "roasted" Copperhill ore outdoors, releasing sulfur dioxide gases. Trees were cut from almost fifty square miles of Copper Basin land to provide the fuel, and the gases killed other vegetation. Erosion of the unprotected topsoil then occurred over several decades. The ravaged hills of the Copper Basin have made a remarkable recovery since the start of a reforestation program in the 1930's. First sponsored by the Tennessee Copper Company, the TENNESSEE VALLEY AUTHORITY, the Civilian Conservation Corps, and others, the program has been continued and expanded by Cities Service.

The Copper Basin operations now employ some 2,000 people, generating a $27 million annual payroll and $50 million annually in purchasing power for the surrounding area. Life in the Copper Basin is closely related to the region's major industry. City Services supports education through scholarships and grants, and the company participates in providing medical and recreational facilities. City Services is also developing the Cherokee Hills Subdivision, an attractive area of modern homes atop the hills surrounding the Basin.

Roy G. Lillard

Refer to: R.E. Barclay, *Ducktown Back in Raht's Time*, Chapel Hill: The University of North Carolina Press, 1946; and articles in the *Cleveland Daily Banner*, April 27, 1871 and July 16 ,1941.

Country Music as a distinct commercial art form emerged in the 1920's and grew out of a number of earlier musical forms that were present in varying degrees in East Tennessee. One of these forms was the traditional folk music of the mountains, the old songs and ballads like "Black Jack Davy", "Pretty Polly", and "The Knoxville Girl" (originally called "The Wexford Girl") which had been brought into the region from 18th century England by English and Scotch-Irish settlers. Another was the rich trove of medicine and minstrel show tunes brought into the mountains by touring show troupes. Yet another influential form was the body of blues and work songs heard from railroad construction crews as they forged their way into remote sections of the mountains in the late 1800's. A fourth consisted of old popular Tin Pan Alley tunes which found their way into the rural areas of East Tennessee years or even decades after their initial publication in sheet music; such songs as "Kitty Wells" and "Wildwood Flower", originally published around the time of the CIVIL WAR, became so much a part of the fabric of mountain culture that they were often collected and studied as genuine folk songs. By 1920, all of these diverse elements were in place and awaited only the modern technology of RADIO and the phonograph record to combine the elements into a new music that was first called "old time", then "hill country", and finally "country" music.

Courtesy National Park Service

Jim Proffitt and Grace Newman, Great Smoky Mountains, ca. 1935.

After the General Phonograph Corporation recorded an Atlanta fiddler named John Carson in 1923 and found that the record was a surprise hit, other companies moved to exploit this new commodity and the new southern market to which it seemed to appeal. One of these other companies was the Aeolian Vocalion Company, and in 1924 their KNOXVILLE representative, Gus A. Nennstiel of the Sterchi Brothers Furniture Company, began to act as a talent scout in locating possible performers and arranging for them to travel to New York to record. In this way, the first East Tennessee country artists made their first records on the Vocalion label. The first Tennesseans to record were two blind Knoxville street singers, Charley Oaks (ca. 1885-1935) and George Reneau (1901-1933), who both sang to their own guitar accompaniment and played a harmonica held in a rack around the neck. Oaks was a native of Kentucky who became a well-known fixture at the Knoxville railroad depot; his early recordings include versions of "Boll Weevil", local ballads like "The New Market Wreck" (chronicling THE NEW MARKET TRAIN

WRECK), and many popular or sentimental songs. Reneau, from JEFFERSON COUNTY, was billed on his records as "The Blind Musician of the Smoky Mountains", but in fact New York record company executives found his voice too rough and untrained, and had Gene Austin—later to become a famous crooner—sing for him on many early records. Reneau taught Austin some of his best tunes, including "Here, Rattler, Here", "Bald-Headed End of the Broom", and "Little Rosewood Casket". Later the company let Reneau record his own voice on selections like "Women's Suffrage" (1925) and "The Sinking of the Titanic" (1925). Uncle Am Stuart (1851-1926), a safe salesman and old-time fiddler from Morristown who had learned his repertoire about the time of the Civil War, became the first East Tennessee instrumentalist to record (also for Vocalion, also in 1924), and the first southern fiddler to broadcast over New York radio.

But Nennstiel's most important discoveries were two singers who had met at the Kentucky School for the Blind and had begun singing duets in 1922: Robert A. Gardner, born in Oliver Springs in 1897, and Lester McFarland, born 1902, who became nationally known as Mac and Bob. Mac and Bob sang in a quiet sweet style, accompanying themselves on mandolin and guitar, and specializing in old sentimental songs, parlor songs from the 19th century, and sacred selections. They became one of the first country groups to fully professionalize themselves on the strength of phonograph records alone. Mac and Bob began recording in 1925, and over the next ten years they recorded over 200 songs for various labels, including hits like "When the Roses Bloom Again", "Twenty-One Years", "Tying the Leaves", and "The Broken Engagement". They began broadcasting over Knoxville station WNOX in 1926, then moved in 1931 to WLS where they became fixtures on the "National Barn Dance". They retired in the 1960's, returning to Oliver Springs.

The practice of bringing rural artists from the hills into New York studios was cumbersome and difficult, so by 1927 record companies were sending out talent scouts to record on location in the South. In this way important pioneering recording sessions were held in BRISTOL (1927, 1928), JOHNSON CITY (1928, 1929), and Knoxville (1929, 1930). The Bristol session of August 1927, headed by Victor's Ralph Peer, was to be the most historic in terms of establishing country music as a national force. Within three days Peer discovered the Carter Family and Jimmie Rodgers, both acts destined to become among the music's most influential. Peer also recorded Charles and Paul Johnson, East Tennessee natives who played Hawaiian style guitar, sang a variety of traditional and vaudeville songs, and were among the first singers to copyright their songs; and The Tenneva Ramblers, a Bristol string band featuring the Grant Brothers. Columbia's recordings in Johnson City attracted even more Tennessee talent and preserved for posterity the vital music of The Roane County Ramblers, who were a square dance band headed by Jimmy McCarroll, a fiddler who played a driving, highly rhythmic style partly influenced by his Cherokee grandmother. Singer and banjoist Clarence Tom Ashley (born in Bristol, 1895) made his classic recording of "The Coo Coo Bird", an ancient English lyric, in Johnson City in 1929. This initiated for Ashley a career that was to continue into the 1960's, when thousands of urban college students rediscovered him and his music. But some of the best music of this early era, when most performers were still gifted amateurs and much of the music was traditional Tennessee folk music, came in the Brunswick - Balke - Collender sessions held in the WNOX studios at the old St. James Hotel in downtown Knoxville in 1929 and 1930. Groups recording here included The Tennessee Ramblers, consisting of the Sievers Family from Clinton, a flashy string band that featured the unusual guitar talents of one of country music's first women guitarists, Willie Sievers; The Southern Moonlight Entertainers, built around the Raney Family from Coal Creek, coal miners who kept alive traditional tunes like "Saro", "Sister Liz", and "Buckin' Mule"; and Ridgel's Fountain Citians, another family band which was possibly the first string band to record with a twelve-string guitar. Unfortunately, many of these records, released at the start of the Depression, sold very poorly and are collector's items today. Indeed, there are a few releases where no copy at all is known to exist.

Other influential East Tennessee musicians went elsewhere to record. Hugh Ballard Cross (1904-ca. 1970), a native of Oliver Springs, recorded extensively in the 1920's, singing novelty and parlor songs in a high tenor voice and dueting with Riley Puckett on the original 1926 hit recording of "Red River Valley". Cross's 1928 recording, with his wife, of "You're as Welcome as the Flowers in May", sold over 74,000 copies, a huge success by 1920's standards. Cross later enjoyed a long radio career, appearing for a time on the Renfro Valley Barn Dance. Charley Bowman (born in Johnson City in 1889) was the most influential East Tennessee fiddler of the time. Bowman gained initial popularity playing with the Hill Billies, a Virginia band that recorded widely. He then appeared in vaudeville and even made movies. Among the tunes he popularized were "East Tennessee Blues", "Governor Alf Taylor's Fox Chase", and a vocal number called "Nine Pound Hammer". This latter number, which has become a folk and country standard, was written by Bowman and recorded by the Hill Billies in 1927; Bowman had heard the skeleton of the tune about 1905 from a Negro railroad section crew. Bowman later recorded with his brothers and his daughters, and he spent twenty years touring around the South with various country bands. Rivaling Bowman in popularity during the 1930's and 1940's was another fiddler, Curly Fox, from GRAYSVILLE. Becoming a star on the Grand Ole Opry in the mid-1930's, and usually appearing with his wife Texas Ruby, Fox featured showmanlike tunes such as "Listen to the Mocking Bird" and "Buckin' Mule", which combined a flair for comedy with excellent musicianship. Curly's 1946 recording of "Black Mountain Rag" was the most popular country instrumental of the era. Dwight Butcher, from OAKDALE, appeared early on Knoxville radio before moving to New York, where his "Old Love Letters" was among the last songs recorded by Jimmie Rodgers, and where he continued to write songs as well as plays, and even did some acting. Andy Patterson, from the Petros area, recorded extensively, eventually teaming up with Warren Caplinger for a long radio career in West Virginia. Patterson was instrumental in preserving and popularizing the famous murder ballad, "The Hills of Roane County".

By the 1930's, radio had replaced records as the prime medium for country music in East Tennessee. Pay was low for radio work, but most performers could thus advertise their personal appearances in local school houses and meeting halls, and so make a passable living by "booking out". Some

Roy Acuff

Courtesy Country Music Foundation Library and Media Center, Nashville, Tennessee artists went on to even greater success; such was the case of East Tennessee's most famous country singer, Roy Acuff. Born in Maynardville in 1903, the son of a Baptist minister, Acuff as a youth learned fiddle tunes from his family and from records by Uncle Am Stuart. After an aborted career as a baseball player, Acuff returned to the fiddle and played in local medicine shows, forming his own band by 1933. By 1936 he was a regular in Knoxville radio and was recording for the American Record Company in Chicago; these recordings included his original "Great Speckle Bird" and "Wabash Cannonball", though the latter featured a vocal not by Acuff but by Dynamite Hatcher. By 1938 Acuff had moved to the Grand Ole Opry, where he completed his switch to a full-time vocalist from a fiddler who occasionally sang. A long series of records and movies followed, and by the end of World War II Acuff was the most popular country singer in the nation. His subsequent career, which included an unsuccessful run for governor in 1948, has earned him the title "The King of Country Music", and he has remained one of the Nashville industry's staunchest defenders of older, more traditional country music forms.

From 1935 to 1957, radio continued to attract country performers to Knoxville and Bristol, and area stations proved to be testing grounds for a number of artists who went on to national fame. Tennessee Ernie Ford, born in 1919 near Bristol, began his career by singing along with Sons of the Pioneers records when he was an announcer at WOPI. He moved to the west coast after the war and enjoyed a huge hit with his

Courtesy Country Music Foundation Library and Media Center, Nashville, Tennessee

Chet Atkins

recording of a COAL MINING lament called "Sixteen Tons". He soon had a national television show, and his strong clear baritone voice appealed to all manner of listeners across the country. Chet Atkins, born in Luttrell in 1924, gained early experience playing his guitar (and even fiddle) over Knoxville radio in the early 1940's. After bouncing around country music for ten years, he landed in Nashville, where his guitar style—a complex type of picking called "western Kentucky choking style"—became extremely popular and was imitated by aspiring guitarists across the country. During the 1950's Atkins became increasingly involved in "session work" in Nashville studios, and by the end of the decade he had emerged as one of the city's key producers, responsible to a large extent for the so-called "Nashville sound" that dominated modern country music for some twenty years. Two singers who in the 1950's became closely associated with the Opry and mainstream country music were Carl Smith (born in 1927 in Maynardville), who carried to a new generation the highpitched forceful mountain style of Acuff, and Jack Greene (born 1930 in Maryville), who began as a sideman for Ernest Tubb before breaking out on his own. Carl Butler (born 1927 in Knoxville) gained fame in the 1950's as a writer and performer of "honky-tonk" songs, before teaming with his wife Pearl in 1962 to begin a duet style based on the success of his biggest hit, "Let Me Cross Over". Kenny Roberts (born 1927 in Lenoir City) achieved fame in the north and northeast as a yodelling cowboy. Comedy became the forte of Archie Campbell (born 1914 in GREENE COUNTY), who worked for years on Knoxville radio before moving to Nashville and the television success of "Hee Haw". Homer Haynes and Jethro Burns (both born in Knoxville in 1920) began their careers as child prodigies, but they eventually became nationally known as Homer and Jethro for their parodies of country hits. After Homer died, Jethro resumed his career as one of the most creative and influential mandolin players in country music.

Other performers remained on the local scene in East Tennessee, where they developed their own following and their own musical styles. BLUEGRASS MUSIC flourished in the area in the late 1940's and 1950's, spurred on by a renewal of recording activity. Such activity was spearheaded by men like Jim Stanton, a Johnson City businessman who founded Rich-R-Tone Records in 1946 when he felt major companies were turning their backs on the kind of music East Tennesseans liked to hear. One of Stanton's best selling artists was Buffalo Johnson from Johnson City. Other local favorites included HOMER HARRIS (The Seven Foot Cowboy), heard for years on a variety of Knoxville area stations; Smilin' Eddie Hill, who worked with Johnny (Wright) and Jack (Anglin) when they were in Knoxville; and Red Malone, popular in the Bristol area. Jack Cassidy has remained a favorite singer and picker among tri-cities fans and has enjoyed a recording career that has spanned three decades. Gospel music, always an influence on country music, has been well represented in East Tennessee by major figures like Fred Maples (born 1910 in GATLINBURG), who was instrumental in forming the Harmoneers, one of East Tennessee's best loved quartets; Pappy Beaver, who has played gospel country music since the 1940's and who today runs a storefront church in Knoxville; and J. Bazzel Mull, a tireless promoter of gospel songs whose colorful "Mull's Singing Convention" radio show was heard throughout the South.

Certainly the most visible East Tennessean on the country scene for the past few years has been Dolly Parton (born 1946 in Sevierville). One of twelve children born into a singing family (her sister and mother have since entered the music business, and the family once produced its own custom gospel LP), Dolly was appearing on Cas Walker's radio and TV shows in Knoxville by the time she was 12. After

Courtesy Country Music Foundation Library and Media Center, Nashville, Tennessee

Dolly Parton

graduating from high school in 1964, she struck out for Nashville, where she had her first hit record in 1967 and joined established star Porter Wagoner as a singing partner. This alliance continued for six successful years before Dolly branched out on her own, enjoying a number of hits that displayed not only her singing talent but her song-writing abilities as well. Her songs often describe her rural East Tennessee background ("My Tennessee Mountain Home", "Joshua", "Daddy was an Old-time Preacher Man"), and in spite of her recent success in mainstream popular music, Dolly Parton has continued to emphasize the "traditional background" in her music.

For the last sixty years, East Tennessee has served as a crucible for country music, yielding as many major performers as any area in the nation. Its rich folk tradition has periodically injected vitality and honesty into mainstream commercial country music, while at the same time helping the local music retain a distinctive regional character. This regional character, rarely found today in any art form, is one of the prime cultural strengths of the area, as well as of the music.

Charles Wolfe

Refer to: Chet Atkins and Bill Neely, *Country Gentleman*, Chicago: Henry Regnery, 1974; Bill C. Malone, *Country Music, U.S.A.: A Fifty-Year History*, Austin: University of Texas Press, 1968; Elizabeth Schlappi, *Roy Acuff: The Smoky Mountain Boy*, Gretna, Louisiana: Pelican, 1978; Cecil Sharp, ed. *English Folk Songs from the Southern Appalachians*, London: Oxford University Press, 1932; and Charles K. Wolfe, *Tennessee Strings: The Story of Country Music in Tennessee*, Knoxville: University of Tennessee Press, 1977.
See also: FRANK PROFFITT

Crab Orchard Stone is CUMBERLAND COUNTY's chief mining resource. It is found only in deposits now known to be in western Roane and Morgan counties and in eastern Cumberland County. The largest deposits lie between the towns of Crab Orchard and Crossville.

Crab Orchard stone in its natural bed.

Courtesy Ruby Hassler

Geologists call the stone "Crossville Sandstone", but other names for it include "Tennessee Quartzite", "Tennessee Variegated Stone", and "Cumberland Mountain Stone". The most common name is "Crab Orchard Stone", given by architect Henry Hibbs in 1927 while walking with Newton Walker along Otter Creek near the Cumberland Mountains.

Crab Orchard Stone is distinct from other sandstone found across the United States. Its layers separate readily, and the stone is hard enough to cut glass. It can be easily quarried, for it is usually found near the surface of the ground, although some of the larger quarries have located marketable stone on deeper ledges. The 95% silica content of the stone gives it excellent weathering qualities along with heat and acid resistance. Crab Orchard Stone contains almost 3% alumina; trace minerals include iron, titanium, and magnesium. These elements produce colors of gray, blue gray, tan and buff, with a blending of yellow, brown, mauve, red and pink. Such secondary colors form swirls, stripes, and various designs in the stone. Crab Orchard stone is categorized into dimension stone, ashlar, flagstone, rough broken stone, and rubble. Uses include roofing, coping, and veneering on both exterior and interior surfaces.

The Crab Orchard Stone Company, formed by John Oman around 1927, first quarried the stone at the Peck Quarry east of Crossville. About the same time, Newton Walker's Cumberland Mountain Stone Company sold "Rainbow Flagging" stone from the old Blakely place southeast of Crossville. There are now three main quarries in operation: Ross L. Brown Cut Stone Company, organized in 1957, Crab Orchard Stone Company, and Turner Brothers Stone Company. These companies quarry their stone in a similar way: bulldozing away the top soil, loosening slabs with an air drill or dynamite, and loading layers from 1/2" to 42" in thickness onto trucks. Strips of 1/2" to 2" thicknesses are used for flagging or paving sidewalks; 2" to 8" thicknesses go for veneer; and stone slabs of greater thickness, ranging from five to fifteen tons, are cut by wire saws at processing plants. An overhead crane moves slabs from the saw bed to the polishing beds. Here, buffing removes saw marks and gives a smooth surface. In the final stage, stone cutters finish each piece with hammer and chisel, pitching the ends and sides to a given line and plane. This produces a bold dramatic face in contrast to the smooth face made by the wire saw.

About 95% of all Crab Orchard Stone is shipped throughout the United States and Canada. The stone has been used in the construction of numerous well-known buildings, including Detroit's United Auto Workers headquarters, Atlanta's Cathedral of St. Philip, Washington's Internal Revenue Service building, and New York's Rockefeller Plaza. Buildings in Cumberland County include two high schools, many homes, and Crossville's post office, jail, and library.

Jenny Wright

See also: CUMBERLAND HOMESTEADS

Craighead Caverns, located between Sweetwater and Madisonville, are known to tourists throughout the Southeast as "The Lost Sea". Geologically, the caverns' most interesting feature is the presence of anthocites or "cave flowers" on the ceilings. Anthocites are clusters of radiating crystals of aragonite whose formation is not well understood. They are rare; perhaps half of the world's known specimens occur in Craighead Caverns.

There is abundant evidence of human use of the caverns. Artifacts found in one large bowl-shaped area indicate that it may have been used by the CHEROKEES as a council chamber. The caverns are named for a Cherokee, Chief Craighead, who owned them during the 1820's.

Early white settlers found the constant 58° temperature ideal for safely storing vegetables, and this practice continued until recent times. During the CIVIL WAR, saltpeter was mined from the caverns. Leaching vats, used by Confederate soldiers in making gunpowder from the saltpeter, are still there. Other uses of the caverns since 1900 have included moonshining and serving liquor, dancing, cockfighting, and mushroom farming.

The Lost Sea itself is an underground lake, 800 feet long by 220 feet wide and as much as 60 feet deep. It was discovered in 1905 by Ben Sands, then a teenager, who crawled through a tiny mud corridor from the Spring Room into what is now the Lake Room. This corridor has since been blasted out with dynamite and lined with manmade stone walls. Lying 140 feet below the surface of the mountain, the Lost Sea is fed from underground springs which can be seen in the Spring Room; its outlet to the Tennessee River has not yet been found. Divers descending beneath the cavern walls have determined that the lake extends at least 750 feet beyond its visible end, but the Lost Sea has still not been fully explored.

Janet B. Thiessen

David Crockett (August 17, 1786 - March 6, 1836), hunter, scout, soldier, humorist, and Congressman, was one of the most famous frontiersmen in United States history. In the late 1820's he captured the heart and imagination of America, and that fascination continues to grow on into the 20th century. This "gentleman from the cane", as a man whom he challenged to a duel called him, was an authentic product of the American frontier. He wooed and won the favor not only of the citizens of the backwoods, but of the eastern establishment and the new national press as well. Crockett has endured as the symbol of the pioneer movement and spirit in America. The exploitation of Crockett's tremendous popularity, initially by the populist press, has virtually obscured Crockett the real man. Scholarly efforts are continuing the process of releasing the real man from the tall tales and romantic hero worship.

In order to understand Crockett the frontiersman, one must first understand the American frontier. The first American settlements were established in Virginia in 1607, and it took over 150 years for the settlers to develop the spirit and resources to begin the westward movement over the Appalachian Mountains. The persons who finally began to cross the mountains and settle the tractless wilderness were six generations removed from their European forefathers who had huddled along the coast. They had to learn a measure of self-sufficiency and independence which enabled them to leave the interdependent, integrated society of their colonial ancestors.

The Crockett family typifies those who settled on the expanding frontier. Of Scotch-Irish descent, the family had migrated to America about 1709 and had then moved from New York to Pennsylvania to Virginia. They arrived in North Carolina in 1771. David Crockett's grandfather, also named David, moved his family in 1775 across the Southern Appalachian Mountains through the Watauga Valley into what is now East Tennessee. The family initially settled near the present town of Rogersville. Two years later, while David's father was serving in the Continental Army, his grandfather and grandmother were killed by marauding Cherokee and Creek Indians. David himself was born on the cutting edge of this turbulent frontier. He was the fifth son of nine children of John and Rebecca Hawkins Crockett, who at this time lived on the waters of Limestone Creek and the Nolichucky River, twelve miles east of the present town of Greeneville.

Any study of David Crockett must depend heavily upon his autobiography, *A Narrative of the Life of David Crockett of the*

Courtesy Tennessee State Library

David Crockett, portrait by S.S. Osgood, acknowledged by Crockett "to be the only correct likeness that has been taken of me."

State of Tennessee, which was published in 1834 and is receiving increasing literary and historical recognition. This narrative begins in GREENE COUNTY in 1794. After his grist mill was washed out, John Crockett moved his family to JEFFERSON COUNTY, where they lived on the south side of the Main Holston Road along the waters of Mossy Creek. This site is today within the present city limits of Jefferson City. Approximately a year later, a sheriff's sale for debts forced the family to move again, this time up the Main Holston Road to a location which is now Morristown. Here John Crockett opened a tavern.

It seems reasonable to surmise, from a close reading of David's autobiography, that much of his early life was spent in a state of POVERTY and deprivation. His father's debts were ever present, and more than once David tells of his father's hiring him out to pay off these debts. In one case, described at length in the *Narrative*, David was indentured at age 12 to a Jacob Siler, who was moving to Natural Bridge, Virginia. After several weeks, in the dead of winter and in knee-deep snow, a homesick David broke away from Siler and made the difficult return journey of approximately 250 miles back home to East Tennessee. Three years later, in order to pay off a debt of $36, David's father prevailed upon him to work six months for an Abraham Wilson, who ran a tavern "where a heap of bad company met to drink and gamble." David agreed to do this because his father promised that he would "discharge me from his service and I might go free."

David ran away from home, with his father in hot pursuit, after a problem with school in 1799. He was gone for two years traveling up through central Virginia as far north as Baltimore. He returned home in 1801. For the next five years, David lived and worked for a Quaker family named Canaday who resided near Panther Springs in the present HAMBLEN COUNTY. John Canaday, (misspelled in the *Narrative* as "Kennedy") was the patriarch of his own family, and his influence on David's early life was profound. David's first love was a half-niece of John Canaday named Amy Sumner. David and his second girlfriend, Margaret Elder, were attendants at the wedding of Amy Sumner and John Canaday's son, Robert. David's only formal education took place over a period of six months in a Quaker school run by one of John Canaday's sons.

While living with the Canadays, David met Polly Finley at a "reaping". David traded his first rifle and some work to one of John Canaday's sons for a horse so that he and Polly could be married. The wedding took place on August 16, 1806, at the home of William and Jean Finley, the bride's parents, at Finley's Gap in Bays Mountain, Jefferson County. David and Polly began married life on a small rented farm within sight of his in-laws' home at Finley's Gap. They had very few of even the most basic material possessions, and after five years of hard work and little progress, David moved his family west in late 1811 to Lincoln County in Middle Tennessee.

The second half of David's life is much better known than the first half. Between 1813 and 1815, he served under Andrew Jackson in the Creek Indian War. He was made a lieutenant in the militia of Lincoln County in 1815. Some months after his return from war in 1815, Polly died, and about the middle of 1816 he married a widow, Elizabeth Patton. He next moved his famly to Lawrence County, further west, where he became a Lt. Col. in the militia, a justice of the peace, a town commissioner, and a court referee. While here he was elected to the Tennessee Legislature for the terms of 1821-1822 and 1823-1824. Carroll County near the Mississippi River was the next stop in his own westward migration, and here he was again elected to the legislature. He had run unsuccessfully for Congress in 1822, but he ran successfully for Congress in 1827, serving continuously — except for the session of 1831-33 — until his defeat in 1835.

In Congress David represented the squatters and the disenfranchised who were settling public lands as he had done. He sought to have these lands deeded over to those who had settled them. The state political powers and Andrew Jackson sought instead to have the lands sold and the proceeds go to fund public education. On this issue, Crockett broke with Jackson and Polk in a bitter fight that lasted until the end of his life. David's tremendous popularity and naive nature made him a useful tool for those opposed to Jackson and his policies. Using David's name, these "allies" gave only token support for his attempts at a land bill. Further, his popularity led to many exaggerations about him being published, and these further obscured the real man and helped give birth to the legend. David's eldest son did follow him in Congress in 1837 and managed to get enacted in 1841 a modified version of his long-fought-for land bill.

After Jackson and his followers successfully defeated him for Congressional re-election in 1835, David declared that the people of Tennessee could "go to hell" and that he himself would go to Texas, which he did. In Texas he aligned himself with the 181 Texas freedom fighters at the Alamo who opposed Santa Anna's forces of 5000 Mexican regulars. David Crockett died at the Alamo in one of the most famous battles in American history. In his life he had become a national figure both in history and in legend. The circumstances of his death canonized him for posterity in both places.

The story of David Crockett is the story of the American Frontiersman. Crockett replaced the Natty Bumppo of James F. Cooper as the real-life ideal of a romantic era. For his struggles he deserves recognition as a man and not only as a legend.

Joe Swann
H. Phillips Hamlin

Refer to: David Crockett, *A Narrative of the Life of David Crockett of the State of Tennessee*, Philadelphia: E.L. Carey and A. Hart, 1834 (Reprinted 1973, Knoxville: University of Tennessee Press, with an introduction and annotations by James A. Shackford and Stanley J. Folmsbee); Stanley J. Folmsbee's articles in *The East Tennessee Historical Society's Publications*, Nos. 28 (1956), pp. 58-65, 29 (1957), pp. 40-78, 30 (1958), pp. 48-74, and 43 (1971), pp. 3-17; and James Adkins Shackford, *David Crockett: the Man and the Legend*, Chapel Hill: University of North Carolina Press, 1956.
See also: DANIEL BOONE

John Cullum (March 2, 1930 -   ), actor, was born in Island Home Park in KNOXVILLE, the youngest of five children. He lived there with his parents until he went to New York in 1956. His father E.V. Cullum, Jr., a native of South Carolina, was prominent in Knoxville's banking, real estate, and insurance business. The Cullum family was active in the Island Home Baptist Church, where John first realized the power of dramatics from the forceful preaching of Rev. Charles E. Wauford. Familiar from youth with the King James version of the Bible, Cullum later found Shakespearean language relatively easy to master. Several church choirs were enhanced by his rich baritone.

John Cullum attended South Knoxville Grammar School, South Junior High, Knoxville High School, and THE UNIVERSITY OF TENNESSEE. He

Courtesy Lee Sanders

John Cullum

acted in all of these schools and at U.T. became the Cadet Commander of R.O.T.C. as well as president of Phi Gamma Delta fraternity and a superb tennis player. After graduating in speech in 1953, Cullum played the European amateur tennis circuit and earned an invitation to Wimbledon. The Korean War, however, interrupted his career for two years. After the war he returned to Knoxville, where he worked with his father in real estate, took graduate work in finance, and was choir director of Dixie Lee Junction Baptist Church. But he was unhappy in Knoxville, and he soon decided to go to New York City and the theater. He once remarked that he felt as "called" to be an actor as his brother Gene was to be a minister. By this time, he had played some thirty major roles in Knoxville theater.

For four years John Cullum was just another scrambling actor in New York City, picking up small roles as he could. His first role was that of a spear carrier in Siobhan McKenna's *St. Joan*. During the summer of 1957, he played the title role (JOHN SEVIER) in *Chucky Jack* at the Hunter Hills outdoor theater in GATLINBURG. There he fell in love with a solo dancer in the play, Emily Frankel. A few years later, after she had won fame for her dancing and choreography, they were married in New York and continued to live there in Greenwich Village.

Cullum's experience with Shakespeare led to his first Broadway show, *Camelot*, in 1960. In *Camelot*, he originated the role of Sir Dinadan and was standby for Richard Burton. Cullum's big break occurred when he replaced Louis Jourdan as the lead in Alan Jay Lerner's musical, *On a Clear Day You Can See Forever*. For this he received the 1965-66 Theater World Award. He appeared again on Broadway in 1967 in the title role of *Man of LaMancha*. In 1970 he was featured in another musical, *1776*, as South Carolina Congressman John Rutledge. For the part of Rutledge, Cullum imitated his own father's southern accent. He recreated Rutledge for the movie version of *1776*. Cullum's other films include *Hawaii* and *All the Way Home*, the latter based on Knoxvillian JAMES AGEE's novel *A Death in the Family*.

The musical *Shenandoah*, which he said "turned my career around," made John Cullum the homespun hero of Broadway. As Charlie Anderson, a Virginia farmer who refuses to take sides in the CIVIL WAR, Cullum drew critical raves for his stalwart acting and brilliant singing. Many called him the best singing actor on the American stage. For *Shenandoah*, John Cullum won the Tony Award as Best Actor in 1975. Three years later, he won a second Tony Award for the flamboyant role of Oscar Jaffee in the musical *On the Twentieth Century*. Cullum also received much acclaim for the 1977 drama *The Trip Back Down*, for the 1979 comedy *Deathtrap*, and for his own *Hamlet*, done in Milwaukee in 1968. While critics have acclaimed his genius in glowing praise, John Cullum himself credits hard work, stamina, and determination as other factors in his success.

Lee Cullum Sanders

See also: GRACE MOORE
PATRICIA NEAL

Cumberland County
Size: 678 Square Miles (433,920 acres)
Established: 1855
Named For: Cumberland Mountain (named for the Duke of Cumberland)
County Seat: Crossville
Other Major Cities, Towns or Communities:
Crab Orchard
Mayland
Ozone
Westel
Pleasant Hill
Homestead
GRASSY COVE
Hebbertsburg
Rinnie
Newton

Refer to: Helen B. and Joseph M. Krechniak, *Cumberland County's First Hundred Years*, Crossville: Crossville Centennial Committee, 1956.
See also: CRAB ORCHARD STONE
CUMBERLAND HOMESTEADS
MAY CRAVATH WHARTON

Cumberland Homesteads, a small CUMBERLAND COUNTY community several miles southeast of Crossville, began in December of 1933 as a subsistence settlement created under Franklin Roosevelt's New Deal administration. The history of the Federally supported Homesteads—the single example of its type in East Tennessee—demonstrates both the power and the limitations of the Federal Government in effecting certain kinds of social change.

The Depression led to a general reevaluation by government planners of the nation's economy and living patterns. Social critics had for years advocated a return from the city to the farm, from the centralized industry and conspicuous consumption of urban areas to the simpler satisfactions and more individually creative activities of rural America. The compromise solution developed by Roosevelt's advisers was the ideal of the "subsistence homesteads", a community which would be rurally situated and agriculturally based, yet attractive enough to host diversified industries and thus decentralize the country's corporate mix. The National Industrial Recovery Act of 1933 provided $25 million in loans for such homesteads, and a new Division of Subsistence Homesteads was soon established within the Department of Interior. The

Division commenced making start-up loans to redistribute unemployed urban laborers and to rehabilitate "stranded groups" living in rural regions. The "stranded groups" homesteads directly affected many people in southern APPALACHIA; three such projects were established in West Virginia, and the fourth came to Cumberland County, Tennessee.

The groups stranded on East Tennessee's Cumberland Plateau comprised several work forces. The first and most numerous were the small farmers, who had never known even relative affluence and who had only been depressed further by the country's economic downturn. There were also the timbermen, the miners, and the mill workers. None of these industries—construction, coal, textiles—fared well during the Depression, and such local businesses as the Harriman Hosiery Mill and the Fentress County Coal and Coke Company forced scores of employees either to strike or to quit. Cumberland Homesteads promised to alleviate the situation by offering families well-paid employment in building their homes, growing crops, and participating in various community ventures. Encouraged by the newly established TENNESSEE VALLEY AUTHORITY, THE UNIVERSITY OF TENNESSEE, and agricultural extension agents on the Plateau, local leaders embraced the advent of the Homesteads.

During the first weeks of 1934, the Cumberland Homesteads project opened an office in Crossville. Project managers bought 10,000 acres from the Missouri Coal and Land Company, and Family Selection Workers screened 1,500 applicants for 250 family homesteads. The rigid process of selection, by which only "hardworking, honest, sober and good citizens" were admitted, allowed a certain amount of favoritism and also lent an air of exclusiveness to the venture. Yet the homesteaders' enthusiasm led to the clearing of 200 acres that first spring, along with the building of roads, fences, a shingle mill, and chicken houses for thousands of baby chicks. Excitement remained high as four-room and even seven-room native stone houses, shingled and panelled in pine, were constructed on plots averaging about 17 acres each. Eleanor Roosevelt, on her way from TVA's NORRIS to Berea, Kentucky, visited in July, and Secretary of Agriculture Henry Wallace followed in October.

The Federal administration of Cumberland Homesteads changed the following spring. The Resettlement Administration, established by Executive Order of the President, was meant specifically for such cooperative communities. RA head Rexford G. Tugwell, a planner *par excellence*, pushed the cooperative concept and used music, arts, and crafts to try to mold a community out of the agglomeration of homesteaders. The Cumberland Homesteaders' Cooperative Association began in December of 1935 to distribute profits from its general store, and within a year it was running a sorghum mill using locally grown sugar cane. A 52-member credit union offered small loans at low interest rates. Later, the Association opened a mine and dug coal cooperatively in Cox's Valley, distributing the fuel at low cost among the Homesteaders. In 1937, a Homesteads canning factory employing 300 workers canned 80,000 quarts of vegetables and fruits.

But problems plagued Cumberland Homesteads. Most analysts of the settlement have emphasized the cross-purposes of the Federal bureaucrats on the one hand and, on the other hand, the Homesteaders themselves. The latter's position was simply stated by honorary mayor Oren Metzger in a 1939 *Crossville Chronicle* editorial; Metzger said that the people only wanted a "normal community with normal facilities." Cumberland Homesteads was hardly that. It was, in fact, a perfect laboratory for the utopian planners, where Washington overseers owned all property and controlled its leasing, maintenance, and general use. The Administration also ran its "cooperative" ventures with a heavy hand, shipping hogs with no feed, forgetting hay for the horses, installing hosiery machines with no power connection. The urban planners' efforts in creating a new form of human interaction, a progressive and perhaps radical response to the Depression, proved incompatible with the rural Homesteaders' more nuts-and-bolts attempts to carve out a home and make a living.

Besides this basic dysfunction, other pressures restricted the Homesteads' course. From the beginning, the relatively few families chosen as Homesteaders were envied and, to an extent, ostracized by surrounding communities. One government worker reported that Cumberland Homestead students stayed away from Crossville High School for fear of unfair treatment. Yet fear extended to government administrators as well. When Tugwell's daughter visited the Homesteads and fell in love with a boy from Cumberland County, her father had her returned promptly to Washington. On a more fundamental level, private business was reluctant to locate in such an atypical setting.

By 1939 the Homesteaders had seen a succession of Federal agencies administer their settlement. In November, the Department of Agriculture's Farm Security Administration offered the Cumberland Homesteaders a chance to buy their homes under a payment schedule that could be completed in as little as five years. Almost all the Homesteaders, anxious to make property and community decisions on their own, entered into purchase contracts. Through the succeeding decades, Cumberland Homesteads settled down to a stable, less frenetic community of approximately 150 residents. Although the 20th century fate of Cumberland Homesteads may not have turned out as grand or special as its Washington founders had hoped, the experiment left a nucleus of sturdy stone homes, a county economy stimulated by government funds and by grass-roots energy, and, in the hearts of many local citizens, a feeling of deep gratitude.

Jim Stokely

Refer to: Patricia B. Kirkeminde, *Cumberland Homesteads as viewed by the newspapers*, Crossville: Brookhart Press, 1977; Helen

CUMBERLAND HOMESTEADS

Bullard Krechniak, *Cumberland County's First Hundred Years,* Crossville: Cumberland County Centennial Committee, 1956 (See appendix for government reports concerning Cumberland Homesteads); Mike Smathers, "Search for the Garden: Planned Communities," in *Southern Exposure*, V.8, No.1 (Spring 1980), pp. 57-63; and Jannelle Warren-Findley, "Musicians and Mountaineers: The Resettlement Administration's Music Program in Appalachia, 1935-1937," in *Appalachian Journal*, V.7, No.1-2 (Autumn-Winter, 1979-80), pp. 105-123.

See also: AGRICULTURE
RUGBY

D

Dandridge, population 1500, county seat of JEFFERSON COUNTY, is the only town in the United States named for Martha Dandridge Washington. The first permanent white settlers came to the area in 1783, making homes along the Nolichucky and French Broad rivers. They included Robert McFarland, Alexander Outlaw, Thomas Jarnagin, James Hill, Wesley White, James Randolph, Joseph Copeland, Robert Gentry and James Hubbard. Others soon followed, attracted by the fertile farmland and the Abingdon-KNOXVILLE stage road. The settlement grew and prospered, even through the days of the ill-fated STATE OF FRANKLIN. On June 11, 1792, WILLIAM BLOUNT issued an ordinance laying off Jefferson County from parts of GREENE COUNTY and HAWKINS COUNTY. Blount also appointed ten citizens as magistrates to organize the new county.

These ten met on July 23, at the home of Jeremiah Matthews. By May of 1793, at their fourth session, they had appointed a committee to locate and lay off the county seat, and had approved plans for building a courthouse, jail, and stocks for the county. Joseph Hamilton was elected clerk, Robert McFarland sheriff, Col. James Roddye register and John Gilliland foreman of a grand jury of fifteen. The first case involved the theft of three yards of linen. The site chosen for the county seat, a neighborhood called "Henderson's Lower Meeting House", was named Dandridge and fifty acres of land were donated by Francis Dean. Samuel Jack surveyed the town; the original plat hangs in the county museum. A capsule history of the town and county may be seen in the excellent museum in the courthouse: Indian artifacts, pioneer utensils, firearms, articles of clothing, CIVIL WAR relics, a sizeable collection of well-preserved documents, letters and newspapers contributed mostly by local citizens, and the original marriage bond of DAVID CROCKETT and Polly Findlay, dated August 12, 1806.

The chief construction material of the period was undoubtedly log, but from 1804 on, brick was also used extensively. Commodious two-story frame houses with shutters and gingerbread trim were common during the 1840's and on into the 1900's. When Dandridge was made a Historic District in 1972, all these houses and other buildings were automatically included in the National Register of Historic Places. The earliest courthouse was probably

Courtesy Jean Bible

Early 20th century Dandridge from the west end of town. Courthouse, with cupola, at upper right.

log, but the first known was a small brick building near the site of the present Greek Revival structure. The latter was built between 1845 and 1848 by the Hickman brothers, who also built the Hickman Tavern, now the Dandridge City Hall. The addition at the rear was made in the 1950's. In its early years, the courthouse also served as a Civil War hospital and as a meeting place for social and civic groups and school graduations.

From the beginning, the churches have been an integral part of community life. The oldest, Hopewell Presbyterian, was organized in 1785. The present building was dedicated in 1872. The French Broad Baptist Church, organized in 1786, was the parent church of the Dandridge Baptist, dedicated in 1845. The present building was dedicated in 1914. Pine Chapel Society of Methodists, organized around 1787, was the forerunner of the present United Methodist Church, which dates back to about 1828. The present building was erected sometime around the turn of the century. The defunct Methodist Episcopal Church, South, had to be demolished because of the building of the Dandridge dike, in order to protect the town from inundation by the waters of the TENNESSEE VALLEY AUTHORITY's

Douglas Lake in the early 1940's.

The first school in Dandridge is thought to have been in a log cabin near the center of town. In 1806, Maury Academy was begun in a simple wooden building, replaced in 1819 by a three-story brick structure, and in 1884 by a new brick building. It was later called Maury High School. In 1929, a new high school was built and the Academy used for an elementary school. This high school was later replaced by another on the opposite end of town, and it became the Dandridge Elementary School. Maury Academy was torn down. With the opening of the new Jefferson County High School in 1975, halfway between Dandridge and Jefferson City, the former Maury High became Maury Middle School.

In 1854 the Bank of Dandridge was incorporated, and two years later the Bank of Jefferson was organized. But the building of the railroad elsewhere in the county, combined with the disastrous effects of the Civil War, slowed progress markedly. Today, with the recreational opportunities provided by Douglas Lake, a favorable tax rate and retirement climate, the development of the Dandridge Industrial Park in 1964, and the tourists attracted by the Historic District, Dandridge has once again begun to grow. Through it all, the town has somehow managed to keep the charm of the old while at the same time taking advantage of the progress engendered by the new.

Jean Bible

Refer to: Weston A. Goodspeed, ed. *History of Tennessee*, East Tennessee Edition, Nashville, Tenn.: Goodspeed Publishing Company, 1887; and James G. M. Ramsey, *Annals of Tennessee to the End of the Eighteenth Century*, Charleston: Walker and James, 1853.
See also: JONESBORO

Charles Frederick Decker, (April 4, 1832 - March 11, 1914). The memory of Charles Frederick Decker, Sr., master potter, remains throughout the Chucky Valley of Tennessee. It was in this valley where the young German immigrant finally settled and built a small family dynasty based on the Decker family trade: pottery.

Charles Decker was born in Langenalb, Germany, and came to the United States while still a teenager. After working for the stoneware manufacturing company of Richard C. Remmey in Philadelphia, Pennsylvania, 25-year old Decker established his pottery firm in 1857. Eight years later, the hardworking proprietor of Keystone Pottery joined his fellow volunteer firemen in serving as honorary pallbearers for the funeral of Abraham Lincoln. During Reconstruction, Decker moved southward. He worked at a pottery six miles north of Abingdon, Virginia, then around 1872 bought about 100 acres of land in the Nolichucky River Valley, approximately six miles south of JONESBORO.

Using deposits of clay which underlay his rich farmland, the German potter promptly reestablished his Keystone Pottery. He built a temporary kiln to make brick for the huge permanent kiln where he would "burn" the many items made by himself, his four sons, and, in later years, as many as 25 employees. The pottery prospered, as did a nearby

Courtesy Beverly Burbage

The Decker family, October 15, 1904. Left to right: William M. ("Uncle Billy") Decker, N.E. Duncan, Dr. Charles F. Decker, Jr., W.F. Decker, Charles F. Decker, Sr., C.H. Decker, F.C. Decker.

store owned by Decker and a man named Davis. In an 1873 Jonesboro newspaper, Decker and Davis proudly advertised "a superior article of Drain Pipe, which every farmer should use to drain their swamp lands, as it will last almost forever." Decker Stoneware was delivered and peddled by wagon throughout a wide area. Jars, crocks, jugs and pitchers, the mainstay of the Keystone Pottery, usually sold for ten cents per gallon of capacity. Various shades of brown with a yellowish tint near the top characterized much of Decker's pottery. In addition to the usual brown or occasional gray glaze, he also used a dark blue glaze for decorative lettering and ornamentation.

Charles Decker's first wife, Catherine, had died just before the CIVIL WAR. His second wife, Sophia Hinch, died in 1886. Decker then married a widow named Susan Elizabeth Broyles Gefellers. Their marriage lasted happily until her death in 1909. During this period of his life, Decker and his family were neighbors to the Taylors of political fame. A buggy used by Republican Alf Taylor, whom Decker supported, was later owned by the latter's youngest son, Richard "Dick" Decker. Dick was a popular fiddler in winter hoedowns at the pottery, events warmed by the roaring wood fire beneath the kiln. Like his three brothers, Dick worked the pottery, store, and farm in exchange for clothes, food, and spending money provided by his father. The oldest son, Charles Jr., studied medicine under an area doctor and later practiced medicine and pharmacy from the family home and store. The next son, "Uncle Billy" to the family, was crippled from infancy but spent his entire life in the pottery.

C.F. Decker, Sr., the skilled old craftsman with a heavy German accent, was the influence that bound together the family industry. He survived both Billy and Charles, Jr., but when his health began to decline shortly after the turn of the century, the pottery ceased production and faded into history. The family patriarch spent his remaining time in his spacious home overlooking the lush river valley and the Keystone Pottery where he and his sons had transformed the valley's clay into lasting memorials to their craftsmanship.

David Kent Miller

See also: COUNTRY MUSIC
BOB AND ALF TAYLOR: KNIGHTS OF THE ROSES

Deer Lodge. As far as is known, a man by the name of Grimes was the first settler on the present site of Deer Lodge, in 1810. Three years later the son of Colonel William Lee Davidson, an early settler in MORGAN COUNTY, purchased a 300-acre tract of land on which the main part of Deer Lodge was later built. In 1845 James Davidson built the first industry in the area, a combined water grist and sawmill. The 300-acre tract was purchased from James Davidson on August 14, 1876, by Peter C. Fox of Jefferson County, Kentucky. Fox erected a double log house and began an open-range sheep ranch. His 150 sheep were soon devoured by wolves and hunters' dogs. In 1884 Abner Ross, former RUGBY settler and

Courtesy Barbara Stagg Paylor

Morgan County Fair, Deer Lodge, 1908. Little Red School at left.

proprietor of Rugby's Tabard Inn, purchased the Peter Fox tract. He brought with him his deer from the deer park at Tabard Inn, and he started plans for his new town of Deer Lodge.

Abner Ross was a short chubby man, a great talker with a jovial manner. He built his home on the site of the Davidson cabin and named it Walnut Knoll. A good many Victorian houses, some patterned after Ohio homes, were constructed nearby. Deer Lodge's first newspaper, *Southern Enterprise* and later *Deer Lodge Newsletter*, began publication in 1888. When the paper ceased operation around 1916, the printing press was sold to the *Morgan County Press* of Wartburg. The Mountain View, built in 1890 and operated by Mrs. J.E. Struble, was the first hotel in Deer Lodge. It was a white square two-story building, with a central staircase running up to the roof and opening into a covered area bordered with benches. The lookout afforded a beautiful view of the Cumberlands. The structure later fell into ruin and was torn down for the lumber. Also during the 1890's, the Summit Park Hotel just east of Deer Lodge served as the outstanding gathering spot for local society. The elite from nearby towns often gathered there and danced, and the hotel was for a while one of the most popular health resorts on the Cumberland Plateau.

Deer Lodge as a town had reached its peak as a busy farming and resort community. Life often centered around Deer Lodge's theater, planing mill, repair shops, band, or local chapters of such clubs as the Grand Army of the Republic, the Women's Christian Temperance Union, and the Independent Order of Odd Fellows. Polish miners and mill workers from Chicago and other northern cities arrived in Deer Lodge and organized more than one Catholic church, one of which was burned in about 1924 by the Ku Klux Klan.

During these early years of the 20th century, many of the Deer Lodge capitalists either died or moved away. Even with renewed advertising and promotion, the town was never the same again. Some adult residents left for better schools elsewhere, or for other work besides farming. Most of their children left for industrial work in Michigan and adjoining states. Although Deer Lodge could make no new provision for industry or recreation in order to keep its young, modern telephone service did arrive in 1957. The Morgan-Scott Project, a broad-based community development initiative supported by the Commission on Religion in Appalachia, came to Deer Lodge in the mid-1970's. Whether Deer Lodge ever reached the expectations of its founder cannot be judged, but the once-bustling town of the 1890's has settled down to a slow-moving — and much different — community.

Brian Stagg

Refer to: Brian Stagg, *Deer Lodge, Tennessee: Its Little-Known History,* 1964.

Deerskin Trade of the Cherokee. From the earliest days of settlement, trade between the English colonists and the native Americans was important to the economic well being of both peoples. This was especially true for the CHEROKEES and the South Carolinians during the colonial years. For southern Indians, deerskins were the most significant item with which they obtained manufactured trade goods. Even prior to making contact with the Cherokee nation, traders from both Virginia and South Carolina engaged heavily in the deerskin trade with the eastern tribes. During the last years of the seventeenth century, the Carolina-based traders established preeminence in the Cherokee trade. In most years 50,000 or more deerskins were sent by packhorse trains to Charles Town. There the skins were inspected, graded, weighed, and packed for shipment to Britain. Because they were an enumerated article, deerskins, by the navigation laws, could only be shipped within the empire.

Most commercial hunting for skins took place during the fall and winter months, with the skins brought down to the low country during the spring. The extensive Cherokee hunting grounds of the western Carolinas, as well as eastern and middle Tennessee, produced large numbers of deer with highly-prized thicker hides. Yet even with these advantages, the Cherokee hunters confronted difficulties in the trade. The excessive slaughter so reduced the deer population that by the middle years of the eighteenth century, hunters had to range further over the hunting grounds. Furthermore, as the Carolina traders enjoyed a virtual monopoly of the Cherokee trade, the opportunities for abuse by unscrupulous dealers were abundant. Even though the total annual harvest of skins was considerable, the individual skin yielded only a small return to each participant while trade goods were relatively expensive. During the early days of the trade a fortunate hunter might bring in sixty pounds during the season (an average buckskin weighed two pounds dressed), but by 1750, twenty-five pounds represented an average year's harvest. The Cherokee hunter thus experienced great economic pressure as he provided an inexpensive commodity, had no alternative markets, and could be overcharged for the trade goods.

With their economy centered on the deerskin trade, it was through this means that the Cherokee obtained not only luxury items, but also articles essential to their living standard and their security. Trade goods obtained in exchange for deerskins included awls, axes, blankets, brass arrowheads, kettles, hoes, cloth, matchcoats, rum, and most significantly, trade guns, powder and lead. Less essential but still important in displaying status were ornaments and cosmetic paints. The trade guns — smaller, lighter, and more cheaply made than most muskets in use at that time — were essential for military survival and for killing the deer with which to buy more trade goods. Although the articles traded to the Cherokee by the English were cheaply manufactured, the primary complaints directed by the Indian dealt with the low quantity rather than the quality. The Cherokee, moreover, recognized that the French traders who sought to make inroads into their trade could not supply them with goods of comparable quality or even of equal quantity at the prevailing English prices. Conversely, the Cherokee were highly regarded as intelligent traders and were envied for their extensive hunting grounds. Both neighboring tribes and the colonists, however, held general contempt for the Cherokee as warriors.

Of the South Carolina traders with whom the Cherokee dealt, little favorable has been written. Separate sources over a span of years labeled them "the very scum of the earth", "a shame to humanity", and "the vilest sort". The Cherokee frequently complained to colonial officials of their treatment at the hands of both licensed and unlicensed traders. Although a few of these traders were reasonably honest, many were completely unscrupulous in their dealings with the Indians. Among the charges most often raised against the traders were that they defrauded the Indians with short measures and dishonest scales, encouraged excessive indebtedness among the Indians, brought in rum illegally, and incited them to violence by ill treatment. The colonial officials recognized these problems and sought by various means to regulate the Indian trade. However, these efforts were at best only partially successful.

If, as some have claimed, the Indian trade was the "spearhead of Great Britain's advance to empire in North America", then the trader, disreputable though he may have been, was an essential agent of British colonial expansion. Without the trade brought among the Cherokee by these men, the influence of France would most likely have prevailed in the trans-Appalachian south. During the colonial period, the deerskin trade was the best means to secure the cooperation of the Cherokee for the British colonies. Through this deerskin trade British imperial interests were extended, a valuable commodity was obtained, the Indians were supplied, and, despite the abuses in the trade, the Cherokee were more firmly attached to the British colonial interest.

Stuart O. Stumpf

Refer to: John Richard Alden, *John Stuart and the Southern Colonial Frontier,* Ann Arbor: University of Michigan Press, 1944; David H. Corkran, *The Cherokee Frontier: Conflict and Survival, 1740-1762,* Norman: University of Oklahoma Press, 1962; Verner W. Crane, *The Southern Frontier, 1670-1732,* Durham, N.C.: Duke University Press, 1928; John Philip Reid, *A Better Kind of Hatchet: Law, Trade, and Diplomacy in the Cherokee Nation,* University Park: Pennsylvania State University Press, 1976, and *A Law of Blood: Primitive Law of the Cherokee Nation,* New York: New York University Press, 1970; and William Shedrick Willis, "Colonial Conflict and the Cherokee Indians, 1710-1760," Columbia University dissertation, 1955.

Samuel Doak (August 1, 1749-December 12, 1830), the leading minister of Presbyterianism and of higher education on the Tennessee frontier, was born in Augusta County, Virginia. At the age of sixteen, he became a Christian and began his studies under a tutor. By trading his part of the family's estate back to his father, Doak produced the money necessary to continue his education at West Nottingham Academy in Maryland. In 1775, he graduated from the College of New Jersey (Princeton University) and became a tutor at Hampton Sydney College. For a short time he was assistant teacher in the school of Reverend Bob Smith of Pesquea, Pennsylvania, and studied theology under his direction.

After being licensed to preach, October 31, 1777, Doak and his wife Elizabeth Montgomery moved to the Holston River settlements in East Tennessee. Leaving Holston after a year, the Doaks bought a farm on Little Limestone Creek in WASHINGTON COUNTY. Here Samuel organized what came to be known as the "Salem Congregation". He also built a log house for a school — the first school west of the Appalachian Mountains — and named it Martin Academy after Alexander Martin, Governor of North Carolina and Doak's fellow West Nottingham graduate. Martin Academy received charters in 1783 from the North Carolina Assembly and in 1785 from THE STATE OF FRANKLIN. Ten years later, by charter of the Territory South of the Ohio River, Martin Academy became Washington College. At "Dr. Doak's Log College", as it was called by frontiersmen, Doak taught such students as J. G. M. RAMSEY, future North Carolina governor Zebulon B. Vance, and the children of JOHN SEVIER. Ramsey considered himself Doak's favorite student and, in his writings, fondly remembered his Washington College days.

Samuel Doak was involved in many important affairs of upper East Tennessee. When area settlers gathered at Sycamore Shoals of the Watauga River, September 26, 1780, to confront the British at Kings Mountain, Doak gave a dramatic sermon and in prayer intoned God's wrath on the enemy. In 1784, Doak helped frame the constitution of the State of Franklin. One year later, he helped form and became first moderator of the Abingdon Presbytery, first presbytery in what is now Tennessee.

Samuel Doak was a serious man, not much for frivolity. But it remained a pleasure to him to impart knowledge to

Portrait of Samuel Doak.

his classes and his congregations. He resigned in 1818 as President of Washington College, only to open, with his son, another private school in GREENE COUNTY. Their Tusculum Academy formed the basis for present-day Tusculum College. At this Academy the elder Doak taught several disciplines, including chemistry and the Hebrew language. It is said that he could hear two or more recitation classes at one time and never miss an error. Samuel Doak touched many minds, and through his contributions to education and RELIGION, left an invaluable imprint on East Tennessee.

Donna Ray Waggoner

Refer to: Pat Alderman, *The Overmountain Men*, Johnson City, Tenn.: The Overmountain Press, 1970; William Gunn Calhoun, *Samuel Doak, 1749-1830*, Washington College, Tenn.: Pioneer, 1966; William Hesseltine, ed. *Dr. J. G. M. Ramsey: Autobiography and Letters*, Nashville: Tennessee Historical Commission, 1954; and Walter Brownlow Posey, *The Presbyterian Church in the Old Southwest*, Richmond, Va.: John Knox Press, 1952.
See also: WASHINGTON COLLEGE ACADEMY

Dragging Canoe (ca. 1740-March 1, 1792), the greatest war chief of the CHEROKEES, was the son of tribal statesman ATTAKULLAKULLA. He received his name when, as a child, he wanted to accompany his father to battle. His father refused to let him go, and the child hid in a canoe. The Cherokee war party discovered him when they reached a portage. Attakullakulla told his son that he could go if he could manage to carry the canoe across the portage. The young boy grabbed one end of the canoe and began dragging it through the sand.

Dragging Canoe came into prominence in March of 1775, at Sycamore Shoals near present-day ELIZABETHTON. There, he strongly protested the Cherokee sale of land to Richard Henderson and the Transylvania Company. Followed by several chiefs, headmen, and other warriors who recognized his leadership, Dragging Canoe stalked out of the negotiations. During the American Revolution, the Cherokees sided with the British against the encroaching settlers. On July 20, 1776, Dragging Canoe and his warriors fought a pioneer force from Eaton's Station at the Battle of Island Flats near present-day KINGSPORT. During the battle, Dragging Canoe thought the Whites were retreating and thundered in pursuit. The pioneers opened fire instead, killing thirteen Indians and wounding many more including Dragging Canoe himself.

From that time on, the "Dragon", as he came to be known to his enemies, followed the Indian style of guerrilla fighting. In the fall of 1776, the Cherokee Council met to debate whether they should move further south and fight on, or save their towns by making terms with the Americans. Although the peace alternative carried the Council vote, Dragging Canoe and his followers split off from the Cherokee Nation and moved south to the foot of Lookout Mountain. Here, along Chickamauga Creek near present-day CHATTANOOGA, they set up their own governing body.

During 1777, while the Cherokee chiefs negotiated treaties with the settlers, Dragging Canoe's Chickamaugans raided throughout the area. By 1779 the states of Virginia and North Carolina felt compelled to move against the rebel Indian settlements. Six hundred volunteers, led by Colonel Evan Shelby, spent two weeks in the Chickamauga settlements burning eleven towns and destroying much property, but the Chickamaugans survived this invasion and moved around the base of Lookout Mountain to various isolated points along the Tennessee River. These Five Lower Towns were well guarded by high mountains and river hazards.

The Chickamauga settlements grew through the 1780's as deserting Cherokees, Creeks, and even refugee Tories joined the ranks. Dragging Canoe received help at various times from the British and the Spanish governments. Also, the warrior was still attempting to rally all the southern Indians in their fight against the frontier Americans. Allied tribes did win several victories, and dances of war and celebration were frequently held among the Chickamaugans. It was after one of these that Dragging Canoe was found dead, perhaps from the frenzied dancing, perhaps from the years of war wounds. He had led his people for nearly two decades with a cry of "We are not yet conquered!" His struggle made possible a firm and relatively fair peace negotiated in 1794 at Tellico Blockhouse. Most significantly, his Chickamaugans carried the standard of Cherokee culture and tenacity which would unfurl again in Georgia during the early 1800's.

Connie J. Green

Refer to: Pat Alderman, *Dragging Canoe: Cherokee-Chickamauga War Chief*, Johnson City, Tennessee: The Overmountain Press, 1978; John P. Brown, *Old Frontiers*, Kingsport, Tennessee: Southern Publishers, 1938; and E. Raymond Evans, "Notable Persons in Cherokee History: Dragging Canoe," in *Journal of Cherokee Studies*, V. 2, No. 1 (Winter 1977), pp. 176-189.
See also: DANIEL BOONE

Dupont Springs, located on the north side of Chilhowee Mountain in SEVIER COUNTY, derived its name from a variation of "dew point" because dew did not form on the mountain at an elevation higher than the area of the iron, sulfur, and freestone springs. In 1901, the Dupont Springs Hotel began receiving guests and became one of the famous resort hotels of the area. Many families from KNOXVILLE took the

Courtesy Marian Oates

Dupont Springs cottagers and hotel guests in front of the Dupont Springs Hotel. Among the vacationers: Frank Oates (standing at upper left in shirt and tie), LaVerne Penland Worden (standing at left center with her hand on her waist), and photographer Jim Thompson (kneeling at lower right).

better part of a day to make the 20-mile trip by horse-drawn hack. Guests stayed anywhere from a few days to the whole summer, and some individuals built or purchased nearby cottages. One early visitor, Theresa Hickman Rostorfer, learned to walk here and now lives in her family's cottage. Vacationers hiked to Green Top, the 3,069-foot summit, or viewed the sunset from such rock outcroppings as the Hotel Bluff, Sunset Rock, Buzzard's Wash, and Lover's Leap.

LaVerne Penland Worden and Ersa Davis recall with great fondness the pastimes enjoyed by children and adults at Dupont Springs: picking huckleberries, group singing, outdoor exploring, horseshoes, croquet, checkers, and cards. On Saturday nights, the tables and chairs in the hotel dining room were pushed aside to provide room for dancing. Many times, music and instruction for the dances came from volunteers living in the valley below. Local farmers supplied milk and fresh vegetables. Since refrigeration was limited to a spring house at Dupont Springs, chicken dressed daily was the most common meat.

The hotel ceased operation around

1913 and later was torn down. After World War II Frank Oates, who as a boy had stayed regularly in one of the cottages, again became interested in the mountain. He and his wife spent several years acquiring property and making Dupont Springs and the surrounding part of the mountain accessible for vacation cottages and permanent homes. There are now over fifty of these dwellings, which stand as a quiet reminder of the active days of the Dupont Springs Hotel.

Marian E. Oates

See also: BEERSHEBA SPRINGS

Wilma Dykeman and James Stokely (May 20, 1920 - ; October 8, 1913 - June 20, 1977), writers, readers and travelers, were a husband-and-wife team with important things to say about their locale and about the human condition. Wilma Dykeman, who writes under her maiden name, is the novelist, speaker and newspaper columnist; James Stokely was the poet, orchardist and gardener. Miss Dykeman was born near Asheville, North Carolina, and was graduated from Northwestern University with a major in speech. Mr. Stokely, son of the co-founder and first president of Stokely-Van Camp cannery, was born in Newport, Tennessee, and was graduated from THE UNIVERSITY OF TENNESSEE with a major in business. They married in 1940 and settled in COCKE COUNTY, where they raised two sons.

The work of Wilma Dykeman might be divided roughly into three categories: first, a concern with early Tennessee history and mountain character; second, a concern for civil rights and human freedom; and third, a kind of reverence for life in the tradition of Albert Schweitzer, yet an affirmation of life which is uniquely her own. In all her works, she is concerned with values and character traits of the highest quality. Her first work, *The French Broad,* was published in 1955 as part of Rinehart's Rivers of America Series. It is an impressionistic history of an area in which her roots are embedded, descriptive of the life of a people who have lived along a river which sweeps through her native Asheville and by Newport, her adopted home. In preparation for her writing, she and her husband pioneered in oral history before it became widely used as an accepted technique for developing historical source material. Traveling up the hollows of East Tennessee and western North Carolina, they sat on many porches and listened to many experiences and much wisdom passed from generation to generation: memories and tradition, powerful forces in history and in its making.

In 1954, against the background of the Brown decision, Dykeman and Stokely addressed themselves to the first of three works probing the causes of racism and celebrating the lives of men who had fought against great odds to reduce its impact. In this work, *Neither Black Nor White,* the authors rejected the stereotype of a monolithic South regarding race. In their investigation, they found black and white bound together by a common land and a common past. *Neither Black Nor White,* winner of the Sidney Hillman Award, led the authors to other individuals who had worked courageously in the early 20th century for human liberty. During the 1960's they published biographies of Southern worker Will Alexander and APPALACHIA worker W. D. Weatherford, plus a Time-Life Library of America volume entitled *The Border States.*

Encouraged by Willis Duke Weatherford, Wilma Dykeman wrote *The Tall Woman*, a popular CIVIL WAR novel published in 1962. A sequel, entitled *The Far Family*, was published four years later; this was a novel concerned with character strengths and weaknesses, and with the senses of family and of place so vividly portrayed in the mountain people. In *Return the Innocent Earth*, her third novel, Wilma Dykeman describes the growth of a small canning company into a corporation of national importance. It is a work in which she reveals a strong conservationist interest. A concern for human resources and the social problems of overpopulation prompted her in 1973 to author a biography of birth control worker Edna Rankin McKinnon.

In 1975, Wilma Dykeman was commissioned to write *Tennessee: A Bicentennial History* as part of the great effort to publish the history of each state in commemorating America's Bicentennial. It is a book eminently readable, full of anecdotes, character study, local color, and moral truth, a book that at once entertains and informs. In an attractive imagery of point, counterpoint, she describes the sights, sounds, smells and tastes of Tennessee as she paints its history. During his wife's work on this book, James Stokely continued to write his poetry, selections of which were published posthumously in memorial issues of *Appalachian Heritage* and *The Small Farm.* Through Wilma Dykeman's and James Stokely's interest in the history of state and region, their concern for human rights and the dignity of the individual, their concern for human and natural resources, and their affirmation of life, they have earned the enduring gratitude of sensitive persons everywhere.

Courtesy Wilma Dykeman

Wilma Dykeman and James Stokely at their home in Newport, 1962.

Sam B. Smith

Refer to: Wilma Dykeman, *The French Broad*, New York: Rinehart, 1955, *The Tall Woman*, New York: Holt, Rinehart and Winston,

1962, *Prophet of Plenty: The First Ninety Years of W.D. Weatherford*, Knoxville: University of Tennessee Press, 1966, *The Far Family*, *Look To This Day*, and *Too Many People, Too Little Love*, New York: Holt, Rinehart and Winston, 1966, 1968, and 1974, and *Tennessee: A Bicentennial History*, New York: W.W. Norton, 1976; Wilma Dykeman and Dykeman Stokely, *Appalachian Mountains*, Portland, Oregon: Graphic Arts Center, 1980; Wilma Dykeman and James Stokely, *Neither Black Nor White*, New York: Rinehart, 1957, *Seeds of Southern Change: The Life of Will Alexander*, Chicago: University of Chicago Press, 1962, and *The Border States*, New York: Time-Life Books, 1968; and James Stokely, "A Selection of Poems", in *Appalachian Heritage*, V.7, No.1 (Winter 1979), pp. 7-14.
See also: APPALACHIAN LITERATURE

E

East Tennessee Development District, established in 1966 by the Tennessee General Assembly, is a cooperative planning and economic development venture of sixteen counties in East Tennessee. ETDD's member counties include Anderson, Blount, Campbell, Claiborne, Cocke, Grainger, Hamblen, Jefferson, Knox, Loudon, Monroe, Morgan, Roane, Scott, Sevier, and Union. Four other development districts—Southeast, South Central, Upper Cumberland, and First Tennessee-Virginia—comprise the remaining counties of East Tennessee.

The purpose of ETDD is threefold. First, the District is to carry on comprehensive planning and development for the region. Second, the District is to assist in developing the region and state in an efficient and orderly manner. Third, the District is to make maximum use of Federal, State and local programs designed to encourage economic development and resource utilization. ETDD's governing Board of Directors consists primarily of elected officials from each governmental body within the district, including county executives, mayors or city managers, one state representative, and one state senator. Policies or projects approved by this Board cannot be implemented until the legislative bodies of the affected areas have granted their approval. ETDD's funding is approximately 75% Federal, with the remaining 25% equally divided between state and local government. The Appalachian Regional Commission provides some funding, in return for which ETDD generates, reviews, and sends locally approved project proposals to ARC.

Over the past fifteen years, ETDD has listed well over two hundred projects worthy of completion by the local governments in the region. The local governments, county and municipal, have committed funds toward completion of almost 90% of the projects endorsed by the ETDD Board of Directors. Among the projects completed have been extensive industrial parks, as well as substantial water and utility projects. The BLOUNT COUNTY Industrial Park and the second phase of the Forks of the River Industrial Park in KNOX COUNTY are two of these development projects. ETDD has contributed to the realization of improved utilities in COCKE COUNTY, the establishment of the ANDERSON COUNTY Utilities Board, the founding of the Tellico Area Services System, and a joint utilities venture between MORGAN COUNTY and ROANE COUNTY.

Some of the larger projects for the future include those related to water, wastewater, and utilities; recreation and open space; tourism; and highway construction. The Big South Fork National River and Recreation Area, for example, is a $140 million project sponsored by the U.S. Army Corps of Engineers and scheduled for completion in 1986. Located on the Cumberland Plateau near the Kentucky state line, the Big South Fork of the Cumberland River has been the object of an exhaustive impact study by ETDD. Further to the east, the construction of dual tunnels under Cumberland Gap will remove Highway 25E from that historic site. A large tourism project endorsed by the District is the 1982 World's Fair in KNOXVILLE. LOUDON COUNTY and MONROE COUNTY have several highway projects, due in part to the TENNESSEE VALLEY AUTHORITY's completion of Tellico Dam in late 1979. The District is also backing several wastewater and water projects, including a $15 million sewage treatment plant for OAK RIDGE and the doubling of capacity for Morristown's water plant.

Mark Davidson

Refer to: Mercy Hardie Coogan, "The Local Perspective: ETDD Weighs Projects in the Balance," in *Appalachia,* V. 13, No. 1 (September-October 1979), pp. 20-27; and David Whisnant, *Modernizing the Mountaineer,* New York: Burt Franklin, 1980, pp. 126-182.
See also: APPALACHIA
POPULATION CHARACTERISTICS

East Tennessee State University is a regional, tax-supported, multi-purpose university located in JOHNSON CITY, in northeast Tennessee. The university was founded in 1911 as East Tennessee Normal School as a result of legislative action in 1909 to improve teacher training in the state. Johnson City and WASHINGTON COUNTY appropriated money to begin construction, and George L. Carter donated 120 acres of land in southeast Johnson City.

The charter faculty numbered twenty-two, and Sidney G. Gilbreath was chosen as the first president. In the beginning, East Tennessee State Normal School's curriculum was a two-year teacher training program. The curriculum was expanded to three years in 1919 and to four years in 1924, at which time the name of the institution was changed to East Tennessee State Teachers College. In 1930 the name changed again to State Teachers College, Johnson City. From 1943 to 1963, the school was known officially as East Tennessee State College. In 1963 the current name was adopted, giving full recognition to the university status of the institution. The university is a member of the State University and Community College System of Tennessee and is governed by the State Board of Regents.

The current curriculum provides for associate and bachelor's degrees in a wide variety of disciplines ranging from the technical to the humanistic. Graduate education is offered in a number of master's degree programs. The university also offers the Ed.S., Ed.D, M.D., and Ph.D. degrees. In seventy years, the university has grown

Courtesy Archives of Appalachia, East Tennessee State University

Trolley between Johnson City and the Normal School (now East Tennessee State University), July 1912.

Students on the East Tennessee State University campus.

Courtesy Archives of Appalachia, East Tennessee State University

from a teacher-training campus of 120 acres and five buildings to a diversified institution of 325 acres and 66 major buildings, as well as centers in KINGSPORT, ELIZABETHTON, BRISTOL, and Greeneville. East Tennessee State University participates in major intercollegiate athletics and is currently a member of the Southern Conference. In earlier years, ETSU belonged to the Smoky Mountain Conference and the Ohio Valley Conference. ETSU is the home of the only indoor collegiate football stadium east of the Mississippi. The Sherrod Library on the main campus houses over 500,000 volumes, and the B. Carroll Reece Museum offers a variety of cultural attractions.

Thomas D. Lane

Refer to: David Sinclair Burleson, *History of the East Tennessee State College*, Johnson City, 1947; and Frank B. Williams, Jr., work in progress.
See also: THE UNIVERSITY OF TENNESSEE

East Tennessee Talk. Where language is concerned, the stereotyped pictures of the southern mountaineer lead to one of two extreme views, the first that of the laconic "hillbilly" (or "ridgerunner" or "briar") who barely has language, the second that of the eloquently articulate and courtly speaker of pure Chaucerian or Elizabethan or Shakespearian English. Neither view is true, though language is a particularly interesting cultural phenomenon to study anywhere in the Southern Appalachian region, because it does display characteristics different from other regions. Researchers talk of "Ozark Folk Speech" and "Appalachian Speech" and "Southern Mountain Speech"; when they do so, they are usually generalizing broadly from personal observation or from studies in one or two counties of one of the states in the Ozarks or in Southern APPALACHIA. Further, they are usually describing rural and relatively uneducated ways of speaking. Actually, there appear to be important differences within the large areas denoted by the labels "Ozark", "Appalachian", and "Southern Mountain".

All speakers of American English have far more in common than any differences they might have, but we generally learn more about the language of a specific area when we focus on that area rather than trying to extend generalizations from other areas. Thus we can theoretically learn more about the way East Tennesseans talk if we confine our attention to people in East Tennessee. The problem is that no detailed linguistic study has been completed in East Tennessee. In the following paragraphs, I will report on the basis of the few completed studies and my own research and observation.

Not everyone in East Tennessee talks alike, of course. For one thing, different age groups use language differently. They do this for two reasons. One is that our culture is marked by a strong tendency toward what sociolinguists call "age-grading"; that is, we think different kinds of behavior (linguistic and otherwise) are appropriate for different age groups. Teenagers everywhere, for instance, use a far greater number of slang expressions than do other age groups. Also, language is always changing; this means that the next generation is sure to use language a bit differently from the preceding one simply because it *is* the next generation.

People use language differently, too, depending upon such facts as whether they grew up in a rural or in an urban environment, how much formal education they and other members of their families have, how much they have travelled, and what their parents' occupations or professions are. These are what are known as sociolinguistic factors, social factors with implications for language use. Other differences are less important; they involve sex, ethnicity, and religious affiliation. We can usefully ignore some of these differences, however, in order to examine some of the broad characteristics of the English language as it is used in East Tennessee. But these characteristics will certainly be found more often in rural areas among less well educated persons.

One way of getting at the truth of the linguistic situation in East Tennessee is to dispel such myths as the one mentioned above, that East Tennesseans speak Elizabethan or Chaucerian English. They don't. They do, however, speak a dialect with some archaisms in vocabulary, in pronunciation, and in grammar. That is, they preserve some older words, some older pronunciations of words, and some older ways of structuring sentences, ways that have changed or died out in other dialects of the language.

It is important to understand that the word "dialect" simply means a variety of a language. As I have pointed out elsewhere,

> dialects are not spoken only in certain parts of the country or only by certain people. A dialect is the speech pattern of a given community and because communities are structured geographically and socially, dialects differ regionally and socially. Each community has its dialect or dialects, and its members speak one or more of these dialects. Consequently, everybody speaks a dialect, and some speakers may speak more than one dialect, particularly if they belong to more than one community. Many highly educated speakers shift back and forth between a fairly formal variety of English (sometimes called Standard English) and the English of their family or home community. (Dumas 1975:24)

Technically speaking, Southern Mountain speech is a subvariety of what linguists call South Midland speech, a dialect that spread, along with the population, southwestward from Pennsylvania, after which it continued to spread westward (ultimately into the Ozarks and as far west as East Texas and eastern Oklahoma) as people migrated further west. It is thus derived from the Scotch-Irish of western Pennsylvania, and in the Southern Mountain region it has changed less than elsewhere because of geographic and social isolation. As this isolation has lessened, language differences have begun to lessen, though the newcomer to East Tennessee can still be quite *pezzled* (*puzzled*) by words like *dope* (for what others know as a *soft drink*, a *sodawater*, a *coke* or a *tonic*), *ramp* (a wild edible plant with a strong and easily identifiable odor), or *poke* (a relatively small cloth or paper container generally used for groceries or other small purchases) *everwhen* (*whenever*) they are used. The absolute newcomer would be hard put to translate the punch line of a story which makes the rounds in KNOXVILLE and which is attributed to a local doctor: "I *hunkered;* my ankle *creeled;* it *bealed* so bad I thought it would *pone.*" (See APPALACHIAN GLOSSARY).

Different dialects use different words; they also pronounce words differently. Of course, newcomers everywhere have to be instructed in the correct pronunciation of place names; in East Tennessee one must be careful to say *Murrville* (*Maryville*), *Tinnessee* (whether one stresses the first syllable or not), *Sevurrville* (*Sevierville*) and *Chatnooga* (not *Chat-ta-noo-ga*). But one may also need to recognize the pronunciation *ingern* for *onion*, that a *jedge* is a *judge*, that it's sometimes hard to tell whether people in Knoxville are saying *Pike* or *Park*, that *deal* sometimes rhymes with *dill* (and that a person named *Neal Hill* never knows how his name is going to be pronounced), that *you* can sound as though it's spelled *y-e*, and that the words *your, his, her, their,* and *our* may all have final *n*'s attached to them, coming out *yourn, hisn, hern, theirn,* and *ourn*. All Southerners know about *y'all* and *you all;* here we have also *you'uns* (and sometimes *we'uns* and *us'uns* and even *we'unses*). *Tennessee* is not the only word that can have an unexpected stress on the first syllable. So can *adult, police, guitar, hotel,* and *motel,* and also the phrase *red light*.

Verb phrases get constructed differently, too. In "standard" English, verbs like "may", "might", "can", "could", "should", "would", and "ought to" are never combined. But in East Tennessee we can combine these modal auxiliaries to produce sentences like "He may can," "She might should," and even "They might should ought to." Also we can dress up our verbs by putting an initial *a-* prefix on the *-ing* forms, producing sentences like "I'm a-going fishin' if it don't rain." This practice was widespread in the language at one time. The *a-* was originally a full preposition, and sentences like "He was on hunting" were once common in the language.

Hit and *hain't* deserve special mention. *Hit* is quite common in the area, *hain't* less so. The first is, of course, a dialect survival of a Middle English pronoun form, which has since become *it* in the standard language. *Hain't* is generally taken to be the contracted form of *has not* or *have not*. In fact, it does double duty with *ain't*. Neither word is used 100% of the time that it might be; i.e., all speakers who use *hit* also use *it*, and all speakers who use *hain't* for *ain't* also use *ain't*. Notions of euphony play a role in determining when *hit* and *hain't* will be used.

Some characteristic usages in this area are common throughout the United States in nonstandard usage; that is, they are not confined to East Tennessee or even to the entire Southern Mountain region. Because these usages convey a good deal of the flavor of spoken English in East Tennessee, I will mention briefly the major categories. Additional examples are contained in the APPALACHIAN GLOSSARY.

Verb Forms. The past and past participle forms of some verbs are different from the standard language. In most cases, the variant forms represent the preservation of competing dialect forms from Middle English. In general, they also represent an attempt to regularize the irregular verbs of English, though they may also represent simplification of principal parts. Examples of irregular verbs that may be regularized are *blow* (*blowed*), *grow* (*growed*), *hear* (*heared*), and *know* (*knowed*). Examples of verbs where the principal parts have been simplified are *do* (*done*), *come* (*come*) and *eat* (*et*). Of course, not all speakers use the variant pronunciations and other features noted above. Some of these usages are highly stigmatized and are avoided by careful speakers.

Noun Plurals. Two classes of nouns frequently have "non-standard" plural forms, those which end in consonant clusters like *-sp, -sk,* and *-st,* and those nouns which in Old English did not require a plural marker. These are particularly common after numerals and are often words denoting measure. Examples of the first are words like *desk, nest, post,* and *wasp,* which produce plurals like *desses, deskes,* or simply *dess* (involving lengthening of the consonant *s*). We may even get forms like *waspers* for the plural of *wasp*. Examples of the second group are *acre, barrel, foot, pound, wagon,* etc. Typical sentences are "It's been two month since he's been here," "I got twenty head of cattle this year," and "He's six-foot-two."

Multiple Negatives. We have all heard the fiction that we should not use double negatives because "two negatives make a positive". That is not so, of course. If it were true, children would be forbidden to read Shakespeare, who freely used multiple negatives as did other writers in the Renaissance, at which time the "rule" was that the more negatives there were in the sentence the more negative the sentence was. The use of multiple negatives characterizes all nonstandard English dialects today. Some particularly interesting usages in Appalachia involve their use with the words "hardly", "anymore", and "ain't". "Can't hardly" may pass muster, simply because "hardly" is not fully accepted as a negative, though its negative force is clear in sentences like "I can hardly lift it," which, however, is indistinguishable in meaning from "I can't hardly lift it." The use of so-called "positive" *anymore* achieves the effect of negation by actually using a "double positive", as in a sentence like "It rains so much anymore that I can't get the crops in." Then there's *ain't*. It is used variously as a contracted form of *am not, is not,* and *are not,* and is common in double negatives like *ain't no, ain't never,* and *ain't none*. Emphasis is achieved by adding a third negative, as in "You ain't got no business over there a-tall" and "There ain't never none there when you need 'em."

Some phrases look different. Others may look the same as in standard English, but have quite a different meaning. Classic is the phrase "don't care to", which in the standard language means "don't want to", but in this area means "don't mind" or "don't object" (as in "I don't care to go to the movies" meaning "I don't mind going to the movies"). This usage retains an older (sixteenth and seventeenth century) meaning and it is still common in Scottish dialect. The potential for misunderstanding here is great. I have heard more than one anecdote illustrating the dangers in the phrase if it is used without care. One involves a traveler from East Tennessee who stopped at a motel on an interstate in the

Midwest to request accommodations for his family and himself for the night. The desk clerk informed him that all he had left was a suite and inquired whether that would be satisfactory. The traveler replied that he didn't care to take a suite for one night. He turned away to inform his wife that they had a room, but when he returned to the desk to claim his room key he discovered that the clerk had assigned the room to another traveler, having interpreted his response as being negative.

Other phrases look different when they're written down, but come out the same when they're spoken. A young man courting a young woman from North Carolina, just across the border from Tennessee, told of occasionally being unable to tell whether she was saying "I want to" or "I won't" when the phrase was followed by a word starting with *d-*. When he proposed to her, she whispered in his ear either "I want to do it" or "I won't do it." He couldn't tell which. He said to her, "Honey, this is important! Which did you say?" They managed to communicate on that subject in spite of a dialect difference.

Another rather strange construction is the retention of what we might call the purposive *for*. It is common in Shakespeare, and in Chaucer (perhaps the best-known use of it is in *The Canterbury Tales,* where the General Prologue alone uses it twice, once in describing the purpose of the pilgrimage, "The holy blisful martyr for to seeke," again in describing the character of the Summoner, who loved "for to drinke strong win reed as blood."), though it has disappeared from the standard literary language. Many of my students recognize this construction when they meet it in earlier literature and muse upon the removal of it from the standard language. One student from Shady Valley in JOHNSON COUNTY recalled using the construction himself (in sentences like "I'm ready for to go") and also hearing his parents, his grandparents, and many other persons use it.

Most of us take our acquisition of language so much for granted that we never stop to look at all the forces that played a role in our learning our native language. The student from Shady Valley mentioned above is one of several students I have taught who have looked back at all the forces that have shaped the language that they heard when they were growing up and since. Another young man, who grew up in Knoxville, devoted a great deal of attention to examining the ways we internalize attitudes as we internalize words, rules for the pronunciation of words, and rules for the construction of sentences. I'd like to quote a few paragaraphs from his study in order to illustrate how social forces and our growing awareness of the importance of people's attitudes toward different linguistic patterns play roles in our use of language. He first describes his background and early years thus:

My mother and her parents lived in the city—their old home is now covered by the Hyatt Regency—and my father and his parents lived in the semi-rural area of Inskip-Norwood. His father worked in a foundry and generally, the family was poor. However, so were many other families during the Depression...The first five years of my life were spent living in Fountain City in a little white duplex on Hiawassee Avenue. My parents were struggling with their careers—my mother was a fashion model and my father was a draftsman—and therefore I spent much time being cared for by my grandmother on my mother's side, and playing with children in this predominantly blue-collar, lower-middle class, neighborhood which was constructed during World War II. Again, it was here during my impressionable years that the East Tennessee vernacular was ingrained upon my mind. My mother and grandmother would scold me for using "ain't", and I learned the taboo of using curse words, by having my grandmother wash my mouth out with soap.

He then comments on his early awareness of his own use of what he now regards as "Appalachian dialect" (though of course he didn't think of it as that when he was learning it):

The characteristics of standard East Tennessee dialect were seen in my father's side of the family, and my two aunts and uncles who lived in CONCORD. The speech of these relatives was used as a stereotype of this dialect. The following are a few examples of this usage: *jedge* (*judge*), *aigs* (*eggs*), *ainch* (*inch*), *fillings* (*feelings*), *rats cheer* (*right here*), *hit* (*it*), *you'uns* (*youall*), 'police (*po'lice*), *'guitar* (*gui'tar*), use of multiple negatives and multiple modals, and a whole host of assimilations such as *gotcha* (*got you*), *hadja* (*had you*), and *mist cha* (*missed you*).

Finally, he concludes by citing an important lesson he has learned about attitudes:

I was always amazed at how my aunts and uncles in Concord were proud of and thoroughly enjoyed their "lazy luxury" of Southern dialect. It was not until I was in college that I learned all the ethnocentric ramifications of this. Both the "educated" and the "semi-illiterate" can display equal amounts of pride in the extreme use of their dialects.

This last point brings us to the consideration of the interesting question of our own attitude toward variation. How should we feel about regional dialects which are different from the standard language? What should our practice as parents, as educators, as writers be? Should we foster difference or should we seek to minimize it? Strong forces work in society to keep language from changing, so there is reason to believe that there is no need to work to preserve dialect differences. At the same time, our larger society in this country is characterized by what many see as an unfortunate tendency toward homogenization, and many people feel that we should act to preserve older cultural patterns, particularly folklore and language. From time to time, in fact, we hear a general alarm to the effect that all the speakers of the dialect are dying out and that we have to hurry if we are to preserve it.

It is true that the remainder of the century is apt to see the demise of most speakers who grew up and acquired their language prior to the technological and cybernetic revolution we are in the midst of. But television, for instance, is not the great leveler many people think it is. It may help to standardize some usages—the *s* sound in *greasy* and *blouse*, for instance, still pronounced by most Southerners with a *z* sound—but it is important to note that since we do not often *interact* with television, it is less potent an influence than it might otherwise be. Indeed, except for the fact that it can standardize pronunciation as well as word choice, its impact seems to be roughly analogous with that of the earliest mail-order catalogues, which had the effect of standardizing some vocabulary items (e.g., *frying pan*, rather than *skillet* or *spyder*).

Where attitudes are concerned, we should remember that as we grow up and acquire language we internalize not only the rules of the language—those patterns which enable us to produce and to understand sentences— but also the attitudes of those around us, including their attitudes toward different varieties of language. We learn to value dialects or languages as we value the people who use them, and our attitudes toward other dialects and other languages are always reflexes of our attitudes toward the people who speak those dialects and those languages. Thus, we will value East Tennessee English and cherish its differences from other linguistic patterns to the extent that we value the people of East Tennessee and cherish the differences we may find between them and people elsewhere.

Bethany K. Dumas

Refer to: Paul D. Bandes and Jeutonne Brewer, *Dialect Clash in America: Issues and Answers*, Metuchen, N.J.: The Scarecrow Press, 1977; Bethany K. Dumas, "Smoky Mountain Speech," in Dolly Berthelot, ed. *Pioneer Spirit 76*, Knoxville, Tenn.: Dolly Berthelot, 1975; Raven I. McDavid, Jr., "What Happens in Tennessee?" in Lorraine Hall Burghardt, ed. *Dialectology: Problems and Perspectives*, Knoxville: University of Tennessee Press, 1971; Cratis D. Williams, "The Southern Mountaineer in Fact and Fiction," New York University dissertation, 1961; and Walt Wolfram and Donna Christian, *Appalachian Speech*, Arlington, Va.: Center for Applied Linguistics, 1976.

Ebbing and Flowing Spring is located three miles east of Rogersville, on the original land grant given to Captain Thomas Amis for his services in the American Revolution. The spring was referred to as "Sinking Spring" in the 1789 grant, for when it ebbs, it appears to sink. When the water reaches its lowest point, it begins to revive rapidly and continues for about ten minutes until the flow reaches its zenith. For the next two and a half hours, it gradually recedes. Then the cycle is repeated and has been known to do so for almost two centuries. Although some scientists believe that an underground cavity stores the water and naturally regulates its flow, no definite reason is known for the behavior of Ebbing and Flowing Spring.

Mary Beal
Syble M. Testerman

Elizabethton. On April 9, 1796, the General Assembly of the newly organized State of Tennessee provided for the creation of CARTER COUNTY out of the northern and eastern sections of WASHINGTON COUNTY. A committee of five—Reuben Thornton, Andrew Greer, Sr., Zachariah Campbell, and David McNabb—decided the location of the county seat. Their choice as a site was a 50-acre tract at the foot of Lynn Mountain and east of the Doe River. Owned by Samuel Tipton, this tract of land was known as "Watauga Old Fields". An act of the legislature on October 23, 1797, officially established Elizabethton, named in honor of Colonel Landon Carter's wife Elizabeth Maclin Carter.

Elizabethton's first courthouse, probably of log construction, stood on the town square for 25 years and was replaced by a two-story building. In April of 1797, William Matlock applied for a license to keep an ordinary and erected the first house. The first newspaper, *Elizabethton Republican and*

Courtesy Archives of Appalachia, East Tennessee State University

Turn-of-the-century Elizabethton from Lynn Mountain.

Manufacturers Advocate, was published by Lyon and Gott until fire destroyed its offices in 1844. Five years earlier, PARSON BROWNLOW published a paper called the *Elizabethton Whig*. In 1878 W.R. Fitzsimmons published *The Mountaineer*, but this was later discontinued. Duffield Academy, named for lawyer George Duffield, began about 1809 and served as a school into the 1900's. Some of the early factories included the Watauga Woolen Mills, Bradley Lumber Company, Jenkins Flour Mill, a large tannery and shoe manufacturing company operated by Colonel John W. Tipton, and the Dixie Chewing Gum factory.

During the CIVIL WAR, the loyalty of the citizens of Elizabethton was divided between the Confederates and the Unionists. The city did not recover from the war until the 1880's and 1890's, when new industries were established with the encouragement of the Cooperative Town Company.The first industry brought to Elizabethton by the Cooperative Town Company was the Line and Twine, established by Martin Clarke and Julian Crandell in 1892. The Elizabethton Shoe Company followed, as did others.

On October 29, 1926, a group of German industrialists started the first spinning machine of the American Bemberg Corporation. The success of the first year's work encouraged the building in 1927 of a second rayon unit, American Glanzstoff. Further good results led the North American Rayon Corporation to locate in Elizabethton. Today, Elizabethton's population numbers over 14,000. The city is operated by a modified City Manager-Council form of government, with seven councilmen elected for four-year terms.

Mildred Kozsuch

See also: BLUEGRASS MUSIC
ELIZABETHTON RAYON STRIKES

Elizabethton Rayon Strikes of 1929, in which about 5,000 workers participated, were the first concrete sign of Southern disenchantment with a textile industry financed by Northern capital and operated in an exploitative manner. As in KINGSPORT, where planners had established an integrated industrial structure—a city benefitting from, yet controlled by, a network of varied industry—business leaders in ELIZABETHTON had successfully fought unionization. Unlike Kingsport, the dominant rayon industry in Elizabethton paid minimal wages and offered its laborers few or no benefits. By March of 1929, almost half the employees of American Bemberg and American Glanzstoff were girls from the valley and mountains of East Tennessee. Most workers worked over 50 hours per week and earned less than 20 cents per hour.

On March 12, when a Glanzstoff foreman lowered the rank of a girl who asked for a raise, 500 of the girls stopped work until the rank could be restored. The incident soon escalated into an effective wildcat strike of Glanzstoff. On Saturday afternoon, March 16, one thousand strikers joined the United Textile Workers union. Supported by CARTER COUNTY sheriff John Moreland, the strikers resisted the denunciations of Arthur Mothwurf, President of both Glanzstoff and Bemberg. On March 25 Mothwurf reluctantly agreed to a small wage increase, averaging about a nickel an hour, and the first strike ended.

The companies, however, had identified most of the strikers and did not rehire several hundred members of the UTW. On April 3, gun thugs kidnapped two union leaders and drove them across the Tennessee state line. Ten days later American Bemberg fired key members of the plant's newly formed grievance committee. This action led, on April 15, to a second and longer strike. Whereas the first two-week strike had concentrated on wages, this second six-week strike demanded improved grievance procedures and an end to company discrimination against members of the union. By May, the Elizabethton strikes had helped influence cotton workers in the Carolina Piedmont to strike for similar changes in working conditions.

Yet the Elizabethton strikes were not successful in the long run. Bemberg reopened on May 6 with a reduced work force. In mid-May, Governor Henry Horton sent 800 National Guardsmen to Elizabethton. These Guardsmen fought the strikers in several skirmishes, including a tear gas confrontation with the female workers. Although a half-hearted settlement of the strike was agreed to on May 25, the company continued to blacklist strikers. By 1930, Bemberg and Glanzstoff were back in firm control of the workers. Still, the 1929 rayon strikes in Elizabethton stand as a first spontaneous challenge against the region's unharnessed industrialization.

Jim Stokely

Refer to: James A. Hodges, "Challenge to the New South: the Great Textile Strike in Elizabethton, Tennessee, 1929," in *Tennessee Historical Quarterly*, V.23, No.4 (December 1964); and *Working Conditions of the Textile Industry in North Carolina, South Carolina, and Tennessee: Hearings before the Committee on Manufacturers, U.S. Senate*, 71st Congress, 1st Sessions, May 8, 9, and 20, 1929, Washington, D.C.: Government Printing Office, 1929.

Daniel Ellis (December 30, 1827 — January 6, 1908) was the best known Union guide in East Tennessee during the CIVIL WAR. Between 1862 and 1865, he piloted thousands of refugees from Confederate-held territory to safety in Kentucky. His life was in constant danger throughout the three years he acted as a pilot.

Ellis was born in CARTER COUNTY and lived in the area until the Mexican-American War in 1846. He then joined the United States Army and fought in several battles against the Mexicans. Ellis found that he did not like army life. He hated war; he hoped that he would never see another one. As soon as his enlistment ended, he returned to Carter County. Ellis worked intermittently as a farmer and a wagon maker for the next few years.

When the Civil War began, Tennesseans were sharply divided in their loyalties. No one could remain neutral. Like his neighbors, Ellis was forced to choose one side or the other. He elected to support the Union. In November of 1861, a group of East Tennesseans loyal to the Union tried to burn all the railroad bridges connecting Memphis and Nashville with Richmond, the capital of the Confederacy. Ellis joined the company which had been selected to burn the Holston River bridge in the town of Union in SULLIVAN COUNTY. Although Ellis's group was successful, the overall plot failed. Many of the bridge burners were captured and either executed or sent to prison. Ellis escaped into the mountains and was hunted by the Confederates. He soon decided that since they were chasing him anyway, he would give them good reason for tracking him down.

Ellis was familiar with almost every trail through the mountains between East Tennessee and Kentucky. He devised a plan to help people escape into Kentucky, and also to make a profit for himself. On August 1, 1862, Ellis left for his first trip from Confederate-held East Tennessee to Kentucky. He co-piloted a group of men who were escaping from Tennessee to join the Union Army. He helped lead the group through the Cumberland Mountains to the Federal forces at Cumberland Gap. The co-pilots returned to Carter County immediately. They began another trek on August 28, 1862. After this second trip, Ellis began to pilot groups on his own. Between August of 1862 and August of 1863, Ellis made ten trips to Kentucky. Many of the people he led paid him for his service, and he was able to support his family in this manner.

Daniel Ellis established extra profitable activities during his piloting. He conducted a regular mail service on his trips, carrying letters and messages back and forth between the people in Tennessee and Kentucky. At the same time, he began a successful horse dealing business. Also during his trips, Ellis made it a practice to steal the enemy's horses. Any horse that belonged to a Confederate was fair game for Ellis. He continued these activities on an independent basis until January of 1865. He then joined Company A, 13th Regiment, Tennessee Cavalry. He was appointed Captain of the company, but he continued to pilot people through the mountains until the end of the war.

When the Civil War ended, Daniel Ellis moved to KNOXVILLE. He received an honorable discharge from the army on September 5, 1865. Thus ended the remarkable career of one of East Tennessee's outstanding Civil War heroes. He alone was responsible for guiding thousands of escaped slaves, prisoners, and soldiers fleeing to the safety of the Union lines. Ellis earned the thanks heaped upon him by many fellow East Tennesseans.

Arthur G. Sharp

Refer to: Daniel Ellis, *Thrilling Adventures of Daniel Ellis,* New York: Harper, 1867 (reprinted 1972, Freeport, N.Y.: Books for Libraries); Ralph Ray Fahrney, *Horace Greeley and the Tribune in the Civil War,* Cedar Rapids, Iowa: The Torch Press, 1936; and Oliver Perry Temple, *East Tennessee and The Civil War,* Cincinnati: Clarke, 1899 (reprinted 1972, Knoxville: Burmar Books).

Embreeville and Bumpass Cove are small mountain communities located in the southeastern corner of WASHINGTON COUNTY and at the northern border of UNICOI COUNTY. The cove, lying between Rich Mountain and Embreeville Mountain, is some four miles long and almost two miles wide. Its watershed is drained by the Bumpass Cove Creek into the Nolichucky River. Numerous remains of the CHEROKEES, where their villages were once located, have been found at the mouth of the cove. This has been one of the richest mineralized areas in East Tennessee—a fact which throughout its history has caused years of great productivity when the mines were active, and years of idleness and financial stagnation when the mines were closed.

The first metal to be mined in the area was lead. Bullets from this source were supposedly fired against the British in 1780 at the Battle of Kings Mountain. Tax lists of the 1780's show William Colyer assessed for 350 acres of land in Bumpass Cove containing a lead mine commonly called "Colyer's Mine".

In 1812 William P. Chester bought 260 acres near the mouth of Bumpass Cove and built a forge for iron ore. He later sold the forge to Elijah and Elihu Embree. The Embrees acquired many additional acres, built forges, furnaces and nail factories, and by 1820 were widely known for their high-quality cast and forged iron products. After the death of Elihu Embree, remembered more as the editor of the first abolitionist publication, Elijah in 1830 formed a partnership—the Washington Iron Manufacturing Company—with Robert L. Blair, John Blair, William Blair, and three others. When Elijah died in 1849, the Blair brothers became sole proprietors. Their "Pleasant Valley Iron Works" soon became the largest producer of iron in East Tennessee. During the CIVIL WAR, Duff Green, a politician and industrial promoter, acquired the iron works. Called the Confederate Iron Works, it proved to be of great value to the East Tennessee campaign. With the collapse of the Confederacy and the paralyzing effect of Reconstruction, the mines reverted to the Blair interests.

In 1890 British capitalists purchased the land and operated under the title of the Embreeville Freehold Land, Iron and Railway Co., Ltd. The Southern Railway built a spur line to the cove to bring coke in for the new furnaces. Elaborate plans were laid out to establish a town. A number of English houses, built during this time, still stand. The financial panic of 1893 caused the furnace to shut down, again forcing a slump period. The Embree Iron Company, created by New York and Chicago interests in 1903, introduced hydraulic mining. The operation was not successful, however, and in 1909 the fires were extinguished for the last time.

Reorganized in 1913, the Embree Iron Company began to mine zinc. Intensive churn drilling to locate deposits of zinc and lead, especially in the area at the end of the cove called Peach Orchard, resulted in the discovery of rich deposits. Large shipments of zinc and lead continued through the post-World War I period. Many pick-and-shovel men were hired to work in the mines. Boarding houses accommodated some of these men, who left their families for the week to walk over the mountains to the mines. Small log houses sheltered other workers and their families, and this area in Embreeville became known as "Poletown". The company built a small track up to Peach Orchard to haul the ore, carry the men to and from the mines, and bring groceries up from the company store. At first, paper coupons called "scrip" were used as a means of exchange at the company store; later, a lightweight metal coin called "doogaloo" was used. Some blacks worked for the company at this time, and evidence of a small cemetery for these workers still exists.

By 1930, the area was again in a slump. It was not until 1935 that more drilling took place. Due to the limiting of imported manganese, companies sought new deposits in this country. In 1939, the Embree Iron Company was the largest producer of metallurgical-grade manganese concentrates in the United States. Yet the ore, mined by power shovel, was quickly exhausted. Some hand mining of zinc, lead and manganese resumed in the Peach Orchard area in the 1940's, but another boom period had ended. Tri-State Mines, owned by Wa Cheng Corporation and under the management of T.K. Lee, bought the mining interests in 1952. Within three years, Tri-State removed most of the remaining ore. By 1960 the last of the mining was finished. All except the families of the older settlers, whose roots were in the area, had left to seek new employment.

In the early 1970's, the Bumpass Cove Landfill was opened for use. For years, several residents had felt that unauthorized waste was being dumped at the site. But it was not until a flash flood in July of 1979 that wider attention was given to the problem. The flood carried waste from the site and unearthed other materials, causing vapor fumes to irritate the lungs and eyes of persons in the area. The landfill was closed, but the problem of the possible hazardous waste remaining in the area still exists.

Jeannette McLaughlin

Refer to: Paul M. Fink, "The Bumpass Cove Mines and Embreeville," in *The East Tennessee Historical Society's Publications*, No. 16 (1944), pp.48-64; Nan Grodi, "Waste Resources Ordered to Clean-up Bumpass Cove," in *Mountain Life and Work*, V.56, No.8 (September 1980), pp.34-35; and Melinda Royalty, "Protest Stops Dumping of Hazardous Wastes" and "Toxic Waste Uncovered in Bumpass Cove," in *Mountain Life and Work*, V.55, No.9 (October 1979), pp.26-28, and V.56, No.3 (March 1980), pp.3-4.

See also: CADES COVE
GRASSY COVE

F

Farragut, located approximately fifteen miles west of KNOXVILLE near Interstate 40, is rich in history. Originally, Farragut was known as Campbell Station, and had its beginning in 1787 when Colonel David Campbell, a Revolutionary soldier, built a house on the west bank of Turkey Creek at Kingston Pike. Campbell Station grew into an important trading post and stopping place for travelers and stock drivers because it was on the main highway from East Tennessee and Virginia to the West. By 1810 the station had more business than Knoxville, including a tavern, a tannery, a wagon shop and a cabinet factory.

Campbell Station was much more than a mere frontier outpost; it was a community which claimed among its residents some of the most influential citizens of KNOX COUNTY. Among these were Alexander Cavet, massacred by Indians near Ten Mile Creek; Charles McClung, author of Tennessee's first constitution; Robertus Love, a miller on Lovell Road; Nicholas Ball, who established a camp on Plumb Creek; and Archibald Roane, second governor of Tennessee. Other residents included the families of Matthew Russell, Jeremiah S. Temple, Alexander

Courtesy C.M McClung Historical Collection, Lawson McGhee Library

David Glasgow Farragut

Campbell, James H. Walker, Dugger Everett, Samuel Martin, Robert Cox, Hugh Smith, P.L. Temple, John Foster, Frederick S. Heiskell, James Swan, and Tom Boyd. Campbell Station lost much of its business prestige with the coming of the railroad. The East Tennessee and Georgia Railroad, built in 1853, bypassed the station by two miles. This brought into being the town of Concord, which now serves as post office to a large surrounding area.

On July 5, 1801, David Glasgow Farragut was born at Campbell Station. After his mother's death, he was adopted by Commodore David Porter. In 1811 David sailed aboard the *Essex* with Porter and spent the remainder of his life in the navy. When the War Between the States broke out, Farragut was living in Norfolk, Virginia, where he was given the command of the *Hartford* with orders to take New Orleans. He did. During August 1864, after his promotion to rear admiral, he captured Mobile Bay in what was his greatest naval victory. Two years later he was commissioned Admiral, the first full Admiral in the U.S. Navy, and was given command of the European Squadron. He died in 1870 at Portsmouth, New Hampshire.

During the CIVIL WAR, a battle was fought at Campbell Station in November 1863. Longstreet and Burnside were the opposing generals. Both sides had to contend with cold and hunger, mud and exhaustion. Longstreet's Confederate reinforcements did not arrive in time to halt Burnside's advance, and Burnside lured Longstreet on to Knoxville. The battle at Campbell Station was one of the decisive factors in the disastrous loss suffered later by Longstreet at Knoxville.

In 1902 eight men of the community met to consider establishing a high school in the tenth district of Knox County. The men were Russell, Miller, McFee, Hackney, Boyd, Tillery, Seaton, and Taylor. The group raised $5,000, and W.A. Doughty donated twelve acres for a schoolhouse with six classrooms and an assembly room. The school opened in 1904 and was named for David Farragut.

James W. Bellamy

Refer to: Mary U. Rothrock, ed. *The French Broad-Holston Country: A History of Knox County, Tennessee*, Knoxville: East Tennessee Historical Society, 1946.

Fauna. The vertebrate fauna of East Tennessee include a wide diversity of fish, amphibians, reptiles, birds and mammals. This diversity is a reflection of the variety of habitats available. Aquatic habitats range from cold swift-flowing mountain streams to springs to warmer and slower waters of larger rivers to natural and artificial lakes and ponds. Terrestrial habitats are encompassed by the Plateau, Ridge and Valley, and Mountain physiographic regions of East Tennessee. East Tennessee accommodates a wide range in elevations and slopes, and such varied GEOGRAPHY results in a diversity of PLANT COMMUNITIES almost unequalled anywhere else in the country. Driving from the foothills of the Great Smoky Mountains to their summit is like traveling from Tennessee to Canada. In a short distance one can visit cove hardwood forests, oak and pine forests, northern hardwood forests, spruce-fir forests, and open fields and heath balds.

This diverse plant life represents the food base for the terrestrial vertebrates of the area. In addition, people have changed these habitats and have had both beneficial and detrimental impacts to some vertebrate species. Those species, such as wolves and mountain lions, that are less tolerant of humans are no longer established residents. Other species such as white-tailed deer, opossums, cottontail rabbits, and a variety of openfield birds and reptiles are likely as abundant or even more abundant than before the influence of people and their land clearing activities. In many instances, such activities opened the forest and created an "edge" effect; this edge in turn provided better food and cover for some species.

The only native species of trout in the waters of East Tennessee is the brook trout; it is found in the higher elevation, colder streams of the mountains. The brown and rainbow trout are two other species that were introduced into East Tennessee. The rainbow trout in particular has thrived well in the mountain streams. Because of siltation, changes in stream characteristics, and competition from rainbow trout, native brook trout are gradually disappearing from their native habitat. Occupying these mountain streams along with trout are a wide diversity of lesser known darters, minnows and other small fish. These species are a vital link in the aquatic food chain of the streams. As the waters of the high elevation streams converge at lower elevations into larger, slower moving rivers, fish such as smallmouth bass and redeye begin to thrive. The warmer waters of major tributaries and lakes are occupied by fish such as catfish, largemouth bass, bluegill, crappie, and carp. Each of these species fills a different niche in the aquatic environment; some are predators, feeding on smaller fish or invertebrates, and others are strictly plant feeders.

The herps (salamanders, toads and frogs, turtles, lizards, and snakes) of East Tennessee are also abundant and diverse. As an example, there are more different species of salamanders in the GREAT SMOKY MOUNTAINS NATIONAL PARK than in any other area its size in North America. The most common species in our area are the slimy and dusky salamanders. Salamanders are semiaquatic vertebrates and range in size from the giant Hellbender, which grows to over 2 $^1/_2$ feet long, to the tiny pigmy salamander at less than two inches in length. All require a relatively moist habitat at some stage in their life cycle.

Common frogs and toads of the region include the terrestrial American toad; and the long musical trell of this toad can be heard frequently on warm summer nights. The spring peeper is a common tree frog whose single piping notes are uttered on warmer days beginning in winter and on into spring. The green frog and bullfrog are the largest of the frogs in our area and inhabit larger, more permanent bodies of water. Bullfrogs are often harvested for the edibility of their legs.

The most common terrestrial turtle of the area is the familiar Eastern box turtle; this species is often seen feeding on berries or earthworms. One of the more common aquatic turtles is the Eastern painted turtle, so-called for its beautiful head and shell colorations. Large bodies of water are inhabited by a variety of turtles. Of these, the largest and perhaps best known is the snapping turtle; this carnivorous species reaches weights of over 50 pounds. The fence lizard and five-line skink are the most frequently observed lizards of the area. Both species occupy relatively dry-open habitats and oak-pine forests. These vertebrates often can be observed sunning on rocks, fences, or logs on warm sunny days from spring until early fall.

There are in East Tennessee two species of poisonous snakes: the copperhead and the timber rattlesnake. Both species are relatively uncommon compared to several nonpoisonous species in our area. Living along stream edges and often mistaken for a copperhead is the common water snake. In terrestrial-wooded habitats the black racer, black rat snake, and garter snake are common inhabitants. These species as well as a number of others eat rodents as part of their diet and thus are quite beneficial to people around their homes, farms and gardens.

Perhaps no other group of vertebrates reflects the diverse habitats of East Tennessee as well as birds. Over 300 different species have been recorded as residents or as simply passing through on their migrations north and south. The spruce-fir forests of the mountains are inhabited by species such as black-capped chickadees, slate-colored juncos, nuthatches, winter wrens, and golden-crowned kinglets. In the northern hardwood forests can be found black-throated blue warblers, rose-breasted grosbeaks, and yellow-bellied sapsuckers. The common and extensive cove hardwood forests are occupied by such common species as tufted titmice, red-eyed vireos, and wood thrushes. In drier forests can be found the Carolina chickadee, downy woodpecker, black-and-white warbler, and yellow-breasted chat. Found in yards and at bird feeders in East Tennessee are mockingbirds, robins, cardinals, bluejays, purple finches, gold finches, Carolina wrens, titmice, Carolina chickadees, and many others. The mockingbird is Tennessee's official state bird. Some of the larger and sometimes more spectacular birds of the area include redtailed hawks, great blue herons, great-horned owls, osprey, and an occasional bald-eagle. Starlings, grackles, crows, and meadowlarks are frequently sighted in more open field-pasture-farm type habitats. Game birds of the area include ruffed grouse, bobwhite quail, mourning doves, and wild turkey. In addition, many different waterfowl species migrate through each year; some of the more common species include the blue-winged teal, mallard, pintail, and Canada goose. The woodduck is a common resident waterfowl species in East Tennessee.

Mammals of East Tennessee range in size from the tiny pigmy shrew (one-twelfth of an ounce) to the black bear (over 300 pounds). The region's only flying mammals, the bats, include more than a dozen different species. All are insectivorous, and two commonly occurring species are the Eastern pipistrelle and the red bat. Arboreal mammals include the red squirrel or "boomer", which is found in the higher elevation coniferous forests of the mountains; the southern flying squirrel, which in reality glides; the common gray squirrel; and scattered pockets of the more rare fox squirrel. A diversity of rodents is found in all habitat types. These rodents range from the more fossorial meadow and pine voles to the beaver; beaver are now beginning to be sighted along several streams in East Tennessee. One relatively large rodent, the muskrat, is quite common along streams in the area and is extensively trapped for its fur value. The cotton rat or "field rat" and white-footed and deer mice are probably the area's most common rodents. Of the Insectivores, the two most common species are the short-tailed shrew and the Eastern mole. Common medium-sized mammals include the red and gray fox, bobcat, Virginia opossum, and raccoon. The raccoon is the official state animal of Tennessee. The Virginia opossum, the only marsupial or pouched mammal in North America, has readily adapted to the presence of humans and their habitat alterations. The most common big game species is the white-tailed deer, and roaming the more remote and protected mountainous areas is the shy, secretive black bear. The black bear is perhaps best representative, or symbolic, of the remaining wilderness-like conditions left in the mountains of East Tennessee.

Michael R. Pelton

See also: FLORA

Fentress County draft board meets with two families. Major Hilton Butler seated on porch; Alvin York gesturing with hand. July 26, 1941.

Courtesy Tennessee State Library

Fentress County

Size: 498 Square Miles (318,720 acres)
Established: 1823
Named For: James Fentress,
Speaker of the Tennessee
House of Representatives
County Seat: Jamestown
Other Major Cities, Towns, or Communities:
Allardt
Grimsley
Wilder
Davidson
Armathwaite
Pall Mall
Clarkrange
Forbus

Refer to: Fran Ansley and Brenda Bell, "East Tennessee Coal Mining Battles," in *Southern Exposure*, V. 1, Nos. 3 & 4 (Winter, 1974); and Albert R. Hogue, *History of Fentress County, Tennessee, the Old Home of Mark Twain's Ancestors*, Nashville: Williams, 1916, 1920.

See also: CONRAD PILE
MARK TWAIN
ALVIN YORK

Festivals and Events

(A Selected List Arranged Chronologically)

Year Round

1. Evening Music, Storytelling, and/or Dancing
Down Home Pickin' Parlor, JOHNSON CITY
Jubilee Center, KNOXVILLE
Red Speeks' COUNTRY MUSIC Theater, Clinton
Starr Mountain Jamboree, Etowah
Wagon Wheelers Square Dance Club, Maryville

February or March

2. Winter Thaw, Roane State Community College, Harriman

The Craftsman's Fair of the Southern Highland Handicraft Guild, Gatlinburg, 1972.

Courtesy TVA

April

3. Cumberland Gap Folk Festival
4. Dogwood Arts Festival, Knoxville
5. Old Oak Folk Festival, Tusculum College, Tusculum
6. Ramp Festival, Cosby
7. Wildflower Pilgrimage, GATLINBURG

April or May

8. Appalachian Music and Crafts Festival, CHILDREN'S MUSEUM OF OAK RIDGE, OAK RIDGE

May

9. BRISTOL Country Music Days
10. Fort Sanders Street Fair, Knoxville
11. The Home Folks Festival, EAST TENNESSEE STATE UNIVERSITY, Johnson City
12. Old Time Fiddling and Bluegrass Festival, Church Hill
13. Old-Time Country RADIO Reunion, JONESBORO
14. Roan Wildflower Tour, Roan Mountain
15. SEVIER COUNTY Music and Arts Festival
16. Spring Folk Lore Festival, Walters State Community College, Morristown
17. Spring Music and Crafts Festival, Rugby Restoration Association, RUGBY
18. Strawberry Bluegrass Festival, Dayton

Summer

19. GREAT SMOKY MOUNTAINS NATIONAL PARK Summer Program
    —CADES COVE, Cosby, and Elkmont Campgrounds: campfire programs, craft demonstrations, and guided nature walks
    —Sugarlands Visitor Center, Gatlinburg: orientation program, guided nature walks, and illustrated evening program
20. Smoky Mountain Hayride, Pigeon Forge

June

21. Bluegrass Festival, Cosby
22. Country Music Days and Singing on Watauga, ELIZABETHTON
23. DANDRIDGE Jubilee
24. Dulcimer Convention, Folklife Center of the Smokies, Cosby
25. Lenoir City Arts and Crafts Festival
26. Midland Center Arts and Crafts Festival, ALCOA
27. Redgate Bluegrass Festival, Maynardville
28. Rhododendron Festival, Roan Mountain
29. Slagle's Pasture BLUEGRASS MUSIC Festival, Elizabethton
30. Tennessee State Square Dance Festival, CHATTANOOGA
31. When You and I Were Young Maggie Festival, Reliance

June or July

32. Historic Jonesborough Days, Jonesboro

July

33. Daddy's Creek Bluegrass Festival, Crab Orchard
34. Gatlinburg Arts and Crafts Festival
35. Nawger Nob Bluegrass Festival, Townsend
36. NORRIS Day
37. The Old Timer and Bluegrass Fiddler Convention, Elizabethton

August

38. Annual Davy Crockett Celebration, Limestone
39. Monteagle Arts and Crafts Show
40. Rugby Pilgrimage

September

41. Bluegrass and Old Time Music

Festival, Bristol
42. Chattanooga-Hamilton County Interstate Fair, Chattanooga
43. Folk Festival of the Smokies, Folklife Center of the Smokies, Cosby
44. The Foxfire Arts and Crafts Festival, Maryville
45. Kiuka Kountry Krafts Fair, Morgan Springs
46. Mountain Heritage Festival, LaFollette
47. Old Timey Music and Mountain Crafts Festival, Jacksboro
48. Tennessee Valley A & I Fair, Knoxville
49. Tennessee-Carolina Fair, Newport
50. Tuckaleechee Cove Arts, Crafts, and Music Festival, Townsend

October

51. Artfest, Knoxville
52. Autumn Gold Festival, Coker Creek
53. Fall Color Cruise and Folk Festival, Chattanooga

Rush Strong Hazen and Thomas Fleming Hazen, *oil by Samuel Shaver, 1860.*

Courtesy Frederick C. Moffatt

54. Gatlinburg Craftsman's Fair
55. HANCOCK COUNTY Fall Festival, Sneedville
56. Mountain Makin's Festival, Rose Center, Morristown
57. National Crafts Festival, Silver Dollar City, Pigeon Forge
58. National Storytelling Festival, Jonesboro

November

59. MUSEUM OF APPALACHIA Fall Festival, Norris
60. OAKDALE Heritage, Arts, and Crafts Fair

December

61. Festival of Christmas Trees and Twelve Days of Christmas, Gatlinburg

Fine Arts. Any regional survey of the fine arts must of necessity begin with the activities of the ubiquitous limner. In ante-bellum years, East Tennessee had its fair share of these itinerant tradesmen. Their laconic appeals appeared infrequently in newspapers, hawking portraits in oil, water color, and in the form of miniature daguerreotypes. Unlike urban sophisticates who beguiled their sitters with the compliment of style, provincial limners sought to reduce the medieval art of "taking a likeness" to a convenient set of mechanical steps.

The timely emergence of portrait photography in the 1850's admirably conformed to this requirement. For example, James Cameron in CHATTANOOGA and Samuel Shaver, the prolific painter-photographer who left portraits in half-a-dozen counties in upper East Tennessee, lent to their subjects a "photographic" intensity by insisting

Courtesy Frederick C. Moffatt

Landscape, *watercolor by Charles Krutch, ca. 1920.*

upon broad patterns of contrasting values and crisp outlines. Shaver's civic guardians appear graceless and implacable, attributes that were perhaps appropriate to their willfully independent lives. Even their unsmiling children seem curiously transfixed when subjected to the limner's penetrating analysis.

Standing somewhat apart from the limner in these same years was the young lady who took up painting as a means for self-improvement. Her primary purpose in depicting delicate fragments of nature and landscape was not so much to document facts as to express the depths of her own sensibility. Sensibility, a capacity for compassion, a willingness to serve, the refinement of character: a whole spectrum of genteel virtues appropriate to womanhood were presumed to be bound up with the simple act of drawing or painting. For this reason, art education in East Tennessee as in many other localities became closely associated with the female institute. Only after 1900 were males enrolled in public schools accorded similar advantages. In retrospect, the genteel mode, particularly as it affected water color painting, seems to have enjoyed a spontaneous existence outside academia, as well. For example, it was

Ross Hahn/Courtesy Charlotte Garrett Burdette

Lloyd Branson surrounded by students.

Hauling of Marble, *oil by Lloyd Branson, 1910.*

Courtesy Frederick C. Moffatt

her impoverishment on Walden's Ridge in Chattanooga, rather than professional training, that around 1890 first inspired the sensitive vignettes of EMMA BELL MILES. In KNOXVILLE, Charles Christopher Krutch's vaporous views of the Smoky Mountains similarly stood as souvenirs of an isolated spirit.

After the CIVIL WAR the fine arts made a slow recovery, but by 1890 Knoxville was well on its way to becoming an art center. The new movement was fed by strains of the limner and genteel traditions, but now pictorial artists were demanding a grand Continental stage upon which to perform. They were encouraged in this brave venture by Lloyd Branson, who resettled in Knoxville around 1880 and with photographer Frank McCrary opened a fashionable atelier on Gay Street. This virtuoso had learned in French studios how compelling design and technical facility could elevate a common scene to sublime dimensions. To such an artist, even regional life bore heroic potential. Branson's example rallied the artists and patrons who formed the Nicholson Art League (1906-1923), the most significant of the study-practice groups that were active in Knoxville from 1900 to 1950.

Until the formation of an art department at the University of Chattanooga in 1928, the cultural climate of that city favored study somewhat more than practice. The Art Study Club, founded in 1913, and the Chattanooga Art Association, established in 1924, emphasized the exhibition and collecting of art, as well as the thorough study of art history. These interests were grandly rewarded

Courtesy Frederick C. Moffatt

Madonna and Child, *tinted photograph by Joseph Knaffl, Sr., 1899.*

in 1951 with the creation of the Hunter Museum of Art.

By the turn of the century, East Tennessee photographers, responding to the national debate over the aesthetic merits of photography in general, firmly repudiated the mechanistic use made of the camera by the limner. This they did by broadening the range of subjects to include landscape and posed narratives, and also by appropriating some of the technical effects long thought to be the exclusive property of painting. In Knoxville, Joseph Knaffl approximated the *sfumato* of Leonardo da Vinci and his Baroque heirs by creating a soft focus for portraits. It was also Knaffl who pioneered in the genre of staged folk narrative, a category exploited in painting by Branson as well. The era of such contrivances subsided in the 1920's with a return to favor of the documentary photograph, a medium perfected in the Knoxville workshops of James E. Thompson. Seen through Thompson's clear lens and from his uniquely devised angles, daily routine took on the characteristics of magic ritual, and the viewer acquired extrasensory perception.

While local painters and photographers puzzled over problems of technique, composition and subject matter, the creation of monumental civic sculpture in East Tennessee was more in the hands of journalists. By successfully conducting public subscription campaigns for the purchase of sculptural fountains, Adolph S. Ochs, president of *The Chattanooga Times*, and George F. Milton, Sr., editor of *The Knoxville News-Sentinel*, introduced their respective communities to the ideal of city beautification. Following disastrous fires, Ochs in 1887 and Milton in 1903 ordered iron figures from the New York firm of J.L. Mott Iron Works. In recommending these works to the public, both newsmen spoke not as artists but as liberal

Interior of Market House, Knoxville, photograph by James E. Thompson, ca. 1935.

Courtesy Frederick C. Moffatt

Courtesy Frederick C. Moffatt

Firemen's Monument, *iron sculpture by J.L. Mott Iron Works (New York), 1888, Chattanooga.*

Marion Greenwood painting The Three States of Tennessee, *oil mural, 1955, The University of Tennessee at Knoxville.*

politicians who required symbols, however inadequate, for their magnanimous views.

However, for the women who erected a large monument over Knoxville's Bethel Cemetery in honor of the slain Confederate soldiers of East Tennessee, such mail-order expedience must have seemed repugnant. In 1891 they secured the services of the versatile Branson, himself a Confederate sympathizer, who in less than a year sculpted the giant sentry standing at the summit of the shaft. It is no accident that Branson's warrior resembles the rustic Saxon, the hero of so many Confederate histories. Underlining their faith in home rule, the patrons insisted that their monument be constructed entirely of Knoxville marble.

As wider travel became possible for more of its members, the Nicholson Art League tended more and more to exchange the homey virtues of East Tennessee life for the timeless image of Rome. Not long after the League's demise and with the advent of the Depression, however, the celebration of home life became a national obsession. So long as it was characteristic of a region, the most uncouth activity or homely artifact became a highly valued token of the heartland. Contrary to some of the publicity attending the development of Regionalism, this did not mean that artists could cease traveling or ignore Renaissance rules of design. The pioneering fine arts program established by muralist Frank Baisden at the University of Chattanooga, for example, depended strongly on drawing from the studio model. Characteristically, one of East Tennessee's foremost monuments of Regionalism, a large mural in the Student Center at THE UNIVERSITY OF TENNESSEE in Knoxville, was created by a New York artist who had studied under Mexico's finest figurative painters.

Courtesy Frederick C. Moffatt and the artist

Fall Fieldflowers, *watercolor by Pauline Wallen, 1979.*

Courtesy Frederick C. Moffatt and the artist

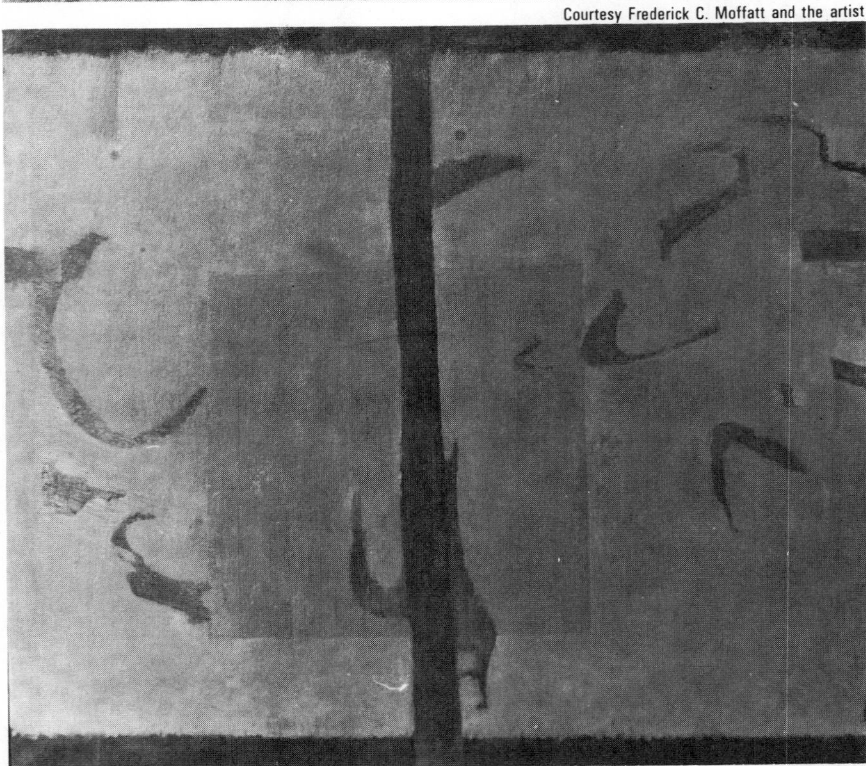

Pond Series II, *oil by Carl Sublett, 1972.*

Another response, directed against academic Regionalism yet nevertheless supporting the general sentiments of the movement, has had a much stronger following in the area. In many respects, Pauline Wallen's minutely-textured water colors depicting decayed barns amid uncultivated fields extend the genteel tradition to the present day. In these works, which are worthy testaments to Andrew Wyeth's extraordinary hold over hinterland artists, the morality of craft and sentiment are met with equal force.

The large band of water-colorists active in East Tennessee today are very much contemporary artists, although in academic circles "contemporary art" usually indicates the condition of "non-objectivity". Carl Sublett's "Pond Series II," painted in 1972, and Philip Nichols' untitled stainless steel sculpture, which was erected on Knoxville's Coliseum Mall in 1978, make no obvious references to human figures or natural objects, but it is arguable whether they can properly be designated as nonobjective. For Nichols and Sublett, the work of art is above all else an object having a specific material existence. Because it represents only itself, the sculpture or painting achieves nominal equality with all other objects existing in the world. But, these artists would also argue, it is precisely this formal objectivity, this independence, that allows such works to free artist and spectator from conventional patterns of vision and thought. Although the rationale supporting abstract art developed before the rise of American Regionalism, it has made a relatively belated appearance in East Tennessee. But this new internationalism would have met with even more resistance had it not been for the enormous expansion of college and university art departments.

Stainless steel sculpture by Philip Nichols, 1978.

Courtesy Frederick C. Moffatt

Frederick C. Moffatt

Refer to: Frederick C. Moffatt, "Painting, Sculpture, and Photography," in Lucile Deaderick, ed. *Heart of the Valley*, Knoxville, Tenn.: East Tennessee Historical Society, 1976, pp. 424-438; and *The Arts of East Tennessee in the Nineteenth Century* (exhibit catalogue), Knoxville, Tenn.: Dulin Gallery of Art, 1971.
See also: ARCHITECTURE
FURNITURE
LEWIS HINE

The First Concrete Highway in Tennessee. The beginning of concrete highways in Tennessee took place in McMINN COUNTY in 1921. A.W. Prater, an Athens businessman, secured a contract for the county to build a fourteen-mile stretch of concrete road from Athens to the Hiwassee River at Calhoun. The roadbed was near, and roughly parallel, to the original Hiwassee Rail Road tracks surveyed in the 1830's.

Kriss & Waldroff, road builders from KNOXVILLE, poured the first concrete on the Fred Perkinson farm 1½ miles south of Riceville. Tom Jones dug and crushed limestone rock for the highway at a quarry which is today Knox Park lake in Athens. Jones loaded the crushed stone into railcars on the Louisville and Nashville tracks formerly built by the Tellico Railroad. The stone was then transferred at North Athens to the Southern Railway. The Southern delivered the cars to a stockpile on the C.E. Smith farm just north of Sanford. There the concrete was mixed and hauled in trucks to the job.

Today, as U.S. Highway 11, this road is still in use from Athens to the Hiwassee River. Most of it was widened after World War II and given a new asphalt surface. But a portion of the road, still in its original condition, serves as the main street through Calhoun.

James E. Burn

Refer to: Charles Fleming Keith, Jr., *McMinn County, Tennessee, 1819-1968*, Athens Tenn., 1968.

Flora. The flora of East Tennessee is unusually rich in number and diversity of species in comparison with PLANT COMMUNITIES from other parts of temperate North America. There are two major reasons for this. The first is the fact that the mountainous and plateau segments of East Tennessee have remained unaffected by either marine waters or continental glaciation longer than any other land area in the Eastern United States. While the Southern coastal plains were under marine waters as late as the early Tertiary Period of our GEOLOGY, and while massive Pleistocene glaciations to the north removed vegetation and soils, East Tennessee was continuously available for plant occupancy.

The second reason for the evolution of new and diverse types of plants was the large number of environments provided by the varied nature of East Tennessee's GEOGRAPHY. Differences in elevation, direction and degrees of slopes, kinds of rocks and soil, air currents, and precipitation provided sanctuaries for many of the new types which would have been eliminated in a region with more uniform topography. Many intermediate plant variations have been preserved in East Tennessee, making it difficult to separate species which appear more distinct in other regions. Examples include the spring beauties (*Claytonia virginica* and *C. caroliniana*), the wood anemones (*Anemone lancifolia* and *A. trifolia*), the *Trillium* species, and the sugar maples (*Acer saccharum*, *A. nigrum*, *A. rugelii*, and *A. floridana*).

The rich flora of East Tennessee exhibits a great variety of interesting geographical relationships with other regions and continents. It must have furnished, for instance, many of the species which moved into the southeastern coastal plains in the wake of marine waters. Some of these species became extinct in Tennessee; others, such as dwarf milkwort and American jointweed, remained in one or two isolated habitats in East Tennessee, but became much more widespread southward. Conversely, many of the species now found in the flora of glaciated terrain must have migrated northward from East Tennessee. Among these species are narrow-leaved gentian, wood sorrel, white cedar, sweet fern, northern bead-lily, and swamp buckthorn.

There are some species, regardless of their origin, restricted to East Tennessee and contiguous areas. The narrowest ranges, limited to the GREAT SMOKY MOUNTAINS NATIONAL PARK, are those of Rugel's Indian plantain, Cain's reed grass, and cloud manna-grass. Somewhat wider ranges include those of southern bead-lily, Fraser's sedge (with no close relative anywhere in the world), southern Appalachian gentian, and American lily-of-the-valley. A few species such as *Magnolia tripetala* and *Saxifraga virginiensis* appear also in the Ozark Mountains, but not in the intervening Mississippi River region. Other members of East Tennessee's flora have varieties or closely related species in the extreme western part of the United States. Among these related forms are the hazelnuts, the bleeding-hearts, the rhododendrons, and the leatherwoods. A very few of East Tennessee's plants, including beargrass and one of the Joe Pye weeds (*Eupatorium maculatum*), occur in the Rocky Mountains and are absent from the intervening grasslands.

There are other species in East Tennessee and contiguous areas which occur also in the highlands of Mexico and Central America. They probably once had a continuous range through the southern United States, but the one or two warm dry periods following the dissolution of the continental glacier permitted grasslands to develop. This effectively eliminated many species from Texas and neighboring areas.

Perhaps the most exciting element in the East Tennessee flora includes those categories which are found not only in the southern Appalachians, but also in parts of eastern Asia. Close relatives of our plants, or the same species, occur in Japan, China, and sometimes as far west as the Himalayan Mountains. Among these plants are umbrella-leaf, *Shortia*, Mayapple, trailing arbutus, cranefly orchid, and ginseng. Some plants occur in northern Latin America as well as southern APPALACHIA and eastern Asia. These include patridge berry, supple-jack, sweetgum, witch-hazel, deciduous holly, jumpseed, yellow jessamine, sourgum, and beech. There are reasons to think that our flowering plants reached the Americas from southeastern Asia, which seems to have been the area in which primitive flowering plants originated. Some must have migrated through eastern and northeastern Asia via Alaska and "fanned out" over much of North America. Later, the continental glaciers and development of the grasslands would have divided their ranges, giving us some of the distributional patterns seen today.

Aaron J. Sharp

See also: FAUNA

Folk Medicine. The problem in following the development of medicine lies in interpreting unwritten history. It seems probable that man discovered, by the process of trial and error, which plants might be used as foods, which were poisonous, and which of them might have medicinal value. For many years, for example, the foxglove plant was used for certain heart conditions. This plant, if given in too large a dose, is very toxic. One of the first major discoveries in herbal medicine occurred in 1785 when William Withering extracted and purified the alkaloid, digitalis, from the foxglove plant. The Indian snakeroot plant (Rauwolfia Serpentina) has been used for 5,000 years, but only with modern chemical methods was the product reserpine extracted. This is used to treat high blood pressure and anxiety. The relaxant effect for anxiety is purely a subjective feeling and would be apparent to the patient, but the effect on blood pressure was not apparent until we learned to measure blood pressure.

These advances were painstakingly passed on by word of mouth. One major factor in the spread of folk medicine was the innate healing power of the human body. There are many wonderful and mysterious defensive mechanisms at work in the body at all times. Most illnesses are self limiting and would eventually clear up if nothing were done. Therefore, if a poultice or decoction were applied or given at the proper time, it was considered curative. The written compilation of herbs, drugs, and chemicals did not follow until many years later.

The first physicians to come to America were British Army doctors. After the Revolutionary War, these doctors were located mainly in the coastal cities. In APPALACHIA folk medicine was about the only kind available. The remedies used consisted mainly of what was available locally, including Indian medicine, plus what the settlers had brought from their homeland. Out of this combination, one herb might have been considered the treatment of choice for several different maladies in different locales. If a drug were considered curative in a diverse array of conditions, it probably was not very good for any of them. One common feature, to be sure, was that the worse a drug smelled or tasted, the more beneficial it was thought to be. Oil of valerian, for instance, probably the vilest smelling of any herbal remedy, was considered very good for hydrophobia, dropsy, serious fever cases, a very wide range of nervous and neurotic disorders, and almost all psychosomatic disorders. Valerian smelled so bad that the patients probably decided to get well in order not to take another dose of the medicine. The common nettle, or stinging nettle, was considered good for chills, colds, poor circulation, anemia, kidney trouble, dropsy, gout, sciatica, senile decay and hemorrhage.

I can remember as a child being treated by my mother and grandmother, even though my aunt was married to a doctor. I was raised in Lebanon, Virginia, a small mountain town of 900 people and three doctors. At about the age of eight I contracted a serious case of dysentery and was treated with vermifuge tea, murdock tea, sassafras tea, paregoric and kaopectate. Nothing worked. I was weak, dehydrated, and very ill. My great-grandmother, who was a teetotaler and frowned on them that did drink, decided that things were getting desperate. She told my mother to give me some "burnt whiskey". They poured about an ounce of whiskey in a cup and lit it with a match. I had to blow out the flame and drink it down in one swallow. What a shock that was to my system—but it worked! Although herbal medicine as an art is slowly dying, I recently had a patient come to my office complaining of an ulcer. He had been treating himself with comfrey tea. He had obtained the comfrey from a lady in Oliver Springs who grew it along with a few other herbs. He had found very little relief and finally came in for more scientific treatment. He was raised in the mountains of North Carolina and remembered being treated with various homemade tonics and cough medicines.

Of the herbs themselves, ginseng is very popular and thus very scarce. It is considered good as a general tonic and for promotion of sexual potency, increased longevity, and relief from high blood pressure and asthma. Some people actually cultivate ginseng for export, even though it takes about six years for the plant to mature. Several old remedies for scurvy, calling for watercress or other plants, contain enough Vitamin C to be effective. Asafoetida is another herb that is still being used in some remote areas. Prepared by mixing the gum of the asafoetida tree with whiskey, it is given for stomach ache. In the past, the vile smelling gum was sometimes encased in a small cloth bag and worn around the neck to ward off evil spirits and diseases. Various areas had their own favorite spring tonic, with some of the most common being sulphur and molasses, sassafras tea or other spice tea.

Almost every household had a basic supply of remedies. There was the usual castor oil for a purgative, plus camphorated oil to rub on the chest for congestion, icthymammol ointment (a black, tarry salve used to "draw boils"), paregoric for diarrhea, and ipepacac for croup as well as an emetic and quinine for fever. Some people believed in rubbing a child with a raw potato or raw onion in order to relieve fever. This has some physiological value in that a liquid residue is applied to the skin, which, on evaporation, will cool the patient. Teeth were cleaned with sassafras twigs or brushed with charcoal or powdered pumice stone. Charcoal was also useful as an antidote in accidental poisonings. A few drops of turpentine or kerosene in boiling water were used for chest congestion. In addition to being used as spices, ferns, marigolds, lily of the valley, mullein, horse radish,marjoram, sage, and thyme have all been used as medicinal herbs. The list is too long to include the multitude of plants, herbs, flowers that have been used as medicines. Most of them, unfortunately, had no real medicinal value. And when the populace was subjected to epidemics of yellow fever, plague, cholera, typhus and influenza, the mortality rate was very high, because no effective remedies were available.

The following is only a partial list of some of the common herbs and their uses. These herbs were usually boiled in water, oil or alcohol to form a decoction or distillate for final use. Some leaves were simply crushed and applied directly to wounds.

adders tongue—*chillblains, cuts, sores, wounds*
agrimony—*tonic, leprosy, jaundice*
arnica—*bruises, sprains*
basil—*upset stomach*

betony—*bad cuts, sores, epilepsy, nerves*
blood root—*adenoids, bronchitis, croup*
boneset—*catarrh, colds, coughs, influenza*
comfrey (called knitbone in the old country)—*bone fractures, tuberculosis, bronchitis, asthma, rheumatism*
cinquefoil—*nervousness, hysteria*
cress—*cleansing blood, purifying the liver, scurvy*
dandelion juice—*warts, cirrhosis of liver, dropsy, ulcers, jaundice, kidney compaints, wine*
elder—*colds, epilepsy, laxative, eye disease, emetic, wine.*

James T. Gillespie, Sr.

Refer to: Arnold Krochmal, *A Guide to the Medicinal Plants of Appalachia*, Washington: U.S. Forest Service, 1971; and Eliot Wigginton, ed. *The Foxfire Book*, Garden City, N.Y.: Anchor Press/Doubleday, 1972, pp. 230-248.

Fort Loudoun was built in 1756 and 1757 by the British colony of South Carolina. It was located along the banks of the Little Tennessee River in what is today MONROE COUNTY. The idea of building a British fort among the Overhill Cherokees was first proposed in 1708, but nothing was done until the outbreak of the French and Indian War. In that struggle the CHEROKEES were allies of the British, and the British wanted Cherokee warriors to fight alongside them on the Virginia and Pennsylvania frontiers. The Cherokees would not go unless a fort was built where Cherokee women and children could take refuge in case the French or their Indian allies attacked the Cherokee towns while the Cherokee warriors were away. The Overhill Cherokees also calculated that a fort would give them direct contact with the British—the source of trade and ammunition—and would thereby enhance the effort of the Overhill towns to gain political supremacy over the Cherokee towns in the Carolinas.

Governor James Glen of South Carolina sent Captain Raymond Demere and the eighty men of his Independent Company of Charleston to garrison the fort. To build the fort, two Provincial militia companies of sixty men each were enlisted. The 200-man expedition was temporarily delayed when Governor Glen was replaced by William Henry Lyttelton, but eventually Governor Lyttelton authorized the expedition to proceed. It reached the Cherokee town of Tomatley about October 1, 1756. Several months before, Governor Glen had sent Ensign John Pearson to the Cherokee county to select a site for the fort, but John William Gerard DeBrahm, the expedition's engineer, disapproved of the site which Pearson had selected. DeBrahm proposed a site about a mile away, but the Cherokees vetoed it. DeBrahm threatened to shoot himself unless his opinion was accepted, but when no one tried to stop him he agreed to a compromise. The site selected was on the south side of the Little Tennessee River above the mouth of the Tellico River.

DeBrahm designed an elaborate European-style fort. It would be diamond-shaped with a bastion projecting from each corner. The bastions would be named in honor of the King, Queen, Prince of Wales, and Duke of Cumberland. Two of the bastions would be on the crest of a hill, but because the hill was not large enough for the entire fort, the rest of the fort would occupy the southern slope of the hill and an adjacent meadow near the river. In all, the fort would enclose about two acres. Each side of DeBrahm's proposed fort was 300 feet long. Outside the projected walls, a ditch would be dug a yard deep and ten feet across, in which would be planted thorny bushes of honey locust. The dirt excavated from the ditch would make the fort's wall: an earthen parapet twenty-one feet thick at the base and sloping upward to a height of about four feet. DeBrahm did not propose to build a palisade. Beyond the main polygon of the fort would be elaborate outer works called Glen's Fort and Lyttelton's Ravelin.

Captain Demere and engineer DeBrahm argued constantly about the design of the fort, which was called Fort Loudoun in honor of the Earl of Loudoun, then the British Commander-in-Chief in North America. In December of 1756, DeBrahm announced that since the fort was nearly finished he would soon return to Charleston. Demere replied that the fort was hardly begun, entirely indefensible, and in no sense near completion. Nonetheless, DeBrahm left one evening and was dubbed by the Cherokees "the warrior who ran away in the night." They derided DeBrahm's fort as a place in which to keep horses, cows, and hogs, but Demere doubted it would hold even them.

Over the succeeding months, Demere continued work on the fort. He generally followed DeBrahm's plan, but incorporated some modifications. A palisade was added inside the parapet, and the grandiose outer works were eliminated entirely. On July 30, 1757, Demere reported that the fort was finished. Around the fort was DeBrahm's dry moat planted with a hedge of honey locusts. There was an ample parapet, though not as high as DeBrahm had proposed. Just inside the parapet was a wall of pointed logs which projected eight feet above the parapet. The logs were angled outward by fifteen degrees for maximum defense. Loopholes were cut in the palisade to permit firing. Each of the four bastions had a platform mounted with three cannon. The cannon had been brought across the mountains on pack horses.

Inside the fort was a row of barracks, a workable drainage system, a powder magazine in the King George bastion, and a large blacksmith's shop which sometimes doubled as a guard house, a chapel, or a council chamber. There were also several storehouses and a number of temporary structures which were later demolished. In November of 1757, two corn houses were built as well as a permanent guard house. Later that year or early in 1758, a large house was built for the fort's commander. The command changed on August 14, 1757, when Captain Raymond Demere turned over the fort to his brother, Captain Paul Demere.

Life at Fort Loudoun conformed to military routine. In the Prince of Wales bastion, the colors were raised every morning and lowered every evening. The drum beat out reveille, parade, and tattoo, and there were many drills and inspections. The guard was changed several times a day, and at night the five large guard dogs were let out of the fort. There were less soldierly activities, too, such as planting and harvesting corn, hunting, fishing, and herding livestock.

Despite the humdrum of military routine, Fort Loudoun bustled with activity. When the Cherokees were not themselves in need, their women brought fish, wild fruits, and vegetables to the fort to barter for trade goods. Indian men came to the fort to have their guns and tools mended by the blacksmith. There were also white women and children in the fort. In August of 1760, there were sixty soldiers' dependents. Occasionally there were visitors like the Presbyterian divines John Martin, who preached at the fort in 1758, and William Richardson, who lived there for several months in 1759. There were parleys between the British and the Cherokees, and the fort's cannon were fired to salute departing war parties and to greet returning ones—especially those which brought in French scalps.

Anglo-Cherokee relations steadily improved after the fort was built. By the summer of 1758, nearly 700 Cherokees were serving alongside the British on the Virginia and Pennsylvania frontiers, But as undisciplined Cherokee warriors passed back and forth from the frontier, they often clashed with backcountry British settlers. The Cherokees stole horses, plundered homes, and frightened frontier families. The settlers retaliated by killing some Cherokees. The Cherokees had a law of blood that demanded a life for a life, so the violence escalated. Angered by the murder of white settlers in the backcountry, Governor Lyttelton imposed an embargo on arms and ammunition going to the Cherokee country. This was effective, but Lyttelton did not wait for it to work. He decided to lead a military expedition against the Cherokees.

When Lyttelton's army reached the frontier, it was devastated by an outbreak of smallpox and was forced to return to Charleston. As soon as the British army was gone, the Cherokees launched a full-scale war against the British colonies of North and South Carolina. An attempt was made to seize Fort Loudoun's cattle, but Demere foiled the attempt, drove the cattle into the fort, slaughtered them, and salted the beef. By January of 1760, Fort Loudoun's supply route had been cut. Beginning on March 20, the Cherokees fired on the fort for four successive days, but at too great a distance to do any harm. The fort's cannon prevented the Indians from coming closer, so OCONOSTOTA, the Cherokee commander, adopted starvation as his tactic.

In response to an appeal from Governor Lyttelton, General Amherst sent an army from New York to Charleston under the command of Colonel Archibald Montgomerie. Montgomerie's 1300 Regulars, joined by about 350 Provincials, marched deep into the Cherokee country, but on June 10, 1760, they were ambushed in a narrow mountain pass near the town of Etchoe. Montgomerie's losses were moderate, but with the mountains looming ahead and no secure line of supply behind, he decided to return to Charleston and so left Fort Loudoun to its fate.

The news of Montgomerie's retreat was a terrible blow to the inhabitants of

Fort Loudoun, but there was still hope that a relief expedition from Virginia would reach them. However, the Virginia troops were not enlisted until June, and they were placed under the command of a man who stopped to build a fort every twenty-five miles and who planned his attack for 1761. In May of 1760, Demere reduced the fort's rations to one quart of corn a day for each man. There was only one month's provisions left, but ATTAKULLAKULLA and those Indian women with husbands in the fort smuggled "pumpkins and Fowles, corn and hogs into the fort." Attakullakulla twice betrayed Oconostota's plans for taking the fort. On June 5 Attakullakulla was expelled from the Cherokee Council and was forced into the woods to live. Thereafter the fort received neither food nor information.

On June 10, the ration was slashed to a quart of corn a day for three men. The last bread was eaten on July 7. Thereafter the people ate four ounces of horseflesh a day plus a few beans and some plums which grew in the ditch. During the first days of August many of the garrison deserted. Demere called a Council of Officers which decided to surrender the fort. On August 7, articles of capitulation were signed. These called for surrender of the fort, its cannon, and supplies to the Cherokees. The inhabitants would be allowed to march unmolested to Virginia or South Carolina. The Indians agreed to furnish a hunting party to provide meat during the march. The garrison could take only such arms and ammunition as they needed for the march.

Early on August 9, the 180 men, and sixty women and children, set out for Fort Prince George, 140 miles away. That night, they camped in a meadow where Cane Creek flows into the Tellico River. The next morning, they were attacked by 700 Cherokee warriors. Three British officers, twenty-three privates, and three women were killed. Captain Demere was scalped alive, made to dance for his captors, his mouth stuffed with dirt, and his arms and legs successively cut off. The scalps of the fallen were beaten in the faces of the survivors as they marched to the various Cherokee towns. A few were tortured to death, but most lived to be ransomed. News of Fort Loudoun's fall was speeded to Fort Toulouse in Alabama, then to New Orleans, and on to Paris by means of a coded message. A French expedition to occupy the fort was stopped only by the Suck of the Tennessee River near CHATTANOOGA.

The Cherokees made peace with the British in December of 1761. The last of the Fort Loudoun captives were returned in the summer of 1762. In that year Lieutenant Henry Timberlake noted but did not describe the "ruins" of Fort Loudoun. It is not known whether the Cherokees destroyed the fort, or if it merely fell into ruin through disrepair. In 1797 Louis Philippe, Duke of Orleans and later King of the French, noted that the site of Fort Loudoun had "only a little rubble and a few irregularities of terrain to mark the fort's existence." Its existence, however brief, had helped to keep the Cherokees from joining the French during the early years of the French and Indian War, when the French were everywhere victorious. A large element of the Cherokees wanted to switch sides, and had they done so, the Creeks and other prominent tribes would have followed suit. The outcome of the war might have been different and the trans-Appalachian west might have remained French. When the Cherokees did turn against the British, it was too late to affect the outcome of the larger struggle. Montreal, the last French stronghold, surrendered within weeks of Fort Loudoun.

A portion of the site of Fort Loudoun was given to the National Society of Colonial Dames in 1917. The entire site was conveyed to the State of Tennessee in 1933. In 1936 the WPA excavated the site and began work on reconstructing the fort, but funding for the project ended in 1937. In the 1950's the Fort Loudoun Association sponsored excavation of the site, and a partial reconstruction of the fort was erected. The Tennessee Division of Archeology excavated the site in 1975-1976 and a new, more complete reconstruction is underway. The original site of Fort Loudoun is now an island in the Tellico Reservoir, formed by the TENNESSEE VALLEY AUTHORITY's Tellico Dam.

James C. Kelly

Refer to: Alberta and Carson Brewer, *Valley So Wild: A Folk History*, Knoxville, Tenn.: East Tennessee Historical Society, 1975; Donald Davidson, *The Tennessee, the Old River: Frontier to Secession*, New York: Rinehart, 1946; Philip Hamer, "Anglo-French Rivalry in the Cherokee Country, 1754-1757" and "Fort Loudoun in the Cherokee War, 1758-1761," in *North Carolina Historical Review*, Volume 2, pp.303-322 and pp. 442-458; Paul Kelley, *Historic Fort Loudoun*, Vonore, Tenn.: Fort Loudoun Association, 1958; and James C. Kelley, "Fort Loudoun," in Ralph Randolph, ed. *Tennessee Forts*, Memphis, Tenn.: Memphis State University Press, 1981.

John Fox, Jr. (December 16, 1862 - July 8, 1919), the regional writer who popularized the mountain people of Tennessee, Kentucky, and Virginia, wrote his first story while working in the COAL MINING business in East Tennessee. "A Mountain Europa" was published in the September-October 1892 issue of *Century* magazine. Fox's best-known novel, *The Trail of the Lonesome Pine*, also has an East Tennessee background.

Fox was born near Paris, Kentucky, and died in Big Stone Gap, Virginia, from pneumonia contracted on a fishing trip in the mountains. In 1878, when he was only 15 years old, Fox entered Transylvania University in Lexington, Kentucky. He transferred to Harvard after two years and was graduated in 1883, the youngest member of his class. He also attended Columbia University Law School in New York for six months. In 1887 he went into the mining business in Big Stone Gap, where his house is now open to visitors as a literary landmark, and where an outdoor production of *The Trail of the Lonesome Pine* is presented each summer.

During the summer of 1882, and on occasional visits during the late 1880's, Fox spent several months in the area of Jellico, Tennessee, near the Kentucky border. By 1890, his brothers Oliver, Horace, and Jim operated mines in Kensee, Proctor, and Wooldridge. While in Jellico, John invited James Lane Allen, his former professor and good friend from Transylvania days, to visit him. When *A Mountain Europa* was published in book form in 1899 by Harper and Brothers, it was dedicated to this author of *A Kentucky Cardinal, The Choir Invisible,* and *King Solomon of Kentucky*. *A Mountain Europa* deals with a mountain girl who rides a bull down the mountain to Jellico. It pictures a mining camp overlooking the Jellico Valley and describes Pine Mountain, the Jellico Spur, and the Cumberland Range. The hero Clayton is considered a "furriner", just as Jack Hale is in *The Trail of the Lonesome Pine*, and Easter Hicks is a forerunner of June Tolliver in that novel. The novelette shows the accurate use of mountain dialect which Fox was to employ in novels like *The Heart of the Hills, The Little Shepherd of Kingdom Come*, and *A Knight of the Cumberland*.

While living at the Florence Hotel in Jellico, Fox became acquainted with a couple who would achieve literary immortality as a result of his most popular novel. Uncle Billy Beam and Aunt Hon lived in a cabin at Proctor, a mining camp just outside Jellico. Fox spent considerable time visiting them and once said that some day he would put them in a book. *The Trail of the Lonesome Pine*, in which they are characters, sold well over a million copies and is still in print. It became a popular stage play and was made into a silent picture in 1916 and again in 1923. In 1936, it was the first all-technicolor film produced entirely outdoors, starring Sylvia Sidney, Fred McMurray, Henry Fonda, Beulah Bondi, and Fred Stone.

The Trail of the Lonesome Pine is dedicated to Fritzi Scheff, the French musical comedy star who married Fox in 1908. When she appeared at the Bijou Theater in Knoxville in 1941 in a play with Talullah Bankhead, Fritzi Scheff told *Knoxville News-Sentinel* columnist Bert Vincent that some of the happiest days of her life had been spent in Big Stone Gap. But only a brief period of mountain bliss it was, for conflicting careers caused the couple to divorce. Readers today find genuine enjoyment in the writings of John Fox, Jr., who gives sympathetic portraits of Appalachian types, presenting them as characters and not caricatures. It is good to know that he received his literary inspiration in East Tennessee, just as MARY MURFREE, another pioneer in local color fiction, did with volumes such as *The Prophet of the Great Smoky Mountains* and *In the Tennessee Mountains*.

David J. Harkness

Refer to: John Fox, Jr., *A Mountain Europa*, New York: Harper and Brothers, 1899; Fox, *The Little Shepherd of Kingdom Come*, New York: Charles Scribner's Sons, 1903; Fox, *The Trail of the Lonesome Pine*, New York: Scribner's, 1908; and Warren I. Titus, *John Fox, Jr.*, New York: Twayne, 1971.

See also: APPALACHIAN LITERATURE
KNOXVILLE THEATRES

Lizzie Crozier French (May 7, 1851 - May 14, 1926). The word "first" is synonymous with the name Lizzie Crozier French of KNOXVILLE. Founder of many women's clubs and societies, educator and principal of a girls' school, candidate for public offices, skilled elocutionist, author and early feminist, Mrs. French left her indelible mark on Knoxville society.

Lizzie Crozier French was educated at a Washington, D.C. convent and at an Episcopal school in Columbia, Tennessee. Her roots extended far into East Tennessee history. Her

Courtesy C.M McClung Historical Collection, Lawson McGhee Library

Lizzie Crozier French

grandfather, Col. John H. Crozier (Knoxville's second postmaster), and her father, Congressman John H. Crozier, were prominent Knoxville lawyers of the early 1800's. Lizzie married W.B. French, a great-grandson of Col. James White, the founder of Knoxville. Tragically, her husband lived only a few months after their marriage in 1872. Mrs. French devoted the rest of her life to raising their son and to making needed changes in society.

Her first challenge to society was in the area of women's education and intellectual development. While she was principal of the Knoxville Female Institute, she and twelve other women braved conservative public opinion to form Ossoli Circle, the first (1885) women's club in Knoxville. It was named for Margaret Fuller Ossoli, a New England transcendentalist and feminist; today, the club is strong and active in community affairs. Even though the group was originally envisioned by Mrs. Crozier-French as a way to "stimulate intellectual growth and moral development," the Ossoli Circle involved Knoxville women in such varied community activities as the Merchants' and Manufacturers' Free Street Fair and Trade Carnival and the Ossoli Story Telling League for children.

Five years after founding Ossoli Circle, Lizzie organized the Women's Educational and Industrial Union (WEIC). In 1894, WEIC and Ossoli Circle united to host the Association for the Advancement of Women in Knoxville. Lizzie and the women in WEIC began organizing a branch of the American Purity Alliance in the city. Through numerous pamphlets and societies such as the White Shield Society, the American Purity Alliance fought legalization of vice and worked for the "physical, intellectual, moral, and spiritual improvement of society".

Far from being a prude, however, Lizzie spoke out often against the double standard. She once was quoted in the newspaper as defending the young people's dances at the old Lyceum building against the charges of being "disorderly".

Mrs. French was quick to see needs in the community and quick to act. In 1890, she influenced the City Council to establish the office of police matron and then helped the matron in rescue work. She persuaded the King's Daughters Society to establish the first kindergarten in Knoxville. She was also responsible for the founding of the first industrial school for boys and girls. During the presidency of Charles Dabney, Lizzie worked to make THE UNIVERSITY OF TENNESSEE co-educational. She also ran for City Council in 1923 and for the office of judge of the juvenile court—a first for a woman in Knoxville.

Many Knoxville organizations such as the Knoxville Pen Women, the Parent-Teacher Association, the Writers' Club, the Women's Suffrage League, and the KNOX COUNTY League of Women Voters owe their inception and much of their original spirit to Lizzie Crozier French.

Mrs. French was a prominent educator as well as a popular elocutionist who gave readings in cities throughout the South. Her civic prominence and speaking ability made her a natural spokeswoman for the women's suffrage movement. She organized the local suffrage and was an active member of the Tennessee Suffrage Association, once serving as the state president.

Lizzie Crozier French remained active in Knoxville social and civic affairs until her death while visiting Washington on behalf of a bill to benefit working women. A newspaper reporter summed up her active and influential life in a succinct understatement: "She has a habit of speaking out on things in which she takes an interest, and doing it in such a way that the services of an interpreter are not necessary to tell what she means."

Diane Bohannon

Friendsville and Friendsville Academy. What is now the city of Friendsville was first settled around 1796. It began with a few families of the Society of Friends who migrated from North Carolina. The nucleus of the Friends Colony included the families of four sisters, daughters of Hugh and Mary Laughlin from near Guilford, North Carolina.

In the early 1800's, these immigrants began making plans to build a school. Following Quaker tradition, they decided to build two separate schools, one for boys, and one for girls. Eventually only a single large building was erected. It had a brick partition and a high stout fence between male and female sides, and carried the simultaneous names of "Friendsville Institute" and "Newberry Female School". The first sessions were held in 1857 with a total of forty-four students. Enrollment grew rapidly as Northern and English "Friends" sent gifts of money and books.

Early industry in the Friendsville area included a gristmill, a sawmill, a tannery, a cotton gin, and a canning factory. Perhaps the most important industry was that of the marble quarries of Knox, Loudon, and Blount counties. The original date of the first quarry is not known, but John J. Craig opened one east of KNOXVILLE in 1880. It became the Great Southern Marble Company in 1884. With the exception of the years 1932 to 1935, the quarries have operated continuously and have shipped marble throughout the United States. Marble from the nearby quarries has been used in many important buildings, including the National Gallery of Art, Washington, D.C.

The CIVIL WAR caused serious strains on the community and the school. Many Quaker settlements in the South disbanded and moved westward. Friendsville did not. At one time there was only one student enrolled, but both the school and the village survived. Their beliefs about war notwithstanding, Friendsville Quakers helped more than 2000 men hide and escape north to join the Union Army. In 1901, the original school building of Friendsville Academy was torn down and a new brick building financed by Elizabeth Farnum of Philadelphia, Pennsylvania. Fire destroyed this structure in 1914, and the present building was then erected. The Academy functioned as a boarding school until 1975, when it was sold to a fundamentalist group and renamed "Christ Academy".

During the 1880's, many Methodist families moved to the Friendsville area. In 1880 they organized their own church. Soon, churches of other denominations were established, including a Baptist church in 1923. The first bank in Friendsville opened in 1908 and closed in 1912 for lack of business. The second bank opened in 1915 and closed in 1936. There was not to be another bank in the community until 1978, when the Bank of ALCOA opened a branch. There was no county school in Friendsville until 1920. In January of that year a grade school opened with approximately eighty students. Today, students are bussed to a consolidated high school. The total population of Friendsville is presently about seven hundred.

Howard Hull

Refer to: Inez Burns, *History of Blount County, Tennessee*, Nashville: Benson Printing Company, 1957.

See also: WASHINGTON COLLEGE ACADEMY

Descendants of Revolutionary soldier James Mathews at marker dedication, Friendsville Quaker Cemetery, June 1935.

Courtesy Will Parham Photographs, C.M. McClung Historical Collection, Lawson McGhee Library

Lewis Hine / Courtesy TVA

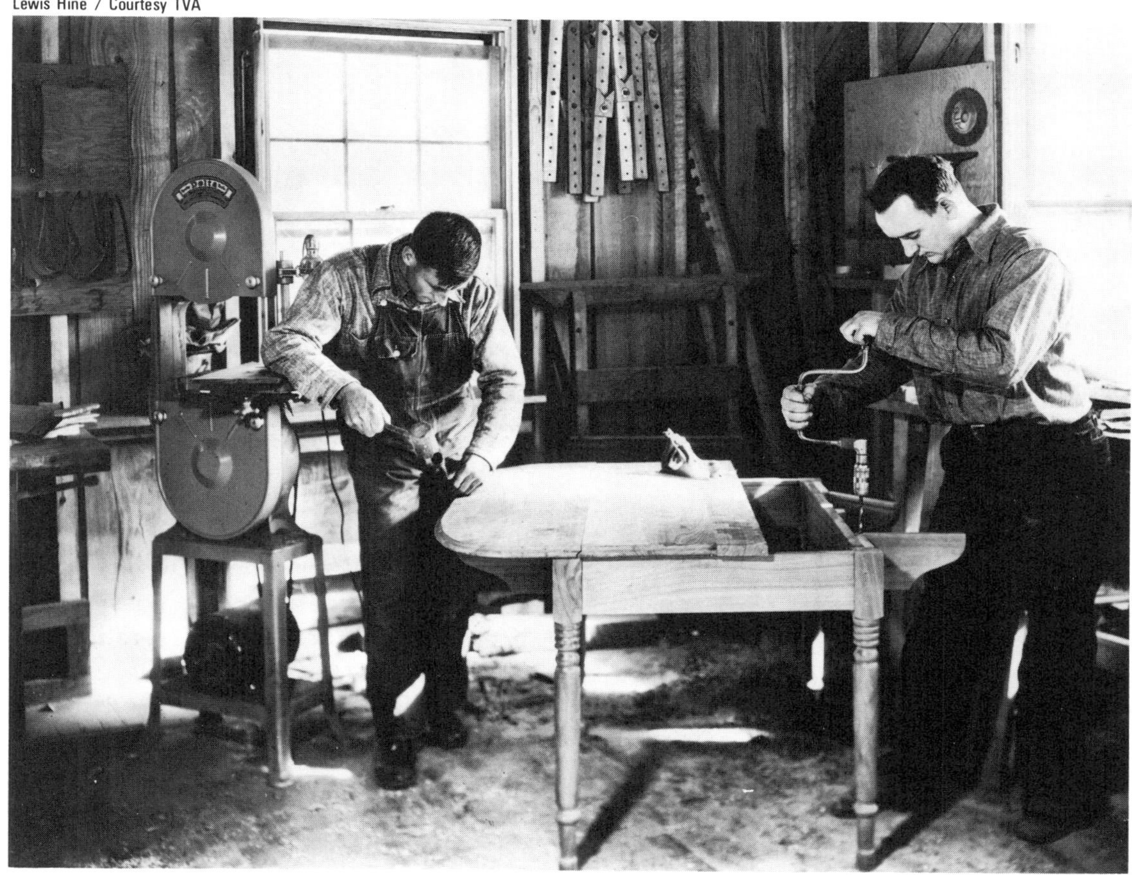

Shop of the Woodcrafters and Carvers, Gatlinburg, November 14, 1933. Richard Whaley, manager, and Charles Huskey work on a drop-leaf table.

Furniture. Many people today in East Tennessee own furniture which reflects the good taste and wealth of its earlier owners. Although the first settlers brought with them only what they could carry, good cabinetmakers soon came to Tennessee from England, the Carolinas, and Virginia. These craftsmen made fine pieces of furniture for those who longed for what they had left behind. As roads improved, more furniture came by wagon from Charleston and other cities, but much of the fine furniture was made locally. Living on the frontier did not cause settlers to give up willingly their former standard of living. Mrs. WILLIAM BLOUNT came to East Tennessee to set up a household that would help her husband live and entertain in the manner appropriate to his position as Governor of the Territory South of the River Ohio. The house now known as Blount Mansion in KNOXVILLE was suitably furnished to enhance his position when the Blounts moved into it in 1792.

Furniture in fashionable East Tennessee houses was often made in the latest styles. Cabinetmakers used pattern books produced by English and American furniture designers; they also copied furniture imported from England or bought in Charleston and other cities on the eastern seaboard. Fashionable furniture at the time of the settlement of Tennessee was in the Federal style, based on the designs of Adam, Hepplewhite, and Sheraton. Its characteristics included tapering legs, flaring bracket feet on chests, urn finials, and the use of inlay. Hepplewhite chairs included heart, shield, or oval backs. Elegant Queen Anne and Chippendale furniture was also made for many years in East Tennessee. Cabriole legs, curved lines, and a variety of types of feet characterized these styles. The claw and ball foot is best known, but trifid feet and club feet were also popular. Much of the simpler furniture in the area was a smaller version of English Elizabethan and Jacobean furniture, made to fit the frontier homes with their smaller rooms and lower ceilings. The use of older styles continued longer in rural areas than in cities. And the furniture of some parts of East Tennessee reflected a strong German influence.

The later Empire style, influenced by the English Regency and French Empire designs, was followed by the Victorian styles. After the Industrial Revolution, much work formerly made with hand tools could be done by machine. For the first time people could buy entire rooms of matching furniture. These buyers moved their older furniture to the kitchen or outbuildings, gave it to slaves or servants, or discarded it in favor of the new. More early East Tennessee furniture was lost or destroyed during the CIVIL WAR. Interest in collecting antiques did not begin in the United States until after the 1876 Philadelphia Centennial Exposition, which featured an exhibit of colonial furniture. It is difficult to identify the makers of early pieces of East Tennessee furniture, because most Southern cabinetmakers did not put labels or marks on their furniture. Use of similar characteristics, such as general form, construction, carving, inlay, or other decorative motifs, is almost the only means of identifying works made by the same cabinetmaker.

East Tennessee had large forests and an abundance of wood varieties, so some furniture makers chose to work in Tennessee because of the possibilities offered by the wood. Traditional mountain "settin' " chairs were often made with different kinds of woods so that the pieces would age to a tight fit without the use of nails or pegs. Maple or ash was usually used for the posts, hickory for the rounds, and white oak splits or hickory bark for the seats. Walnut and cherry were the woods most often used for the more elaborate pieces of furniture, while poplar and pine were usually used as secondary woods. Inlay on furniture in East Tennessee often consisted of holly. Combinations of wood were apparently more prevalent in furniture in Tennessee than in other areas.

The earliest settlers in mountainous areas had to be self-sustaining and produce most of their own furniture. Some skilled workers made not only their own furniture, but enough to sell or barter in their neighborhood. The 1820 Census of Manufactures lists 44 cabinetmakers, nine chairmakers, and one cabinetmaker/chairmaker working in Tennessee. T. McAffry, Knoxville, who employed three men in his "cabnite maker shop", had on hand cherry, walnut, and pine planks as well as 60 locks and 120 knobs. During the previous year, he had made two sideboards at $130 each, five "bureaus mahogany front" at $50 each and ten at $24 each, seven sets of tables at $45 each, two square tables at $4 each, and 12 bedsteads at $10 each. Secretaries, china presses, and circular bureaus were among items made by James Bray of KNOX COUNTY in 1820. Chairs valued at $2572 were made by Jas. S. Bridges, Knoxville, maker of Windsor and fancy chairs.

By 1976, over 20,000 people with a payroll of almost $140,000,000 were employed in the manufacturing of household furniture in Tennessee. Among the largest companies in East Tennessee are Forest Products Division of Ludlow Corporation and Berkline Company, both of Morristown; La-Z Boy Chair Co., Dayton; Kroehler Manufacturing Co., Newport; Athens Furniture Co.; and Cleveland Furniture Co.. In counterpoint to the large manufacturing companies, some area individuals are still making and selling traditional mountain chairs, while cabinetmakers such as Robert G. Emmett and Grover W. Floyd II are using traditional tools to make furniture in Queen Anne and Chippendale styles. Westel and GATLINBURG furniture makers continue to produce furniture which has brought them a wide reputation for many years. The future of furniture making in East Tennessee should be as interesting as its past.

Mary Frances Crawford

Refer to: Ellen Beasley, *Made in Tennessee: An Exhibition of Early Arts and Crafts*, Nashville: Tennessee Fine Arts Center, 1971; Richard Harrison Doughty, *Greeneville: One Hundred Year Portrait (1775-1875)*, Greeneville, 1975; Robert R. Madden and T. Russell Jones, *Mountain Home: The Walker Family Farmstead, The Great Smoky Mountains National Park*, Washington: National Park Service, 1977; and Alice Winchester, ed. *Antiques in Tennessee*, New York: Antiques Magazine, 1971.

See also: FINE ARTS

G

Hattie Harrison Gaddis (October 1, 1894 - March 6, 1972), midwife and herself one of eleven children, was born in GREENE COUNTY. She learned midwifery from her mother, who was a Cherokee Indian. Hattie married Jess Gaddis, a tobacco farmer, and they had four daughters and two sons. Hattie Gaddis was known by most people in the county as "Mammy" Gaddis. She is said to have delivered, during a time span of approximately 45 years, over 700 babies with the loss of only two. Greeneville physicians recognized her as a highly respected midwife and referred indigent pregnant women to her. She also cared

Hattie Harrison Gaddis and husband standing on the porch of their home, along with neighbors and children delivered by her or staying with her temporarily.

Courtesy Ruby Dayton

for persons who were ill or dying, and she dressed out corpses for funerals.

Usually, Mammy received no fee for her services. Instead, husbands of her patients helped "Pap" Gaddis for a day on their 30-acre farm in eastern Greene County. Although the three-room farmhouse had no running water or electricity, Hattie constantly kept children of those who were sick or recuperating from surgery. Itinerant preachers and revival speakers came and invariably spent the night. And Hattie's 20 grandchildren and 23 great-grandchildren frequently stayed with her.

Remembering the much harder times of her youth, Mammy Gaddis felt that she "had it made". She sewed her clothes and made her own SOAP, brooms, canned fruits, sausage, and meat. Since she was accustomed to making even her own mops, she considered it a great treat once to buy a mop. Her small home always had freshly scrubbed wood floors and smelled of lye soap. It was literally an open house to the world.

Ruby Dayton
Jeanne Holloway-Ridley

See also: CHEROKEES
PRIMARY HEALTH CARE CENTERS

Gatlinburg, a mountain resort with 3,000 permanent residents, plays host to as many as 30,000 people per night during the summer tourist season. It all started back in the early 1800's when Widow Martha Huskey Ogle and her seven children, accompanied by her brother Peter Huskey and his children, came from South Carolina to this valley of the Little Pigeon River. Besides the Ogles and Huskeys, other pioneers included the McCarters, Reagans and Whaleys. Soon to follow were the families of Bohannon, Clabough (later Clabo), King, Maples, Conner, Bradley, Ownby, Watson, and Trentham.

The original name of the town was White Oak Flats. Radford Gatlin, the Confederate supporter who left his name on the town after a brief stay, came to the White Oak Flats community in 1854. After several feuds and disputes over land and loyalties, he departed, friendless.

Education in the community owes its beginning to the subscription school in existence before 1830. A public school was established after the CIVIL WAR, followed in 1912 by the PI BETA PHI SETTLEMENT SCHOOL. At first the mountain people suspected this invasion by "furriners". Although they desired better advantages for their children, the settlers were afraid that charity was involved or that religious propaganda might be started. Gradually, however, the young settlement workers were accepted in the community.

In the early days before road machinery or automobiles, the mountaineers had to work those wagon or sled roads which were located nearest their homes. The law prescribed work for six days or payment of a $3 annual poll tax. But this was to change. After the GREAT SMOKY MOUNTAINS NATIONAL PARK was authorized and the Park's initial land purchases completed during the 1930's, Gatlinburg found itself the front door neighbor of the Park. A great awakening began to occur

Courtesy Gatlinburg Chamber of Commerce

A shopping mall in Gatlinburg, 1980.

in this little mountain village as descendants of the pioneers saw their vision of a summer resort coming true. Andy Huff, for example, gave strong support to the Park movement and established the first hotel in Gatlinburg. His Mountain View Hotel became the first headquarters for the Park and for the Bureau of Public Roads. The Mountain View lives on under the ownership of Huff's descendants.

Residents and visitors alike take part in yearly events to enjoy the beauty of the entire area. During the fall, mountain people begin gathering their wares for the craft fairs that are the highlight of this season. With the coming of the winter months, Gatlinburg celebrates the "Twelve Days of Christmas" and "Festival of Trees". A spring "Wildflower Pilgrimage" was started in 1950 and is held the last full week in April.

Emily Nixon

Refer to: Jeanette S. Greve, *The Story of Gatlinburg*, Strasburg, Virginia: Shenandoah, 1931; and Jerome E. Dobson, "The Changing Control of Economic Activity in the Gatlinburg, Tennessee Area, 1930-73," University of Tennessee dissertation, 1975-6.
See also: FESTIVALS AND EVENTS

Geography. East Tennessee is characterized by three kinds of more-or-less mountainous landscapes that are crossed on any east-west line. The approximately 12,500-square-mile area contains three major divisions: the

Cumberland Plateau and Mountains, drained by both the Tennessee River and the Cumberland River; the Ridge and Valley, referred to here as the Valley or Great Valley, and drained by the Tennessee River with a small area in the south drained via the Conasauga River to the Gulf; and Unaka Mountains, referred to here as the Mountains, which include the Great Smoky Mountains and are drained by the Tennessee and again to a slight extent by the Conasauga.

The Cumberland Plateau is a flat to rolling area extending as a continuous tableland from MARION COUNTY north through western MORGAN COUNTY and SCOTT COUNTY. Southward it lies at elevations of about 2000 feet; northward the surface lies at about 1400-1600 feet. The surface is in places much dissected by gorges extending down to 1100 feet elevation, and even to about 600 feet where the Tennessee flows south from Marion County. The southern half of the Plateau is bisected by the Sequatchie Valley, a spectacular canyon which extends from northern BLEDSOE COUNTY south to the Tennessee River and is matched in Alabama by a similar valley extending north to that river. East of the Sequatchie Valley, the Plateau is referred to as Walden Ridge. Low mountain ranges (to about 3000 feet) protrude above the surface of the Plateau near the northern end of the Sequatchie Valley. These ranges include Hinch Mountain, Brady Mountain, the Bear Den Mountains, and Crab Orchard Mountains. In CUMBERLAND COUNTY, two outstanding bowl-shaped valleys have been formed: Crab Orchard Valley and GRASSY COVE. The latter has no external stream drainage at all!

The Cumberland Mountains of Tennessee extend from eastern Morgan and Scott counties eastward to the Cumberland escarpment and include western ANDERSON COUNTY, western and northern CAMPBELL COUNTY, and northwestern CLAIBORNE COUNTY. In this rugged mountain area, peaks extend to 3643 feet (Cross Mountain), and valleys are cut as low as about 1000 feet.

The Great Valley area of East Tennessee is one in which ridges and valleys alternate east-west across the landscape in more-or-less regular fashion, trending in a northeast-southwest direction. To the south, toward CHATTANOOGA, the valley floor lies at about 800-900 feet along the Tennessee River; ridges extend upward to about 1400 feet. North toward KNOXVILLE, valleys and ridges are at about 900-1000 and 1100-1300 feet. Near KINGSPORT, they average about 1200 and 1600-1800 feet. Three sets of high ridges occur in the Great Valley: Powell Mountain, in Claiborne County and HANCOCK COUNTY, extending to 2400 feet in elevation; Clinch Mountain, in GRAINGER COUNTY, HAWKINS COUNTY, and Hancock County, extending to about 2200 feet (an isolated extension occurs at HOUSE MOUNTAIN in KNOX COUNTY); and the Bays Mountain, in GREENE COUNTY, Hawkins County and SULLIVAN COUNTY, extending to about 2200 feet.

The Unaka Mountains of East Tennessee lie in parts of all of the counties forming the eastern edge of the state. The whole group lies in the Blue

Ridge, extensively developed in North Carolina and elsewhere. Part of the Unakas are the magnificent mountains of special interest, reserved in the GREAT SMOKY MOUNTAINS NATIONAL PARK. Several mountains stand out prominently along the western edge of this strip at its contact with the Great Valley. These are the Chilhowee-Bean-Starr Mountains in POLK COUNTY, MCMINN COUNTY, and MONROE COUNTY; Chilhowee Mountain in BLOUNT COUNTY and SEVIER COUNTY; English Mountain at the junction of Sevier County, COCKE COUNTY, and JEFFERSON COUNTY; Stone, Meadow Creek, Bald and Cherokee Mountains between Newport and JOHNSON CITY; and Holston Mountain in the northeastern corner of Tennessee. These ridges again trend to the northeast; the highest peaks and ridges lie at about 2800-4800 feet.

The main block of the Unakas may contain great masses of mountains in close proximity, or more-or-less isolated peaks with their spur ridges. To the south, in Polk County, Big Frog and Little Frog Mountains illustrate the second case. Northward, in Monroe County, the Unicoi Mountains occur as an approximately 500-square-mile mountain group (more than half in North Carolina). Northward, the Great Smoky Mountains are a much larger group oriented almost east-west with peaks to 6643 feet. Between the Pigeon River and the French Broad River another complex mass, the Bald Mountains, have peaks to 4200 feet. North of the French Broad, this elongate mountain mass culminates in Roan Mountain (6283 feet). Lower mountains extend north of this, sheltering such beautiful sites as Shady Valley.

H. R. DeSelm

See also: GEOLOGY AND SOILS
THE THREE STATES OF EAST TENNESSEE

Geology and Soils. The bedrocks of the Unaka Mountains of East Tennessee are extensively folded and faulted. Stream erosion has reduced the perhaps once very high folds to their present size. Bedrocks vary from conglomeritic sandstones to metamorphic rocks such as slates, gneisses, schists and a few patches of granite. These weather to chiefly steeply sloping, rocky, sandy, acid, infertile, shallow to deep soils. In a few places, the more ancient bedrocks underlying the Unakas have been pushed over the dolomites of the Great Valley, and erosion has exposed the dolomites on the valley floors and lower slopes. These valleys (windows) are unique sites within the western fringe of the Unakas; Shady Valley, Stony Creek Valley, Bumpass Cove, Tuckaleechee Cove, CADES COVE, Wear Valley and Happy Valley are examples.

Bedrock pattern in the Great Valley is indeed complex. Ancient pressures from the southeast caused the formerly flat-lying rocks to fold; some faulted (broke) and overrode others to the northwest. The folds have been long since eroded to the present ridge-valley system: the valleys are underlain chiefly by soft shales, limestones and dolomites; the ridges are underlain chiefly by cherty dolomites or sandstones. Soils developed on this variety of bedrocks vary. On the dolomite they vary from shallow to deep, from near neutral to acid, and clayey and often stony. On sandstone they vary from shallow to more often deep, from acid to somewhat calcareous, and are sandy and more-or-less rocky. On shales they vary from shallow to deep, from slightly to quite stony, and are clayey and neutral to acid. On the purer limestones they vary in their stone content, and are clayey, usually shallow, and slightly acid to neutral or calcareous. The high ridges are capped by sandstones with characteristic sandy, acid, stony, and shallow to deep soils.

The flat to rolling surface of the Cumberland Plateau is underlain by sedimentary, chiefly flat-lying rocks of ancient age which occur as sandstones, siltstones, shales and coals. Soils developed from these surface rocks are usually shallow, sandy and acid. The lower half to two-thirds of the deep valleys and large gorges of the Plateau surface exhibit chiefly ancient flat-lying limestone bedrocks. These bedrocks are usually at least partly covered by sandstone colluvium from the upper slopes. Soils here may be acid, sandy, rocky as is the colluvium, or may be more calcareous, higher in clay, and vary both in depth and stoniness.

H. R. DeSelm

Refer to: Edward T. Luther, *Our Restless Earth: The Geologic Regions of Tennessee*, Knoxville: University of Tennessee Press, 1977.
See also: GEOGRAPHY
PLANT COMMUNITIES

Nikki Giovanni (June 7, 1943 -), poet, speaker and columnist, daughter of KNOXVILLE COLLEGE graduates Gus and Yolande Watson Giovanni, grew up in KNOXVILLE and Cincinnati. She attended 10th and 11th grades at Austin High School, skipped 12th grade, and in 1967 graduated with honors from Fisk University in Nashville. At Fisk, she edited the college literary magazine and fought for the 1964 reinstatement of the campus chapter of the Student Nonviolent Coordinating Committee (SNCC). Her first major collection of poems was published in 1970 as *Black Feeling, Black Talk, Black Judgement.*

With these poems, plus her "Extended Autobiographical Statement" entitled *Gemini* (1971), Nikki Giovanni vaulted into national prominence. During 1974 and 1975, she was awarded Honorary Doctorates of Literature from Ripon University, the University of Maryland, and Smith College. Since then she has continued to record poetry albums and to publish poetry collections for adults and children, as well as conversations with James Baldwin and Margaret Walker. Nikki Giovanni also serves as editorial consultant for *Encore American* and for *Worldwide News Magazine.* Through her writings and talks, she has always advocated individual responsibility—the necessity for each person to grasp firmly and to proceed courageously with his or her own education, vocation, life and destiny.

Jim Stokely

Refer to: Nikki Giovanni, *Black Feeling, Black Talk, Black Judgement,* New York: Morrow, 1970; *Gemini: An Extended Autobiographical*

Statement on My First Twenty-Five Years of Being a Black Poet, Indianapolis: Bobbs-Merrill, 1971; and *My House,* New York: Morrow, 1972.
See also: CHARLES CANSLER

Grainger County
Size: 282 Square Miles (180,480 acres)
Established: 1796
Named For: Mary Grainger, wife of William Blount
County Seat: Rutledge
Other Major Cities, Towns, or Communities:
Bean Station
Washburn
Powder Springs
Puncheon Camp
Blaine
Thorn Hill
Joppa
Buffalo Springs

See also: MUSICAL INSTRUMENTS

Rutledge, county seat of Grainger County, 1920's.

Courtesy Thompson Photographs, C.M. McClung Historical Collection, Lawson McGhee Library

Grassy Cove, in CUMBERLAND COUNTY on Highway 68 east of Crossville, is about two miles wide and five miles long. The cove, completely encircled by mountains, was a lake, and its fossils and shells are widely studied. There are also traces of Indian habitation. Grassy Cove's Cove Creek empties into a large limestone cave, sinks underground, and reappears in the upper Sequatchie Valley to form the Sequatchie River.

The first families said to have settled

Jim Stokely

Grassy Cove, November 2, 1978.

in Grassy Cove came from Virginia in 1801. They were John Ford, Sr., Reuben Ford, William Loden (originally Logan), John Nail, John McKinney, James Gibson, William Newton, John Walker and others. John Ford, Sr., a Revolutionary War veteran, established the first store. He donated ground for the first church and school in 1803. Five years later the church had 48 members. Other settlers soon came from Virginia and the Carolinas. In 1828 the Gordon road was constructed through the cove from ROANE COUNTY on its way across the Cumberland Plateau to Middle Tennessee. The stagecoach used that road and stopped regularly at Stockmans Inn. The old Kentucky Stock road also passed through Grassy Cove.

Saltpeter Cave, the best known cave in the cove, was used during the CIVIL WAR by Richard Matthews and Andrew Kemmer to make gunpowder. During the late 1860's the petrified body of a Confederate soldier was found in the cave. He was dressed in what had been new clothing and appeared to have died of natural causes. The discovery received wide publicity and created much interest. Although he was given a formal burial, people grew superstitious about the corpse. A group of men finally disinterred the body and reburied it in an unmarked grave. They swore to each other never to reveal the site and, as far as is known, they kept that vow.

Grassy Cove families were divided by the Civil War and so experienced much sadness and hardship. After the war Presbyterians established the Grassy

Cove Academy, which operated until 1906. Today Grassy Cove is a farming community with a population of approximately 85. It has retained its unique blend of hillside forests and rich grazing lands.

Patricia B. Kirkeminde

Refer to: Cora S. and Nettie M. Stratton, *And This Is Grassy Cove,* Crossville, TN: Chronicle Publishing Company, 1938.
See also: CADES COVE

The Grassy Fork String Band. There are still communities in the Southern Appalachian mountains where the life styles and folkways of the residents—because of lack of contact with the contemporary world—remained unchanged from the traditions of the original settlers until less than a generation ago. Only with the coming of RADIO, television, and widespread recreational travel have the formerly unspoiled ways of living, speaking, and music-making in these remote areas become influenced and changed by modern ways.

Grassy Fork, in COCKE COUNTY, was one such community. The Grassy Fork String Band, as I knew it, was made up of three such residents: Leola Black, lady fiddler, Haskell Williams, guitarist, and Rolfe Ford on banjo. They played the oldtime southern mountain music in the oldtime way, just as they learned it from kinfolk and friends in the community. Of all the performers and string bands I've heard, none has performed the old-timey music with more faithfulness to the traditional string band sound—and with less obvious influence from the corrupting effects of the modern-day world—than these good folks from Grassy Fork.

Leola passed away in June of 1973 and is sorely missed, but Rolfe and Haskell still get together as often as possible to make music with other friends for the neighbors and kinfolk. Many's the good evening, in Leola's time and since, that we've spent in the company of the Grassy Fork String Band, playing the old tunes and enjoying ourselves in the general good fellowship of people who like one another and have something to share. Of course, no special excuse is needed for such a musical evening, but some of the best of our memories of good times happen through gatherings at our local community center. These occur, on the average, about once a month, beginning with a covered dish, pot luck supper. Better food doesn't exist than what we eat there, where good country cooks show off their specialties, followed by several hours of oldtime music making, mountain dancing, and folk games.

Jean Schilling

See also: APPALACHIA
COUNTRY MUSIC

Graysville is a small semi-urban community similar to the hundreds of other country towns characteristic of APPALACHIA. The community is located in the southern part of RHEA COUNTY, approximately two miles north of the HAMILTON COUNTY line. Rugged ridges, typical of the eastern Tennessee Valley, surround the town. Lone Mountain to the north and Black Oak

Ridge to the east form two sides of a rough triangle around Graysville, while Walden's Ridge on the west closes the triangle. Roaring Creek flows along the southwestern side of Graysville, and just to the east lie the tracks of the Cincinnati, New Orleans and Texas Railroad.

The town takes its name from William Gray, one of its earliest and best known residents, who arrived after the CIVIL WAR. The post office was established in 1875 with William Gray as postmaster. After the coming of the railroad, the community experienced an influx of population from all points of the compass. In 1884 Henry and William Fox organized the Fox Coal Company, which opened mines in the side of Walden's Ridge. In addition to coal, a large deposit of tile clay was mined from an adjoining range of hills. A bank and two hotels were established the same year. In 1885, the Dayton Coal and Iron Company began operations a few miles to the north and created an additional demand for coal. Funded by European investors, Dayton Coal and Iron operated 375 coke ovens which converted coal into coke. This coke fueled two large blast furnaces with an annual production capacity of 90,000 tons of foundry and forge pig iron. After 1900 the Durham Coal and Iron Company acquired Fox Coal Company, expanded it, and established a large coke oven complex near Roaring Creek.

The industrial development and intense prosperity of Graysville entered a decline following World War I and were completely crushed by the economic depression of the 1930's. Most of the mines shut down. The bank was consolidated with the Dayton Bank, the hotels closed, and the people began to leave. The present population of Graysville is less than 1000. As is often the case in the Southern Appalachians, Graysville has no clearly defined boundary between the urban and the rural. There are no paved streets or business districts. Sprinkled haphazardly among frame dwellings are two general purpose "grocery" stores, a television repair shop, a small library, a barber shop, three automotive repair shops, and one service station. The community has a school and eight Protestant churches, four of which are Baptist. There is no local industry. The economy of Graysville is geared toward small-scale farming, mining, and pulpwood cutting, supplemented by sporadic industrial employment outside the area.

E. Raymond Evans

Refer to: E. Raymond Evans, "The Graysville Melungeons: A Tri-Racial People in Lower East Tennessee," in *Tennessee Anthropologist,* V. 4, No. 1 (Spring, 1979), pp. 1-31.
See also: COAL MINING
RAILROADS (SOUTHEASTERN)

Great Smoky Mountains National Park. The finest mountain wilderness resource in the eastern United States is the Great Smoky Mountains National Park. The park serves as a genetic storehouse for many plant and animal species in this part of the country. Although the move to establish the GSMNP began in 1923, the park was not officially established until June 15, 1934. It now consists of more than a half-million acres about equally divided between East Tennessee and western

Courtesy Thompson Photographs, C.M. McClung Historical Collection, Lawson McGhee Library

Photographs like this, taken during the 1920's by Jim Thompson, helped persuade Federal officials to locate part of the Great Smoky Mountains National Park in Tennessee.

North Carolina, lying between the Pigeon River on the northeast and the Little Tennessee River on the southwest. The Appalachian Trail winds about seventy miles over the highest peaks and ridges of the Great Smokies. The southern terminus of the Blue Ridge Parkway, administered by the National Park Service to provide extensive motoring in a mountain environment, is also located within the park. It joins the existing transmountain highway between GATLINBURG, Tennessee, and Cherokee, North Carolina.

About 160,000 acres of the park form virgin forest, existing today as it has for centuries. Most of the remaining acreage was timbered during the late 19th and early 20th centuries. This timbering, part of the long human history in the Smokies, was discontinued with the establishment of the park. The disturbed area has since made a remarkable recovery from abusive logging practices, due primarily to this region's mild CLIMATE, abundant rainfall, and long growing season. Today, the Smokies constitute an area which represents in superlative form the vegetation and wildlife that a mountain environment can support. It is an ecological standard against which man's modification of his environment can be judged.

The unique character of the Smokies resides in the wide variety of plants and animals which inhabit the park. Luxuriant PLANT COMMUNITIES can be found, from the rich mixture of the cove hardwoods—the highest expression of the deciduous forest—through the hemlock hardwoods of the mid-altitudes, to the spruce-fir forests of the higher slopes and ridges. In the GSMNP, there are almost as many kinds of native trees as in all of Europe. This diversity of habitat and species has led to designation of the park as an International Biosphere Reserve. Twenty-eight IBR's exist in the nation, but only four are located in the populous East. Botanists have listed more than 1300 kinds of flowering plants, about 2000 species of fungi, nearly 350 mosses and liverworts, and 230 lichens. There are at least fifty mammals which are native to these mountains, the largest of which is the black bear. Numerous species of reptiles find a home here, including an outstanding array of salamanders. About 200 kinds of birds have been seen within the park's borders.

Before the Great Smoky Mountains National Park was established, loggers and other mountaineers had cleared many miles of pathways and dirt roads along the streams and ridges of these mountains. But for the most part, these were unsuitable as an interpretive trail system for a national park. Once abandoned, they were quickly reclaimed by nature. Under the directions of the National Park Service in the mid-1930's, the Civilian Conservation Corps constructed bridges, fire towers, trail shelters, and several hundred miles of trails. More than 600 miles of horseback and foot trails are now interlaced throughout the park, providing ready access to its most outstanding features.

Wilderness is the essential endowment of the Great Smoky Mountains National Park. But without legal Wilderness Area designation, it can never be guaranteed that this sanctuary will continue intact through future generations. It is the responsibility of this generation to preserve this great biological reserve. Future generations will then look to these mountains and wonder why we have set them aside to be left as they are for all time. Out of curiosity they will go, and they will find the wilderness—and, perhaps, themselves.

Ray Payne
Russ Manning

Refer to: Carlos C. Campbell, *Birth of a National Park in the Great Smoky Mountains,* Knoxville: University of Tennessee Press, 1960 (revised edition, 1970); Wilma Dykeman and Jim Stokely, *Highland Homeland: The People of the Great Smokies,* Washington: National Park Service, 1978; National Park Service, *Draft General Management Plan for the Great Smoky Mountains National Park,* Washington, 1978; and Arthur Stupka, *Notes on the Birds of Great Smoky Mountains National Park,* 1963, and *Trees, Shrubs, and Woody Vines of Great Smoky Mountains National Park,* 1964, Knoxville: University of Tennessee Press.

See also: CADES COVE
FAUNA
FLORA
STATE PARKS

Greene County

Size: 613 Square Miles (392,320 acres)
Established: 1783
Named For: Nathanael Greene, General

in the American Revolution

County Seat: Greeneville

Other Major Cities, Towns, or Communities:

Mosheim
Baileyton
Tusculum
Rheatown
Mohawk
Caney Branch
Warrensburg
Camp Creek

Refer to: Richard Harrison Doughty, *Greeneville: One Hundred Year Portrait, 1775-1875*, Greeneville, Tenn., 1975; and Allen E. Ragan, *A History of Tusculum College, 1794-1944*, Greeneville, Tenn.: Tusculum Sesquicentennial Committee, 1945.

See also: BLUEGRASS MUSIC
DAVID CROCKETT
HATTIE HARRISON GADDIS
ANDREW JOHNSON
THE STATE OF FRANKLIN

Grundy County

Size: 358 Square Miles (229,120 acres)

Established: 1844

Named For: Felix Grundy, U.S. Senator from Tennessee

County Seat: Altamont

Other Major Cities, Towns, or Communities:

Tracy City
Monteagle
Palmer
Beersheba Springs
Coalmont
Laager
Gruetli
Cumberland Heights

See also: BEERSHEBA SPRINGS

H

Halls Crossroads is located eight miles north of KNOXVILLE on Highway 33. The 200-year-old community is bounded on the south by Black Oak Ridge and on the north by Copper Ridge. The eastern boundary is Brown's Gap Road, and the western boundary is Dry Gap Pike. Halls encompasses parts of Beaver Creek Valley and Hine's Valley, an area of approximately 36 square miles. The settling of this area, originally called the Beaver Creek Settlement, was accelerated by the existence of trails passing westward down Beaver Creek Valley. In 1788, the various sections of trail were joined and widened by the North Carolina militia, thus forming the Emory Road. This road became part of the Cumberland Road, used by many settlers en route to the Cumberland Settlements in Middle Tennessee.

One of the early pioneers in the Beaver Creek Settlement was Thomas Hall, a veteran of the Revolutionary War. During the siege of Charleston, Thomas Hall had been captured and imprisoned by the British. For his services during the war, he received a land grant from his native state of North Carolina. It was this grant which brought Thomas Hall to Tennessee in 1796. According to family legend, Thomas Hall's grandson, Pulaski, returned from the California gold fields in the early 1860's. With his stake from a gold strike, he established a general store at the junction of Emory Road and Andersonville Pike. The name Halls Crossroads originated from this store and crossroads. Although it included grist mills, saw mills and distilleries, the area remained primarily an agricultural community until the mid-20th century, when Knoxville's growing population began to expand outward. Halls Crossroads has now become a suburb of Knoxville, with a population of approximately 16,000.

The community now has over one hundred small businesses. The oldest of these is Avondale Farms, which supplies dairy products to much of East Tennessee. Two other businesses owned by decendants of early settlers are Mynatt Brothers Hardware and Tindell Building Supplies. Halls Crossroads embraces several churches including Beaver Dam Baptist Church, organized prior to 1786, one of the two oldest Baptist churches in KNOX COUNTY. To educate its growing population, Halls Crossroads has a high school, a middle school, three grammar schools, and an area vocational school. The early settlers of Halls Crossroads saw the woodlands slowly give way to pasture fields and farmlands. Today's settlers are seeing the pasture fields and farm lands give way to subdivisions.

Dorothy Kelly

Refer to: Calvin Trillin, "U.S. Journal: Knoxville, Tennessee," in *The New Yorker*, March 12, 1979, pp. 110-117.

Hamblen County
Size: 155 Square Miles (99,200 acres)
Established: 1870
Named For: Hezekiah Hamblen, a leading citizen of HAWKINS COUNTY
County Seat: Morristown
Other Major Cities, Towns, or Communities:
Russellville
Whitesburg
Lowland
Alpha
Springvale
Roe
Hales Crossroads
See also: COMMUNITY COLLEGES
COUNTRY MUSIC
MELVILLE MILTON MURRELL

Hamilton County
Size: 550 Square Miles (352,000 acres)
Established: 1819
Named For: Alexander Hamilton, the U.S.A.'s first Secretary of the Treasury
County Seat: CHATTANOOGA
Other Major Cities, Towns, or Communities:
East Ridge
Red Bank
Soddy-Daisy
Signal Mountain
Collegedale
Tiftonia
Lookout Mountain
Ooltewah
Sale Creek
Refer to: Gilbert E. Govan and James W. Livingood, *The Chattanooga Country, 1540-1951: From Tomahawks to TVA*, New York: Dutton, 1952 (Revised 1963, Chapel Hill: University of North Carolina Press; Third edition, 1977, Knoxville: University of Tennessee Press).
See also: EMMA BELL MILES
TVA NUCLEAR PLANTS

Hancock County
Size: 230 Square Miles (147,200 acres)
Established: 1844
Named For: John Hancock, first signer of the Declaration of Independence
County Seat: Sneedville
Other Major Cities, Towns, or Communities:
Kyles Ford
Treadway
Evanston
Mulberry Gap
Luther
Big Creek
See also: BLUEGRASS MUSIC
ALEX STEWART

George Washington Harris (March 30, 1814 - December 10, 1869), creator of *Sut Lovingood's Yarns*, is recognized today as perhaps the most gifted of the humorists of the Old Southwest and, increasingly, as one of the great comic geniuses of America. He was born in Alleghany City, Pennsylvania, the son of George W. and Margaret Glover Bell Harris. In 1819, he moved to KNOXVILLE under the custody of his half-brother Samuel Bell. As a young man Harris served as an apprentice to his half-brother, who operated a metalworking shop in Knoxville at the corners of Main and Prince Streets. He achieved considerable skill in this trade, and even built a working model of a steamboat. Upon completion of his apprenticeship at the age of nineteen, he became captain of the steamboat *Knoxville.* In 1835 he married Mary Emeline Nance, daughter of Pryor Nance who was owner of the Knoxville race track.

In 1839 Harris bought 375 acres of land in BLOUNT COUNTY, but left farming in the early 1840's to open a metalworking shop in Knoxville. During this time he began to submit political articles to the Knoxville *Argus* and "sporting epistles" to William T. Porter's *Spirit of the Times.* The first Sut Lovingood Yarn, "Sut Lovengood's Daddy 'Acting Horse' ", appeared in the *Spirit* in 1854. The character Sut was supposedly based upon was Sut Miller, whom Harris had met while working near THE COPPER MINES of southeastern Tennessee.

An ardent secessionist, Harris submitted anti-Lincoln sketches to the *Nashville Union and American.* During the CIVIL WAR he lived in several southern cities. His one book, the *Yarns,* was published in 1867, the same year of the death of his first wife. He remarried in October 1869 to Jane E. Pride and died mysteriously in December following a railroad business trip to Lynchburg, Virginia. The manuscript *High Times and Hard Times,* which Harris had taken with him to inquire about printing costs at the Lynchburg *Republican,* has never been found.

The *Yarns,* on which Harris's fame is based, is characterized by the brilliant use of metaphor and an irreverent form of satire reminiscent of Rabelais and Swift. Mark Twain admired Harris's writing and included one of the tales in his *Library of Humor.* Throughout the *Yarns* Sut, the hero, is practical joker, archetypal trickster, and hillbilly rolled into one. He more than adequately illustrates "universal onregenerit human nater" in himself and others. William Dean Howells, reflecting the proper attitude of the Genteel Tradition, found the ribald Lovingood stories coarse, but following the praise by such renowned critics of American culture as Bernard DeVoto, Walter Blair, and F.O. Matthiessen, there has been a revival of interest in Harris that now seems certain to last indefinitely. Even detractors of Sut Lovingood acknowledge Harris's unusual skill as a craftsman. Edmund Wilson, for instance, called the *Yarns* "the most repellent book of any real literary merit in American Literature." Recent critics such as Noel Polk consider the *Yarns* to be a major work of art of the nineteenth century. With the new emphasis on Appalachian Studies, Harris's reputation, already well-established, is sure to grow.

Robert J. Higgs

Refer to: Milton Rickels, *George Washington Harris,* New York: Twayne, 1965; and M. Thomas Inge, ed. *Sut Lovingood Yarns,* New Haven, Conn.: College and University Press, 1966.

See also: APPALACHIAN LITERATURE
STEAMBOATS, FLATBOATS, RAFTS AND CANOES

Homer Harris, Stardust, and Old Martin Guitar (May 18, 1909 -). Homer Harris, known as the seven-foot

Courtesy Mrs. Clarence Bowling

Homer Harris on WBIX radio in Muskogee, Oklahoma.

cowboy of RADIO, television, stage and screen, was born along Big Creek in COCKE COUNTY, between Del Rio and Hartford. His parents were David M. and Debbie Laws Harris. In 1936 he won a talent contest in Dallas, Texas, where he paid $55 for a Martin Guitar. The next year, he landed a job singing on WBIX radio from the mezzanine of Montgomery Ward department store in Muskogee, Oklahoma. Homer Harris moved to California in 1938 and played at dude ranches and night clubs, including a six-week engagement at Club Fortune in Reno, Nevada. He acted as an extra in several Hollywood westerns and entertained in Palm Springs at Shirley Temple's sixth birthday.

During World War II, Harris participated in many GI shows. He lost his Martin Guitar near Paris, but it was found in 1945 with other special service equipment at Karlsrue, Germany. After the war, Homer returned to East Tennessee and joined Lowell Blanchard's "Mid-Day Merry-Go-Round" radio show on WNOX. Harris's guitar was stolen twice from the radio station; each time, he found it in a pawn shop and redeemed it for $15. In 1949, Homer moved to Cas Walker's radio show on WIVK-WROL. He bought from Cas a 3-year old trick horse named Stardust, known in later years for such feats as playing the Martin guitar with his nose.

After more radio work in Lexington, Kentucky, Harris moved to JOHNSON CITY in 1953 and joined the "Bonnie Lou and Buster Show" on WJHL-TV. He went on to tour across the South with his horse and guitar, then returned to KNOXVILLE as part of Cas Walker's television shows on WATE and WBIR. During the 1960's, Homer Harris and Stardust entertained at elementary schools throughout the region. Stardust died in 1973 at the age of 29, but 3-year old Stardust, Jr. took over. Four years later, Homer Harris underwent open-heart surgery, an operation which gave him a light stroke and partial loss of finger mobility. He was forced to curtail his guitar playing and retired in 1978.

About the same time, Harris accidentally ran over his Martin guitar with the wheel of his horse trailer. The Martin's hard top case saved it from being crushed. Since then, the guitar has been restored as a collector's item. Says Harris: "It sounds better now than it did when it was new."

Dorothy H. Bowling

The Harris Mill. David M. "Doc" Harris (1873 - 1953) of COCKE COUNTY, saddlebag doctor, schoolteacher, and Old Harp singer, was the son of Rev. William Logan Harris from Parrottsville. While a teenager, David once carried a sack of corn on his shoulder all the way from the Fifteenth Community along Big Creek across Hog Back Mountain to a grist mill at Edwina. During this trek, he conceived the idea of building a water wheel and grist mill on the Gulf Fork of Big Creek. In about 1900, Harris bought 30 acres on Gulf Fork, where he taught school and lived as a bachelor until he married Debbie Laws in February of 1906. They raised five children: Nora, Homer, Oscar, Dorothy, and Oran.

In 1915 David Harris, carpenter W.C. Duckett, and other community residents completed a dam across Big Creek; a 2,000 foot waterway or "race" made at various points of rock and cement, earth, or wood; an overshot water wheel almost twenty feet high,

The Harris mill. Left to right: Mrs. Black and son, Mrs. Harris holding son Oscar, Homer, Nora, Canada Duckett with brace and bit, and Mr. Harris.

Courtesy Mrs. Clarence Bowling

run by water from the race pouring into "buckets" at the top of the wheel; and the mill itself, a maze of cogs and gears operating a pair of millstones three feet thick. Later, Harris added a sawmill and a shingle mill which also derived power from the main shaft turned by the overshot wheel.

The Harris mill ground mostly corn. A gallon of "toll" or payment, measured from a half-gallon wooden box, was taken from each bushel ground. Because Doc Harris's other duties took him frequently away from home, Mrs. Harris operated the mill most of the time. Some individuals brought in rye grain to be ground to "cap" their moonshine stills. In these cases, it was necessary for Mrs. Harris to grind some of her toll corn to clear the rye from the mill and from the next person's "turn".

To keep the water wheel from freezing in winter, the race would be closed off at the dam. Mrs. Harris frequently broke ice at the dam in order to raise the millrace gate and service a customer. In warmer seasons, the children loved to walk up the buckets on the wheel and ride as fast as they could. About once a year, the local millwrights removed the top millstone and sharpened both rocks with hammer and chisel, recutting the grooves that fanned out from the center hole.

During the 1930's, Harris hooked a generator to a smaller, companion mill. The generator supplied power for electric lights and RADIO, but power on this small scale soon gave way to other means. When the children joined the armed services or moved to KNOXVILLE and other towns, the Harris family mill like many mills just faded away.

Oran Harris
Dorothy Harris Bowling

See also: ALFRED BUFFAT HOMESTEAD AND MILL
HOMER HARRIS, STARDUST, AND OLD MARTIN GUITAR
OLD HARP SINGING

Mildred Haun (January 6, 1911 - December 20, 1966), writer and editor, was born in HAMBLEN COUNTY. Until the age of 16, she lived with her family in Haun Hollow in the Unaka Mountains of COCKE COUNTY. Daughter of James Enzor Haun and Margaret Ellen Haun, Mildred Eunice grew up amidst the folklore—the music, superstitions and tales—of southern APPALACHIA. In 1927, intending to become a trained midwife and return to the mountains, she left Cocke County to live with an aunt and uncle near Nashville. She attended Franklin High School and then Vanderbilt University. At Vanderbilt, Mildred studied under such teachers as John Crowe Ransom and Robert Penn Warren. She began writing stories set in the mountain world of her childhood. After graduating from Vanderbilt in 1935, she continued to write stories while teaching at Franklin High. Also during this time, and under Donald Davidson's direction, she edited her extensive master's thesis entitled "Cocke County Ballads and Songs".

By the end of the 1930's, with the aid of a fellowship to the University of Iowa, Mildred Haun had assembled a book-length collection of her mountain stories. She gave these stories a unifying point of view in the character of midwife Mary Dorthula White.

Bobbs-Merrill published *The Hawk's Done Gone* in 1940. Through the next decade, Mildred Haun reviewed books for *The Nashville Tennessean*, assisted Allen Tate in editing *The Sewanee Review*, and helped her mother farm back in Haun Hollow. From 1950 to 1957, she worked in the Technical Data Division of the Arnold Engineering Development Center in Middle Tennnessee. Until her death in Washington, she wrote technical releases and papers for such agencies as the U.S. Department of Agriculture. But Mildred Haun's fiction was the great achievement of her life. Her stories combine rural realism with a harrowing sense of superstition, witchcraft, and fatalism. Her faithful attention to dialect, and her sensitive treatment of such subjects as the MELUNGEONS, remain in Haun's stories as part of her powerful preservation of East Tennessee life and culture.

Jim Stokely

Refer to: Herschel Gower, ed. *The Hawk's Done Gone and Other Stories*, with an Introduction by Herschel Gower, Nashville: Vanderbilt University Press, 1968; Mildred Haun, "Cocke County Ballads and Songs," Vanderbilt University thesis, 1937; and Stephen Glenn McLeod, "The Bottom of the Night: A Study of Mildred Haun," Vanderbilt University thesis, 1973.

See also: APPALACHIAN LITERATURE
HATTIE HARRISON GADDIS

Hawkins County

Size: 480 Square Miles (307,200 acres)
Established: 1786
Named For: Benjamin Hawkins, North Carolina representative in the Continental Congress
County Seat: Rogersville
Other Major Cities, Towns, or Communities:
Church Hill
Mount Carmel
Surgoinsville

Rogersville, county seat of Hawkins County, 1875.

Courtesy Rowan Studios, Rogersville

Courtesy Rowan Studios, Rogersville

The International Card and Label Company's plant in Hawkins County, formerly the Rogersville Knitting Mill.

BULLS GAP
PRESSMENS HOME
Mooresburg
Stanley Creek
St. Clair
Grassy Fork

Refer to: Hawkins County Bicentennial Committee, *200 Years, The Bicentennial Celebration of the U.S.A. — Hawkins County*, Rogersville, 1976

See also: AUSTINS MILL
BLUEGRASS MUSIC
EBBING AND FLOWING SPRING
TVA NUCLEAR PLANTS

Hawkins County mail carriers, 1902, responsible for the first free rural delivery of mail in the United States. Left to right: W.S. Armstrong, F.L. Shanks, Ed Lee, S.D. Mitchell.

Courtesy Rowan Studios, Rogersville

Courtesy Rowan Studios, Rogersville

Early well digging in Hawkins County.

Courtesy Rowan Studios, Rogersville

The Frank Hale Oil Company, Hawkins County, 1912.

Highlander Research and Education Center. In 1933, shortly after the first adults came to the Highlander Folk School, Highlander director Myles Horton was arrested in Wilder, Tennessee, during a bitterly fought coal strike. He was charged with "coming here, getting information, and going back and teaching it." Horton, now retired, would be the first to attest to the accuracy of the charge, for it very neatly describes the educational philosophy which has always guided the activities of Highlander. Over the years, the Highlander Research and Education Center has changed its name, location, staff and primary focus, but it has remained dedicated to the belief that education can be used as an active force to change society.

Begun in 1932 as a community school near Monteagle, Tennessee, on the southern end of the Cumberland Plateau, Highlander soon became singularly devoted to the labor union movement. Highlander published union newspapers, helped organize farmer unions in the South, and served as a center for training rank-and-file local leaders and shop stewards in southern unions. During the 1950's and 1960's, the school became actively involved in the civil rights movement. The 1970's were a period in which Highlander's focus shifted to community organizing in the Appalachian mountains. Throughout most of its history, Highlander has had to face red-baiting and racist attacks, arsons, arrests, and evictions, including investigations by the House Un-American Activities Committee and prosecution by the state of Tennessee in 1959.

Today, located on a 104-acre farm near New Market, Tennessee, the Highlander Center is both a meeting place for Appalachians who have particular grievances and a place where information about APPALACHIA's exploiters is assembled, publicized, and utilized. Frequent workshops are held at the Center, in a facility which can comfortably accommodate 30 participants overnight. The subjects of the workshops include community-controlled health clinics, food cooperatives, rural housing, mining and flood disasters, occupational health and safety, strip mining, and the economic issues surrounding energy and land control. The participants are usually mountain people who exchange ideas based on first-hand experience. In 1977 and 1978, 66 separate workshops and residential meetings were held at Highlander involving an estimated 1500 people.

Highlander's Resource Center has developed an active program of helping community and labor groups acquire the information resources they need for effective democratic action. Collective research, for example, has served as a basis for challenging the low taxation of vast coal company reserves. Portable videotaping has enabled groups to take their message to others. Educational programs in such environs as United Mine Workers health clinics and the Amalgamated Clothing and Textile Workers' KNOXVILLE headquarters have encouraged union members to confront environmental, occupational, and administrative problems. In all these efforts, Highlander's emphasis remains on training and information rather than manpower and organization. The result of such an emphasis is a set of activist research programs bound together by the notion that information is power.

In addition to providing technical skills, Highlander uses history, music, and culture to support and encourage the continuing struggle for labor justice. Highlander's ultimate goal is to build a unified movement for change in the mountains, a movement that would recognize the need and have the ability to reach out to groups in other parts of the country. Some critics charge that Highlander's methods are too incremental and fragmented to create such a movement; they argue that direct political action is the most efficient educational tool. But Highlander has never tried to answer such criticsm by claiming credit for changes in the South or in Appalachia. Highlander's supporters firmly believe that those who furnish ideas are as important in the process of change as those who put the ideas in practice.

Steve Fisher

Refer to: Frank Adams with Myles Horton, *Unearthing Seeds of Fire: The Idea of Highlander,* Winston-Salem, N.C.: John F. Blair, 1975; Guy and Candie Carawan, *Voices from the Mountains,* New York: Alfred A. Knopf, 1975; Steve Fisher, ed. *A Landless People in a Rural Region: A Reader on Land Ownership and Property Taxation in Appalachia,* New Market, TN: Highlander Center, 1979; and Helen Lewis, Linda Johnson and Donald Askins, eds. *Colonialism in Modern America: The Appalachian Case,* Boone, N.C.: The Appalachian Consortium Press, 1978.

See also: AGRICULTURE
BROADSIDE TV
COAL MINING
THE CONVICT LABOR (COAL CREEK) WARS
PRIMARY HEALTH CARE CENTERS
THE THREE STATES OF EAST TENNESSEE

Lewis Wickes Hine (September 26, 1874 - November 4, 1940). The photographs which Lewis Hine made in East Tennessee in 1933 vividly portray rural life and the early work on Norris Dam. In its first months, the TENNESSEE VALLEY AUTHORITY hired the nationally known photographer to document the dambuilding and its impact. During the fall of 1933, Hine took over one hundred pictures in Anderson and Union counties as well as some in Hawkins, Sevier and Sullivan counties. When bureaucrats wanted more technical shots, the assignment (Hine's last real work) did not continue. The most cohesive and eloquent group of photographs was taken around the UNION COUNTY community of LOYSTON, about to be inundated by Norris Lake. Hine recorded persisting folkways and strong family units, frequently gathered at the hearthside. The sturdy and numerous Stooksburys furnished some of Hine's best images. In contrast to the defeated Alabama sharecroppers photographed by Walker Evans for *Let Us Now Praise Famous Men* (1939), Hine's East Tennesseans appear as a self-reliant people.

Born in Oshkosh, Wisconsin, Hine began his photographic career just after the turn of the century. His first subjects were immigrants at Ellis Island and on New York's Lower East Side. Working for the National Child Labor Committee over the first two decades of the century, he crusaded against the exploitation of children in industry. Sometimes assuming disguises, Hine photographed children working under appalling conditions in cannery, mill and mine. After recording war-destroyed Europe, Hine in the 1920's selected as his theme dignity and craftsmanship among American workers. His most famous "work portraits" are those shot one hundred floors up at the Empire State Building, under construction in 1930.

A quarter century after his death, Hine's work began to attract attention nationally once again. In the late 1970's, TVA, the Tennessee State Museum and others began making Hine's East Tennessee photographs more widely known.

Anne Dempster Taylor

"W.R. Cole and family at home. Mr. Cole is night watchman for the new bunkhouses at Norris Dam. The Cole home is situated on land that will be utilized for the town of Norris. October 23, 1933."

Lewis Hine / Courtesy TVA

"Esco Glandon, a renter, lives at Bridges Chapel on land that will be islanded by the Norris Dam reservoir. His son has developed some talent in drawing. Note the drawings along the mantel. October 31, 1933."

Lewis Hine / Courtesy TVA

Lewis Hine / Courtesy TVA

"Family group of Fletcher Carden, Andersonville, also a night watchman. His home, also on the Norris site, will be moved. Carden has 12 children. He is shown here repairing shoes at the fireside. November 8, 1933."

"The home of Mrs. Jacob Stooksbury, Loyston. Many of the furnishings are characteristic of the homes in the region—the oil lamps, the spinning wheel, the wickerwork chairs, the embroidery on the mantel. November 23, 1933."

Lewis Hine / Courtesy TVA

Refer to: Judith Mara Gutman, *Lewis W. Hine and the American Social Conscience*, New York: Walker and Company, 1967.
See also: FINE ARTS

Ben W. Hooper (October 13, 1870 - April 18, 1957). Bennie Walter Wade, the illegitimate son of Sarah Wade and of Dr. Lemuel Washington Hooper, was born in Newport, Tennessee. Soon after Bennie's birth, the Wade family moved to DANDRIDGE, then to Mossy Creek (present-day Jefferson City), then to New Market, then to the slums of KNOXVILLE. Sarah Wade was persuaded by a Knoxville resident to place her son in St. John's Orphanage, an institution affiliated with St. John's Episcopal Church. There he received his first formal academic and religious instruction. Dr. Hooper located his son in the orphanage, adopted him and changed the boy's name to Ben Walter Hooper. Ben Walter Hooper later became the 35th governor of the state of Tennessee.

Hooper attended Newport Academy and graduated from CARSON-NEWMAN COLLEGE in 1890. He read law under Newport attorney Horace Nelson Cate, was elected in 1892 as state representative from COCKE COUNTY, and gained admission to the bar two years later. The same year, Hooper's constituents reelected him as their representative. He served as captain in the Spanish-American War of 1898-9, then married Anna Belle Jones in 1901. Hooper's Newport law practice was interrupted five years later, when he

Ben Hooper speaking in front of Mossy Creek Bank, Jefferson City, early 1910's.

Courtesy William E. Tate

was appointed Assistant U.S. Attorney for the Eastern Tennessee District. He continued in this office until he resigned in 1910 to run for governor.

Ben Hooper's gubernatorial campaign originated almost by accident. Tennessee at that time was hotly debating prohibition, and Newport became the site of debate between two candidates for the Republican gubernatorial nomination. Hooper was scheduled only to introduce Arch Hughes, the prohibitionist, but when candidate Jesse M. Littleton denounced both Hughes and Hooper, the latter vigorously answered Littleton and denounced the entire state political machine controlled by liquor Democrats. It was the effectiveness of this reply, recognized by Sevierville newspaper editor William Montgomery, which seriously introduced Hooper's name as a candidate.

Exploiting factionalism in the Democratic Party, Ben Hooper defeated Robert L. Taylor by 133,976 votes to 121,694 votes and was inaugurated in Nashville's Ryman Auditorium. Hooper was reelected as governor in 1912, but was defeated by Thomas C. Rye in 1914. Governor Hooper supported paroles for deserving prisoners, bank regulation, temperance legislation, and judicially ordered enforcement of existing legislation. He opposed such practices as the issuance of free railway passes to public officials.

Hooper and his family returned in 1915 to Newport, where he resumed his practice of law. In 1916 and 1934, he ran for U.S. Senator, but Kenneth D. McKellar defeated him each time. In 1920 President Warren G. Harding appointed Hooper to the United States Railroad Labor Board in Chicago, a position from which Hooper averted a major Class I railway strike called for October 30, 1921. In 1926 the Hooper family again returned to Newport. Ben Hooper became a chief land buyer for the nascent GREAT SMOKY MOUNTAINS NATIONAL PARK. He also wrote his autobiography, became active in community clubs, and in 1953 was elected vice-president of Tennessee's Limited Constitutional Convention. He died of pneumonia.

Edward R. Walker III

Refer to: Everett Robert Boyce, ed. *The Unwanted Boy: The Autobiography of Governor Ben W. Hooper*, Knoxville: University of Tennessee Press, 1963.
See also: CORDELL HULL
ESTES KEFAUVER
BOB AND ALF TAYLOR: KNIGHTS OF THE ROSES

House Mountain, 2100 feet high, rises in solitary splendor from the Great Valley of East Tennessee. It is located eight miles northeast of KNOXVILLE, about midway between the communities of Mascot and Corryton. Erosion has separated House Mountain by over three miles from Clinch Mountain, its mother ridge. Animals on House Mountain range from migrating hawks and warblers to small mammals such as raccoons, squirrels, chipmunks, and rabbits. Plants include mountain laurel, huckleberry, trailing arbutus, pigeon-wheat moss, sedge and bluestem grasses, and more than twenty species of trees.

In 1971, the Tennessee General

Assembly passed a Natural Areas Act providing for a system of state nature preserves. Some preserves, such as Savage Gulf on the Cumberland Plateau, were classified as scientific-educational in nature, while Sewanee Natural Bridge and other areas satisfied scenic-recreational demands. Throughout the 1970's, various naturalists and planners supported by many Knoxille citizens and school groups worked to have House Mountain preserved as a scenic-recreational area. This activity clashed with the desires of those local landowners unwilling to sell their land to the state. Advocates of purchase countered that "the land" is not inherited from grandparents, only borrowed from grandchildren.

Jim Stokely

See also: FAUNA
FLORA
GEOGRAPHY
STATE PARKS

Sam Houston, the Liberator of Texas, spent his teenage years in BLOUNT COUNTY and in the nearby Cherokee villages. While his family was living in Virginia, his father selected a frontier farm a few miles south of Maryville. Relatives of the family had already located in the area, but Major Houston died before he could execute the move to the Tennessee home. His widow, however, made the move in 1807 with her nine children, when Sam was fourteen years old. During his first year in Blount County, Houston had brief ventures as a pupil in Porter Academy and as a clerk in a family store. He was dissatisfied with both experiences and found frontier farm life uninspiring. He left home at age fifteen to live for three years with the CHEROKEES in their village along the Little Tennessee River. This was in keeping with Houston's later self-evaluation that he had been a "wild and impetuous" youth. The Cherokees treated him kindly, named him "The Raven", and formally adopted him.

During his sojourn with the Cherokees, Sam Houston contracted debts with white traders. In order to pay these debts, he decided to become a schoolmaster. About six miles northeast of Maryville, there was a log cabin which the frontiersmen had built for school purposes in 1794. It was near a spring which discharged about one hundred gallons of water per hour, a real blessing for pupils and teacher during the summer months of school. The patrons of the community selected Houston as schoolmaster for the term which ran from May through November, 1812. The tuition rate for the whole term was eight dollars per pupil, to be paid partly in cash and partly in such items as corn and calico. Because of the outbreak of the War of 1812, Houston taught only one term. Today, the school site is listed officially on the National Register of Historic Places as the Sam Houston Schoolhouse.

In 1813, at the age of twenty, Houston left East Tennessee to become a volunteer in Andrew Jackson's army. He fought with Jackson at the Battle of Horseshoe Bend. As a political protege of Jackson, Houston was elected Governor of Tennessee in 1826. After a stint as government trader to the Cherokees, then living in the Territory of Arkansas, Houston left for the Mexican province of Texas in 1833. Two years later, he became Commander-in-Chief of the newly organized Texas Army. One month after the Mexican Army overwhelmed the Alamo in March of 1836, Sam Houston's forces launched a surprise attack against the Mexicans at San Jacinto River near the present-day city of Houston. Within fifteen minutes, the Americans had captured the Mexican President. The independent Republic of Texas was soon established, and Sam Houston became its first President. After Texas was admitted to the Union in 1845, Houston became one of the state's first U.S. Senators and served in that capacity for nearly fourteen years. He was elected Governor of Texas in 1859, was deposed from this position in 1861 because he declined to take a Confederate oath, then retired to private life until his death in 1863.

Lowell Giffen

Refer to: Donald Day and Harry H. Ullom, eds. *The Autobiography of Sam Houston*, Norman: University of Oklahoma Press, 1954; and Marquis James, *The Raven: A Biography of Sam Houston*, Indianapolis: Bobbs-Merrill, 1929.
See also: THE ONE-ROOM SCHOOL

Cordell Hull (October 2, 1871 - July 24, 1955). The "Father of the United Nations", winner of the Nobel Peace Prize in 1945, Cordell Hull was born in a rented log cabin in the western foothills of the Cumberland Plateau, near the line between Pickett and Overton counties. The third of five sons, he learned early in life that hard work and self-reliance were the keys to success. His father William Hull was a farmer, logger, and storekeeper who put Cordell to work piloting LOG RAFTS down the Obed and Cumberland rivers to Nashville. It was in Nashville where Cordell read his first newspaper and decided that he wanted a career in public affairs. He attended Montvale Academy in Celina, county seat of Clay County, and went on to college in Kentucky and National Normal University at Lebanon, Ohio. He passed his bar exam in 1891 and opened a law office in Celina.

Cordell Hull was elected to the state legislature in November of 1892, at the age of 21. During the Spanish-American War, he served three months in Cuba as a captain. Upon returning to Tennessee, he moved his law office to Gainesboro, county seat of Jackson County, and was soon appointed by the governor to fill a vacancy of the Fifth Judicial District. While a judge, Hull ran for U.S. Congress and won. With the exception of one term, he served as a U.S. Representative from 1907 to 1931. Through daily study, he developed an expertise in the field of tariff and taxation. He wrote, in 1913, the Federal income tax law and was also responsible for the graduated inheritance tax. Hull saw these taxes as a way of equitably distributing the tax burden, and of replacing revenue lost from a lowered tariff. As a member of Congress he was instrumental in lowering tariffs, which he felt helped special interest groups at the expense of the common man.

From 1921 to 1924, Cordell Hull was

chairman of the Democratic Party. He was Tennessee's favorite son for President in 1928. Two years later, he was elected to the U.S. Senate. In February of 1933, President Franklin Roosevelt appointed him Secretary of State. Secretary Hull improved relations with Latin America and, in the pursuit of free trade, authored the Reciprocal Trade Agreements. His work on plans for a United Nations led to the Nobel Prize. In the fall of 1944, Hull resigned his position. He spent his next eleven years writing his memoirs and visiting friends and relatives. He died of a stroke.

The Cordell Hull Birthplace and Memorial on State Highway 53 near Byrdstown contains a reconstruction of the log house in which Hull was born, along with many relics from his years in political life. The museum is open to the public during the summer months.

Jewel Tabor Jean

Refer to: Harold B. Hinton, *Cordell Hull, a Biography*, New York, 1942 (reprint, Garden City, N.Y.: Doubleday, 1942); and Cordell Hull with Andrew Berding, *The Memoirs of Cordell Hull,* 2 V., New York: Macmillan, 1948.

See also: BEN W. HOOPER
ESTES KEFAUVER
BOB AND ALF TAYLOR: KNIGHTS OF THE ROSES

J

Jack and the Beanstalk. *(This tale was told by Oscar Cotton, age 97, Paint Rock Route, Oneida, Tennessee. It was collected by Mrs. Flora Mae Hicks, Elk Valley, Tennessee, who says of it: "This is an old version I've never heard before. This man lives far into the mountains. I took a jeep to his mountain cabin December 31, 1954, and had him tell me this. He was very feeble.")*

Once upon a time there was a mother and her son Jack living alone in wealth. One night a great giant come to their house and took from them a bag of gold, their magic harp, and their little hen that laid golden eggs. All they had left was an old brown cow.

One morning his mother sent Jack to market to trade the old brown cow for some grub. Just at dusk one evening Jack returned home. His mother was anxious about Jack because they was no food in the cabin and she was hungry. When she saw Jack coming she went to the paling fence to wait for him. When he come near to her she said, "Jack, what did you get in trade for the old brown cow?"

Jack said:

I traded my cow for a little red calf
And in that trade I lost just half;
I traded my calf for a little pink pig
It wasn't worth much 'cause it wasn't very big;
I traded my pig to a little white mouse,
He wouldn't say please and he wouldn't keep house;
So I traded by mouse for a little white bean,
The prettiest bean you have ever seen.

Jack's mother was so angry she threw the little white bean through the window into the yard.

Next morning, when Jack looked out the window, he saw a great beanstalk growing in the yard, stretching up and up into the sky as far as he could see. Jack began to climb the beanstalk while his mother was gone in the woods to see if she could find something for them to eat. He climbed and climbed and climbed until he come to the top of the beanstalk. He saw such a tall building he decided it must be a giant's land. Jack walked up to this giant castle and knocked on the door. As soon as the door was opened Jack knew it was the giant's house and this was Mrs. Giant facing him. Jack said, "Good morning, Mrs. Giant. My name is Jack."

"Jack, you are a brave boy to come here," said Mrs. Giant as she listened for a moment. Then she whispered softly, "Jack, hide in this kettle quickly. I hear the giant coming!"

In come Mr. Giant, saying:

Fee, fie, foe, fum,
1, 2, 3, and here I come
Fum, foe, fie, fee,
Here I come, 1, 2, 3,
Bring my little hen

That lays the golden eggs!

Mrs. Giant brought the little hen that began to sing:

Cack, cack-a-dack,
Cack, cack-a-dack.

As the hen sang, the giant went to sleep.

Jack hopped out of the kettle and grabbed the little hen and away he ran. The little hen recognized Jack and she began to sing for him. This awoke the sleeping giant who chased Jack. Jack hurried home with the little hen. He ran in the house and said, "Look, mother, I've brought back the little hen that giant stole from us." The little hen sang for mother.

While mother was talking to the little hen, Jack climbed back up the beanstalk. When Mrs. Giant saw Jack at the door again she said, "Jack, the giant is very angry with you and he will soon be here. Hide in this kettle quickly."

Jack just had got in the kettle when he heard the giant saying:

Fee, fie, foe, fum
1, 2, 3, here I come,
Here I come, 1, 2, 3,
Bring me my magic harp!

Mrs. Giant brought the harp and it began to sing:

Harper, harper, where are you?
Come and play a tune or two;
In the summer or in the spring
Play the strings and I will sing!

As the harp sang these words the giant fell asleep.

Jack hopped out of the kettle and grabbed the harp and away he ran. The harp was so happy it began to sing louder. This woke the giant up and he began to chase Jack. Jack climbed down the beanstalk and ran to his mother and said, "Look, mother, I've brought back the golden harp the giant stole from us." The harp and the little hen were so glad to be home they sang together.

Then Jack started to climb the beanstalk again. He climbed right up to giant's land again. Jack heard the giant coming so he ran into the house and jumped in the kettle. The giant came in, saying:

Fee, fie, foe, fum,
1, 2, 3, and here I come;
Fum, foe, fie, fee,
Here I come, 1, 2, 3.
Bring me my money bag!

Mrs. Giant brought him the money bag. The giant said:

Money, money, sing to me!

The money sang:

Diamonds, rubies, emeralds too
Sparkling like the silver dew;
Count them over one by one
Sparkling like the sun.

This made the giant go to sleep. As soon as Jack heard him snoring, he jumped out of the kettle and grabbed the money bag off the table and ran. The money bag began to sing louder, and this woke the wicked giant. He was so angry with Jack that he intended to kill him this time. He was going to follow Jack home. Jack climbed faster and faster but he could see the old giant gaining on him. When Jack got near the ground he dropped the money bag so he could climb down faster. As he reached the ground his mother saw the giant after Jack so she ran and got an ax and Jack cut the beanstalk down with a great crash. The giant bounced back up into Giant's land.

They never saw him again, and Jack and his mother lived happily ever after.

Leonard Roberts

See also: LOG RAFTS
THE UNINVITED

Courtesy William E. Tate

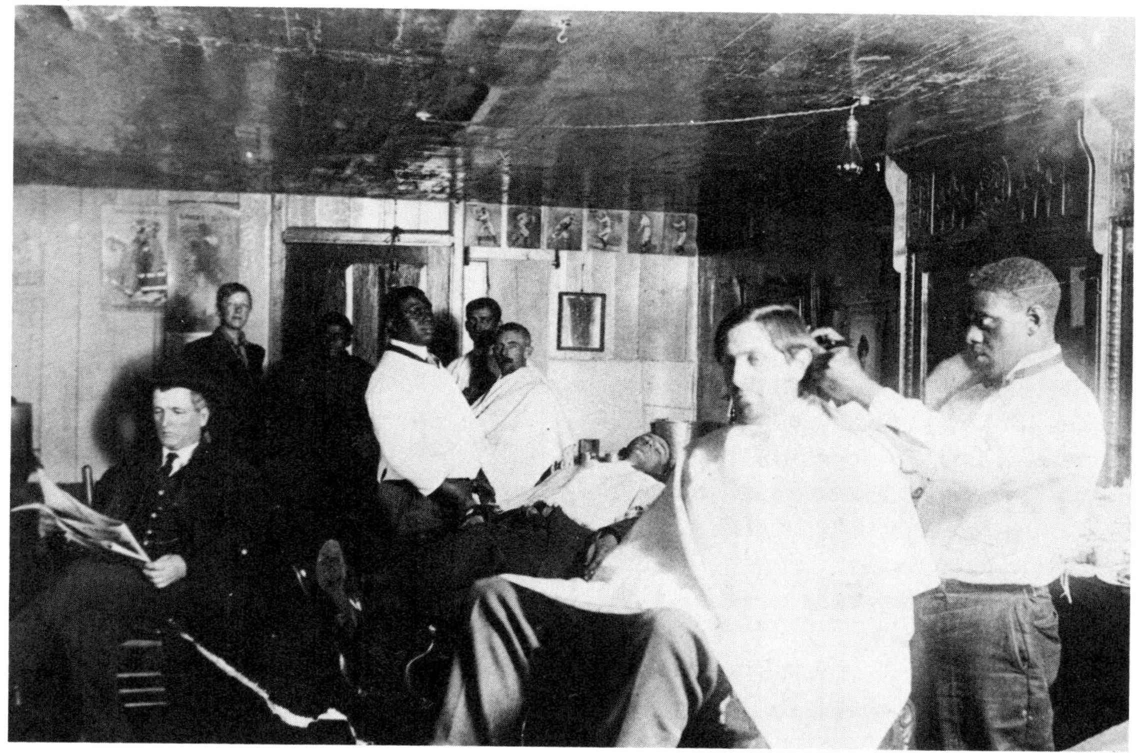

Louis Ingram's barber shop, Jefferson City, ca. 1911. The barber in the foreground is Roy Ingram, a veteran of the Spanish-American War. Roy's brother Louis, holding the razor strop, stands at the center of the group. The third barber is "Kid" Patterson; next to him, in front of the door, stands shoe shiner D.K. Mills. The man reading the newspaper is Chief of Police Hodge. At Louie's in those days, according to Jefferson City resident William E. Tate, baseball was all the talk.

Jefferson County

Size: 274 Square Miles (175,360 acres)

Established: 1792

Named for: Thomas Jefferson, author of the Declaration of Independence and the U.S.A.'s first Secretary of State

County Seat: DANDRIDGE

Other Major Cities, Towns, or Communities:

Jefferson City
White Pine
New Market
Chestnut Hill
Strawberry Plains
Willardtown
Mount Horeb

Refer to: The Bicentennial Committee of Jefferson County, Tennessee, *Heritage—Jefferson County,* Jefferson City, 1976.

See also: FRANCES HODGSON BURNETT
CARSON-NEWMAN COLLEGE
HIGHLANDER RESEARCH AND EDUCATION CENTER
JEFF DANIEL MARION
THE NEW MARKET TRAIN WRECK

The Jellico Explosion. On Friday, September 21, 1906, just before 8:00 a.m., a terrific explosion of a carload of dynamite left nine dead, two hundred injured, and property damage of a million dollars. At 5:30 that morning a Pennsylvania freight car, loaded with 450 boxes holding more than ten tons of high explosives, had arrived in Jellico from KNOXVILLE. Consigned to Rand Powder Company in Clairfield, the car had been sidetracked to the joint yards of the Southern Railway and the Louisville and Nashville, about a hundred yards from the Union Station.

Just after breakfast, a tremendous explosion demolished every house on the Kentucky side of Jellico and many on the Tennessee side. About 500 of the population of almost 2,000 were left homeless. The sound of the blast was heard for twenty miles. The explosion broke nearly every piece of glass within a mile and wrecked every business house on both sides of the state line. The Union depot was shattered into splinters. The hole where the car had stood measured about thirty feet in diameter and fully twenty feet deep.

Some of the dead men were so badly mutilated that it was impossible to identify them. A railway spike was driven through the center of a watch. Special trains of doctors were sent from Knoxville and Williamsburg, Kentucky. No one ever determined the cause of the explosion, but there were many rumors. One story held that three men were shooting at a mark and a bullet went wild. Another story had it that Walter Rogers, who was killed, was shooting at a bird and the shot hit the car. Another version said that a carload of pig iron was switched into the explosives car. Spontaneous combustion was also blamed. Some observers, noting that the saloons had been nearer the disaster center, believed it an act of God.

Mae Walker

Courtesy Archives of Appalachia, East Tennessee State University

Andrew Johnson

Andrew Johnson (December 29, 1808 - July 31, 1875), seventeenth President of the United States, was born in Raleigh, North Carolina. His father, Jacob Johnson, died when Andrew was three years old. At the age of ten, having never had a day's instruction at school, he was apprenticed to James J. Selby, a tailor in Raleigh. His apprenticeship precluded any hopes of schooling. During this period, however, Andrew received his first incentives to seek an education. A gentleman of Raleigh made a practice of sitting in the tailor shop and reading to the workmen from *The American Speaker*. These readings included selections from the great orators and writers of England and America. Speeches of Pitt, Burke, Fox and others excited great interest in the young apprentice. He set about the laborious task of learning to read. With difficulty he acquired the alphabet, and by assistance from his fellow workmen and neighbors, he progressed so far as to read with ordinary ease.

In 1824, just before the termination of his period of service, young Johnson left Raleigh and secured work in Laurens Courthouse, South Carolina. There he remained about twenty months. Johnson then returned to Raleigh and offered reparation to Selby, who required a bond of indemnity. Johnson could not give this, and he soon departed for the West and Tennessee. On a Saturday afternoon in September of 1826, a primitive one-horse wagon drawn by a blind pony entered the town of Greeneville, Tennessee. In the wagon or accompanying it were Mary McDonough Dougherty, mother of Andrew Johnson, her second husband Turner Dougherty, and Andrew himself, eighteen years of age.

On May 17, 1827, the young tailor married Eliza McCardle, the only child of a Scottish shoemaker. Mordecai Lincoln, magistrate and kinsman of Abraham Lincoln, conducted the wedding ceremony in nearby Warrensburg. Soon after, Johnson bought a tailor shop and rolled it from its location on Main Street to its present location on the corner of College and Depot. At the rear of the shop, Johnson constructed a two-room cabin. This cabin served as the Johnsons' first home in Greeneville.

Andrew Johnson became prominently identified with a debating society composed of leading townspeople—principally lawyers—and students from Greeneville College. In 1829 an election for aldermen was held in which the more aristocratic elements of Greeneville, the merchants and slave owners, were opposed by the mechanics and artisans. To the surprise of all, Andrew Johnson, a tailor, Blackstone McDannel, a plasterer, and Mordecai Lincoln, a tanner, were elected. This election led Johnson, a Democrat and successor to Andrew Jackson, into a series of public offices: Mayor of Greeneville (1834-35, 1837-39), State Representative (1835-37, 1839-41), State Senator (1841-43), and U.S. Representative (1843-53). Johnson used his time in Washington in studying at the Library of Congress rather than in "doing society". He remained in Congress for five terms and continued to improve his mind in all aspects.

Elected for two terms as Governor of Tennessee (1853-57), Johnson secured an act levying higher taxes for schools than ever before and thus earned the title of "The Father of Public Education in Tennessee". He supported the establishment of a Bureau of Agriculture, the building of RAILROADS, reforms in the banking and judicial departments, and the purchase of Andrew Jackson's home, The Hermitage, as a state shrine. In 1857, Johnson was elected by the Tennessee Legislature as United States Senator. The fateful election of 1860 saw Johnson and his followers come out for the Southern Democrat, John C. Breckinridge of Kentucky. With the election of Lincoln and the secession of South Carolina followed by the other Deep South states, the issue of secession arose in Tennessee.

On May 30, 1861, a convention assembled in KNOXVILLE for the purpose of keeping East Tennessee in the Union. On the second day of the meeting, Senator Johnson spoke for three hours, denouncing the Secession Party and eloquently appealing to the people to stand by the Union. The convention adjourned to reassemble June 17, 1861, in Greeneville. On June 8, Tennessee voted to leave the Union and join the Confederate States of America. Soon after, urged by his friends, Johnson left Greeneville for Washington by way of Cumberland Gap and Cincinnati. He was the only Southern Senator to retain his seat during the CIVIL WAR. For his loyalty to the Union, President Lincoln appointed Johnson to be Military Governor of Tennessee, with the rank of Brigadier General in the United States Army. Lincoln also chose Johnson as his Vice Presidential running mate in the 1864 presidential election. On the National Union ticket of that year appeared the names of Abraham Lincoln, a Republican, and Andrew Johnson, a War Democrat. Elected in November, Johnson had hardly been sworn in as Vice President when the assassination of Lincoln brought him to the highest office of the land.

As President, Andrew Johnson worked to carry out Lincoln's conciliatory theory of reconstruction. Johnson's bitter feud with the Radical Congress led to his impeachment and trial from March to May, 1868. The vote of Senator Edmund Ross of Kansas against conviction saved Johnson's Presidency. The Johnson family vacated the White House on the inauguration of Grant in 1869, and Johnson's farewell reception was a great personal triumph. It was said that thousands of people passed through the Executive Mansion to shake hands and extend farewell. Johnson's return to Greeneville was cause for great celebration in his hometown as well.

Shortly after his return to East Tennessee, Andrew Johnson plunged again into an active political career. In 1875, the Tennessee Legislature elected him once more to the U.S. Senate. After serving a short term in the Senate, Johnson returned to Greeneville and on July 28, 1875, went to CARTER COUNTY to visit his daughter Mary. Stricken with paralysis there, Johnson died three days later. On August 1, his body was brought back to Greeneville by rail, and on the next day, his funeral was attended by five thousand people. He was buried on Signal Hill, a gravesite he had picked at a much earlier time. His body was wrapped in the American flag, and his head was pillowed on his well-worn copy of the United States Constitution. Today, Greeneville harbors the Andrew Johnson National Historic Site, including the tailor shop, two residences and the burial place, now a National Cemetery.

Richard Harrison Doughty

Refer to: LeRoy P. Graf and Ralph W. Haskins, eds. *The Papers of Andrew Johnson*, 10 Volumes (projected), Knoxville: The University of Tennessee Press, 1967 to present; and Hans L. Trefousse, *Impeachment of a President: Andrew Johnson, the Blacks, and Reconstruction*, Knoxville: The University of Tennessee Press, 1975.

Johnson City, an urban center of northeastern Tennessee with an

Courtesy Archives of Appalachia, East Tennessee State University

The "Rag Time Opera" fair, downtown Johnson City, early 1900's.

estimated population of over 40,000, was not chartered under its present name until after the Civil War. The immediate area had been settled as early as the 1760's by some of the first pioneers of the region. These pioneers came into the area through the gap in the Stone Mountains now known as the Trade community in Johnson County. They followed buffalo trails and usually camped at the spring now located at the entrance to the Tipton Haynes historical site. Many travelers, including Daniel Boone, came via this route to other parts of present-day Tennessee and Kentucky. The settlers of the Johnson City area were part of both The Watauga Association in 1772 and The State of Franklin in the 1780's.

The first post office in the area was established at Green Meadows in 1832, with Henry Johnson the first postmaster. A second office at Blue Plum, about two miles from the Carter County line, followed in 1849. This post office was discontinued in 1859 and a new one established at Johnson's Depot. Ten years later, Johnson City received its charter from the state and named Henry Johnson its first mayor. It is not known where the first city hall was located, but for years city government was administered from a large brick building at the present site of *The Johnson City Press-Chronicle*. The entire

Courtesy Archives of Appalachia, East Tennessee State University

A residential street in Johnson City, 1920's.

downstairs of the former building was originally a market, with an auditorium and offices upstairs. Later, City Hall moved to East Main Street.

RAILROADS made Johnson City the principal city in WASHINGTON COUNTY. The East Tennessee and Virginia Railroad, completed in 1858, ran from KNOXVILLE to BRISTOL through Johnson's Tank. The East Tennessee and Western North Carolina Railroad, chartered after the Civil War, hauled iron ore from Cranberry, North Carolina, to the blast furnace in Johnson City. By 1908, what is now known as the Clinchfield Railroad constructed another line across the Blue Ridge Mountains of North Carolina. Transportation within Johnson City was handled by streetcars, which ran from the Carnegie Section through Main Street and eventually on to East Tennessee State Normal School. All the railroads carried passengers, but this service has been replaced by buses, airplanes, and private cars.

Both industry and general business have shown marked growth in Johnson City. The first large industry was a tannery established in 1882, followed the next year by Johnson City Foundry and Machine Works and by the Carnegie Furnace Company. Lumbering was also an early industry. Exum Furniture Company and Harris Manufacturing pioneered in the making of furniture and wood products. The first ice cream parlors were opened on Market Street by Tom Cox, a white man, and by Horace Ryan, a black man. Two early grocery stores, located on Main Street and operated by Jim Worley and by Evans and Hill, have given way to a variety of super markets. The New York Bargain Store and the Old Beehive have been replaced by such national department store chains as K-Mart, Sears, Parks-Belk, and J.C. Penney. Johnson City now has a diversified industrial and retail base.

Schools and churches multiplied as well. The Sinking Creek Baptist Church, organized in 1782, boasts the oldest church building in Tennessee. At one time, Baptists and Presbyterians worshipped together in a building on Main Street. The first school in Johnson City started on Rome Hill in 1864. Science Hill Male and Female Institute opened three years later above Knob Spring on land donated by Tipton Jobe, a pioneer of the area. This later became Science Hill High School. The East Tennessee State Normal School opened in 1911 with less than a hundred students and evolved by 1963 into EAST TENNESSEE STATE UNIVERSITY.

Cultural and recreational facilities have progressed from early horse racing and Jobe's Opera House on Main Street, through the Little Theatre, to almost every type of activity including water and winter sports. The first public library was started in one room by the Monday Club and staffed entirely by volunteers. With the help of Samuel Cole Williams, the Mayne Williams Library was built and led in turn to the new Johnson City Public Library. The first RADIO station, WJHL, started in 1938. WJHL was followed by three other radio stations and, in 1953, by the first television station: WJHL-TV. By public subscription, the John Sevier

Johnson City lumber yard, 1920's.

Courtesy Archives of Appalachia, East Tennessee State University

Courtesy Archives of Appalachia, East Tennessee State University

Interior of the Mathias William Jackson store, Mountain City, ca. 1902.

Hotel was opened in 1924 and now serves as a senior citizens center. Johnson City continues to be the center of what Landon C. Haynes, the first lawyer of the community, referred to as the "Beautiful Land of the Mountains".

May Ross McDowell

Refer to: Cordelia Pearl Archer, "History of the Schools of Johnson City, Tennessee, 1868-1950," East Tennessee State University thesis, 1953; and Samuel Cole Williams, *History of Johnson City and Its Environs*, Johnson City: Watauga, 1940.
See also: BLUEGRASS MUSIC
BROADSIDE TV
COUNTRY MUSIC

Johnson County
Size: 293 Square Miles (187,520 acres)
Established: 1836
Named For: Thomas Johnson, a leading citizen of CARTER COUNTY
County Seat: Mountain City
Other Major Cities, Towns, or Communities:
Butler
Doeville
Shady Valley
Laurel Bloomery
Trade
Bakers Gap

See also: FRANK PROFFITT

Jonesboro in WASHINGTON COUNTY played a central role in the early settlement of the frontier west of the Appalachian Mountains. After THE

Billy Glenn / Courtesy TVA

Main Street in Butler, June 13, 1947. Nearby Watauga Dam, under construction throughout 1947, forced the evacuation of Butler. The Watauga reservoir inundated Butler in 1948.

WATAUGA ASSOCIATION was subsumed in the Washington District, and after the District in turn became Washington County, North Carolina, a seat of justice was needed for the county. Local leaders chose a site with a good water supply, centrally located between the existing settlements of Watauga and Nolichucky. They named the new town "Jonesborough" after Willie Jones of Halifax, North Carolina, who had long favored recognition of western settlers. Chartered in 1779, with a town plan and building codes, Jonesboro became the first planned community in the United States west of the mountains. For a time Jonesboro served as capitol of THE STATE OF FRANKLIN, but the western territory eventually joined the Union in 1796 as the State of Tennessee. The Tennessee State Seal was designed in Jonesboro.

Jonesboro prospered from the start due to its prominent location on the Great Stage Road. The famous Chester Inn, built in 1797, was only one of several architecturally significant stage inns built in Jonesboro. The town attracted many future state and national leaders, including Andrew Jackson, who in 1788 was admitted to the practice of law in Jonesboro. A number of Federal and Greek Revival residences were constructed, as well as three magnificent Greek Revival churches during the 1840's. With the influx of people and ideas came a deep concern for important social issues. The first abolitionist paper in the United States, Elihu Embree's *Manumission Intelligencer*, began publication in Jonesboro in 1819. And strong-willed PARSON BROWNLOW, later Reconstruction Governor of Tennessee, published a newspaper in Jonesboro in the 1840's.

The greatest period of growth in Jonesboro was spurred by the coming of the East Tennessee and Virginia Railroad. This line, completed in 1858, connected Jonesboro with major cities in the North and East. During the CIVIL WAR, the town suffered severe shortages. The building from which salt was rationed, for example, is still called the "Salt House". Yet Jonesboro survived the war intact, with only a few minor skirmishes. After the war, the Victorian period saw a number of sophisticated Gothic Revival and Italianate houses built in Jonesboro, as well as most of the existing storefronts on Main Street. Wealthy merchant James H. Dosser built three majestic Italianate houses as wedding gifts for his children! Such local artisans as George Sprinkle added elaborate wooden porches to many older Federal buildings. A later return to the classically symmetric style produced, in 1913, the beautifully proportioned Washington County courthouse.

Jonesboro's buildings, in fact, portray

Main Street in Jonesboro, summer 1979.

Courtesy TVA

the whole historical range of ARCHITECTURE in East Tennessee: rustic log houses, fine Federal buildings with distinctive stepped gables, magnificent Greek Revival churches, picturesque Victorian storefronts and residences, and Neo-Classical commercial and public buildings. During the 1960's, private citizens and government officials realized that the pressures of modern development threatened to destroy Jonesboro's historic treasure. By 1970, they succeeded in making Jonesboro the first historic district in Tennessee and placing it on the National Register of Historic Places. Today, the non-profit Jonesboro Civic Trust promotes the preservation effort by working with both public and private sectors. A Historic Zoning Commission reviews all proposed changes in the District. Many buildings have been stabilized, some fully restored, and brick sidewalks, limestone curbs, and street lamps reconstructed. Jonesboro has remained a living vigorous town by building its future upon its past.

Ed Johnson

Refer to: Paul M. Fink, "The Rebirth of Jonesboro," in *Tennessee Historical Quarterly*, V.31 (1972), pp. 223-239.

K

Estes Kefauver (July 26, 1903 - August 10, 1963). Estes Kefauver was born in Madisonville, Tennessee. He developed an interest in public life at a very young age, due in part to the fact that his father was the mayor of Madisonville. The elder Kefauver also ran a hotel, where Estes heard many lawyers and politicians discussing the events of the day. At age nine, young Kefauver worked in his first political campaign—for Woodrow Wilson. He attended MONROE COUNTY public schools, then graduated from THE UNIVERSITY OF TENNESSEE. While attending the university, he served as president of the student body and editor of the school newspaper, and also starred on the football and track teams.

For a year after graduation, Estes Kefauver taught high school math and coached football in order to earn enough money to attend Yale Law School. He graduated with distinction in 1927 and practiced corporate law in CHATTANOOGA. In 1935 he met Nancy Pigott of Scotland, who was visiting her aunt in Chattanooga. When she returned to Glasgow, he followed. They were married in 1936. Three years later, Governor Prentice Cooper appointed Kefauver as State Revenue Commissioner, in which position Kefauver cut the state debt by $50 million while reducing taxes.

Estes Kefauver resigned his post as Commissioner and was elected Congressman from Tennessee's third district. By 1948 he was ready to run, contrary to his father's advice, for the U.S. Senate against the powerful political machine of Ed Crump. Kefauver won the election and gained recognition in the Senate as Chairman of the Crime Investigating Committee. Kefauver conducted exhaustive hearings of underworld characters and public officials which resulted in thousands of bookies being put out of business. Kefauver also supported the 1954 Supreme Court ruling on school desegregation and was considered a maverick by his fellow southern Senators. Many of these colleagues worked for his election defeat.

Kefauver's liberal stand concerning race relations helped earn him the disfavor of his party's hierarchy. In 1952, although Kefauver entered 16 Democratic presidential primaries and won 14, Adlai Stevenson was nominated at the convention. Kefauver was selected in 1956 as Stevenson's Vice Presidential running mate, but Dwight

Estes Kefauver

Eisenhower was reelected President.

Quickly rebounding from these defeats, Estes Kefauver returned to the Senate to work on what he seemed to do best: championing the cause of the little man, and working for more cooperation among nations of the world. He served on numerous committees which studied the causes of inflation and juvenile delinquency. He campaigned against pornography and opposed the seniority system in Congress. He supported consumer protection and federal aid to education. He was a staunch friend of the TENNESSEE VALLEY AUTHORITY and wanted to extend to other areas the idea of river control. In international affairs, he supported the reciprocal trade agreements, foreign aid programs, and the North Atlantic Treaty Organization. At the time of his death by massive heart attack, Estes Kefauver was investigating professional boxing and the high prices of prescription drugs. He was buried in the Kefauver family plot in Madisonville.

Jewel Tabor Jean

Refer to: Estes Kefauver, *Crime in America*, Garden City, N.Y.: Doubleday, 1951; Joseph Bruce Gorman, *Kefauver: A Political Biography*, New York: Oxford University Press, 1971; and Charles L. Fontenay, *Estes Kefauver: A Biography*, Knoxville: University of Tennessee Press, 1980.

See also: BEN W. HOOPER
CORDELL HULL
BOB AND ALF TAYLOR: KNIGHTS OF THE ROSES

Kingsport is a Southern Appalachian industrial city located on the Holston River in Sullivan and Hawkins counties of Upper East Tennessee. Instead of the planned town for 50,000, it is, as of 1975, a part of the new JOHNSON CITY-BRISTOL-Kingsport Standard Metropolitan Statistical Area that in 1977 had a population of more than 400,000 and rank of eighty-eighth among the SMSA's in the country. Kingsport's population alone in 1977 numbered only 33,860.

The modern city of Kingsport was an offshoot of the Carolina, Clinchfield & Ohio Railroad project, launched by George L. Carter of Hillsville, Virginia, and eventually completed under the direction of John B. Dennis of Blair and Company, New York City. Although Carter had recognized the potential of Kingsport's future location, he disposed of his land in Sullivan and Hawkins counties in 1914. The next year the Kingsport Improvement Corporation was chartered and acquired property from Kingsport Farms, Inc., for the establishment of the town. John B. Dennis held the principal interests in both companies, and it was he who financed the establishment of Kingsport. He also enlisted J. Fred Johnson, originally from Hillsville and Carter's brother-in-law, to become the principal promoter.

Dennis's prime consideration was the development of an industrial city that would create traffic for the railroad. While Dennis envisioned, financed, and directed the establishment of Kingsport, J. Fred Johnson, the native mountaineer, was the man with the ideas and ideals to made the plan a reality. Their expectations for success rested on the availability of raw materials, the completion of the railroad, the existence of an adequate

Church Circle, Kingsport, November 14, 1979.

Courtesy Tennessee Eastman

labor supply, and the concept of interlocking industries—that is, industries that cooperated with and complemented each other while developing non-local markets. Even with these advantages, they expected to create more than just a company town; they anticipated a diverse industrial community with a pleasant social and physical environment.

The "Kingsport spirit" was the term applied to the sense of community that Dennis and Johnson fomented. The city's inception as a planned industrial center contributed to the pervasive opinion among the early residents of the town that Kingsport was special, unique, and destined for greatness. Johnson and Dennis recruited an interesting array of experts to advise them. For the physical plan, they hired Dr. John Nolen; for the ARCHITECTURE, several reputable professionals including Clinton MacKenzie, Thomas Hastings, Grosvenor Atterbury, and Evarts Tracy. To enhance the beauty of the physical plan, Johnson and Dennis employed Lola Anderson (later Mrs. John B. Dennis), a graduate of the Landscape Art Course at Cornell University, to maintain a nursery and provide free advice for all residents of the town. To draft a model charter, the K.I.C. had their lawyers prepare the articles of incorporation, submitted the articles to several Southern authorities for comments, and finally asked the Bureau of Municipal Research in New York City to revise the document. To foster the development of education, the Improvement Company looked to Columbia University to help and organized a school system based on that of Gary, Indiana, incorporating the work, study, and play program of William Wirt. To safeguard the public health, Dennis and Johnson sought the cooperation of the Tennessee Board of Health, and Dr. T.B. Yancey was put at their disposal.

Dennis and Johnson arranged for the incorporation of Kingsport in 1917. After this establishment of a city manager-board of mayor and aldermen government, and the sale of property from the original 1,100-acre site, much of the responsibility for the city's future lay with public officials. Ten years after incorporation, Kingsport had ten industries, employing 3,383 workers, and two other factories under construction. By 1930, the census recorded 11,914 inhabitants. As the "model city" faced the grim years of the 1930's, it already had in operation one particular company—TENNESSEE EASTMAN—that would make Kingsport an enigma: an industrial city experiencing growth while the nation was in the throes of economic depression. During the decade of the 1940's, when Johnson and Dennis both died, Kingsport was still growing, partly as a result of the influx of construction workers and employees for the Holston Army Ammunition Plant.

The post-World War II situation in Kingsport is a common one in American urban history, marked by a deteriorating downtown, industrial pollution, the mushrooming of a "Golden Mile" of discount stores and fast food chains, annexation battles, shopping malls, and the absence of dynamic public leadership. But the picture is not entirely bleak, for

Kingsport has much to commend it: pleasant neighborhoods, service clubs and churches, a sound economic base, and renewed interest in the downtown area on the part of public officials, architects, businessmen, and other concerned citizens.

Margaret Ripley Wolfe

Refer to: Lisa Alther, *Kinflicks* (novel), New York: Knopf, 1976; Edward L. Ayers, "Northern Business and the Shape of Southern Progress: The Case of Tennessee's 'Model City'," in *Tennessee Historical Quarterly*, V.39, No.2 (Summer 1980), pp. 208-222; Kingsport Environmental Health Study Group, "Smells Like Money," in *Southern Exposure*, V.6, No.2 (Summer 1978), pp.59-67; Howard Long, *Kingsport: A Romance of Industry*, Kingsport: Sevier Press, 1928; and Margaret Ripley Wolfe, "J. Fred Johnson, His Town, and His People: A Case Study of Class Values, the Work Ethic and Technology in Southern Appalachia, 1916-1944," in *Appalachian Journal*, V.7, No.1-2 (Autumn-Winter 1979-80), pp.70-83.

See also: KINGSPORT PRESS
TENNESSEE EASTMAN

Lewis Hine / Courtesy TVA

Gaines McGlothin, farmer and Kingsport Press employee, cutting index tabs, November 10, 1933.

Kingsport Press, the nation's largest book manufacturing plant, was the brainchild of KINGSPORT planners John B. Dennis and Colonel James Blair, and of Joseph Sears, former president of the Appleton publishing house. Located near a plentiful supply of timber, many sawmills, a pulp mill owned by the Mead Corporation, and a new paper mill, Kingsport Press began book production in January of 1923. Its first run was the New Testament.

After researching the American book market, Press managers decided to produce hundreds of time-honored classics. By the spring of 1925, Kingsport Press had printed approximately thirty million ten-cent copies of 116 different classics. This output has been termed "America's biggest bargain in culture." The process of "perfect binding", developed at Kingsport Press, cut costs greatly by substituting glued for sewn pages. Today, customers of the Press include the nation's leading publishers.

Donna Ray Waggoner

Knox County

Size: 508 Square Miles (325,120 acres)
Established: 1792
Named For: Henry Knox, the U.S.A.'s first Secretary of War
County Seat: KNOXVILLE
Other Major Cities, Towns, or Communities:
Karns
Mascot

Outing of relatives and friends at Lyons Spring in Knox County, summer 1896. Crawford Gibson, Jean Crawford, and Hugh Ragsdale on mule, with Colonel and Mrs. S.B. Crawford at extreme right.

Courtesy C.M McClung Historical Collection, Lawson McGhee Library

Solway
Mount Olive
HALLS CROSSROADS
Trentville
Skaggston
Corryton
FARRAGUT
Riverdale

Refer to: Betsy Beeler Creekmore, *Knoxville*, Knoxville: University of Tennessee Press, 1958 (Second Edition, 1967; Third Edition, 1976); and Mary Utopia Rothrock, ed. *The French Broad-Holston Country: A History of Knox County, Tennessee*, Knoxville: East Tennessee Historical Society, 1946.

See also: ALFRED BUFFAT HOMESTEAD AND MILL
CONCORD
J.G.M. RAMSEY
SAWYERS FORT
THE SOUNDS OF RAILROADING

Knoxville lies in the heart of the Valley of East Tennessee, along the Tennessee River about five miles below the confluence of the Holston and French Broad rivers. It is approximately equidistant between the Great Smoky Mountains to the east and the Cumberland Range to the west. It is surrounded within thirty miles by six TENNESSEE VALLEY AUTHORITY lakes on the Tennessee River and its tributaries. Knoxville's corporate area is 77 square miles. Its estimated corporate population in 1979 was 182,000.

Knoxville became the focal point of European settlement in East Tennessee after the Revolutionary War. The first settlers on the site of Knoxville were the family of James and Mary Lawson White

Community night at Lonsdale in Knox County, late 1920's.

Courtesy Thompson Photographs, C.M. McClung Historical Collection, Lawson McGhee Library

Courtesy Thompson Photographs, C.M. McClung Historical Collection, Lawson McGhee Library

Downtown Knoxville, looking south on Gay Street, ca. 1915.

in 1786. General White had first explored the area two years earlier and purchased from North Carolina approximately two square miles in the present area of downtown Knoxville. At the time of White's exploration and settlement, Knoxville was under the jurisdiction of the self-declared STATE OF FRANKLIN.

In 1790 the site of Knoxville came under the jurisdiction of the Territory South of the River Ohio, commonly known as the Southwest Territory, and under the governorship of WILLIAM BLOUNT. The territorial capital was moved from Rocky Mount, near present JOHNSON CITY, to the site of Knoxville in 1791. Knoxville is considered to have been founded as a town in 1791, the year that streets and lots were laid out and sold in the vicinity of James White's fort, but Knoxville was not incorporated until 1815. Knoxville was the state's capital from Tennessee's admission to the Union in 1796 until 1811 and then again for approximately one year in 1817-1818. However, no state capitol building was ever erected in Knoxville.

Although Knoxville was the center of population, commerce, government, and culture in East Tennessee from the time of its first settlement, its population growth and economic growth were still very slow until the CIVIL WAR. Its handicap was lack of good transportation to the outside world. Its overland connection to the east coast was long and arduous, and it was cut off from North Carolina by mountains. It did not have dependable through river transportation to New Orleans because of Muscle Shoals in northern Alabama. Growth had to await the arrival of the East Tennessee and Georgia Railroad in the 1850's.

The new railroad, the Tennessee River, and a concentration of Union supporters in the Knoxville area made the city a focal point in the Civil War. Many Knoxvillians were involved in an attempt by East Tennessee in 1861 to secede from the Confederate State of Tennessee and become a separate state in the Union. The Confederates occupied Knoxville during the first half of the war. Union forces moved into the city in mid-1863 when the Confederates left it fairly unprotected. The Confederacy soon obtained reinforcements from CHATTANOOGA and placed Knoxville under a siege which imposed severe hardship on the populace. The Confederates attacked the Union fortress of Fort Sanders in a small-scale but bloody suicide assault on November 29, 1863. The defeated Confederate forces then withdrew from Knoxville for the duration of the war.

Knoxville began to flourish as a city soon after the Civil War. The main initial impetus for the growth was a network of RAILROADS to nearby Southern Appalachian coal fields. There was enough iron ore in the region to establish the Knoxville Iron Works, the city's first real industry which is still in Knoxville today. Marble and lumber were both available nearby in large quantities and Knoxville built up substantial extractive industries from these sources. The major industrial thrust in Knoxville came in the 1880's with a wave of cotton and woolen textile mills, supplied by cheap labor from the hills and mountains of Southern APPALACHIA. Concurrently, Knoxville was developing, with its rail network, into one of the leading wholesale centers in the South. The pulse of progress became so tremendous that Knoxville hosted in 1910 and 1913 major Appalachian Expositions which attracted national attention. Knoxville experienced a continuing commercial and industrial boom into the 1920's. In the late 1920's, however, when motor transport began to erode Knoxville's rail wholesale business, the city's marble, textile, and lumber industries declined.

When the Tennessee Valley

Knoxville resident.

Courtesy Thompson Photographs, C.M. McClung Historical Collection, Lawson McGhee Library

Courtesy Thompson Photographs, C.M. McClung Historical Collection, Lawson McGhee Library

Textile workers, Knoxville, early 20th century.

Authority was created in 1933 in the depth of the Great Depression, the Board of Directors chose Knoxville as its administrative headquarters, partly because of its intent that the construction of nearby Norris Dam be TVA's first major engineering project. The agency remains in downtown Knoxville today and is housed primarily in modern twin edifices on the crown of prominent Summit Hill. The electric power from dams built by TVA in the 1930's led to two major nearby wartime developments. The first was the expansion of the ALUMINUM CORPORATION OF AMERICA's plant at ALCOA into one of America's largest aluminum manufacturing centers. The second development, which had an even greater impact on Knoxville, was the choice of OAK RIDGE as the research and industrial site for the development of atomic bombs during World War II.

Immediately after World War II, the economy of Knoxville depended heavily on the continuing program under the Atomic Energy Commission at Oak Ridge, the expansion of THE UNIVERSITY OF TENNESSEE, and the growing economic activity induced by the new GREAT SMOKY MOUNTAINS NATIONAL PARK. The TVA program was rather slack until 1949 when TVA launched a huge program of construction of coal-fired generating plants. But private business in Knoxville remained primarily under the domination of historical family ownership and management. During the 1950's, Knoxville began developing industrial parks, encouraging the entry of national and regional firms into the

Charlie Krutch / Courtesy TVA

Pawn shop on Central Street, Knoxville, February 1935.

Knoxville economy, and exploring ways to preserve business in downtown Knoxville. During the 1960's and 1970's, Knoxville experienced a new economic surge with urban development projects, the opening of a civic center, and a general population expansion as a wide variety of industrial, scientific, and commercial establishments moved into Knoxville. The city was also expanding as a convention and tourist center.

Knoxville's diversified industrial economy includes the following major manufacturing establishments: Standard Knitting Mills, which processes raw cotton into finished knitted products, 2600 employees; Allied Chemical Corporation Automotive Products Division, which manufactures seat belts, 2000 employees; Fulton Sylphon Division of Robertshaw Controls, Inc., which manufactures automotive temperature and emission controls and bellows assemblies for numerous industries, 1300 employees; Rohm & Haas Tennessee Inc., which manufactures plexiglass, emulsions, and resins, 850 employees; and Dempster-Dumpster Systems Division of Carrier Corporation, which manufactures refuse handling equipment, 850 employees. There are numerous other companies encompassing textiles, chemicals, fertilizer, metals, and food processing industries. Knoxville is the national management headquarters of the Magnavox Corporation. Energy is a major component in the city's economy. For more than a century Knoxville has been a major center for the ownership, management, financing, and marketing of Appalachian coal. It is the headquarters for the Blue Diamond Coal Company. TVA, Oak Ridge, and The University of Tennessee have contributed heavily to a phenomenal increase in the production of electrical and nuclear energy.

The Knoxville area AGRICULTURE is diversified. Its distinctive crop is burley tobacco, of which the annual volume on the Knoxville market is about ten million pounds. Knoxville's external transportation facilities include the Southern Railway System, the Louisville & Nashville Railroad, Interstate highways I-40 and I-75, the navigation channel of the Tennessee River, and several passenger and freight airlines. Knoxville is an air international port of entry.

From its early founding, Knoxville's population has been bi-racial. The white population has historically been highly of Anglo-Saxon origin. However, the city's population has become more cosmopolitan during the 1960's and 1970's, drawing from numerous United States sources. Knoxville is still relatively low in ethnic groups of European, Latin-American, and Oriental origin. Knoxville's black population before the Civil War included both free blacks and slaves, and the city was the center of a manumission movement for slaves in the early nineteenth century. Blacks have throughout Knoxville's history constituted ten to fifteen percent of the urban population. The cultural influence of blacks on Knoxville continues primarily through KNOXVILLE COLLEGE, founded in 1875, and the Beck Cultural Exchange Center, founded in 1975.

Knoxville's primary historical attractions are the James White Fort, the WILLIAM BLOUNT Mansion, the JOHN SEVIER State Historical Park, the 1797 Ramsey House, the Confederate Hall of the United Daughters of the Confederacy, the former City Hall, and the former County Court House. Cultural attractions include the Dulin Art Galley and the Audigier Art Collection at The University of Tennessee.

Lowell Giffen

Refer to: Lucile Deaderick, ed. *Heart of the Valley: A History of Knoxville, Tennessee,* Knoxville: East Tennessee Historical Society, 1976; and Mary U. Rothrock, ed. *The French Broad-Holston Country: A History of Knox County, Tennessee,* Knoxville: East Tennessee Historical Society, 1946.

See also: JAMES AGEE
BLUEGRASS MUSIC
HARVEY BROOME
PARSON BROWNLOW
CHARLES CANSLER
COUNTRY MUSIC
JOHN CULLUM
LIZZIE CROZIER FRENCH
NIKKI GIOVANNI
GEORGE WASHINGTON HARRIS
KNOXVILLE THEATRES
JOSEPH WOOD KRUTCH
CORMAC McCARTHY
DAVID MADDEN
MAPLEHURST PARK
PATRICIA NEAL
RADIO
GEORGE AND ELIZABETH ROULSTONE

Aerial view of Knoxville, looking east, ca. 1960.

Courtesy Thompson Photographs, C.M. McClung Historical Collection, Lawson McGhee Library

Knoxville College, founded in 1875 and chartered by the State of Tennessee in 1901, is the outgrowth of the missionary effort of the United Presbyterian Church of North America to promote religious, moral, and educational leadership among the freedmen. The Freedman's Board of that denomination, recognizing that without qualified teachers and ministers there could be no significant answer to the problem of effectively educating millions of blacks, sent representatives to explore the South for a suitable location. They chose KNOXVILLE as the best site for a normal school, because of its prospects for good race relationships and its opportunity for blacks. Longstreet's Hill, still scarred with rifle pits and trenches from the CIVIL WAR, was chosen as the permanent site of the school. The first building was completed and dedicated in 1876.

Knoxville College set out initially to serve the most immediate and obvious needs of its students through elementary, trade, and high school training, as well as the normal school curriculum. The college began its wider service to the community by establishing a home and school on its campus for orphaned black children. By 1883 the institution offered twelve full years of schooling and by 1898, an additional four years in the medical and literary departments.

In 1890 Knoxville College was designated by the State of Tennessee to provide industrial training for black students. With funds provided under the Morrill Act, the College built and equipped facilities for training in mechanical arts and in AGRICULTURE. This arrangement lasted until 1913, when the State of Tennessee established a land-grant college for blacks in Nashville. By 1914 Knoxville College had a fully organized College of Arts and Sciences. It maintained an academy until 1931.

From the 1920's through the 1940's teacher-education emphasis remained primary. The training of ministers gradually declined, to be replaced by an expanding liberal-arts orientation in keeping with gradually widening professional opportunities for the institution's graduates. In 1957-58 Knoxville College was one of the first group of predominantly black institutions admitted to full membership in the Southern Association of Colleges and Schools. The College's official charter was amended in 1962 to remove legal racial admission restrictions, though it is clear that from its beginnings children of white faculty members had been among its students. Knoxville College has always maintained a bi-racial faculty and has been one of Knoxville's leading centers of black-white cultural exchange and joint participation in academic, social, and religious functions.

During the decade of the 1960's the college expanded its physical plant, diversified its program, and broadened its recruiting efforts to reach potential students from a wider geographic area and a greater range of backgrounds. Through cooperative relationships with THE UNIVERSITY OF TENNESSEE and OAK RIDGE National Laboratories, students have access to a number of major programs and individual courses which would have been otherwise unavailable in a small private college. Knoxville College offers bachelor's degrees in science, mathematics, education, sociology, psychology, political science, history, food and lodging administration, the humanities, music, business and commerce. It offers specialized training in computer science and pre-professional programs in medicine, law, theology, nursing, dentistry, and medical technology. Two-year programs leading to the Associate of Arts degree are available in pre-health biology and food biology and in general, legal and medical secretarial work. Students in pre-physical therapy can train a year past the Associate of Arts degree.

In 1979-80 Knoxville College enrolled 670 students from 27 states and five foreign countries. Its alumni have distinguished records of achievement in such professional fields as education, ministry, law, medicine, science, public administration, athletics, journalism, and business. The 1979 appraised value of the land and physical facilities of Knoxville College was in excess of twenty million dollars. The annual budget of the college in 1979-80 was $4,351,000. The plant includes a modern fine arts center, library, science hall, student center, and numerous dormitories.

Lois N. Clark
Lowell Giffen

See also: CHARLES CANSLER
NIKKI GIOVANNI

Knoxville Theatres, 1872-1942. Many theatres have played a part in KNOXVILLE's entertainment history. However, only three stand out as buildings of real architectural significance: Staub's, the Bijou, and the Tennessee. Several others were also important enough to deserve special mention.

Knoxville's first theatre to be erected was Staub's Opera House, which opened October 1, 1872. Built by Peter Staub, the impressive four story brick structure housed several stores on the Gay Street level with the theatre occupying the upper floors. Reports vary on the theatre's seating capacity, which was probably about 400 initially. The opening show was *William Tell, the Hero of Switzerland.* Appropriately, the house curtain depicted a scene of Switzerland near Staub's birthplace. Double cone reflector lights in the ceiling illuminated a fresco of Shakespeare looking down serenely upon the audience. When Peter Staub was called to the stage after the gala opening, he spoke only these words: "Ladies and gentlemen: I can build a house, and I can make a coat; but I cannot make a speech." Staub's Theatre, as it was then called, was remodeled in 1885. The orchestra floor was lowered to the Gay Street level, increasing the seating capacity to 900 or 1,000 according to newspaper accounts. Curiously, a seating chart in E.W. Crozier's *Knoxville Blue Book of 1894* shows only about 462 seats counting the four boxes. There were 18 rows in the orchestra, 4 aisles and 19 to 30 seats to a row. The top rows in the horseshoe balcony only held 88 seats. The theatre reopened September 21, 1885, with *Martha* starring Emma Abbott. Following her rendition of "The Last Rose of Summer", the packed audience gave her 18 curtain calls, a house record that still stood in 1901. Fritz Staub assumed management of the theatre in 1885, when his father was appointed Consul to Switzerland.

In 1901 Staub's was again enlarged. The entire interior was completely rebuilt when the auditorium was widened and balconies added. Only the Gay Street facade and north side wall were retained. The theatre now claimed 1,800 seats, although the actual capacity was probably closer to 1,500.

Staub's closed in September of 1919 when Marcus Loew assumed control of the house. A $100,000 remodeling program of the historic theatre included the installation of a 3-manual 16-rank Moller pipe organ for accompanying silent films, complete redecorating of the interior, and modernizing the exterior with a new marquee and entrance. It reopened as Loew's on February 20, 1920. However, only nineteen months later it changed hands again. A company headed by E.A. Booth reopened the theatre on October 3, 1921, as the Lyric. During the depression years, it became used less and less as it fell into a growing state of disrepair. It also became a fire hazard, and as the Bijou was being used now for touring shows, the Lyric became the weekend home of wrestling matches. In the 1940's the WNOX Tennessee Barn Dance was a regular Saturday night attraction. Plans for a new Knox Theatre on the Lyric site were announced by Wilby-Kincey in 1949, but never materialized. Demolition of the historic old house began in August, 1956, and by the end of October only brick rubble remained where such legendary names as Maude Adams, Ethel Barrymore, Sarah Bernhardt, John Drew, Otis Skinner and the Four Cohans once appeared.

In 1888, two theatres briefly opened in existing buildings. People's Theatre and an early Bijou opened at 26 Reservoir (Commerce) and 255 Crozier (Central), respectively, but these were gone by the following year. The first small movie theatres appeared in 1907. The Edison Theatorium, later known as the Marvel, Ole Bull and Grand, lasted until 1917. The Theoto, however, closed within the year. In rapid succession, 1908 saw the Columbia (renamed Empire in 1910), Crystal, Arcade and Lyceum (later Majestic) open, followed by the Bonita in 1910 and the Gay in 1911. The Gay, renamed the Strand in 1917, remained a downtown landmark until it closed in 1949. Of several small black theatres opening on Vine and Central from 1908 to 1913, none lasted for long except for the Gem. The Gem opened at 102 Vine in 1913 and did not close until 1962. Other magic names to cinema audiences were the Rex, Queen, Dixie, and Picto (renamed Liberty, Central, Cameo, Joy and Center). Most were converted "store front" theatres located on Gay Street. The Strand, remodeled in 1938, featured reruns and always a western and serial on weekends. It seated about 900 people on orchestra and balcony levels.

In May of 1908 construction began on the Bijou Theatre in the rear of the Auditorium Hotel, with extensive

Courtesy Wallace Baumann

The Bijou, ca. 1920.

remodeling of the front portion of the hotel being undertaken to provide the theatre with its handsome entrance and outer lobby. Built by C.B. Atkin, W.G. Brownlow and Jeanette Cowan at a cost of $50,000, the theatre was leased to the Bijou Company of Richmond, Virginia, operated by Jake Wells. Wells had joined Fritz Staub three years earlier in a company leasing and operating Staub's Theatre directly across Gay Street, and they decided that Knoxville was large enough for another modern theatre.

Wells's Bijou Theatre opened Monday, March 8, 1909, at 8:15 p.m., with George M. Cohan's musical production *Little Johnny Jones* featuring 70 singing and dancing people. Admission prices were 15¢, 25¢, 35¢ and 50¢. According to newspaper accounts, the theatre seated 1,503 people (565 seats on the orchestra floor, 448 seats in the balcony, 418 seats in the gallery, and 72 seats in the four loggias and six boxes). It was designed by Oakley, of Montgomery, Alabama, and contained a stage ample for any road productions: proscenium width 35 feet, height 27 feet, depth (footlights to rear wall) 32′8″. The theatre was almost an exact duplicate of Atlanta's Lyric Theatre, considered the handsomest theatre in the south. Special attention was given to the theatre's acoustics, sightlines to the

Courtesy Wallace Baumann

The Riviera and Gay Street, ca. 1923.

stage, and lighting. Many consider the Bijou's acoustics the finest in Knoxville even today. The decorative scheme featured predominant colors of olive green, gold and white, accented with buff trimming. Delicate fresco work of olive green and gold adorned the ceiling. The boxes, balcony and gallery were tastefully treated in white with gold accents, and the carpet and draperies in the boxes were of olive green cast in keeping with the artist's color conception of the house. Twelve dressing rooms with hot and cold running water, proper lighting, mirrors and wardrobes, adjoined the stage.

By 1911, movies were often shown on the bill with vaudeville and were occasionally the main attraction. B.F. Keith vaudeville was often featured, beginning in 1914, and the Peruchi Players began appearing at the Bijou on July 4, 1921, returning frequently for lengthy engagements until the Bijou closed in 1926. During the next six years, the house was dark; used cars were stored on the stage and auditorium ground floor. The Peruchi-Booth Company reopened the theatre briefly on September 5, 1932, but on December 23 the Bijou began a new policy of showing movies only. Wilby-Kincey leased the theatre from 1935 until December 10, 1964. During this time,

Courtesy Wallace Baumann

Interior of the Tennessee Theatre, October 1928.

the theatre was used as a second-run house and in 1947 began holding over the first-run films from the Tennessee. It was late in the 1930's that some of the greatest Broadway stars began appearing on the theatre's stage, now that the old Lyric had fallen from grace due to old age. Such memorable stars as Ethel and John Barrymore, Alfred Lunt and Lynn Fontanne, Tallulah Bankhead, Maurice Evans, Clifton Webb, Paul Lukas, Louis Calhern and Dorothy Gish appeared during a ten year span from 1937 to 1947. The seating capacity was now 1,237, not counting box seats. During the 1940's and early 1950's, the Bijou was the home of the Knoxville Symphony, the Knoxville Civic Music Association, and THE UNIVERSITY OF TENNESSEE Theatre productions. It was used briefly in 1963 by Simpson Theatres as a first-run house while the Riviera was being rebuilt after a fire. From April, 1965, until it closed in 1975, the Bijou showed "adult films". Knoxville Heritage purchased the historic building in 1976, saving it from threatened demolition. Today, a restored Bijou is once again an important part of Knoxville's entertainment scene.

Tennessee Enterprises, Inc. opened the Riviera on December 6, 1920, calling it "The Shrine of the Silent Art".

Knoxville's newest "movie theatre" cost $200,000, seated 1,006 on one floor, and boasted of the city's first Wurlitzer pipe organ. Stage shows were also featured on its small shallow stage during the 1920's and 1930's. The theatre was destroyed by fire on June 23, 1963, but was rebuilt and reopened January 23, 1964. In the rebuilt house, the stage was eliminated, curtains draped all walls, and new spacious seating reduced the capacity to 756 seats. The Riviera ended its 55-year life on January 7, 1976, with a film appropriately titled *Adios Amigos*. It was always a long narrow house with little distinctive architectural detail.

The late 1920's saw the opening of the Rialto (1927-1935) at 313 N. Gay, which moved to Market Square; and two neighborhood houses: the Rivoli (1928-1958), later the Gay, in Burlington, at 3811 McCalla, and the more impressive Booth (1928-1957) on West Cumberland Ave. The Booth was of Spanish design, seated 738 people, and was the only neighborhood house with an orchestra pit and stage to feature live acts during its early years. From 1935 it was operated by Wilby-Kincey, and its usual rerun movie fare was occasionally interspersed with first-run and foreign films.

A new era in Knoxville's theatre history dawned on Monday, October 1, 1928, at 12:30 p.m., when Publix Theatres proudly opened the doors of the palatial Tennessee Theatre. Designed by the Chicago firm of Graven & Mayger, it cost $1,000,000 to build and equip. Of Spanish-Moorish design, it seated 2,000 people and was advertised as "The South's Most Beautiful Theatre". One passes through an inner vestibule into the Grand Lobby over two stories in height, 34 feet wide and extending over half a city block to the orchestra foyer. Five huge chandeliers light the ornately designed hall with its green and coral terrazzo floor, at the end of which are impressive carpeted stairways on each side leading to the balcony. Many fine pieces of antique furniture and original oil paintings decorate the orchestra and balcony foyers, as well as the lower lounge areas.

The ceiling of the unusually wide auditorium features a large eliptical dome within a much larger one encircled by Moorish figures and griffens, silhouetted by striking cove lighting around the entire perimeter which changes color to create different moods. Of primary interest to theatregoers has always been the $50,000 3-manual, 14-rank Wurlitzer Pipe Organ. The large red and gold French console of Arabic design is on a lift at the left side of the orchestra pit. The 1,125 pipes and toy counter are located in ornately framed chambers on either side of the elaborately designed and lighted proscenium arch. The well equipped stage, with its 42 lines and three levels of dressing rooms, was termed "a paradise for theatre folk". The stage's proscenium width of 54 feet made it easily adaptable to the 48 foot Cinemascope Screen installed in October, 1953.

The opening show on October 1, 1928, featured Jean Wilson at the golden voiced Wurlitzer, Don Pedro and his Melody Boys orchestra and the stage show "Joy Bells", and on the silver magnascope screen Clara Bow in *The*

Fleet's In, with Vitaphone specialties. Admission prices for all of this were only 10¢ and 40¢ for matinees and 15¢ and 60¢ in the evenings. A special section in *The Knoxville Sunday Journal* heralded "Tennessee Theatre Palace of Splendor". An article proclaimed "Magnificent temple of amusement launches Knoxville into a new theatrical era," and a bank ad congratulated Publix on "the South's 'Little Roxy'—a veritable temple of pleasure!"

Some of the famous stars and shows to appear on the Tennessee's stage have been Van Arnham's Minstrels in 1932; Gene Austin, Tom Mix and Tony, Nick Lucus, and the Dan Fitch Revue in 1933; the A.B. Marcus Revue, Ray Teal and his Floridians, and Earl Carroll's Vanities in 1934; and Broadway touring shows *3 Men On A Horse*, *Mary of Scotland* with Helen Hayes, Philip Merivale and Pauline Frederick, *Ziegfeld Follies* with Fanny Brice, and Ben Blue in 1935. Glenn Miller and Vaughn Monroe came later with their bands, and Desi Arnaz, John Payne and Donald O'Connor made personal appearances in the 1940's. Several World Premieres have been held at the Tennessee, including *So This is Love* in 1953 with Kathryn Grayson, Walter Abel, Joan Weldon and Merv Griffen in attendance; *All The Way Home* in 1963 with Robert Preston and producer David Susskind present; and *The Fool Killer* in 1965 with stars Tony Perkins, Henry Hull and Arnold Moss adding lustre to the occasion.

Many famous organists have played the Tennessee's Mighty Wurlitzer Pipe Organ, including C. Sharpe Minor and Johnny Winters in the early years, and Lee Erwin and Lyn Larsen in the latter ones. Probably the organist best remembered by Knoxvillians is Billy Barnes, who was house organist from October 1, 1937 to March, 1942, and whose RADIO broadcasts from the theatre during these years and also from 1946 to 1950 were heard daily Monday through Friday.

On December 14, 1966, the theatre was closed for two weeks for refurbishment and reseating. Care was taken to preserve the original beauty and design of the theatre, which reopened Christmas Day with 1,545 seats. ABC Southeastern Theatres ended its operation of the Tennessee on November 1, 1977, and the house became dark for the first time in 49 years. A brief six-month operation in 1978 failed, and now William W. Akers has assumed the management of the theatre for the owner, Atkin Realty Co., presenting Hollywood classic movies and occasional stage shows. The grandeur of the past remains today, and views of Spanish balconies, stained glass windows, and the huge blue dome echoing the tones of the mighty organ still give one the feeling of having enjoyed a real experience.

Although the 1930's were years of economic depression, a surprising number of stage shows appeared at Knoxville theatres during these years. On occasion, the Tennessee, Riviera, Bijou, Strand, Roxy, Booth and Rialto all featured live entertainment. The Roxy (1933-1959) ended its 4-a-day vaudeville shows at 413-15 Union Avenue after fourteen continuous years. It was said to be the last theatre south of the Ohio River with daily stage shows. Cotton and Webfoot Watts were headliners for years, and many young moviegoers slipped in to see the Roxy's live acts knowing their parents would not approve.

Other movie houses opening in the 1930's and early 1940's were a second Rialto, on Market Square (1930-1945), the Palace, 4231 N. Broadway (1936-1948), the State, 1505 Washington Ave. (1937-1954), the Broadway, 2411 Broadway (1939-1957), the Park, 2301 Magnolia (opened 1938, now Studio One), the Sunset (later Ritz, Savoy and Booker-T), 1301 Western Ave. (1941-1946), and the Lee, 137 Tennessee Ave. (1942-1956).

A new time of theatre building followed World War II, with new neighborhood houses prospering until the advent of television caused their demise. Today, movie audiences find their cinema fare in compact movie complexes built in the 1970's along Kingston Pike. Two "real theatres" still remain on Knoxville's Gay Street: The Bijou and the Tennessee. One hopes these Knoxville institutions will be preserved as reminders of Knoxville's illustrious entertainment past.

Wallace W. Baumann

Joseph Wood Krutch (November 25, 1893 - May 22, 1970), the youngest of three sons of Edward and Adelaine Wood Krutch, was born in KNOXVILLE. His early interest in science was reflected in his reading at the local library and his pursuit of various simple experiments. The touring companies which brought vaudeville and drama to Knoxville provided his introduction to the arts, and his earliest published writings were reports of Knoxville box office receipts for *The Footlight* (in return for which he enjoyed a press pass to every show). In 1911 he entered THE UNIVERSITY OF TENNESSEE, where he concentrated in mathematics and busied himself extra-curricularly by holding editorial positions on the student newspaper and the undergraduate literary magazine. His memories of his Knoxville youth can be found in his autobiography, *More Lives Than One* (1962).

In 1915 Krutch left Knoxville for New York City, where he enrolled as a graduate student in English at Columbia University. His graduate studies were briefly interrupted by stateside service in the Army Psychological Corps, but by 1919 he had begun his dissertation on Restoration drama. A Columbia fellowship supported his research abroad; and during 1919-20 he travelled in England and France, accompanied by Mark Van Doren, a Columbia classmate who was to be a distinguished poet-critic and one of Krutch's closest lifelong friends.

Having completed his graduate studies, Krutch in 1920 joined the English faculty at Brooklyn Polytechnic Institute. His success as a teacher was modest. Hoping to write himself free of the academy, Krutch began to contribute essays and book reviews to periodicals of general circulation. His work appeared frequently in such distinguished journals as *The Literary Review* and the *Nation*. In 1924 he resigned his teaching position to become the *Nation*'s drama critic and Associate Editor. The following year he returned to Tennessee as the magazine's correspondent at THE SCOPES TRIAL in Dayton. His dispatches, highly critical of the intellectual and political climate which had led to the trial, earned him the notice of the *Knoxville Sentinel* which, in an editorial, said: "Knoxville will not reserve for him any niche in their future halls of fame."

In 1923 Krutch had married Marcelle Leguia, a Basque who some years before had come to the United States for nursing training and had been unable to return to France because of the War. Her professional training helped Krutch through the various illnesses which plagued him throughout his life, and her devotion to him remained undivided for nearly fifty years. One of her earliest gifts was the suggestion that they rent a summer home in Cornwall, Connecticut, whither to retreat from the urban bustle of Greenwich Village. Free from the distractions of literary journalism, Krutch there completed his first major book, the psychoanalytic biography *Edgar Allan Poe* (1926), which was well received. During summers in Cornwall, Krutch also wrote a series of essays which were collected as *The Modern Temper* (1929). Drawing together the insights that Krutch had gained during several years of book and drama reviewing, the book was widely acclaimed at publication and remains a classic statement of the spiritual and intellectual currency of its period.

At Cornwall, Krutch also developed an interest in nature. There, as later when he moved to Redding, Connecticut, he kept journals in which he recorded his minute observations of the FLORA and FAUNA around him. It would be many years before his interest in nature found literary expression. Meanwhile, Krutch's career floundered. The successes of the 1920's were not followed by equal successes in the 1930's. Two books of literary criticism—one a study of the novel; the other, an extended essay in aesthetics—received cool receptions. The radical politics of the decade were none Krutch could embrace, and his critiques of Communism appeared in the *Nation* as well as in *Was Europe a Success?* (1934). Nor was he any more enthusiastic over the political drama of the 1930's, which he encountered in his continued role of drama critic.

Disillusioned by the literary and intellectual world of the day, Krutch in 1937 reduced his commitment to the *Nation* and accepted a professorship of English at Columbia, where he taught courses in drama. The leisure of his professorship allowed him to write two fine literary biographies: one of Samuel Johnson (1944), the other of Henry David Thoreau (1948). His longstanding interest in nature and a more recent interest in nature writing inspired Krutch to try his own hand at the genre. He soon completed the essays for *The Twelve Seasons* (1949), his first book of nature essays. That book and another, *The Best of Two Worlds* (1953), celebrated the natural world of New England.

Meanwhile, Krutch was also discovering the Southwest. Partly for reasons of health, Krutch resigned his Columbia and *Nation* posts and in 1952 moved to Tucson. A prolific writer now that he was living wholly by the earnings of his typewriter, Krutch published numerous essays about nature in general and desert plants and animals in particular. He gleaned four books from this material. Krutch was also appearing regularly in such periodicals as the *Saturday Review* and the *American Scholar* with familiar essays, often tinged with social criticism. Two volumes in this vein were *Human Nature and the Human Condition* (1959) and *The Measure of Man* (1954). The latter reconsidered the pessimistic conclusions of his earlier *Modern Temper* and argued that man has capacities not fathomed by positivist, behaviorist science. For this book, Joseph Wood Krutch won the National Book Award. During his Tucson years, Krutch enjoyed many other honors and awards as well as a broad and admiring readership. When he died there in 1970, he was recognized as one of the leading men of letters of his day.

John D. Margolis

Refer to: Joseph Wood Krutch, *The Measure of Man*, Indianapolis: Bobbs-Merrill, 1954, *The Modern Temper*, N.Y.: Harcourt, Brace, 1929, and *More Lives Than One*, New York: W. Sloan, 1962; and John D. Margolis, *Joseph Wood Krutch: A Writer's Life*, Knoxville: University of Tennessee Press, 1980.
See also: FRANCES HODGSON BURNETT

L

Lee College in Cleveland, Tennessee, was founded by the Church of God on January 1, 1918. The Bible Training School, as Lee College was then known, occupied the council room of the church's general offices on Gaut Street. Mrs. Nora Chambers taught the twelve students who registered. The second term, which started in November, was greatly affected by the influenza epidemic then raging. Of seven students enrolled, one died of the dreaded disease.

After World War I, the school outgrew its facilities and moved twice within the town. Under the leadership of J.H. Walker, Sr., a high school was added in 1930 and the music program expanded. Enrollment included 131 regular students and 123 in the "musical normal school". By 1938 the school had outgrown its accommodations in Cleveland, so the 63-acre campus of Murphy Collegiate Institute was purchased and the school relocated in Sevierville, Tennessee. For the first time, the school enjoyed facilities constructed specifically for educational purposes. By 1941 enrollment had reached 385, with the larger number of students in the religious education division. That same year a junior college was begun, one of the first institutions of higher education started by a Pentecostal group. The school continued its growth and was soon taxing its quarters at Sevierville.

The school was relocated in Cleveland in 1947 on the newly purchased Bob Jones College campus, whose 20 acres had housed Centenary Female College, a Methodist institution, as early as 1885. The new college, with 28 buildings, was named in honor of Flavius J. Lee, a former president and leader in the Church of God. The high school received accreditation in 1948, as did the junior college twelve years later. In 1953, the school added a Bible College, which was fully accredited by 1959. Plans were initiated in 1965 — the same year the high school program was terminated — to expand the junior college into a four-year college of liberal arts and education. The Tennessee State Department of Education approved the proposal in 1968, and the Bible College and the College of Liberal Arts were combined into a single school comprised of three divisions: Arts and Sciences, Religion, and Teacher Education. One year later Lee College received full accreditation, reaffirmed in 1973 for a ten-year period.

Throughout succeeding years, Lee College has continued a long-range building and remodeling program which included a new science building, new dormitories, and the Charles W. Conn Center for the Performing Arts and Christian Ministries. Projected buildings include a field house for physical education and athletic events, and a joint library to be shared by Lee College and the Church of God School of Theology. A Continuing Education Program, jointly sponsored by Lee College and the Department of General Education of the Church of God, was initiated in 1976 to appeal to adults and lay workers who might otherwise not be able to attend college. With the current faculty nearing 70 full-time members, approximately 55 percent hold earned doctorate degrees in the areas of their teaching specialty. A nursing program is in the advanced planning stages, and students are expected to be actively enrolled for the program by 1981.

William R. Snell

See also: CARSON-NEWMAN COLLEGE
TENNESSEE WESLEYAN COLLEGE

Lenoir Car Works, once the most important industry in LOUDON COUNTY, began in 1904 in an area south of Lenoir City. The site, between the Tennessee River and Southern Railway's main line south from KNOXVILLE, had been designated for industrial use when the town was laid out in 1890. The Car Works, which built and repaired freight cars, was purchased in 1905 by Southern Railway. The railroad company later purchased a neighboring foundry that made train wheels. By 1907, the Car Works covered 33 acres, produced 10 to 12 cars per day, and employed about 500 men. Records of the period show that 75 percent of the people in the area depended on the plant for their living. Principal early buildings included the machine and blacksmith shops, the wood shop, the erecting shop, and a boiler and engine house.

The Lenoir Car Works labor force reached a peak of 2,700 men during World War I. In the mid-1920's, wooden freight cars were declared unsafe and orders began to decrease. Foundry operations were increased, so that even during the Depression, about 700 men worked in the brass foundry, the steel foundry, the grey iron foundry and a wheel foundry which produced 400 to 500 wheels per day. During World War II, the machine shop was turned into a second steel foundry. Much of its top-secret production consisted of castings necessary for freight ships and other craft.

The grey iron and steel foundries, which made castings for steam engines, were forced out of business in the late 1950's by the advent of the diesel engine. Steel and wrought iron wheels replaced iron wheels and caused the wheel foundry to close its doors in January of 1963. Early in 1980, the Sarten Metal Reclaiming Company purchased thousands of patterns and molds from the original pattern shop. Sarten moved many of the one-of-a-kind pieces to the Tennessee Valley Railroad Museum in CHATTANOOGA. Lenoir Car Works now employs less than twenty persons in assembling glued joint rails and producing brass journal bearings.

Patricia Boatner

See also: RAILROADS

Will G. and Helen H. Lenoir Museum. Not many of us live with a sense of being a part of history in the making. Will G. and Helen Hudson Lenoir did. Early in their married life, they began saving and collecting glass, FURNITURE, tools and Indian relics that were rapidly slipping into the past. They furnished their home in Philadelphia, Tennessee, with these items. Will G., a descendant of General William Lenoir who fought at the Battle of Kings Mountain, farmed and ran a gas station at Philadelphia. Helen Hudson, daughter of a Sweetwater postmaster and dairy farmer, was a school teacher and artist.

The Lenoirs also kept tourists in their home. When the Depression arrived, tourists stopped coming. Helen Hudson, like her fellow teachers, was paid in IOU's, and the highway was relocated behind Will G.'s gas station. At great sacrifice, the Lenoirs held together most of the collection because of their appreciation for the ingenuity and artistry that had produced the items. After the TENNESSEE VALLEY AUTHORITY opened up a new job at NORRIS, the Lenoirs moved there and

Wheel floor outside the wheel plant of the Lenoir Car Works, 1943.

Courtesy Ross Lee

had a sixth child. A favorite family pastime became driving through the countryside, inquiring whether "you have anything old you'd sell—old dishes, old bottles, old furniture, old tools." Most trips netted something, and often someone would be found only too glad to sell discarded "junk" from his smokehouse or barn to "that man who'd buy anything old."

The Lenoirs dreamed of a museum, but Helen died in 1960. Will G. continued to collect and keep alive the idea of permanent housing for the Lenoir Collection. During the 1960's, state officials agreed to accept the collection and put it on permanent public display in a building designed for that purpose. In 1975, about 10 years after the first offer to the State, the Will G. and Helen H. Lenoir Museum opened its doors at Norris Dam State Park. The 5000-piece Lenoir collection of traditional East Tennessee material culture is currently displayed in a number of settings to demonstrate various uses of the items. These Museum settings include an early kitchen, dining room, and bedroom, a section for farm tools and dairy utensils, a home fabric production center, cabinets for china and glass, and a country store.

Sarah Lenoir Hilten

See also: CHILDREN'S MUSEUM OF OAK RIDGE
MUSEUM OF APPALACHIA
MUSEUMS

Libraries. Sometimes, in the late afternoon when her third-grade class became too restless to study, Miss Sue Ellen Wolf would stop the drone of her lessons, ask one of the larger boys to poke up the fire a bit, and then say, "If you'll be quiet, I'll read to you for a while." Miss Wolf's library consisted of only two books. The favorite was *Miss Minerva and William Green Hill*, a tale about a small boy, his aunt, and a goat. The other was *Black Beauty*. She read both books over and over again. The children never tired of them. In fact, it never occurred to most of the children that other books existed, except the Bible. Miss Wolf taught in the St. Clair Grammar School, a one-story, wooden structure which had been converted from a house to serve the youngsters in the Holston Valley communities in HAWKINS COUNTY.

The time was 1930, and books and libraries were not highly regarded then in most parts of the Tennessee Valley. The high school at St. Clair was only a little better off for books than Miss Wolf's third grade. The ladies from the high school PTA had collected some damaged and imperfect copies of books from the KINGSPORT PRESS in nearby KINGSPORT. The books contained novels by Sir Walter Scott, Dickens, Hawthorne, Cooper, and George Eliot. Printed on thin paper in fine print, they often had a number of pages left out in assembly. But the PTA mothers apparently figured that if only 32 pages out of 480 were gone, they would hardly be missed. To this day, some of the students are probably still wondering whatever happened to Rowena in Scott's *Ivanhoe*.

The St. Clair School was quite typical of most rural and many urban areas of the Tennessee Valley in the early

1930's. Teachers taught by textbook, and the famous "Blueback Speller" had not entirely disappeared from the land. Public libraries existed in the major cities—KNOXVILLE and CHATTANOOGA. Some of the more progressive county seat towns had small public libraries, most of which had been started by women's clubs in an effort to preserve local histories and that intangible they called "culture". But very few school libraries existed, and those that did were limited almost entirely to the colleges and a few of the larger high schools.

In that day, "book learning" was regarded as important only insofar as it was practical. The three R's were practical for keeping and reading board feet of lumber, deeds, store accounts, taxes and the Bible. Most parents in the Tennessee Valley sacrificed sweat and bread to keep their children in school, at least through the eighth grade. But too much education—high school and beyond—was oftentimes regarded as

Library in tool box of a horse-drawn wagon on a TVA reservoir clearance job near Rockwood, September 17, 1940.

Courtesy TVA

impractical, if not downright dangerous. School often meant the loss of children from the farm and community. When the TENNESSEE VALLEY AUTHORITY came to the Tennessee Valley in 1933 and began building Norris Dam, it hired workmen primarily from the vicinity. The Authority determined that it had to get into the business of education, because education was basic to improving the "economic and social well-being of the people" as well as to developing the highly skilled labor force necessary for construction and operation of a complex series of dams.

Mape Phillips was typical of the thousands of workers TVA hired in the early days. He had gone through the sixth grade at Choptack School and then, when his father was hurt while logging on the side of Clinch Mountain, had quit to take over the family farm. That was in 1928. In 1934, he got a job as a laborer at NORRIS, a job which guaranteed him good steady wages. But Mape soon found out that his pay as a laborer was the lowest on the books. He

Library truck at Philadelphia, July 14, 1943.

Billy Glenn / Courtesy TVA

also found out that if he knew more arithmetic and could read better, he could get a better job. He saw the books which TVA made available from the Norris Library and decided to use them to advance his education. After gaining sufficient academic background, he enrolled in a skilled trades training course offered by TVA, became a millwright, and followed his trade for 31 years while raising a family and sending four of his seven children through college.

TVA realized from the beginning that continuing education for its own employees was a necessity. Soon after it was organized, and even before moving its headquarters to the Valley, TVA formed a technical library as a means toward this end. TVA planners further reasoned that if a technical library were necessary for the Authority's own administrative and engineering staff, would not libraries be essential to employees located at the construction projects? And, if experience showed them to be beneficial at the construction projects, would they not be just as valuable for the people of the Valley? Thus TVA developed its concept of the use of libraries as a vital and practical tool in education. This concept, expanded and demonstrated over and over again, formed the basis for today's modern library systems in the Valley and over much of the United States.

The Norris construction project offered an ideal laboratory for testing this concept and, therefore, became the first area of TVA's library activity. At Norris, two libraries were established: one for the Norris School, and one to serve the residents of the town and the construction workers housed at the site. From the latter library, books were dispatched—in a system which later developed into the now familiar bookmobile—to the remote reaches of the reservoir area where TVA crews were at work. Construction workers then usually lived together, away from their families, in camps or barracks near their work. The workers could check out practical books to help them gain additional knowledge useful in helping them advance in their jobs. Or they could choose books to be read for entertainment during their idle evening hours. In the Norris School, the library replaced the traditional textbook as the main tool for learning. Through the library, students pursued topics of interest to them.

Seeking to use and strengthen public libraries where they existed, TVA contracted with Lawson-McGhee Library in Knoxville for services to workers at Fort Loudoun and Watts Bar dams. Under TVA supervision, Lawson-McGhee Library provided the same kind of services which TVA itself had been providing, both for TVA employees and for the residents of the surrounding areas. The elements of a cooperative regional library system—matching the resources of the State Library with the combined resources of several adjacent counties—began to evolve with the Watts Bar Dam project, started in 1939. There, the State Library assumed administrative responsibility and Lawson-McGhee provided the service. Bookmobiles were sent out into the surrounding rural communities, stopping at designated schools, country stores and private homes to pick up and deliver books on a regular schedule. For many rural residents, this was their first contact with books and libraries.

Once the dam construction was completed, TVA continued to contract with the libraries to provide the new service to the communities for a period of time to allow the counties to determine whether they wanted to assume permanent responsibility. Citizens, once exposed to the service, were reluctant to see it dropped. One library patron in MEIGS COUNTY, for example, told the county court that, since there were no newspapers or telephones in the county, the library provided her only link with the outside world. Under the regional library concept, two or more counties, with state assistance, could combine to provide better library service cheaper and more efficiently than one county could alone.

The guiding hand behind TVA's library activities was Miss Mary Utopia Rothrock, who served as TVA library specialist from 1933 to 1951. She seized upon the opportunities which TVA's early construction projects provided to fashion a regional system for getting books into the homes of Valley residents who had never had them before. To coordinate and promote library development throughout the seven Valley states, TVA invited representatives of various types of libraries to Knoxville in the early 1940's. This group organized the Tennessee Valley Library Council. As an aid to further library development, the council sponsored a comprehensive survey of existing library systems in the Southeast—the first such survey ever made. Information was gathered and evaluated on the number of libraries, locations, services offered, budgets, personnel, buildings and equipment, strengths, and weaknesses.

Since that first survey, many changes have occurred: the post-war years brought considerable industrialization and urbanization; the Federal library programs directed changes in collections, services, and library aims; the Southern Association of Colleges and Schools incorporated library evaluation into its accreditation program and adopted standards which had to be met; individual states developed extensive library services; library education became available at several colleges and universities; states developed school library systems and programs for school library development; and the Southeastern Library Association (which absorbed the Tennessee Valley Library Council) grew into a strong professional organization. Libraries, even in rural elementary schools of the Tennessee Valley, have come a long way from Miss Wolf's meager two-book collection in 1930. Citizens have come to recognize both the value of education and the practical role which libraries can play in providing access to current information. Better libraries, therefore, have contributed significantly to improving the "economic and social well-being of the people" of the Tennessee Valley.

Jesse C. Mills

See also: MUSEUMS

Lincoln Memorial University, created as a living memorial to Abraham Lincoln, was chartered by the State of Tennessee on February 12, 1887. It is a liberal arts co-educational college located at Harrogate, within sight of historic Cumberland Gap. The Reverend A.A. Myers, a Congregationalist minister, came to Cumberland Gap in 1890 and opened The Harrow School. His interests in education led to discussions with local leaders about the establishment of a university. General O.O. Howard, who had served under Lincoln during the CIVIL WAR, was visiting in the area to deliver a lecture on Lincoln, and he joined Myers and others in the creation of a board of directors, the purchase of the elaborate Four Seasons Hotel property, and the establishment of the institution.

Through the years, Lincoln Memorial University has maintained a consistent dedication to the principles exemplified in the life of the great American President whose name is synonymous with humanitarianism, individual liberty, and an appreciation for the common man. As extensive program of scholarships, grants, work aid, and loans has been important to the institution in fulfilling its purposes and in illuminating its claim as a "college of opportunity" for students without reference to social status or financial ability. In addition to one hundred acres of the campus proper, which includes residence halls, instructional, administrative, health and recreational facilities, the University owns approximately nine hundred acres of farmland.

A major collection of books, pamphlets, manuscripts, pictures, sheet music, paintings, sculpture, and other memorabilia of Abraham Lincoln is housed in the Lincoln Museum at the entrance to the campus. Scholars from throughout the world use the collection for research purposes. A supplement to this is the collection of historical reference material related to the Civil War period. Alumni of Lincoln Memorial University have distinguished themselves in professional careers, community leadership, politics and government, and in nearly every aspect of American life. Particularly noteworthy are Jesse Stuart, James Still, and Don West, classmates and students in 1929 of accomplished author and teacher Harry Harrison Kroll. Stuart and Still later became two of APPALACHIA's most famous writers, while West went on to help found Highlander Folk School in East Tennessee and to direct the Appalachian South Folklife Center in Pipestem, West Virginia. Another alumnus, newspaper editor and regional historian Robert L. Kincaid, served as President of Lincoln Memorial University during the 1940's and 1950's.

Student enrollment has varied significantly over the years. Students have traditionally been from the Appalachian region, but many are enrolled from other states. By 1980, total enrollment had climbed to more than one thousand.

William H. Baker

Refer to: Joe Clark and Jesse Stuart, *Tennessee Hill Folk*, Nashville: Vanderbilt University Press, 1972; Robert L. Kincaid, *The Wilderness*

Courtesy National Park Service

With the help of six oxen, George Washington Shults and neighbors snake logs through the forest.

Road, Indianapolis: Bobbs-Merrill, 1947; "Don West, Poet and Preacher," in *Goldenseal: A Quarterly Forum for Documenting West Virginia's Traditional Life*, V. 5, No. 4 (October - December 1979); and "Learning for Dollars," *Forbes*, March 19, 1979.
See also: APPALACHIAN LITERATURE

Log Rafts. Throughout the 19th century, many loggers in East Tennessee sent much of their timber to market via log rafts. These rafts, made of the actual logs to be transported and sold, floated down such rivers as the Holston and the Clinch to Clinton, KNOXVILLE, Rockwood, CHATTANOOGA, and other towns and landings. High tides in winter and spring made river rafts a cheap and effective method of getting the timber to market. The frequent use of STEAMBOATS, whatever the season, was too risky in the relatively low waters of the Tennessee River's tributaries. As late as 1917, before the improvement of roads and the thinning of the timber, one observer on the Clinch counted thirteen rafts passing in one day.

Walnut, white oak and poplar were prize timbers for the construction industries of the larger cities. The most acceptable size for these logs was between 30 and 48 inches in diameter, and twelve feet in length. Loggers "snaked", or dragged, the logs to the

Courtesy Gene Branam

Logs in transit from creek to river.

river, laid them parallel, and fastened them together with "binders", or cross pieces, of hickory or black gum saplings. Wooden pegs held the binders to the logs.

The rafters had three men on both ends of the raft, each crew working a pole with a paddle attached to keep the raft in the middle of the river. They usually cooked their meals in the center of the raft, sometimes on a small man-made bank of dirt and rocks, sometimes on a piece of tin laid under a rough shelter. Some rafters employed such singers as the brothers Jess and Ed Baldwin for entertainment during the floating. The longer raft trips lasted several weeks. Sent off by family and friends, the men stopped occasionally to buy eggs and vegetables, eat a meal, or spend the night in a nearby inn or hayloft. When they reached their destination, they took the raft apart and sold the lumber. Before the RAILROADS came, the rafters walked home.

Such adventure gave rise to many stories and legends of voyages south and return trips. There was the story of a black man, working for the Gillenwater family, who loved to run. He was said to run from Rogersville to Knoxville and back, a distance of about 120 miles, in one day. One hungry steersman ate a meal in a city restaurant

The Lenoir Car Works and Lenoir City, ca. 1905.

and said, "The sample of food is fine; bring me a meal of the same." One rafter who sold his logs in Chattanooga took pay in gold. He returned by train to Whitesburg, Kentucky, and set out on foot to Sneedville. As he walked, the weight of the coins became heavier and heavier. He told his sons, "Had I needed to go another mile, I would have gladly thrown those coins away."

The families, waiting at home during the raft trips, had their share of experiences. Three-year old S.W. Banard, for example, lived with his family on a small farm in HANCOCK COUNTY. One day in 1864, while his father was away on a raft to Chattanooga, his mother laid on top of their pig pen a chicken which had just died. Returning later to bury the chicken, she found a starving Cherokee Indian pulling feathers from the chicken, preparing to eat it raw. Not knowing what the Indian wanted, Banard's mother hid the children under the floor boards of the house. She quickly ran to the log smoke house and watched the Indian through a crack in the logs. Seeing that the Indian wanted only the dead chicken, she stood in the doorway and motioned for him to leave, which he did (with the chicken).

Elizabeth S. Smith
Lois Maxwell Mahan and Joseph L. Mahan
Ruby L. Johns and Porter Johns

Refer to: Cordell Hull, *The Memoirs of Cordell Hull* (2 V.), New York: Macmillan, 1948; p. 20; and John Rice Irwin, *The Story of Marcellus Moss Rice and His Big Valley Kinsmen*, Montevallo, Alabama, 1963, pp. 60-62.
See also: AUSTINS MILL

Loudon County

Size: 237 Square Miles (151,680 acres)
Established: 1870
Named For: FORT LOUDOUN, an early British fort on the Little Tennessee River
County Seat: Loudon
Other Major Cities, Towns, or Communities:
Lenoir City
Philadelphia
Greenback
Eaton Crossroad
Clear Prong

M.L. Stanley / Courtesy Ross Lee

Bookmobile users, Philadelphia in Loudon County, July 14, 1943.

Billy Glenn / Courtesy TVA

Fort Loudoun Lake, Loudon County.

Luttrell
Jena

See also: JOHN BOWERS
LENOIR CAR WORKS
RICHARD MARIUS
NATIONAL CAMPGROUND

Lower Windrock Mining Camp. The Windrock Coal and Coke Company, a subsidiary of the Bessemer Coal, Iron and Land Company of Birmingham, Alabama, began the development of the Windrock coal mines in 1903. These operations consisted primarily of two camps: Upper Windrock and Lower Windrock, both in ANDERSON COUNTY, Tennessee. Components of Upper Windrock consisted of the entrance to the underground mines at about 2500 feet elevation, a short tram road to the upper tipple, a powerhouse, maintenance shops, a commissary, a church/school, a baseball diamond, and approximately 105 houses for the miners' families.

Lower Windrock consisted of the main tipple; the L & N Railroad tracks; a commissary, church, school, and baseball field; numerous garages; and approximately 65 residences. Upper and Lower Windrock were connected by a one-mile incline track used primarily for the hauling of coal in ten-ton cars. Many workers lived outside the lower camp at Khotan, The Cove, Piedmont, Tuppertown, Oliver Springs, and other communities. At its peak, Windrock Coal Company employed about 350 men. During the 1940's automation cut employment in half. In June of 1961, due to the poor economics of deep mined coal, Windrock Coal and Coke Company closed its operations. The later advent of surface or strip mining of coal marked an end to "life in the camps".

During its heyday, a center of that life was the commissary. The commissary was stocked with merchandise to serve not only the people of Lower Windrock Camp, but also the numerous company employees who lived in peripheral areas as far away as Oliver Springs. The stock included groceries, flour, meal, cow feed, overalls, shoes, shovels, picks, carbide for the miners' lamps, chewing tobacco, ladies' dresses and shoes, needles, lace, ribbons, beans, loose crackers, sour pickles in the barrel, soft drinks, and, of course, candy. Meats were refrigerated by ice-boxes at first, then by a kerosene-powered gadget called an "icy-ball", and finally by electric refrigerators.

Like most coal companies who maintained commissaries, Windrock Coal Company made use of scrip. Scrip was first issued in paper, then in coin-like pieces of aluminum with an inscription of the company name and a number indicating the value of the piece. As an example of its use, a miner could go to the commissary and request to "draw" ten dollars in scrip. The manager or clerk would phone the company bookkeeper to see if the miner had worked enough to have ten dollars or more "coming to him". If the answer was yes, the miner would receive the ten dollars in scrip. If the miner traded for only six or seven dollars worth of goods, he could take the balance home for him (or his wife) to spend later at the commissary.

The scrip system was a convenience for the miner and his family, but it worked in favor of the company by insuring future trade at the high-priced company commissary. In some instances, because of prior arrangements, the scrip could be traded at Sienknechts Store in Oliver Springs, but this was discouraged by the company's practice of discounting a certain percent for redeemed scrip. Peddlers who accepted scrip in payment for produce could usually trade it out at the commissary. Of course, scrip found other uses. A thirsty miner could always find someone who would sell him a quart of "mountain dew" or a bottle of "Strutt Street medicine" for pay in scrip. Scrip was tried in coin vending machines. Scrip was also prominent in most poker games, and found its way into the collection plate at church meetings.

All the buildings in the camp except the church and school were of box construction. The houses were made of wide unplaned poplar or pine planks nailed in a vertical position to form the outside walls. The cracks between the wide boards were covered by strips two or three inches wide. The ceiling and inside walls were of wooden bead-ceiling construction which could be painted or papered. The rough outside walls were periodically given an ample coat of lime whitewash, which discouraged insects and gave the house a shining immaculate appearance. Wire or picket fences protected the lawns and flower or vegetable gardens from ranging animals. Hedgerows were used as sub-dividers. Many of the houses were shaded by oak, hickory, or ash trees.

All of the houses and buildings that made up the Lower Windrock Mining Camp are now gone except the church, one dwelling house where Roger Cox now lives, and the two-room schoolhouse which has been remodelled and is now the home of Ramsey Lively. Roads have been changed, water pumps no longer operate, the L & N tracks have been abandoned, and former house sites are overgrown with bush and bramble. Nevertheless, the compactness of earlier camp life brought about a spirit of fellowship and neighborliness which blossomed into lasting friendships that strongly prevail unto this day.

Snyder Roberts

See also: BROWNTOWN
COAL MINER'S SON
COAL MINING

Loyston. As the TENNESSEE VALLEY AUTHORITY closed the floodgates of Norris Dam in 1936, the slowly rising waters submerged more than 35,000 acres of land. More significantly, however, the waters of Norris Reservoir covered things incalculable in merely quantitative terms — memories, fondly remembered landmarks, patterns and habits of rural and communal life — all were equally inundated by the inexorable advance of the waters which represented, for better or worse, the march of technological progress in the Tennessee Valley. For families which had to be relocated to escape the rising waters, the uprooting from communities where many had lifetime ties constituted a journey whose magnitude cannot be calculated in miles.

One area affected by the inundation was Loyston, a typical farming community of some 70 persons. Although little more than a crossroads settlement, Loyston had its own general stores, filling station, cafe, grist mill, barber shop, and Delco lighting system, which served a few homes and stores in the center of town. State Highway 61, a dirt road, was the main street, providing a link to the county seat, Maynardville, and to the more distant urban center of KNOXVILLE, 30 miles to the south. Loyston, despite its small size, was a focal point for many of the farmers of UNION COUNTY.

The Stooksburys were regarded as one of the leading families of the Loyston area. They were typical in their family ties, their life styles, and their attitudes of the thousands of farm families of the Loyston area and of East Tennessee. Self-sufficient farming was the way of life for the Stooksburys and most of the families in the Loyston community. Only two tracts were not used for farming — one homesite and a lot used for a general store in Loyston. The tracts were relatively small, averaging 50 acres each, although eight of the families owned more than one tract.

All the Stooksburys raised food for the consumption of their families. Grain was taken to Loyston to be ground at a Stooksbury-owned mill located behind one of the local stores. Sorghum was boiled off for syrup; hogs were slaughtered each fall for the staple pork meat which was consumed in large amounts; and the garden plots supplied beans, tomatoes, potatoes, and other vegetables which the family ate. Butter, lard, milk, eggs, and cream came from the family livestock. Many possessed bee gums to obtain honey for their own use and for sale to others.

By modern standards, the cumulative adjusted gross farm income of the Stooksburys of Loyston seems pitifully small — $13,196, over two-thirds of which was accounted for by the cash value of food consumed on the farm. But, by 1933 standards, theirs was somewhat above the average for small East Tennessee farmers. The outlook was not too encouraging either. Lack of out-migration, limited employment off the farm, and constant population pressure on a fixed amount of land were inhibiting economic factors characteristic of Appalachian AGRICULTURE even to this day.

Life for the residents of Loyston was not easy, and modern conveniences were almost unknown. Homes varied in size and construction from a primitive log cabin with two rooms, an earthen floor and an attached lean-to for cooking to spacious and attractive frame or brick houses of eight rooms or more. Heat was supplied by wood-burning fireplaces, although a few were equipped with coal-burning grates. The coldness of East Tennessee winter nights in the shadow of the Cumberlands and the inadequacy of heating facilities are attested to by the considerable number of quilts possessed by each family. Aesthetically attractive and socially valuable for the quilting bees that brought neighbors and friends together, the quilt was a family necessity as well.

Possessions most highly prized in the rural areas of the Tennessee Valley in the 1930's were those which either diminished the drudgery of farm labor, enhanced a family's mobility, or provided entertainment beyond the irregular church outings, sorghum boilings and other infrequent community gatherings. Trucks and cars, sewing machines, cream separators, and phonographs and radios all fell within these categories.

The educational requirements of the Stooksburys and most other families of the Norris Reservoir area were met by THE ONE-ROOM SCHOOL. Many of the Stooksbury children attended Union County School, also known as Loyston Elementary. Others attended Oakdale School, a small, bleak, and somewhat cramped frame building heated in winter by a stove provided with wood cut by the families of attending children. School attendance was sporadic, depending on distance, weather, and the

Loyston's main street.

Courtesy TVA

Marshall A. Wilson / Courtesy TVA

The "Last Roundup" of Big Valley residents at Loyston School, Sunday, October 14, 1934. This was a farewell gathering of kinfolks before the Norris Lake impoundment forced them to move from the basin area.

amount of farm work requiring the labor of the older children.

Mining and timber cutting, two important sources of outside non-farm income, had dried up by 1930. But with the coming of TVA, many working sons found employment on work related to Norris Dam. Ironically, the forces disrupting the generations-old habits of Union County farmers and necessitating their removal from the land where many had spent their lives were also beneficial because of the jobs they provided in the area. A few young men taught school, but for the Stooksburys, at least, teaching was apparently daughter's work. Six Stooksbury daughters were employed teaching in local schools.

RELIGION played an important role in the lives of the Norris Reservoir families, whether seen in terms of spiritual sustenance or in the more secular role of providing social cohesion. The most preferred religion among the Stooksburys was Methodism, in contrast to the majority of Union County families who showed a preference for the Baptist church in either its primitive or missionary branches.

During 1934 and 1935, as work on Norris Dam progressed, the slow progress of appraisal, purchase, and relocation went relentlessly onward. TVA's Reservoir Family Removal Section and THE UNIVERSITY OF TENNESSEE's Agricultural Extension Service worked to ease the pain for those directly involved. Where did the Stooksburys go after leaving Big Valley? Nine of the 17 families for which there are records moved to KNOX COUNTY, three to BLOUNT COUNTY, three to LOUDON COUNTY, and two to ANDERSON COUNTY. In no case did any move farther than 60 miles from their former homes.

The Stooksburys, like most families in the Norris area, met the prospect of moving with a mixture of anxiety, regret, and anticipation, tinged for some with bitterness. Anxiety over obtaining a "good price" for the land was uppermost in their thoughts as well as sorrow at leaving friends and neighbors in a community where deep roots had been sunk. Some residents, however, asserted that, despite relocation and the attendant discomfort, the progress of TVA was "good for the country," and at least half anticipated the prospect of a "fresh start" with new opportunities.

As the waters of TVA's Norris Reservoir closed over what was once Loyston, more than the center of a rural community disappeared. The life styles of the Stooksburys and other Union County landowners like them became equally submerged in the changing patterns of existence and accelerated pace so prevalent since the Depression years of the 1930's — changing patterns in no small measure due to TVA's presence in East Tennessee.

Michael J. McDonald
John Muldowny

M

William Anderson McCall (January 9, 1891 -) was born in the East Tennessee hamlet of Wellsville, about twelve miles south of Maryville. His father, originally a farmer, moved the family to coal mines across the state line in Red Ash, Kentucky, where William followed his father into the mines at the age of nine. Until he was twenty, William worked a part of each year in the mines. During this period the McCall family lived in twenty-nine different houses, most of them in coal camps, in Red Ash and in the vicinity of Jellico, Tennessee.

McCall attended Highland College (later absorbed by Cumberland College) in Williamsburg, Kentucky, where Highland's president, recognizing McCall's potential, told him: "Under no circumstances must you not be allowed to finish college." McCall was graduated with a bachelor's degree in 1911. He taught for two years at LINCOLN MEMORIAL UNIVERSITY, where he earned a second bachelor's degree, then went on to Teachers College, Columbia University. There, while earning a third bachelor's degree, a master's and a doctorate, he came to the attention of two giants of American education, Dr. E.L. Thorndike and John Dewey.

McCall remained at Teachers College for twenty-five years in a distinguished career as teacher, researcher and test designer. He devised ways of measuring intelligence, of testing teacher efficiency and pupil achievement, and of evaluating educational systems. With a colleague he devised the McCall-Crabbs Standard Test Lessons in Reading, used by generations of American school children and still in regular use. In an afterword to McCall's delightful *I Thunk Me a Thaut*, a journal he began in 1891 on his eighth birthday, Helen Dudar calls him "one of the architects of modern education."

Jim Wayne Miller

Refer to: William A. McCall, *I Thunk Me a Thaut*, New York: Columbia University Teachers College Press, 1975.
See also: PHILANDER PRIESTLEY CLAXTON
COAL MINER'S SON

Cormac McCarthy (July 20, 1933 -), writer, son of Joseph and Gladys McGrail McCarthy, was born in Providence, Rhode Island. The McCarthys moved to south KNOX COUNTY when Cormac was a small child. His father was Chief Legal

Counsel to the TENNESSEE VALLEY AUTHORITY in KNOXVILLE before joining a private law firm in Washington, D.C. Young Cormac attended parochial schools in Knoxville, including Catholic High School, before entering THE UNIVERSITY OF TENNESSEE for one year. He then joined the U.S. Air Force for four years, but returned to U.T. for three more years. He left the University in 1959 without a degree, a formality he considered unnecessary.

McCarthy is a critically acclaimed master of "Southern Gothic" fiction. His work is populated mostly by members of the rural lower classes of East Tennessee. His characters struggle to survive in a dark sordid world of hopeless POVERTY, violence, and ignorance. McCarthy's anti-heroes often engage in murder, incest, necrophilia, and other forms of degredation. Their occupations are those frequently associated with the rural poor of East Tennessee: commercial fishing, hunting, moonshining, and small farming.

The novels of Cormac McCarthy are set in Knoxville and the surrounding countryside. *The Orchard Keeper* is a well-woven tale of moonshining, murder, and revenge. In *Outer Dark*, Culla and Rinthy Holme have an incestuously conceived child, and each goes on a violence-filled journey: she to find the infant her brother has given to a passing tinker, he to find his sister. The central character of *Child of God* is Lester Ballard, a poor white who loses his farm and his mind, and who turns to murder, rape, and transvestitism in his role as a crazed avenging angel. *Suttree*, McCarthy's first urban novel and his longest, takes place mainly in the downtown Knoxville of the early 1950's. Cornelius Suttree, U.T. graduate and scion of a good Knoxville family, leaves his wife and child for the life of a commercial fisherman. He resides in a dilapidated houseboat on Fort Loudoun Lake between the Gay Street and Henley Street bridges. Many Knoxville landmarks appear in this work, including Regas Restaurant, Comer's Pharmacy, the Farragut Hotel, and the Huddle Tavern.

Much of McCarthy's fiction is allegorical in nature, using mythical structures in its plots. McCarthy achieves many of his best stylistic effects by joining together his narrators' highly sophisticated vocabulary with the unrefined dialect of his native East Tennessee characters. In addition to writing novels, McCarthy has also authored short stories and "The Gardener's Son", a screenplay produced by National Educational Television. Cormac McCarthy has won the Faulkner Foundation Award (for *The Orchard Keeper*), an American Academy of Arts and Letters fellowship for European travel, and a Guggenheim Fellowship.

J. Michael Pemberton

Refer to: Cormac McCarthy, *The Orchard Keeper, Outer Dark, Child of God, Suttree,* New York: Random House, 1965, 1968, 1973 and 1979; and William J. Schafer, "Cormac McCarthy: the Hard Wages of Sin," in *Appalachian Journal*, V. 4 No. 2 (Winter 1977), pp. 105-119.
See also: APPALACHIAN LITERATURE

McMinn County
Size: 432 Square Miles (276,480 acres)
Established: 1819
Named For: Joseph McMinn, Governor of Tennessee
County Seat: Athens
Other Major Cities, Towns, or Communities:
Etowah
Englewood
Niota
Calhoun
Riceville
Carlock
Pine Grove
Rogers Creek
Spring Creek

Refer to: Theodore H. White, "The Battle of Athens, Tennessee," in *Harper's*, January 1947, pp. 54-61.
See also: FIRST CONCRETE HIGHWAY IN TENNESSEE
TENNESSEE WESLEYAN COLLEGE
WOMEN GET THE VOTE

David Madden (July 25, 1933 -   ), author and teacher, was born in KNOXVILLE, a city which would become the subject for many of his novels and stories. Madden was the son of James and Emile Merritt Madden. After attending public schools in Knoxville, Madden enrolled in THE UNIVERSITY OF TENNESSEE in 1951 and later attended Iowa State Teachers College. He graduated from The University of Tennessee in 1957, earned an M.A. from San Francisco State University in 1958, and studied further at Yale Drama School (1959-60). Madden's college years were interrupted by his travel in this country and abroad, including a stint at sea as a merchant sailor and service in the army during 1954-55. In 1956 he married Roberta Young, and four years later a son, Blake Dana, was born. Madden has successfully combined careers in university teaching and writing, having taught at Centre College (1960-62), the University of Louisville (1962-64), Kenyon College (1964-66), Ohio University (1966-68) and Louisiana State University (1968-present).

While David Madden has also written poetry and drama, he is best known for his fiction — in particular for the novels *Cassandra Singing*, *Bijou*, and *The Suicide's Wife*. His collection of short stories, *The Shadow Knows*, won an award from the National Council on the Arts. Madden's writing has touched on a broad range of subjects, and he has written with much success in a variety of styles and genres. In *Bijou* he looks with nostalgia on his youth in the 1940's in Knoxville. *The Suicide's Wife* enters the consciousness of a confused, struggling middle-aged widow living in a present-day university town in West Virginia. *Cassandra Singing* traces a high school senior awakening to the responsibilities of adulthood. Like the youthful protagonist in *Bijou*, Lone McDaniel of Harmon, Kentucky, carries the innocence of a young man from rural American origins and values into the temporarily overwhelming moral vacuum of the modern urban scene. The severing of human ties with the past is enforced by the grandfather's refusal to speak to his son, and by the imminent destruction of the family home in Harmon by the encroaching interstate highway.

A similar depiction of the young man's loss of innocence occurs in *Bijou* with thirteen-year old Lucius

Hutchfield, usher at the Bijou Theatre in Cherokee, Tennessee. As a first-generation urban family with roots in rural APPALACHIA, the Hutchfields preserve many traditional forms of communication, including storytelling at family gatherings. But as the family structure succumbs to the pressures of an urban environment, Lucius Hutchfield gradually replaces the sheltering innocence of his lost family with the assuaging fantasy of film and category fiction. At the conclusion of the novel Lucius makes his way to the home of Thomas Wolfe, the true model for his own experience of the mountain boy's confused and painful encounter with modern America.

A similar protagonist appears in *The Beautiful Greed* in the case of Alvin Henderlight, a youth from Knoxville with ancestral origins in CADES COVE. Signing with a merchant ship bound for Chile, Henderlight comes to know the depths of human malice and pettiness, and the need for self-control as a response to it. Throughout the novel, his search for new adventures is frustrated and his taste for sophisticated pleasures sours in comparison with his memory of mountain innocence at his grandfather's farm in Cades Cove. He finally realizes that he has not been in control of his own life; his decision to face the crew's enmity and not to desert ship marks his emerging sense of responsibility. Similar young men appear in Madden's less successful novel, *Brothers in Confidence.*

In his recent novel *On the Big Wind,* David Madden experiments with a narrative which chronicles the life of its protagonist from 1968 to 1979. During these years, Big Bob Travis loses his job as a prominent radio announcer in Nashville, is deserted by his wife, and descends through a series of lesser radio and promotion positions, only to pull his life together as an ABC news reporter. At the conclusion of the novel, Travis finds himself returning to his dying mother in the COAL MINING hollows of eastern Kentucky. East Tennessee becomes once again the setting for Madden's novel in progress, *Knoxville, Tennessee,* an epic of the CIVIL WAR.

Madden has written or edited several important books of non-fiction, including *Tough Guy Writers of the Thirties* (1968), *The Poetic Image in Six Genres* (1969), *American Dreams, American Nightmares* (1970), and *Remembering James Agee* (1974). His critical book on *Wright Morris* describes Morris's achievement as "bringing into focus a representative part of America" and seeking the "meaning of the legends, myths, and realities of America as they survive and prevail today in the minds of common men." This description might apply equally well to Madden's own fiction.

Jeffrey Folks

Refer to: David Madden, *Bijou, Cassandra Singing, The Shadow Knows,* and *The Suicide's Wife,* New York: Crown, 1974, 1969, 1970, and 1978; and David Madden, *Wright Morris,* New York: Twayne, 1964.
See also: APPALACHIAN LITERATURE

Maplehurst Park is a small residential area located between downtown KNOXVILLE and THE UNIVERSITY OF TENNESSEE. It is bounded to the south by the Tennessee River, to the north by 1982 World's Fair development and Church Street Methodist Church, to the east by Henley Street, and to the west by Second Creek and the University. In its evolution from wilderness to farmland to elegant estates to suburban development to deteriorating student quarters to, perhaps, revitalized downtown dwelling space, the neighborhood has much to say, generally, about changing social patterns typical to older American cities and, specifically, about the families, forces of history, and economic conditions unique to Knoxville.

It is not quite clear when the land became incorporated into the City of Knoxville. Certainly by 1831, when the city charter was amended to include all properties between First and Second Creek, it had joined the original sixteen blocks established in 1791 and the fourteen blocks added in 1795 to become part of the city proper. Neither is it certain when or how the property passed into private ownership. By 1825, railroad developer Campbell Wallace owned the major part of the area and had built a large home there. Knoxville banker John Churchwell became the second owner of the house, but financial failures preceding the CIVIL WAR forced him to sell in 1858.

On the eve of the War, ironically, the area entered into its "golden age" under the successive ownership of two of Knoxville's most important families. James Hervey Cowan, nephew of pioneer merchants and a civic leader, purchased the house and six acres of land from Churchwell. For a few short years the estate, called River Lawns, provided elegant residence for Cowan and his ten children. With Knoxville's population at only a few thousand, the leading families frequently intermarried and were closely knit both socially and commercially. The Cowans were related by marriage to the Whites, Humes, Dickinsons, and Estabrooks and were business associates of the McClungs, who, in turn, were related to the Whites and so on. Most of these families lived within walking distance of their businesses, their churches, and each other, and it is easy to romanticize that life then, at least for the privileged few, was serene and secure.

But River Lawns, along with the rest of Knoxville, was soon embroiled in the troubles and tragedies of the Civil War. Its location, on a hill above the Tennessee River and on the outskirts of town, exposed it to pressures from both sides of the conflict. In 1862, Confederate Major General Edmund Kirby Smith established headquarters in the Cowan's home as Commander of the District of East Tennessee. A Cowan family member later remembered that, during the worst of the war, troops camped on the terraced grounds, and dead horses were left to lie in the gardens. Knoxville's fortunes improved during Reconstruction, as did Cowan's. In 1870 he spent $10,000 rebuilding River Lawns into one of Knoxville's finest showplaces.

James H. Cowan died the next year, leaving the house and property to his unmarried daughter Mary. She sold the estate in 1883 to Edward Jackson Sanford, a Connecticut native and a successful Knoxville businessman. Sanford renamed the house

Courtesy C.M. McClung Historical Collection, Lawson McGhee Library

Maplehurst, and it once more became home to a young family. E.J. Sanford's sons, the young men who played among the maple trees that lined the drive and gave the estate its name, matured along with Knoxville and, in the early twentieth century, became the city's most prominent citizens. Edward T. Sanford, the eldest, became a Justice of the United States Supreme Court, Alfred F. Sanford became publisher of the *Knoxville Journal*, and Hugh W. Sanford, the youngest, became one of Knoxville's wealthiest businessmen.

After E.J. Sanford's death in 1902, the estate was subdivided and sold off, as residential lots in Maplehurst Park. Although soon there were dozens of residences including apartments and townhouses surrounding the Sanford mansion, the neighborhood remained very fashionable. Throughout the teens and twenties, many of Knoxville's socially prominent citizens built large comfortable homes in Maplehurst Park and along adjacent West Hill Avenue. The first incursion by University students into the Park took place in the early 1910's, when the Sanford mansion became home to the Kappa Sigma Fraternity. A fire in 1932 destroyed the roof of the old place, and the fraternity was forced to seek other quarters. With the worsening of the Depression, Maplehurst Park began a gradual downhill slide. City directories from the next four decades record first an increase in vacant properties, then an ever-accelerating rise in the number of apartments as the big houses were

Courtesy C.M. McClung Historical Collection, Lawson McGhee Library

Opposite: "River Lawns", rebuilt by James Cowan in 1870-71 on the southwest corner of Hill and High streets, Knoxville.

Maplehurst Park, ca. 1930's, showing old Cowan-Sanford House and present houses.

parcelled into furnished rooms. Even the townhouses were divided into one, two, and three room flats. The empty mansion was eventually dismantled to make room for a parking lot.

During the sixties and early seventies, Maplehurst Park was home to two distinct groups: a large transient student population, and a smaller but more stable community of retired persons. Among University students, Maplehurst Park became a desirable place to rent. The Park's older but well-kept apartments and tree-shaded yards offered a pleasing contrast to either newer apartment complexes or the more raucous and deteriorated student quarters of the Fort Sanders neighborhood.

Nationwide, the late seventies saw a new appreciation for urban living bring middle class and professional people back to downtown areas. Maplehurst Park reflected this trend. More and more college students decided to remain in the Park after graduation. Many young people who worked in Knoxville's central business district were eager to move into a pleasant neighborhood located only a two-minute walk away from Main Street. Professors and other University personnel also discovered the amenities of Maplehurst Park.

The important issue now is whether or not those amenities can be maintained. The major landlords of the Maplehurst area are to be commended for their seeming affection for the Park, and it is hoped, especially among residents, that neither runaway urban renewal nor the new popularity for downtown living will prompt the deed holders to cash in their urban gem.

Jeff D. Johnson

Refer to: Mary U. Rothrock, ed. *The French Broad-Holston Country: A History of Knox County, Tennessee,* Knoxville: East Tennessee Historical Society, 1946, 1972; and Lucile Deaderick, ed. *Heart of the Valley: A History of Knoxville, Tennessee,* Knoxville: East Tennessee Historical Society, 1976.

Jeff Daniel Marion and His Poetry: Mapping The Heart's Place. East Tennessee is a special place. I can't name the thing that makes it special, but I know it's there — and I know how to find it. First, get a map. Read aloud the names of the towns: White Pine, Chestnut Hill, Strawberry Plains, Sweetwater. Locate the rivers: Nolichucky, Holston, Hiwassee, French Broad. Upstream, look for mountains: Roan, Unaka, Big Bald, Tricorner Knob. The next step is to travel. In town, head for the oldest store. Sit close to the coal stove and listen. At the river, throw a stick to the current. Wait till it disappears. On the mountain, make your own trail to a small spring. Drink. This is it.

This is East Tennessee in its natural — and best — state. It's the East Tennessee that endures: earth, water, and the ways and places of men. For me, no place on earth is more important. That's why I like the poetry of Jeff Daniel Marion. Here is a writer who knows East Tennessee and, more than that, knows its value. Marion's instincts are true: his poems center on the richness of this land and the details of this life. In Marion's poems, East Tennessee transcends GEOGRAPHY and becomes a place for the spirit, home for the heart.

But the poems say it best. Consider "Arrival II", which describes a scene so common that it's usually overlooked and forgotten:

To come on fields like these—
cattle black, browsing:

a mist is rising beneath them,
lapping their legs.
They are figures of darkness
deeper than the falling dark.
Here, they seem not to move
caught in this stillness
that lies beyond me.

I turn toward the hills,
waves about to break.

In eleven lines, Marion recreates a field of cattle and discovers more than the scene itself. Mist rises, darkness falls, and stillness overtakes the land. Marion senses the magic of that moment, the energy in the air and in the hills, "waves about to break." Reading Marion, I know the land — and myself — a little better.

Water is also important to Marion. In "Ebbing & Flowing Spring", he remembers the unusual rising and falling waters of EBBING AND FLOWING SPRING near Rogersville, his hometown. Returning years later, Marion is struck by the changes at the spring, the dipper gourd gone and the springhouse unused. He is struck too by the unchanging pattern of the waters, still rising and falling. As he waits for the waters to rise once more, he listens:

It's a quiet beginning
but before you know it
the water's up & around you
flowing by.
You reach for the dipper
that's gone, then
remember to use your hands
as a cup for the cold
that aches & lingers.
This is what you have come for.
Drink.

This is Marion at his best, affirming the natural and human life of the region.

In his poetry and in his life, Marion is close to the land. On his farm near DANDRIDGE, he raises chickens and cattle and plants a big garden every spring. When he's not writing or farming, he teaches English at CARSON-NEWMAN COLLEGE in Jefferson City. He also finds time to edit a poetry magazine called *The Small Farm*. He started the magazine in 1975, and it soon became one of the best "little magazines" in the country. Marion's own work has been published in many poetry journals and in several anthologies. He has written two chapbooks, *Watering Places* and *Almanac*, and a full-length collection entitled *Out in the Country, Back Home*. His newest book, *Tight Lines*, was published in 1981 by Iron Mountain Press. In addition, Marion has completed but not yet published a collection of prose sketches and poems called *By the Banks of the Holston*.

From the Holston to Mt. LeConte, Marion enlarges the East Tennessee experience and informs it with his vision. For Marion, writing is an act of self-discovery, a way of finding what he calls "a map of the heart's true country." For his readers, Marion's poems are a source of renewal, a way of sharing the vision:

Yoked in these lines
I mean to work this land.
What comes up won't be wasted
& what's between the rows
is welcome, too.
Maybe occasionally a green heron
will visit my pond.
I'm always at home here
still believing
the reward of this labor
is vision
honed to the blue sharpness
of ridges.

John Coward

Refer to: Jeff Daniel Marion, *Out in the Country, Back Home*, Winston-Salem, N.C.: The Jackpine Press, 1976; and *Tight Lines*, Emory, Virginia: Iron Mountain Press, 1981.

See also: APPALACHIAN LITERATURE
NEW MARKET TRAIN WRECK
POETRY MAGAZINES
THE WAYSIDE GRILL

Marion County

Size: 506 Square Miles (323,840 acres)
Established: 1817
Named For: Francis Marion, "The Swamp Fox", Brigadier General in the American Revolution

County Seat: Jasper
Other Major Cities, Towns, or Communities:
South Pittsburg
Whitwell
Kimbal
Victoria
Sequatchie
Griffith Creek
Sulphur Springs
Haletown
Battle Creek

See also: STATE PARKS

Richard Marius (July 29, 1933 -), historian, teacher, and writer, was born in northeast LOUDON COUNTY. He grew up on a farm at Dixie Lee Junction on Loudon County's border with KNOX COUNTY. His mother, Eunice Henck Marius, daughter of a Methodist preacher, had as a child moved with her family from BRADLEY COUNTY to KNOXVILLE. Marius's father, Henri Marius, son of a Greek tobacco merchant, had studied at the University of Ghent and had been severely wounded in World War I before emigrating to the United States. In 1918, while working at the LENOIR CAR WORKS in Lenoir City, Henri Marius had met and married Eunice Henck, then a reporter for *The Knoxville News*.

On the family farm, Mrs. Marius regularly read aloud to her children from the King James version of the Bible and from Charles Dickens, Rudyard Kipling, Edgar Allen Poe, and MARK TWAIN. Richard also listened to tales told fresh or retold by his mother's sisters and brothers. These tales included ghost stories and accounts of the CIVIL WAR, in which Richard's great-grandfather had been a Union scout. Years later, Marius the writer would refer to his "treasury" of childhood memories and experiences as one of the three major influences on his fiction. The other two influences have been his love of English and his work in the profession of history.

Marius graduated from THE UNIVERSITY OF TENNESSEE in 1954. Swayed by his mother's devotion to RELIGION, he entered the seminary, where he spent four unhappy years in New Orleans and Louisville before receiving a Bachelor of Divinity degree from the Southern Baptist Theological Seminary. He then took a train to New Haven, Connecticut, where he entered Yale University's graduate program in history. After four "disorganized and happy" years there, he earned his Ph.D. in Reformation history.

In 1962, the same year he received his Yale degree, Richard Marius wrote a novel. He later burned the manuscript as an apprentice effort. Meanwhile, he taught history at Gettysburg College. In 1964 he began a fourteen-year career with The University of Tennessee, where he became one of the most popular professors on campus. By studying history, he told a student reporter, "We see how many different kinds of human good there are. I like to think the real study of history leads us to a greater tolerance of one another." In 1969, while still at U.T., Marius published *The Coming of Rain*, a powerful historical novel set in Bourbonville (Lenoir City), Tennessee. Marius's first Yale University Press volume of the works of Thomas More, for which

Marius is co-editor, followed four years later. Since 1973, Marius has published a biography of Martin Luther and a second novel, entitled *Bound for the Promised Land.* In 1978, Richard Marius left East Tennessee to become head of the Expository Writing program at Harvard University.

Jim Stokely

Refer to: Patty Brooks and Franklin Jones, "Marius: Religio Historici," in The University of Tennessee *Daily Beacon*, June 23, 1978; and Richard Marius, *Bound for the Promised Land*, New York: Knopf, 1976, *The Coming of Rain*, New York: Knopf, 1969, *Luther*, New York: Lippincott, 1974, and "The Middle of the Journey," in *The Sewanee Review*, V.85, No.3 (Summer 1977), pp. 460-467.
See also: APPALACHIAN LITERATURE

Maryville College, located in Maryville, Tennessee, is a liberal arts, coeducational, non-sectarian institution related to the Presbyterian Church. The institution began as Southern and Western Theological Seminary, authorized by the Presbytery of Union on October 8 and formally opened October 19, 1819. Isaac Anderson opened this first seminary in the South, only twelve years after Princeton Seminary, with five students in a frame house. Among the first three percent of American colleges and universities founded, the institution was incorporated in 1842 as Maryville College. Except for five CIVIL WAR years, it has been in continuous existence.

From its inception, the college has served many publics. Initially, it provided college preparatory training, regular four-year college work, and three-year seminary education. Open to all races, it counted Indians and blacks among its students. It was, in 1867, among the earliest U.S. institutions to open itself to coeducation. Seminary services were dropped upon incorporation, and in 1925 the century-old preparatory school was terminated. Only the liberal arts college remains. When the Civil War interrupted the school's operation, 250 students had graduated. The faculty and student body split almost evenly between the Union and Confederacy. Both Northern and Southern forces brought destruction to the college buildings and necessitated a second founding on a new campus nearby.

College plant and campus grew significantly from the initial two-story brick building of 1820. In the pre-Civil War era, a two-story frame building was built and later replaced by a three-story brick college destined to remain unfinished until destroyed by the war. The half-lot campus was enlarged to two lots, and a 200-acre farm was later acquired and sold. Endowment reached $16,000, with a library of 6,000 volumes. Reopened in 1866 through the efforts of Professor Thomas J. Lamar, Maryville College undertook a vigorous campaign for funds and buildings. Present buildings number 24 on a 375-acre campus.

Stated purposes of the College have changed in time but have embodied an "intention of academic excellence and one which produces in its students Christian belief, Christian character, and Christian service motivation." Framed in terms of broad expectations that "millions (be) made happy on earth, and heaven peopled with multitudes," the first statement of purpose sought to prepare men for the ministry. To accomplish this, the institution had to devote energy to literary subjects and general education. President Samuel Tyndale Wilson (1901-30) succinctly defined the purpose as "the Maryville Spirit," composed of four qualities: "Breadth of Human Interest, Thorough Scholarship, Manly Religion, and Unselfish Service." More recent years have given more attention to the liberal arts as a foundation for vocational and career objectives while continuing to affirm that the College is "not a university or professional school."

The student body increased from 5 to 98 in pre-Civil War years, dropped to 13 in 1866, and reached its highest total in 1920 with 1003 students in preparatory and college departments. The largest number in the four-year college alone was 949 during the 1947-48 academic year, when enrollment was swelled by returning veterans. During the 1970's, enrollments hovered around 600. Today, most students are housed in dormitories, and they originate from a wide geographic area.

Arda S. Walker

Refer to: Ralph Waldo Lloyd, *Maryville College: A History of 150 Years, 1819-1969*, Maryville: Maryville College Press, 1969.

Meigs County

Size: 191 Square Miles (122,240 acres)
Established: 1836
Named For: Return Jonathan Meigs, Indian agent for the Cherokee Nation
County Seat: Decatur
Other Major Cities, Towns, or Communities:
Peakland
Union Grove
Big Spring
Sewee
Goodfield
East View

See also: TVA NUCLEAR PLANTS

Melungeons The term "Melungeon" is used in reference to a few of the some two hundred mixed racial groups inhabiting the eastern half of the United States. Considerable attention devoted to the "mysterious" Melungeons of Hancock and Hawkins counties, Tennessee, has obscured the fact that Melungeon groups have been identified in Morgan, Rhea, and Roane counties as well, and in the states of Kentucky, Ohio, and Virginia.

A dark tawny skin, blue eyes and straight black or blond hair served, at one time, to distinguish the Melungeons from the predominantly Anglo-Saxon population that surrounded them. Their anomalous physical appearance and unknown racial heritage stimulated numerous mystifying theories about their origin. Various observers have suggested that the Melungeons are descendants of Gypsies, a "lost" tribe of Israel, a group of shipwrecked Portuguese sailors, Arabs, Sir Walter Raleigh's "Lost Colony", or "Welsh-Indians". The very word "Melungeon" has been reported as being derived from the French "melange", meaning "mixed"; from the Portuguese

Courtesy TVA

Postmistress and librarian at Ten Mile in Meigs County, ca. 1943.

"melungo", meaning "shipmate"; or from the Greek "melan", meaning "colored".

Genetical studies done in HANCOCK COUNTY strongly support the theory that the Melungeons are but one of the many mixed racial populations formed in the late 1700's as a result of admixture among three racial groups: European White, Indian, and Negro. Census data and other historical documents indicate that those people in Hancock County who have such Melungeon surnames as Goins and Mullins are probably descendants of "mixed bloods" who migrated before 1800 from the Piedmont area of North Carolina and Virginia. No reliable evidence to date verifies the assumption that there was ever a distinctive Melungeon culture; Indian and Negro traits were more than likely intentionally discarded in an effort to identify with the Whites. Ethnographic work in Hancock and Rhea counties clearly shows that the people identified as Melungeon share a complex of cultural patterns (e.g., RELIGION, social organization, custom, dress, foodways, and folklore) identical to that which characterizes rural Whites throughout Southern APPALACHIA.

As with other mixed racial isolates, the Melungeons endured a long history of ostracism and denigration. Whites perceived them to be lazy, stupid, hostile, promiscuous, and untrustworthy. Because of the negative connotations associated with being a Melungeon, people deeply resented being so labeled. As a result of intermarriage with Whites over many generations, the Melungeons have undergone nearly complete racial dissolution. Such is the case in Hancock County, where the majority of people who claim to be or are said to be Melungeon are no different in physical appearance from native Whites. It may very well be that within a generation or two, there will be no Melungeons, only memories and myths about them.

Anthony P. Cavender

Refer to: Jean Patterson Bible, *Melungeons Yesterday and Today*, Rogersville: East Tennessee Printing Company, 1975; E. Raymond Evans, "The Graysville Melungeons: A Tri-Racial People in Lower East Tennessee," in *Tennessee Anthropologist*, 1979; Edward T. Price, "The Melungeons: A Mixed-Blood Strain of the Southern Appalachians," in *Geographical Review*, 1951; and Jesse Stuart, *Daughter of the Legend*, New York: McGraw-Hill, 1965.
See also: CHEROKEES

Migrant Workers. Each spring and summer, hundreds of Spanish speaking migrant workers travel to East Tennessee from Texas and Florida. In East Tennessee, they work in the preharvest and harvest of strawberries, tomatoes, tobacco and apples. Most workers are provided housing, utilities, and transportation to the fields at no cost. Government grants and church groups have established some day care centers and schools for children of the migrants. Wages, paid on a unit or piece rate basis, average about $5 per hour, with top production bringing as high as $12 per hour. Tomato stakers, tyers, and pruners are paid per hundred feet, strawberry pickers per eight-quart carrier, tomato pickers per 35 pound bucket, and apple pickers per 38 pound bushel.

Although there is no way of exactly counting the number of migrant workers in East Tennessee, the following estimates for 1980 were fairly accurate:

June 15: 250 (125 from Texas via Florida, 125 from Texas)
July 15: 455 (255 from Texas via Florida, 200 from Texas)
August 15: 440 (225 from Texas via Florida, 215 from Texas)

The total number of migrants in the area, including nonworkers, would be at least two or three times the figure for workers on any given day. Most workers have homes in Texas, but work Florida vegetables during the early part of the year and migrate on up the eastern seaboard. They work the crops in East Tennessee and elsewhere, then migrate back to the Florida area for the fall vegetable crops. The balance of the workers come directly from their home base in Texas, work the East Tennessee crops in the summer, and return to Texas when school starts.

David R. Kirkham

Refer to: Robert Coles, *Migrants, Sharecroppers, Mountaineers,* Boston: Atlantic-Little, Brown, 1971.

Emma Bell Miles (October 19, 1879 - March 19, 1919), writer, artist, and naturalist, was born in Evansville, Indiana. She was the only child of schoolteachers Benjamin Franklin Bell and Martha Ann Mirick Bell. The Bell family moved to Walden's Ridge, just north of CHATTANOOGA, in 1891. There young Emma roamed the woods, learning to identify birds and plants, and largely educated herself by reading *Harper's Magazine.* In 1899-1900 and 1900-01 Emma attended the St. Louis School of Art with the aid of wealthy friends, and she seemed destined for a brilliant career as an artist. But while in St. Louis she turned from art to literature, and particularly to the writings of Thoreau, which only increased her homesickness for the mountain and for her suitor, Frank Miles. She returned to Walden's Ridge and married Frank Miles on October 30, 1901, against her father's wishes.

Twin girls were born to Emma and Frank in the fall of 1902, and three more babies followed in rapid succession. Nonetheless, Emma continued to paint and write. As early as 1904, she began to publish her poems, articles, and short stories in prominent magazines. Her book, *The Spirit of the Mountains,* appeared in 1905. It was a nonfiction account of mountain life, with much of the material supplied by her husband's relatives. Horace Kephart quoted extensively from the book in his *Our Southern Highlanders,* which appeared a few years later.

Emma's poem "After Reading Thoreau" (*Century,* October 1906) inspired Anna Ricketson, daughter of Thoreau's friend Daniel Ricketson, to initiate a correspondence that lasted ten years. Emma also corresponded and collaborated with the MacGowan sisters, who had moved to the writers' colony at Carmel, California. Some of Emma Bell Miles's best stories appeared in *Harper's, Putnam's, Craftsman,* and *Lippincott's* between 1908 and 1912. They included "The Common Lot", "The Homecoming of Evalina", "Three Roads and a River", and "At the Top of Sourwood". All dealt with mountain themes and contained the finely drawn descriptions of nature that were characteristic of Emma's writing.

In the fall of 1913 Emma moved to Chattanooga, and in April of 1914 she began working as a staff writer for the *Chattanooga News.* During this time she wrote a regular column entitled "Fountain Square Conversations". In the fall of 1915, she learned that she had tuberculosis and entered Pine Breeze Sanatorium. She returned to Walden's Ridge in the early spring, but her condition worsened, and she was forced to enter the sanatorium for the second and last time in September of 1916. She continued to write while a patient at Pine Breeze, publishing *Our Southern Birds* just before her death at the age of 39. After a funeral at Christ Episcopal Church, she was buried in the Hamilton Memorial Gardens (White Oak Cemetery) in Chattanooga.

Kay Baker Gaston

Refer to: Emma Bell Miles, *The Spirit of the*

Mountains, New York: James Pott and Co., 1905 (reprinted 1975, Knoxville: University of Tennessee Press), and *Our Southern Birds*, Morristown, Tenn.: Globe Book Co., 1922; and Abby Crawford Milton, ed. *Strains from a Dulcimore*, Atlanta: Bozart Press, 1930.
See also: APPALACHIAN LITERATURE

John Mitchel (November 3, 1815 - March 20, 1875) was a famous Irish patriot and revolutionary whose life tangentially but significantly touched East Tennessee in the 1850's. A graduate of Trinity College, Dublin, Mitchel first became an attorney. In 1845 he abandoned this profession and turned to journalism as a more effective means of opposing Britain's continuing oppression of Ireland. Increasingly dissatisfied with the moderate nationalists, he joined the Young Ireland party in 1846, a much more extremist movement which opposed any policy of compromise toward or gradual concessions from Britain. Mitchel was an incisive writer and an effective polemicist. In 1848 he began publishing the *United Irishman* in Dublin, dedicated to the cause of Irish independence.

This paper and his highly inflammatory articles brought Mitchel to trial for seditious libel in March, 1848. Under a new British law, the Treason Felony Act, he was convicted without jury and sentenced to exile for fourteen years. After excruciating hardships and suffering he ended up in a penal colony in Australia, from which he effected an escape with his family to the United States in 1853. In both San Francisco and New York, Mitchel met with an enthusiastic welcome.

In New York he began another newspaper, *The Citizen*, which opposed both abolitionism and the Know-Nothing party. American nativism, represented cholerically in the Know-Nothing party, temporarily disillusioned Mitchel with Americans. In 1855 he went to KNOXVILLE, seeking an isolated locale to indulge his misanthropy. However, Know-Nothingism was alive and well even here. Its Tennessee spokesman was the irascible, frenetic PARSON BROWNLOW, editor of the Knoxville *Whig*. Brownlow offered an ungracious welcome to the Irish stranger, warning him that East Tennesseans would not tolerate any newcomer who presumed to *dictate* to them!

Feeling that Knoxville was neither town nor country, in May of 1855 Mitchel moved his family to a 132-acre farm in Tuckaleechee Cove (present-day Townsend). Although his family lived under primitive conditions in a rude, two-room log cabin, he was enchanted by the beauty of this cove. The CLIMATE was temperate, deer were plentiful, and Mitchel was able to grow an abundance of pioneer crops in addition to enjoying an excellent orchard. In this edenic environment his old geniality and sociability gradually returned. Yet the isolation of the cove and the lack of close neighbors of comparable background or education weighed heavily on Mrs. Mitchel. For this reason, Mitchel returned to Knoxville with his family in the fall of 1856, although not without lamenting "that I should never again call my own so lovely a spot on earth."

Despite his dislike of progress and rapid commercial development in

Knoxville, Mitchel did find many intellectual and well-educated friends there. With one of these, William G. Swan, he entered into partnership to begin publishing the *Southern Citizen* in October, 1857. This newspaper was dedicated to states' rights, a defense of slavery as a positive good, and advocacy of reopening the African slave trade. Nothing seems more ironic today than the prospect of an Irish revolutionary, dedicated to freeing his own country from British tyranny, advocating Negro slavery on this side of the Atlantic. To publish such an anti-abolitionist organ in East Tennessee was a mistake even Mitchel soon realized, and he consequently moved the *Southern Citizen* to Washington, D.C. in 1858.

The key to understanding why Mitchel saw "the South as the Ireland of this continent" lies in the fact that he equated British commercialism and industrialism with similar patterns of development in the American North. In contrast, Southern civilization seemed superior because it was agrarian, nonindustrial, and largely uncommercial. In some respects Mitchel's arguments anticipated the Nashville Agrarians of the twentieth century. His argument that slavery was a positive good echoes John C. Calhoun.

However misguided in his defense of slavery, Mitchel embraced the cause of the Confederacy during the CIVIL WAR as fervidly as he had earlier fought for Irish independence. Unable to serve in the Confederate army, he edited a rebel newspaper, the *Enquirer*, and later wrote articles for the *Examiner* in wartime Richmond. Two of his sons were killed while serving in the Confederate army; a third son lost his right arm in a battle near Richmond.

Regardless of the cause, Mitchel fought fearlessly for what he believed, and few doubted the sincerity of his convictions. His brief sojourn in East Tennessee perhaps alleviated local distrust of foreigners, but few East Tennesseans embraced his defense of slavery. Mitchel left with an acute appreciation of the scenery, some insight into Knoxville's shortcomings and potential, and several lifelong friends. He died in Ireland in 1875, characteristically fighting the British Parliament to honor his recent election to that body as representative of Tipperary.

Durwood Dunn

Refer to: William Dillon, *Life of John Mitchel*, 2 Vols., London, 1888; and Samuel Cole Williams, "John Mitchel, The Irish Patriot, Resident of Tennessee," in East Tennessee Historical Society's *Publications*, No. 10 (1938), pp. 44-56.

Monroe County

Size: 660 Square Miles (422,400 acres)

Established: 1819

Named For: James Monroe,
President of the United States

County Seat: Madisonville

Other Major Cities, Towns, or Communities:

Sweetwater
Tellico Plains
Mount Vernon
Vonore
Coker Creek
Citico Beach
Hopewell Springs
Acorn

Charlie Krutch / Courtesy TVA

Water-powered sawmill between Madisonville and Tellico Plains in Monroe County, May 1938.

Refer to: Robert L. Hilten, *The Hiwassee Story*, Madisonville, Tenn., 1970.
See also: CRAIGHEAD CAVERNS
FORT LOUDOUN
ESTES KEFAUVER
PRIVATE EDUCATION IN SWEETWATER

Grace Moore (December 5, 1901 - January 26, 1947), the "Tennessee Nightingale", opera singer and popularizer of grand opera in America, was born in the Harmony Grove community about three miles south of Del Rio in COCKE COUNTY. Her father, Richard L. Moore, had come as a young man from Murphy, North Carolina, to trade in lumber and store merchandise. Her mother, Tessie Jane Stokely, was a descendant of John Stokely, John Huff, Russell Jones, and other pioneer settlers in the Del Rio area. About 1906, Richard Moore moved his family to KNOXVILLE, then forty miles north to Jellico, where he entered the wholesale dry goods business. Later, the Moores moved south to CHATTANOOGA, where Richard Moore owned Loveman's department store.

It was Jellico that Grace knew and loved as a young girl. She is remembered there as a vivacious and energetic child. She once rode through town on an elephant during a circus parade, and she played on the high school basketball team. Grace also began singing in the choir of the First Baptist Church in Jellico. She went on to Ward-Belmont College in Nashville. During this time, her idol Mary Garden gave a Nashville concert, and Grace was allowed backstage for a few words. Later encouragement and influence by Mary Garden helped Grace Moore attend the Wilson-Green School of Music in Washington, D.C. At the close of her first term at Wilson-Green, she was selected to give a solo concert. Critics' praise led her to New York City, where her first job was at the Black Cat Cafe. Next, she accompanied a touring company through the West. Her first major theatrical performance, in "Up in the Clouds", was followed by her first Broadway appearance as an understudy to star Julia Sanderson in the musical, "Hitchy Koo".

But opera was her desire, and in hopes of fulfilling that desire, Grace spent a year in Paris. She met Irving Berlin, who offered her a role in the "Music Box Revue" of 1923. At the conclusion of that season she auditioned for the Metropolitan Opera, but was told her voice was not ready. She continued in the "Music Box Revue" of 1924 and 1925, then returned to Paris for eighteen months of further study. After another audition for the Met, Grace Moore was granted a contract on June 13, 1927, with the Metropolitan Grand Opera Company. The following February, she made her debut as Mimi in "La Boheme". Other operas in which she later played included "Tosca", "Faust", "Carmen", "Romeo and Juliet", "Tales of Hoffman", and "The Love of Three Kings."

In July of 1931, Grace Moore married

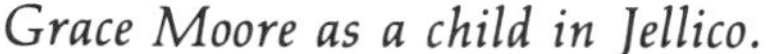

Grace Moore as a child in Jellico.

Courtesy Grace Moore Foundation, University of Tennessee

deMeyer / Courtesy Grace Moore Foundation, University of Tennessee

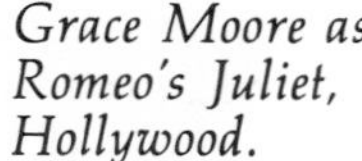

Grace Moore as Romeo's Juliet, Hollywood.

Valentin Parera of Madrid. They maintained homes in France and Sandy Hooks, Connecticut. Succeeding years saw Grace Moore star in a series of movies, a medium which she felt could take grand opera to a large public. *One Night of Love* (1934) was her most successful film; for it, she received a fellowship and a gold medal awarded by the Society of Arts and Sciences. Other films were *A Lady's Morals*, *New Moon*, *Love Me Forever*, and *I'll Take Romance*. After her stint in Hollywood, Grace joined the Chicago Opera Company. Following a post-World War II concert in Copenhagen, Grace Moore died when her airplane crashed and exploded during take-off. Memorial services were held for her at New York's Riverside Church and at Chattanooga's First Baptist Church. She was buried in Forest Hills Cemetery in Chattanooga.

Edward R. Walker III

Refer to: Grace Moore, *You're Only Human Once*, Garden City, N.Y.: Doubleday, Doran and Co., 1944; and Ruth Webb O'Dell, *Over the Misty Blue Hills: The Story of Cocke County, Tennessee*, Newport, Tenn., 1951.
See also: JOHN CULLUM
PATRICIA NEAL

Morgan County

Size: 539 Square Miles (344,960 acres)
Established: 1817
Named For: Daniel Morgan, Brigadier General in the American Revolution
County Seat: Wartburg
Other Major Cities, Towns, or Communities:
Petros
Sunbright
OAKDALE
Coalfield
DEER LODGE
Lancing
RUGBY

Refer to: Ethel Freytag and Glena Kreis Ott, *A History of Morgan County, Tennessee*, Wartburg: Specialty Printing Company, 1971.
See also: WILLIAM R. NELSON

Carl Holder, farmer, near Wartburg in Morgan County, May 1967.

Paul Moore / Courtesy TVA

Mary Noailles Murfree (January 24, 1850 - July 31, 1922) was born into a wealthy and socially prominent Tennessee family on a plantation in Rutherford County about thirty miles southeast of Nashville. Her mother's sister married John Bell, presidential candidate of the Constitutional Union Party in 1860. Her father, William Law Murfree, was a distinguished lawyer and grandson of Hardy Murfree, for whom Murfreesboro had been named in 1811.

Despite dislocation caused by the CIVIL WAR, Mary lived a sheltered life and was initially encouraged to write by her father, a scholarly man who spent hours reading the novels of Scott to his children. Educated at home by a private tutor, then at the Nashville Female Academy, and later at the exclusive Chegary Institute in Philadelphia, her initial interest in writing seemed a natural outgrowth of both her temperament and environment. Her first published work, an essay on genteel society, was published in *Lippincott's Magazine* in 1874. Some critics suggest that had Murfree continued writing in this vein of social satire, her ultimate artistic accomplishment would have been much greater.

In 1878, Murfree launched her career as one of the pre-eminent local color writers of nineteenth century America with the publication of "The Dancin' Party at Harrison's Cove" in the *Atlantic Monthly*. From 1878 until 1920, she wrote ten novels and thirty-five short stories about the mountains and mountaineers of the Cumberland Mountains and the Great Smoky Mountains. Her other works are comparatively insignificant. As a child, Murfree had spent fifteen summers at BEERSHEBA SPRINGS, a mountain resort in GRUNDY COUNTY on the Cumberland Plateau. Here she saw and took note of natives who would later populate her fictional world. During the 1870's, she made frequent trips with her family to the Great Smoky Mountains in East Tennessee, whose scenery and coves were likewise incorporated into her fiction.

Murfree's best works are *In The Tennessee Mountains* (1884), a collection of short stories, and *The Prophet of the Great Smoky Mountains* (1885). During the 1880's, her novels about Tennessee mountain life brought her critical acclaim in both England and the United States. Revelation in 1885 of her true identity as a genteel Southern spinster — she had heretofore used the pseudonym Charles Egbert Craddock — created quite a sensation in the American literary world.

By the 1890's, critics were complaining increasingly about Murfree's episodic plots and overblown descriptions of mountain scenery. Her novels seemed to repeat the same plot over and over with only minor variation, always using her stock characters — the beautiful maiden, scolding old woman, tyrannical infant, and mountain men ridiculous in their obtuseness and quaint speech. By the twentieth century, public interest in her writings had largely vanished, and her reputation among literary critics was eclipsed. Sympathetic biographers argued that she nevertheless had performed a valuable service by preserving an accurate portrait of

Tennessee mountain society in the 1870's and 1880's.

Historians disagreed. Cultural historian Henry Shapiro argues that Murfree left a highly selective and grossly distorted image of Tennessee mountain life. Through her fiction she transformed APPALACHIA into a strange land inhabited by quaint and peculiar people. Tragically, this enduring stereotype of Southern mountaineers isolated and retarded within an otherwise homogeneous and unified America continues today to impede any real understanding of the historical realities of Appalachia.

Murfree saw her mountaineers as *sui generis,* a people so separated and backward they could never be integrated into modern industrial America. The caste system she subsequently championed would permanently preclude progressive change or assimilation into the twentieth century, according to historian Robert Love Taylor, Jr. Careful study of CADES COVE, whose environs and scenery Murfree used extensively in her fiction after 1885, indicated that she completely failed to comprehend the lives or lifestyle of the people there. Despite her assumption of a static, unchanging society, Cades Cove was far from static and actually entered into a period of great progressive change following its postwar recovery. In her fiction, Murfree also indiscriminately mixed customs and speech patterns of the Cumberland Mountains with those of the Great Smoky Mountains. Scholars challenge her assumption that a homogeneous dialect ever existed in either region.

Courtesy Tennessee State Library

Mary Murfree

Most literary critics find little intrinsic merit in Murfree's writings today. Largely unread, she occasionally occupies space in an anthology illustrating local colorists. Historians generally agree that her stereotypes of the Tennessee mountaineer have done irreparable damage to an accurate assessment of the inhabitants of Southern Appalachia from the end of the Civil War until 1900.

Durwood Dunn

Refer to: Richard Cary, *Mary N. Murfree,* New York: Twayne, 1967; Durwood Dunn, "Mary Noailles Murfree: A Reappraisal," in *Appalachian Journal,* V. 6, No. 3 (Spring 1979), pp. 196-204; Edd Winfield Parks, *Charles Egbert Craddock,* Chapel Hill: University of North Carolina Press, 1941; Henry D. Shapiro, *Appalachia on Our Mind: The Southern Mountains and Mountaineers in the American Consciousness, 1870-1920,* Chapel Hill: University of North Carolina Press, 1978; and Robert Love Taylor, Jr., "Mainstreams of Mountain Thought: Attitudes of Selected Figures in the Heart of the Appalachian South, 1877-1903," University of Tennessee dissertation, 1971.

See also: APPALACHIAN LITERATURE
EAST TENNESSEE TALK
JOHN FOX, JR.

Melville Milton Murrell (November 9, 1855 - February 20, 1933), inventor and minister born in Panther Springs, Tennessee, obtained a patent in 1877 for "The Great American Flying Machine". When Wilbur Wright was ten and Orville was five, Murrell was watching his machine fly down a hillside near Panther Springs. At the age of five, Murrell had made his first attempt to fly. According to family legend, he took two of the largest cabbage leaves in his mother's garden and climbed on top of a stone wall in front of the house. He jumped off the wall with a leaf in each hand, flapping them as hard as he could. After he fell, he climbed to the top of the wall and tried again.

Murrell's parents were Colonel Marcus Rufus Murrell of the state militia and Mary Rebecca White Murrell, sister-in-law of U.S. Senator W.T. Senter. The Colonel ran a general store, sold tickets for the stage, engaged in farming, and gradually accumulated a large agricultural estate. During the CIVIL WAR, Colonel Murrell sympathized with the North yet played host to both Union and Confederate forces, depending on who was in command of the area. When Confederate General James Longstreet retreated from KNOXVILLE in late 1863, he and his army camped the winter in Morristown. On October 27, 1864, Union forces under General Gilliam attacked the Confederates at Panther Springs. The Murrell house stood in the armies' line of fire, and Melville and his brothers had to hide in the fireplace for protection.

After the war the Murrell family moved to Morristown, where the Colonel sold farm machinery. In 1869 the father became secretary-treasurer of the Cincinnati, Cumberland Gap, and Charleston Railroad, which was then being built through Morristown. The family later moved back to the Panther Springs farm and a comfortable style of life.

As a teenager, young Murrell spent many hours designing his flying machine. On December 4, 1876, he sent a model of his invention to the Patent Office. "I finished it Saturday night," he wrote in a letter to a friend. "I can now say: 'Eureka, Eureka' for it works like a charm." His patent became the fourth ornithopter patent issued, but Murrell's machine was the first airplane in America built to carry a man. It was a hand-driven type made of canvas and wood. The wings were hinged and arranged to flap like those of a bird; they were controlled by a series of cords over pulleys and hand-manipulated cranks. The tail, which guided the machine, could be turned horizontally or vertically. Strapped in his seat, the operator maneuvered the machine with both hands and feet.

Several leading businessmen of Morristown, including the Rev. W. C. Hale, John Mathes, F. Roger Miller, J.N. Fisher, and Henry Mullins, witnessed the launch of Murrell's machine. With the aid of 300 feet of guide wires, it took off from the top of a hill on the Murrell farm and flew for several hundred yards down the hillside. Operator Charlie Cowan, a hired man, repeated the performance many times, but he could not manage to keep the machine aloft for very long. A Mr. Fisher once offered Murrell $60,000 for his patent rights, but Melville rejected the offer on the advice of his father.

Five years after his "Flying Machine" attempts, Murrell embarked upon a 45-year career as a Methodist circuit rider. He never attended a seminary, and the most formal schooling he had ever received was at the old Panther Springs Academy. But through his reading, he became well informed in law and the Bible. In 1885, Murrell married Matilda Miller from Rogersville and had five children. He became a skilled brickmason, carpenter, and blacksmith.

Melville Murrell continued his interest in invention. He created many industrial devices, including a manure spreader, a broom-tying machine, and a railway water pump which ran automatically when the yard engine approaching the tank released a system of weights and pulleys.

About 1912, Murrell made another attempt at a flying machine by incorporating the engine from his son's motorcycle. The motor proved too weak to lift the plane, and Murrell discontinued his experiments. In 1928, at the age of 73, unknown to his family and with the help of a hired man, Melville Murrell carried the pieces of his "Great American Flying Machine" into a field and burned them. Only a small wing fragment was preserved. Perhaps he felt his attempts had been failures. Perhaps he disliked the way the airplane had been used during World War I. Perhaps, finally, Murrell deserves little credit as a contributor to aeronautical science, but he does deserve recognition for his native inventive genius.

Becky Jo Weesner Moles

Refer to: Genius of the Hills, 16mm film, 11 minutes, Bob Mabry and Phil Hardison, East Tennessee State University, 1979.
See also: RELIGION
RAILROADS (NORTHEASTERN)

The Museum of Appalachia, *located on eighty acres at I-75 near the town of* NORRIS, *was begun in 1969 by John Rice Irwin. Called by the official* Tennessee Blue Book *"the most authentic and complete replica of pioneer Appalachian life in the world," the museum now contains well over 200,000 items. Its more than thirty log buildings—all authentically furnished—include an 1840 church, a cantilever barn, the Arnwine Cabin (listed on the National Register of Historic Places), an early schoolhouse, and a completely restored nineteenth-century farm homestead. The pioneer setting features early methods of farming and gardening, along with various types of farm fowl and animals.*

On a spring morning in 1962, shortly after I was elected Superintendent of Schools in ANDERSON COUNTY, I attended a public auction of the household and farm items of the old Miller place on the banks of the Clinch River, a few miles below Norris Dam. I shall always remember driving that morning down the tiny dirt road, which ended at the Miller place, and seeing the varied assortment of ancient relics and artifacts which had been dragged from the old house, the barn, the smokehouse, and several other outbuildings. Here were the reminders and the authentication of a pioneer-frontier culture and heritage I had revered since childhood. The fact that I was descended from the Miller family added to the profundity of my impression.

There were old wheat cradles, the ox yoke used by the first settlers to break the virgin ground, a wooden bucket which had been fished from the Clinch during the great Barren Creek flood, and massive hand-forged fish gigs to spear the mammoth-sized catfish which were once plentiful. There were the beautiful old cupboards, tables, handmade maple chairs with bottoms of hickory bark, and indeed a thousand items, each capable of filling a niche in history. Needless to say, I purchased many of these relics as the country auctioneer continued the sale throughout the day. From that time on, the collection of these intriguing mountain artifacts became an obsession with me.

But it would be less than accurate to indicate that my interest in collecting started so suddenly and simply. I had the good fortune to have been brought up in the company of my four grandparents, who had been born in UNION COUNTY in the 1860's and 1870's and who were familiar with and highly interested in

Museum of Appalachia.

Courtesy John Rice Irwin

the pioneer-frontier customs. They were the grandchildren of those first pioneers who had settled the wilderness by migrating down the valleys from Pennsylvania through Virginia, or by crossing over the formidable Smoky Mountains from North Carolina. I listened intently to their stories of those frontier days: stories of families who lived all winter on nothing but parched corn; of grown men who traveled barefoot through the snow; of marauding bears and panthers. But mostly I liked to hear detailed descriptions of what I perceived to be a great, gentle, colorful and ingenious people—venerable, yet rugged.

My first interest was the people themselves, and from them came my interest in collecting their relics, artifacts and tools. Even today, the intrinsic value of an item is not as important to me as its history. The fact for example, that a plow was made by Little Lige Collins in a dark cave while hiding from the Yankee soldiers during the CIVIL WAR, so that his woman could plow the corn crop, deepens the meaning of that implement. A child's sled takes on new meaning and beauty when one learns that old Marion Fisher had stopped his plowing for a day to make the crude wooden toy for his little four-year-old girl, who he thought might be dying of diptheria. And there is something very meaningful about gripping the handle of a wooden plane which was long ago held and used by the hand of great, great Grandpa Rice. In addition to my parents and grandparents, I sought out the company of the old people of the community. I hunted and trapped with them and listened to their stories of "the old-timey ways".

Our own lifestyle in the depression years of the 1930's employed many of the frontier-related customs and philosophies as well as the same types of plows, tools, baskets, FURNITURE, bed covers, and other items as those of frontier times. We used mules for all our farming, kept cows for our milk, made our butter, raised virtually all our food, and lived without the use of telephones or electricity. I remember well, for instance, the first time I talked on a phone at Uncle Eli's house; I was fourteen years old. And we carried water from the big hand-dug well at my Grandpa Irwin's place. Realizing my intense interest in these matters, my grandparents would occasionally give my brother and me some "old-timey" item. Grandpa Rice, I remember, once stated: "You boys ought to start a sort of little museum sometime with these old relics our people had."

So the Miller sale, though the beginning of my serious collecting, was by no means the beginning of my interest. But at that time, in 1962, I started collecting in earnest. Although the job of County Superintendent, with 8,000 students and several hundred employees, was a most strenuous one, I managed to find time. When we finally started closing the office on Saturday, I made the best of it. Leaving home long before daylight, I would go literally from one mountain home to another. I would often be gone from 16 to 20 hours, and on several occasions for a full 24-hour period. As the years passed, I became acquainted with many hundreds of the mountain folk, people whom I greatly admired and respected. I learned the most difficult art of quickly getting invited into the attics, the smokehouses, and every "nook and cranny" in my search for the varied remnants of the past. In later years I have spent considerably more time in this most interesting quest, leaving home often for days at a time.

As my garage became full and overflowing with the items I had collected, *The Knoxville News-Sentinel* published the fact that I would like to find a home for them. But after several months of "talking" with representatives of the Federal government, and with other agencies, it appeared that their plans were nebulous and illusive and would never materialize. At this point, I acquired a large log house from the Tennessee Land and Mining Company and reassembled it behind my home near Norris. It was soon filled, and I next bought and reassembled the Arnwine Cabin, which was later included in the National Register of Historic Places. My wife Elizabeth and I began to have several visitors and a few school groups—not many, but enough to create some problems. At that point, I decided to open the two cabins to the public and to charge a small admission. This was in the summer of 1969.

The very first people who came to our small museum saw the admission sign and promptly left, as did most of the others. In those first few months, we would have one or two couples on a pretty weekend. I installed a service station bell so that my wife could know when someone drove in the driveway. About this time, the *News-Sentinel* reported that I had opened the collection to the public; that weekend, a total of fourteen people "flocked" out to tour the collection. Since then, the structures have multiplied to more than thirty, with a 10,000 sq. ft. display barn housing over 150,000 items. The land area has increased from less than two acres to approximately 80 acres, and a 12,000 sq. ft. gift shop - music barn has recently been completed. To say that the growth and acceptance of the Museum of Appalachia has exceeded my boldest dreams is a great understatement. In the beginning I was highly pleased, even exuberant, with the fourteen people who came in a single day. But during our first Fall Festival, in November of 1980, there were about 10,000 visitors in a two-day period.

My emphasis now is to document more fully the relics now on hand, describing their former owners, the makers, and as much history as possible. I also want to have more of the old-timey farming practices carried on, and to increase the number of farm animals. Emphasis is being placed on continuing such activities as making molasses, lye SOAP, hominy, brooms, picking ducks and geese, SPINNING AND WEAVING, basketmaking, food preserving, shingle splitting, chair bottoming, blacksmithing, corn grinding, and many other traditional "crafts". An extension of this action-oriented approach is the increased emphasis on the traditional and mountain music which will be featured on a regular basis. I would be less than grateful if I did not credit the hundreds of unselfish people who in so many ways have assisted in the growth of the Museum: my mountain friends, the family, the news media, and many throngs of strangers who have helped promote us. Without the help of these countless friends, the Museum of Appalachia would never have happened.

John Rice Irwin

See also: APPALACHIA
MUSEUMS
MUSICAL INSTRUMENTS
RIFLES
TANNING AND LEATHERMAKING

Museums. East Tennessee caught the museum fever, as did the rest of the state, in the early part of the 20th century. Since that time many museums in East Tennessee have been established and dedicated to furthering knowledge about the cultural, historical and scientific aspects related to the area, preserving what has been entrusted in their care, and, when appropriate, presenting a broader view of the world through their exhibits, research, study collections, and other programs.

The development of museums in East Tennessee reflects a trend that began in Charleston, South Carolina in 1773, when a group of inspired citizens formed the first public museum in America, the purpose of which was to preserve objects of nature and the past. Quality objects and local artifacts were collected to encourage study and improve public taste. By the end of the 19th century smaller communities had begun to support their own local museums, state-funded museums were operating, the first Historic House Museum was established in Newburgh, New York, natural history societies had museums associated with them, and universities were being given large gifts to endow museums and build collections. The 20th century saw planned methods of acquiring specimens rather than simply being repositories of countless "curiosities" or "menageries". The museum had begun its educational role as teacher and interpreter of knowledge for the public.

In 1895 George Brown Goode, assistant secretary of the Smithsonian Institution in Washington, D.C., defined museums as institutions "for the preservation of those objects which best illustrate the phenomena of nature and the works of man, and utilization of these for the increase of knowledge and for the culture and enlightenment of the people." More recently, most museums have tried to meet certain additional criteria to qualify as museums. Since it was founded in 1906, the American Association of Museums has provided the necessary professional standards and quality guidance for museums in the United States. To supplement the AAM's program, some states have established their own state museum association that functions state-wide and administers to local museum needs and concerns. In Tennessee, the Tennessee Association of Museums (TAM) fills that role as an organization encouraging high museum standards and involved with the total museum resources across the state. TAM works in cooperation with the AAM, the American Association for State and Local History, and the regional Southeastern Museum Conference in steadily striving for improved quality.

The AAM has defined a museum as "An organization and permanent non-profit institution essentially educational or aesthetic in purpose which owns or utilizes tangible objects, cares for them, and exhibits them to the public on some regular schedule." There are numerous types of museums. According to the AAM, there are some 84 categories that vary in size and comprehensiveness. Included are types of Art, Children's, University, General, History, Science, and Specialized Museums. Museums can also be classified as State, County, and City Museums, depending on their scope and location. East Tennessee has a representative sampling from these major categories, and predictably the majority of them are History Museums. It should be noted, however, that often a museum can qualify for more than one category. Overlaps are generally due to a broad range of interest that may embrace Art, History and Science.

In the main, Art Museums in East Tennessee have been set up in existing historically significant houses or institutional buildings, often already outfitted with a core collection. Some offer a wide choice of art subjects in one facility, as well as special traveling or loan exhibitions and art education programs. For example, the Hunter Museum of Art in CHATTANOOGA, founded in 1951, includes a 1904 mansion and a modern wing built in 1975. The Hunter's collections of fine FURNITURE, decorative arts, American paintings, drawings and sculpture of the 18th through 20th centuries are exhibited here, along with temporary exhibitions as supplements to the permanent collections on display. The Dulin Gallery of Art in KNOXVILLE was founded in 1962 and mainly functions as a gallery of changing traveling and loan exhibitions. The Dulin's Neo-classical mansion, listed in the National Register of Historic Places, was designed by the architect John Russell Pope and completed in 1917.

Also in Knoxville, the 1834 "Crescent Bend" Armstrong-Lockett House has been a Decorative Arts Museum since 1977. Owned by the Toms Foundation, "Crescent Bend" contains the W.P. Toms memorial collection. Another Decorative Arts Museum in Knoxville is Speedwell Manor. Built around 1830, it houses 18th and 19th century furnishings along with Western and Oriental decorative arts. "Hopecote", a house architecturally styled in the manner of an English cottage, was completed in 1924. Located on THE UNIVERSITY OF TENNESSEE campus, it was opened in 1979 as a "teaching laboratory" and for other functions. Although considered a Historic Village Museum, the MUSEUM OF APPALACHIA in NORRIS is a Folk Art Museum as well. The Museum of Appalachia presents a wide selection of American pioneer objects shown in restored structures within a farm-like setting.

Universities have art galleries in existing campus buildings. The Elizabeth Slocumb Gallery of contemporary art and crafts is associated with EAST TENNESSEE STATE UNIVERSITY in JOHNSON CITY. Opened in 1965 and named to honor the first chairperson of the Department of Art, it is primarily a teaching gallery. The Frank H. McClung Museum at The University of Tennessee in Knoxville has the Eleanor Deane Audigier art and antique collection on exhibit; it also possesses a gallery for contemporary art

George Baker / Courtesy Hunter Museum of Art

Hunter Museum of Art, Chattanooga.

exhibitions.

Children's Museums developed out of the need for highly imaginative museum experiences scaled to and for children. These have become centers of joyful activity and involvement, places where children can exercise their sense of touch, learn new skills, and experience alternative types of learning. A relatively new one in East Tennessee is the CHILDREN'S MUSEUM OF OAK RIDGE, opened in 1973, which in addition to its exhibition program offers multifarious educational activities that include dance recitals, arts festivals and hobby workshops for children as well as adults. The Students' Museum in Knoxville, both a Children's Museum and a Natural History Museum, has collections of rocks and minerals, insects, shells, birds and other animal life. It includes interpretive history and science exhibits as well as a planetarium that was opened in 1976 with funds raised by the Akima Club of Knoxville. Formerly called the Andrew Jackson School Children's Museum, the Estelle Carmack Bandy Children's Museum in KINGSPORT provides exhibits that deal with the history of the museum, Indian heritage and natural history; it also has pioneer furniture, tools and clothing on display. Children are encouraged to touch objects and attend special historical dramas, and resource people are invited to the museum to teach and demonstrate crafts.

According to the 1981 *Official Museum Directory*, there are about 451 College and University Museums in the United States. They serve both "town and gown" and function differently from public museums, serving mainly as teaching and research supports for related departments. Most of them evolved from collections associated with academic departments. Predictably, therefore, the collections and programs of those in East Tennessee are diversified, focusing either on art, science, history or a combination of subjects. The University Gallery at The University of Tennessee at Chattanooga features paintings and graphics; the Joseph B. Wolffe Gallery at The University of Tennessee at Knoxville exhibits sports sculpture; the Institute of Archaeology at The University of Tennessee at Chattanooga is primarily concerned with local prehistoric and historic archaeological material; and the History Museum at LINCOLN MEMORIAL UNIVERSITY in Harrogate houses Abraham Lincoln memorabilia. The B. Carroll Reece Museum at East Tennessee State University in Johnson City and the Frank H. McClung Museum at The University of Tennessee at Knoxville have collections and programs in several subject areas. The latter museum has the largest collection of southeastern Indian archaeological material in the United States, as well as collections in art, history and science.

Company Museums continue to mushroom throughout the country and serve to record the vast dimensions of industry and commerce that might otherwise be overlooked. There seems to be almost as many kinds of Company Museums as there are actual businesses. East Tennessee has the distinction of being the home of one that is unique. The Ancient Brick Museum of the General Shale Products Corporation in Johnson City is the only museum in the world that exhibits the history of brick-making, tracing 10,000 years of development by using the company's extensive collection of bricks gathered from the far reaches of the globe.

History Museums outnumber all other types of museums. Since the past has always had great fascination for people of all ages, History Museums help to suggest what other periods in time might have been like, and, in some measure, serve to satisfy this curiosity. Historic Houses, Buildings and Site Museums serve to honor the persons who lived there, to commemorate the local occurrence of important historical events, to preserve significant ARCHITECTURE, or to combine more than one of these types. One of the first History Museums in East Tennessee, ANDREW JOHNSON's Tailor Shop, opened in 1923. It is now part of the Andrew Johnson National Historic Site in Greeneville, which includes a museum of interpretive exhibits, Johnson's nearby home, cemetery, homestead and the Tailor Shop. Founded in 1942, the museum complex seals the memory of the Greeneville tailor whose humble beginnings did not hinder his rise to the Presidency of the United States.

Probably the earliest recognized Historic House Museum in East Tennessee is Blount Mansion in Knoxville, founded in 1926. A National Historic Landmark, it was built in 1792 for WILLIAM BLOUNT, Governor of the Territory South of the River Ohio. In Harrogate, Lincoln Memorial University's History Museum and Library, housed in a special room provided in 1928, furthers the ideals of the Great Emancipator Abraham Lincoln. Its rich collection of Lincolniana has become the most extensive in the world. A relatively new History Museum is Beck Cultural Exchange Center in Knoxville, a museum of black culture that opened in 1975 to preserve, collect, research and exhibit material related to the achievements of Knoxville's black citizens since the early 19th century. The restored 1783-1815 farmhouse at Marble Springs in Knoxville represents the home of "Tennessee's greatest civil military hero", Governor JOHN SEVIER. Several miles away, a restored handsome red granite and blue limestone house, designed by the architect Thomas Hope and built in 1797 for Colonel Francis Alexander Ramsey, was the boyhood home of Tennessee's historian Dr. J.G.M. RAMSEY. During the CIVIL WAR, Confederate as well as Union forces used as their headquarters the premises of the Cravens House on Lookout Mountain overlooking Chattanooga. The area was the scene of numerous skirmishes between the forces. In Knoxville, the Confederate Memorial Hall ("Bleak House"), an antebellum mansion affiliated with the United Daughters of the Confederacy, served as General James Longstreet's headquarters during the siege of the city in 1863.

There are several architecturally significant houses and buildings in East Tennessee, but one of the finest examples of the Second Empire architectural style in Tennessee is Glenmore, a Historic House Museum in Jefferson City. The 18th century John and Landon Carter House in ELIZABETHTON probably has one of the most attractive classic interiors anywhere. The Netherland Inn House Museum and Boat Yard Complex in Kingsport is a Historic House and Site erected 1802-1818 and comprised of several houses and cabins. The city intends to build a Flatboat Museum at the Boat Yard site as part of a three-mile-long Historic District riverfront park, which will include 18th century Cherokee campgrounds as well as fort and battle sites. Rocky Mount, the Historic House and Site in Piney Flats, was the capital of "The Territory of the United States of America South of the River Ohio" from 1790 to 1792. Here, Governor William Blount administered his affairs before Knoxville became the territorial capital in 1792. A separate museum building has exhibits that interpret numerous historic frontier objects.

History Museums often have an exhibit building or interpretive center associated with them. The SAM HOUSTON School House, restored in 1954 and situated in BLOUNT COUNTY, is a one-story log cabin where the great soldier, statesman, and Governor of Tennessee taught school in 1812. On the grounds is a building exhibiting early school and pioneer objects. WILL G. AND HELEN H. LENOIR MUSEUM in Norris, opened in 1975 and operated by the Norris Dam State Park, contains 18th-19th century collections of early farm implements, pioneer furnishings, and a general store. A nearby grist mill, built in 1798 on Lost Creek in Union County, was moved to Norris Dam State Park in 1935. Visitors can observe corn and wheat still being stone ground. High above the Tennessee River on Lookout Mountain in Point Park is the Ochs Observatory and Museum, built as a memorial to Adolph S. Ochs, conservationist and publisher of the *Chattanooga Times* and *New York Times*. The site affords a broad vista of the battlefields where the fierce Battle of Chattanooga was fought in 1863. The small museum, built on the mountainside and administered by the National Park Service, has exhibits that relate the entire story of the battle.

Sometimes Historic Sites have reconstructions and restorations built at or near the spot of the original structure. Near Vonore is FORT LOUDOUN, a reconstructed stockade with log gates and replicas of colonial cannons. It represents the original fort that was built in 1756-1757 by South Carolina provincial troops to stop the French and increase English dominance in the Mississippi Valley during the French and Indian War. An orientation museum at the site includes exhibits interpreting the history of the Tennessee Valley. In Knoxville, James White's Fort, named for Knoxville's founder, is a reconstruction of the early stockade built as protection against possible Indian attacks. The Crockett Tavern Museum near Morristown, founded in 1958, is a reproduction of the tavern of the 1790's established and run by John and Rebecca Crockett, parents of the famous pioneer and political figure DAVID CROCKETT. A replica of his birthplace is near Limestone in GREENE COUNTY. Brazelton Cabin in New Market was built about 1832. This restored brick cabin was an outbuilding of Brazelton Place, a grand Georgian home built in 1832, and is used to exhibit Civil War material.

Whole towns or sections of cities are Open-Air Museums that also preserve aspects of an area's historical and cultural roots. Unique JONESBORO, the first town in Tennessee (charted 1779), was a transportation center bustling with commerce and strategically located on the "Great Stage Road". Today, it represents "a living museum of regional 19th century architecture of the Southern Appalachians." Rugby Colony in RUGBY was a small rural community established in 1880 by Thomas Hughes, educator and author of *Tom Brown's School Days*, to promote progressive economic, social and educational value systems. Seventeen remaining structures with Gothic Revival and Italianate architectural forms are reminders of a faded ideal. CADES COVE Open Air Museum near GATLINBURG was first granted legal settlement in 1821 to pioneers who wanted to settle on good grazing land. Now part of the GREAT SMOKY MOUNTAINS NATIONAL PARK, Cades Cove has been "set aside to exhibit mountain culture" and to preserve significant characteristics of early rugged frontier life. Historic Districts as Open-air Museums are numerous in East Tennessee and include Elizabethton, Greeneville, Rogersville, DANDRIDGE, Blountville and Church Circle District in Kingsport. Most Historic Districts have structures dating back to the 18th century.

Science Museums are not as numerous as History Museums, but they are far more diversified. Since some interpret their material from a historical viewpoint, they can be considered both Science and History Museums, while certain objects from ethnological and archaeological collections can be interpreted as fine art. From anthropology to zoology, a growing number of Science Museums keep the general public in touch with the meaning applied and natural science can have for them as individuals. Located in OAK RIDGE, the American Museum of Science and Energy brings the history of energy to life. The exhibit program includes machines, gadgets, devices, demonstrations and other activities designed as instructional tools to teach and involve the public in scientific progress and its relevance. At The University of Tennessee at Chattanooga, the Institute of Archaeology offers exhibits based on its collection of pre-historic material. The Institute also does research in historic and industrial ARCHAEOLOGY. The Medical Museum at the Knoxville Academy of Medicine was begun in 1952 as a permanent memorial to former medical practitioners. The renovated 1908 Nolichucky Powerhouse in Greeneville serves as an interpretive center for the TENNESSEE VALLEY AUTHORITY's Nolichucky Environmental Education Project.

The University of Tennessee Arboretum in Oak Ridge is a Science Museum, but with a living collection of native plants being the exhibit and research feature. The major collections of American holly, willow, pine, juniper and dogwood are in test gardens, so that scientists can observe their ability to adapt to local environmental conditions. Zoos, aquariums, wildlife refuges, and bird sanctuaries are also Science Museums of living exhibits and study collections; the Knoxville Zoological Park and the Nolichucky Waterfowl Sanctuary and Environmental Study Area in Greeneville are only two of many. Nature Centers are also considered museums. The Ijams Audubon Nature Center in Knoxville is a 26-acre park owned by the city with two miles of marked wildflower gardens and nature trails. The Chattanooga Nature Center, located on a site associated with the Battle of Chickamauga, has an active program that includes an exhibit hall, laboratory, traveling exhibitions, and collections of Tennessee wildlife, rocks, and minerals. Visitor Centers include Sugarlands Visitor Center, begun in 1961 near Gatlinburg in the Great Smoky Mountains National Park. In addition, some LIBRARIES that have collections other than books and exhibit areas are considered museums.

As the name suggests, Specialized Museums concentrate on one specific subject. The 1981 *Official Museum Directory* lists 35 different kinds, starting with Agriculture and Antiques and ending with Religious, Transportation, and Village Museums. The Tipton-Haynes Living Historical Farm in

Johnson City was founded in 1965 and comprises several late 18th century houses, a slave quarter, and a mid-19th century law office. In Chattanooga, the Houston Antique Museum is noted for its fine collection of early American, French and English glass and 19th century decorative arts and furniture. The Harris Swift Museum of Religion and Ceremonial Arts and Library of Rare Books in Chattanooga has exhibits and collections that pertain to all faiths. The Tennessee Valley Railroad and Museum, founded in 1961 in Chattanooga and offering steam train excursions, is devoted to preserving railroad artifacts and researching the history of RAILROADS. Locomotives, train cars, and a 1920 depot are on exhibit at the museum site. As mentioned earlier, the Museum of Appalachia in Norris is a Village Museum of 30 restored pioneer log structures.

As might be predicted, those cities in East Tennessee with the largest populations have the greatest number of museums. Knoxville, settled about 1786, provides the most museums; it is followed by Kingsport and Chattanooga. In terms of East Tennessee as a whole, the majority of museums were founded after 1950, and most of these in the 1960's—a time of prosperity and governmental stability in the state, in spite of racial unrest. Museums continue to emerge. One of the newest is the Newport-COCKE COUNTY Museum, opened in 1980 in the Newport Community Center. The Museum exhibits 19th century interiors, early farm and shoemaker's tools, quilts and other historic material. The JEFFERSON COUNTY Historical Museum, located in the Dandridge Courthouse in Dandridge (second oldest town in the state), continues to perfect its operation. The Scottish Rite Temple in Knoxville plans to expand its modest exhibit area and library of objects and material pertaining to its fraternal order of Freemasons.

The new Kingsport Fine Arts Center, now located in a former First Methodist Church, is a civic art and culture center for all the arts. Located on the historic 18th century Daniel Boone Trail, the Center is attempting to develop an art collection of its own. In HANCOCK COUNTY, the Old Jail—built around 1860 and listed in the National Register of Historic Places—is believed to be the oldest building in Sneedville. When plans for a new jail are completed, the Old Jail will become a museum. The same will undoubtedly be true for the 1905 SCOTT COUNTY Jail in Huntsville, a prison that can hold 33 offenders and has kept a perfect record of no escapees! In Knoxville, the new East Tennessee Historical Center—formerly the Custom House, built 1870-1874—houses the archival McClung Collection and will include exhibits on Tennessee history. The restoration of Elizabethton's Carter House and the construction of its new visitor center have been completed. At Rocky Mount, a new visitor center and museum extension have opened with exhibits about the early history of Tennessee. In Chattanooga, plans have been made to open the museum of the National Knife Collectors Association. The Jonesboro History Museum will open in 1982. The future of museums in East Tennessee looks bright.

Elaine Altman Evans

Refer to: Edward P. Alexander, *Museums in Motion*, Nashville: American Association for State and Local History, 1979; *America's Museums: The Belmont Report*, Washington, D.C.: American Association of Museums, 1968; Lawrence V. Coleman, *College and University Museums* and *Historic House Museums*, Washington, D.C.: American Association of Museums, 1942 and 1933; Federal Writers' Project, *Tennessee: A Guide to the State*, New York: Viking, 1939 (reprinted 1949; New York: Hastings House); Herbert and Marjorie Katz, *Museums, U.S.A.*, Garden City, N.Y.: Doubleday, 1965; *The National Register of Historic Places*, Washington, D.C.: National Park Service, 1976; and Alma S. Wittlin, *Museums: In Search of a Usable Future*, Cambridge, Mass.: MIT Press, 1970.

Musical Instruments. The first musical instruments in East Tennessee were those made and used by the prehistoric Indians. Archaeologists have found a few effigy pottery whistles, modelled mainly on animals and birds, in excavations of mounds and village sites. These early Indians must have had other instruments made of wood, cane or gourd which did not survive the centuries. During the early eighteenth century, the CHEROKEES became the dominant tribe in East Tennessee. These Indians used both rattles and drums with their dances. Rattles were made from dried gourds or turtle shells with beans, corn, or pebbles placed inside. Sometimes they were decorated with rattlesnake rattles or hawk feathers. The drums were either simple hide-covered tom-toms or water drums. One water drum at the Museum of the Cherokee Indian in Cherokee, North Carolina, is barrel-shaped with a covering of groundhog hide. Such a drum would have been partially filled with water to produce a special tone.

The first Europeans in this area were the members of Hernando DeSoto's 1540 expedition, but it is not known if they brought any musical instruments with them. It can only be guessed that they, like the English and French soldiers who came later, must have used traditional European military fifes and drums in their long marches. The first white settlers in East Tennessee came mainly from central Pennsylvania, western North Carolina and Virginia, bringing only the bare necessities for survival in the mountainous wilderness. They also brought with them a love for music and a knowledge of several instruments which are associated today with APPALACHIA: the fiddle, mouthbow, dulcimer, banjo, and guitar. Carving out a new life was so difficult for the first several generations of settlers that there was rarely any spare time or proper tools to make musical instruments in the traditional European styles. Because flutes and other wind instruments were too difficult to make without certain tools, the mountain folk improvised stringed instruments with gourds, boxes, syrup buckets, and other spare materials. The MUSEUM OF APPALACHIA at NORRIS displays an extensive collection of these crude instruments as well as instruments of more traditional designs.

It is the opinion of John Rice Irwin, owner of the Museum of Appalachia, that the fiddle has been the most widely owned and played instrument in the mountains. Certainly East Tennessee has, over the years, produced some talented fiddlers and fiddle makers. The area has long encouraged the art of fiddling by holding regular fiddling contests and Saturday night musical parties. In the late nineteenth century, A.L. Cassady and Evart Acuff started making fine quality traditional fiddles in UNION COUNTY. Today, that tradition continues in the workshops of Charles Gene Horner of Westel (CUMBERLAND COUNTY) and Clyde Cox of Karns (KNOX COUNTY). These and other craftsmen have generally used locally grown curly maple for the back and sides of their fiddles, and spruce for the top. There is no difference in design between a fiddle and a violin. The difference in names comes with the type of music played and the way the instrument and the bow are held. The violinist tucks the instrument securely under his chin, while the fiddler leans it against his chest.

Although not as widely found as the

Guitarist, violinist, and mandolin player, Cocke County, ca. 1910. The violinist is playing in the manner of a fiddler. The European-style mandolin, with a bulge in the back, resembles the back of a Colorado potato beetle and is called a "tater bug" in East Tennessee.

Courtesy Gene Branam

fiddle, the mouthbow has been played for many generations in East Tennessee. Local tradition holds that the Indians taught the early settlers to play it. Since mouthbows (also called musical bows) are found in every part of the world except Europe, this tradition may indeed be true. The instrument looks like a simple hunting bow and was often carved of cedar or hickory and strung with whatever fine wire was available. The musician places one end of the wooden arc against his slightly opened lips and plucks the string with either the fingers or a pick. Variation in the "twangy" tone are produced by changing the shape of the mouth, as when playing the Jew's harp. ALEX STEWART of Union County has made mouthbows as well as many other items and tools.

One of the great misconceptions about East Tennessee's early musical instruments is that everyone knew about and played the dulcimer. Actually, the dulcimer was not very common in this area. Recent research by Ralph Lee Smith suggests that there were fewer than 1,000 dulcimers in all of Appalachia before the 1940's. The origins of the dulcimer reach as far back as ancient Persia, yet it is still a mystery how the mountain dulcimer developed in East Tennessee. Peter Cohan, a dulcimer maker in OAK RIDGE, believes that the Pennsylvania-German settlers who came into East Tennessee knew about the German zither and built the dulcimer as a kind of simple zither. The wide variations in shape attest to the folk origins of the mountain dulcimer. Small ripples of interest in the dulcimer in the 1940's grew to a great wave of enthusiasm by the late 1960's. The autumn craft shows throughout the area usually manage to include Jean and Lee Schilling of Cosby, Peter Cohan and Johnny Tigue of Oak Ridge, James Luther of Maryville, and several other dulcimer makers.

The banjo made its way into the East Tennessee mountains about the turn of this century. Most musicians made their banjos with four long melody strings and a fifth short thumb string. Their choice of wood for the neck and rim ranged from white oak to walnut, hickory, maple, or poplar. Tanned groundhog hide was preferred for making the banjo head, but large squirrel and wildcat hides were also used. Sometimes thin strips of wood or metal, called frets, were placed under the strings to indicate where the picker should place his fingers while playing. Other makers omitted the frets. These fretless banjos have lately become popular collector's items both in America and England. Today most banjos are commercially made, but some are still made by the hands of such craftsmen as Thurman Tindell of Knox County and Gene Horner of Cumberland County.

The guitar became popular in East Tennessee in the early twentieth century, perhaps when the mountain boys were introduced to guitar music during their military service. When the mailorder catalogues from Chicago advertised cheap guitars, hard-earned dollars were quickly spent for these shiny new "git-tars". With the advent of commercially recorded COUNTRY MUSIC, the guitar's popularity continued to spread until it has become

Doris Ulmann / Courtesy Doris Ulmann Foundation, Berea College

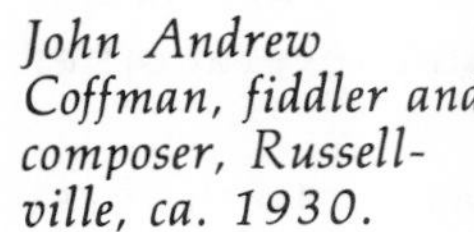

John Andrew Coffman, fiddler and composer, Russellville, ca. 1930.

perhaps the most popular folk instrument in the area. With the rise in string bands, the mandolin was also introduced to this region. Known locally as the "tater bug" because of the resemblance between its striped rounded back and the potato beetle, it became an important member of the popular bluegrass bands of the area.

Although stringed instruments were very popular with East Tennessee folk, they were seldom played by women and were rarely used in religious services. Great emphasis was placed on vocal music and the rudiments of music learned in the annual singing schools, so that the church folk could sing loud praises to the Lord without the secular distraction of fiddles and such. When the Methodists, Baptists, and Presbyterians finally allowed organs into their churches, they were the small harmoniums or pump organs. Circuit-riding ministers even had portable free-reed pump organs. Ornately carved harmoniums commanded an important spot in the fine parlors of the area during the 1920's, only to give way later to the still popular electronic organs. The most spectacular organ in East Tennessee today is the "Mighty Wurlitzer", which was installed in the Tennessee Theater in KNOXVILLE in September of 1928. This three-manual (triple keyboard) instrument has twelve hundred pipes in fourteen ranks plus two sound chambers. Chinese red and trimmed in gold, this Wurlitzer is one of the few theater organs in America still in fine playing condition.

The first piano in East Tennessee may have been brought in by Colonel Whiteside, owner of the Bean Station Tavern in GRAINGER COUNTY. In the early 1800's, Whiteside had a small German-made Stein piano brought by wagon over the mountains for his inn. The square piano—actually rectangle, but still referred to as "square" style—had two legs damaged during the CIVIL WAR, but it has otherwise survived intact. Two similar pianos are on public display in Knoxville, at the Armstrong-Lockett House on Kingston Pike and at Blount Mansion on Hill Avenue. During the 1920's, the JFG Coffee Company of Knoxville gave a miniature piano, custom-made in Japan, to each grocer who ordered at least three cases of JFG Coffee. Although this gift piano looked like a child's toy piano, it was actually designed like a standard piano, complete with hammers and dampers for the strings. One such piano is on display at the Lynn Sheeley Piano Company in Knoxville.

East Tennessee now boasts a wide variety of musical instruments and musical organizations. This area has ten symphony orchestras as well as college and public school bands, bluegrass bands, rock and dance bands, handbell choirs, and countless keyboard and other soloists. Musical instruments have continued to be an important part of life for the folk of East Tennessee.

Peggy Flanagan Baird

Refer to: John Rice Irwin, *Musical Instruments of The Southern Appalachian Mountains*, Norris, Tenn.: The Museum of Appalachia Press, 1979; Jean Schilling, *Old Time Fiddle Tunes for the Appalachian Dulcimer*, Cosby, Tenn.: Crying Creek Publishers, 1978; and Charles K. Wolfe, *Tennessee Strings*, Knoxville: University of Tennessee Press, 1977.

See also: BLUEGRASS MUSIC
OLD HARP SINGING

N

The National Campground, located in LOUDON COUNTY between Lenoir City and Greenback, was established in 1873, eight years after the CIVIL WAR, "to promote the cause of our great Redeemer and unite the different denominations in Christian fellowship; also to allay the feuds engendered by the late national difficulties." First known as Union Campgrounds, the assembly was

Interior of the National Campground tabernacle, built 1874, now listed on the National Register of Historic Places.

Patricia Boatner

made up of Presbyterians, Cumberland Presbyterians, Baptists, Methodists, Southern Methodists and Friends. Founders incorporated the organization, elected a mayor, and set up laws to govern the campus. Drinking, stealing, and destroying trees were listed among the worst crimes.

Organizers held a tent meeting in 1873, but by the fall of the next year, the tabernacle was completed at a cost of $600. The shed, open on all four sides, was supported by massive hand-hewn oak posts, roof joists and overhead beams held together by wood pegs. A cabin known as The Preacher's Camp was later built to house the visiting ministers, and a dining hall was constructed near one of the two springs on the site. The largest crowds attended before the advent of modern transportation. Hundreds came by horse or wagon and camped for two weeks or more. The "camp meeting" not only provided spiritual renewal; it was also the major social event of the year. Today, a week-long camp meeting is still held each August. Worshipers sit on the original benches, sing the old songs, and listen to the same summoning bell which rang in 1873.

Patricia Boatner

See also: RELIGION

Patricia Neal (January 20, 1926 -), actress, was born in Packard, Kentucky. Her family soon moved to KNOXVILLE, where Patricia attended Park City-Lowery Elementary School. After seeing a monologist perform at a church program, Patricia begged her parents for drama lessons. Within a few years she became well-known in her hometown as an entertainer. Patricia graduated from Knoxville High in 1943, went on to study drama at Northwestern University, and trained further at the Barter Theater in Abingdon, Virginia. She moved to New York and gained recognition in Lillian Hellman's Broadway play, *Another Part of the Forest*. Soon after her successes in New York, Patricia Neal moved to Hollywood to star in such movies as *John Loves Mary* (her first, with Ronald Reagan) and *The Fountainhead* (with Gary Cooper). In 1952 she returned to Broadway, where she appeared in *The Children's Hour, A Room Full of Roses*, and *Cat On A Hot Tin Roof*. Patricia Neal reached a pinnacle in her career when she won an Academy Award in 1963 for her role alongside Paul Newman in *Hud*.

Patricia and her family were in California two years later, during the filming of *Seven Women*, when she suffered a massive stroke. With the help of her husband, Welsh author Roald Dahl, Patricia Neal recovered remarkably and signalled a dramatic comeback as an actress by starring in the 1968 film, *The Subject Was Roses*. She has since become an outstanding spokeswoman for people suffering from severe debilitations. A proud hometown played host to her in October of 1978, when Knoxville held the Patricia Neal Homecoming Festival at the Tennessee Theatre and dedicated the Patricia Neal Rehabilitation Center at Fort Sanders Presbyterian Hospital.

Jim Stokely

See also: JOHN CULLUM
KNOXVILLE THEATRES
GRACE MOORE

William R. Nelson of MORGAN COUNTY, my grandfather, used to tell tales to us grandchildren and sing us the old English ballads. But the stories he told of witches and "hants" were what held us spellbound and quaking in delighted terror. Grandpa had grown up at a time when CHEROKEES still lived in cabins among the white settlers of the Cumberland Plateau. He told of an old Indian woman who lived in a cabin near him when he was about ten years old. Most of the others in the area avoided her, for it was a well-established fact that she practiced witchcraft. She had a humped back, wild straggly hair, dark leathery skin, and soul-piercing black eyes.

For some unexplained reason, perhaps because he sometimes helped her with her chores, the Indian woman "took a liking to" little Bill Nelson. One day some of the other neighbor boys taunted her and threw rocks at her house. In retaliation, she cast a spell on their only milk cow. The cow's milk immediately became unfit to drink, foul and rancid in both odor and taste. This went on for a few days, and the baby of the family was in desperate need of fresh wholesome milk. So Bill made a good fire in his mother's cook stove, filled a large pan with the tainted milk, then set it on the range. As the boiling milk spilled across the red hot stove, the smoke and the stench were almost overpowering. Very soon the aged Indian woman came hobbling up the hillside as fast as her wizened legs would

Courtesy June Wortley

William R. Nelson

carry her. Very nauseated, she all but fell inside the cabin door, pleading with the little boy to stop burning the milk as he was killing her. Little Bill consented to do so, if she would take the curse off the neighbor's cow. She agreed, and by next milking time the cow's milk was again pure and sweet.

This witch did not always perform black magic. Sometimes she did good deeds for people. For instance, she had the power to remove warts and to "put back" boils and abcesses. Before the old lady died, she passed on this power to my grandfather. During the time when I lived with him and my grandmother, a week rarely passed when one or two people did not come to him to have boils or abcesses or warts removed. He did not like to treat a boil or an abcess unless it was in a place chafed by clothing. Otherwise, he said, the flaw was a sign of bad blood and might pop up somewhere else.

When I was in my early teens, I had three ugly seed warts appear on the inside of my arm about midway between by wrist and elbow. They were painful as well as repulsive, for I was constantly bruising them on some object. I was living in Indiana then and asked a doctor there to remove them. He said that if he cut them out, it would leave a scar; furthermore, the warts might return. A few weeks later I came to Morgan County to visit my grandparents. My grandfather merely passed his fingertips across the warts. I determined to keep my eye on them, but one cannot sit and watch warts forever, so eventually I looked away. The next time I looked at my arm, it was as smooth as silk with no scar and no sign of where the warts had been. Grandfather always said that before he died he would pass this power on to someone else in the family. But he died suddenly in his sleep, and the power was forever lost.

Grandpa also told us about a cabin he had once lived in when he was a boy which, to his way of thinking, was haunted. He said that many times in the night the family would hear the sound of horses' hooves clattering up the wooden steps, across the porch and into the house, followed by the sound of dishes and pots and pans crashing to the floor. Yet when the family would rush pell mell down the stairs, all would be serene, in perfect order on the first floor. Perhaps you, my reader, do not believe in the supernatural, but I, perhaps due to early conditioning, will keep an open mind on the subject.

June Byrd Wortley

See also: THE UNINVITED

New Market Train Wreck. September 24, 1904: Twelve year old H.J. Wilson wandered from his father sitting on a store bench, talking, there in Strawberry Plains, taking the mid-morning leisure of the fine polished blue clarity and warmth of a September day. But more interesting to little Red Wilson was the world of trains. So he sauntered over to the nearby depot. Leaning in the doorway, he saw John Hayes, a telegraph operator, and his assistant, Adam Douglas. It was Hayes who, a few seconds later, suddenly looked up and shouted to Douglas: "My God, the trains are going to run together! No. 15 had orders to take siding at New Market for No. 12 to pass. No. 15 didn't do it."

Aboard a day coach on west-bound No. 15 on her way from Talbott's Station to visit kin in KNOXVILLE, Miss Suzie Haynes delighted in the cool breezes and the morning's scenery from her open window: acres of rolling farmland in a fertile valley, not too far off there on a hillside some farmer with his team of horses plowing. Suddenly, from behind her, the porter rushed to her window, leaned out to stare down the tracks: "If they stay on the track we'll meet them!"

Two funnels of black smoke drawing nearer: Joe Whitaker looked up from his plowing to watch the trains pass, but before words could reach his lips to say the inevitable, the crash occurred. Standing there on the hillside above the tracks at 10:18 a.m., he saw the two engines rearing, then cars piling on top of cars, telescoping, heard the crack and snap of wood splintering, saw debris flying all directions, heard the screams of passengers.

Word spread slowly. By shortly past 12 noon one hundred workmen were sorting through the debris, removing bodies, caring for the injured. From the surrounding communities of New Market and Friends Station every available wagon and buggy was employed to carry the injured and the dead.

Over in DANDRIDGE, some twenty miles from the scene of the accident, J.B. Gass, a merchant, heard the news. His wife and his recently married daughter had earlier traveled to Knoxville to select FURNITURE and were to be returning on the No. 12 train from that city. Hitching his horse to his buggy, he began the journey across dirt roads. Fearing the worst, he drove the horse faster and faster, until it fell exhausted. Gass ran on by foot, begged rides with others on their way to the disaster. When he arrived late in the afternoon, his worst fears were confirmed: his wife and daughter had died in the accident.

Alfred Sanford, publisher of the *Journal and Tribune* in Knoxville, tried to sort through the jumble of reports and stories he was receiving of the accident. To gather news for his paper's story firsthand, Sanford decided to make the trip by automobile to New Market, although it was a thirty mile journey on dirt roads. Arriving in the afternoon amid the confusion of workmen sorting through debris, families of the dead and injured mourning, and a claims man sent by Southern Railway officials with $30,000 to settle all claims on the spot, Sanford gathered his facts: Train No. 15 traveling west from BRISTOL and engineered by W.D. Caldwell had orders to take the siding at New Market to let pass No. 12, engineered by Dick Parrott and eastbound from Knoxville. Both trains, estimated to be traveling in excess of 70 mph, collided near Friends Station. Of the 300 or so persons on the two trains, 64 were killed and 152 injured. The injured were removed to Old Knoxville General Hospital.

A few days later Red Wilson and several of his friends walked the eight miles up the tracks from Strawberry Plains to the site of the wreck. Although most of the wreckage had been removed by then, there were still reminders: stray pieces of clothing, remnants of suitcases and trunks, a few toys strewn here and there. But above all, Red Wilson says, "there was an odor I'll never forget. An odor like no other odor, odor of bits of human flesh and blood that has been ground into the earth."

Jeff Daniel Marion

Refer to: Jefferson County Standard-Banner, September 20, 1979, p. 9-A.
See also: THE JELLICO EXPLOSION
RAILROADS (NORTHEASTERN)

Norris. With varying degrees of accuracy, Norris has been called "Model Town", "The First Planned Community", "The First All-Electric Town", and even "Little Lord Fauntleroy Town". Born in the New

Deal era out of the need to house workers at Norris Dam, Norris was designed as a demonstration in techniques of new town planning and development. As a result, Norris has become a showcase for visitors from the United States and abroad.

In the chronology of new-town development in the United States, Norris (1933-1935) stands between Stein and Wright's Radburn (1928-1929) and the Resettlement Administration's greenbelt towns (1935-1938). Norris was the first new town in America to completely utilize the greenbelt principle, which had been used in the earlier British new towns. As early as 1934, Norris was intended as a permanent community with a capacity of 1,500 family units (approximately 5,000 people). The town would function as satellite to KNOXVILLE but would have some small, light industries and offices. The first 150 houses would be used to demonstrate electric heating and facilities, and the community as a whole would have streets, utilities, and other services equal to those of a large town. The greenbelt, a strip of open land around the community, would be used for protection of the town water supply, a town forest, a recreation area and garden space. The overall result was to be a town of modest homes set in a community which gave attention to the natural features of the landscape and provided an interesting and livable environment.

As part of the Norris Dam project, the TENNESSEE VALLEY AUTHORITY also

TVA hiring at Steiner's Store for Norris Dam construction, 1933.

Lewis Hine / Courtesy TVA

Charlie Krutch / Courtesy TVA

Norris cafeteria during the building of Norris Dam, ca. 1934.

constructed a 21-mile freeway which crossed the dam and connected two important highways leading out of Knoxville: U.S. 25W on the west and State Highway 33 on the east. Designed as a scenic highway with a 250-foot right-of-way and with access and sign control, it became Tennessee's first freeway-type highway. For Norris, the Freeway helped overcome some of the isolation of the townsite and proved important to the orderly transition of the construction village to a permanent town within the greater Knoxville region.

The sometimes eccentric ideas of the first TVA board chairman, A.E. Morgan, and of his wife Lucy, strongly influenced early Norris. Morgan had a high regard for the people and culture of Southern APPALACHIA, and he saw TVA's role as preserving the individualism of the region while strengthening it economically. With Norris in mind, he had TVA architects inspect and measure existing houses in the region. One result was that the hill country "dog trot" house was one of a dozen basic house designs used with exterior variations—brick, board, native stone, cinder block, and shingles. Chimneys and fireplaces went into Norris homes along with wiring for electric heat. Hand-riven oak shingles covered roofs. All had open porches with screens. Each household was assigned a plot of the common land for gardening.

Norris was a testing ground for new building ideas. Improved insulation with mineral wool and aluminum foil helped cut the cost of electricity for home heat and also helped keep houses cool in summer. Norris pioneered in large-scale electric home heating. Ceiling heat, now a common method, was first placed in two Norris homes. A special "hillside" house was planned to fit steep sites, avoiding deep land cuts and wholesale tree cutting. Because the original town plan indicated no private lots, homes literally nestled into hills and among trees in random patterns, often in semicircles around open green spaces. Roads also curved to fit the contours of the land. Native stone lined gutters along natural drain channels in lieu of roadside curbs.

Few East Tennesseans moved into the Norris homes. Construction workers, housed largely in dormitories without their families, left when the dam was finished. Many went on to other TVA projects. The people who moved into the town were the young idealistic, enthusiastic New Dealers from all parts of the country who were to guide TVA's wide range of resource development. These Norris citizens had broad interests. There was an excellent Little Theater, and the total list of community organizations numbered 21 by 1942. The cavernous community building with its natural log columns was Norris's activity center, with space for ball games, ping pong, a commissary, a gift shop, offices, and a stage. A Sunday school class, open to all denominations, met there from the first and later grew into the Norris Religious Fellowship Church, still nondenominational. Its existence did not prevent critics from dubbing Norris "a Godless town" because it had no separate church building for nearly 20 years.

The food store in the town center was originally "The Norris Cooperative Society", in which shares sold for $10 with one vote to a member regardless of the size of investment. The store delivered to homes twice daily and consistently lost money. By taking on a filling station business, then in a gray stone building at the town entrance, the cooperative finally became solvent before it was dissolved in 1938 in favor of a private lessee. The Norris Creamery had become the first private business under lease in 1937. But the cooperative idea was prevalent in early Norris. Stone masons who wanted a share of construction formed a cooperative to contract with TVA for building six fieldstone houses. Teenagers formed a co-op to share such chores as lawn mowing and car washing.

In the school, a cooperative taught mathematics. Grades six through nine formed the Norris School Produce Company with capital of $50 raised by floating bonds at 10 cents each. The teenagers grew crops on a $4^1/_2$-acre plot and handled advertising, selling, and production. This was typical of experimental teaching methods in the TVA-operated school, much publicized as one without report cards where the "don't" system of discipline was outlawed. Children studied through

Courtesy TVA

Norris drugstore, mid-1930's.

projects rather than texts. Teachers "guided" instead of ruling.

TVA gave up operation of the school in 1941. It was operated by THE UNIVERSITY OF TENNESSEE until 1948, when it became a part of the ANDERSON COUNTY school system. Even so, for many years Norris residents contributed money to provide their children with extra courses, generally in the arts, which were not then a part of the county curriculum. One county official said students who went through the early Norris school "nearly always flunked English in college because they hadn't been taught spelling," but they were so bright they usually survived despite that.

From earliest days, the school was a major point of contact between Norris residents and county people. More than half of its students were Tennesseans. But no real amalgamation took place for years. Even communication came slowly. Norris women did not understand that when a domestic worker said, "I don't care to," it meant she did not object. County people thought Norris cooking was odd: "They just run some beans through boiling water and call 'em done!"

During the TVA years, Norris was a relatively protected East Tennessee village with preferential rents, water, and electricity rates. Residents were completely free of responsibility for upkeep of their rented homes. TVA had a maintenance crew of at least 17 painters, carpenters, and electricians which was ready to answer any need from replacing light bulbs to repairing frozen plumbing. As early TVA policies changed to permit non-TVA people to live in Norris, wartime activity at nearby OAK RIDGE fed the Norris housing demand. During the war, one-third of the town's working people were Oak Ridge commuters. Meanwhile, Norris residents were pushing TVA for more say in the management policies and service levels of the town. Congress, for its part, required TVA either to make Norris self-supporting or to dispose of it.

In 1946, TVA decided to sell Norris. On June 15, 1948, the town was sold as a unit at public auction. A corporation of Norris citizens submitted a bid of $1,900,000, but the successful bidder was Henry D. Epstein, who headed a group of Philadelphia investors. Sale price was $2,107,500. Sale provisions gave existing tenants a year's occupancy right and a preference in the purchase of individual homes. The greenbelt was excluded by TVA from the town sale pending the establishment of a municipality or other local entity which could represent local interest in these lands. Norris was chartered as a Municipal Corporation by a special Tennessee Act of April 1949. The Epstein group sold off existing houses and then in 1953 sold their remaining real estate holdings to the Norris Corporation for $280,000. Thus the citizens of Norris finally achieved their goal of self-determination.

Today, Norris is no longer a cultural island. More native Tennesseans are there, and the cultural blending has been fed by marriages between Norris families and the county residents. Consolidation of schools and areawide athletic competition have erased the old distinction between Norris children and those in the surrounding area. New generations can appreciate cornbread cooked the Southern way with vegetables cooked the Northern way without stopping to think of the distinction. The present Norris population of 1400 is expected to double in 20 years, and Norris's greatest challenge remains that of preserving its unique physical setting while finding ways to continue to provide and pay for the high level of community services.

Alberta Brewer
Aelred J. Gray

See also: ARCHITECTURE

O

Oak Ridge, with a population of almost 30,000, came into existence as a result of the U.S. Government's decision to harness the capabilities of atomic fission into a "super weapon" that could be used against the enemy in World War II. The Manhattan Project, the code name given to this intense secret effort, was established on August 13, 1942, while war raged in Europe and the Pacific. The Army Corps of Engineers was given a three year time limit to perfect the atomic bomb.

In September 1942 War Department officials decided that a rural area approximately 25 miles northwest of KNOXVILLE would be an ideal location for construction of the huge facilities necessary for project research and development. The Government immediately began negotiations with approximately 1,100 families who owned the 93 square miles of land needed for the "war effort". The area residents were ordered to leave their homes no later than January 1, 1943. The Oak Ridge site was selected for a variety of reasons. Planning specifications called for an inland site in an area removed from major population centers, accessible by water and rail. A major consideration was the enormous amount of power the plants would consume. Less than a decade before, the TENNESSEE VALLEY AUTHORITY had begun to harness the region's rivers, thereby providing a ready source of hydroelectric power.

Edward Westcott

Oak Ridge laborer, 1943. During the first years of Oak Ridge, coal from the nearby Cumberland Plateau was the only fuel used for heat. A coalburning steam plant in the town proper piped steam for heating through miles of overhead pipe to most public buildings. Workmen like this one delivered coal to the homes.

Edward Westcott

Oak Ridge, December 13, 1944. Workmen at the top-secret K-25 Gaseous Diffusion Plant listen to a plea from Sergeant Mike Miller, a wounded soldier back from the war in Germany, to stay on the job and get the job done. Note the lack of hard hats worn by the workers in those days. Manhattan District intelligence officers censored this photograph by cutting the negative at the point that showed the uranium production facility. The right section of the photograph remained classified until after World War II, and only the left portion was cleared for publication.

TVA's presence in the area was also an aid in keeping the Government's new project from causing undue curiosity. East Tennesseans had grown accustomed to having "government men" surveying, buying land, and hiring local residents as construction workers. The War Department placed under contract a Boston firm, Stone and Webster Engineering Corporation, to handle site construction. On February 1, 1943 construction began on what was then called Clinton Engineer Works. Armed guards at "gates" or checkpoints along area roads enforced security around the project. Mounted patrols provided security along the natural barrier of the Clinch River. The site for the actual town was bordered by a ridge called Black Oak. In the summer of 1943, CEW employees were asked to submit suggestions for the new town's name. Oak Ridge was chosen as appropriate, not only because of the

Edward Westcott

Oak Ridge, February 1945. The largest family living in early Oak Ridge was that of Mr. and Mrs. Melvin Otto Sportsman, from Little Rock, Arkansas. The family of 12 inhabited an expandable trailer at 615 Detroit Way, Gamble Valley Trailer Camp. Seated beside Mrs. Sportsman is her daughter-in-law, wife of the pictured Marine and eldest child Charles Sportsman.

natural landmark, but also because the administration of the Manhattan Project thought the name's rural connotation would aid in disguising the sophisticated nature of the project's mission.

Research at the Oak Ridge facilities centered on the problem of producing U-235, known as enriched uranium, from the more plentiful element U-238. U-235 was the vital component for creating the atomic bomb. Three methods were developed for the enrichment process: thermal diffusion, electromagnetic separation, and gaseous diffusion. Three major facilities were built at Oak Ridge to fulfill specific needs. The first atomic bomb was made from material separated at the Y-12 plant, also the site for production of U-235 electromagnetically. Later research showed the electromagnetic process to be relatively inefficient. As a result, Y-12 evolved into a machining and metallurgical facility for nuclear weapon components, the function it serves today. The K-25 plant, now known as the Oak Ridge Gaseous

Diffusion Plant, produced U-235 by the gaseous diffusion method. This process for uranium enrichment proved to be the most efficient. Today K-25, along with two other similar plants in the United States, produces more than 80% of the enriched uranium available for use in nuclear power plants in America and the Free World. Clinton Laboratories became known as X-10 and is now called the Oak Ridge National Laboratory. This facility still houses the world's first full-scale nuclear reactor. The Graphite Reactor was built over an eleven-month period and was placed in operation on November 4, 1943. Today ORNL is recognized around the world as a center for energy research of all types.

The Oak Ridge facilities have consistently been operated by the U.S. Government, though the administrative chain of command has varied over the years. In 1947 the Army relinquished control of the facilities to the newly formed Atomic Energy Commission (AEC). Oak Ridge operations (ORO) was established as part of the AEC to oversee the development of nuclear energy for peacetime purposes. ORO has continued to operate the installations, although its governmental parent agency has changed. In 1975 the duties of the AEC were taken over by the Energy Research and Development Administration (ERDA), which in turn became part of the newly created Department of Energy (DOE) in 1977.

Underneath this shifting governmental hierarchy, private contractors have from the beginning played an active role in the development and operation of the Oak Ridge facilities. In 1943 TENNESSEE EASTMAN, a subsidiary of Eastman Kodak, entered into a contract with the Manhattan Project. Their personnel, along with the employees of Stone and Webster and the University of California, were hired to furnish technical expertise for equipment design and service for the Y-12 plant. Many other private firms and institutions held government contracts or provided needed expertise during the early stages of Oak Ridge's development. Union Carbide, which had originally been contracted to design and operate the gaseous diffusion plant (K-25), took over operation of Y-12 in 1947. One year later, when Carbide assumed responsibility for ORNL (X-10), all three of the major facilities were finally under the management of a single corporation. Union Carbide Corporation's Nuclear Division is responsible for the operation and management of these government-owned facilities.

Today, a wide range of energy-related activities are conducted at Oak Ridge. The single largest item of production is still enriched uranium. When used to fuel TVA NUCLEAR PLANTS, U-235 can generate twenty to thirty times more energy than was required for its production. Research at Oak Ridge has led to a new, highly efficient means of uranium enrichment through a gas centrifuge technique. This process requires only 4 percent as much electricity as the currently used gaseous diffusion method. Another promising area of research centers around fusion energy, a process which utilizes hydrogen, one of the earth's most plentiful elements. Major research is also being undertaken in energy production using non-nuclear sources such as solar, geothermal, and coal. Research conducted at the Oak Ridge facilities will continue to be of increasing importance in our energy-conscious world.

Patricia L. Hudson

Refer to: Charles W. Johnson and Charles O. Jackson, *City Behind a Fence: Oak Ridge, Tennessee 1942-1946*, Knoxville: University of Tennessee Press, 1981; George O. Robinson, *The Oak Ridge Story: The Saga of a People Who Share in History*, Kingsport, Tenn.: Southern Publishers, 1950; and Martha Cardwell Sparrow, "The Oak Ridgers," Mississippi State University thesis, 1980.

See also: CHILDREN'S MUSEUM OF OAK RIDGE
WHEAT

Oak Ridge, August 14, 1945. As in towns across the country, residents of Oak Ridge came out in large numbers to celebrate Japan's surrender and the end of World War II. Just one week earlier, Oak Ridgers had learned of their part in making the bomb dropped on Hiroshima. On this V-J Day, the crowd shouted and danced in the streets all night.

Edward Westcott

Courtesy Oakdale Heritage Society

Looking north along the Oakdale rail yard, ca. 1905. Babahatchie Inn, constructed 1892, at left. Passenger depot at central right; freight depot opposite rail cars. Behind the depots, company-built housing for the railway workers.

Oakdale. The city of Oakdale lies nestled in a low valley of the Cumberland Plateau along the eastern foothills of Walden Ridge. Oakdale's population is approximately 300, but it has been as high as 2,500 during the economic boom of railroading. By 1785 the Honeycutt family was pioneering on the east bank of the Babahatchie River, later named Emory River, which today flows through the center of town. Active settlement of the area commenced soon after the Third Treaty of Tellico in 1805. The town carried the name of Honeycutt until the late 1800's.

During the late 1870's, Oakdale came into its own as the main Southern Railroad switching point between Cincinnati, CHATTANOOGA, and KNOXVILLE. The determining factor for this was the steep grade between Oakdale and Somerset, Kentucky; large steam locomotives simply could not pull long trains up such grades. The Southern Railroad thus purchased from the Honeycutt family a 2-mile strip of land on the east bank of the Emory River. Workers on this strip, known as the north yards, saw a train every three minutes and serviced a phenomenal amount of railroad traffic. Here trains were switched, broken apart, maintained, refueled, and restructured for the long grades north. The river, and local mines, guaranteed a ready supply of water and coal for the voracious boilers of steam locomotives. Workmen on the north-south route, faced with 26 tunnels between Oakdale and Somerset, were referred to as the "Rat Hole Division".

Oakdale's most imposing building was the Babahatchie Inn, a huge Victorian structure with a large cupola, serving as a hotel for the many train crews laying over in Oakdale. Under new management, the Inn became the largest railroad Y.M.C.A. in existence. Later it was torn down and replaced by a brick building. A major flood in 1929 and subsequent smaller floods destroyed town property, as did fire and general decay during the 1940's and 1950's. But the replacement of steam by diesel power spelled the economic demise of Oakdale. The steep grades north that were the nemesis of the steam locomotive proved to be no challenge to the powerful diesel engines. The last steam locomotive pulled out of Oakdale in 1953, and the north yards became utilized for only limited switching.

Oakdale remains primarily a railroad town, but its ancillary shops and buildings are gone. Even the distinctive depot has been torn down. Gone also is the busy passenger service, except for an occasional excursion train for nostalgic reasons. Nevertheless, Oakdale lives on. Oakdale School has an enrollment of 620 students from the surrounding area. There is an active city government and a well-stocked library. Three churches serve the community, as do various civic and social groups. Recently the Oakdale Heritage Society was formed to preserve the town's rich railroading history. Long-range goals include a museum and a community center. Quietly Oakdale stands today, a constant reminder of a bygone era, the ribbon of railroad tracks serving their original purpose, moving trains north and south.

Barbara Oakley Hayes

See also: COUNTRY MUSIC
MUSEUMS
RAILROADS (NORTHEASTERN)

Oconostota, a Cherokee chief, was born about 1712, possibly at Chota. He grew to be "a strong, athletic, large man" of "great bodily powers" whose face had been scarred by smallpox as a youth. He was not among the seven Cherokees who went to England in 1730, and he first appears in the written records in 1736 when he joined the pro-French faction of the CHEROKEES. According to tradition, he became Great Warrior of Chota in 1738, which made him the war leader of the Overhill towns, located along the Little Tennessee River. In 1753 his jurisdiction was extended to the entire Cherokee nation.

Finding that the French could not supply the Cherokees adequately, Oconostota gradually warmed to the British. In 1753 he aided the pro-British Chickasaws in their war with the pro-French Choctaws by raiding the Choctaw towns along the Tombigbee River. In 1755 he took five French prisoners during a campaign in the Illinois-Wabash region. That year he also led the unprecedented number of 500 Cherokee warriors to a decisive victory over the Creeks at Taliwa, Georgia. When war broke out between Great Britain and France, Oconostota led an expedition against Fort Toulouse in the Alabama country and took six

French scalps and two prisoners. Later he participated in an expedition against the French on the lower Ohio River.

Oconostota was not among the hundreds of Cherokees who in 1758 went to the Virginia and Pennsylvania frontiers to fight alongside the British. Many Cherokees who did go clashed with backcountry British colonials. The violence escalated, and finally South Carolina declared an embargo on Cherokee trade. In order to get the embargo lifted, Oconostota led a party to Charleston, where Governor Lyttelton made prisoners of the Cherokees and forced them to accompany his army on its march to the Cherokee country. ATTAKULLAKULLA secured the release of Oconostota from captivity. Both chiefs then signed a treaty with the British. Oconostota did so insincerely. He launched war against the British as soon as Lyttelton's army had returned to Charleston. On February 16, 1760, Oconostota appeared at Fort Prince George in upper South Carolina and asked to parley with its commander. When Lieutenant Coytmore came out, Oconostota signalled to a party of concealed gunmen, and Coytmore fell dead. The garrison retaliated by killing all of the Cherokee hostages in the fort.

Oconostota then laid siege to FORT LOUDOUN. He planned a night attack, but Attakullakulla betrayed it to the British. Leaving conduct of the siege to Ostenaco, Oconostota hurried off to intercept the British punitive expedition which General Amherst had sent from New York. On June 27, 1760, Oconostota ambushed Colonel Archibald Montgomerie's army in a narrow mountain pass. Montgomerie's losses were severe, and he decided to return to Charleston. Montgomerie's retreat insured the fall of Fort Loudoun. The inhabitants were guaranteed safe passage to South Carolina, but on August 10 the Cherokees fell upon them and massacred many. Oconostota was not present at the massacre, but probably he gave the signal for it. Soon afterward Oconostota made peace overtures, but when news of the massacre reached Charleston the British could think only of revenge. Oconostota went to New Orleans to ask for assistance, but he came back empty-handed except for a handsomely engrossed captain's commission in the French army.

On June 10, 1761, Oconostota attacked a new British expeditionary force under the command of Colonel James Grant. Grant had learned from Montgomerie's mistakes, and Oconostota was unable to repeat his success of June, 1760. Grant then destroyed most of the Cherokee towns in the Carolinas and was poised to march on the Overhill towns. He would only negotiate with Oconostota, who would not again entrust his person to the British. Finally the pro-British Attakullakulla was recalled to power to negotiate the peace. Despite its unsuccessful conclusion, the war enhanced Oconostota's position. He was associated in the Cherokee mind with some of the most signal victories in Indian annals—the defeat of Montgomerie and the capture of Fort Loudoun. Those successes, together with his "personal bravery and other superior abilities", made him the single most powerful Cherokee chief after 1760, as Attakullakulla had been the single most powerful chief immediately preceding the war.

Oconostota was not among the Cherokees who visited England in 1762 and 1765, and he was only gradually reconciled to the British. In 1764 he did take eight scalps from Pontiac's Indians, who were in rebellion against the British. In 1767 he and Attakullakulla traveled to upstate New York to make peace with the Iroquois. Oconostota complained of the encroachments which whites made on Indian lands after 1763, but he did not want to fight the whites again. In 1770 and in 1773 he rejected offers to join an Indian confederacy to drive out the whites. By personally preventing a Cherokee-Shawnee alliance, he kept the Cherokees out of the unsuccessful Indian insurrection known as Dunmore's War. In 1773 Oconostota did make war on the Chickasaws and was decisively defeated at Chickasaw Old Fields.

Oconostota's power waned as he aged and grew apart from DRAGGING CANOE and other young warriors, who were the dynamic force in Cherokee society. He outraged them in 1775 by agreeing to sell 20,000,000 acres to the whites in the so-called Transylvania Purchase. He later protested that he had been tricked into it. He had not been. He simply reversed himself in response to the criticism of the young warriors and British officials. At the outbreak of the American Revolution, Oconostota happily conformed to the initial British policy of keeping the Cherokees out of the contest. The young warriors, however, saw a split of the whites as too good an opportunity to be missed. In 1776, they won over the Council to a war policy against the American settlers.

Oconostota did not participate in any of the campaigns, but he helped to make peace with the Americans in July of 1777 at the Long Island of the Holston River. In Williamsburg he promised to be faithful to the American cause. He was invited to General Washington's camp, but he did not go. By 1780 Oconostota was again alienated from the Americans. He authorized new attacks against them which were repulsed. The Americans captured his baggage in January of 1781. He fled to the mountains and in July of 1782 resigned his position as Great Warrior. He spent the winter of 1782-1783 with Joseph Martin, North Carolina's Indian Agent. In the spring, sensing death, Oconostota asked Martin to accompany him to Chota. There Oconostota died and was buried by Martin in a canoe. His probable remains were recently discovered.

James C. Kelly

Refer to: John P. Brown, *Old Frontiers*, Kingsport, Tenn.: Kingsport Press, 1938; David Corkran, *The Cherokee Frontier: Conflict and Survival 1740-1762*, Norman: University of Oklahoma Press, 1962; James C. Kelly, "Oconostota", in *Journal of Cherokee Studies*, V. 3., No. 4 (Fall 1978), pp. 221-238; Duane H. King, "Oconostota's Grave," in *Early Man: Magazine of Modern Archeology*, Summer 1979, pp. 17-20; and William MacDowell, ed. *Colonial Records of South Carolina*, series 2, *Documents Relating to Indian Affairs, 1754-1765*, Columbia: South Carolina Historical Commission, 1962.

Old Harp Singing is a traditional American religious art form extirpated from all but the southeastern United States. Harp singing, called "Old Harp Singing" in the central East Tennessee counties, and "Sacred Harp Singing" in southeastern Tennessee and the Deep South, is the present manifestation of two sequential American innovations: the singing school and shaped notes.

Singing schools were begun in the mid-18th century in New England. As the colonial population grew, psalm tunes and hymns gained in popularity. A small number of native tunesmiths emerged, including Samuel Holyoke and Oliver Holden. Psalms were set to popular secular tunes as well as to new melodies, but the quality of congregational singing was not equal to the popularity of the practice. Impromptu schools to teach "the rudiments of music" were convened by men (no records have been found of female singing masters or tunesmiths at that time) who fancied themselves knowledgeable of such things. Both as a vehicle toward religious expression and as a social outlet, these schools became extremely popular. The singing masters soon found that they could prosper further by using and selling their own compilations of hymns and tunes, often including secular songs.

At the turn of the 19th century, a new innovation was contrived to take advantage of the older tradition of singing syllables in the octave. William Little and William Smith, in 1802, introduced variously shaped noteheads to conform with the syllable scale of fa-sol-la-fa-sol-la-mi-(fa). Through this device the singer was better able to "read" his part, especially after practice of the various intervals between notes or syllables. This form of notation, also called buckwheat notes, patent notes (some systems were patented) or character notes, became popular, especially in rural areas. All popular systems used identical symbols for fa, sol, and la: the triangle, circle, and square, respectively. Most systems used the diamond for mi, and some systems spelled fa as "faw". During the mid-1800's, shaped notes saw little acceptance in the more urban Northeast, but thrived in the rural West (Pennsylvania, Indiana, etc.) and South, eventually retreating to only limited enclaves in the southern mountains and across the Gulf Coastal states.

Although now buried in historical obscurity, it would seem certain that pioneers moving south into Tennessee from the Shenandoah Valley of Pennsylvania and Virginia had access to contemporary shaped note tunebooks by the likes of Wyeth, Davisson, St. John and others. In mid-century, two Knoxvillians, W.H. and M.L. Swan, were pursuaded to gather their own compilation. *The Harp of Columbia*, to which W.H. Swan added several tunes of his own composition, was first published and printed in KNOXVILLE in 1848.

W.H. Swan, probably the father of Marcus Lafayette Swan, was a singing school master. Presumably influenced by J. B. Aiken's *Christian Minstrel*, which had introduced *seven* noteheads to conform with the newer do-re-mi-fa-sol-la-ti-(do) solmization, the Swans used a unique set of noteheads for do, re, mi and ti. The book ran through several printings before W.H.'s death. After the CIVIL WAR, M. L. Swan revised the collection, publishing *The New Harp of Columbia* in 1867 and substituting for several of the previous tunes a number by Lowell Mason and others. It is this book which has been in continual use until the present day.

Without dispute, the greatest advocate and apologist for harp singing was George Pullen Jackson, a language professor at Vanderbilt University. Captivated by what he called "southern white spirituals", he travelled throughout the region gathering data on the songs, the books and the people of the tradition. He became convinced that many of the tunes could be traced to English, Scottish or Irish folk tunes of ancient lineage, and he sought to prove the idea in a series of seminal books on the subject. They have become known as the Jackson trilogy. Jackson's interest and experience were centered in Alabama and Georgia singing, however, and he wrote relatively little about the East Tennessee tradition. The musicology of *The New Harp of Columbia* has been explored by Dorothy Horn in *Sing to Me of Heaven.*

The ritual of a present-day sing is relatively set, but for the uninitiated it is not easily discerned. The four parts are placed in a square; in southeastern Virginia the singing is aptly called "singing on the square". The general host selects individual song leaders who, with the help of a tuning fork or pitchpipe, "set the tone", or find the pitch best suited for the piece. Most songs are pitched lower than written, for the original key was set usually at the convenience of the printer, not the singer. Individual songs are occasionally referred to as lessons—an echo of the singing school tradition—and the assembled group is called the "class" for the same reason. After all singers have found their notes, the leader calls them to "chord", or sound the initial harmony, and then to "sing the sounds". The entire song is carolled in syllables, and only then are words, usually known as "the poetry", introduced. Most songs are well-known to the participants, and the correct sequences of verses are sung by tradition. In the sings of central East Tennessee, no. 107 ("Holy Manna") starts the sing, and no. 95 ("Parting Hand") closes it.

Most present-day sings are afternoon affairs, but in their heyday of the 1920's, up to 200 singers joined for "all day singing and dinner on the ground". A special periodical, called *The Harp Singer's Review* and produced by the Reverend Bandy in Greeneville in the late 1910's, contained portraits of singing masters and reports of sings in the area. Just across the mountains from CARTER COUNTY, in North Carolina, a small group sang and still sings from White's *Christian Harmony*, a seven-note book using the Aiken notation. Some Tennesseans must have used the book as well. In far southeastern Tennessee, *Christian Harmony* sings are still held. As far north as CLEVELAND, Tennessee, the *Original Sacred Harp (Denson Revision)* is used. These sings are an extension of the very popular practice in Georgia, Alabama and other Gulf Coast states. The largest gatherings in East Tennessee at this time are in Wear's Valley in SEVIER COUNTY on the fourth Sunday in September and the first

Sunday in October.

Ronald H. Petersen

Refer to: Dorothy D. Horn, *Sing to Me of Heaven: A Study of Folk and Early American Materials in Three Old Harp Books*, Gainesville: University of Florida Press, 1970; George Pullen Jackson, *White Spirituals in the Southern Uplands*, Chapel Hill: University of North Carolina Press, 1933 (reprinted 1965, New York: Dover Publications); Jackson, ed. *Spiritual Folk-Songs of Early America* and *Down-east Spirituals, and Others*, New York: J.J. Augustin, 1937 and 1943, and *Another Sheaf of White Spirituals*, Gainesville: University of Florida Press, 1952; and M. L. Swan, *The New Harp of Columbia*, Nashville, Tenn.: Methodist Episcopal Church, 1867 (reprinted 1978, Knoxville: University of Tennessee Press, with an Introduction by Dorothy D. Horn, Ron Petersen, and Candra Phillips).
See also: COUNTRY MUSIC
RELIGION
ROBERT EMMETT WINSETT

The One-Room School. The history of the one-room school parallels the history of early public education in many parts of East Tennessee. Rugged mountains, wild meandering rivers and poor transportation dictated isolation. Blue Springs, Oak Grove, Tiger Creek, Walnut Mountain—each little community was nestled around a one-room school and a one-room church which combined to serve as the community's center for educational, social, political, and spiritual activities.

Often economics decreed that the school and church be housed in the same building. Whether separate or together, the two institutions worked hand-in-hand to exert an unwavering moral influence on the community.

Community revivals saw school dismissed to enable students to attend a special morning service held especially for them. A stair-step procession paraded off to church, with toddling first-graders leading the way and gangling eighth-grade boys bringing up the rear. Off to the right or left, a paddle-wielding teacher supervised the march. At church, student behavior would be under careful community scrutiny. The teacher was being evaluated as well as the students, and the paddle was a reminder that no nonsense would be tolerated.

Not all school functions were as solemn as revivals and disciplinary actions. Recess and dinner (lunch) were fun times when teacher and pupil could commune in a more relaxed atmosphere, although school rules were still in effect. At recess, the playground resounded with the excitement of laughing children in games such as whoopee hide, dare base, crow hop, yankee over, and all sorts of rope jumping activities, intermingled with ball games for the bigger boys.

School let out an hour for dinner, sometimes longer. Students could walk home or bring their food in a bucket or paper bag, commonly called a "poke". The dinner bucket was often a lard or syrup bucket with nail holes punched in the lid to keep the food from sweating. Jars of "sweet milk" were stashed away in some cool place outside. Dinner was a time for barter. Fried apple pies were traded for a piece of Fannie Estep's chocolate cake; children who had become tired of country ham traded for store-bought fineries such as peanut butter.

On rainy days, the students were permitted to eat at their desks. But on sunny days, the whole school ground became a dinner table. Some students would eat under the oak tree, some would slip under the floor, and others might even build a secret playhouse they could slip away to. The girls mostly ate under the big sweetgum tree, where the teacher could watch and keep the boys from pestering them.

Two special days were anticipated by the students, although neither was marked on any official school calendar. Once a year, the stovepipe would fill with soot and a gust of wind would send puffs of dirty, black smoke pouring out of the nostrils of the potbellied stove. The teacher would dismiss class, and two of the older boys would take the stovepipe outside and beat it clean. The oiling of the floor was another holiday. The teacher would arrange for a local grocer to save about five gallons of used motor oil. Students would bring a few grass sacks to be used as mops and the older boys would oil the floor.

As important as they were, dinner, recess, revivals, and the oiling of floors were only brief interludes from the one-room school's main business, the business of educating youngsters. The teacher demanded that learning take place; the community expected learning to take place; and periodically the district supervisor would pay a visit to the school to see if, in fact, learning was taking place. To check on the quality and quantity of learning in "his" school, the supervisor would drop in for a surprise visit. He'd stand at the back of the room a few minutes observing classroom procedure, then he'd march to the front and begin asking students random questions on a variety of subjects. Nervously, the teacher kept her fingers crossed, hoping the supervisor would ask questions she'd covered in class and that he would ask them of her brightest students.

The teacher in those one-room schools of yesteryear faced an awesome task as she went about the business of educating her students. The school's enrollment usually consisted of some 15 to 30 students, which wasn't a large pupil-teacher ratio even by today's standards. However, these numbers included a few students in each grade, one through eight. Therefore, the teacher was faced with the task of teaching eight grades at once.

Somehow, they seemed to get the job done. Older students would look after younger students, and bright students would tutor slow students. Students in seven grades would do desk work while the other class sat around the potbellied stove and recited their lessons. This afforded students the opportunity to listen in on any level of instruction that matched their needs or abilities. A bright third-grader could learn a difficult spelling word being studied by the sixth grade, or an over-aged youngster who was repeating the eighth grade could review some arithmetic he missed a year earlier.

The one-room, one-teacher school was a study in interdependence. Each student became an intricate part of a dynamic community. Eighth-grade girls looked after first-grade toddlers and thus gained valuable experience for a future role they were most likely to play. Certain boys became benefactors of weaker or younger students and protected them from the school bully or made sure they didn't wander down to

Lewis Hine / Courtesy TVA

Oakdale School, Loyston, October 23, 1933. All recognizable faces in photograph identified by Tressie Stooksbury: Teacher, Dora Stooksbury; front row (left to right), George Stooksbury, Earl Irwin, Helen Stooksbury, Edith Sharp, Ruth Stooksbury, Glenmore Stooksbury, Homer Stooksbury; second row, Anna Rucker, Rowena Stooksbury, Ulysses Stooksbury, Grady Stooksbury; third row, Mossie Stooksbury (face hidden behind stovepipe), Mary Nell Stooksbury, Carlock Stooksbury, Eli Stooksbury; fourth row, Sue Simmons, Earnest Wright, Rastus Simmons; fifth row, Rothal Stooksbury, Nellie Anderson, Goodlow Stooksbury, Worley Stooksbury; sixth row, Parlie Graves, Gladys Anderson, Irdell Wright, Carl Simmons; seventh row, Tressie Stooksbury, Mildred Stooksbury, Lester Sharp, Lester Stooksbury.

the ever dangerous river. Even the lad who had failed grades a time or two contributed to the close community. Gladly he'd sacrifice his geography lesson and go to the woods and gather rich pine kindling so his classmates would have a warm fire the next morning.

As the isolation of decades was broken by new roads and easier transportation, the one-room schools, which had provided the only public education thousands of students had ever known, slowly disappeared from the landscape. The demise was gradual, but steady. In 1931, the Tennessee Department of Education reported 3,112 one-room, one-teacher schools in the state. By 1948, 2,095 were still operating. That number was cut by more than half, to 904, by 1955. Then, in 1957, the Tennessee Department of Education published a strong finding against one-room schools that "the instruction program, the physical setting, furnishings, and equipment of elementary, secondary, and combination schools with fewer than eight teachers are inferior to those in larger schools." Following this report, consolidations accelerated, reducing the number to 567 in 1958 and to 92 in 1966.

But the one-room school, for all its supposed educational shortcomings, can be applauded for its durability. A strict discipline and a demand that the basics be learned characterized many of these one-room schools that produced the teachers, doctors, farmers, mechanics, and community leaders who were to guide the destiny of the region for several generations.

Dan Crowe

P

The Pea Huller. The first automobile appeared in Dayton during the first decade of the 20th century. It was Dr. Gillespie's bright red two-seater, and the noise it created in running soon gave it the nickname of "Pea Huller". The atmosphere of the whole town was one of curiosity, interest, and also fear. Horses attached to buggies, surries, or wagons often became frightened at the new monster, rearing up and causing runaways or general danger to drivers and people on the streets.

If a horse driver heard the "Pea Huller" down the street or somewhere close, he would in all haste turn down a cross street to avoid meeting this new invention. Even Dr. Gillespie had real trouble in learning to start it and drive it, for there were no self-starters—just the outside crank to turn and turn and hope the engine would begin to chug. Most of the time Dr. Gillespie just returned to his old "tried and true" horse and buggy. But he was determined not to let failure conquer. Periodically, he would get out the "Pea Huller" and try again. He did not dare go out on country roads at first, because he was afraid of getting stuck in the mud or otherwise stranded until some farmer could bring him in by more dependable transportation.

Gradually, a few other cars were bought by venturesome and "modern" citizens and the "Pea Huller" became less of a novelty. For several years horses were afraid of cars, but after a while they seemed to learn that these monsters were not as bad as they sounded. Many of Dayton's more conservative citizens still lamented that automobiles would bring undesirable features into our quiet country town. They could not know the extent of that first car's influence.

Martha Campbell Meek

See also: THE SCOPES TRIAL

Pearling. Tennessee pearls, famous for their color and luster, occur naturally in mussels in almost all East Tennessee rivers. Prehistoric Indians, the first pearl fishers, gathered mussels by hand from riverbeds while wading in the shallows. Mound builders inhabiting this area left veritable MUSEUMS full of fresh-water pearls. In 1540, DeSoto took "two bushels of Pearls" from Georgia Indians. Early 17th century journals state that no Indians in North

America made as extensive use of pearls as did the Virginia and Tennessee tribes.

By the late nineteenth century, the accepted method for working deeper mussel pools was trolling from small boats equipped with bars. From the bars were hung a series of chains with prongs and small knobbed tips. Because mussels face upstream, the boats drifted downstream. As the prongs touched the mussels, the latter clamped shut and were hauled from the river. Clinton, county seat of ANDERSON COUNTY, became a center of pearling in East Tennessee. Jewelers from New York City regularly visited Clinton and purchased area pearls. Local dealers included Vic Cagle and Sam and Ross Hendrickson.

By the turn of the century, the thriving pearl industry in the Tennessee River Valley employed about 11,000 workers. Groups of men working in partnership earned two dollars each per day as they harvested and sold both pearls and shells. Casual family associations, such as the James Peach family, became professionalized into The American Shell Company, or Gem World International of KNOXVILLE. Beginning in the 1930's, however, the cold water of TENNESSEE VALLEY AUTHORITY lakes killed much of the mussel population. The growing use of

Cooking mussels to separate the shells from the meat. Chickamauga Lake, August 1964.

Charlie Krutch / Courtesy TVA

plastic buttons caused a decline in the pearl button market and led to the closing of Knoxville's Lane Street Pearl Button Plant. Industrial water pollution, COAL MINING in the headwaters, and overharvesting in the shallows furthered the slump in the pearling industry.

Today in East Tennessee, pearls have become more of a by-product of the commercial uses of mussel shells for buttons and for shell exporting to Japan. Common names of the commercially valuable shells include pig toe, pocketbook, white heel splitter, monkey face and Higgins eye, an endangered species. In 1979-80, Tennessee sold 288 commercial musseling licenses and maintained five mussel sanctuaries.

Phyllis Michael

Refer to: Joan Dickinson, *The Book of Pearls*, New York: Crown, 1964; Katherine Hoskins, *Anderson County*, Memphis, Tenn.: Memphis State University Press, 1979, pp. 49-51; Cormac McCarthy, *Suttree*, New York: Random House, 1979, pp. 306-331; and W.E. Myers, "Pearl Fisheries of Tennessee," in *Tennessee Academy of Science Transaction*, V.2, January 1914, pp. 19-25.

Peters Hollow. In the spring of 1823, the Taylors of Rome Hollow claimed their hen's eggs were harder than those of the Peters Hollow hens. That challenge resulted in a yearly Easter Sunday egg-fighting event held along Stony Creek in CARTER COUNTY's Peters Hollow. When the railroad began its run from ELIZABETHTON up Stony Creek to a logging camp at Buladeen, the festival grew. Today it brings thousands of people to the valley between Holston and Iron Mountains, reuniting families near and far who have come to compete or just observe.

Throughout the history of the Peters Hollow event, Easter Sunday has begun with a sunrise service and has progressed to an egg fight which still begins with the traditional challenge, "I'll fight ye," or, "Come hit me." According to Tom Peters, unofficial mayor and native of Peters Hollow, "The eggs are held cupped in the hand, small end up, and tapped with the small end of the challenger's egg. If the challenger's egg cracks, he is allowed to turn it to the large end and try again. If that end cracks, his opponent then accepts a challenge from someone else or goes on to challenge another person." One year, an egg "borrowed" from someone napping broke eight hundred other eggs. But the hard-shelled eggs of Ray Lowe's little red hen made him champion for a period of years. This ended one day when, as Tom Peters tells it, "Lowe tied the hen up on his front porch and she fell off and hung herself."

In earlier years, the eggs came from each family's own hens. Friends and neighbors arrived at Peters Hollow on horseback, in wagons, and on foot, with their food baskets and hard-boiled eggs. In those days, before commercial dyes, the eggs were colored with coon root, onion hull, rye, and other grasses. Currently, fifteen thousand or more eggs are purchased at area grocery stores, brightly dyed with commercial dyes, and carried to Peters Hollow in wash tubs, wheelbarrows, baskets, and car trunks.

June M. Boone

See also: FESTIVALS AND EVENTS

Pi Beta Phi Settlement School - The Arrowmont School of Arts and Crafts. The Pi Beta Phi Sorority, a national organization of college women, has done much for education and for crafts in East Tennessee. In 1912, this Sorority established a settlement school in GATLINBURG, with dormitories for children who lived too far away for daily commuting. At that time mountain schools were poor, lasted only for short terms, and were taught by largely unqualified teachers. Lack of passable roads prevented some mountain children from getting to school at all. Terms at the Pi Beta Phi Settlement School were of normal length, and the curriculum included home economics and weaving for girls, AGRICULTURE and manual training for boys.

Inside many mountain cabins, teachers and other visitors from the school found beautiful items: household FURNITURE and utensils made of wood, baskets, brooms, quilts, and handwoven "kiverlids" and cloth. The newcomers encouraged the mountain people to make these things in quantity, sell them through the school, and thus augment family incomes. Initially, various chapters of Pi Beta Phi marketed the crafts, but in 1926 a shop named Arrowcraft was opened on the school grounds. A hundred mountain weavers worked in their homes to supply the shop. Arrowcraft still flourishes in Gatlinburg, selling fine mountain crafts, and mountain women still weave for it.

In 1945, Pi Beta Phi, in collaboration with THE UNIVERSITY OF TENNESSEE, opened a summer craft school. Students soon came from all parts of America and from foreign countries. This school, now called Arrowmont School of Arts and Crafts, was one of the country's earliest craft schools and has always been one of the best. Studios, exhibit halls, auditorium, dormitories, and offices are presently housed in a handsome complex of buildings, complete with fine equipment and excellent teachers. The summer term has more than doubled in length to over twelve weeks, and Arrowmont's facilities are used during the rest of the year for workshops, conventions, and conferences. The Settlement School, no longer needed as county roads and schools improved, was gradually phased out. It has been this adaptability, this willingness to change with the times, which has contributed to the Sorority's success. Pi Beta Phi has always found new ways to serve the community, whether it be the small community of Gatlinburg or the world community of crafts.

Bernice A. Stevens

Pickett County
Size: 158 Square Miles (101,120 acres)
Established: 1879
Named For: Howell L. Pickett, State Representative from Wilson County
County Seat: Byrdstown
Other Major Cities, Towns, or Communities:
Static
Chanute
Midway
Oak Hill
Robbins

Travisville

Refer to: Tim Huddleston, *Pioneer Families of Pickett County, Tennessee,* Collegedale: College Press, 1968.
See also: CORDELL HULL

Conrad Pile (March 16, 1766 - October 14, 1849), better known as "Old Coonrod", great-great-grandfather of ALVIN YORK, was born in Chester County, Pennsylvania. His ancestors had migrated from Wiltshire, England, to Pennsylvania in 1683. Conrad's father, John Pyle, was a highly skilled physician. In 1768 the family moved to Orange County, North Carolina, where John doctored both sides in the American Revolution. After the Revolution, Conrad obtained a land grant based on a 1797 warrant issued by North Carolina to the heirs of veteran Hezekial Swain. The next year, Conrad entered the previously unsettled valley of the Wolf River in what is now FENTRESS COUNTY. Until he built a home, he lived in a sheltered cave near the York Spring.

The first deed conveying land in Fentress County was Henry Rowan's to Conrad Pile, September 22, 1780, concerning a tract on Caney Fork of Wolf River. Pile built a one-room house a few hundred yards from the cave. He slept there, accompanied by his long rifle and a pitchfork with the tines straightened. He traded with the CHEROKEES and often acted as an arbitrator between them and the white man. He kept gold coins in a keg with furs thrown over it. On August 15, 1808, Pile was issued a grant by Governor JOHN SEVIER for land on Rottens Fork of Wolf River. "Old Coonrod" became a wealthy and powerful man, owning a general store and a flour mill operated by slaves. He and John Clemens, father of MARK TWAIN, were the largest landowners of the Wolf River Valley.

Conrad Pile married and had eight children. On his deathbed, he tried unsuccessfully to tell his family where he had hidden his gold. Rumors ran wild, and one hollow was extensively dug, but the gold was never found. Pile's estate was divided among his eight children and his oldest son's eleven children. The money did not go very far, but these nineteen children and grandchildren inherited much land. During the CIVIL WAR, bushwhackers murdered two of Pile's grandsons. Rod Pile, a non-combatant sympathizing with the North, was arrested in 1863 and shot by members of Champ Ferguson's band. Jefferson Pile was killed on the Byrdstown Road by Tinker Dave Beatty's men. These deaths started a series of East Tennessee feuds, sometimes known as the war feuds.

Jana Humphrey

See also: APPALACHIA

Plant Communities. The many plant species of East Tennessee have been heavily influenced by the GEOLOGY and the GEOGRAPHY of the area. During the ice ages, for example, the tropical element of our FLORA and FAUNA was virtually eliminated. Species which now range north to Ohio, the Great Lakes and even Canada migrated to

Tennessee. The high mountains and the Plateau were an avenue of this migration. Of the 1500 - 2000 kinds of native vascular plants that occur here, some have had their origin here and some have migrated here under the impact of changing CLIMATE. In the past two hundred years, some new plants have been deliberately or accidentally introduced. The great number of native species have persisted in the many combinations of soils, bedrocks, and climates of our area.

The rural landscape of East Tennessee comprises several kinds of gross vegetation patterns. One is the agricultural pattern of road edges. Interspersed in these open areas are weed-shrubs such as elderberry, vines such as Japanese honeysuckle, and trees such as cedar, Virginia pine, hackberry, elm, sassafras, tulip, sumac and mimosa. These plants invade the road and lane edges and fencerows. In fields or pastures which have been abandoned, one sees a second pattern: "old field succession", i.e., successive invasions of vegetation. The crop weeds of newly abandoned fields or fescue pastures are invaded by broomsedge, and this later by blackberries, catbriars, honeysuckle and sumacs. This "shrub-vine" stage is in turn invaded by sassafras and persimmon, cedar and/or pine or tulip trees. After as long as 50 or 100 years, these various communities are invaded by many other tree types such as oak, hickory, beech and sugar maple, whose seedlings are better able to endure their own shade. This patchwork of

Woodland floor.

Courtesy TVA

successional stages is commonly seen in our area.

The third vegetation pattern is that of forest, which is usually clearcut or selectively cut at twenty to forty year intervals. This gives large forest areas a patchwork aspect of their own; the cuttings encourage species with high light needs and usually eliminate the rare species with very special site requirements. Succession after cutting rarely proceeds long enough to produce a community which is more-or-less stable, whose seedlings can survive in the shade of the canopy and can tolerate their own or their neighbors' chemical inhibitors. Less disturbed forests, of course, are usually more stable. In the section of the essay which follows, I describe vegetation communities in East Tennessee which are apparently stable (self-reproducing).

Stream Borders

Throughout much of the eastern United States, including East Tennessee, the gravel and sand bars of slow-moving streams are covered by a small herb known as water willow. These dense stands further slow the water, and stream-carried sand, silt, and even clay are dropped around the stems. As the level of this material rises and drainage improves, a small tree known as sand bar willow invades in dense stands. These stems further impede water movement, and the bar is built higher. As drainage improves further, black willow invades, to be invaded in turn by sycamore and green ash. During high water of the winter season, the water willow and perhaps the sand bar willow may be uprooted and carried downstream. In more violent floods, the entire sequence is washed away and the whole successional series begins anew.

Boulder bars of middle-size Cumberland Plateau streams are vegetated by strongly rooted, flood tolerant and light requiring shrubs like alder, as well as grasses, sedges and other herbs. Along streams where the bank is steeper, river birch and alder grow together. On the Plateau, the river birch shares dominance with holly and red maple. Without such disturbance as logging or flooding, the maple may become the sole dominant, since the birch is intolerant of shade.

Ponds and Wide Valley Flats

In the Unaka Mountains, valley flats are almost all in cultivation now, but small surviving stands include willow, sycamore, and green ash. A pond in CADES COVE is forested at its border by sweetgum and red maple. In the Great Valley, a particularly wet site near CHATTANOOGA is dominated by overcup oak; at neighboring sites, with a little improvement of drainage, cow oaks, willow oaks, and white oaks become important. Around small ponds on the Plateau, buttonbush gives way to red maple and black gum, and this to white oak in the drainage sequence. Swamps along larger, slower-moving streams throughout East Tennessee once had a heavy understory of cane, long since eliminated by grazing.

Marshes

Just how many marshes occurred on the natural East Tennessee landscape is not known. They must have been few, for they are scarcely mentioned by early explorers and diarists. The marshes and the swamps, which occurred on the flattest and most fertile sites, were drained by the first settlers and put into cultivation early. However, a few ponds with marsh borders which may be natural are known in the Valley. At Amnicola marsh in HAMILTON COUNTY, the open water is being covered by a floating mat of plants: scattered shrub-sized willow, rose-mallow and hawthorne growing on a dense mixed stand of smartweed, cutgrass, sedges, cattail and bedstraw. In one ALCOA marsh, cattail with sedges and rushes in the deepest water is bordered by rose-mallow, and this bordered by a willow forest. In another Alcoa marsh, the deepest water is covered by a mat of cutgrass, sedges and such plants as cattail, peppermint and watercress. The border is a distinctive community dominated by willow and green ash; the shrubs buttonbush and rose are interspersed in an understory which includes cutgrass, sedges and the climbing beans: ground nut and hog peanut.

On the Plateau, the swamp fringing ponds usually has a canopy dominated by red maple, black gum and sweet gum. The understory is a diverse mixture of ferns, grasses, and sedges, but under the trees closest to the central carr or marsh, the moss *Sphagnum* covers the ground. Under the tree branches that extend farthest over the marsh, a mixed sedge zone of sedges, rushes, grasses and other herbs occurs. This usually surrounds a similar area extensively covered by buttonbush, and this zone surrounds one in yet deeper water dominated by manna-grass or the three-way sedge. This zone surrounds one covered by the rooted floating mermaid-weed, and this surrounds small pools with pondweed or water-milfoil and bladderwort in the deepest water.

Cove Hardwood Forests

In the rugged area between Cumberland and Pine Mountains of CAMPBELL COUNTY and CLAIBORNE COUNTY, and extending north into Kentucky, there once occurred extensive forests of mixed hardwood composition. This type of forest, occupying protected slopes along with moist but well drained and aerated soils of valley bottoms, has been called the cove hardwood forest. In the Cumberlands this forest type was reported as extensive and rich, with more than twenty tree species sometimes dominant and 30-35 canopy trees altogether. Trees of great size obtained, and dozens of kinds of wild flowers brightened the forest floor. Peripheral to this center of diversity, the cove hardwood forests occurred in such restricted sites as the gorges and some high ridges of the Plateau, ravines in the Valley, and the coves of the mountains.

The most typical dominants in all these areas are sweet buckeye, basswood and sugar maple. Many stands in the GREAT SMOKY MOUNTAINS NATIONAL PARK are of this type. Other stands are dominated by tulip, beech, hemlock and silverbell. In the Valley, certain sub-types occur: the beech-white oak, the sugar maple-hickory, and the beech-sugar maple-basswood-buckeye. About two dozen cove hardwood forest types have been seen on the Plateau. Dominance is shared among hemlock, sugar maple, tulip, beech, white oak, basswood, northern redoak, buckeye, shagbark hickory, white ash, and red maple. Many other trees, such as dogwood, occur less often in the canopy or as small trees. The ground flora is typically showy and rich in species.

Hemlock-Northern Hardwood Forests

In the Mountains the cove hardwood forests pass, with increased elevation and the accompanying increased precipitation and lower temperatures, into forests often called hemlock-northern hardwood. The more typical cove species become less important, and sweet birch, yellow birch, red maple, and sugar maple increase in importance.

Oak Forests

Most of the forest area of East Tennessee was once covered by oak forest vegetation—certainly more than two-thirds and perhaps as much as 80 percent. These forests once had an associate, the American chestnut, which was an important food source for wild game and also made excellent construction timber for early settlers. With the death of the chestnut by blight, our oak forests are changing. Most are now simply oak or mixed oak dominated, but some share dominance with hickory, other hardwoods, or pines.

Of our oak forests, the most important and widespread types are those dominated by white oak. On the surface of the Plateau, white oak forests occupy the lower slopes of gentle to rolling topography and, mixed with scarlet oak and chestnut oak, dominate middle and upper slopes of broad ridges. In the Valley, white oak forests have been found on virtually every major bedrock type and associated soil group: shales, sandstones, limestones, dolomites and terraces. They occur on most aspects of both ridge and draw. Many other tree species occur with them, although black oak is the most common associate. In the Mountains, white oak forests generally occur on the lower slopes of coves, and at higher ridge elevations on well-lit southern slopes.

Stands dominated by northern red oak are uncommon in East Tennessee, but forests dominated by chestnut oak, usually mixed with pines, are common here. Chestnut oak forests occur on rocky or steep middle to upper slopes; typical Valley stands cover shale, sandstone, and limestone, and the Mountain understory commonly consists of laurel, blueberry or huckleberry. Post oak and blackjack oak forests occur extensively on shallow soils of the Plateau.

Pine Forests

Pine vegetation is certainly as familiar as any forest type to anyone who has been outdoors in East Tennessee. In the release of fields from crops or pasturing, pines invade these lands. During stages lasting from fifteen to perhaps a hundred years, pines are the dominant trees. This successional community occurs on virtually all disturbed sites of low to middle elevation.

White pine stands occur with probable stability on ridge tops, with other pines and oaks. The white pine can tolerate more shade than can other pines, and so occurs widely as an associate with various forest types. It reaches great size and age. The yellow pines have a more acidic litter. Shortleaf pine and Virginia (scrub) pine occur everywhere in the Valley and on the Plateau, and at lower elevations in the

Mountains. Pitch pine and table mountain pine are common in the Mountains, less so in the Valley and on the Plateau. Loblolly pine, extensively planted for pulping or for ornamentation, is native to dry forests from MEIGS COUNTY southward.

Tulip Tree (Tulip Poplar) Coves

Like the white pine, the tulip tree reaches great size and age, and produces prodigious numbers of an easily blown winged "seed". It is not confined to coves, but invades disturbed areas in adjacent oak forests or pine stands. Nearly pure stands of tulip tree exist in cut-over coves and adjacent slope positions throughout our area. These stands are often called "tulip coves".

Rocky Glades

Rocky glades occur on flats of both limestone and dolomite in the Valley, and on the hard sandstones of the Plateau surface. Certain limestone and dolomite strata are relatively pure carbonates and so weather to very thin soil. In addition, these strata go into solution in rain water, eroding into bedrock cracks and caves. The shallow soils and severe underdrainage result in sites too dry for good tree growth. Resultant openings in the forest are covered by lichens, mosses, and a great variety of both annual and perennial grasses and other herbs. In spring, the herbs make the glade an area of great beauty. On somewhat deeper soils, the glade is surrounded by cedar and/or pine stands.

Barrens

Extensive barrens sometimes occur in East Tennessee, chiefly on soil of about three to six inches depth in the Valley and on the Plateau. These areas, similar to midwestern prairies, are dominated by tall perennial grasses including the bluestems, the broom sedges, the Indian grasses, the dropseeds, the poverty grasses and needle grass. Barrens occasionally exist in strips adjacent to rocky glades. Ecologists have not been able to explain why these areas, discovered so many years ago, were not forested and are not forested now. Some barrens, in fact, are currently succeeding to thicket and forest.

Spruce-Fir Forests

At Mountain elevations over 5800 feet, and on ridges exceeding 4500 feet, slopes are covered by the Appalachian boreal forest. At about 4500 feet, the ridges' dominant hemlock is replaced by red spruce and yellow birch. Between about 5000 and 6000 feet, spruce and Fraser fir dominate the forest. Above about 6000 feet, small fir trees dominate. This mainly coniferous vegetation extends northward to Canada.

Heath Slicks

Interspersed in the high forest of the Mountains are heath slicks or balds on ridges and peaks. Here the forests give way to a dense shrub vegetation dominated chiefly by members of the heath family: rhododendron, laurel, sand myrtle, blueberry, azalea, trailing arbutus and wintergreen. The roots of these plants grow in a fibrous peat of up to 30 inches depth. Theories suggesting why these areas are not invaded by forest vary from drought to soil acidity to chemicals produced by the heaths which inhibit seed germination or seedling growth.

Grassy Balds

The grassy balds have also caused

much argument among ecologists. Their origin remains shrouded in mystery, but one geographer offers good circumstantial evidence that they are all clearings made by the first few generations of settlers and herders in the Mountains. The balds, currently growing over to shrubs and trees, are places of great beauty and spectacular views. The azaleas on Gregory Bald in the Great Smoky Mountains offer flower colors ranging from white through yellow to orange. Roan Mountain bald is being invaded by the purple rhododendron, massed in extensive areas. On both of these balds, the June flowering time offers a beautiful spectacle.

H.R. DeSelm

Poetry Magazines. A few years ago Donald Hall remarked in "The Mass Content" that "maybe poetry thrives on an audience which is local and intense....Printed poetry thrives in personal magazines and in the efforts of one-man publishers, not in magazines which need a huge circulation. We almost hand our poems around the way they did it in the seventeenth century."

Certainly John Coward, a native of East Tennessee and editor of *Puddingstone* and Southbound Books, illustrates the truth of Hall's words. Coward started *Puddingstone* in 1974 with the belief that "publishing the work of good writers is like my civic responsibility." Coward has also noted that he "felt that there was something important in existing in the Appalachian region. I wanted to express that in some form.... I started with little forethought; we just put something together and we've been putting it together ever since on a very haphazard sort of schedule. It is a personal enterprise; my wife helps me. I like to keep the magazine open to all kinds of writers....I feel that one of the miracles of the small press world is discovering fine poets." The six issues of *Puddingstone* to date have included poems by Jim Wayne Miller, Marita Garin, John Wills, Malcolm Glass, Dave Smith, Anne Roney, Rodney Jones, George Ellison, Robert Morgan, and a variety of others. Southbound Books, which evolved from the Puddingstone Press, has published the following chapbooks by area poets: Rodney Jones, *Going Ahead, Looking Back;* JEFF DANIEL MARION, *Watering Places,* and Jim Stokely, *Mummy Truths*. Coward has also published a poetry pamphlet, *Letter To My Brothers,* by Anne Roney, a resident of KNOXVILLE.

In 1975 Jeff Daniel Marion, native of Rogersville, founded *The Small Farm,* a poetry magazine designed to provide a "ground", a small acreage for poets and poems to grow, poems whose roots are in the earth. Marion's purpose as editor of *The Small Farm* was to "offer poems that take our earth consciousness in new directions, to publish poems that leave us marked, changed by the experience of the poem." Further, Marion adds, "We believe in the importance of the creative act as a means of self-renewal, as a vital connection with the organic flow of all life processes. Too, we see poetry as a striving to clarify the life we're living right now. We prefer in poetry a language that is alive, springy, a surface that is deceptively simple, underneath which are all the profundities, mysteries. We want a poetry that speaks to us now in a language that renews earth realities and possibilities, a poetry coming from and committed to specific places." Although the twelve numbers of *The Small Farm* have emphasized poets from the Appalachian region—such as Robert Morgan, Jim Wayne Miller, Fred Chappell—much attention has been devoted to poets from outside the region. Double issue Number 9 & 10, for example, was devoted entirely to the work of Oregon poet William Stafford. Whether emphasizing poetry from East Tennessee, Oregon, or the Appalachian region, Marion's purpose is best summarized in his statement: "If I can bring the writers and readers together, into contact with one another as a kind of community, I'm convinced the region/place/persons will be richer for the sharing, the interchange, the stimulus."

Jim Stokely, native of Newport, started his poetry pamphlet *Touchstone* in 1977, as he says, from the experience of a single poem: "It was actually one particular poem that got me started. The poem is by a former student from Berea College, Yvonne Williams. When I read her poem, I thought that it was the sort of thing that needed to be shared and read, so I built my first issue around it." Although *Touchstone* grew from the experience of a single poem, Stokely in a broader perspective says, "You make a magazine like *Touchstone* because it is a strand of life that is one of those essential threads tying it together." In its ten issues, *Touchstone* has published poems by Fred Chappell, James Still, Jim Wayne Miller, Bennie Lee Sinclair, George Ellison, John Quinnett, Rickey Beene, and others. Stokely is especially aware of the connections between place and poetry. He says, "There is a special spirit in East Tennessee with which people approach writing in general and poetry in particular. Since a person cannot make money with a small magazine, it provides a good weaning process, a way to wean oneself from a dependency on the fluctuations of the marketplace. You do what you think will add to the spirit of the place and to the metaphysical quality of such a beautiful place as the Southern mountains....In the long run, more possibilities exist in a place like the Great Valley, rather than an urban, more populated place. The Great Valley has the kind of rural farmland, almost an English countryside, that I think is one of the spawning grounds of poetry—where people made their living *not* by writing things on paper but by farming the land, coopering, engaging in all sorts of crafts that were necessary trades at that point. It was a world where people could find a day's work and go to a tavern and engage in the sorts of discussions, in the sorts of imaginative discourses, that would lead naturally to a poetry based on the oral tradition, on people talking to one another. That spirit of what poetry can mean in someone's life is what the small press is all about." Further, Stokely notes that *Touchstone* "was not designed or meant to exist in a vacuum; it was meant to exist in an environment which also included magazines as *The Small Farm* and *Puddingstone*, works which represent a kind of base of a region's output."

Perhaps, then, here in East Tennessee

we do hand our poems around—we share them in a spirit of community, a felt need of an individual self to connect with other lives and through that connection to come away richer, deeper, for the sharing.

Jeff Daniel Marion

Refer to: The Mossy Creek Journal (Carson-Newman College), No. 3 (Spring 1979); and "Right Where You Are," in *Tennessee Librarian*, V.31, No. 1 (Winter 1979).
See also: APPALACHIAN LITERATURE
GEORGE SCARBROUGH

Polk County
Size: 434 Square Miles (277,760 acres)
Established: 1839
Named For: James K. Polk,
Governor of Tennessee
County Seat: Benton
Other Major Cities, Towns, or Communities:
Copperhill
Ducktown
Ocoee
Wetmore
Reliance
Conasauga
Turtletown
Parksville

See also: THE COPPER MINES
VINELAND

Store and post office at Parksville, Polk County, before Ocoee Dam No. 1 was built, ca. 1910.

Courtesy Tate Kimbrough Photographic Collection

Population Characteristics

	Total Population 1980	Median Years of School Completed 1970	Median Family Income 1969	Number of Active Physicians 1979
ANDERSON	66,878	12.2	8,554	78
BLEDSOE	9,182	8.7	4,736	2
BLOUNT	77,828	11.2	7,898	64
BRADLEY	66,695	10.0	7,922	46
CAMPBELL	34,269	8.3	4,389	21
CARTER	50,051	9.8	6,194	18
CLAIBORNE	24,516	8.4	4,273	9
COCKE	28,711	8.6	5,436	5
CUMBERLAND	28,305	8.7	5,475	23
FENTRESS	14,757	8.1	3,937	3
GRAINGER	16,676	8.4	5,085	3
GREENE	54,157	9.3	6,182	44
GRUNDY	13,559	8.4	4,181	1
HAMBLEN	48,911	10.3	7,219	39
HAMILTON	282,291	12.0	8,608	467
HANCOCK	6,873	7.9	2,683	1
HAWKINS	43,662	8.8	6,299	10
JEFFERSON	31,176	9.6	6,295	13
JOHNSON	13,753	8.6	4,984	8
KNOX	318,391	12.0	8,194	555
LOUDON	28,421	9.1	6,900	12
McMINN	41,567	9.2	6,868	26
MARION	23,607	8.7	6,117	9
MEIGS	7,432	8.5	5,311	0
MONROE	28,585	8.5	5,921	12
MORGAN	16,829	8.8	5,363	4
PICKETT	4,332	8.3	4,607	2
POLK	13,525	8.7	6,678	5
RHEA	24,100	8.9	5,704	7
ROANE	47,715	10.0	7,401	25
SCOTT	19,268	8.3	4,172	5
SEQUATCHIE	8,432	8.8	6,108	3
SEVIER	41,293	8.9	6,377	16
SULLIVAN	143,178	11.3	8,372	209
UNICOI	16,341	9.2	6,485	6
UNION	11,670	8.4	5,004	1
VAN BUREN	4,696	8.5	6,014	1
WASHINGTON	88,635	10.8	7,259	148

Refer to: County and City Data Book, Washington, D.C.: Bureau of the Census, 1972.

See also: KNOXVILLE

Poverty. What is poverty?

Let us be very specific and precise. It is of the senses. Poverty is a smell. It is the cooking smell of old grease used and re-used, saturated into clothes and hair and rotting upholstery; the sleeping smell of beds crowded with ill-nourished bodies, and threadbare blankets soaked with odors of sickness and staleness; the smoking smells of cheap tobacco rolled into brown paper cigarettes, or lumps of grimy coal spreading from grate or cookstove. Gutter-sewers, overripe garbage, dust and heat in summer, cold and permeating dampness in winter. A stifling, nauseating, omnipotent smell.

Poverty is a sound. It is the sound of perpetual crying: an infant mewling, a mother mourning, an old man moaning. The sound is of shrieks in the night, noise the day long. Shuffling feet, hacking coughs, rustling vermin, insistent leaks and drips and crackings. Conflict, disintegration, more deafening in its constancy than its loudness: this is the sound-track of poverty's grind.

Poverty is a sight. It is the sight of slumped shoulders, useless hands stuffed into empty pockets, averted eyes. The scene is of land ill-used—barren, blasted, junkstrewn wasteland—or of streets that are blighted wildernesses of asphalt, brick, steel, and random-blowing trash. The sight is of faces pinched by years of need, guarded permanently from hope; and it is the raw ugliness of crowded, unscreened, fly-specked rooms, and of faded clothes too large or tight or threadbare for the body they conceal. Glaring, nerve-wracking city lights outside; and inside, the dim, dingy, ceiling bulbs that cast shadows but no illumination. Unrelieved, lifelong ugliness: this is the face of poverty.

Poverty is a feeling—through the pores, in the belly, on the feet. Cold so sharp it burns and heat so sweltering and oppressive it chills with a clammy sweat. The feeling of poverty is dull aches, twinges, pangs, brief satisfactions, creeping numbness. Pain.

Poverty is a taste. It is the taste of hot saliva boiling into the mouth before nausea, of dried beans and chicken gizzards and hog skins and too many starches and too few fruits. Stale bread and spoiling vegetables, cheap coffee and the sweet momentary fizz of soft drinks that allay but do not alleviate hunger pangs. The taste is compounded of snuff, tobacco, decaying teeth, flour gravy, headache powders, raw whiskey, bitterness.

This is the poverty of the body.

It gnaws at individuals one by suffering one.

But poverty is more than the sum of its physical parts. It is not only hunger today but fear of tomorrow. Not only present chill but future freeze. Not only daily discomfort but accumulations of illness. It is fear, but fear made impotent by the enormity of today's demands and an insufficiency of energy to forestall tomorrow's defeats.

Poverty is of the mind, too. And its root and flower is apathy. Apathy so total that the body is drained of all but the dullest perception, and the mind is drugged to all but the most primitive hungers. The light of reason—curiosity, search, comparison, logic—flickers feebly.

This is poverty of the mind.

It gnaws at people singly and in groups, stifling them, condemning them to living death.

Then there is poverty of the spirit. This is the darkest, subtlest, most widespread deprivation of all. For this is the poverty that afflicts those who have money as well as those who have none. Its need is deeper than flesh and more craving than thirst. It witnesses tears but does not weep, permits pain and never winces, indulges ignorance without protest, hears cries for help and remains unmoved. It denies the human capacity for empathy and the creative necessity for imagination.

This is poverty of the spirit, malnutrition of vision.

It can destroy civilizations.

Wilma Dykeman

See also: WILMA DYKEMAN AND JAMES STOKELY

Pressmens Home, a small community three miles north of Rogersville, was from 1912 to 1967 the headquarters of the International Printing Pressmen and Assistants' Union. A health resort named Hale Springs had been established there in the early 1800's.

George L. Berry, native of the Clinch Valley in Tennessee, became President of the IPP & AU in 1907. Soon after, he launched a site search for a tuberculosis sanatorium for union members. After exploring the Asheville area in North Carolina, Berry revisited his boyhood home near Rogersville and spent a night at Hale Springs. His union purchased the hotel and 3,000 acres along Little Poor Valley Creek.

Pressmens Home became a complete "little town" within itself, including hotel, apartments, chapel, administration building, power plant, sanatorium, and technical trade school. In the early days Marie Berry, George Berry's wife,

Pressmens Home post card.

Courtesy Thompson Photographs, C.M. McClung Historical Collection, Lawson McGhee Library

rode horseback over Pine Mountain to Rogersville for the weekly payroll. A new trade school was built in 1948, the year George Berry died. Students from throughout the United States and Canada came to learn the latest techniques in printing on the most modern equipment in the printing trade. Two union magazines and many correspondence courses were printed there. In December of 1967, the headquarters of the IPP & AU moved to Washington, D.C. Pressmens Home was purchased as a real estate venture and its name was changed to "Camelot". Since then, the property has changed hands several times.

Alix Wohlwend Brooks

Primary Health Care Centers. East Tennessee is not unlike other rural areas in its shortage of health care services, but East Tennessee has distinguished itself in its response to this common rural problem. Beginning in the early 1970's, many small communities in East Tennessee began to organize health clinics to provide services in areas that had lacked such resources for as many as 25 years. Several of these citizen groups were assisted by medical and nursing students from the Vanderbilt University Student Health Coalition. The students provided various health screening and education programs during week-long health fairs. The health fairs helped identify and document health needs and inspired the organization of local health councils.

These health councils began the task of raising money to build facilities and equip them. Quilt sales, pie suppers, baseball games, gospel sing-ins, cake walks and benefit concerts gave everyone a chance to contribute to a community-wide effort. Many communities petitioned their county courts for support. Many received help from the TENNESSEE VALLEY AUTHORITY, local churches, and private foundations. Two public agencies also played a major role in the development of the clinics: the East Tennessee Regional Public Health Department, and the East Tennessee Human Resource Agency. All these groups created a network of clinics which by 1980 numbered 19, serving over 40,000 people a year.

The model chosen by most of the health councils—a primary health care center with a nurse practitioner or physician assistant serving as the primary provider—was also a pioneering effort. The nurse practitioner or physician assistant provides basic health care services in joint practice with a physician who visits the clinic approximately one day per week. Together, the nurse practitioner or physician assistant and the physician establish a protocol for patient care under which the NP/PA functions in the physician's absence. The NP/PA also provides patient teaching along with community education services and places a strong emphasis on preventive health services.

The efforts of consumers and providers in East Tennessee have inspired expansion of these ideas to other parts of Tennessee and America. The Student Health Coalition concept

Robert Kollar / Courtesy TVA

Stoney Forks Community Health Center, Campbell County, 1978.

which began in East Tennessee has now been adopted by university students in North Carolina, Georgia, Alabama, Texas and Ohio. And the primary care center model has spread throughout the state. There are now over 80 primary care centers in Tennessee, the vast majority of which are staffed by nurse practitioners or physician assistants. Tennessee has more primary care centers than any other Southern state and is now considered a national leader in the development of health care services in medically underserved areas.

Caryl Carpenter

See also: PUBLIC HEALTH SERVICES

Private Education in Sweetwater. The location of the town of Sweetwater was made possible by the Hiwassee Purchase, negotiated with the Overhill CHEROKEES in the period 1819 - 1820. Soon after this transaction, the area north of the Hiwassee River was settled rapidly; Sweetwater took its name from the Indian name for the area. The town plan was primarily the work of I.T. Lenoir, and the town slowly grew to a community of some consequence. Sweetwater's first educational effort was begun by John Fine, who arrived in 1821. He conducted school in a building erected for that purpose on his own land just west of the Cannon Spring, which is now part of the grounds of the Sweetwater High School.

On the death of Mr. Fine in 1857, the

citizens of the town recognized the necessity for an increased effort in the field of education. That same year, they erected for $1,500 a building on a lot now occupied by the Sweetwater Hospital. This institution, called Union Institute, was organized as a stock company, for which interested citizens paid $20 per share. E.E. Taylor, I.T. Lenoir, and S.J. Rowan were elected trustees with Professor Gabriel Ragsdale as the first school administrator. The upper portion of the school was devoted to the education of females, and the lower portion to males. From 1858 to the end of the CIVIL WAR, Union Institute continued in operation largely under the supervision of the qualified ladies of the town, the male administrators having been called to fight. During Reconstruction, the school was operated by various instructors drawn from the graduates of Hiwassee College.

In 1874, the Rev. J. Lynn Bachman took over the administration of Union Institute. Ten years later the name of the school was changed to Sweetwater College. The school moved into a new building, financed in large part by Sweetwater citizens, at the intersection of College Street and East North Street. Sweetwater College engaged in elementary, preparatory, and college level instruction. By 1898, the enrollment of Sweetwater College had increased to the point that the "Bachman Building", as it was called in later years, had become too small. The trustees bought back the old Union Institute building, which had been remodeled in 1896 to accommodate the Baptist operated Sweetwater Seminary for Young Ladies. There is evidence that during the period from 1898 until 1902, the school was operated under the name of Sweetwater Military College. Dr. Bachman continued to serve as school administrator until 1902.

In 1902 Col. O.C. Hulvey took over the primary responsibility of administration. About that time, the school became known as Tennessee Military Institute. Two events during Col. Hulvey's 13-year administration were of great significance. The first was the completion in 1909 of a new large and commodious building. The program of the school became definitely military and devoted to the college preparatory education of young men. Col. Hulvey also made a great contribution to TMI in that he was one of the first educators in the eastern half of the nation to begin an adequate advertising program to attract students to the school. As a result, the school changed from one which served primarily the local community to one with a student body composed of students from throughout the eastern half of the United States.

Col. C.R. Endsley, Sr., former Headmaster of Castle Heights Military Academy in Lebanon, Tennessee, served as Superintendent of Tennessee Military Institute from 1919 to 1956. Assisted by L.U. Ragsdale, Reese Neese, and C.W. Price, Col. Endsley made great strides in raising the graduation requirements and establishing an efficient disciplinary control of the school. During the period from 1919 to 1926, the school also added dormitory space and built an adequate infirmary to take care of the physical needs of the students. In 1936, a new gymnasium was added.

In the spring of 1956, Col. Endsley, Sr. suffered a disabling stroke, and the administration of the school passed to his son, C.R. Endsley, Jr. Col. Endsley, Jr. continued to lead and guide the school from that year until 1971. During this period the school experienced its most rapid building program ever, and the academic program was upgraded. The school reached a maximum enrollment of 260 students, drawn primarily from the eastern half of the United States and several foreign countries. Also during this period, five major additions to the buildings and grounds were completed.

At the time of the retirement of Col. Endsley, Jr., the enrollment of the school began to decline, due primarily to the aversion of the American public to things military as a result of the Vietnam War. This trend continued unabated until 1975. During that year, the Board of Trustees recognized the impossibility of continuing the school under its current management and policy; and as of August 1, 1975, the school property and equipment were purchased by Sanford Gray. Mr. Gray at that time also assumed responsibility for accumulated debt from the previous administrations. Mr. Gray had first come to the school in 1955 as a coach, and had gradually worked up in the organization from teacher and coach to Director of Athletics and Vice President of the school. He was thoroughly informed on the requirements for operating a school of this type. The school at this time reverted to a proprietary status, being wholly owned by Mr. Gray and his family, and it became TMI Academy.

Mr. Gray immediately instituted a program to increase the enrollment of the school, which has shown gains during each year from 1975 to date. He also added to existing school property to make it more adequate to meet the needs of a non-military, co-educational, college preparatory school. TMI Academy continues not only to serve the town of Sweetwater, East Tennessee, and the eastern half of the United States, but it also educates a number of students from foreign countries.

C.R. Endsley, Jr.

Frank Proffitt (June 1, 1913 - November 24, 1965), one of America's finest interpreters of traditional mountain ballads, was born in Laurel Bloomery in JOHNSON COUNTY. His grandfather John Proffitt, who had fought for a Tennessee Union regiment during the CIVIL WAR, had moved the family soon after the war from western North Carolina to Johnson County. Frank lived there for at least a year, then moved with his parents a short distance across the North Carolina border into Watauga County. As a young man, Frank Proffitt farmed and also worked as a part time carpenter. He saw a town for the first time when he was 16, barefooted in Tennessee, after crossing the Unaka Mountains to Mountain City. He learned many of the old songs from listening to relatives and neighbors, including his father Wiley and his aunt Nancy Prather. When Frank C. Brown came soliciting North

Carolina folklore for a now-famous collection, Frank Proffitt contributed eleven songs. The latter also married Bessie Hicks, member of a large Beech Mountain family with a great knowledge of mountain music and tales.

In the spring of 1938, Bessie's father Nathan Hicks made a dulcimer for Frank and Anne Warner of New York City. The Warners visited the Hicks family in June and heard the accomplished singing and guitar playing of Nathan's son-in-law Frank. Frank Proffitt sang, among other songs, the locally popular "Hang Down Your Head, Tom Dooley", a ballad based on a murder and hanging which had occurred in Wilkes County in 1868. According to musicologist Sandy Paton, "Tom Dooley" was "the first song Frank Proffitt ever heard his father pick on the banjo." Excited by their trip to the North Carolina mountains, the Warners returned in 1940 and recorded Frank Proffitt on an early disk-and-groove recorder. Through the 1940's, the Warners reshaped the "Tom Dooley" ballad—shortening it, altering the melody, putting the verses in chronological order—and included it in a 1950 record album.

Frank Proffitt, meanwhile, was following a course of employment similar to that of many residents in the Southern Appalachian mountains. During the Depression, he had earned money working under the Works Progress Administration. In early 1942 he was planning to return to East Tennessee to help with the construction of the TENNESSEE VALLEY AUTHORITY's Douglas Dam in SEVIER COUNTY, but he actually spent the final War years doing carpentry in OAK RIDGE. After World War II, Proffitt joined thousands of mountaineers in a general job-seeking migration to northern cities. He labored mainly in a spark plug plant in Toledo, Ohio, and also hired on with more temporary road building and carpentry crews.

In 1959 Frank Proffitt heard and saw, on his new television set back in North Carolina, the Kingston Trio singing their own pop version of "Tom Dooley". Proffitt later wrote that he walked out of his house onto the ridge and, gazing toward Wilkes County, cried. The Kingston Trio and Capitol Records sold three million copies of "Tom Dooley", helped create the folk music wave of the 1960's—and collected almost all the income from the song. Although Frank Proffitt received minimal royalties for his vital role in the ballad's popularity, he did receive recognition in folk music circles. Pete Seeger and other musicians ordered fretless banjos and dulcimers from him, for he had begun making instruments as his father Wiley had done. In 1961, accompanied by Frank Warner, Frank Proffitt participated in the first Folk Festival at the University of Chicago and came to national attention. He soon recorded two folk albums and taught at the Pinewoods Folk Music Camp near Plymouth, Massachusetts. He spent the bulk of his last four years farming in Watauga County, and touring up and down the East. He died on Thanksgiving morning and was buried in a family plot on a hill near his North Carolina home.

Frank Proffitt's full legacy comprises more than stories in *Time* or *Life*, or even the particular strains of "Tom Dooley".

Utilizing an excellent memory and a close rapport with fellow mountaineers, he collected many traditional songs—saving them from possible extinction—as the occasions arose: "Young Hunting" on a visit to his aunt; "Wild Bill Jones" from timbermen just returned from West Virginia; "Moonshine" at the age of 17, near Chilhowie, Virginia, at a party. Although his formal education extended only to the sixth grade, Frank Proffitt wrote many eloquent letters to friends throughout the country. Perhaps most importantly, he was a devoted father and a man of sincerity, a craftsman and a humanitarian who referred to himself simply as "a mountain man".

Jim Stokely

Refer to: Frank and Anne Warner, "Frank Noah Proffitt: A Retrospective," in *Appalachian Journal,* V.1, No.3 (Autumn 1973), pp. 162-198; *Frank Proffitt Sings Folk Songs,* Folkways Records (FA 2360), 1961; *Frank Proffitt of Reese, North Carolina,* Folk-Legacy Records (FSA-1), 1962; and *Frank Proffitt Memorial Album,* Folk-Legacy Records (FSA-36), 1968.

Public Health Services. Although Tennessee became a state in 1796, only years later would organized public health and preventive medicine be initiated. In 1862 wounded men during the CIVIL WAR were sent to CHATTANOOGA, where they filled hospitals, churches, and private homes. The women of the town organized to nurse these wounded. This is the first record in Tennessee of what could be considered public health nursing service. After the battles of Missionary Ridge and Chickamauga, the women of Chattanooga again nursed the wounded. In July of 1881, three years before the typhoid bacillus was first isolated, and four years before water-borne typhoid fever first attracted widespread attention in America, the fever appeared in RUGBY colony. Originating in the Tabard Inn's well water, it attacked several guests of the hotel. Rugbeians quickly disinfected the Inn, boiled all drinking water, and terminated the outbreak. Tabard Inn reopened on November 7, 1881.

Tennessee, like other states, benefitted from the services of voluntary health agencies prior to a time when such services could be assumed by the government. Examples of such early agencies include The Tuberculosis Association, Metropolitan Life Insurance Company, and the Red Cross. The first public health nurse working in a Tennessee county health department program was employed in 1919 in BLOUNT COUNTY and paid by the American Red Cross. Four years later, the state General Assembly created the Tennessee Department of Public Health with divisions of administration, local organization, epidemiology, vital statistics, laboratories, sanitary engineering, child hygiene, public health nursing, and health education. Current public health services in East Tennessee are comprehensive and change with the needs of the people. These services, which are available to citizens who contact their county, district, or regional health departments, include control of tuberculosis and venereal disease, child health and education projects, emergency

Courtesy Thompson Photographs, C.M. McClung Historical Collection, Lawson McGhee Library

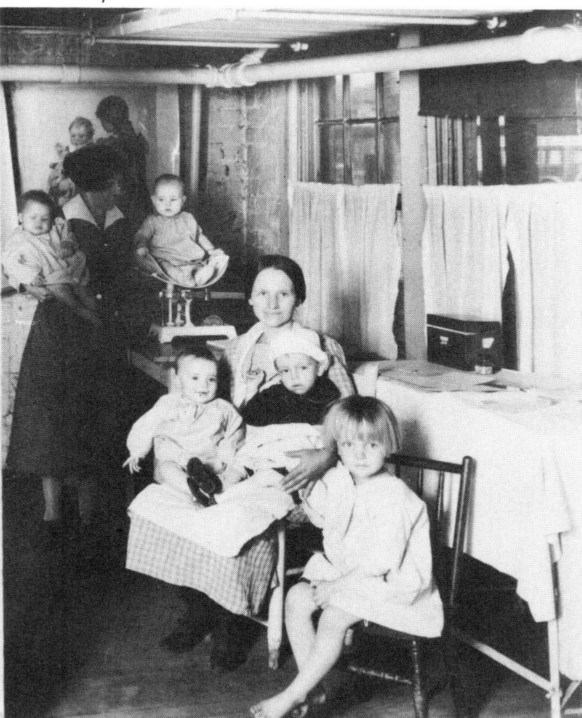

Red Cross clinic, Knoxville, 1920's.

medicine, family planning, home health care, physical and occupational therapy, environmental sanitation, immunization, dental treatment, and programs in nutrition, speech and hearing.

Margaret Lagerstrom
James D. Harless

Refer to: Sadie Carter, *Public Health in Tennessee; The First Hundred Years,* Nashville: Tennessee Department of Public Health; and Margaret Lagerstrom, *History Public Health Nursing in Tennessee 1910-1960,* Nashville: Tennessee Nurses' Association, 1960.

See also: PRIMARY HEALTH CARE CENTERS

R

Radio has been a political and cultural force in East Tennessee for over fifty years. Early network affiliations and electrical transcriptions allowed Tennesseans access to the overall popular culture of the nation, and a strong tradition of local programming allowed them to explore the rich diversity of their own regional culture. Although there were relatively few stations in East Tennessee before World War II, their influence was widely felt in an era of poor roads and no television. The 1978 *Broadcasting Yearbook*, by contrast, listed over seventy stations broadcasting regularly in East Tennessee, ranging from tiny 250-watt stations reaching a radius of twenty miles to powerhouse stations of 100 kilowatts blanketing the entire region.

In 1932, at the dawn of the radio era, a listener in East Tennessee could hear only four local stations: KNOXVILLE's WNOX, affiliated even then with the Columbia network and broadcasting at 1,000 watts; BRISTOL's WOPI, an independent station broadcasting at 100 watts; Knoxville's WROL (11 watts); and Knoxville's WFBC (50 watts—hardly the power of a typical mobile unit in radio today). In that age before cluttered airwaves, many listeners would also tune in on distant stations like WSM in Nashville, WLS in Chicago, and, depending on where the listener lived, WWNC, the powerful voice of Asheville, North Carolina. Throughout most of the 1930's and 1940's, it was WNOX and WOPI that came to set the pace for most of the local programming in East Tennessee.

WNOX first went on the air in 1921 as one of Tennessee's first stations and one of the first ten stations in the nation. The original call letters were WNAV. The station was first owned by the First Baptist Church, then by the People's Telephone Company, and later by the Liberty Mutual Insurance Company. Its broadcasting studios were located first in the basement of the Sterchi Brothers furniture store, then at the top of the St. James Hotel, later at the top of the Andrew Johnson Hotel, and finally in 1955 in the Whittle Springs Hotel. Starting in the mid-1920's, the station began to attract local musical talent, including the jazz orchestra of Maynard Baird as well as early COUNTRY MUSIC entertainers like Mac and Bob (McFarland and Gardner), Hugh Cross, Otis Elder, and a band called The Smoky Mountain Ramblers, who had a regular program sponsored by a Knoxville

Courtesy Archives of Appalachia, East Tennessee State University

A young Tennessee Ernie Ford as the WOPI radio announcer, Bristol, 1939.

"painless dentist". WNOX's success at programming local live music led in part to the station's hosting Knoxville's first commercial recording sessions, in 1929 and 1930. Music thus recorded ranged from the hot jazz of Maynard Baird (one of his original tunes was called "Postage Stomp") to the sedate strains of the "U-T Trio", and from the gospel quartet to the dynamic blues stylings of Loudon's Will Bennett, with a rich variety of "southern mountain tunes" in between.

In 1935 Scripps-Howard purchased WNOX, making it the first broadcast facility owned by that newspaper chain. In May 1937 the station increased its power, making it East Tennessee's strongest station, and that same year it played a major role in relief work during the 1937 Ohio River flood. In 1945 the station played a similar role in documenting and organizing relief efforts for a mining disaster in Pineville, Kentucky. That same year, the station was the first to broadcast from OAK RIDGE with news of the atomic bomb. During World War II, the station sponsored war bond tours featuring station entertainers. Cliff Allen's "Farm Show" attracted a wide variety of listeners in the late 1940's. In 1960 the station dropped its long-standing CBS affiliation, returning to original programming and a contemporary music format.

Perhaps the best-remembered show of WNOX was a daily program initiated in January of 1936 called "Mid-Day

Merry-Go-Round", a live "barn dance" variety show. The program began in station studios at the Andrew Johnson Hotel, but growing crowds soon made it necessary to move the show to the municipal auditorium. The station eventually built new studios on Gay Street, which included a 600-seat auditorium in addition to offices and studios. The emcee and founder of the program was Lowell Blanchard (1910-1968), a native of Palmer, Illinois, who in 1935 came to the station fresh out of the University of Illinois. Blanchard was a song writer and singer, but he was first and foremost an organizer. He coordinated the artists for the program as well as announcing and presiding over a melange of talent that ranged from the blackface comedy of "Kentucky Slim" (Charley Elza) to the jazz-pop stylings of the String Dusters, a band featuring a young Chet Atkins. Most of the music, however, was country, and a number of major country stars gained early experience on the show.

Soon after Blanchard started the "Mid-Day Merry-Go-Round", he also began a Saturday night music program, "Tennessee Barndance", broadcast live from the Lyric Theater. During the heyday of live local entertainment, as many as sixty performers appeared on one broadcast of "Tennessee Barndance", and many of the sponsors for it and the "Merry-Go-Round" could boast of affiliations going back some twenty years. By the early 1940's, the station was broadcasting well over a hundred half-hour country music programs per week. From this high-water mark, live programming gradually declined during the 1950's and 1960's. Both the "Mid-Day Merry-Go-Round" and the "Tennessee Barndance" survived into the early 1960's before succumbing to changing times.

The prime competition for WNOX in the 1930's and 1940's was Knoxville station WROL, dominated by the colorful grocery entrepreneur Cas Walker. Walker found as early as 1935 that he could sell groceries by sponsoring country music shows, and he proceeded to do both with panache and gusto. Walker was especially fond of BLUEGRASS MUSIC, and WROL was for a time the home of Flatt and Scruggs, the Bailey Brothers, and even the Osborne Brothers. Walker called bluegrass "jumping up and down music." He was pleased to note that residents of Knoxville began to go into radio supply stores to ask for "the Cas Walker" tube or "the Lowell Blanchard" tube when a radio failed.

Further east, in Bristol, station WOPI went on the air in 1929. WOPI was the brainchild of W.A. Wilson, Sr., a native of GREENE COUNTY, who was an expert in telegraphy and chief operator at the Bristol office of Western Union. Wilson himself hosted a program called "The Saturday Night Jamboree", featuring live talent from the hills around Bristol and including a few performers who sang old ballads in the ancient unaccompanied style. Early favorite performers included black-face comedian J.H. Phipps ("Chitlins"), female guitarist and singer Zada Leonard, and the Routh Sisters, a vocal trio. Dozens of local string bands appeared, including the Roe Brothers and Tenneva Ramblers. WOPI soon built a Radiotorium seating 350 for live shows, and the station continued with a rich variety of local programming, including a regular "cooking school" and a popular "Breakfast Club". For years the station also broadcast various news programs and, through WLW in Cincinnati, "The Ohio School of the Air". In 1945 the station was destroyed by fire, but was quickly rebuilt. In fact, in 1946 Wilson started the first FM station in the region, with transmitters located atop Virginia's White Top Mountain reaching a range of 100 miles in each direction.

Other tri-cities stations also made important contributions to the music and regional culture of the area. WJHL (JOHNSON CITY and ELIZABETHTON) took to the air in the late 1940's and featured a country music program called "Barrel of Fun", an informal Saturday morning gathering presided over by "Turtle" Tolbert. WCYB in Bristol boasted of a two-hour daily show called "Farm and Fun Time", which became perhaps the country's most important crucible for the newly-developing bluegrass music. The Stanley Brothers, Flatt and Scruggs, and Carl Story all spent important years on WCYB. The radio culture of East Tennessee, though sparsely documented by historians, made a lasting impact on the people of the area. It reached into the most remote hollows and valleys, bringing into countless homes a rich mixture of

Studio audience at WOPI radio in Bristol, late 1930's.

Courtesy Archives of Appalachia, East Tennessee State University

information, ideas, and entertainment.

Charles Wolfe

See also: THE SCOPES TRIAL

Railroads (Southeastern Tennessee). The first railroad construction in Tennessee was in southeast Tennessee, and two major systems now serve the area. The Southern Railway System includes the line of the first operating railroad in East Tennessee, which in the early 1850's connected southeast Tennessee with KNOXVILLE to the north and with Dalton, Georgia, to the south. In 1888, Athens in MCMINN COUNTY was connected with Tellico Plains in MONROE COUNTY; and in the 1890's, another Knoxville-to-Georgia line traversed southeast Tennessee. Today, these latter two lines are part of the Louisville and Nashville Railroad system.

The Hiwassee Rail Road, chartered in 1836, reorganized in 1848 as the East Tennessee and Georgia Railroad, and merged in 1894 into the Southern Railway Company, was the first railroad put under construction in Tennessee. Through the efforts of Senator James Hayes Reagan of McMinn County, the General Assembly of the State of Tennessee passed, on February 19, 1836, "An Act to incorporate the Hiwassee Rail Road Company...for the purpose of facilitating...transportation from Knoxville, East Tennessee through the Hiwassee District to...the southern boundary of Tennessee." The Act stipulated that unless two-thirds of the $600,000 capital stock were subscribed before January 1, 1837, and actual work started before January 1, 1838, the charter would be forfeited. Last minute subscriptions by six McMinn County citizens for $280,000 of the $400,000 minimum stock saved the charter. Solomon D. Jacobs of Knoxville was elected President, with Asbury M. Coffey of Athens as Secretary-Treasurer. A brick building, still standing on North Jackson Street in Athens, was built as the company's headquarters.

John C. Trautwine of Pennsylvania, chosen as the Chief Engineer, directed the location and surveying of the roadbed. On June 4, 1837, the Directors entered into a contract with Kennedy Lonergren for the grading of the roadbed from Calhoun on the Hiwassee River to Blair's Ferry (now Loudon) on the Tennessee River, a distance of 41½ miles. In a letter dated August 17, 1837, Trautwine wrote that "the grading of the Hiwassee Rail Road has commenced at a point two miles below the town of Athens." This was the first actual construction work done on a railroad in Tennessee.

Financial problems beset the Hiwassee Rail Road, however, and a deed of trust was executed in the summer of 1842 in an effort to save the project from complete bankruptcy. This led to a lawsuit against the company, filed by the Attorney General of Tennessee in October 1842, asking for forfeiture of the charter. All rail line work halted pending an investigation by the state. When construction was suspended, 66 miles of roadbed had been built, the roadbed had been graded and readied for placing the ties, wooden ties had been bought and placed along the roadbed, and a bridge had been built over the Hiwassee River at Calhoun. The cost had been $936,329, or 50% more than the total authorized capital. During the four-year investigation, the grades and fills eroded, the wooden ties rotted, and the roadbed and Hiwassee River bridge were used as a toll-free turnpike.

On January 1, 1847, after being cleared by the investigation, the company was reorganized and T. Nixon Van Dyke elected President. Toward the end of 1847, with company debt reduced by about 80%, the Directors asked the Tennessee General Assembly for a revision of the charter. On February 4, 1848, the Hiwassee Rail Road became the East Tennessee and Georgia Railroad Company with capital stock increased to $2,000,000. In January 1849, the Directors let a contract to Duff Green for building the railroad from Dalton. Ground was broken in Dalton in June 1849, and by October of 1850, the roadbed had been finished and ties laid all the way to the Tennessee state line. Here the new roadbed connected with the roadbed previously built by the Hiwassee Rail Road.

In a change from previous plans, the East Tennessee and Georgia contracted with the English firm of Bailey and Company for 8,000 tons of improved T-pattern rails, to be made of Welsh iron and weighing approximately 57 pounds per yard. The first thousand tons were shipped August 17, 1850, and the actual "laying down" of the rails commenced in December of 1850. After doing considerable work, Duff Green failed, but a new contract was made with William Grant and Company. Grant completed the line to the Hiwassee River bridge. At this point, President Van Dyke called on the people of McMinn County for $15,000 of additional stock subscriptions to finish the line through McMinn County. McMinn citizens again met the challenge, and J.G. Dent and Company completed the line from Calhoun to Blair's Ferry (now Loudon). The railroad reached the Mouse Creek area (now Niota) in February of 1852. On July 23, *The Athens Post* announced a regular schedule between Loudon and Dalton, Georgia, to be effective on August 10, 1852.

After the construction of a bridge over the Tennessee River at Loudon, the first train arrived in Knoxville in mid-June of 1855. On June 27 a special $4.00 round trip fare, effective July 3rd, 4th and 5th from Knoxville to Dalton, was announced as part of the great "Railroad Jubilee and Fourth of July Celebration". A 39-mile branch line from CLEVELAND to CHATTANOOGA, completed in 1858, allowed direct access to Chattanooga instead of going on to Dalton, then switching to the Western and Atlantic Railroad and returning northward. In 1869, the East Tennessee and Georgia Railroad Company merged with the East Tennessee and Virginia Railroad Company to form the East Tennessee, Virginia and Georgia Railroad Company. Twenty-five years later, the Southern Railway Company acquired the lines of the East Tennessee, Virginia and Georgia.

The Louisville and Nashville, the second major railroad system to serve southeast Tennessee, began as the Knoxville and Southern Railroad Company. At Blue Ridge, Georgia, in the 1890's, the Knoxville and Southern connected its tracks from Knoxville with those of the Marietta and North Georgia Railroad from Atlanta. The two companies merged in 1896 to form the Atlanta, Knoxville and Northern Railroad. In 1902 the Louisville and Nashville Railroad Company, then operating in Middle Tennessee, acquired the AK & N. Desiring a more direct route to Atlanta than through the Hiwassee River gorge and the mountains of North Georgia, the L & N decided to build a new line from McMinn County to Cartersville, Georgia. Construction on the roadbed began in 1904 and was completed in 1906.

The town of Etowah, platted in 1905 at the northern terminus of the new line, became headquarters of the Atlanta Division of the L & N. Railroad shops and terminal facilities for the Atlanta Division were constructed there. In 1925, over twenty trains a day passed through Etowah. But the Knoxville and Atlanta Divisions merged five years later, and the new District offices were located in Knoxville. During the 1960's the L & N discontinued passenger service between Knoxville and Atlanta.

Several short lines in southeast Tennessee, all now abandoned, were used in various COAL MINING and timber operations. The Babcock Lumber Company operated two lines in MONROE COUNTY until the early 1930's. The Athens and Tennessee River Railroad, along with the Rockwood and Tennessee River Railway, was a part of a rail-barge-rail operation which moved ore to the Roane Iron Works at Rockwood in ROANE COUNTY. Still in use is a $22^1/_2$-mile line built in 1888 between Athens in McMinn County and Tellico Plains in Monroe County. First incorporated in 1887 as the Tellico Railroad Company, the railway was acquired in 1911 by the Louisville and Nashville. The point where the Tellico's tracks crossed the line of the Knoxville and Southern Railroad became known as Tellico Junction, then in 1908 as Englewood. Today, the connector line is in service almost daily from Athens to Englewood, and the spur to Tellico Plains continues to offer weekly service.

James E. Burn

Refer to: James Burn, "The Hiwassee—East Tennessee and Georgia Railroad," in *The Daily Post-Athenian*, June 10, 1969, pp. A-4 and A-14; Stanley J. Folmsbee, "The Beginnings of the Railroad Movement in East Tennessee," in *The East Tennessee Historical Society's Publications*, No. 5 (1933), pp. 81-104; Kincaid A. Herr, *The Louisville & Nashville Railroad, 1850-1942*, Louisville, Ky.: L & N Magazine, 1943; and James W. Holland, "The East Tennessee and Georgia Railroad, 1836-1860," in *The East Tennessee Historical Society's Publications*, No. 3 (1931), pp. 89-107.

Railroads (Northeastern Tennessee). The first railroad to enter East Tennessee was the Western and Atlantic, built by the State of Georgia, extending north out of Atlanta and reaching CHATTANOOGA in 1850. The next railroad line completed in East Tennessee was the East Tennessee and Georgia Railroad connecting Dalton,

Georgia, with Loudon, Tennessee, in 1852. It was extended north through KNOXVILLE three years later. The East Tennessee and Virginia Railroad reached BRISTOL in 1858 and connected there with a line extending on to Petersburg and Richmond. During the CIVIL WAR, this rail line was of vital military importance. It was the only direct connection between Atlanta, the arsenal of the Confederacy, and Richmond, its capitol. Union sympathizers in upper East Tennessee constantly sabotaged the line to disrupt the war efforts of the Confederacy. After the war, the combined East Tennessee, Virginia and Georgia Railroad was absorbed by the Southern Railway Company.

The late 1870's brought a railroad with an unusual origin and purpose into East Tennessee. The City of Cincinnati, Ohio, was an important river port with railroads extending to the north, east and west. City leaders believed that a railroad extending to the south would contribute further to the growth of Cincinnati. As there were no prospects of such a railroad being built, the City itself undertook it. It became the Cincinnati Southern Railroad. This line crossed the Ohio River into Kentucky and then into Tennessee, serving Harriman and Rockwood and terminating at Chattanooga. There it connected with other railroads and with river port facilities. The Cincinnati Southern developed into a very busy,

Southern Railway depot, Johnson City, ca. 1930. Present location of the downtown traffic loop.

Courtesy Archives of Appalachia, East Tennessee State University

high tonnage transportation link. It is today leased and operated by the Southern Railway System.

One of the unique railroads of the eastern United States had its beginning in East Tennessee in 1879. The East Tennessee and Western North Carolina Railroad, later known as the "Tweetsie", was headquartered in JOHNSON CITY. It extended eastward to ELIZABETHTON and Hampton, then up through the rugged, precipitous, and beautiful Doe River gorge. The main purpose of building the ET & WNC was to provide an outlet for the rich iron ore deposits in the Cranberry, North Carolina, area. Hundreds of thousands of tons of the ore were transported to Johnson City, where it was processed at the Cranberry furnace. Timbering developments and tourism followed. The guests of the popular 166-room Cloudland Hotel atop Roan Mountain arrived, for example, by way of the ET & WNC Railroad.

The peculiar feature of this road was its "narrow gauge", that is, its three feet between rails as compared to the 4′-8$^{1}/_{2}$″ between rails for standard gauge. Also, the tracks of the ET & WNC reached an elevation of 4,110 feet above sea level at Linville Gap, North Carolina, the highest point reached by a common carrier in the eastern United States. As the iron ore deposits and timber reserves were depleted, and as modern highways were constructed in the 1920's and 1930's, traffic declined. In 1950, the line section east of Elizabethton was abandoned. The section from Johnson City to Elizabethton had been standard gauged in 1918 by adding a third rail on the outside; this section remains in operation today as an industrial switching line.

The twenty years from 1885 to 1905 formed the period of greatest railroad building in East Tennessee. In 1888, the Tennessee Central was built from Monterey to Harriman, connecting there with the Cincinnati Southern to provide an outlet for coal deposits in CUMBERLAND COUNTY. Also in the late 1880's, the Knoxville, Cumberland Gap and Louisville Railroad was built from Knoxville to the American Association development at Middlesboro, Kentucky. This railroad provided Middlesboro an outlet to the south. The Tennessee Central line into Harriman, as well as the Knoxville, Cumberland Gap and Louisville, is now a part of the Southern Railway System.

By 1902, the Louisville and Nashville Railroad Company operated a line south out of Knoxville to Atlanta, plus a line from northern Kentucky south to Jellico near the Kentucky-Tennessee state line. The advantages of connecting the two lines were obvious. The link from Jellico to Knoxville was completed in 1904. This made a continuous rail line from Cincinnati to Atlanta.

During the 1880's, there came another railroad that would have a great impact on the development of upper East Tennessee. In 1886 the Charleston, Cincinnati and Chicago Railroad (called the "3-C" Railroad) was chartered. This railroad company laid over a hundred miles of track in the Carolinas to the foot of the Blue Ridge Mountains near Marion, North Carolina. The northern headquarters, established in Johnson City, supervised construction north and south of that city. By 1893 the road had

Courtesy Gene Branam

Southern Railway excursion train at the Falls of the French Broad River, 1970, steaming from Newport toward North Carolina.

been extended south to Erwin and north to the Watauga River. That year, however, the company financing the venture went bankrupt, and the assets were sold at foreclosure. In 1902 George L. Carter acquired the railroad and completed construction six years later, under the names of the South and Western and later of the Carolina, Clinchfield and Ohio. It is the present-day Clinchfield Railroad serving KINGSPORT and Johnson City with headquarters in Erwin.

Other railroads constructed during that period were the Knoxville and Ohio, from Clinton to Jellico; the Knoxville and Sevierville; and the Virginia and Southwestern extending from Appalachia, Virginia, through Bristol to Elizabethton and Mountain City. The Cincinnati, Cumberland Gap and Charleston Railroad from Morristown east through Newport to Asheville, North Carolina, was completed in 1882. A line from Knoxville to Clinton, built prior to the Civil War by the Knoxville and Kentucky Railroad, was later extended to Harriman and OAKDALE. Yet the completion of the Clinchfield Railroad in 1908 marked the end of major railroad construction in East Tennessee. There have since been some alignment improvements and double-tracking, but no new railroads have been built.

J.A. Goforth

Refer to: Riley Oakey Biggs, "The Cincinnati Southern Railway: A Municipal Enterprise," in *The East Tennessee Historical Society's Publications*, No. 7 (1935), pp. 81-102; Lou Harshaw, *Trains, Trestles & Tunnels: Railroads of the Southern Appalachians*, Asheville, N.C.: Hexagon Company, 1977; James W. Holland, "The Building of the East Tennessee and Virginia Railroad," in *The East Tennessee Historical Society's Publications*, No.4 (1932), pp. 83-101; and Francis Ehl Ward, "A Historical Study of the East Tennessee and Western North Carolina Narrow-Gauge Railroad," Appalachian State University thesis, 1958.

See also: THE JELLICO EXPLOSION
THE NEW MARKET TRAIN WRECK

J.G.M. Ramsey (March 25, 1797 - April 11, 1884). James Gettys McGready Ramsey, M.D., Tennessee historian, doctor, and businessman, was born six miles east of KNOXVILLE at Swan Pond. His father, Francis A. Ramsey, was a surveyor who had migrated from near Gettysburg, Pennsylvania, in 1783. J.G.M. Ramsey's mother, Peggy Alexander, was the daughter of John McKnitt Alexander, secretary of the Mecklenburg Convention of May 1775. James Ramsey regarded the Mecklenburg Resolves as the first American declaration of independence.

Ramsey was raised in an atmosphere of culture and Presbyterian doctrine. He attended Ebenezer Academy in KNOX COUNTY and at the age of 19 graduated from SAMUEL DOAK's Washington College. Ramsey read medicine under Dr. Joseph Strong of Knoxville and went on to the University of Pennsylvania medical school for a year. He practiced medicine intermittently all of his life. Ramsey married Margaret Barton Crozier in 1821. He built his home, Mecklenburg, at the confluence of the Holston and French Broad rivers. In 1858, Ramsey became president of the Knoxville branch of the Bank of Tennessee. One of his major interests was RAILROADS. He believed that the future of East Tennessee depended on railroad connections with the Atlantic seaboard. He helped form the East Tennessee and Georgia Railroad and is generally regarded as one of the most important figures in the early history of Tennessee railroads.

Ramsey's friendship with historian Lyman Draper bolstered Ramsey's determination to preserve Tennessee's historical heritage. The result of this determination was *The Annals of Tennessee to the End of the Eighteenth Century*, published in 1853. In *The Annals*, Ramsey combined scholarly research with personal knowledge of people and events. The volume depicts, with a sure hand and an exacting mind, stories of Indian warfare, details of pioneer life, and the careers of such men as JOHN SEVIER and WILLIAM BLOUNT.

J.G.M. Ramsey was a states'-rights Democrat and an ardent supporter of the South. During the CIVIL WAR, he served as Confederate tax collector and disburser of funds. He devoted his medical skills to soldiers and civilians, and his sons fought in the Confederate Army. Arsonists burned Mecklenburg, including a 4,000-volume library and priceless historical papers. When the

Union Army reached Knoxville, Ramsey carried funds to Atlanta, Savannah, and Augusta. At the end of the war he went to Charlotte, North Carolina, to join his wife. Aged 68 and 64, with $42 between them, the Ramseys began a new life on a rented farm called "Exile's Retreat". Ramsey worked on his autobiography and resumed medical practice with a borrowed horse and saddlebags. He was indicted for treason in Tennessee, but received amnesty from President ANDREW JOHNSON.

Ramsey returned to Knoxville in 1871. He helped organize the Tennessee and East Tennessee Medical Societies, drafted Knoxville's first sanitary ordinance, and was a trustee of Blount College, Washington College, and Tusculum College. He helped reorganize the Tennessee Historical Society. Most importantly, he completed his autobiography, a moving account of a Southern family beset by hardships during the Civil War.

Eunice Begun

Refer to: J.G.M. Ramsey, *The Annals of Tennessee to the End of the Eighteenth Century*, Charleston, South Carolina: Walker and Jones, 1853 (Reprinted, Knoxville: East Tennessee Historical Society, 1967, with annotations by Stanley J. Folmsbee and an index by Pollyanna Creekmore and Marie Quinn); and Ramsey, *Autobiography and Letters*, ed. by William B. Hesseltine, Nashville: Tennessee Historical Commission, 1954.

See also: APPALACHIAN LITERATURE
STEAMBOATS, FLATBOATS, RAFTS AND CANOES

Rattlesnake Springs. Despite the adoption of a constitutional government, a written language, a bilingual newspaper, and other tangible evidence of rapid acculturation, the CHEROKEES were subjected in the early nineteenth century to relentless demands for their land. The Treaty of Removal (Treaty of New Echota) was signed December 29, 1835, at New Echota. Of the 300 Indians who signed, only 79 were legal voters, and the treaty has been called the "Ocoee Steal" by some Cherokees. Although the treaty was repudiated by all but a small minority of the Cherokees, the U.S. Senate approved it on May 23, 1836, by a one vote margin. By this treaty the Cherokees ceded all their lands east of the Mississippi in exchange for five million dollars and the right to occupy lands in modern Oklahoma. They agreed to move west within two years.

The Ross party countered with a protest reputedly signed on February 22, 1838, by 15,665 Cherokees. Governor George Gilmer of Georgia threatened to use state troops against the Federal Government if removal were not completed immediately. The round-up of the Cherokees began on May 26, 1838, under the direction of General Winfield Scott. Detention camps or stockades, possibly numbering as many as 29, were located at all the large springs in the vicinity of the Cherokee Agency. Rattlesnake Springs, located about three miles south of what is now the town of Charleston in BRADLEY COUNTY, was the major camp. On the site of Charleston stood Fort Cass, an important gateway to the Cherokee domain in East Tennessee, western North Carolina, northern Georgia and northern Alabama. A short distance to the east, the Great Indian War Path connecting the tribes of the east with those of the south and west crossed the Hiwassee River near old Columbus. Prior to their trek west in the autumn of 1838, some 13,000 Cherokees were grouped at Rattlesnake Springs under the supervision of United States troops. But for the fact that it was the scene of the beginning of one of the most tragic and melancholy migrations in the history of the United States, Rattlesnake Springs would no doubt remain forever unknown beyond its own immediate area.

By Council resolution, Chief JOHN ROSS was made superintendent of emigration. Thirteen detachments of about equal size were organized along lines of family ties and kinship, and each group was placed under the custody of two qualified Cherokee officers. In this way about 13,000 Cherokees, including Negro slaves, were put in readiness for the long journey. John Ross started the final removal on October 1, 1838, by leading the first detachment in prayer, after which a bugle sounded and the wagons started rolling. Peter Hildebrand led the last group to arrive in the West, on March 25, 1839. Few Cherokees were adequately prepared for the trip. Although there is some disagreement on mortality figures, about 4,000 died during capture, detention, removal, and as a direct result of the removal. On the trip, Quatie, Chief Ross's wife, contracted pneumonia and died, and her uncoffined body was buried in a shallow grave as the remaining numbers of the party moved on. There can be little doubt as to the injustice of the Cherokee removal. The march of the Cherokees westward to their new home is known as "The Trail of Tears". Rattlesnake Springs has been placed on the National Register of Historic Places.

Roy G. Lillard

Refer to: James F. Corn, Sr., *Red Clay and Rattlesnake Springs*, Cleveland, Tenn., 1959; and John M. Wooten, *A History of Bradley County*, Cleveland, Tenn.: Bradley County Post 81, The American Legion, 1949.

Red Clay Council Ground. Beginning in 1828, the State of Georgia moved swiftly and relentlessly to suppress the Cherokee Nation existing within its borders. Georgia law annexed all Cherokee lands, annulled all laws and ordinances of the Cherokee Nation, closed Cherokee courts, and forbade all political gatherings or assemblies. In 1832 the national assemblies or councils were moved to the council ground at Red Clay. From 1832 to 1838 the Red Clay Council Ground, located in the extreme southwest corner of BRADLEY COUNTY just north of the Tennessee-Georgia state line, served as the site for the national meetings of the Cherokee Nation.

Red Clay has been called the last eastern capital of the CHEROKEES before their removal beyond the Mississippi River. Earlier, the site had been called Hicks' Village, Sleeping Rabbit's Village, and Fortville. During the 1830's, a number of the national leaders lived nearby. The national treasurer issued and paid bills from Red Clay. The Cherokee Supreme Court met there, as did the Committee and Council of the nation. Around Red Clay were enacted some of the most interesting events in

Cherokee history. At a full council held in October of 1835, a proposed treaty with the United States providing for removal of the Cherokees to the west was overwhelmingly rejected. And it was from Red Clay that the Cherokee Government, led by Chief JOHN ROSS, vainly maneuvered to have the fraudulent treaty of New Echota annulled.

The only natural landmark at Red Clay Council Ground is the Council Spring, a large limestone spring which rises in a deep pool near the western edge of the valley and which has a daily flow of over 400,000 gallons. Brigadier General John E. Wool and his detachment of troops camped at a spring about one-fourth mile east while observing meetings of the Cherokees in Council. The council house stood just east of the great Council Spring. Records indicate that as many as four or five thousand Cherokees attended some of the Council Meetings. Fifteen head of cattle were said to have been killed every day, and a proportionate quantity of Indian corn used to feed those present. Twenty-four native families were employed in cooking and setting tables three times a day. The councils varied greatly in duration, scope and attendance, but transactions of the Government were completely public, and officials deliberated in the Council House as the people stood around outside the building and listened to the proceedings. The councils were as much social and religious in nature as they were political. Sermons and hymn singing formed as much a part of the activities as did the Council deliberations. Among other actions, the Cherokees gave the vote to males 18 or older, so that 18-year olds were voting in Tennessee as early as 1828. Near the Council Ground is the tomb of Sleeping Rabbit, a famous Cherokee veteran of the War of 1812.

The Red Clay Council Ground has been placed on the National Register of Historic Places. This historic site was preserved through the efforts of Col. James F. Corn, Sr., and is now composed of approximately 275 acres. In 1979 the Tennessee Department of Conservation completed the development of the Red Clay Historic Area as one of Tennessee's STATE PARKS. This development includes the James F. Corn, Sr. Interpretative Center (museum), visitors' center, council house, trails, Council Spring, a Cherokee farm house and barn, picnic area and shelter, amphitheater, observation platform, and ranger's residence. The Red Clay area will also serve as the location or trail head of the legislatively designated Trail of Tears State Scenic Trail.

Roy G. Lillard

Refer to: Bryan Butler, "The Red Clay Council Ground," *Journal of Cherokee Studies*, Winter 1977, V.2, No.1; James F. Corn, Sr., *Red Clay and Rattlesnake Springs*, Cleveland, Tennessee, 1959; Roy G. Lillard, *Bradley County*, Memphis, Tenn.: Memphis State University Press, 1980; William R. Snell, *The Councils of Red Clay Council Ground, 1832-1837*, Cleveland, Tenn.: Modern-Way Printing Co., 1980; and John M. Wooten, *A History of Bradley County*, Cleveland, Tenn.: Bradley County Post 81, The American Legion, 1949.

Religion has always been of fundamental social importance in East

Courtesy Thompson Photographs, C.M. McClung Historical Collection, Lawson McGhee Library

Church Street Methodist Church in Knoxville, a neo-Gothic structure completed in 1930.

Tennessee and the southern mountain country. Mainline denominations came into the area with the first settlers. Histories of imported frontier denominations include William Warren Sweet's *Religion on the American Frontier: The Baptists, 1783-1820* (New York: Holt, 1931), Richard Nye Price's *Holston Methodism From Its Origin to the Present Time* (Nashville: Methodist Episcopal Church, South, 1903-1913), Walter Brownlow Posey's *The Presbyterian Church in the Old Southwest, 1778-1838* (Richmond: John Knox Press, 1952), and Charles Willis Cassell, W.J. Finck, and E.O. Henkel, eds. *History of The Lutheran Church in Virginia and East Tennessee* (Strasburg, Va.: Shenandoah, 1930). Also helpful for any study of the Baptists in East Tennessee are James Jehu Burnett's *Sketches of Tennessee's Pioneer Baptist Preachers* (Nashville: Marshall and Bruce, 1919), Lawrence Edward's "The Baptists of Tennessee with Particular Attention to the Primitive Baptist of East Tennessee" (University of Tennessee thesis, 1940), and Glenn A. Toomey's *The Sesquicentennial History of the Nolachucky Baptist Association and Its Affiliated Churches, 1828-1977* (Morristown, Tenn.: Nolachucky Baptist Association, 1977).

The Great Revival, a frontier product with long-lasting influence, is explored by John B. Boles in *The Great Revival, 1787-1805: The Origins of the Southern Evangelical Mind* (Lexington: University Press of Kentucky, 1962). Dickson D.

Bruce *(And They All Sang Hallelujah: Plainfolk Camp-meeting Religion, 1800-1845,* Knoxville: University of Tennessee Press, 1974) traces the direct imprint of the Revival upon many antebellum worship services.

Loyal Jones's bibliographical essay in *Appalachian Journal* ("Studying Mountain Religion," V.5, No.1, Autumn 1977, pp. 125-130) lists relevant religious song books as well as introducing religious movements native to APPALACHIA. These movements include the smaller, and usually more rural, churches or sects. The Disciples of Christ, an important denomination begun by Alexander Campbell in the 1840's (see Alfred DeGroot and Winfred Ernest Garrison, *The Disciples of Christ: A History,* St. Louis: Christian Board of Publication, 1948), gave rise in turn to the Church of Christ and the Christian Church. The Cumberland Presbyterians, an offshoot of the Presbyterians, prompted Benjamin Wilburn McDonnold's *History of the Cumberland Presbyterian Church* (Nashville: Cumberland Presbyterian Church, 1888). The history of the Church of God, based in CLEVELAND and claimant to the first Pentecostal-Holiness church in America, is the subject of Charles W. Conn's *Like a Mighty Army Moves the Church of God* (Cleveland, Tenn.: Church

Congregation leaving Sharps Station Methodist Episcopal Church near Loyston, Sunday afternoon, October 29, 1933. Norris Lake later submerged this church.

Lewis Hine / Courtesy TVA

of God, 1955).

The fortunate propensity of preachers, especially Methodist preachers, to keep journals or to write their autobiographies has given us a continuity of insight into the daily workings of the church. Such ministerial records include those of Francis Asbury (Elmer E. Clark, J. Manning Potts, and Jacob S. Parton, eds. *Journal and Letters*, 3 Volumes, Nashville: Abingdon, 1958), Peter Cartwright (W.P. Strickland, ed. *Autobiography of Peter Cartwright, the Backwoods Preacher*, New York: Hunt and Eaton, 1856; reprinted 1956, Nashville: Abingdon), THE BLACKSMITH PREACHER Thomas Sexton (*From the Anvil to the Pulpit: Thirteen Years in the Wilderness of Sin and Seventeen Years in the Land of Beulah*, Knoxville, Tenn.: S.B. Newman, 1906), D. Sullins (*Recollections of an Old Man: Seventy Years in Dixie*, Bristol, Tenn.: King Printing, 1910), Frank Richardson (*From Sunrise to Sunset: Reminiscence of Bristol, Tennessee*, Bristol: King, 1910), G.C. Rankin (*The Story of My Life: Or, More Than a Half Century as I Have Lived It and Seen It Lived*, Nashville: Smith and Lamar, 1912), and Isaac Patton Martin (*A Minister in the Tennessee Valley for Sixty-seven Years*, Nashville: Parthenon, 1954), all of whom were active in East Tennessee.

Individual church histories are even more numerous than the memoirs. Two, selected from many, describe particularly powerful churches in KNOXVILLE: Isaac Patton Martin's *Church Street Methodists, Children of Francis Asbury: A History of Church Street Methodist Church, Knoxville, Tennessee, 1816-1947*, (Knoxville: Methodist Historical Society of Holston Conference, 1947), and Charles M. Seymour's *A History of 100 Years of St. John's Episcopal Church in Knoxville, Tennessee* (Knoxville: Vestry of St. John's Parish, 1947). The home mission movement, which during the 19th and early 20th centuries established rural churches, schools and clinics throughout the southern mountains, has spawned studies as eulogistic as Robert S. Wightman's "The Southern Mountain Problem: A Study of the Efforts to Solve a Great Unfinished Task" and Lewis A. Wenrick's "Teaching the Mountaineers of Tennessee" (both in *Missionary Review of the World*, V.45, 1922, pp.120-126 and 811-812), as critical as Henry D. Shapiro's *Appalachia On Our Mind: The Southern Mountains and Mountaineers in the American Consciousness, 1870-1920* (Chapel Hill: University of North Carolina Press, 1978).

The Church's relationship with the State was radically defined in East Tennessee at least as early as PARSON BROWNLOW's heyday (see William Gannaway Brownlow, *Ought American Slavery to be Perpetuated? A Debate between Rev. W.G. Brownlow and Rev. A. Pryne*, Philadelphia: J.B. Lippincott, 1858). Beryl Flake Maurer examines 20th century cases in his "The Rural Church and Organized Community Activity: A Study of Church-Community Relations in Two East Tennessee Communities" (University of Tennessee thesis, 1953). Recent analyses of church conditions and responsibilities include Will D. Campbell, *Up to Our Steeples in Politics* (New York: Paulist Press, 1970); Elma L. Greenwood, *How Churches Fight Poverty: 60 Successful Local Projects* (New York: Friendship Press, 1968); and *CORA: Our*

Christian Commitment in Appalachia (Knoxville, Tenn.: Commission on Religion in Appalachia, 1971).

Jim Stokely

See also: BRUCE BARTON
CATHOLICISM
CIVIL WAR
(CIVILIAN LIFE AND INSTITUTIONS)
SAMUEL DOAK
THE SCOPES TRIAL
UNITARIAN UNIVERSALISTS

Rhea County

Size: 312 Square Miles (199,680 acres)
Established: 1807
Named For: John Rhea,
U.S. Representative from Tennessee
County Seat: Dayton
Other Major Cities, Towns, or Communities:
Spring City
Morgantown
Grandview
Evensville
Washington
Morgan Springs

Refer to: Thomas Jefferson Campbell, *Records of Rhea: A Condensed County History,* Dayton: Rhea Publishing Company, 1940.
See also: GRAYSVILLE
THE PEA HULLER

Women sorting strawberries at Chickamauga Products Company in Dayton, county seat of Rhea County, June 5, 1944.

Billy Glenn / Courtesy TVA

THE SCOPES TRIAL
TVA NUCLEAR PLANTS
ROBERT EMMETT WINSETT

Doris Ulmann / Courtesy Doris Ulmann Foundation, Berea College

Mary Ownby at her home near Gatlinburg, 1933, rifling the barrel for a mountain rifle. Photograph taken by Doris Ulmann for Allen H. Eaton's Handicrafts of the Southern Highlands *(New York: Russell Sage Foundation, 1937; reprinted 1973, New York: Dover).*

Rifles. The first firearms to enter Southern APPALACHIA were carried by the "long hunters". These firearms, of the Pennsylvania type, were long and slender with a rifled octagonal barrel and a full stock. These rifles provided essential food and protection to the early hunters. The rifles had to be dependable and accurate. They typically cost the equivalent of several months' wages. Later, as families began to move into Appalachia, they brought another kind of firearm. These were the "smooth bore" or fowling pieces which

Laura Thornborough / Courtesy National Park Service

Squirrel hunter William Ramsey with pump gun, Great Smoky Mountains, late summer, ca. 1927. Leggins protected Ramsey against briers, thorns and snake bites.

were of a large caliber and could shoot either "shot" or a large ball.

Accompanying these early settlers were a few gunsmiths and blacksmiths/gunsmiths. By the late 1700's, the Pennsylvania rifle makers were entering their golden age of gunsmithing, with relief-carved gun stocks, intricate metal working, and engraving. The Appalachian gunsmiths, without the resources of their northern counterparts, turned to the more available bar-and-sheet iron, and to walnut wood, in order to build their guns. These plain looking rifles evolved into what is now a distinct and recognized class called Tennessee or Southern Mountain rifles. The Bean family from KINGSPORT were perhaps the most widely known of these early gunsmiths. Many excellent rifles were also made by others, but all gunmakers did not sign their work. Some gunmakers made only a few rifles per year because their main vocation was blacksmithing.

Soldiers returning home from the CIVIL WAR introduced another kind of firearm. The rifled musket had been the standard shoulder weapon for the North and South. It was typically 58 caliber (with a bore .58 inches in diameter) and ruggedly built so that it could be used as a club. The veterans usually shortened these rifles and reamed out the rifling, essentially converting the rifled musket for use as a shotgun. Some of these may still be seen from time to time, gathering dust over fireplace or door. By the early 1900's in Appalachia, cartridge firearms had replaced most of the muzzle-loading rifles and shotguns. However, some people continued to make the Tennessee rifles. Hacker Martin from JONESBORO was perhaps best known and helped to bridge the gap between the demise of muzzle-loading firearms and their resurrection in recent years.

Today, there are many excellent gunmakers in southern Appalachia. Their rifles provide endless hours of pleasure for the black powder buffs, and they create a direct link with our ancestors of Appalachian heritage. The Pennsylvania or Kentucky rifle is still characterized by a full-length "tiger striped" maple stock with brass or silver buttplate, patchbox, thimbles, nosecap,

Courtesy Gene Branam

A Cocke County fox hunter with hounds, horn, pet fox, corncob pipe and double barrel shotgun.

and trigger-guard. The barrel is octagonal and varies from 28 caliber to over 50 caliber, with different numbers of lands and grooves (rifling), and different lengths (sometimes over 40 inches). The Tennessee or Southern Mountain rifle, on the other hand, has a straightgrain walnut stock with iron buttplate, iron thimble, and a trigger guard made of sheet iron bradded or welded together. Some have a plain iron "banana" patchbox, but many have only a hole drilled in the side of the stock to hold grease. These also vary in caliber, barrel length, and type of lock and rifling. Both styles of rifles are also called "hog-eye" or "squirrel" rifles.

Tom Humphrey

Refer to: John G.F. Dillin, *The Kentucky Rifle*, Washington: National Rifle Association of America, 1924; and John Rice Irwin, *Guns and Gunmaking Tools of Southern Appalachia: The Story of the Kentucky Rifle*, Norris, Tenn.: The Museum of Appalachia Press, 1980.

See also: SOAP
SPINNING AND WEAVING
TANNING AND LEATHERMAKING

Roane County

Size: 350 Square Miles (224,000 acres)

Established: 1801

Named For: Archibald Roane, Governor of Tennessee

County Seat: Kingston

Other Major Cities, Towns, or Communities:
Harriman
Rockwood
Oliver Springs

Looking east down Race Street in Kingston, Roane County, late 1860's. Race Street was part of the Old Stage Road from Knoxville to Nashville. The sign reads "Exchange House By D.T. Peterman". The famous East Tennessee inn was located on the site of Robert King's original house and tavern (1799). This particular structure, built about 1840, burned in 1929.

Courtesy C.M McClung Historical Collection, Lawson McGhee Library

Elverton
Paint Rock

Refer to: Elsie Staples Burkett, ed. *Historical Review: Rockwood's Centennial Year, 1868-1968*, Rockwood: *Rockwood Times*, 1968; and Walter J. Pulliam, *Harriman: The Town That Temperance Built*, Maryville, Tenn.: Brazos Press, 1978.
See also: BROWNTOWN
COMMUNITY COLLEGES

John Ross (October 3, 1790-August 1, 1866) served as Chief of the CHEROKEES for thirty-eight years. One who knew him personally said, "He appeared to center his mind and soul in the welfare of the Cherokees." In remembrance of John Ross, one of the nine districts of the Cherokee Nation has been called by his Indian name, Coweescoowe or Kooweskowe. He was born near Lookout Mountain, Tennessee, the son of David and Mary (McDonald) Ross. Both parents were Scottish, John himself but one-eighth Cherokee blood. At the age of nineteen, he was sent by the United States Indian agent on a mission to the western Cherokees, and during the War of 1812 he served as adjutant of a Cherokee regiment in the army of Andrew Jackson and fought against the Creeks in the battle of Horseshoe Bend.

John Ross was named to the Cherokee council in 1817 and became president of that body two years later. In 1827 he was named assistant chief, and he assisted in drafting both Cherokee constitutions. Ross became principal chief of the Cherokees in 1828, a position he held until his death. John Ross led the Cherokee party which opposed removal to the west, but even when his efforts failed, the United States Government asked him to lead his people to their new home in Oklahoma. He did so. As the CIVIL WAR approached, Ross attempted to follow a policy of neutrality. In 1861 the Cherokees signed a treaty of alliance with the Confederacy, but this was repudiated in 1863.

Courtesy National Portrait Gallery

Lithograph of John Ross.

In 1813 John Ross married a full blood Cherokee woman, Quatie, who died in 1839 at Little Rock, Arkansas, during The Trail of Tears on the way to Indian Territory. In 1845, Ross married Mary Bryan Stapler, a white woman of the Quaker faith. It is said that he was of aristocratic training and manner and that his home near Park Hill, resembling the mansion houses of the Old South, was surrounded by fields cultivated by his numerous slaves. John Ross's last home east of the Mississippi was in BRADLEY COUNTY, located at Flint Spring near the RED CLAY COUNCIL GROUND. There, in November of 1835, Chief Ross and his guest John Howard Payne, author of "Home, Sweet Home", were arrested by Georgia authorities and taken to Spring Place, Georgia, where they were imprisoned and held for several days.

That John Ross had great ability as a statesman and diplomat cannot be questioned, and the fact that he was for nearly forty years the head of his nation is evidence that he possessed the confidence of a majority of his people. Governor SAM HOUSTON put John Ross in the same class with Clay, Webster and Calhoun for eloquence and statesmanship. Henry A. Wise of Virginia, in a sensational speech in Congress over the Cherokee question, said that Ross was in no wise inferior in intellect and moral honesty to the distinguished John Forsyth, Georgia's leading statesman. Ross's greatest achievements were the development of political and social cohesion of the Cherokee Nation, and his greatest efforts were made to safeguard tribal lands from the white man's encroachments.

John Ross died in Washington, D.C., where he was assisting in making the Cherokee treaty of 1866. Resolutions were passed for bringing his body from Washington at the expense of the Cherokee Nation and for providing suitable obsequies, in order that his remains should rest among those he so long served. One resolution stated, "Blessed with a fine constitution and a vigorous mind, John Ross had the physical ability to follow the path of duty wherever it led. No danger appalled him. He never sacrificed the interest of his nation to expediency. He never lost sight of the welfare of his people." Dr. George F. Mellen of THE UNIVERSITY OF TENNESSEE has written that John Ross "unquestionably is the finest character and the most powerful figure in Cherokee annals." The name of this great chief is inseparable from Cherokee history.

Roy G. Lillard

Refer to: Rachel Caroline Eaton, *John Ross and the Cherokee Indians*, Menasha, Wisc.: George Banta Publishing Company, 1914; Roy G. Lillard, "John Ross, Principal Cherokee Chief," in *Cleveland Daily Banner*, 1976; Gary E. Moulton, *John Ross: Cherokee Chief*, Athens, Ga.: University of Georgia Press, 1978; and Gertrude McDaris Ruskin, *John Ross, Chief of an Eagle Race*, Chattanooga, Tenn.: John Ross House Association, 1963.

George and Elizabeth Gilliam Roulstone. In the dreary November days of 1791, a young printer who had moved his press from North Carolina on horseback and flatboat to a crude log hut at Hawkins Court House (now Rogersville) carefully set his type by hand and inked the entire page. Using the hand-powered lever, he slowly pressed copy after copy of what he called the *Knoxville Gazette*. Absorbed in the excitement of a new venture, George Roulstone was probably unaware of the importance of the moment: he had just produced the first newspaper in Tennessee.

The three-column, four-page paper, printed on scarce paper imported from Philadelphia or North Carolina, was to be issued at KNOXVILLE, but Indian trouble at the newly designated capital kept Roulstone from moving to Knoxville until October of 1792. Roulstone and a partner named Robert Ferguson had accepted an invitation from Governor WILLIAM BLOUNT to publish a newspaper in the rapidly growing territory of East Tennessee. The 30,000 settlers were hungry for information, and influential politicians such as Blount and JOHN SEVIER recognized the importance of the press in keeping the public informed. Of course, neither were they unaware of the power of the press for promoting their own political points of view.

Printing a newspaper did not pay well since many people paid for the subscriptions in food or household necessities. In September of 1794, to help Roulstone make ends meet, Gov. Blount had him appointed as the public printer to the state at the impressive salary of $600. Besides printing all government forms, Roulstone regularly printed the journals of the legislative sessions. Many of his original books are now in THE UNIVERSITY OF TENNESSEE (Knoxville) Library.

George Roulstone was born on October 8, 1767, to George and Mary Stevens Roulstone of Boston, and he grew up during the time the Revolutionary War was being waged. Some have suggested that Roulstone's nearness to the Revolution may have made him acutely aware of the importance of the press in a free country. Whatever the reason, he became a printer and published his first newspaper, *Chronicle and Essex Advertiser*, in Salem, Massachusetts. This venture lasted only a few months.

The southern states were vigorous and growing in the late 1700's, so young Roulstone headed for North Carolina. He printed the *North Carolina Gazette* in Hillsboro and the *Fayetteville Gazette* and the *North Carolina Chronicle* in Fayetteville, but he did not have the financial backing to make these papers a success. He and Robert Ferguson met in North Carolina and became partners in the new Knoxville venture until 1793, when they dissolved the partnership. Ferguson seemed to be more of a financial backer than a printer.

The young and energetic Roulstone became fairly active in the growth of Knoxville and East Tennessee. Besides being appointed as the public printer, he was appointed in 1794 as the clerk of the territorial legislature and appointed in 1796 as the clerk of the Senate of the

Paper boy Kelly McCarter, fourteen years old, on the Newfound Gap Highway route in the Great Smoky Mountains National Park, February 7, 1935. Photographer Carlos Campbell recorded in his notes: "He said he makes $2.00 a week."

Carlos Campbell / Courtesy National Park Service

first General Assembly in Tennessee. He also began two other weeklies in Knoxville. From 1798 to 1800 he published the *Register,* and he also published *The Genius of Liberty* (actually a sub-title to the *Register*) along with John Rivington Parrington. In 1799, the *Knoxville Gazette* was combined with George Wilson's *Impartial Observer* for a few years.

Recognized as a person of growing importance in Knoxville, George Roulstone was elected as one of the first trustees of Blount College, which later became The University of Tennessee. Roulstone was also appointed in 1794 as Knoxville's first postmaster. He had earlier hired a rider to made trips between East Tennessee cities to take mail to subscribers along with copies of his newspaper. For many East Tennesseans, Roulstone's paper was the only access to news.

One of Roulstone's most noteworthy achievements was the printing of what has been regarded as the first book printed in Tennessee. The book, printed in 1793, was entitled *Acts and Ordinances of the Governor and Judges, of the Territory of the United States of America South of the River Ohio*. It was referred to more informally as *Laws of the State of Tennessee* or *Roulstone's Code*. The book was a laborious compilation of Tennessee laws in an inexpensive and portable form. Roulstone collected, indexed, and printed the laws in this volume more as a public service than as a money-making venture. Each of the 320 pages was set in type, inked, and pressed by hand. All of the approximately 100 copies were then bound by hand. Many errors have since been discovered in the book, but it was a massive and important individual undertaking at that time.

In 1794, George Roulstone married Elizabeth Gilliam, a daughter of Devereaux Gilliam and Edith Ellis Gilliam. After the Revolutionary War, Col. Gilliam and his family had moved from Amherst County, Virginia, to Tennessee and had established Gilliam's Fort on the land where the Ramsey House now stands. Elizabeth Gilliam Roulstone was an intelligent woman who worked every bit as hard as her husband in their struggle to earn a decent living in a pioneer setting. She ran a boarding house and simultaneously raised her family. Elizabeth had to be a strong woman, for nine years after her marriage she was left a widow. An elaborately worded eulogy in the August 15, 1804, edition of the *Knoxville Gazette* informed readers that George Roulstone was stricken on August 5 with a violent fever and pains in the chest. Five days later he died, leaving Elizabeth expecting their fifth child.

Elizabeth took over her husband's printing work while continuing to run the boarding house. She was elected to fill her husband's office as public printer; this made her the first female officeholder in Tennessee. One of Elizabeth's lodgers in the difficult years following George's death was Col. William Moore, a veteran of the Revolutionary War. He and Elizabeth were married, and he learned the printers' trade. In 1809, the family (with the addition of two little girls) moved to Carthage, Tennessee, where Moore and his stepson James published the *Carthage Gazette*. The Roulstone influence on journalism and general development in

Tennessee can still be felt.

Diane Bohannon

Refer to: John Dobson, *The Lost Roulstone Imprints,* Knoxville: The University of Tennessee Library, 1975; Joseph Hamblen Sears, *Tennessee Printers, 1791-1945,* Kingsport: The Kingsport Press, 1945; and Samuel Cole Williams, "George Roulstone: Father of the Tennessee Press," in *The East Tennessee Historical Society Publications,* 1945.
See also: J.G.M. RAMSEY

Rugby began as a dream in the heart of a young Englishman who yearned to help others as he had seen others helped, and as he himself had been helped. Thomas Hughes had reached the top in fame and popularity as a philanthropist, jurist, and writer. He had told his own story in *Tom Brown's School Days,* the short classic for which he was best known. He had told about his eight years of growing up under the spell of the brilliant young schoolmaster, Thomas Arnold, at the prestigious old school at Rugby, England.

Hughes was a student at Oxford when he learned of the death of his beloved schoolmaster from Rugby. Shocked and grieved at the news, he felt compelled to follow in his footsteps by helping other young men. He chose to devote his efforts to a certain group of young Englishmen whom he considered underprivileged.

To one standing on the outside looking in during the late eighteenth and early nineteenth centuries, being born into British Royalty was a sure ticket to life's highest privileges. But Hughes had come to know that this was not always true. The fortune of the son depended on his being first born. Enslaved by this custom, many of England's best educated and most capable young men found open to them a choice of only three professions that were considered respectable enough for the sons of royalty. Like it or not, it must be medicine, law, or the priesthood; and many, of course, were blessed with neither love nor aptitudes for any one of the three. These often went through life struggling in pursuit of wealth and happiness.

Thomas Hughes's dream became a plan to establish a new colony where young Englishmen would find a chance to turn to careers of manual labor that encompassed creativity and the showing of new initiative. On a visit to America in 1870, he realized that this country was the proper setting for his project. His search for the right location for his new colony ended with the purchase of wilderness acreage in the northern Cumberland Mountains of Tennessee. He chose the name Rugby in honor of his alma mater.

In 1877, construction of the new Rugby began. Beautiful trees were felled from the virgin forests and made into building materials for both homes and fine FURNITURE. English ARCHITECTURE was given a special slant and made unique by the unusually high quality of panelling cut from the sturdy oaks, walnuts, and cedars of the area. Furnishings that could not be made according to elaborate specifications were brought from the homeland to insure exquisite taste in both homes and public buildings.

Christianity was one of the cornerstones upon which Rugby was

Courtesy Rugby Restoration Association

Thomas Hughes Public Library, Rugby, 1882.

established. Thus the spire of Christ Church Episcopal arose amid the treetops early in the construction period. The charming Carpenter's Gothic structure of native pine and walnut was furnished with a rosewood organ built in London in 1849, altar hangings made in England in 1884, and collection plates carved by Henry L. Fry, who carved one of Queen Victoria's thrones.

Education and culture were next in priority. The Hughes Public Library was quickly built and equipped with 7,000 volumes of the finest Victorian literature in America. Some of the volumes date back to the 1600's. Tabard Inn, namesake of the Southwark hostelry in Chaucer's *Canterbury Tales*, was a copy of an English club with its excellent dining room, billiard tables, tennis and croquet courts. It was a delightful place much used for social gatherings by Rugbeians; and visitors from the highest ranks of all parts of the world sat by the hour on the beautifully ornamented verandas, gazing at the surrounding mountains or the Clear Fork River below. Rugby had gained so much popularity that it was considered "the" place to go for vacationers and travelers.

News of the colony's progress spread across this country by newspaper and crossed the waters to Britain with every passing ship. The famous sons of

England did, indeed, work with their hands, and they grew to be skilled at many crafts. But here, as in their homeland, they continued to put first their pursuit for pleasure and happiness. Enterprise and survival came last. Subsidies received from "home" encouraged their leisurely attitudes. Early in the workday, men would lay down the tools of their crafts (axes, hoes, rakes, hammers), bathe, and don their boiled and starched shirts to join their ladies for formal tea at Tabard Inn. Then they would stroll on the lawns while listening to orchestral music floating from the windows. This relaxation was followed by formal dinners, dancing to the music of the Rugby orchestra, or perhaps a concert or literary discussion.

Not all Rugbeians were Englishmen. Indeed, only about 80 of 200 colonists in 1880 were British. Another 80 came from other American states, and the remaining 40 were native East Tennessee mountaineers. Thomas Hughes did believe strongly in hard work, and the colonists made serious efforts at farming and canning. But winters were harsh; unpleasantries came often. Hotel and house fires were not rare. An outbreak of typhoid dampened Rugby's original allure. Perhaps most significantly, several Rugby investors quarrelled over leadership of the colony, while Hughes himself unsuccessfully attempted to guide Rugby in absentia. By 1890, many of the families had given up and had returned to their British homes. Others had drifted away to more prosperous parts of America. The residence of English aristocracy in East Tennessee quickly became a sojourn.

Today, the Rugby Restoration Association, made up of people within the area (some are descendants of Rugby's original inhabitants), are keeping Rugby very much alive in nineteenth century style. With some help from the Federal Government, members of the Association have arranged for Rugby to be seen today as nearly as possible as it was in the beginning. Regular worship services are held in Christ Church, just as they have been since it was first built in the 1800's. And the Thomas Hughes Library, with its rich collection of Victoriana, presents literally the same appearance as the day the doors first opened in 1882. Rugby now stands, in fact, as a memorial to the man who devoted his life to helping mankind.

Vera T. Dean

Refer to: John Egerton, *Visions of Utopia*, Knoxville: University of Tennessee Press, 1977; Thomas Hughes, *Rugby, Tennessee, Being Some Account of the Settlement...*, New York: Macmillan, 1881 (reprinted 1973, Rugby, Tenn.: Rugbeian Press); and Brian L. Stagg, *The Distant Eden*, Knoxville: Paylor Publications, 1973.

S

Sawyers' Fort. John Sawyers was born in Virginia in 1745. Shortly after his marriage in 1776, he and his wife moved to present-day SULLIVAN COUNTY to make a permanent home. For his service in the Battle of Kings Mountain, John Sawyers was given a land grant of 1,000 acres in what is now northeast KNOX COUNTY, between Clinch Mountain and HOUSE MOUNTAIN. In 1785, eleven years before Tennessee became a state, John Sawyers and his family moved to this land. Here, along Big Flat Creek where it crossed what would become Emory Road, Sawyers erected a log house and several out-buildings surrounded by a log stockade.

Although Sawyers' Fort never came under direct attack, it did serve, during several Indian uprisings, as a shelter for the Sawyers Family and their neighbors. The first log cabin was replaced in 1805, as Colonel Sawyers became a Justice of the Peace and Knox County's State Representative. In 1831, Sawyers died in his home at the site of the original fort.

Dorothy Kelly

Refer to: Mary U. Rothrock, ed. *The French Broad-Holston Country: A History of Knox County, Tennessee,* Knoxville: East Tennessee Historical Society, 1946, p. 350.
See also: CHEROKEES

George Scarbrough (October 20, 1915 -), teacher in high schools and colleges for eighteen years, poet for a lifetime, is a fascinating study in contrasts. Born and raised on tenant farms in POLK COUNTY, he is a country boy to the bone, dedicated as his writing so lyrically testifies to his iris and tomatoes, to the neat rows of preserves in his white-washed basement, and to ramblings and blackberry pickings in the hills and valleys of his beloved Tennessee, which he has never wished to leave for long. As a child, Sunday walks in the woods were the only recreation allowed by his stern, part-Cherokee father.

But George has since learned the more sophisticated pleasures of the Renaissance man. He has traveled widely in America and in Europe, where he taught in G.I. schools. He is discriminating in his love of good wine, music, art, and the fine prints, books and antiques which crowd his small OAK RIDGE house. He is knowledgeable in many areas of the sciences and passionate in his devotion to the English language.

Raised in a family of six boys and one girl, George was the only child who yearned to go to college or even high school. His mother, who gave him her love of nature and books, was the one person—aside from a few teachers—who understood his potential or his need. His ambition grew stronger after he won several national writing contests for students. With painfully long breaks for farm labor and for teaching he ultimately attended THE UNIVERSITY OF TENNESSEE, the UNIVERSITY OF THE SOUTH (on a literary scholarship), LINCOLN MEMORIAL UNIVERSITY, and the University of Iowa, where he pursued doctoral work in 1957 at the Writer's Workshop.

Scarbrough's third published book of poems, *Summer So-Called*, was written as a master's thesis at The University of Tennessee. Selected by the *The New York Times* as one of the year's best, this book thrust him into the national limelight. Other honors followed, including the 1961 Borestone Mountain Award and the 1964 Mary Rugeley Ferguson Award from *The Sewanee Review*, as well as grants from PEN, The Author's League, and the Carnegie Fund for Authors. After a lapse of some years, *George Scarbrough: New and Selected Poems* appeared in 1977. This volume brought him renewed attention from such notables as Allen Tate, who called him "one of the few genuine poetic talents to appear in the South in the past generation." He was honored the following year by the Governor's "Outstanding Tennessean Award".

Much of *New and Selected Poems* was written after the poet took an early retirement from teaching in order to care for his stroke-affected mother. He has since contended with near-poverty and severe health problems. Yet he remains a man who will mow the neat flower-filled yard around his spotless white house, wash his mother's laundry, and afterwards walk some three miles to her nursing home. His work in progress includes *Hymns from the Home Country*, a collection of poems and photographs, and an autobiographical novel entitled *A Summer Ago*. We have not heard the last from George Scarbrough.

Pat Benjamin

Refer to: George Scarbrough, *Tellico Blue*, New York: Dutton, 1949; *The Course is Upward*, 1951; *Summer So-Called*, 1956; and *George Scarbrough: New and Selected Poems*, Binghampton, N.Y.: Iris Press, 1977.
See also: APPALACHIAN LITERATURE

The Scopes Trial. Few people in history have become so widely known—so closely identified with a movement, a cause or an event—that their last name alone is a familiar part of the language, synonymous with the time and place and source of their fame. A modest high school teacher in a small town in East Tennessee achieved such distinction. Scopes.

In July of 1925, John Thomas Scopes stood trial in Dayton for presenting the theory of the simian descent of man to a high school biology class in violation of a recently passed state law forbidding any teacher in any publicly supported state school to teach such a theory. The trial was such a blend of controversy and expediency, commercialism and buffoonery, eloquence and ridicule, that it has provided raw material for generations of journalists, has enlivened many an otherwise dull history, and has spawned a highly successful Broadway play and Hollywood movie. Only recently have serious attempts been made to understand the context in which the trial took place. The circus aspects on the surface of this happening yield to a deeper drama of profound social change involving strong faith, tradition, and unexpressed fears. To understand the national issues and regional antagonisms aroused by this so-called "evolution controversy", it is necessary to know something of the time and the place.

The year was 1925. Calvin Coolidge was President of the United States. The Ku Klux Klan was in resurgence, not only in the South but across the nation, especially in the Midwest. Many cities, including KNOXVILLE, had recently suffered racial riots. World War I had forever disrupted accepted social patterns, and in the turmoil of change, the entire nation seemed often to be clutching at a world without change. Racial, religious, ethnic tensions abounded. Chicago Mayor Big Bill Thompson crusaded against the history textbooks used in the city schools. European colonialism had a firm grip on large portions of Africa and Asia. Something called RADIO was gaining popularity and changing the character of public communication. Although Columbia, Tennessee, was still the mule capital of the world, automobiles were becoming familiar vehicles and were changing the pace and style of life across the country. Bobbed hair, short skirts, prohibition hip-flasks, and Rudolph Valentino imitations were outer symbols of deep and often disturbing changes.

A dry statistic from the 1920 census reveals the dimensions of one vast alteration in American life. For the first time in the nation's history, there were more people living in the cities than in the country. Small town dwellers, farmers, crossroads people began to feel a sense of threat from, and resentment against, a society that seemed too quick to question established traditions, too eager to embrace change. In this period of upheaval, the South changed most slowly, remained predominantly rural, and clung to tradition—some of it strong and humane, some of it destructive and unworthy of a proud culture. In a time of profound tension, one thing alone seemed to provide stability for great numbers of people, especially Southern people. That refuge was RELIGION and the church.

During the quarter-century before the Dayton trial, many colleges and universities were centers of controversy over Darwinism. Professors were sometimes terminated because of "scientific doctrine". In southern California in 1910, a militant group began publishing a series of pamphlets called "The Fundamentals", and their doctrine brought the word "fundamentalist" into popular usage. State legislatures wrestled with resolutions that forbade teaching "the theory that denies the story of divine creation as taught in the Bible." The religious unease and controversy from which the Dayton trial stemmed was not an isolated local aberration, although the sensationalism surrounding it often made it seem so. It was part of a nationwide anguish which sometimes bordered on frenzy in its longing to reduce inquiry and complexity to quiescence and simplicity.

This, then, was the time. The place, Dayton, was the seat of RHEA COUNTY and had some 1,800 citizens. Coal mines in the nearby mountains had been important at the time of its founding in 1820. Small textile plants had eventually become the central industry. And one center of social life, as was the case in small towns across America, was the Main Street drug store. Here, at Robinson's on the afternoon of April 5, 1925, a little group congregated most accidentally. They were: Walter White, superintendent of county schools; lawyers Herbert and Sue Hicks; proprietor Frank Earl Robinson; and a man named George Washington Rappleyea. Rappleyea, a tough, unkempt, argumentative native of New York who had come south as a surveyor and had married a Tennessee girl, was vehemently opposed to the "anti-evolution" bill recently passed by the legislature. Others in the gathering more or less favored the bill, but they were intrigued when Rappleyea mentioned a newspaper article in which the American Civil Liberties Union of New York offered to support a test case involving the new law.

Rappleyea asked, "Why not have a test case right here in Dayton? It would put Dayton on the map."

As they discussed this bright possibility, it was discovered that a young science teacher substituting for the regular biology teacher had taught from a text explaining the theory of evolution and praising Charles Darwin. His name was John Thomas Scopes. Scopes, then 24 years old, had been born in Illinois and had grown up in Kentucky, where he had graduated from the state university. He had gone on to Tennessee to teach and to coach athletics. That afternoon in 1925, he was interrupted in a tennis game, came to the drug store, and heard the proposition that he should be arrested and test the law. Scopes agreed and returned to his tennis match. Rappleyea, exultant, sent a telegram to the Civil Liberties Union. Drug store owner Robinson and his wife, who were local correspondents of *The Chattanooga Times*, sent a brief dispatch to that newspaper.

By the next afternoon the Civil Liberties Union had assured cooperation in the case and inquiries had come to Robinson from six other newspapers, including one in New York. The Scopes case, the Monkey Trial, was under way. In the sweltering July heat, it seemed that the eyes of the world were focused on the Dayton courthouse and the lawn to which the trial was eventually moved. Chicago's radio station WGN made the nation's first remote control broadcast from Dayton. Robinson's drug store sold a Monkey Fizz, and palm leaf fans brought a premium price. The postman had to deliver Scopes's mail to him in #3-size washtubs. The heart of the scene, however, was the confrontation between William Jennings Bryan and Clarence Darrow. Each had numerous distinguished and colorful associates in defense and prosecution of the case, but it was the clash between the Great Commoner and the Great Defender that provided high drama.

Each man was eloquent and fierce. Bryan represented much of the best of traditional, rural America. He had been born in 1860 in Salem, Illinois, in the same town that later saw the birth of John Scopes. His career had included law, journalism, teaching, real estate, leadership in the Presbyterian Church, and three unsuccessful candidacies for the presidency of the United States. His Cross of Gold speech was already famous in the annals of political oratory. Although political enemies in Nebraska likened him to the river Platte—"a mile wide at the mouth but only six inches deep"—Bryan had led boldly in several progressive and even radical causes. He had advocated the establishment of a U.S. Department of Labor, popular election of U.S. Senators, anti-trust legislation, and women's suffrage. Three years older than Bryan, a native of Ohio, Clarence Darrow was the product of a tradition almost precisely the opposite of Bryan's. As the son of a village eccentric, Darrow had grown up with an awareness of all that was narrow and confining in small town and rural life. As a brilliant lawyer and one of the wily debaters of his time, Darrow had become famous as a champion of the underdog, a religious agnostic, and an opponent of capital punishment.

These two big, rumpled, conscientious orators were brought face to face near the close of the trial. Judge John T. Raulston barred expert testimony concerning the validity of the Darwinian theory, and Bryan agreed to offer himself for examination as an expert witness on the Bible. In his famous cross-examination, Darrow asked Bryan if he believed in each of the miracles exactly as described in the King James Bible: Jonah and the whale, the sun standing still, and others. Bryan said that he did. During close questioning on precisely how long Biblical Creation had required, Bryan became self-contradictory and finally angry. By this time the court was being held outdoors, the audience had waited ten days for this personal jousting and tilting, the heat bore down with the summer fierceness, and Bryan rose from his chair shouting that Darrow's purpose was "to cast ridicule on everybody who believes in the Bible." Darrow growled in reply: "We have the purpose of preventing bigots and ignoramuses from controlling the education of the United States and you know it, and that is all."

A short while later Bryan accused Darrow of using a court in Tennessee to slur the Bible and its believers. Darrow roared, "I am examining you on your fool ideas that no intelligent Christian on earth believes." And the crowd exploded. One report said that they voiced "amazement, amusement, sorrow, triumph, rage, disappointment" in accordance with their own measure as true believers. Judge Raulston adjourned court. The great debate was over. As for "winning" or "losing", John Scopes was found guilty and fined $100 and costs. Tennessee did not repeal its Butler Law until 1968. On July 26, 1925, a few days after the close of the trial, William Jennings Bryan died. It was the end of an era.

The Monkey Trial. Stereotypes identified with the area and its people during this world-publicized event still afflict this corner of APPALACHIA. Perhaps the native humor (or good humor, wherever it surfaced) displayed during and after that fierce hot summer is characterized by a story that circulated through the town and surrounding hills. Some time after the trial was over, a tourist passing through Dayton stopped to ask directions. He gazed curiously around the courthouse square and asked the mountain man with whom he was talking, "Are there any monkeys here?"

Without cracking a smile, the squire replied, "No, but a lot of them pass through."

Wilma Dykeman

Refer to: Fred C. Hobson, Jr., *Serpent in Eden: H.L. Mencken and the South,* Chapel Hill: University of North Carolina Press, 1974; John Thomas Scopes and James Presley, *Center of the Storm: Memoirs of John T. Scopes,* New York: Holt, Rinehart and Winston, 1967; Mary Lee Settle, *The Scopes Trial,* New York: F. Watts, 1972; and *The World's Famous Court Trial: Tennessee Evolution Case. A Complete Stenographic Report of the Famous Court Test of the Tennessee Anti-evolution Act at Dayton, July 10 to 21, 1925, Including Speeches and Arguments of Attorneys, Testimony of Noted Scientists, and Bryan's Last Speech,* Cincinnati: National Book Company, 1925.
See also: AGRICULTURE
THE PEA HULLER

Scott County
Size: 544 Square Miles (348,160 acres)
Established: 1849
Named For: Winfield Scott,
General in the Mexican War
County Seat: Huntsville
Other Major Cities, Towns, or Communities:
Oneida
Robbins
New River
Winfield
Elgin
Glenmary
Isham
Norma
Lone Mountain

Refer to: Esther Sharp Sanderson, *County Scott and Its Mountain Folk,* Huntsville, 1958.
See also: BRUCE BARTON
STATE PARKS

Sequatchie County
Size: 273 Square Miles (174,720 acres)
Established: 1857
Named For: Sequatchie Valley
(named for a Cherokee chief)
County Seat: Dunlap
Other Major Cities, Towns, or Communities:
Lone Oak
Cagle
Mount Airy
Fredonia
Cartwright
Lewis Chapel

Refer to: J. Leonard Raulston and James W. Livingood, *Sequatchie: A Story of the Southern Cumberlands,* Knoxville: University of Tennessee Press, 1974.
See also: COAL MINING
GEOGRAPHY

Sequoyah or George Gist (1771-August 1843), inventor of the Cherokee alphabet or syllabary, was born in the village of Tuskegee, Tennessee, near FORT LOUDOUN. He was the son of an Indian mother, Wurteh, and of Nathaniel Gist, white soldier and scout.

Courtesy Tennessee State Library

Sequoyah

While a youth he moved to a small farm near Willstown, Alabama. Sequoyah never attended school; he could neither read nor write. He is said to have conceived his idea of a Cherokee alphabet when a nephew returned from a distant school and wrote English words. Sequoyah believed that if the white man could make "talk" on "leaves of paper", then the Indian could do this, too. He also observed that if the CHEROKEES were to take their place with the white man, they must have a written language.

Sequoyah started to work on his alphabet in 1809. He fought in the War of 1812 against the Creek Indians, taking part in the Battle of Horseshoe Bend. He married Sally Benge in 1815. In addition to farming, Sequoyah became a skilled silversmith. At about this time he became crippled in one leg due to accident or disease. In 1818 six thousand Cherokees, including Sequoyah, exchanged their shares of ancestral land in Southern APPALACHIA for acreage in the Arkansas territory. Sequoyah at this time was working hard on his alphabet. He withdrew to a cabin apart from his house. He endured the ridicule of neighbors and was suspected of being a witch. He finally evolved an alphabet of 86 letters, including a number of English letters he had found in a spelling book. The alphabet was completed in 1821. It is also called a syllabary because the letters stand for syllables.

By means of Sequoyah's alphabet, many Cherokees became literate in a matter of months. They taught each other in their cabins or by the roadside. The alphabet strengthened, through letters, the ties between families of the western and eastern Cherokees. In 1824 the Cherokee Nation presented a medal to Sequoyah in honor of his "talking leaves". Through the efforts of missionary Samuel Worcester, the Cherokees acquired a printing press. The Bible, school books, hymnals, and the constitution and laws of the Cherokee nation were printed with Sequoyah's alphabet. In 1828 Elias Boudinot began publishing the first Indian newspaper, the *Cherokee Phoenix*, in New Echota, Georgia. Also in 1828 the U.S. Congress appropriated $500 to Sequoyah in honor of his alphabet. But in spite of his fame, Sequoyah remained a modest man, reserved in manner and with an innate dignity.

About this time, the Cherokees in Arkansas were removed to the Oklahoma territory. Sequoyah lived with his family in what is now Sequoyah County, Oklahoma, farming and teaching his alphabet in a Cherokee school. When the eastern Cherokee survivors of The Trail of Tears arrived in Oklahoma during 1838-39, Sequoyah did much to settle disputes between factions and to establish a secure tribal government. Upon hearing of injustices suffered by Cherokees in Texas and Mexico, Sequoyah resolved to visit them and bring them back to their rightful home. In August 1842 he set out with several companions and his son, Tessee. Sequoyah became ill on the journey. This illness and the hardships of the trail were too much for him. He died in San Fernando, Mexico.

A statue of Sequoyah stands in the Hall of Fame of the U.S. Capitol and represents, along with that of Will Rogers, the State of Oklahoma. Sequoyah's name is perpetuated in the redwood trees (Sequoia sempervirens and Sequoia gigantea), named in his honor by German botanist Stephan Endlicher. But Sequoyah's enduring fame rests in the Cherokee alphabet, one of the most remarkable literary achievements in the history of mankind.

Cherokee writing.

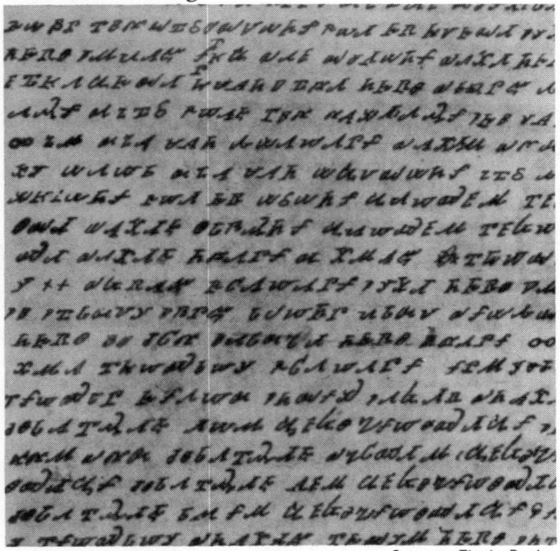

Courtesy Theda Purdue

Eunice Begun

Refer to: Grant Foreman, *Sequoyah*, Norman: University of Oklahoma Press, 1938; and Jack F. Kilpatrick, *Sequoyah, of Earth and Intellect*, Austin, Texas: Encino Press, 1965.

John Sevier (September 23, 1745-September 24, 1815), one of the founders of THE WATAUGA ASSOCIATION, hero of the Battle of Kings Mountain, well known Indian fighter, Governor of THE STATE OF FRANKLIN and the first Governor of Tennessee, was born near Harrisonburg in Rockingham County, Virginia. His emigrant father Valentine Sevier was a well-to-do landowner, merchant, and miller. John attended school in Staunton, Virginia, and later at Fredricksburg Academy. It is thought that through his acquaintance with Lord Fairfax he met George Washington, and that from Washington's dreams of independence from England sprang Sevier's purpose to move to the frontier country of Watauga, in what is now upper East Tennessee, to be away from the yoke of English oppression.

In 1771 Sevier, his father, mother, brothers and all their families made the move into the upper Holston country. In 1776 they moved on south into the Watauga country near what is now ELIZABETHTON. John Sevier became heavily engaged in all civil matters pertaining to settlement. He was also, from the first, enmeshed in battle with the CHEROKEES. He lost his first wife, Sarah Hawkins, in a wintry flight from an Indian attack. Sevier also lost three nephews, sons of his brother Valentine, Jr. Notwithstanding these facts, Sevier showed the Indians as much mercy as possible. In thirty-five battles against the Indians, his forces killed fewer than two hundred. He undertook to dissuade his troops from cruelty, especially toward women and children.

Probably the most important feat in his illustrious military career was when Colonel Sevier and his friend, Colonel Isaac Shelby, led the now famous Overmountain Men across the tortuous mountain trails from Watauga to Kings Mountain, South Carolina. En route they were joined by Cleveland, McDowell, Winston, Campbell, Candler, Hill, Lacey, Hawthorne, Hanebright, Graham, and Williams, who commanded the Virginians, North Carolinians, South Carolinians, and a small detachment from Georgia. On October 7, 1780, this force of 1,840 men attacked the British troops of General Cornwallis, under the command of Colonel Patrick Ferguson. The British troops, who held the crest of Kings Mountain, were soundly defeated in a battle lasting only a few hours. Three hundred enemy were killed or wounded, and 810 were taken prisoner, with all their arms and supplies falling to the victors. This outstanding victory closed the back door of the Revolution and, in the opinion of many experts, turned the tide of America's fight for independence.

The voters, not knowing of his death in 1815, reelected "Nolichucky Jack" to the Congress of the United States, "in absentia", during his mission to the Creek Indians in what is now Northern Alabama. John Haywood, author of the first authoritative history of the State of Tennessee, asked that the fame of Sevier and of his illustrious comrades be perpetuated with a commemorative monument. The monument asked for by Haywood may be seen at the final resting place of John Sevier and his widow "Bonnie Kate", on the grounds of the old KNOX COUNTY Courthouse in KNOXVILLE, Tennessee.

John Sevier Courtesy Tennessee State Library

George A. Bauman

Refer to: Carl Driver, *John Sevier*, Chapel Hill: University of North Carolina Press, 1932; John Haywood, *The Civil and Political History of the State of Tennessee, from its Earliest Settlement up to the Year 1796*, Knoxville, Tenn.: Heiskell and Brown, 1823; and Sevier Papers, Tennessee State Archives, Nashville, Tennessee.

Lewis Hine / Courtesy TVA

Farmland along main highway near Sevierville, October 22, 1933.

Sevier County
Size: 597 Square Miles (382,080 acres)
Established: 1794
Named For: John Sevier, former Governor of The State of Franklin
County Seat: Sevierville
Other Major Cities, Towns, or Communities:
- GATLINBURG
- Pigeon Forge
- Pittman Center
- Kodak
- Harrisburg
- Wears Valley
- Seymour
- Boyd's Creek
- Jones Cove

Refer to: Ethelred W. Crozier, *The White-Caps: A History of the Organization in Sevier County*, Knoxville, Tenn., 1899 (reprinted 1963, Sevierville, Tenn.: Brazos).
See also: PARSON BROWNLOW
DUPONT SPRINGS
GREAT SMOKY MOUNTAINS NATIONAL PARK

Soap. Without soap, life today would be very different. In the United States, nearly three billion pounds are manufactured annually. The chief producing centers are located in Indiana, Illinois, Ohio, New York, California, Pennsylvania and Missouri. Although Tennessee is not among the major soap

Lewis Hine / Courtesy TVA

Mr. and Mrs. Jo Stinnett, tenant farmers, at Seymour in Sevier County. October 21, 1933.

producing states, much soap is manufactured in Tennessee's larger towns and cities. As late as the early 1900's, almost every household made its own soap. Homemakers made use of home-produced fats and oils and usually made their own lye in ashhoppers. The fats were usually byproducts of hog butchering for the winter meat supply. The lye was made by allowing water to flow through hickory ash accumulated from fireplaces and stoves.

The soap making process was very demanding for the product to be the kind of soap that would meet most of the family's needs for cleansing agents. The soap had to cleanse properly and not burn the skin or damage the fabrics. The ingredients had to be correctly balanced with just enough fat and an exact amount of lye (alkali) for saponification to take place, producing a superior product. Soap making usually took place in the backyard of the home. The large black iron kettle that served many purposes was cleansed and prepared to hold the soap mixture. After filling the kettle half full of water, a fire was built around it to bring the water to a rolling boil.

Adding the fat meant that the stirring process had to start to keep the fat from settling to the bottom of the kettle. To this boiling mixture, regularly and constantly stirred, a measured amount of lye was added. This mixture was to boil exactly fifteen minutes with no interruptions in stirring. At this point, the soap makers added a cup of borax to give the soap a firmer consistency and to make it more usable in hard water. Some people added spice to give the soap a distinctive fragrance. When all the fire had been removed from around the kettle the soap mixture, looking like chicken gravy, was ladled into wooden trays lined with cloth to prevent the liquid soap from running through the cracks. These flats were covered and set aside to cool and harden overnight. The next morning, the soap was cut into cakes or bars and stored to be used for all the family's cleaning needs for the year. Some of the best might be entered in the county fair, and some might be shared with neighbors.

Most of the soap we use today is made in factories where large steel vats holding as much as 150 tons are heated by steam coils. Ingredients are added through inlet pipes, and the finished mixture is beaten smooth by paddles in what is called a crutcher. Then the mixture flows into frames to dry, harden and be prepared for cutting into sizes for marketing. Dyes are added to the liquid mixture to add color, and perfumes are added to give fragrance. Soap is manufactured and marketed in many forms, such as shaving soap, shampoos, antiseptic and deodorant soaps, and liquid and powdered soaps. These products are so widely advertised on television in afternoon dramatic shows that the programs have been given the name of "soap operas". The viewing audience for these shows is tremendous.

Claire Gilbert

Refer to: "Soapmaking" in Eliot Wigginton, ed. *The Foxfire Book*, Garden City, N.Y.: Anchor Press/Doubleday, 1972, pp. 151-158.

See also: RIFLES
SPINNING AND WEAVING
TANNING AND LEATHERMAKING

The Sounds of Railroading. I remember when RAILROADS were in their heyday. Whistle sounds and train noises were the background music in our homes. We reckoned time by the goings and comings of trains, and we determined our daily schedules by whistles and timetables. We were a railroad family, and Oakwood was a community of Southern Railroad engineers, conductors, firemen and shop men. Local trade revolved around the twice-a-month paydays.

I loved to lie in bed and listen to the night trains. I learned to distinguish passenger trains from freight trains, and my daddy taught me to recognize the engineer by a certain whistle sound. He said that engines had personalities because they were possessed by the men who ran them.

The passenger train far, far away: I'd listen to the wail of its whistle as it announced itself to Powell Station or to Heiskell or to Clinton. Then there'd be the steady rumble of the fast freight. I'd count the chuggins of the engine in labor. The Black Oak Ridge was a demanding challenge, but when the top was scaled, the speed, the mood, and the sound of the train would change. I could hear the increase in speed, the giant wheels racing with confidence on rails of steel. The midnight flyer on a cold snowy night had a sound of sadness. Its soulful refrain would carry on for miles and miles and spread out across the valley between the ridges. It could conjure almost more loneliness than I could stand. My spine would tingle and I'd shiver and scoot down beneath the bed covers. I would be filled with awe, but I would savor the effect because I liked it.

There were daytime sounds of railroading, switch engines and such, but they never meant much to me. It was the nighttime noise that I liked. It was carried into my home live from the sound track; but alas, its only remaining glory is in memory.

Amy C. Goforth

See also: CLERKING FOR THE L&N

Spinning and Weaving are crafts basic to every civilization. In this country's colonial days, they were home industries, with almost every woman knowing how to operate a spinning wheel and a loom. Both wheel and loom were often made by the men in the family. With the coming of the industrial era, these home arts were abandoned. For many years hand spinning and weaving almost disappeared. Today, however, these are far from being lost arts. Both crafts are well known in East Tennessee.

Spinning, whether done by machine or by hand, is the twisting of wool, cotton, flax, or other raw fiber into thread. In hand spinning, the raw material must first be cleaned and carded—combed between two currycomb-like tools until it is free of foreign materials and the fibers are smooth and straight, rolled into soft rolls. It is then spun into yarn or thread on the spinning wheel. In the early days in East Tennessee, the large wheel, which is turned by hand, was used more than the small wheel, which is run by foot power, because the larger one was easier for the mountain woodworker to make.

Cloth, or any woven material, consists of two sets of fibers: a longitudinal set called the warp, and a transverse or horizontal set called the weft or woof. The warp threads are fastened to a loom to keep them in place and to allow finished cloth to be rolled on a beam while more warp is unrolled to be woven. The weft is a continuous thread that is passed over and under the warp threads by means of a shuttle on which the warp is wound. Most looms are operated by treadles, whose action lifts one set of warp threads and lowers another so that the shuttle can pass between them.

Because our mountain area was so isolated, such crafts as weaving and spinning persisted much longer than elsewhere in the country. When, in the early years of the 20th century, interest in handcrafts began to revive, some mountain women were still weaving and spinning. Many who had abandoned these crafts and were using machine-made cloth still had spinning wheels or looms stashed away in attic or shed, along with weaving drafts (patterns) their mothers and grandmothers had used.

In such centers as the PI BETA PHI SETTLEMENT SCHOOL in GATLINBURG, teachers and workers recognized the beauty of the old weavings and encouraged the women to weave as a means of adding to meager family incomes. The centers marketed the weavings and helped design products that would sell to outsiders. Pi Beta Phi employed a designer and operated its own shop, Arrowcraft, where weaving and other native crafts were and still are sold. This center has often employed over a hundred mountain women as weavers.

Weaving had always been chiefly a utilitarian craft, with weavers producing such items as coverlets, tablecloths, place mats, rugs, and yard goods, although some wall-hangings were made. In its early revival, weaving followed this tradition and to some extent still does. But a change was coming. During the 1950's and 1960's there was a steady growth in crafts, with more and more young people entering the field professionally. Many of these had trained at college or art school. Crafts, and especially weaving, began to acquire a new look.

Mrs. James Watson, 65 years old and a spinner of wool yarn for the weavers at Pi Beta Phi Settlement School, at work in her mountain cabin near Gatlinburg. November 14, 1933.

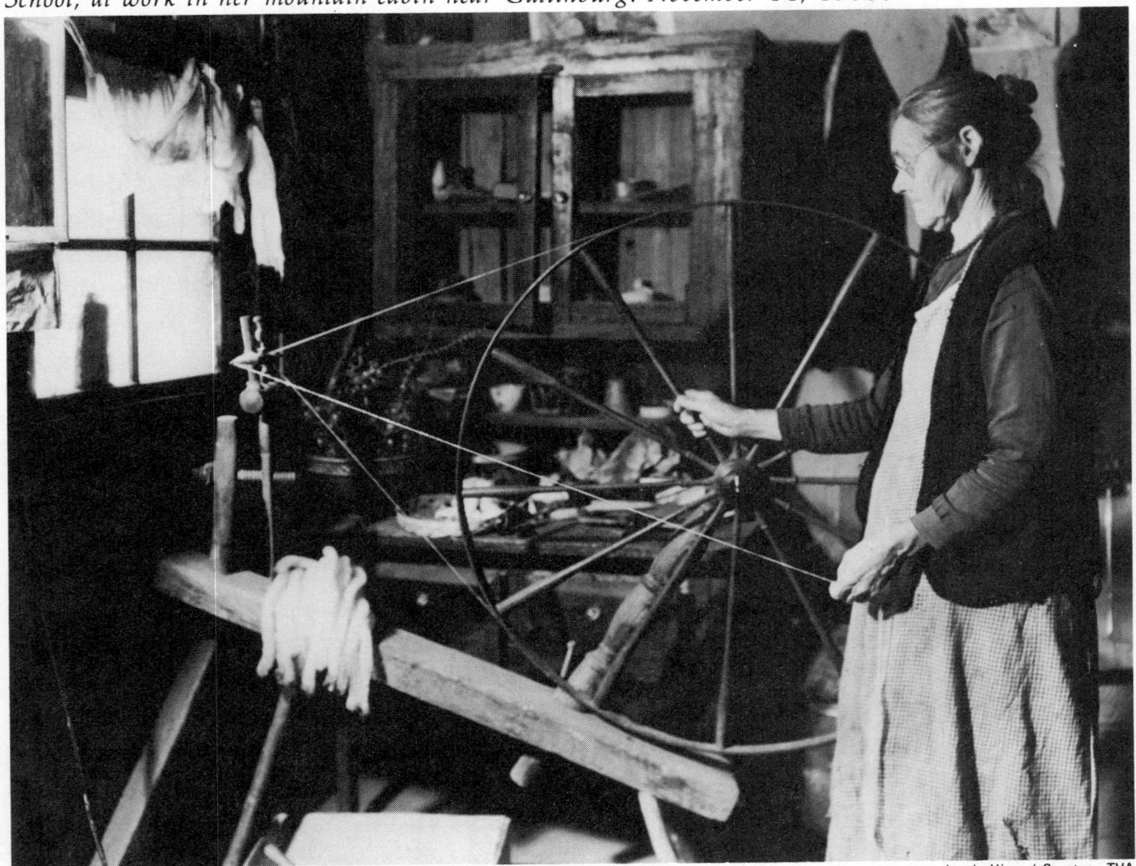

Lewis Hine / Courtesy TVA

In this new revival of crafts, weaving was popular, and it ceased to be exclusively traditional and utilitarian in nature. Today much weaving is experimental and purely ornamental. Even the utilitarian, in the hands of many craftsmen, has taken on a bold new look, and pillows and ponchos may be exciting in design. Off-the-loom weaving and three-dimensional weaving are becoming more and more popular and are included in exhibits. Traditional weaving, however, still holds its own among many craftsmen. Much weaving, even the conservative, is now made more interesting by the use of man-made fibers and even of leather, wood, and various native materials in addition to the usual wool, cotton, and linen.

Hand-spinning was not revived as vigorously or as early as weaving. In the late 1950's and the early 1960's, it was hard to find a hand spinner in the southern mountain area. Now, however, many craftsmen are involved in spinning and its sister craft, vegetable (or natural) dyeing of threads and yarns. These two crafts as well as weaving are alive and well in East Tennessee.

Bernice A. Stevens

See also: RIFLES
SOAP
TANNING AND LEATHERMAKING

The State of Franklin, an independent political entity from 1785 to 1789, was at one time seriously considered as a candidate for the 14th state in the early union of states. The State of Franklin remained centered in what is now northeastern Tennessee throughout its existence, although its proposed boundaries fluctuated to include part of present-day Virginia, Kentucky, Middle Tennessee, and northern Alabama. The rise and fall of this state took place in a fluid atmosphere of political growth, testing, and intrigue.

The thirteen colonies that entered the Revolutionary War with England in 1776 were only loosely bound by their common purpose. The change to self-rule was sudden, and each of the thirteen new states slid into debt. The relatively landless states of the North insisted that Virginia, North Carolina, and Georgia cede their unappropriated western territory to Congress. This western territory was extensive. Virginia claimed land west to the Mississippi River, including the Northwest Territory beyond the Ohio River. North Carolina also claimed land west to the Mississippi, including all of present-day Tennessee. Georgia claimed lands covering parts of present-day Alabama and Louisiana. In September of 1780, the northern states introduced into the Continental Congress a motion that this unsettled territory be considered as common property of the proposed Confederation. The southern states strongly opposed this move, and Maryland's insistence on Virginia's cession of the Northwest Territory delayed ratification of the Articles of Confederation until March of 1781.

Meanwhile, settlers on the western fringes of the southern states were exploring ways to organize and better govern themselves. Arthur Campbell, for example, living on the Holston River in southwest Virginia, was exerting great effort to create a new state which would include a portion of southwest Virginia and the upper territory of present-day East Tennessee. At the same time, such pioneer land speculators as WILLIAM BLOUNT, Richard Caswell, John Donelson, Stockley Donelson, Joseph Martin, and JOHN SEVIER stood ready in the North Carolina territory to ride the shifting sands of land ownership and acquire large tracts for themselves. In 1783, for example, William Blount helped push what is now known as the "Land Grab Act" through the North Carolina legislature. The legislators, knowing that they would soon have to cede their unappropriated western land, established the Armstrong Land Office in Hillsborough in order to appropriate or sell as much of the western land as possible. The land office operated seven months and conveyed vast acreages to a small clique of speculators.

The North Carolina legislature reluctantly ceded what was left of its western lands in the spring of 1784. News of the cession soon reached the overmountain settlements along the Holston, Watauga, and Nolichucky rivers. Many of the transmountain people realized that they would have neither governmental protection against Indian attacks nor orderly enforcement of civil, criminal, and military law. They moved at once to name county delegates to meet in a general convention and adopt needed measures. WASHINGTON COUNTY selected eighteen delegates, GREENE COUNTY thirteen, and SULLIVAN COUNTY nine. The forty delegates met in Jonesborough (JONESBORO) in late August, elected John Sevier their president, and advocated a new state. Although North Carolina repealed its own cession in November, the news was slow in reaching the overmountain country. In December, another convention at Jonesborough established the State of Franklin and adopted a provisional constitution similar to the constitution of North Carolina.

Though ready to rejoin North Carolina when he heard of that state's repeal of the cession, John Sevier could not stop the separatist movement. In March of 1785, he was elected Governor of the State of Franklin. Lacking currency, the state paid its officers in animal pelts, clothing, tobacco, and other produce. In May, commissioner William Cocke presented Franklin's cause to the Congress. Several states favored acceptance of North Carolina's cession and, presumably, the admission of Franklin as the 14th state, but the vote for the State of Franklin fell short of the nine necessary for approval.

North Carolina never recognized the State of Franklin and began a slow but successful campaign against Franklin officials by offering them places in the North Carolina government. A vicious internal split among the Franklinites surfaced at a 1785 constitutional convention at Greeneville, as Sevier contended with rival John Tipton and his "Tiptonites". Tipton generally supported North Carolina and feuded with Sevier's family into late 1788. Sevier himself, attempting to extend Franklin's boundaries against the CHEROKEES and for the good of his own land holdings, negotiated the Treaty of

Dumplin Creek and even made overtures to Spain concerning the western land. But the legal situation remained confused. Many land owners were fearful for their titles, and political rivalries rendered nearly useless the initial potential of Franklin's government. By 1789, the State of Franklin was drained of support. Sevier was elected to the North Carolina state senate in August. In December, the North Carolina legislature again voted for cession, thus paving the way for the establishment of the Northwest Territory. Although the State of Franklin failed, its leaders were destined to become the moulders of that territory and of the 16th state, Tennessee.

Pat Alderman
Jim Stokely

Refer to: Thomas Perkins Abernethy, *From Frontier to Plantation in Tennessee*, Chapel Hill: University of North Carolina Press, 1932; and Samuel Cole Williams, *History of the Lost State of Franklin*, Johnson City, Tenn.: The Watauga Press, 1933.
See also: THE WATAUGA ASSOCIATION

State Parks. For more than 10,000 years, man's presence has been felt in the Appalachian region of Tennessee. Today, this heritage is preserved through historical, archaeological, and natural sites known as state parks. The TENNESSEE VALLEY AUTHORITY helped pave the way for many of Tennessee's parks, and the first one to be placed under the administration of the Division of State Parks was Harrison Bay in HAMILTON COUNTY, leased from TVA on June 16, 1938. During the state park boom of 1920-1940, it became evident that state parks were not the same as national parks or the then more popular municipal parks. Falling in the middle of the scale, state parks dealt more with conservation while national parks were centered around preservation and municipal parks geared development toward recreation.

Some 18 parks represent East Tennessee. A few are classified as Rustic, or basically primitive with nothing more than bare essentials to disturb natural areas. Several parks are Day Use only, while Resort parks are those with exceptional vacation facilities. East Tennessee has two Scenic River parks: one in POLK COUNTY along the narrow rock-strewn Hiwassee River, and the other in COCKE COUNTY bordering the historic French Broad River. Several parks, such as Frozen Head State Park near Wartburg, emphasize Environmental Education. There are also several Historic parks, born from the need to preserve our Indian and pioneer heritage. All of the East Tennessee parks offer excellent recreational opportunities, including year-round camping, hiking, and picnicking. Many offer a whole spectrum of activities such as swimming, boating, horseback riding, golf, and winter sports. Some have restaurants open all year, and four offer year-round cabins.

Big Ridge State Rustic Park (3640 acres) sprawls along the shores of Norris Lake in UNION COUNTY. One of the first parks developed by TVA as a demonstration area, Big Ridge was acquired by the State Division of Parks in 1949. Focal points include the nature exhibit, visitor center and a peninsular-beached swimming area.

Booker T. Washington State Day Use Park (356 acres) lies along Chickamauga Lake in Hamilton County. Bought from TVA for the nominal sum of one dollar, this facility is today a gold mine for fishermen, boaters, and other outdoor enthusiasts.

Cove Lake State Day Use Park (1,465 acres) was developed in 1938 with a 92-acre tract of land purchased from Caryville citizens. Today the site, situated in the northern Cumberland Plateau in CAMPBELL COUNTY, provides a 27-room white-stone motel and restaurant. A special treat for winter visitors is the several hundred Canadian geese that make this natural woodland a feeding ground.

Cumberland Mountain State Rustic Park (1,529 acres), also on the Cumberland Plateau, lies 2000 feet above sea level in CUMBERLAND COUNTY. The park was deeded to Tennessee by the U.S. Department of Agriculture after being developed as the CUMBERLAND HOMESTEADS by the Farm Security Administration. It was originally designed to be an integral part of the homestead plan and to provide subsistence for some 250 families in the general area. Today, cabins, campsites, and a restaurant overlook a 50-acre lake and scenic stone bridge.

Davy Crockett Birthplace (13 acres) is a historic area near the present town of Limestone in GREENE COUNTY. Maintained as a memorial to the Tennessee pioneer, it marks the spot of DAVID CROCKETT's birth with a replica of his parents' log cabin. The park should not be confused with David Crockett State Day Use Park in West Tennessee. The facility offers picnic and year-round camping facilities.

Fall Creek Falls State Resort Park (16,029 acres) in BLEDSOE COUNTY and VAN BUREN COUNTY is the second largest in Tennessee and is one of the least developed. It features Fall Creek Falls, which falls 256 feet in a crescendo of natural beauty.

French Broad Scenic River slices through Cocke County toward confluence with the Holston River near KNOXVILLE.

Frozen Head Natural Area (10,218 acres) in MORGAN COUNTY offers a wide variety of trails to the backpacker or day hiker.

Harrison Bay State Day Use Park (1,321 acres) clings to 39 miles of Chickamauga Lake shoreline in Hamilton County. With a claim to the most complete boat docking facilities in the TVA lake system, this facility is a multiple recreation area.

Hiwassee State Scenic River in the southeasternmost corner of Tennessee is one of America's most naturally beautiful waterways.

Indian Mountain State Camping Park (311 acres) is located in Campbell County between Jellico and the Kentucky border. Used primarily for camping, this park has the distinction of being the first to be developed on abandoned strip-mined land.

Norris Dam State Resort Park (2,321 acres) lies in ANDERSON COUNTY near TVA's massive Norris Dam. The park features tracts of virgin forest, an 18th century grist mill, and the WILL G. AND HELEN H. LENOIR MUSEUM.

Panther Creek State Day Use Park (1,289 acres) in HAMBLEN COUNTY is a relatively new park with the latest in modern facilities and a network of hiking opportunities.

Pickett State Rustic Park (831 acres) in PICKETT COUNTY contains many natural bridges and geological formations.

Red Clay State Historic Area (315 acres) includes RED CLAY COUNCIL GROUND. Its reconstructed Indian village and model Cherokee farm depict life as it was in BRADLEY COUNTY and other parts of East Tennessee during the 1830's. A museum and cultural center offer visitors historically important materials about the CHEROKEES.

Roan Mountain State Resort Park (2,104 acres) in CARTER COUNTY contains part of the famous Appalachian Trail, plus hundreds of acres of blazing rhododendron for summer visitors.

Sycamore Shoals Historic Area (26 acres), also in Carter County, recalls the history that led to expansion of America's western boundry. A museum reproduction of Fort Watauga offers daily visitors a glimpse of our past.

Warrior's Path State Day Use Park (1,355 acres) is located in upper East Tennessee's SULLIVAN COUNTY. Fort Patrick Henry Lake provides the setting for a golf course and other recreational opportunities.

In addition to the state parks, seven state forests are located in East Tennessee. Central Peninsula State Forest in Union and Campbell counties comprises 24,329 acres; Lone Mountain in Morgan County, 3,597 acres; Franklin-Marion in MARION COUNTY, approximately 6,000 acres; and Mt. Roosevelt in ROANE COUNTY, 9,205 acres. Counties containing forests bearing the county name include SCOTT COUNTY (3,182 acres), Pickett County (11,177 acres), and Bledsoe County (6,656 acres).

Patricia A. Hope

Refer to: Bevley R. Coleman, "A History of State Parks in Tennessee," George Peabody College for Teachers thesis, 1963; and *Master Plan for the Tennessee Outdoor Recreation Area System*, Nashville: Tennessee Department of Conservation, 1974.
See also: GREAT SMOKY MOUNTAINS NATIONAL PARK

Steamboats, Flatboats, Rafts and Canoes. The tributaries and the headwaters of the Tennessee River system provided the first paths both for land and for water transportation in East Tennessee. These small mountain streams were too turbulent, however, for any craft but light canoes. Henry Timberlake, who in 1761 went by canoe from the Long Island of the Holston (KINGSPORT) to the vicinity of the site of FORT LOUDOUN for the purpose of gaining a thorough knowledge of the navigation conditions of the river, useful in case of war with the Indians, has left an excellent description of the Indian craft:

> Their canoes are the next work of any consequence; they are generally made of a large pine or poplar, from 30 to 40 feet long, and about 2 broad, with flat bottoms and sides, and both ends alike; the Indians hollow them now with the tools they get from the Europeans, but formerly did it by fire: They are capable of carrying about 15 or 20 men, are very light, and can by the Indians, so great is their skill in managing them, be forced up a very strong current, particularly the bark canoes; but these are seldom used but by the northern Indians.

This particular type of dugout canoe

Courtesy Neal O'Steen, University of Tennessee

The "City of Knoxville" steamboat, 1902, docked on the Tennessee River below The University of Tennessee.

was called a *pirogue* by the French and a *piragua* by the Spanish

As traders and explorers emerged from the wilderness with glowing descriptions of the country beyond the mountains, the eastern people became increasingly encouraged to go into this new region. Settlers, however, could not travel as the hunters and traders did, with small amounts of goods; they were burdened with household effects, cattle, farming implements, and the other necessaries for starting a new life in the wilderness. As the settlers came upon the broader and less turbulent rivers of the Tennessee system, they envisioned their use for transporting families and household goods. The first requisite of an emigrant's craft was its ability to carry downstream whole families and their effects. In the evolution of craft for the westward trek the emigrant did not attempt to improve upon the speed of the current and had no interest in developing a craft to go upstream.

Several types of boats were used by the settlers. One device was to join two *pirogues* by means of planks fastened across them, thus making a sizable raft which traveled with the current and could be kept off the banks and rocks by means of poles. Next evolved the skiffs or bateaux, coffin-shaped, intended for longer voyages than could be made on the *pirogues*. Perhaps the most useful of all the types developed, however, were the flatboats, called variously broad horns, Kentucky boats, and arks. These vessels could be knocked to pieces at the end of the journey and the lumber used to build the first houses of the emigrants. A boat of this kind cost from $1 to $1.25 per running foot. It was oblong, with sides boarded up and a roof curved to shed the rain, about 15 feet wide and from 20 to 25 feet long. The timbers of the bottom were massive, intended to be of great strength and capable of carrying heavy loads. Large "sweeps" or oars were used to help direct the course of the boats, to keep them clear of rocks, snags, and sawyers (partially submerged trees).

During this period one of the most famous immigrant parties to descend the river was the flotilla under the leadership of John Donelson, which went from the Watauga settlements down the Holston and Tennessee Rivers and up the Ohio and the Cumberland to the present site of Nashville. It took from December 22, 1779, to April 24, 1780, to make the journey. Most of the vessels were flatboats and dugout canoes. Donelson's boat, the *Adventure*, had been built and fitted out at the Boatyard (now Kingsport) on the Holston.

Kingsport was the nominal head of flatboat and keelboat navigation on the Holston and regularly sent goods to and received goods from KNOXVILLE. An illustration of the character of this river traffic is found in a notice in the *Knoxville Register* of November 30, 1831, which states that two keelboats arrived from Kingsport with bagging, rope, tobacco, and nails, and took back coffee, hemp, sugar, and dry goods.

With the development of local two-way trade came the necessity for some means of carrying products upstream. A partial answer to this need was found in keelboats, which began to appear on the rivers and streams and eventually took their place in the commerce of the Tennessee, Ohio, Mississippi, and Mobile river systems. The keelboat was long and slender, pointed or rounded at bow and stern, and built on a heavy keel that was capable of resisting the impact of collision with submerged rocks and logs. It was built to carry from 10 to 50 tons. Planks laid along the gunwales provided a walkway the complete length of the boat along which the crew passed toward the stern as they pushed on the long poles by which the boat was shoved against the current. It required one man for every 3,000 pounds of freight, and the work was so tiring that it was necessary for the men to rest every hour. A trip of 14 to 30 miles a day was considered very good. Needless to say, such transportation was expensive.

Various other methods were used to help propel keelboats upstream. One was to tie a "cordelle", or rope, to the vessel, by which the boatmen towed it as they walked along the banks of the river. Where there were no towpaths the rope would be fastened to a tree along the shore and the men would pull the boat up toward the tree, repeating the process on upstream. This method was known as "warping". "Bushwhacking" consisted of pulling the boat upstream by hauling on the branches of trees and bushes as the boat coasted along the shore to avoid the full force of the current. The upstream freight of the rivers was always considerably smaller than the downstream freight. In spite of the expense of operating keelboats, they remained the best means for transporting freight upstream until the advent of the steamboat.

The *Clermont*, built for Robert Fulton and Robert Livingston, made its first successful trip up the Hudson River in August 1807. It demonstrated the practicability of steam navigation on inland waterways and brought new hopes to the Middle West for the development of steam navigation. Hope for service on the upper Tennessee was aroused in the spring of 1825 when some Knoxvillians, in view of the mutual dependence of northern Alabama and East Tennessee, attempted to arrange to run a steamboat between Knoxville and Muscle Shoals. The idea, however, did not materialize.

The passage of a steamboat over Muscle Shoals and up the Tennessee to the confluence of the Holston and French Broad Rivers was a momentous occasion for the people of East Tennessee. The first boat known to accomplish this was the *Atlas*, designed according to the ideas of Henry Shreve and owned by Messrs. Connor, Rider, and Turner. By February 6, 1828, it had ascended the Shoals, and on March 3 it arrived in Knoxville. The arrival of the boat in Knoxville was the occasion of great celebration, and $640 was presented as a gift to the three owners. Fresh hopes for the establishment of steamboat service on the upper Tennessee River arose in the minds of citizens of East Tennessee.

The next day the boat steamed up to the junction of the Holston and the French Broad Rivers, just above Knoxville. Dr. J.G.M. RAMSEY was chosen to address the crowd that assembled there. He took occasion to express his personal opinion that navigation should not be promoted on the upper Tennessee because the area would then attract outsiders, which would bring about a subsequent deterioration of the East Tennessee region.

Following the appearance of the *Atlas* on East Tennessee waters, enthusiasm for river navigation reached a point of action despite the opposition of Dr. J.G.M. Ramsey. A steamboat company was immediately organized at Knoxville, and W.B.A. Ramsey was sent to Cincinnati to superintend the building of a boat. The steamer was named the *Knoxville*, in honor of the city that started the movement to bring the first regular river service to the upper Tennessee. There were some who greeted the news of steamboat service with regret, believing, as did Dr. Ramsey, that navigation of the river would injure the country by encouraging further exploitation and exhaustion of its resources. Others, however, saw navigation as an auxiliary to AGRICULTURE and industry, an opportunity for each person to specialize in his own kind of work and to leave the transportation of produce and goods to market to someone engaged solely in that business. Such an arrangement, they believed, would permit the producers time to engage in new activities or to improve those already undertaken.

River trade was increasing on the upper Tennessee owing to the development of CHATTANOOGA. Ross's Landing, as it was called by the

CHEROKEES, was incorporated as Chattanooga on December 20, 1839. Chattanooga was the chief stopping place for steamboats plying between Muscle Shoals and Knoxville. It was also the source of supplies for much of the area above the Shoals. Grain, coal, iron ore, and lumber were shipped down from north of Chattanooga to be distributed, and finished goods were sent from the city to the people up the river.

Many boats operated on the river as the demand arose, without having regular schedules. In the year 1880, 553 steamboat landings were made at Chattanooga in addition to 308 landings by flatboats. On the upper Tennessee, from above Knoxville, goods were formerly brought down on both the French Broad and the Holston rivers on flatboats or rafts. In the winter of 1885-86 a total of 300 flatboats loaded with freight came down the Holston. A general demand for steam navigation resulted in several attempts to use light-draft steamboats on the Holston, but with slight success.

The French Broad was more successful than the Holston in obtaining river improvements, and after its navigability had been improved the steamboat *Lucille Borden* was built to run regularly on the river. In 1891 this boat made a total of 96 trips for a distance of 40 miles up the river. DANDRIDGE came to be the most practical landing point on the French Broad. Traffic on the river declined after 1900 because no improvements were made in the channel. Steamboats seldom ventured up the Clinch River except on high water, at which time it was possible to reach Clinton. In 1884, in addition to 1,000 rafts of lumber, 250 flatboats came down the river laden with other products. Steamboats plied the Hiwassee River as far as Charleston, 20 miles above the mouth. In 1896 a boat line, known as the Chattanooga and Hiwassee River Packet Co., was established to operate on the Hiwassee River. Until 1918 it owned one of the largest packets operated on the river, but tonnages decreased soon after 1900. In the latter year one steamboat reported 81 trips from Chattanooga to Charleston, Tennessee.

Steamboat excursions furnished a pleasant diversion from the regular routine of navigation. Many such excursion trips were made on the Tennessee in the early days of steamboating. Sometimes a trip lasted only a day, and again it might stretch out into a period of three or four days or even longer. Frequently the boat towed a barge for dancing, although it was also carried to safeguard passengers in the event of an explosion or other accident. These excursions have given to steamboating a romantic aspect which has never completely left the minds of the people living on and along the inland waterways.

As the country developed, a new counterforce had to be met by the water carriers since the channels of trade changed with the coming of the RAILROADS and the integration of their services. The wave of popular interest in railroads during the era of railroad expansion did much to lessen the agitation for river development. Wages on the river went down, employment became irregular, and uncertainties as to the future of rivermen diverted interest to other fields of business. The papers that were once replete with river news and with editorials urging people to become active in supporting improvements of the Tennessee River gradually turned their attention to the railroads and other topics. Consequently, the river and its needs were neglected.

To take care of the type of commerce that was still on the river, rivermen turned to towboats and barges, because one towboat could carry a cargo equal to that transported by several ordinary steamboats. Steelhull steamers were first built successfully in 1881, and they finally replaced the heavier wooden vessels. With the invention and perfection of the Diesel engine, boatmen used it as motive power for boats and found it invaluable, with the result that its use for this purpose has become extensive. Another type of boat developed for river trade was the gasoline launch. This was a small boat, and was especially suitable for use on tributary streams where short hauls and small lots of freight were involved.

After the recession of popular interest in river transportation, there came renewed enthusiasm at various times. There were at all times, however, some groups interested in an improved

Surgoinsville Ferry, ca. 1940's, reported to have been the last operating ferry in Hawkins County.

Courtesy Rowan Studios, Rogersville

channel for the Tennessee River, and many of these groups were extremely active in pressing Congress to recognize the importance of the river and in arousing enthusiasm among others in this behalf. The demand for an effective improvement of the Tennessee River system, prolonged though it was, finally culminated in comprehensive action by Congress. A consideration by Congress of all water-control and water-use factors presented by the Tennessee River system led to the passage of the legislation now comprising the Tennessee Valley Authority Act. In the light of what has been accomplished since the creation of the TENNESSEE VALLEY AUTHORITY, one may venture the opinion that the citizens of the Valley and contiguous areas utilize a type of water-transportation facilities of which their forefathers could not even dream.

J. Haden Alldredge
Mildred Burnham Spottswood
Vera V. Anderson
John H. Goff
Robert M. LaForge

Refer to: Robert T. Quarles and Robert H. White, eds. *Three Pioneer Tennessee Documents* (including John Donelson's journal), Nashville: Tennessee Historical Commission, 1964; Tennessee Valley Authority, *A History of Navigation on the Tennessee River System*, Washington: Government Printing Office, 1937; and Samuel Cole Williams, ed. *Lt. Henry Timberlake's Memoirs, 1756-1765*, Johnson City, Tenn.: The Watauga Press, 1927.
See also: LOG RAFTS

Alex Stewart. To the early settlers of APPALACHIA, wooden vessels such as buckets, churns, barrels and kegs were as important as farm tools and livestock. Settlers depended on them for such chores as carrying water, milk and meal; gathering vegetables; feeding the chickens; churning butter; and storing items like nails and salted meat. Men who made the vessels were called coopers. They were indispensable to early communities on the frontier. Over the years, however, metal and then plastic began to replace wood as the principal material used in vessels, and the role of the cooper declined. Like the blacksmith and other classic traditional craftsmen, the cooper has all but disappeared. Only a very few still practice coopering "the old way".

One such man is Alex Stewart, a 90-year-old master craftsman and cooper who lives in a remote corner of HANCOCK COUNTY in upper East Tennessee near Sneedville. Alex's grandfather, Boyd Stewart, established the first cooperage in the area during the mid-1800's. Boyd Stewart, who had nine children, passed his skills on to one of his sons, Joe Stewart; and he in turn taught one of his sons, Alex. Thus, in the fullest sense of the meaning, Alex is a traditional craftsman. He made his first vessel in 1912. For the past several years Alex has been teaching his grandson (Rick Stewart) and a close personal friend and fellow craftsman (Bill Henry) how to make vessels the way his "pap" and "grandpap" made them, so that the art will not die out.

Alex Stewart does not believe that traditional crafts will disappear altogether. "I think people will go back to it," he says earnestly. "They're interested in how the old folks come up." He believes that young people

Robert Kollar

Alex Stewart

especially should have a chance to see how the old folks came up. And he is getting his wish. A number of MUSEUMS now offer extensive exhibits of early Appalachian life and culture. One of the most comprehensive of these is John Rice Irwin's MUSEUM OF APPALACHIA at NORRIS, Tennessee. Here, visitors come face to face with authentic, reconstructed, furnished cabins; a cantilevered barn; a church and other buildings representative of pre-industrial Appalachia. Nearly every traditional craft and occupation, including coopering, is represented in a large exhibit hall. Irwin has spent most of his adult life locating items for his collection. Alex's work is well represented.

Like many traditional craftsmen, Alex made his own tools. For example, he forged metal tools in his own blacksmith shop, then made handles for them on a foot-powered, spring-pole lathe. He has used the lathe for 60 years. He uses no power tools.

"I tried to use power tools, but I couldn't do no good. I can do a lot better work with my foot than I can with a motor."

When Alex Stewart was growing up, wooden vessels were still used on the farm. But demand began to slacken 30 or 40 years ago. By the early 1960's, thinking his talents were no longer useful, he had laid aside his tools. Wood for his vessels, which he had gathered mostly from his own farm, was becoming harder to find, and the years were advancing on him. Retirement, it seemed, was imminent. No new challenges or adventures seemed to be waiting to spark the creative fire of this man who in his lifetime had been cooper, blacksmith, farmer, carpenter, cook, furniture maker, logger, miner, sawmill operator, trapper, weaver, tanner, and stonecutter.

But retirement was not be be his lot—at least not yet. This 72-year-old mountain man was about to discover a whole new reason to keep going. A chance exchange in 1963 between Irwin and Ellis Stewart, a cousin of Alex's, provided the spark that put Alex back to work. Irwin wanted to purchase, for his museum collection, a particularly fine cedar bucket that he found at Ellis Stewart's. Stewart said he didn't want to sell it, but directed Irwin to the home of the bucket's maker, Alex Stewart. Irwin asked Alex to resume production of his wooden vessels. He told him he would provide good cedar if Stewart would make the vessels for him. Alex agreed, and thus was born a new partnership beneficial to both men. Alex was using his skills again, and the Museum of Appalachia had a steady supply of buckets, piggins, churns and other vessels.

This was just the beginning. In 1968, Stewart met master whittler Bill Henry of OAK RIDGE, who became his close friend and later his apprentice. Promoted by Irwin, stories on Alex and his work began to appear in Tennessee newspapers. An article in the popular *Foxfire* magazine (from a referral by Bill Henry to editor Eliot Wigginton) soon made Alex one of Tennessee's best known craftsmen. By 1976 his reputation was reestablished. Wigginton, in his *Foxfire 3* book, devoted a full chapter to Alex and his churnmaking, and the National Geographic Society featured Alex on the cover and in a two-page spread in its *The Craftsman in America*. The TENNESSEE VALLEY AUTHORITY sponsored a month-long formal apprenticeship program for Bill Henry with Alex Stewart in January of 1976, then featured the two craftsmen in a cover story in the Summer 1976 issue of *Tennessee Valley Perspective* magazine.

It was in the summer of 1976, at the age of 85, that Alex Stewart took his first airplane ride. At the invitation of Ralph Rinzler, Alex and Bill Henry flew to Washington, D.C. to participate in the Festival of American Folklife. During their stay, the two men toured the Capitol, White House, several government buildings, and the National Geographic Society headquarters, where Alex saw a lifesize color photograph of himself hanging in the lobby. There was some initial concern about whether Alex could make such a long and arduous trip at his age. Alex never thought about not going. "I meant to go if I came home in a box," he said. "I wanted to see all them foreigners." Today, Alex lives in the pleasant white frame home on Panther Creek he built for his family. Behind him rises Newman's Ridge where his grandfather built his first house. In front of Alex's house across the road to Sneedville stretches Panther Creek Valley. His coopering shop has been moved from the old tobacco barn behind his house to a shop alongside his son's nearby house, and the road to Sneedville has been paved. Otherwise, things have changed little over the years. At 90, Alex the cooper has finally slowed down a little, but Alex the man has lost neither the twinkle in his eye nor the humanity that prompted Bill Henry to write this tribute:

> Wise beyond all eighty-nine years, curious as a cat, tough as a pine knot, independent as a hog on ice, industrious as a honey-bee, and as handy as the pocket on your shirt. He is also a bit of a paradox; frugal as a Scotchman, yet he would give you the shirt off his back. If you gave him just cause, he'd knock you down then help you up and dust you off.

Alex's work is now a part of the permanent collections of the Museum of Appalachia, THE WILL G. AND HELEN H. LENOIR MUSEUM near Norris, the Foxfire Museum in Rabun Gap, Georgia, and the CHILDREN'S MUSEUM OF OAK RIDGE. His place in history has been assured. As his father and grandfather live on in his hands and his work, Alex Stewart, too, will live on through the work of his grandson and his friend. He has preserved the art of coopering "the old way" for another generation.

Robert Kollar

Sullivan County

Size: 413 Square Miles (264,320 acres)
Established: 1779
Named For: John Sullivan, Major General in the American Revolution
County Seat: Blountville
Other Major Cities, Towns, or Communities:
KINGSPORT
BRISTOL
Morrison City
Sullivan Gardens
Bluff City
Hillcrest
Ruthton

Refer to: Oliver Taylor, *Historic Sullivan: A History of Sullivan County*, Bristol, 1909 (reprinted 1971, Nashville: Elder).
See also: ANNE W. ARMSTRONG
THE STATE OF FRANKLIN

Sunset Gap Community Center is located at the southwestern end of the English Mountain range, on the county line between Cocke and Sevier. It began in 1923 when Sara Cochrane and the Presbyterian Church founded an elementary school on a few acres of donated land. Since then, Sunset Gap has given way to educational consolidation, but has continued to confront personal, family, and community needs on a variety of levels. It has retained its local commitment by becoming an active meeting place, complete with baseball teams and scouting troops, pre-school classes and pot-luck suppers.

The Center was first conceived in 1908 when Miss Cochrane, then a student at Massachusetts' Northfield Seminary, wrote an essay about Southern APPALACHIA and became interested in this unique land. Though originally from New Jersey, she accepted a postgraduate teaching offer in Kentucky's isolated Harlan County. Sara Cochrane taught there for three years, then travelled to Arizona, where at Ganada Mission she organized and opened one of the first Navajo schools. But time found her back among the mountains of old; in 1916, the Presbyterian Board of Missions sent her to East Tennessee to supervise the gradual closing of one of their schools.

The school was located in SEVIER COUNTY, along Wilhite Road, and was called Juniper. There happened to be a woman from the upper Wilhite community, the wife of Ance Williams, who was not satisfied with Juniper's going out of existence. The school had taught eleven of her children to read and write, and she wanted the same for their children. So Betty Williams contacted Sara Cochrane in 1923 and donated to the Presbyterian Church 10 acres of new land at the head of Wilhite, on the county line. Upon hearing the news that a school might indeed remain in the area, J.D. Williams and D.T. Templin

Jim Stokely

Mountain valley adjoining Sunset Gap Community Center, November 1975.

from COCKE COUNTY gave several acres on the other side of the line.

Miss Cochrane responded heartily to this generosity. She decided to build a schoolhouse squarely across the county line so that children from both counties could attend. She also decided not to build a church, because she realized that the people of the nearby communities already attended their own churches. However, she did hold Sunday School classes to supplement the outside services. During the fall of 1923, as the Teacher's Cottage was being constructed, Sara Cochrane lived in a tent. But soon she was witness to an even greater effort: the building of the main class room center. Families from miles around donated lumber and labor for the imposing structure. A visitor later sat upon its front porch in the evening, watched day fade into night, and coined a name for the school: Sunset Gap.

The elementary school was a good one, among the best in the entire state. One of its first teachers was a young Pennsylvania-born girl named Josephine Burrows, just out of college in New York and Massachusetts, fresh from summer work in Kentucky with Mrs. Mary Breckinridge, one of the founders of the Frontier Nursing Service. Miss Burrows knew that Sunset Gap needed either a trained nurse or a home economics teacher, and although she was neither, she learned before long that professional titles made little difference. She taught physical education, then weaving, for Miss Cochrane had begun a weaving class with a $700 contribution. Many of the girls in this class worked their way through Washington College near JONESBORO. Other graduates later went to North Carolina's Warren Wilson College.

As years went by, names changed and expansions were made. Sara Cochrane retired in 1948, but not before she had organized a PTA chapter. The new director, Elizabeth Wright, added a recreation room, a weekly family night, and a Home Demonstration Club. By 1952, when Miss Wright retired, Sunset Gap had grown into a community center. Today, the grassroots strength of Sunset Gap shows itself in a rich assortment of ways. A strong Scout program involves boys and girls with service projects, decision-making responsibilities, and annual trips to other areas of North America such as Canada or the southwest. Sunset Gap helps organize a baseball league each spring. Local residents also participate in Sunday School classes, a weekly sewing club, a biweekly thrift sale, and a weaving club. The Center maintains a year-round Pre-school for 3-5 year olds, and it offers supplemental reading and lessons for grade-school children having trouble with English or arithmetic. Through these efforts, Sunset Gap touches the lives of approximately 125 families annually. The Center also sponsors summer and spring work-study camps, during which high school volunteers from Pennsylvania to Michigan to Florida come for a week or ten days. They live on campus and combine painting and carpentry or yard work with a chance to compare communities and ways of life.

Jim Stokely

Refer to: Jim Stokely, *To Make A Life: Settlement Institutions of Appalachia*, Berea, Kentucky: SIA, 1977.

See also: PI BETA PHI SETTLEMENT SCHOOL
PRIMARY HEALTH CARE CENTERS
WASHINGTON COLLEGE ACADEMY

T

Tanning and Leathermaking. The production of leather is recognized as one of man's earliest arts. Hundreds of years ago, men made garments and tents from the hides of the animals they killed for food. Egyptian murals from about 1450 B.C. depict the activities of leather tanners and dressers. Some specimens of 3000-year old alum-tanned leather have been discovered in China. American Indians had their unique way of preparing a variety of essential leather products. Buckskin is one of their best known specialities that has continued to be prized until the present time. Until the twentieth century, farmers and ranchers maintained small tanneries producing leather items needed for their own use. They often bartered with their neighbors and with merchants, exchanging their tanned leather for food, FURNITURE, clothing, livestock and other essentials. The farmers used improvised equipment and products from their farms, such as tannic acid from the bark of chestnut or oak trees, for the tanning solutions. The local stores furnished the salt, lime, neat's-foot oil and borax, usually in exchange for a piece of leather.

The process of tanning leather at home is a long and arduous one, requiring manual labor, patience, and continuous watching and manipulation. All skins can be tanned, but most of the leather used today is made from the hides of cattle, pigs, sheep and goats. Some horse hides are tanned, as are the skins of smaller animals. The hides must go through many processes that preserve them and make them pliable and water resistant. The procedures used are determined by the use to be made of the leather. The farmer first salts the hides to preserve them until weather conditions make possible the tanning procedures. The flesh and hair must be removed carefully and the hides cleaned and made flexible.

Vegetable tanning is the process used for making leather for shoe soles, cases, straps, harnesses, belts for heavy industrial machinery, upholstery, book binding and other products requiring body. Vegetable tanning produces a firmer, heavier and more water-resistant leather. The tanning solution, made of vegetable products such as bark, provides color to the hides and continues the process of making them flexible. The procedures are long and tedious even in the factories. In the mid-1950's, some innovative practices were

Doris Ulmann / Courtesy Doris Ulmann Foundation, Berea College

Tanner Covey Odom at home in Luther, Tennessee, ca. 1933.

introduced that have cut the time required appreciably and have improved the product. Chrome tanning, which takes a shorter time than vegetable tanning, derives its name from the chromium-containing chemicals used. This has come to be the method used throughout the world for producing practically all upper shoe leather, clothing, gloving and other specialized leathers that must be resistant to perspiration and high temperatures. Chrome tanning results in more elastic leather.

When the tanning has been completed, the leather must be finished, or treated with oils, soaked in water, and manipulated to bring about the pliability, resilience, strength and degree of softness required. This involves numerous kinds of operations meticulously selected and efficiently carried out to produce the great number of varieties of leather needed. Numerous factories, employing many persons, produce an immense amount of leather annually in the United States and in Tennessee. According to the 1977 Census of Manufacturing, the leather industry in Tennessee employed 3.6 per cent of the total employees engaged in manufacturing. This provided jobs for almost 18,000 Tennesseans. The tannery in CHATTANOOGA is the largest in the state, employing about 200 persons when in full operation. This city also manufactures ladies' slippers, saddlery and work gloves. CLEVELAND factories make handbags for ladies. Tennessee Handbags has a large factory in DANDRIDGE. When in full operation, this company produces 100,000 ladies' handbags each month.

Claire Gilbert

Refer to: "Hide Tanning" in Eliot Wigginton, ed. *Foxfire 3*, Garden City, N.Y.: Anchor Press/Doubleday, 1975, pp. 55-78.
See also: RIFLES
SOAP
SPINNING AND WEAVING

Bob and Alf Taylor: The Knights of the Roses. Few politicians in the United States have equalled the Taylor brothers for conducting colorful and entertaining campaigns. Alf (Alfred A., 1848-1940) was Governor of Tennessee for one term and was a United States Congressman for three consecutive terms. Bob (Robert Love, 1850-1912) served as Governor of Tennessee for three terms and was a United States Senator for one term. Both brothers were born in Happy Valley in western WASHINGTON COUNTY. They were brought up in a home with divided political loyalties, their father being a Whig and their mother a Democrat. Alf and Bob attended Princeton Preparatory School, Milligan College, and the University of Chattanooga at Athens, Tennessee.

Newspapers were not easily obtainable in Happy Valley. The Taylor brothers' greatest source of reading materials was *The Washington Intelligencer* (later *The Congressional Record*), to which their father subscribed. Both boys were avid readers and for amusement would carry on the debates where the congressmen in Washington left off. This was the basis for their interest in politics and may partially account for

Frank Leslie's *feature coverage of the 1886 campaign for the governorship of Tennessee.*

Courtesy TVA

Courtesy Archives of Appalachia, East Tennessee State University

The Taylor home, ca. 1910, with Alf and Bob sitting in front of their porch.

the fact that each embraced a different political party, Alf becoming a Republican and Bob a Democrat. But in spite of their political differences, they were devoted brothers. They became known as "The Knights of the Roses" following a remark by Bob that, although they were roses from the same garden, Alf was a scarlet rose while he, Bob, was a rose of purest white.

In 1886, the Taylors opposed each other for the office of Governor of Tennessee. This campaign became known as "The War of the Roses". For the most part they campaigned together, covering the state by horse and buggy, each lashing the other's political convictions in heated debate, then sharing the same bed in a local hotel. These were the days of torchlight parades, hard-hitting speeches, and afternoon and evening political entertainment. One evening, crowds of people followed their band to the hotel at which the brothers were staying. Quickly Bob stepped onto the balcony and began his speech with a verse, as was his custom. Then he launched forth into the body of his speech. By this time Alf appeared at a window to listen to his brother. At first he could not believe his ears as he recognized his own speech which he had spent hours that day composing. He ran to his room and confirmed that his speech was missing. That night, Alf spoke without notes when he addressed the same crowd.

Alf had his revenge several days later, when a delegation from 'Possum Creek came to talk to Bob. They were misdirected to Alf's room, and not knowing the brothers personally, assumed that Alf was Bob. Hot and tired, the delegation members expressed a desire for strong drink. Alf, pretending to be Bob, acted outraged. "Gentlemen," he said, "I am a temperance man. I abhor liquor even more than I abhor a Republican. Before I would be instrumental in polluting your lips with one drop of this hellish stuff you call for, I would give up the race entirely and allow Alf Taylor to be elected Governor of Tennessee." The delegation left, each member expressing his disappointment and disgust in his former idol.

Alf again bettered Bob after both had ascended one day to the same makeshift stage. Alf was holding forth in one of his flowery flights of oratory, and Bob was sitting on a bench awaiting his turn to speak. Several of Bob's admirers, who had been drinking, joined him on the bench. They became a little too exuberant, and their end of the bench broke down. Alf stopped his speech until the commotion was over, then turned back to his audience and raised his hand. "Hold on, fellow citizens," he said. "Don't get alarmed. That's just the Democratic platform collapsing as usual."

Grace Mauer

Refer to: Dan M. Robinson, "The Political Background of Tennessee's War of the Roses," in *The East Tennessee Historical Society's Publications*, V.5 (1933), pp. 125-141; and Robert L. Taylor, Jr., "Mainstreams of Mountain Thought: Attitudes of Selected Figures in the Heart of the Appalachian South," University of Tennessee dissertation, 1971.

See also: BEN W. HOOPER
CORDELL HULL
ESTES KEFAUVER

Tennessee Eastman. Probably more than any other single industry, Tennessee Eastman Company can be credited with the founding and survival of the planned industrial city of KINGSPORT. The first major manufacturer to build a facility after the town was begun in 1917, Tennessee Eastman opened its initial plant in 1920 for the manufacture of wood alcohol, distilled from forest byproducts abundantly available in the nearby Appalachian Mountains, for use in the making of photographic film by the parent Eastman company in Rochester, N.Y. By 1945, when the original distillation process ceased, Tennessee Eastman had added an array of chemical products including acetate yarns, plastics, and acetate dyes. During World War II Tennessee Eastman managed, for the Federal Government, both the Holston Ordnance works in Kingsport, producer of conventional explosives, and a section of the Clinton Engineering Works in OAK RIDGE which produced U-235 for atomic bombs.

In the years following the war, modern technology and research made Tennessee Eastman a leading U.S. producer of chemicals, plastics, and chemical fibers. By 1980, the company was manufacturing over 350 different products and employing nearly 15,000 workers in the Kingsport area. An industry of this magnitude necessarily has immense impact on economic, social, cultural, and political life in the relatively small city of Kingsport, and over its history Tennessee Eastman has been both praised and condemned for its paternalism toward employees and its active encouragement of political leadership by managerial personnel. Like other extractive industries in East Tennessee, the Eastman Company has, almost since its inception, experienced opposition from environmentalists and conservationists.

Sharon Macpherson

Tennessee Valley Authority. Since its creation in 1933, the Tennessee Valley Authority has grown into a large Federal agency exerting large impacts in several important areas of East Tennessee and regional life. A sufficient knowledge of the history and effects of the TVA requires acquaintance with much more than the Authority's annual reports. This brief bibliographical essay gives only a bare introduction to the literature, meaning, and research challenges of the Tennessee Valley Authority.

Beyond such standard New Deal accounts as Arthur M. Schlesinger, Jr.'s *The Age of Roosevelt*, V.3 (*Power for the People,*

Tennessee Eastman and Kingsport, September 1976.

Courtesy Tennessee Eastman

Boston: Houghton Mifflin Company, 1960, pp. 362-376), an excellent in-depth study of the beginnings of the TVA is Preston J. Hubbard's *Origins of the TVA: The Muscle Shoals Controversy, 1920-1932* (Nashville, Tenn.: Vanderbilt University Press, 1961; reprinted 1968, New York: Norton). The extremely important policy struggle within the first TVA Board of Directors—between David Lilienthal and Arthur Morgan, and finally won by Lilienthal—is chronicled in Thomas K. McCraw's *Morgan vs. Lilienthal: The Feud Within the TVA* (Chicago: Loyola University Press, 1970). Insights into the visions and activities of these two powerful individuals can be gained from Arthur E. Morgan's *The Making of the TVA* (Buffalo, N.Y.: Prometheus, 1974) and from David E. Lilienthal's *TVA—Democracy on the March* (New York; Harper and Brothers, 1944) and his *Journals*, V. 1 (*The TVA Years, 1933-1945*, New York: Harper, 1964).

The TVA's successful control of floods and navigation in the Tennessee River Valley is told by Wilmon Henry Droze in *High Dams and Slack Water: TVA Rebuilds a River* (Baton Rouge: Louisiana State University Press, 1965). Examinations of the inception of TVA's power program can be found in Victor Carr Hobday's *Sparks at the Grassroots: Municipal Distribution of TVA Electricity in Tennessee* (Knoxville: University of Tennessee Press, 1969) and in Thomas K. McCraw's *TVA and the Power Fight* (Philadelphia: J.B. Lippincott, 1971). Virtual in-house assessments of TVA's record into the 1950's and 1960's include former TVA General Manager Gordon R. Clapp's *The TVA: An Approach to the Development of a Region* (Chicago: University of Chicago Press, 1955), Roscoe C. Martin, ed. *TVA: The First Twenty Years. A Staff Report* and John R. Moore, ed. *The Economic Impact of TVA* (Knoxville: University of Tennessee Press, 1956 and 1967), and former TVA Director Frank Smith's *The Politics of Conservation* (New York: Pantheon, 1966).

Dick Bodenheimer / Courtesy TVA

Linemen bringing electricity to a rural couple, Fort Loudoun, Tennessee, April 22, 1947.

Henry Billings's *All Down the Valley* (New York: Viking Press, 1952) is only one of many volumes expressing post-New Deal liberal support for TVA. Conservative opposition, represented in 1964 by Republican Presidential candidate Barry Goldwater, had been summarized twenty years earlier by

Robert Kollar / Courtesy TVA

TVA Fisheries biologist Gary Hamilton holds a snail darter found in the Little Tennessee River, October 1979. The snail darter was at the center of a late 1970's national controversy between proponents and opponents of the Tellico Dam. Refer to: Eugene Kinkead, "Our Far-flung Correspondents (The Snail Darter)," in The New Yorker, *January 8, 1979; and Peter Matthiesson, "How to Kill a Valley," in* The New York Review of Books, *February 7, 1980, pp. 31-36.*

Frederick Lewis Collins (*Uncle Sam's Billion-dollar Baby*, New York: Putnam's, 1945). On a less political level, two professors in the 1940's completed influential studies using the Authority as a test case. Charles Herman Pritchett's *The Tennessee Valley Authority: A Study in Public Administration* (Chapel Hill: University of North Carolina Press, 1943) explored the administrative potential of a Federal agency headquartered not in Washington, but in KNOXVILLE, at a proximity to the "grass roots". Philip Selznick, in *TVA and the Grass Roots: A Study in the Sociology of Formal Organization* (Berkeley, Calif.: University of California Press, 1949; reprinted 1966, New York: Harper and Row), delved behind Lilienthal's theory of "democracy at the grass roots" to discover "co-optation" and other complexities at work in TVA's early agricultural program.

Recent evaluations of TVA's overall program have ranged from highly supportive to highly critical. An example of the former is Marguerite Owen's *The Tennessee Valley Authority* (New York: Praeger, 1973), whose pictures suggest a TVA-engineered transformation of East Tennessee from a natural and cultural wasteland to a green and vibrant paradise. North Callahan's positive *TVA: Bridge Over Troubled Waters* (San Diego, Calif.: A.S. Barnes, 1980) is counterbalanced by James Branscome's basically negative section on TVA in *The Federal Government in Appalachia* (New York: The Field Foundation, 1977, pp. 14-22). Like Branscome, David Whisnant finds much fault with post-World War II TVA (see *Modernizing the Mountaineer: People, Power and Planning in Appalachia*, New York: Burt Franklin, 1979, pp. 43-69). More detailed examinations of recent TVA policies, personnel and programs are sorely needed.

Jim Stokely

See also: TVA DAMS
TVA NUCLEAR PLANTS

TVA Dams. The fourteen major dams built by the TENNESSEE VALLEY AUTHORITY in East Tennessee to control the Tennessee River and its tributaries constitute the bulwark of the Authority's plan to develop all the resources of this fourth largest river in the United States. Mandated by Congress in 1933 and largely completed by 1953, this construction of dams is the first instance in history of an entire river being completely developed for navigation, flood control, power, and such other uses as water supply and recreation.

Norris Dam, the first TVA dam to be built (from 1933 to 1936), was named after Senator George Norris of Nebraska, the father of the Congressional Act creating TVA. Located just below the confluence of the Clinch and Powell rivers, Norris Dam is still one of the most visited and one of the most outstanding engineering achievements of its time. Although its construction had been initiated by the U.S. Corps of Engineers just prior to the creation of TVA, Congress in 1933 specifically ordered the building of the dam to be taken over by TVA and pursued with all possible speed. This

Lewis Hine / Courtesy TVA

Some of the workmen at the Norris Dam site, November 3, 1933. In the rear are the warehouse under construction and the foundation cribs for a heavy-duty bridge over Clinch River.

giant building project would, it was felt, provide employment in an area hard hit by the Depression.

In order to expedite construction of Norris Dam TVA assigned the design of the concrete gravity structure to the experienced Bureau of Reclamation in Denver. TVA also decided to build the dam with its own labor, an unusual procedure meant to get the work under way without waiting a year or more for the design to be completed and bids taken from contractors. TVA quickly hired thousands of supervisory and construction personnel, who started work even as the design drawings were being produced. So successful and economical was this policy that TVA used it on all other dams. Another construction innovation used on Norris Dam and subsequently on almost all TVA Dams was the policy of providing housing for the families of the workers, instead of just barracks for the workers themselves. This resulted in the Authority's establishing a village near the dam, called NORRIS, which lived on after the dam was completed.

The unified development plan that TVA devised for the Tennessee River involved two types of dams: storage dams on the major tributaries to store

Courtesy TVA

Norris Dam

the heavy rainfall, mostly in the winter, to prevent downstream floods; and high dams on the main river to increase depths for navigations. The storage dams also aided navigation by releasing water to augment low water flows in the summer. The river dams, conversely, were provided with gates to store rainfall for flood control, as well as with locks to pass shipping from one level to the next. Both types of dams were equipped with hydroelectric generators to produce power from water releases otherwise going to waste.

TVA has built ten storage dams on the six main tributaries of the Tennessee River: the Holston, French Broad, Hiwassee, Little Tennessee, Clinch and Powell. TVA has built four East Tennessee dams on the main river, called "run-of-the-river" dams. Of these four, Nickajack Dam just below CHATTANOOGA replaced an earlier dam, the Hales Bar dam, in the same general location. This dam was acquired from the Tennessee Electric Power Company early in TVA's life, but it leaked so badly that efforts to repair it were futile. TVA finally abandoned it and replaced it with a superior dam. In 1939, TVA purchased from TEPC a total of five power dams, including Ocoee Nos. 1 and 2.

Courtesy TVA

Kingston Steam Plant

The potential for large amounts of cheap electric power served as the impetus for rapid expansion and completion of the TVA system of dams. Confronted with the need, during World War II, for vast amounts of power for industry and for the atomic plants at OAK RIDGE, the U.S. Congress called on TVA to supply this demand. Three emergency programs not only speeded up construction of three dams already underway, but also started construction of nine additional dams. All these dams were substantially completed in time to contribute to the war effort. The TVA power system as a whole has since become the largest in the country, operating a total of some 35 hydroelectric plants in addition to the TVA steam plants and the TVA NUCLEAR PLANTS.

All the TVA dams are long-lived structures with lives estimated normally at 100 years. With the constant maintenance provided by TVA, however, their lives will be even longer. Measurements indicate that silting of the reservoirs will not endanger the dams for much longer periods of time, perhaps as much as 1000 years. The question is often raised as to why TVA does not build more dams. The answer is that all of the economical sites have already been used.

If the cost of energy continues to rise, some few sites not now economical may become so. But they would be small in size, on minor tributaries, and would have little impact on the economy of the region.

The following is a list of TVA dams built in East Tennessee:

Main River Projects	Construction Completed	Lake Area (acres)	Generating Capacity (Kilowatts)
Chickamauga	1940	35,400	117,000
Watts Bar	1942	39,000	159,900
Fort Loudoun	1943	14,600	139,140
Nickajack	1967	10,370	100,350

Tributary Projects	Construction Completed	Lake Area (acres)	Generating Capacity (Kilowatts)
Norris	1936	34,200	100,800
Cherokee	1941	30,300	135,180
Ocoee No. 3	1942	480	28,800
Douglas	1943	30,400	120,600
Watauga	1948	6,430	50,000
South Holston	1950	7,580	35,000
Boone	1952	4,310	75,000
Fort Patrick Henry	1953	872	36,000
Melton Hill	1963	5,690	72,000
Tellico	1979	15,860	(23,000)

(indirectly via increased flow through Fort Loudoun generators)

Harry Wiersema

TVA Nuclear Plants. The TENNESSEE VALLEY AUTHORITY was created in 1933 as a regional resource and development agency. Its major purpose was to construct a system of dams and reservoirs that would promote navigation of the Tennessee River and its tributaries, provide flood control, and produce electrical power in the hydroelectric facilities at the dams. By 1945, after many TVA DAMS had been built, the power-producing potential from hydroelectric facilities was about completed. As electrical energy demands continued to grow, TVA began a program of construction of large coal-fired steam-electric plants. Four coal-fired units in East Tennessee, with three times the generating capacity of all East Tennessee TVA dams, were placed in service near Watts Bar Dam, near Kingston, near Cherokee Lake, and near KNOXVILLE and OAK RIDGE.

In the early 1960's, TVA management concluded that nuclear power had a slight economic advantage over coal-fired plants. The Authority decided to add nuclear power to its electrical production system. In July of 1966, TVA applied to the Atomic Energy Commission for permits to construct the Browns Ferry plant in northwest Alabama. Since Browns Ferry, three nuclear power plants have been undertaken in East Tennessee. These are Sequoyah on Chickamauga Lake in HAMILTON COUNTY, Watts Bar on Watts Bar Lake in RHEA COUNTY, and Phipps Bend on the Holston River in HAWKINS COUNTY.

Each of these nuclear plants has a nuclear boiler rather than the conventional coal-fired boiler. The nuclear boiler uses enriched uranium in its core as a fuel. When the uranium atoms are made to fission, or split, the heat given off then generates steam. The turbine generators in the nuclear plants are essentially the same as those in the coal-fired plants. Various safety systems in the nuclear plants provide for emergency cooling of the nuclear core in case the water surrounding the core accidentally leaks out.

Construction on the two-unit Sequoyah plant, located about ten miles northeast of CHATTANOOGA, started in 1970. In September of 1980, the Nuclear Regulatory Commission approved full-power operation of Sequoyah. This plant is located on a peninsula extending into Chickamauga Lake, so that cooling water can be taken in on the northeast side of the plant and returned to the lake on the south side. Cooling towers cool the water before it is discharged into the lake. Diffuser pipes distribute the warm water into the lake.

Construction on the two-unit Watts Bar plant, like Sequoyah a pressurized water type plant, started in 1973. The local economy was stimulated by the creation of new jobs and the influx of construction workers associated with the project. Rhea County experienced growth in the housing industry, and neighboring MEIGS COUNTY incurred increased mobile home park development. In 1976, 41% of the movers lived in houses, 37% in mobile homes, 16% in apartments, and 6% in sleeping rooms. Approximately 69% of the movers brought families, including 341 school-age children. Construction activity peaked in June of 1977, with 3275 workers at the site. Wages paid during construction are estimated to total a third of a billion dollars.

Construction on the Phipps Bend plant, a boiling water type plant designed for 1233 megawatt capacity, started in 1977. During the planning of Phipps Bend, alternate sites were considered in Tennessee and Alabama. Due primarily to fewer socio/economic impacts of plant construction, Phipps Bend of the Holston River became the actual site. The other major reason was Phipps Bend's proximity to greater electrical demand.

Fred Heddleson

Tennessee Wesleyan College traces its origins to 1857, when the trustees of Athens Female College transferred ownership of their campus to the Holston Annual Conference of the Methodist Episcopal Church, South. At that time, the campus consisted of two acres in the town of Athens and an incomplete three-story building later known as Old College. The Methodists secured this school primarily to extend the church's evangelical mission into higher education, but also as a means of increasing denominational prestige and of keeping students loyal to the southern branch of their recently (1844) divided church.

Despite an auspicious beginning, Athens Female College shared in the devastation wrought throughout East Tennessee by the CIVIL WAR. Union sentiment had always been strong in this section, and after Federal forces were again in control, loyal Methodists agitated for their own separate church. This reorganized Methodist Episcopal Church, reflecting the intense bitterness of its pro-Union ministers, obtained the college property in 1866 from its now prostrate rival, the Methodist Episcopal Church, South.

In 1867 a new charter was obtained from the state legislature for East Tennessee Wesleyan College. In the following year, the college became coeducational and adopted the title of university. Regardless of changes in name, however, the institution remained firmly under the control of Methodists loyal to the Union. Indicative of this strong Unionism is the fact that the three postwar presidents of the college—Percival C. Wilson, Nelson E. Cobleigh, and James A. Dean—were all born in the North and educated at Northern colleges. This continuing pro-Union sentiment was again clearly expressed when in 1866 the college changed its name to Grant Memorial University.

The years following the Civil War saw two patterns emerge which would continue to characterize the college's future. First, academic instruction in both the classical and scientific curriculum was of a uniformly high quality. Most of the faculty were dedicated Methodists educated in leading Northern colleges. Second, because of the great POVERTY of the surrounding region, the board of trustees adopted the fateful policy in 1872 of providing free tuition to all students needing aid. Such an eleemosynary tradition, however commendable in itself, would keep the college in perpetual financial difficulty.

Largely to alleviate continuing fiscal problems, the college at Athens merged in 1889 with Chattanooga University under the new title of U.S. Grant University. Almost from the beginning, this union was plagued with jealousies, strife and contention. By 1906, the Athens branch had been reduced to only a preparatory department and a two-year normal school. In 1925 a complete separation from the University of Chattanooga was effected. Tennessee Wesleyan College, chartered under a name very similar to its post-Civil War predecessor, returned to fully accredited collegiate status, although the school remained a junior college until 1954.

The college survived the Depression

years of the 1930's under the able leadership of President James L. Robb, who successfully attracted large contributions from philanthropists—notably Mr. and Mrs. Henry Pfeifer of New York City. The end of World War II brought a heavy influx of veterans to the campus, a situation which contributed to the college's decision to again become a four-year liberal arts college in 1954.

By the 1970's, Tennessee Wesleyan's campus reflected major changes in the number and size of new buildings surrounding the original Old College. But the college's long commitment to excellence in liberal education and to Methodism—United Methodism by 1939—remained unaltered.

Durwood Dunn

Refer to: Albea Godbold, *The Church College of The Old South*, Durham, N.C.: Duke University Press, 1944; and LeRoy A. Martin, *A History of Tennessee Wesleyan College, 1857-1957*, Athens, Tenn., 1957.
See also: CHATTANOOGA
RELIGION

The Three States of East Tennessee. Many analysts recognize the "three states" of Tennessee—East, Middle, and West—which have long influenced Tennessee's politics and culture. But few observers are aware of a similar subdivision within the eastern third of the state. The GEOGRAPHY of East Tennessee leads naturally to the following breakdown: the Unaka Mountains (including the Great Smoky Mountains) along the North Carolina border; further to the west, the Great Valley stretching southwestward from BRISTOL to KNOXVILLE to CHATTANOOGA; and, on the far west, the Cumberland Plateau. The characteristic resources and history of each of these three subregions have affected each area in characteristic ways.

Extensive timber, water, and forest reserves throughout the Unaka range spill over from North Carolina to the bordering tier of Tennessee counties: Johnson, Carter, Unicoi, Greene, Cocke, Sevier, Blount, Monroe, and Polk. The presence here of the GREAT SMOKY MOUNTAINS NATIONAL PARK, the Cherokee National Forest, and various state and local preserves gives to these far eastern counties an unusually large share of public recreational acres (see accompanying map). This acreage provides the base for an imposing and still growing tourist industry all along the Unaka tier.

The Great Valley of Tennessee has always offered settlers a milder terrain than the mountains to both east and west. The relatively flat and fertile valley, fought for bitterly by CIVIL WAR armies, is broken only by such orderly wrinkles as Bays, Clinch, and Powell Mountains, and Copper, Newman, and Wallen Ridges. Residents of the Great Valley have developed urban centers, diversified industry, and other traditional signs of national progress at a much faster rate than their neighbors of either the Unakas or the Cumberlands. Indeed, the valley has for a long time drawn to it the more ambitious, mainstream-minded sons and daughters of Unaka and Cumberland mountaineers.

Since 1933, the TENNESSEE VALLEY AUTHORITY has come to symbolize and

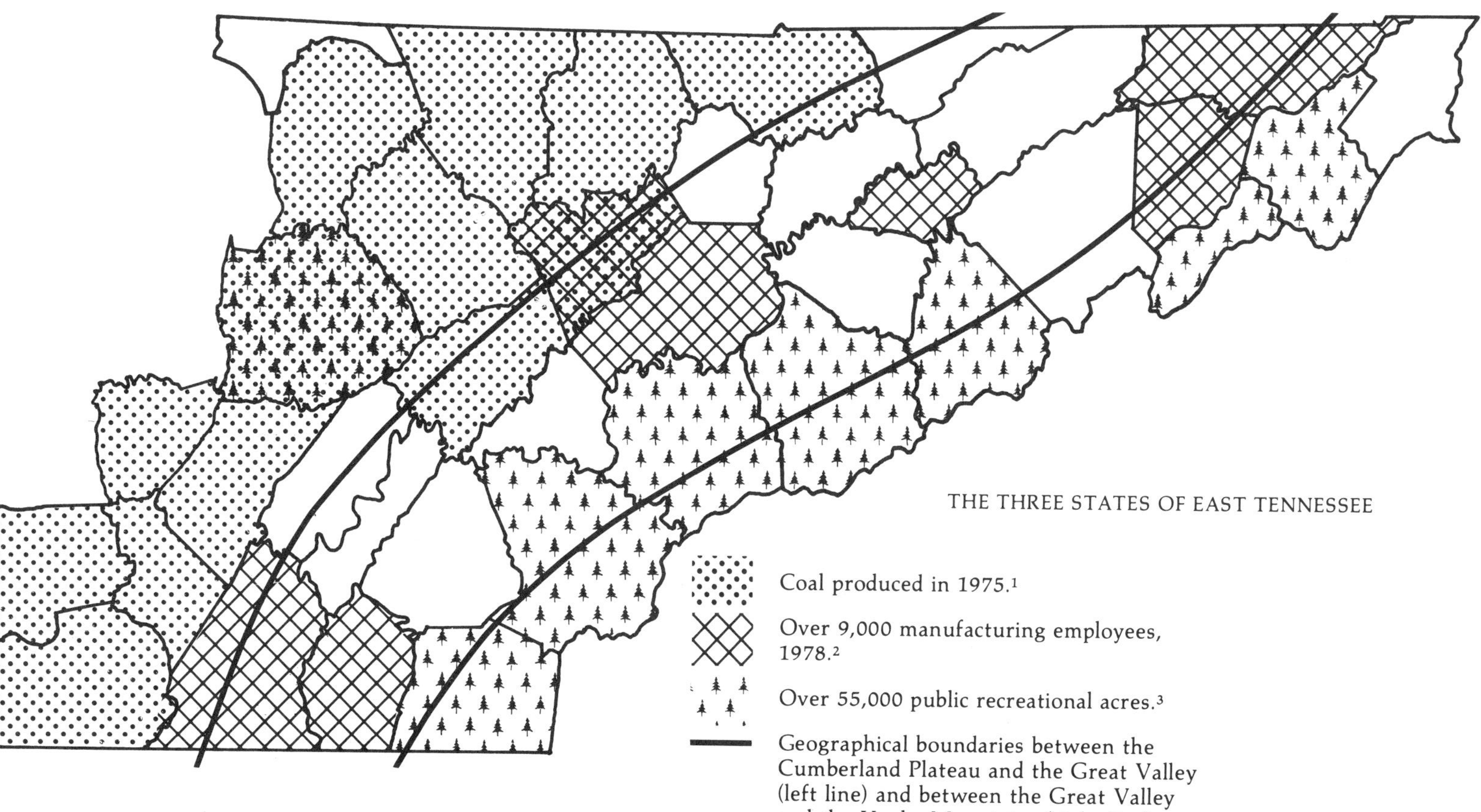

[1] Appalachian Regional Commission, *Appalachia — A Reference Book*, Washington, D.C., 1979, 2nd ed.

[2] Tennessee Department of Economic and Community Development, *Tennessee Directory of Manufacturers*, Nashville, 1978.

[3] Appalachian Regional Commission Development Districts, Recreation Plans, 1972, 1973, 1975, 1978.

stand at the heart of this area's development. It is no coincidence that TVA's headquarters are located in Knoxville, East Tennessee's largest city, or that power-hungry OAK RIDGE lies virtually adjacent to important TVA installations like Bull Run Steam Plant. The Authority has played a fundamental role in the urbanization of the Great Valley, in the distinctive growth of its manufacturing base (see map) and the support of such population centers as Chattanooga, KINGSPORT, Bristol, JOHNSON CITY, Morristown in HAMBLEN COUNTY, and CLEVELAND in BRADLEY COUNTY.

Further west, heralded by the long slanting bluffs of Walden's Ridge and Cumberland Mountain, lies the Cumberland Plateau. Coal, lying in extensive veins from the northern fields surrounding New River to the southern fields surrounding the Sequatchie Valley, has been the watchword of Plateau history. Like other portions of central APPALACHIA, the Tennessee Plateau has long suffered the great irony of harboring an incredibly rich natural resource along with a relatively impoverished human population. The instruments of that irony, from the Civil War to the BROAD-FORM DEED to mammoth corporations, are too complex to discuss here. But the fact remains that coal defines the Plateau counties as a distinct realm (see map). For the forseeable future, coal and COAL MINING will continue to play a dominant role in that realm's definition.

The vital social issues affecting East Tennessee spring directly from the dilemmas facing its subregions. The Unaka counties must not let the financial promise of tourism or logging or water rights overwhelm the small-farm, small-town landscape which has served them well in the past. Rural leaders can learn much in this regard from small indigenous institutions such as SUNSET GAP COMMUNITY CENTER and The Folklife Center of the Smokies in COCKE COUNTY. The Great Valley counties must combine stable non-exploitive industry with decentralized communities. These Valley counties must temper a looming megalopolis with self-contained neighborhoods which emphasize quality of life as much as efficiency of livelihood. East Tennessee's leadership, centered in the Great Valley, might well consider the ongoing social efforts of HIGHLANDER RESEARCH AND EDUCATION CENTER, or East Tennessee Community Design Center in Knoxville, or dozens of other talented groups working for the betterment of their region.

Finally, the county governments of the Cumberland Plateau must not sell their birthright of coal and local privilege for an untaxed mess of environmental ravages and human negligence. Organizations like Save Our Cumberland Mountains, based at Jacksboro in CAMPBELL COUNTY, have for years been fighting against just such a sale. School systems, health delivery systems, industrial parks, and all the other tools of social development must be attended to on the Plateau and throughout East Tennessee. The three states of East Tennessee are in reality one region, one small area of America for us to improve and preserve.

Jim Stokely

Refer to: East Tennessee Community Design Center, *Inner Connections and Open Spaces,* Knoxville, 1980; John Gaventa, *Power and Powerlessness: Quiescence and Rebellion in an Appalachian Valley,* Urbana: University of Illinois Press, 1980; Theodore Schmudde, "The Making of Recreational Places in East Tennessee," in Ole Gade, ed. *Planning Frontiers in Rural America,* Washington: U.S. Senate Committee on Agriculture and Forestry, 1976; and David E. Whisnant, *Modernizing the Mountaineer: People, Power, and Planning in Appalachia,* New York: Burt Franklin, 1980.

The Treaty of Holston. In the fall of 1790, when WILLIAM BLOUNT of North Carolina was appointed by President George Washington to govern the newly established United States Territory South of the River Ohio, one of the first problems to be dealt with was the Cherokee Indian situation. Since the 1770's, when white settlers had begun occupying Cherokee lands in what is now upper East Tennessee, the CHEROKEES had been restless and often hostile. They resented the white intruders building cabins and forts on their hunting grounds, stripping the land of trees to plant crops and make roads, and hunting the bear, deer, and other animals which the Cherokees felt belonged to them.

For twenty years the Cherokees and white settlers had fought, and many on both sides died. Now it was up to Governor Blount to do what he could to bring peace to the troubled land. When Blount sent word to the Cherokee chiefs that he wanted to talk, they at first refused. Other treaties, especially the Treaties of Dumplin Creek and Hopewell, both signed in 1785, had brought neither peace nor restitution for stolen lands. The Cherokees were suspicious and apprehensive. But in early spring of 1791 James Robertson, a prominent leader among the settlers, went to talk with the Cherokee chiefs. Many of the Cherokees had known and traded with General Robertson for years. Eventually the chiefs agreed to come to White's Fort, now KNOXVILLE, to meet Governor Blount and discuss a treaty.

During the last week of June, 1791, the Cherokees began assembling in a wooded field just south of James White's fort, near First Creek's confluence with the Holston (now Tennessee) River. Within a few days approximately 1200 Cherokees had arrived, among them 42 principal chiefs. The negotiations were a ceremonious affair. William Blount is said to have sat under a marquee surrounded by military officers and prominent local leaders including several white and Indian interpreters. The Cherokee chiefs were introduced to him one at a time in order of age. Many of the braves wore eagle feathers on their heads signifying their rank, and all had come unarmed. For three days discussions continued in a dignified manner. The Cherokees observed the orderly procedures they used in their most important council meetings, where one chief at a time spoke standing while others sat attentively in a circle around him.

Finally, on July 2, the Treaty of Holston was agreed to and signed. Among the most important provisions of the treaty was the establishment of a new boundary between the United States of America and the Cherokee Nation. The boundary ran from the North Carolina border northwest along the ridge dividing the Little River and the Little Tennessee River watersheds, up to the Clinch River, then north to Cumberland Mountain. The treaty further provided that white settlers could travel on the Tennessee River without fear of attack, and that a road could be built through Indian territory from the settlements in East Tennessee to those along the Cumberland River in Middle Tennessee. In return, the Cherokees received various goods, including agricultural implements, and a guaranteed payment of $1000 a year which was later raised to $5000 a year. The United States Government also agreed to send instructors to teach the Cherokees new methods of farming and animal husbandry. Other gifts were promised to be delivered at a later time.

Although the peace that Blount had hoped for was not to come for three more years, the treaty assumed great importance in opening up vast areas of land for American expansion. Most of East Tennessee from the North Carolina boundary west to the Clinch River and beyond was made available for settlement. Today, a million and a half people live within the boundaries of what was once the Treaty of Holston. Countless others have moved on from this soil to populate nearly every corner of this country and world.

Michael McCormack

Refer to: Rudolph C. Downes, "Cherokee-American Relations in the Upper Tennessee Valley, 1776-1791," in *East Tennessee Historical Society Publications*, V.8 (1936), pp.35-53; Henry T. Malone, *Cherokees of the Old South: A People in Transition*, Athens: University of Georgia Press, 1956; J.G.M. Ramsey, *The Annals of Tennessee to the End of the Eighteenth Century*, Charleston, S.C.: Walker and Jones, 1853 (reprinted 1967, Knoxville: East Tennessee Historical Society, with annotations by Stanley J. Folmsbee and an index by Pollyanna Creekmore and Marie Quinn); and Charles C. Royce, "The Cherokee Nation of Indians," in *Nineteenth Annual Report*, Washington: Bureau of American Ethnology, 1887 (reprinted 1975, Washington: Smithsonian Institution Press).

Mark Twain (Samuel Langhorne Clemens, November 30, 1835 - April 21, 1910). Though born in Florida, Missouri, Sam Clemens barely missed being a native of what he was to call the "Knobs of East Tennessee". His father John Marshall Clemens, and his mother, Jane Lampton Clemens, of Virginia and Kentucky families, married in Columbia, Kentucky, in 1823. About two years later they moved south to Gainesboro, Tennessee, where they lived for a short time and where their oldest child, Orion, was born. About March, 1827, the Clemenses moved eastward to the newly established FENTRESS COUNTY and its county seat of Jamestown. Appointed one of the county commissioners, John Marshall Clemens drew up the specifications for the courthouse and jail, became the first circuit court clerk of the county, acted as attorney general, and maintained his law practice. If we may believe his famous son, he was "honored and envied as the most opulent citizen of Fentress County."

John Marshall Clemens owned land on both sides of the courthouse square. His own house—said to have been "unusual for its style and elegance"—was located one block north of the block northeast of the courthouse, at present the site of the Jamestown post office. Across the street from the site of the house is the "Sand Spring", where the Clemens family got its water. Since 1938 the spring has been located in a small park, the spot having been restored and beautified by the Jamestown Garden Club with the assistance of Mark Twain's daughter, Clara Clemens Gabrilowitsch (later Samossoud). The street between the home site and the spring is now called Mark Twain Avenue, not the only occurrence of the name in Jamestown, for a cafe and motel on the square bear it as does the local American Legion post.

During their stay in Fentress County the Clemenses also lived at Pall Mall, where the elder Clemens served as postmaster from 1832 to 1835. Four children were born while they lived in Fentress County: Pamela, Pleasants Hannibal, Margaret, and Benjamin. Only Pamela, best known as the model for "Mary" in *The Adventures of Tom Sawyer*, survived to adulthood. John Marshall Clemens' most significant act during his stay in East Tennessee was the purchase of some 75,000 - 100,000 acres of Fentress County land in the belief that it would make his heirs fabulously wealthy. Purchased over a period of about twelve years in parcels seldom larger than 5,000 acres, the land was bought for $400 — $500. The Clemens family retained at least some of the land throughout the nineteenth century, and Orion Clemens paid several visits to Jamestown in attempts to sell it. It was, however, Sam Clemens who reaped the greatest benefits from the land, when he used it as a major plot element in his first novel, *The Gilded Age* (1873), written in collaboration with his Hartford, Conn., neighbor, Charles Dudley Warner. Twain renamed Jamestown "Obedstown" and had "Si Hawkins" go through the experience of buying the land and then moving to Missouri, as John Marshall Clemens had done in May of 1835, the year in which Sam was born.

East Tennessee's JOHNSON COUNTY served as the setting for a short piece called "Journalism in Tennessee" (1869), describing Mark Twain's alleged experiences as associate editor of the *Morning Glory and Johnson County War Whoop*. A footnote in chapter 49 of *Life on the Mississippi* reprints a press dispatch concerning the killing of Joseph A. Mabry, Joseph A. Mabry, Jr., and Thomas O'Connor on Gay Street in KNOXVILLE, October 19, 1882. A cancelled chapter of that book would have lauded Knoxville for its efforts at preserving law and order.

Allison R. Ensor

Refer to: Allison R. Ensor, "The Tennessee Land of *The Gilded Age*: Fiction and Reality," in *Tennessee Studies in Literature*, 1970; Charles Neider, ed. *The Autobiography of Mark Twain*, New York: Harper, 1959; Rachel M. Varble, *Jane Clemens: The Story of Mark Twain's Mother*, Garden City, N.Y.: Doubleday, 1964; and Dixon Wecter, *Sam Clemens of Hannibal*, Boston: Houghton Mifflin, 1952.

See also: APPALACHIAN LITERATURE
CONRAD PILE

U

Unicoi County
Size: 185 Square Miles (118,400 acres)
Established: 1875
Named For: Unaka Mountains
(a corruption of the Indian name)
County Seat: Erwin
Other Major Cities, Towns, or Communities:
- Banner Hill
- Unicoi
- Rocky Fork
- Flag Pond
- Ernestville
- Marbleton
- Limestone Cove
- Bumpass Cove

See also: EMBREEVILLE AND BUMPASS COVE

The Uninvited. One of the loveliest of the old homes in RUGBY is called "Roslyn". It stands staunch and square, with green-shuttered windows and white settles on either side of the entrance stoop. There is a wide veranda at the rear looking out over a beautiful

Unicoi County, ca. 1950. Dave Farnor, a mill customer on horseback from nearby Murry Branch, has just given Ben Tilson a "turn" of corn.

scene of mountains. Huge old oak trees form a backdrop at the rear. A sweeping circular drive leads from the road, and the grounds are kept in immaculate order.

Lord John Boyle of Scotland, President of the Rugby Board of Aid, built Roslyn in 1888 and named it after Castle Roslyn in his mother country. In the early days of the house a dashing young man named Jesse Tyson often drove a tally-ho, laden with young people and drawn by a fine team of horses, up and down the road. At that time Roslyn was renowned for its gala parties and for a great deal of entertaining among the young people.

One snowy night in January, about 1970, when Roslyn was owned by Brian Stagg and his mother Dorothy, Brian heard a sound outside the house. He stepped out on the stoop to investigate. He distinctly heard the hoof beats of a team of horses and the sound of carriage wheels on the ice-covered driveway. The sounds circled the driveway, pausing for a moment at the door, then moving on. Brian called his mother to come and listen, and they heard muted sounds of laughter and gaiety, as if a group of young people were out for a joy ride.

This visitation occurred twice during the winter months. After the Staggs had lived at Roslyn for about a year, a former owner of the house asked if they had heard any strange or unexplained sounds. Brian and Dorothy conceded that they had, and the former owner admitted that she, too, had heard such sounds when she lived there. She had hesitated to tell them, she said , for fear they might not want a house which had uninvited visitors, and which was perhaps the scene of return by joyful spirits to the happier times of their youth.

June Byrd Wortley

See also: JACK AND THE BEANSTALK
LOG RAFTS

Union County

Size: 212 Square Miles (135,680 acres)
Established: 1850
Named For: local pre-CIVIL WAR sentiment in favor of the Union
County Seat: Maynardville
Other Major Cities, Towns, or Communities:
Luttrell
Condon
Paulette
Sharps Chapel
Mossy Spring
New Loyston

Refer to: Kathleen George Graves and Winnie Palmer McDonald, *Our Union County Heritage: A Historical and Biographical Album of Union County*, Josten's, 1978.
See also: COUNTRY MUSIC
LOYSTON
STATE PARKS

Unitarian Universalism. With the opening of APPALACHIA to settlement, it was inevitable that both Unitarians and Universalists would find their way there. These movements were themselves maturing in the early nineteenth century, and theological issues were read and hotly debated throughout the country. There are traces of a Universalist congregation at Limestone in WASHINGTON COUNTY as early as the 1830's. Despite the failure of

Lewis Hine / Courtesy TVA

Sherman Stiner homestead, Lead Mine Bend, Union County, November 8, 1933.

a Unitarian church in KNOXVILLE following the CIVIL WAR, minister Seth Saltmarsh remained there to become a well-known physician. The paucity of permanent results reflects the vigor of the revivalist tradition in Appalachia, which scorned the Universalists as "Hell-Redemptionists". It probably also reflects the small number of immigrants from New England, where the liberal church flourished.

The 1890's witnessed a spurt of activity for both Unitarians and Universalists. Under the patronage of Ferdinand Schumacher, a Universalist church was one of the first to be built in Harriman in 1891. Its seventy-five foot tower, the highest point in town for many years, departed from the steeple tradition by offering the public a platform from which to view the town. Both Unitarians and Universalists also attempted congregations in Knoxville and CHATTANOOGA.

Though all these efforts failed to have permanent significance, several fascinating personalities can be glimpsed. Physician William Hale (1838-1906) served in the Union Medical Corps during the Civil War, was captured, and almost died in a successful escape. Convinced of Universalism by his father and his uncle Aman Hale (who had once preached for the Methodists), William was licensed as a Universalist minister in 1877. As such he travelled widely, going great distances to participate in religious debates. He also preached regularly (one Sunday out of four) near his home at Free Hill, where Universalists shared in a union meeting house. Through it all, he kept high public esteem for his continuing medical practice. LIZZIE CROZIER FRENCH, Annie McGhee McClung, and Mrs. J. C. Tyler (grandmother of JAMES AGEE), all active in the struggle for women's suffrage, were alienated by the anti-suffragette stance of the existing churches. As a result, they attempted to organize a Unitarian church in Knoxville in the 1890's. Mrs. McClung also started the first kindergarten in Knoxville and was a founder of the Florence Crittenton home. When the Knoxville church experiment failed she took herself and her children to the Universalist church in Harriman.

In the pattern of "home missions", the Association of Universalist Women maintained until the mid-1940's an educational program attached to Inman Chapel on the Pigeon River in North Carolina. College students from northern churches came for the summer to teach literacy and other basics. A small library and a clinic for the county visiting nurse were also provided. The establishment of congregations of significant strength and durability was to require yet a third creative period and yet another "migration"—this one accompanying World War II. Today, strong congregations can be found in at least the major cities in East Tennessee: OAK RIDGE, Knoxville, Chattanooga and KINGSPORT.

Unitarianism historically questioned the Trinity as a formula and moved slowly to a belief in a human Jesus who taught humanitarian concerns. Universalism historically read the New Testament as promising ultimate salvation to *all*, a minority interpretation which still agitates contemporary religious circles. The two movements increasingly influenced each other and merged in 1960. Universalist opinions were also held by many German Dunker congregations which moved south from Pennsylvania, but these never became part of the English speaking liberal religion.

Howard Box

Refer to: Ida Metz Hyland, *Unitarian-Universalism in East Tennessee,* Johnson City,1979; Russell E. Miller, *The Larger Hope: The First Century of the Universalist Church in America,* Boston: Unitarian Universalist Association, 1980; and Walter T. Pulliam, *Harriman: The Town that Temperance Built,* Maryville: Brazos Press, 1978.
See also: RELIGION

The University of the South. On the lower Appalachian plateau stands the college town of Sewanee at an altitude of 2,000 feet. The site was determined in the 1850's, when the railroad of the Sewanee Mining Company was completed up the mountain from the main line at Cowan. It was the steepest railroad in the world at the time. The company, which had been given 140,000 acres of coal-rich land by the State of

Tennessee for industrial development in a virtually uninhabited area, served its own and the public's interest by donating 10,000 acres to a budding educational enterprise. The University of the South was founded in 1857 and received its charter in 1858. Its cornerstone was laid in 1860, it was reclaimed from an over-grown wilderness in 1866, and its first nine students were admitted in 1868.

Packed in those eleven years is one of the most dramatic stories in American education, and within the period covered by those years, the most exciting, bloody, and tragic event of the nation's history. Between 1857 and 1868 the nation divided. A new nation was born, flourished briefly, and died, leaving the Southern land wasted. Sewanee, as the University is frequently referred to, is thus the child of two eras: one of them the rich, confident, aristocratic South of the 1850's, and the other the beaten, emaciated, poverty-wrung South of Radical Reconstruction.

Bishops James Hervey Otey, Leonidas Polk, and Stephen Elliott were the principal founders of the University of the South. Each was a convert to the Episcopal Church. Bishop Otey had been a teacher, Polk a soldier, and Elliott a lawyer. In that order they became the first bishops of Tennessee, Louisiana, and Georgia; in that order they served as the first, second, and third chancellors of the University. These men realized that schools were a generative force in modern Christianity. Especially was there a need for training clergy. Thus it was that proposals outlined by Polk were received eagerly by nine Southern bishops meeting in Philadelphia at the triennial General Convention of 1856. Together the bishops would succeed where singly they had failed. Their university would be the first in America to be created complete, not piece by piece, and for it they were prepared to raise the largest sum of money ever raised up to that time for an American educational institution.

Distinguished leaders of church and state from all over the South came to the elaborate cornerstone exercise on October 10, 1860. Eight bishops marched in the procession, four abreast, to the slab of Tennessee marble which was to be the six-ton cornerstone of a building "not unlike the capitol at Washington." Eyewitnesses said there were 5,000 present. Certainly there were more people at Sewanee then than ever again came voluntarily. Three years later, over 50,000 Confederate soldiers came across the domain in July as General Braxton Bragg retreated with his Army of Tennessee before General Rosecrans toward the heroic and pathetic actions of Chickamauga and Missionary Ridge.

After the CIVIL WAR the newly-elected second bishop of Tennessee, Charles Todd Quintard, and his collaborator, George Rainsford Fairbanks, visited the wasted campus in March of 1866. The buildings were gone, the cornerstone destroyed, and the endowment lost. The forest had crept back to reclaim the cleared land. The supporting Church was destitute, and the South was ruined. In these circumstances, Bishop Quintard and George Fairbanks with a few friends and workmen gathered in the woods and erected a rude cross twelve feet high, cut from saplings. They said some prayers, and Bishop Quintard announced that the University of the South was reestablished. Bishop Quintard, after trying unsuccessfully to raise money in the starving South, went to England. There, preaching 250 times in 180 days, he was able to bring back 2,500 pounds—enough to construct a few frame buildings and hire some faculty.

The university opened on September 18, 1868. Four teachers and nine students assembled in the wilderness for services in the first St. Augustine's Chapel. Writing of the early period in Sewanee's history, Bishop Thomas Frank Gailor of Tennessee said, "They set a standard of scholarship and life at Sewanee which influenced the whole South. For ten long years, from 1869 to 1879, Sewanee was the forlorn hope of higher education in the South.... It is only common justice to give credit to Sewanee which made the first stand for higher education and held the banner high when governments were paralyzed with the desolation of the War." As to Sewanee's traditions, the composite character of the institution had been firmly established by the time the first degrees were awarded in 1874. This tradition represented the coming together of five influences: those of the Old South, of West Point, of Oxford and Cambridge, of the Graeco-Roman culture, and of the encompassing tradition of the Episcopal Church.

During its first hundred operative years, Sewanee alumni included four governors, four senators, five admirals, a score of generals, and fifty bishops. More than ten percent of all Episcopal clergy in America received all or part of their training at Sewanee. Perhaps the University's greatest success lay in developing a body of citizens with a sense for civic responsibility. Its most outstanding single group of alumni was its businessmen, among whom it numbered not only presidents of Standard Oil, National Broadcasting, American Airlines, and Coca-Cola, but also heads of hundreds of smaller firms, banks, manufacturing plants, and merchandising establishments. Also during its first hundred years, until Federal scholarship funds became available, the University charged people in the county nothing for tuition. Despite this there have been few takers, with notable exceptions such as two state Supreme Court justices, an attorney general, and a number of other award winners. Similarly, the Episcopal Church, through its mountain missions, has made little headway. Only the hospital at Sewanee has truly won the confidence and whole-hearted appreciation of the people living on the Cumberland Plateau.

During that first century, 3,318 earned degrees were awarded. The University could note that it ranked highest in the South in the proportionate production of Rhodes, Danforth, Woodrow Wilson, and Fulbright scholars, and that better than one out of each hundred degree winners had attained one of those academic distinctions. In 1980, the University of the South enrolled 1,000 young men and women in its College of Arts and Sciences; 200 in its preparatory school, the Sewanee Academy; 80 in its

Courtesy University of the South

The University of the South campus.

theological seminary; and over 3,000 in its international Theological Extension Department. Summers annually bring 200 young artists playing in the Cumberland Orchestra and the Sewanee Symphony, which have been in continuous operation since 1956. The University of the South has an endowment of $25 million, while its lands and buildings are worth twice that much. With its system of leasing rather than selling lots, it maintains control over its domain—23 miles in circumference—and operates its own police department, fire department, and forestry service. The University has been called the capital of its church in the South, and a point of pilgrimage for all Episcopalians.

Arthur Ben Chitty

Refer to: Arthur Ben Chitty, "Sewanee: Then and Now," in *Tennessee Historical Quarterly*, V. 38, No. 4 (Winter 1979), and *Reconstruction at Sewanee: The Founding of the University of the South and Its First Administration, 1857-1872*, Sewanee: University of the South Press, 1954.

The University of Tennessee is virtually as old as the sociological region surrounding it. The University's history follows the same pattern as the history of East Tennessee. In 1794 a group of ambitious residents of the three-year old town of KNOXVILLE, capital of the Territory of the United States South of the Ohio River, created one of the first institutions of higher learning west of the Blue Ridge Mountains. Blount College had a character as distinctive as the people it served. Not only was it begun without the financial security of a large endowment; Blount College was also founded as a private non-sectarian school in an era when most colleges had a religious affiliation. This new institution even admitted women, although their number totalled only five, and they did not stay long enough to receive degrees. After these five, the school did not admit women again for a hundred years. But this one distinction did make Blount College the first coeducational college in the nation.

The names of the first leaders and trustees of the college read like a roster of present-day East Tennessee counties: WILLIAM BLOUNT, JOHN SEVIER, William Cocke, Archibald Roane, Joseph Anderson, David Campbell. But the name "Blount College" was not to endure. Only twelve years after its founding, it was converted into a public institution and renamed East Tennessee College. During the early years of the college, financial support was quite lean. One fund-raising scheme proposed a lottery for the benefit of the school. Officials of Blount College went so far as to write to Thomas Jefferson at Monticello for his help in distributing lottery tickets. Jefferson declined to participate, but he wrote in some detail how the campus of the college should be organized: "I consider the common plan followed in this country, but not in others, of making one large and expensive building as unfortunately erroneous. It is infinitely better to erect a small separate lodge for each separate professorship with only a hall below for his class, and two chambers above for himself; joining these lodges by barracks for a certain portion of the students opening into a covered way to give a dry communication between all the schools, the whole of these arranged around an open square of grass and trees would make it, what it should be in fact, an academical village, instead of a large and common den of noise, of filth, and of fetid air."

In 1826 East Tennessee College moved to a new location. Previously situated east of Knoxville, the college paid $600 for forty acres on top of a hill—known since as "The Hill"—located at that time on the western outskirts of town. Here was erected Old College, the principal building of the institution until it was replaced in 1921 by Ayres Hall. Another name change came in 1840. Bolstered by the sale of a land grant for about $34,000, the institution grew into East Tennessee University. This sale was the only support that the state government gave its East Tennessee school from the time of its founding until 1903.

The CIVIL WAR was devastating to East Tennessee University. From 1862 until 1865 the university's campus was taken over by first the Confederate and then the Union Army, and it was closed during this time. It reopened in 1866 under President Thomas W. Humes, with twenty students enrolled. In 1869 East Tennessee University was offered and promptly accepted the opportunity to become the Federal Land Grant College of the State of Tennessee. This designation required the school to serve people in all specialized areas of knowledge, and to broaden its horizons to encompass many new programs in addition to the conventional classical and professional studies. The new status granted the school $272,000 derived from the sale of Federal lands under terms of the Morrill Act of 1862. Ten years later, the State Legislature recognized the institution as Tennessee's official state university and named it The University of Tennessee.

The University of Tennessee was now responsible for the educational needs of the entire state, and for the establishment of new programs in AGRICULTURE and "the mechanic arts" as part of the new approaches to higher education and research required by the Federal Land Grant Act. Ironically, the establishment of the University's agriculture program—now recognized as one of the best and largest in the nation—was one of the most difficult projects the University faced. With a faculty and administration of principally classical scholars, the University was slow to move ahead with its agriculture curriculum, and it received harsh criticism from the State Legislature and from state farmers' organizations. Dr. Charles W. Dabney became president of the University in 1877. He made great strides toward fulfilling the University's role as a Land Grant institution, including establishing a strong program in agriculture. Dr. Dabney reopened the school to women in 1893, a radical move

Interior of student room at The University of Tennessee, 1890's.

Courtesy Neal O'Steen, University of Tennessee

Courtesy Neal O'Steen, University of Tennessee

Registration at The University of Tennessee, Knoxville, 1948.

that created controversy for several years.

The University of Tennessee entered the twentieth century characterized by steady if not spectacular growth. In 1903, the school began receiving state support: $10,000 in that year, increasing to over $130 million in 1980. Between 1909 and 1965, the University acquired campuses in Memphis, Martin, Nashville, and CHATTANOOGA. The Agricultural Extension program continued its growth and spread throughout the state. Following World War II, veterans swelled college enrollments nationwide. This period was the beginning of unparalleled growth for the University. President Andrew Holt led the institution through a major reorganization in 1968, which made it a university system with five primary campuses and other research and educational centers throughout the state. Dr. Holt retired in 1970 with the University's statewide enrollment approaching 50,000. Today, the University attracts students from every state in the nation and from over seventy foreign countries. Distinguishing the institution in every field are more than 100,000 alumni throughout the world, who with their gifts generously support The University of Tennessee.

Jill Bell

Refer to: Stanley J. Folmsbee, "Blount College and East Tennessee College, 1794—1840: The First Predecessors of the University of Tennessee," in *East Tennessee Historical Society's Publications*, V. 17 (1945), pp. 22—50; Folmsbee, *East Tennessee University, 1840—1879, Predecessor of The University of Tennessee* and *Tennessee Establishes a State University: First Years of The University of Tennessee, 1879—1887*, Knoxville: *University of Tennessee Record*, V. 62, No. 3 (May 1959) and V. 64, No. 3 (May 1961); Thomas Jefferson, letter to Hugh L. White, May 6, 1810, University of Tennessee Special Collections; and James Riley Montgomery, *The Volunteer State Forges Its University: The University of Tennessee, 1887—1919*, Columbia University dissertation, 1961, and *Threshold of a New Day: The University of Tennessee, 1919—1946*, Knoxville: *University of Tennessee Record*, V. 74, No. 6 (November 1971).

A portion of The University of Tennessee campus, looking west from the Hill, late 1970's.

David Luttrell

UNIVERSITY OF TENNESSEE

See also: BIG ORANGE FOOTBALL
WILLIAM BLOUNT
JOHN BOWERS
HARVEY BROOME
PHILANDER PRIESTLEY CLAXTON
WILMA DYKEMAN AND JAMES STOKELY
GEORGE AND ELIZABETH ROULSTONE

V

Van Buren County
Size: 254 Square Miles (162,560 acres)
Established: 1840
Named for: Martin Van Buren, President of the United States
County Seat: Spencer
Other Major Cities, Towns, or Communities:
Cummingsville
Bone Cave
Lonewood
Piney
Laurel Cove

See also: STATE PARKS

Vineland, or The Old Dutch (Deutsch) Settlement, was located in Sylco Valley, less than a mile west of Pace Gap, at the head of Dutch Creek and at the foot of Hogback Mountain and Wolf Ridge. It was sometimes called Bayer's Settlement. In 1837 Dr. Gerald P. Troost described the area as recalling "to my memory the Alpine scenery of Switzerland." Sometime during the 1840's, Miss Rosine Parmentier and her sister and brother-in-law, Adele and Edward Bayer of New York City, purchased about 50,000 acres of land in the mountains of POLK COUNTY. At the turn of the century, Parmentier still owned approximately 26,000 acres.

N.E. Guerin, who became director of the settlement, recruited settlers from the Baden, Germany area. Two or three dozen people, composing some ten families, arrived in 1849. The majority of the settlers were German, with a sprinkling of French and Italians. It is said that a few Swedes resided in the settlement for a brief time. Names of the settlers included: N.E. and Loschuk Guerin; Andrew and Katherine Weber; Jacob and Caroline Lindner; Framer, Chevira, and Louise Gianelley; Alphonso A. Chable, who later became director of the settlement; C.N. Dietzsch and family; Varnus Miller (Muller); L.D., Alley, and Bandic Nocherina; Ferdinand, Catherine, Raimond, Benedict, and Augusta Beckler (Bachle); and Francis, Catherine, Crepin, and Louis Miolane. Other Europeans living near the settlement included Curbows and Muncks.

The purpose of the settlement is unknown. Perhaps the best explanation is that the Germans were intrigued by the possibility of establishing profitable vineyards, as well as having a place where natural FLORA might be investigated and collected. The owners of the settlement were very much interested in botany and at one time owned a botanical garden in New York City. The name Vineland indicates the major interest of the settlers; they planted grapevines along with vegetables, flowers, and apple and peach trees which they may have brought from Europe. According to local lore, considerable wine was produced and exported by the early 1850's. But this venture seems not to have been successful, perhaps due to both transportation difficulties and the quality of wine produced. In 1857, however, during the first fair held in BRADLEY COUNTY, N.E. Guerin received four prizes, including best display of grapes and best specimen of native wine. There were at least four winemakers living in the settlement.

It has been suggested that the owners of Vineland might have been interested in planting a Catholic colony. All members of the settlement were of the Catholic faith, and there was certainly a strong vein of missionary zeal among the owners. Rev. M. Jacquet of the Dominican Order did visit the settlement, but there is no evidence of any attempt made by settlers to convert their neighbors. In later years, many of the settlers' descendants joined local Protestant churches. There is some evidence to suggest that the community was organized as an experiment in social living. It was referred to as a model community, and state officials reported that they would like to see additional settlements of this type established in Tennessee. The owners stated that other suitable sites for additional settlements had been located in the vicinity.

During the early years, the members of Vineland did not mix with the local citizens. The German settlers operated their own government and provided their own school and church. They built a mile or more of good road, planted flowers alongside it, and constructed their houses along this one main street. Though some of their houses were the usual square log cabin, many were made of wide short blocks pinned together end to end, making a round or circular house. The round warehouse for the settlement was used to store products to be sent to market. N.E. Guerin, settlement director and also operator of a mill, reported an estate of $1,000 in 1850, and of $6,000 ten years later. Most of the settlers were artisans, with sons often following the occupations of their fathers.

In 1852, the three owners from New York City made a six-week visit to the settlement. Miss Rosine Parmentier kept a diary of their journey by boat, train, and wagon, and this diary is still in existence. With the coming of the CIVIL WAR, several of the young men of the settlement joined the Confederate Army. Alphonso A. Chable, whose father had served under Napoleon, rose to the rank of captain. Legend has it that Rosine Parmentier was in love with this young Frenchman. However, Chable later married a local girl and named two of his daughters for the owners of the settlement—Rosine and Adele. Following the war, some of the soldiers did not return to Vineland. The population decreased, and some members of the second generation intermarried with the local citizens and moved to other locations. Miss Parmentier may have deeded some of the property to various families of the settlement. The last family, Mr. and Mrs. William Beckler, left Vineland in 1927. After the turn of the century the property was purchased by the U.S. Forest Service, and today only a few grave stones and perhaps a few foundation stones mark the site.

Roy G. Lillard

Refer to: James D. Clemmer, "The Dutch Settlement", and John S. Shamblin, "Old Dutch Settlement in Polk County Recalled," in "J.D. Clemmer's Scrapbooks, 1884, 1934," Microfilm typescript, Tennessee State Library and Archives, Nashville; and Ben H. McClary and LeRoy P. Graf, eds. "Vineland in Tennessee, 1852 : The Journal of Rosine Parmentier," in *The East Tennessee Historical Society's Publications*, No. 31 (1959), pp. 95-111.

See also: RUGBY
CATHOLICISM

W

Nancy Ward (Nanye'hi) was born in Chote, the capital of the Cherokee Nation, in 1738. Her mother, Tame Doe, was the sister of ATTAKULL-AKULLA, civil chief of the Cherokee Nation. As a young girl she was given the nickname Tsist-u-na-gis-ka (Wild Rose) due to her rose-like complexion. Nancy married Kingfisher and had two children, Five Killer and Catherine, before her husband was killed in 1755 in the Battle of Taliwa with the Creeks. When he was shot and killed, Nancy was at his side, chewing the lead bullets for his rifle. She took up the weapon and rallied the Cherokee to victory.

Because of her valor, the clans chose her as Agi-ga-u-e, "Beloved Woman" of the CHEROKEES. Her words carried much weight in the tribal government, for the Cherokees believed that the Great Spirit frequently spoke through the Beloved Woman. As Beloved Woman, Nancy headed the Women's Council and sat on the Council of Chiefs. She had complete power over prisoners. Sometimes known as "War Woman", she also prepared the warriors' Black Drink, a sacred ritual preparatory to war.

Brian Ward, an English trader who had fought in the French and Indian War, came among the Cherokee and married Nancy in the late 1750's. Ward already had a wife who had not yet arrived in this country; however, Norma Tucker writes: "the Cherokee did not consider marriage to be a life-long institution." Brian Ward and Nancy lived in Chote for a time. A daughter, Elizabeth, was born. Then Ward moved back to South Carolina, where he lived the remainder of his life with his white wife and family. Nancy Ward visited his home on many occasions.

Nancy Ward was respected and well known by White and Indian alike. James Robertson visited her home. JOHN SEVIER owed much of his military success to her; on at least two occasions, she sent Isaac Thomas to warn Sevier of impending Indian attacks. She once stopped the warriors at Toqua from burning Mrs. William Bean, wife of Tennessee's first permanent white settler, at the stake. She kept Lydia Bean in her home for a time, then allowed her to return to Watauga. However, Nancy made good use of having the white woman in her home, for she learned from Mrs. Bean the art of making butter and cheese. As soon as she could manage it, Nancy Ward bought cattle and introduced dairying into the Cherokee economy.

Nancy Ward was the first and perhaps the only Cherokee woman to participate actively in treaty negotiations. She spoke powerfully in 1781, and at the Treaty of Hopewell in 1785 she made a dramatic plea for continued peace. But the Cherokees were forced to give up still more of their land. During the last decade of the 18th century, Nancy Ward continued to live at Chote and provide for orphans and the homeless. In the beginning of the 19th century, she came to be known as Granny Ward, because of the many children who were so much a part of her life.

But, as Ben Harris McClary has written, Cherokee life was changing: "As Nancy Ward had hoped, the Cherokees were learning the ways of the settlers, now so geographically close to them. They were becoming farmers and cattle raisers...the old system of clan-tribal loyalty was giving way to demands for a republican form of government....Under the new government, there was no place for a 'Beloved Woman'."

The Hiwassee Purchase of 1819 forced Nancy Ward to abandon Chote. She moved south and settled on the Ocoee River near present-day Benton. There she operated an inn on the Federal Road until her death in 1822. Her grave is located on a nearby hill, between the graves of her son Five Killer and her brother Longfellow.

There is a story sworn by her great-grandson that when she died "a light rose from her body, fluttered like a bird around the room, and finally flew out the open door. It was watched by the startled people in attendance until it disappeared, moving in the direction of Chote. Thus," McClary writes, "Nancy Ward passed from life into legend."

David Ray Smith

Refer to: Ben Harris McClary, "Nancy Ward: The Last Beloved Woman of the Cherokees," in *Tennessee Historical Quarterly*, V. 21 (1962), pp. 352-364; Norma Tucker, "Nancy Ward, Ghigau of the Cherokees," in *Georgia Historical Quarterly*, V. 53 (1969), pp. 192-200; Samuel Cole Williams, *Tennessee During the Revolutionary War*, Nashville: Tennessee Historical Commission, 1944; and "Some Recollections of Jack Hildebrand as Dictated to Jack Williams, Esq., and M.O. Cate, at the Home of Hildebrand in the summer of 1908," typescript, Cleveland Public Library, Cleveland, Tennessee.

Washington College Academy, founded by SAMUEL DOAK about 1780, was originally called Martin Academy. Martin Academy received college status in 1795 when the Assembly of the Territory of the United States South of the River Ohio passed an act establishing a college at Salem. Among the incorporators were the Reverend Doak, General JOHN SEVIER, Colonel Landon Carter, and John Tipton. College work soon began, and James Witherspoon and John W. Doak were the first graduates. For many years, Washington College continued as the foremost institution of classical learning on the western frontier.

The CIVIL WAR brought many hardships to the college. Buildings were burned, equipment and books stolen, classes suspended, and the present girls' dormitory used as a barracks for soldiers and a stable for their horses. As Washington College became one of many institutions of higher learning, the school faced financial problems. By the turn of the century, the institution adapted to the mountain region it served and established a self-help program. Under this program, children who did not otherwise have the opportunity to attend a good school could live at Washington College and work to pay for their education.

In further adaptation to the educational needs of the area, Washington College began in 1920 to provide secondary education for local WASHINGTON COUNTY students. In 1923, the college curriculum was terminated, although the college charter has been retained. After two new county high schools were built in 1971, Washington College reverted to its private status and emphasized its self-help program for both boarding and day students. Seventh and eighth grades were added to the program in 1978. Today, the school is known as Washington College Academy. New buildings have been built, older ones renovated, and the endowment and scholarship funds strengthened. An active alumni organization, local civic groups, and individual friends of the school support the Academy through gifts of money, equipment, and time.

Shirley H. Dellinger

Refer to: Howard Ernest Carr, *Washington College: A Study of An Attempt to Provide Higher Education in Eastern Tennessee*, Knoxville, Tenn.: S.B. Newman, 1935; and Isabelle Foster, "Washington College and Washington College Academy," in *Tennessee Historical Quarterly*, V. 30 (1971), pp. 241-258.
See also: FRIENDSVILLE AND FRIENDSVILLE ACADEMY

Highway between Johnson City and Bristol, Washington and Sullivan counties, 1920's.

Courtesy Archives of Appalachia, East Tennessee State University

Washington County
Size: 323 Square Miles (206,720 acres)
Established: 1777
Named For: George Washington, Commander-in-Chief of the Revolutionary Army
County Seat: JONESBORO
Other Major Cities, Towns, or Communities:
JOHNSON CITY
Mount Carmel
Gray
Sulphur Springs
EMBREEVILLE
Washington College

Refer to: Samuel Cole Williams, *Dawn of Tennessee Valley and Tennessee History, 1541 - 1776*, Johnson City: Watauga, 1937.
See also: CHARLES FREDERICK DECKER
SAMUEL DOAK
THE STATE OF FRANKLIN
BOB AND ALF TAYLOR
WASHINGTON COLLEGE ACADEMY

The Watauga Association. DANIEL BOONE and scores of hunters began exploring the overmountain country during the 1760's. They found the rich valleys of the Holston, Watauga, Nolichucky, and Clinch rivers teeming with wildlife. Their tales of this utopia free from British taxes soon spread from settlement to settlement. Although English authorities had guaranteed this territory to the CHEROKEES, excited pioneer settlers ignored the King's Proclamation Line of 1763 and began pouring into this land of the western waters.

William Bean of Virginia, in 1769, was the first known permanent settler in the new country. James Robertson from North Carolina soon led some sixteen families across the mountains to the Watauga Valley. The Robertson settlement is known today as ELIZABETHTON. Jacob Brown and several families from South Carolina followed Robertson and established claims on the Nolichucky River. Evan Shelby from Maryland built a home and fort on the Holston River, thus establishing the beginnings of BRISTOL. Also in 1771-1772, John Carter and partner Joseph Parker built a trading post in what is now known as Carter's Valley near the present town of Rogersville.

The Cherokees complained to English officials about the increasing number of whites encroaching on lands guaranteed to the Indians. Alexander Cameron, Deputy British Superintendent to the Cherokee Nation, ordered the new settlers off Indian land west of the Proclamation Line of 1763. This warning from Cameron created a critical situation for all four pioneer settlements, as most of their cabins were built more than fifty miles inside the Cherokee boundary. They were not under the jurisdiction of either Virginia or North Carolina and therefore could not legally purchase the land. Decisions had to be made; the settlers could leave or fight. John Carter moved his family to Watauga for safety. Jacob Brown and the Nolichucky families also moved to the security of the larger settlement.

After much discussion, the family heads decided to send representatives to Chota, Capital of the Cherokee Nation, to hold talks with the tribal chiefs. James Robertson and John Bean were chosen for this mission. The Wataugans, surprisingly granted a meeting with the chiefs, presented gifts to the Cherokees.

A white trader interpreted Robertson's talks. The younger chiefs opposed any arrangement with the Wataugans, but Robertson finally persuaded the majority of the chiefs to grant a 10-year lease with monetary considerations. ATTAKULLAKULLA was delegated to visit the Wataugans and negotiate the details of the lease. Jacob Brown later met in North Carolina with some 300 Cherokees, headed by Chief John Watts, and worked a similar agreement for his Nolichucky holdings.

The Wataugans realized the immediate need for an organization to handle legal matters, to file claim papers, and to hold court. Family heads met and set up their own judicial and civil body in May of 1772. Their written articles of association, simple yet adequate, were fashioned after Virginia laws. The Wataugans elected a sheriff, a clerk, and, as a court, five commissioners. These five were empowered to settle questions of debt, probate wills, record deeds, determine rights of property, issue marriage licenses, and hang horse thieves. Unfortunately, a copy of the articles has not been preserved. Historians differ widely in their interpretations of the Watauga Association, placing it at various points along a spectrum from a fairly typical frontier thrust toward law-and-order to the first written constitution adopted by a free and independent people in America.

The organization of the Watauga Association did not end the problems of the settlement. Newcomers disregarded the boundary limits of the lease agreement. When Henderson negotiated his Transylvania agreement with the Cherokees in 1775, the Wataugans and Jacob Brown managed to retain deeds to their holdings. In July of 1776, Cherokee warriors led by DRAGGING CANOE invaded all four white settlements, but without much success. Realizing that they needed help, the settlements successfully petitioned North Carolina to be accepted as part of that state. Twenty years later, after several changes of nomenclature, the Wataugans were included in the new State of Tennessee.

Pat Alderman

Refer to: Stanley J. Folmsbee, Robert E. Corlew and Enloch L. Mitchell, *Tennessee: A Short History*, Knoxville: University of Tennessee Press, 1969; and Archibald Henderson, *The Conquest of the Old Southwest*, New York: The Century Co., 1920.
See also: JOHN SEVIER
THE STATE OF FRANKLIN

The Wayside Grill. Located on Highway 11-W, the Wayside Grill in Rogersville was a local gathering place for teenagers and a favorite lunch spot for workers from the nearby Card & Label Plant. The "goings-on" there were legendary.

AT THE WAYSIDE

Coming back in the fall dark
somehow I still expect to find
it the same: enter through
a screen door & there you are
lodged behind the counter, taking
arms against the last remaining
flies, swatter in hand
& eyes focused on the stock
market pages, dreaming of gold &
Cadillacs.

Already at 14 that very day
our dreams had rounded to perfection:
the Yankees win again & Don Larsen
has pitched the perfect game:
now it is the evening
Speedy turns full volume on the radio
replaying each strike, the blast of voices
beside the steaming black coffee on the
counter
till he forgets the paper route that has
mapped
35 years of his life.
It is the evening Buford Ray
leaves 5 games racked on the
pin-ball, leaps onto the counter
beside the radio, his hands cupped
to his mouth & puts Johnny
Weissmuller
to shame in the best Tarzan yell
this side of the Roxy Theatre.
It is the evening Donnie Roy gooses
the waitress Evelyn Lee in the ribs,
frogs her arm & spins her out onto
the floor near the jukebox where
already
Buford Ray has slugged the juke
as Kitty Wells' record whines,
the overhead fan whirls,
and the dancers spin & spin & spin with
the world,
the sounds of feet, music, hands
clapping
going out into the dark
searching the distances of stars & moon
until finally Mrs. Mapes looks up
over the stock market section of her
Journal
& for the first time in nearly 15 years
a broad grin stretches her wrinkled
cheeks
before she smacks her swatter on the
cash
register and says, "Now boys."

And now I enter.
A face I've never seen before
rises, floats moon-like in the mirror
behind the register.
Youth glistens in the hard light,
disguised only by a blond mustache:
"What for you, good buddy?"
"Change—change for a dollar," I say,
squinting into the light,
"just some change."
Past a still overhead fan,
past a door no longer screened,
I turn back to the waiting
dark, cold & starless.

Jeff Daniel Marion

See also: APPALACHIAN LITERATURE
KNOXVILLE THEATRES
JEFF DANIEL MARION

May Cravath Wharton (August 18, 1873 - November 19, 1959), came to CUMBERLAND COUNTY in April of 1917. She had spent her youth on the plains of Minnesota where her family were homesteaders, living a vigorous outdoor life, doing many of the farm chores and herding the domestic animals on the unfenced wild pasture. After graduating from Carleton College in Minnesota, May Wharton continued her education at the University of North Dakota and set her heart on a teaching career. She graduated from medical school at the University of Michigan, and when a medical missionary post failed to materialize, she went to Atlanta to begin private practice. There she met her future husband, a social worker who in 1917 received a call to go to Pleasant Hill Academy in the plateau country of East Tennessee.

The Whartons had true missionary spirit and decided it was a challenge they could not abandon. Mrs. Wharton's intention was primarily to assist her husband in his work with the young underprivileged mountaineers of the community. When they arrived in Crossville, May Wharton was disturbed by the lack of simple health practices and by the need for medical care for both children and adults. She began to answer health calls near the academy, going to homes of families with sick children and to the old and infirm. Since there were few automobiles at that time, mostly T-model Fords which were no match for the precipitous, gullied, washed-out mountain roads, May Wharton rode a saddled mule. She carried her instruments and medicines in saddle bags and in a pack behind her. As her services became more extensive and valuable, she later procured a good horse that could be ridden or harnessed to a buggy. As the years passed, and roads improved to accommodate the growing number of cars, Dr. Wharton finally acquired an automobile and a driver who could maneuver it through the rural terrain.

Dr. Wharton often gave her services free or accepted exchanges of food and labor. To maintain an inventory of medicines, dressings, and equipment, she often had to rely for help on her own meagre resources, her moneyed relatives, and eastern friends or church groups. In 1920 the sudden death of her husband entangled her affairs and changed her service. She had relied on him heavily to run the Academy. She made plans to leave Pleasant Hill, but a community group met and offered her a sizeable tract of land if she would stay and manage a health facility which they would build. Together with Elizabeth Fletcher and Alice Ashead, a nurse from Canada, May Wharton continued her practice out of a makeshift hospital. The three taught nursing, organized clinics, and sought surgical attention for those in need.

In 1950, due in large part to the efforts of May Wharton, the Cumberland Medical Center was dedicated in Crossville, Tennessee. Seven years later marked the opening of Uplands, a model nursing home and retirement community at Pleasant Hill. Dr. Wharton died in 1959. She must surely see now the continued service that the two health facilities give to the Cumberland Plateau. Truly she envisioned an Uplands of tomorrow.

John H. Dougherty, Sr., M.D.

Refer to: J.M. and Helen Bullard Krechniak, *Cumberland County's First Hundred Years*, Crossville: Centennial Committee, 1956; and May Cravath Wharton, *Doctor Woman of the Cumberlands*, Pleasant Hill: Uplands, 1958.
See also: HATTIE HARRISON GADDIS
PRIMARY HEALTH CARE CENTERS
PUBLIC HEALTH SERVICES

Wheat, until 1942, was a rural community northeast of Clinch River in ROANE COUNTY. Wheat community names appeared on petitions for the establishment of Roane County in 1799 and in 1801, when the petition was granted. The Wheat community was known as Bald Hill before 1881. The first school was the Robertson School, so well established by 1850 that it was used as a call point in land transactions.

Courtesy TVA

Community fair near Wheat, mid-1930's.

A Cumberland Presbyterian minister, William H. Crawford, founded Poplar Creek Seminary at Bald Hill in 1877. Crawford remained President of the school for twelve years. In 1878 and 1879 two benefactors, J.W. Pyatt and Baptist minister George Jones, gave more than 250 acres to the school. Families were permitted to live rent-free in campus houses, with fuel furnished, so long as there was a Poplar Creek student within the family or an adult employed by the school.

Postal service had been available in the Wheat area as early as 1838, but the first Post Office came in 1881. Henry Franklin Wheat was appointed postmaster, and the community took its new name from him. Although Wheat population was scattered, the center of the community consisted of three general stores, two churches, and Poplar Creek Seminary. In 1886 the Seminary changed its name to Roane College and offered the usual four-year collegiate courses as well as a full teaching curriculum. Roane College continued to function until 1908, when the property was deeded to the Roane County Board of Education. Thereafter, the school was known as Wheat High School.

After Norris Dam was built, the TENNESSEE VALLEY AUTHORITY brought electric power to the community. In cooperation with THE

Courtesy TVA

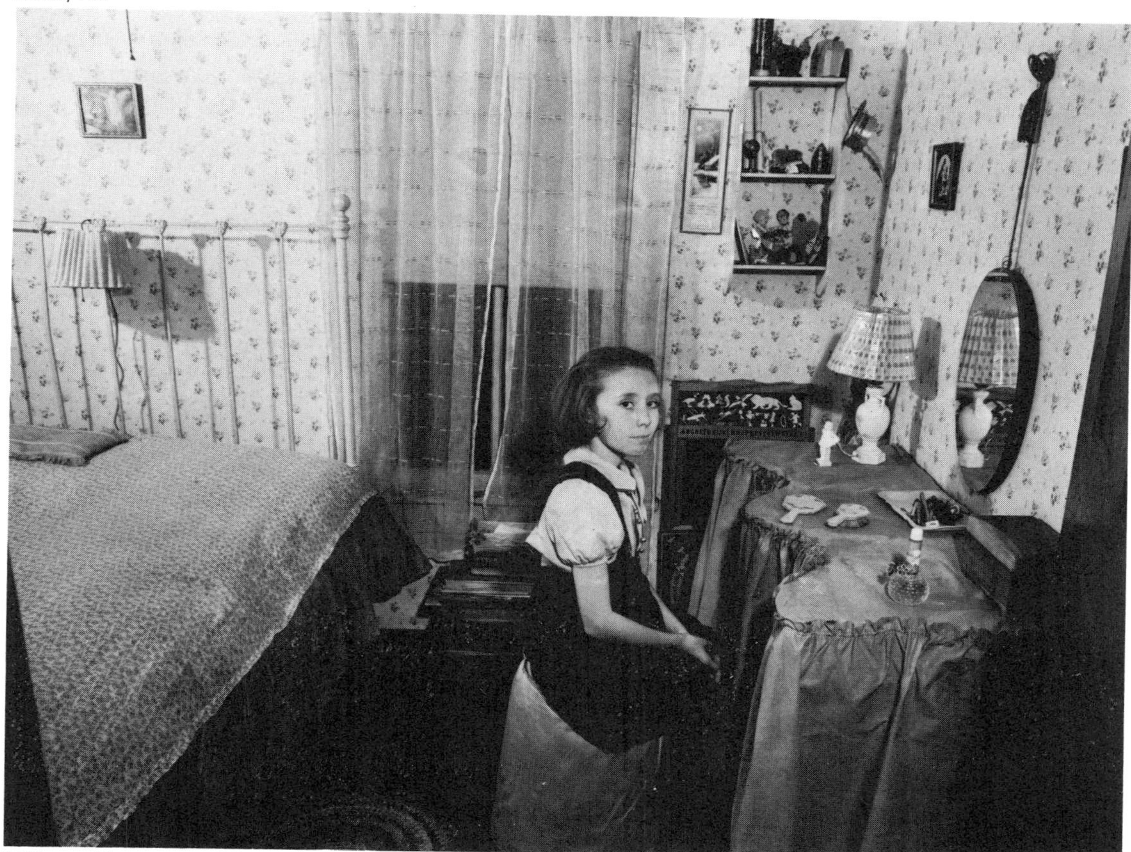

Wheat, Tennessee, November 1939.

UNIVERSITY OF TENNESSEE Agricultural Extension Services, TVA selected the Wheat area as a demonstration project in farm improvement. In January of 1937 Wheat organized into a cooperative with a board of 14 trustees under the supervision of the Assistant Roane County Farm Agent and the Home Demonstration Agent. Through the cooperative, telephone service and a community center came to Wheat. Land improvement was achieved through a fertilizer program, while cooperative seed buying and crop sales improved local economic growth.

On October 6, 1942, land in and around Wheat was condemned by the U.S. Government for national defense purposes. The present OAK RIDGE Gaseous Diffusion Plant is located in the area. Wheat Homecoming is held the first Sunday of each October at the George Jones Memorial Baptist Church, the only building left standing from the previous Wheat Community.

Dorathy S. Moneymaker

Refer to: Dorathy S. Moneymaker, *We'll Call It Wheat,* Oak Ridge: Adroit, 1979.
See also: AGRICULTURE

Robert Emmett Winsett (January 15, 1876 - June 26, 1952), born in rural BLEDSOE COUNTY, Tennessee, was one of the South's leading composers and publishers of gospel music. His Winsett Music Company at Dayton remains one of East Tennessee's oldest sources for paperback shape-note song books. As a young man, Winsett studied under a number of influential figures in Southern gospel music, including A.J. Showalter and J.M. Bowman. Though he taught music from 1896 until 1938, he was always interested in composing as well, and he reportedly wrote his first song at age seven.

In 1903 Winsett began publishing song collections in inexpensive paperback formats, using the seven-shape note system then current among Southern singing conventions. By 1908 he had published his most famous collection, *Songs of Pentecostal Power*, a book which proved so popular among rural churches in the South that it still remains in print today. From 1908 to 1928 he was located in East CHATTANOOGA, and for a time he owned and operated the Dixie Recording Laboratory, one of the first regional record companies in the nation. In 1929 he moved his business to Dayton, where it remained. In Dayton, Winsett's song books continued to sell throughout the world, though he became increasingly interested in providing "church books" (collections of older songs for use in church services) instead of "convention books" (collections of newer songs for singing conventions). Over the years Winsett wrote hundreds of gospel songs, including "When I Take My Vacation in Heaven", a favorite of singing groups in the 1920's; "The City on the Hill", which has gone into folk tradition in East and Middle Tennessee; and "Will You Meet Me Over Yonder". Perhaps his most famous song is "Jesus Is Coming Soon", written on the eve of World War II and now sung as a standard in many mid-South churches and gospel groups.

When Winsett died in 1952, leaving a wife and nine children, his business was continued first by his wife Ruth Winsett and later by their son Harold Winsett. Faced with mounting economic pressures and shifting musical tastes, the family sold the company in 1979 to Ellis Crum of Sacred Selections in Kendallville, Indiana, who announced plans to retain the company name and keep in print several of the most popular books.

Charles Wolfe

Refer to: R.E. Winsett, ed. *Sacred Jewels*, Dayton, Tenn.: R.E. Winsett, 1939.
See also: OLD HARP SINGING
RELIGION

Women Get the Vote. When Tennessee Governor Albert Roberts called the General Assembly into a special session in August of 1920, thirty-five states had ratified the Nineteenth Amendment to the Constitution of the United States. Ratification by only one more state was needed for the Amendment to become law. The Tennessee Senate quickly gave its approval, leaving the question of ratification entirely with the House of Representatives. Polls indicated the House vote would be close, so close that arguments were advanced by both sides for delaying the vote until after the November elections. One simple but effective way to postpone any action would be to "table" the resolution to

Courtesy The Daily Post - Athenian / Used by permission Mrs. Harry T. Burn, Sr.

Harry T. Burn on the steps of the capitol in Nashville after ratification of the 19th Amendment, August 18, 1920. Top row, left to right: Banks P. Turner, Gibson County Representative; Catherine M. Flanagan and Anita Pollitzer, National Woman's Party; Harry T. Burn. Bottom row: Thomas O. Simpson, Representative of Humphreys and Perry counties; and Betty Gram and Sue White, National Woman's Party.

concur with the Senate vote.

Speaker of the House Seth Walker had promised to support the Amendment. After the Legislature convened, however, he personally led the fight against ratification. After several stormy sessions, Walker offered on August 18 a motion to table the resolution. The vote was a 48 to 48 tie, which meant a failure to table the resolution. A second roll to check the tally resulted in the same 48 to 48 tie. This apparently convinced many Representatives that no one could be persuaded to change and break the deadlock. Seth Walker then called for a vote on the resolution itself, knowing that a tie vote would defeat it.

Harry T. Burn, 24-year old Republican Representative from Niota in McMINN COUNTY, had not intended to support ratification at the Special Session. He had, in fact, caucused with the Opposition, and he wore the red rose of the Anti-Suffragists. But on August 18, when he arrived at the capitol, a letter from his mother was delivered to him. In the letter, Mrs. J.L. Burn wrote, "Hurrah and vote for Suffrage, and don't keep them in doubt," closing with the admonishment, "Don't forget to be a good boy, and help Mrs....Catt with her 'Rats'. Is she the one who put the rat in ratification." (Mrs. Carrie Chapman Catt was an active Suffragist who had come to Nashville to work for ratification.)

On both 48 to 48 roll calls, young Burn voted to table. In the vote on the resolution itself, however, having to go on record for or against ratification, Burn voted for the adoption of the resolution. The tally was now 49 to 47 in favor of the motion to concur and ratify the Amendment, thereby enfranchising 26,883,566 women in the United States. Before the results were announced, Seth Walker switched his vote to "yes", making the final vote 50 to 46.

Questioned later about his crucial change, Harry Burn said, "I know that a Mother's advice is always the safest for her boy to follow, and my Mother wanted me to vote for ratification." Fifty years later, he said, "I am glad that I was able to do something for the millions of fine American women. If I had it to do over, I would do it again."

James E. Burn
Harry T. Burn
William J. MacArthur, Jr.

Alvin York (December 13, 1887 - September 2, 1964) was born in FENTRESS COUNTY, Tennessee, not far from the Kentucky line. His parents had little money but eleven children, so the boy began working on the family farm before he was six. Schools in the region were poor, and with the demands of providing for such a large household, York received only some three years of formal education. Instead, he learned farming and blacksmithing from his father and, since hunting was still important for supplying food, became an excellent shot with both rifle and pistol.

As a young man, York was caught up in the usual vices of drinking, gambling, and brawling, but a religious experience in 1915 changed the course of his life and made him a devout fundamentalist Christian. He became an elder in the Church of Christ in Christian Union, a small sect that imposed strict discipline on its members. Because the church was opposed to violence, York requested deferment as a conscientious objector when the United States entered World War I in 1917. His numerous appeals were denied, however, and he was drafted in November of 1917.

Throughout his training period, York was torn between his sincere religious convictions and the call of patriotism. Unable to reconcile the two, he finally took his dilemma to his commanding officer, who tried to use the Bible to show York that Christianity approved the use of force in a just cause. After a short leave to think things over, York returned to camp convinced that America was fighting God's battle in the Great War and that his Christian duty demanded he take up arms. York's faith and patriotism became mutually reinforcing drives that transformed him into a soldier of the Lord.

York sailed for France with the 82nd Division in May, 1918, where he won international acclaim for his single-handed shoot-out with a German machine gun battalion in the Argonne Forest. With the rest of his unit pinned down behind him, York killed 25 German soldiers, captured 132, and in the process silenced 35 machine guns. For this feat, which Allied Supreme Commander Marshal Ferdinand Foch called "the greatest thing accomplished by any private soldier of all the armies of Europe," York was promoted to sergeant and given the Congressional Medal of Honor.

An article in the *Saturday Evening Post*

made York a national figure, and he returned home to a tremendous welcome. Offered thousands of dollars in show business contracts and product endorsements, he refused everything, saying "Uncle Sam's uniform" was not for sale. York returned to Fentress County to resume the life the war had interrupted, although the Rotary Clubs of Tennessee did raise the money to buy him four hundred acres of farmland.

After the war, York gave much of his time to community service. His concern for education prompted him to undertake lecture tours to raise the money to build what became the York Institute, a large modern high school that still serves the people of Fentress County. York also worked to bring better roads to the area and, in the 1940's, became involved in oil drilling in the Cumberland Mountains. On the eve of World War II, when friends convinced him that his story would inspire patriotism in those difficult days he finally capitulated to pesistent requests that he permit a motion picture to be made of his life. York also wanted to build an interdenominational Bible school for the mountains, and he believed that income from the film would make its construction possible. *Sergeant York* was a great success and won an Academy Award for its star, Gary Cooper.

York's last years were hard ones. A 1954 stroke left the old hunter bedridden, while the $150,000 he made from the film involved him in trouble with the Internal Revenue Service. Inexperienced in handling such sums and plagued by bad advice, his tax bill with interest reached $172,723.10 before the IRS agreed to settle for $25,000 in 1961. Speaker of the House Sam Rayburn led a drive to raise the money by popular subscription, and industrialist S. Halleck du Pont created a trust fund to give York an income for the rest of his life.

Courtesy Tennessee State Library

Alvin York

The real importance of Sergeant York lies in his role as a symbol. In the context of 1919, when he first became prominent, he was a reassuring figure. To a nation returning from a frightening war fought with mass armies and destructive machinery, his achievement reaffirmed the value of the individual in the industrial age. This perception was enhanced by the fact that York was a "citizen-soldier" who literally returned to the plow when the fighting ended. At a time when many Americans feared foreigners and radical ideas, York seemed a genuine pioneer restored to life to uphold the virtues of home, patriotism, and piety. In a broader sense, York represented a set of values and a lifestyle that Americans continued to honor even as they rejected them. He was a farmer at a time when a majority of Americans lived in urban areas. While American society generally was becoming more materialistic, York showed his indifference to material concerns by rejecting opportunities to enrich himself. Alvin York represented not what Americans were, but what they wanted to think they were. As a result, he won a special place in the American imagination that lingered long after "the war to end all wars" had become an empty phrase.

David D. Lee

Refer to: Sam Cowan, *Sergeant York and His People*, New York: Funk and Wagnalls, 1922; Thomas Skeyhill, *Sergeant York: Last of the Long Hunters*, Chicago: John C. Winston, 1930; and Alvin York, *Sergeant York: His Own Story*, New York: Doubleday, 1928.

See also: AGRICULTURE
BRADLEY COUNTY WAR HEROES
RELIGION
RIFLES
THE SCOPES TRIAL

Contributors

PAT ALDERMAN is an author and local historian living in Erwin.

J. HADEN ALLDREDGE, MILDRED BURNHAM SPOTTSWOOD, VERA V. ANDERSON, JOHN H. GOFF, and ROBERT M. LaFORGE formed the original Transportation Economics Division of the Tennessee Valley Authority, Knoxville.

FRAN ANSLEY is a lawyer living with her family in Knoxville.

PEGGY FLANAGAN BAIRD is a music teacher living near Clinton.

WILLIAM H. BAKER is Dean of University Development at Tennessee Technological University, Cookeville.

GEORGE A. BAUMAN, Jefferson County Historian, is a resident of Dandridge.

WALLACE W. BAUMANN is President and General Manager of Woodruff's, Inc., Knoxville.

MARY BEAL, owner of Ebbing and Flowing Spring, lives in Rogersville.

EUNICE BEGUN is an active volunteer worker for such Oak Ridge organizations as the YMCA and the AAUW.

BRENDA BELL is a local coordinator for "Threads", a joint education program of the Amalgamated Clothing and Textile Workers Union and the National Endowment for the Humanities, and is living in Blount County with her family.

JILL BELL is Public Affairs Director for WUOT-FM, The University of Tennessee's public radio station.

JAMES W. BELLAMY is Principal of Farragut High School.

PAT BENJAMIN is a poet living in Oak Ridge.

JEAN BIBLE is Co-Historian of Jefferson County and lives in Dandridge.

PATRICIA BOATNER is Today's Living Editor of the *Lenoir City News*.

DIANE BOHANNON is a high school teacher living in Knox County.

JUNE M. BOONE is a writer living in Oak Ridge.

DOROTHY HARRIS BOWLING, sister of Homer Harris and daughter of David and Debbie Harris, lives in Knoxville and works for the Tennessee Valley Authority.

HOWARD BOX is minister of the Oak Ridge Unitarian Church.

ALBERTA BREWER is a writer living in Norris.

ALIX WOHLWEND BROOKS is a retired IPP & AU employee living in Rogersville.

ANNE BROOME, widow of Harvey Broome, lives in Knoxville.

CHARLES F. BRYAN, JR. is Assistant Editor of The Papers of Andrew Jackson, The Hermitage.

HARRY T. BURN, son of Harry Thomas Burn, is a librarian at Oak Ridge Associated Universities.

JAMES E. BURN, McMinn County Historian, is an employee of The Dycho Company in Niota and operates a nearby dairy farm.

CARYL CARPENTER is Administrator for Valley Health Services, LaFollette.

HARRY M. CAUDILL is a lawyer and writer living in Whitesburg, Kentucky.

CONTRIBUTORS

ANTHONY P. CAVENDER is an Instructor in Anthropology at The University of Tennessee, Knoxville.

ARTHUR BEN CHITTY is historiographer and former Alumni Director of the University of the South.

LOIS N. CLARK is Head Librarian and an Associate Professor at Knoxville College.

AMELIA COPENHAVER, former postmaster of Bristol for 39 years, is President of the Sullivan County Historical Society.

JOHN COWARD edited the poetry magazine *Puddingstone* and now teaches at Emory and Henry College, Emory, Virginia.

MARY FRANCES CRAWFORD is Home Economics Reference Librarian at The University of Tennessee, Knoxville.

DAN CROWE is a teacher and local historian living in Elizabethton.

MARK DAVIDSON is an English teacher at William Blount High School near Maryville.

BEULAH A. DAVIS is an Assistant Professor of English at Roane State Community College, Harriman.

LILLIAN PERRINE DAVIS was a retired teacher, editor, welfare agent, and efficiency inspector living in Knoxville before her death in 1980.

RUBY DAYTON is an artist living in Knoxville.

VERA T. DEAN is Senior Secretary of the Classics Department at The University of Tennessee, Knoxville.

SHIRLEY H. DELLINGER is Librarian of Washington College Academy.

HENRY R. DeSELM is a Professor of Ecology at The University of Tennessee, Knoxville.

JOHN H. DOUGHERTY, SR. is a doctor living in Fairfield Glade.

RICHARD HARRISON DOUGHTY is a teacher at Greeneville High School.

BETHANY K. DUMAS is an Associate Professor of English at The University of Tennessee, Knoxville.

DURWOOD DUNN is Chairman of the Department of History at Tennessee Wesleyan College, Athens.

WILMA DYKEMAN is a writer and speaker living in Newport.

C.R. ENDSLEY, JR., former Superintendent of Tennessee Military Institute, lives in Sweetwater.

ALLISON R. ENSOR is an Associate Professor of English at The University of Tennessee, Knoxville.

E. RAYMOND EVANS is a contract archaeologist living in Chattanooga.

ELAINE ALTMAN EVANS is Curator of Collections at the Frank H. McClung Museum, The University of Tennessee, Knoxville.

GEORGE F. FIELDER, JR. is a Historical Archaeologist with the Tennessee Historical Commission, Nashville.

STEVE FISHER is an Associate Professor of Political Science at Emory and Henry College, Emory, Virginia.

JEFFREY FOLKS is a Professor of English at Tennessee Wesleyan College, Athens.

KAY BAKER GASTON is a free-lance writer living on Signal Mountain just north of Chattanooga.

LOWELL GIFFEN is a retired employee of the Division of Personnel at the Tennessee Valley Authority, Knoxville.

CLAIRE GILBERT, a retired teacher, is Coordinator of Ministries with Older Adults in the Knoxville District of the United Methodist Church.

JAMES T. GILLESPIE, SR., M.D., is a physician practicing in Oak Ridge.

AMY C. GOFORTH is a housewife living in Knoxville.

J.A. GOFORTH is Chief Engineer of the Clinchfield Railroad Company, Erwin.

AELRED J. GRAY is a Professor in the Graduate School of Planning at The University of Tennessee, Knoxville.

CONNIE J. GREEN is a writer and former teacher living on a farm in Loudon County.

ALFRED K. GUTHE is a Professor of Anthropology at The University of Tennessee, Knoxville.

H. PHILLIPS HAMLIN is an Assistant Professor of Philosophy at The University of Tennessee, Knoxville.

DAVID J. HARKNESS recently retired as Director of Library Services at The University of Tennessee, Knoxville.

JAMES D. HARLESS is Environmental Health Supervisor at the Oak Ridge Health Services Department.

ORAN HARRIS, brother of Homer Harris and son of David and Debbie Harris, lives in White Pine and works for American Enka Corporation.

FRED HEDDLESON, a consultant to the Nuclear Safety Information Center of Oak Ridge National Laboratory, is an employee of JBF Associates, Knoxville.

BILL HENRY is a craftsman and an employee of Union Carbide Corporation, Oak Ridge.

ROBERT J. HIGGS is a Professor of English at East Tennessee State University, Johnson City.

F.A. HILENSKI is Assistant to the Dean of Liberal Arts at The University of Tennessee, Knoxville.

SARAH LENOIR HILTEN, daughter of Will G. and Helen H. Lenoir, lives in Norris.

JEANNE HOLLOWAY-RIDLEY is a writer and photographer living in Knoxville.

PATRICIA A. HOPE is a free-lance travel writer living in Oak Ridge.

PATRICIA L. HUDSON is a Reference Librarian at The University of Tennessee, Knoxville.

HOWARD HULL is an Assistant Professor of Arts and Music Education at The University of Tennessee, Knoxville.

JANA HUMPHREY is a wife and mother living in Oak Ridge.

TOM HUMPHREY is a manager of manufacturing at EG&G ORTEC, Oak Ridge.

EDITH WILSON HUTTON is a genealogical researcher living in Knoxville.

JOHN RICE IRWIN is Executive Director of the Tennessee-Appalachia Educational Cooperative, Oak Ridge, and owner-operator of The Museum of Appalachia, Norris.

JEWEL TABOR JEAN is a teacher of history and geography at Halls High School.

RUBY L. JOHNS and PORTER JOHNS are farmers living near Sneedville.

ED JOHNSON is Executive Director of the Jonesboro Civic Trust.

JEFF D. JOHNSON, a resident of Maplehurst Park, is Assistant Director of An Appalachian Experience at the Children's Museum of Oak Ridge.

DOROTHY KELLY is a radiologic technologist at St. Mary's Medical Center, Knoxville.

JAMES C. KELLY is Chief Curator of The Tennessee State Museum, Nashville.

PATRICIA KIRKEMINDE is a bookseller living in Crossville.

DAVID R. KIRKHAM is Area Representative for Rural Manpower Services, Tennessee Department of Employment Security, Harriman.

ROBERT KOLLAR is Chief Publications Photographer at the Tennessee Valley Authority, Knoxville.

MILDRED KOZSUCH is Head Processor at the Archives of Appalachia, East Tennessee State University, Johnson City.

MARGARET LAGERSTROM is a former chairman of the Tennessee Nurses Association, Nashville.

THOMAS D. LANE is an Associate Professor of English at East Tennessee State University, Johnson City.

DAVID D. LEE is an Associate Professor of History at Western Kentucky University, Bowling Green.

ROY G. LILLARD, Polk County Historian, is Chairman of Social Sciences at Cleveland State Community College, Cleveland, Tennessee.

MICHAEL A. LOFARO is an Assistant Professor of English at The University of Tennessee, Knoxville.

WILLIAM J. MacARTHUR, JR. is head of the McClung Historical Collection at Lawson McGhee Library, Knoxville.

MICHAEL McCORMACK is an account executive with S.B. Newman Printing Company, Knoxville.

J.H. McCRARY is a retired lumberman living in Bristol.

MICHAEL J. McDONALD is an Associate Professor of History at The University of Tennessee,

Knoxville.

MAY ROSS McDOWELL is President of Johnson City Foundry and Machine Works, Inc.

JEANETTE McLAUGHLIN is a graduate student in Museum Education at George Washington University, Washington, D.C.

SHARON MACPHERSON is Associate Editor of The Papers of Andrew Jackson, The Hermitage.

LOIS MAXWELL MAHAN and JOSEPH MAHAN are retired teachers living in the Karns community.

RUSS MANNING is a writer and editor living in Knoxville.

JOHN D. MARGOLIS is a Professor of English, and Associate Dean of the College of Arts and Sciences, at Northwestern University, Evanston, Illinois.

JEFF DANIEL MARION is a poet and an Associate Professor of English at Carson-Newman College, Jefferson City.

GRACE MAUER is a free-lance writer living in Knoxville.

MARTHA CAMPBELL MEEK, widow of the former Chancellor of The University of Tennessee at Martin, lives in Martin.

PHYLLIS MICHAEL is a voice and piano teacher living in Oak Ridge.

DAVID KENT MILLER was a student at East Tennessee State University, Johnson City, before his death in 1977.

JIM WAYNE MILLER is a Professor of German Language and Literature at Western Kentucky University, Bowling Green.

JESSE C. MILLS, a student in Miss Wolf's third grade class in 1930, is Chief Librarian at the Tennessee Valley Authority, Knoxville.

FREDERICK C. MOFFATT is an Associate Professor of Art at The University of Tennessee, Knoxville.

BECKY JO WEESNER MOLES, great-granddaughter of Melville Milton Murrell, lives in Bean Station.

DORATHY MONEYMAKER is a local historian living in Oak Ridge.

JOHN MULDOWNY is an Associate Professor of History at The University of Tennessee, Knoxville.

EMILY NIXON is a tourist director working for the Gatlinburg Chamber of Commerce.

BARBARA OAKLEY-HAYES is an artist living in Oakdale.

MARIAN E. OATES is Executive Director of the Tanasi Girl Scout Council, Knoxville.

JOHN ALFRED PARKER, owner and resident of the Buffat homestead, is clerk of the Tennessee Supreme Court and Courts of Appeal.

RUSSELL D. PARKER is a Professor of History at Maryville College.

JAMES PATRICK is Academic Dean of The University of Dallas, Irving, Texas.

RAY PAYNE is a Design Engineer at the Oak Ridge National Laboratory.

MICHAEL R. PELTON is a Professor in the Department of Forestry, Wildlife, and Fisheries at The University of Tennessee, Knoxville.

J. MICHAEL PEMBERTON is an Assistant Professor of Library Science at The University of Tennessee, Knoxville.

RONALD H. PETERSEN is a Professor of Botany at The University of Tennessee, Knoxville.

JEAN PHILLIPS is a grocery store manager in Robbins.

LEONARD ROBERTS is Director of the Appalachian Studies Center at Pikeville College, Pikeville, Kentucky.

SNYDER ROBERTS is a local historian, writer, and retired high school teacher living in Oliver Springs.

LEE CULLUM SANDERS, sister of John Cullum, lives in Knoxville.

JEAN SCHILLING is co-founder, with her husband Lee, of The Folklife Center of the Smokies, Cosby.

DOROTHY SENN, a free-lance magazine writer and photographer, is a writer and columnist for *The Oak Ridger*.

AARON J. SHARP is Professor Emeritus of Botany at The University of Tennessee, Knoxville.

ARTHUR G. SHARP is a Civil War buff living in Connecticut.

PATRICIA A. SHIRLEY is Senior Bookkeeper for the Physics Department at The University of

Tennessee, Knoxville.

JAMES HAYDEN SILER, a native of Campbell County, is a retired teacher living in Oak Park, Illinois.

TOM SILER is a sports columnist for the *Knoxville News-Sentinel.*

DAVID RAY SMITH is a planner-estimator in the maintenance division at Union Carbide's Y-12 plant, Oak Ridge.

ELIZABETH S. SMITH is a retired Hawkins County and Knoxville schoolteacher living in Clinton.

SAM B. SMITH is a Professor of History at Tennessee State University in Nashville and Co-editor of The Papers of Andrew Jackson.

WILLIAM R. SNELL is an Associate Professor of History at Lee College, Cleveland.

BRIAN STAGG was Executive Director of the Rugby Restoration Association before his death in 1976.

JO STAFFORD is a writer living in Harriman.

BERNICE A. STEVENS is a craftsman, teacher, and writer living in Gatlinburg.

JIM STOKELY is Director of An Appalachian Experience at the Children's Museum of Oak Ridge.

STUART O. STUMPF is an Associate Professor of History at Tennessee Technological University , Cookeville.

ALLEN D. SWANN is a local historian living in Florida.

JOE SWANN is President of Cherokee Lumber Company, Maryville.

ANNE DEMPSTER TAYLOR is Director of Alumni Affairs at The Webb School, Bell Buckle.

JEROME G. TAYLOR is a Professor of History at Cleveland State Community College.

SYBLE M. TESTERMAN is Executive Director of the United Way of Hawkins County.

JANET THIESSEN is a writer living in Oak Ridge.

IVAN M. TRIBE is an Assistant Professor of History at Rio Grande College, Rio Grande, Ohio.

ROBERT RANDOLPH TURNER is a Professor of English at Carson-Newman College, Jefferson City.

RUTH OSBORNE TURNER is an Assistant Professor of English at Carson-Newman College, Jefferson City.

DONNA RAY WAGGONER is a housewife living in Knoxville and a writer for *Knoxville Lifestyle* magazine.

ARDA S. WALKER is Chairman of the Department of History at Maryville College.

EDWARD R. WALKER III, Cocke County Historian, is a teacher in the Cocke County school system.

MAE WALKER, daughter of S.B. and Lula Stepp Walker, is a writer living in Knoxville.

HORACE V. WELLS, JR. is Publisher of the *Clinton Courier-News.*

LARRY WHITEAKER is an Associate Professor of History at Tennessee Technological University, Cookeville.

HARRY WIERSEMA is retired from his TVA position as Assistant to the Chief Engineer.

CRATIS WILLIAMS is Special Assistant to the Chancellor of Appalachian State University, Boone, North Carolina.

JOHN WILSON is a staff writer with the *Chattanooga News-Free Press.*

VERLIN A. WILSON, a Maryville resident, is a retired employee of the Louisville and Nashville Railroad Company.

CHARLES WOLFE is an Associate Professor of English at Middle Tennessee State University, Murfreesboro.

MARGARET RIPLEY WOLFE is an Associate Professor of History at East Tennessee State University's Kingsport University Center.

JUNE BYRD WORTLEY is a local historian living in Lancing.

JENNY WRIGHT is co-owner of Penny Craft Shoppe, Rockwood.

JAMES A. YOUNG edits the *Nuclear Division News,* an employee publication of Union Carbide Corporation, Oak Ridge.

INDEX

Prepared by Jane Barnes Alderfer
and Shirley Ann Gadd

Italicized numerals refer to photographs.

A

INDEX

B

D

E

INDEX

F

G

H

I

J

K

L

M

N

O

P

R

S

T

U

Z

85°
84°
PICKETT
FENTRESS
SCOTT
CAMPBELL
MORGAN
ANDERSON
CUMBERLAND
ROANE
VAN BUREN
BLEDSOE
RHEA
LOUDON
MEIGS
MONROE
GRUNDY
SEQUATCHIE
MC MINN
HAMILTON
BRADLEY
MARION
POLK
Byrdstown
Jamestown
Oneida
Huntsville
La Follette
Jacksboro
Wartburg
Clinton
Oliver Springs
OAK RIDGE
Crossville
Harriman
Kingston
Rockwood
Lenoir City
Loudon
Spencer
Pikeville
Dayton
Decatur
Madisonville
Athens
Sweetwater
Dunlap
Cleveland
CHATTANOOGA
Jasper
South Pittsburg
Soddy-Daisy
Etowah
Alcoa
WALDEN RIDGE
CHEROKEE NATIONAL FOREST
UNICOI MOUNTAINS